The Salmon

Their Fight
for
Survival

The Salmon

Their Fight for Survival

ANTHONY NETBOY

Illustrated with photographs
Maps by Samuel H. Bryant

HOUGHTON MIFFLIN COMPANY BOSTON

1974

The poem on page 364 is used with the kind
permission of the University of Washington Press.

First Printing v

Library of Congress Cataloging in Publication Data
Netboy, Anthony.
The salmon: their fight for survival.

Bibliography: p.
1. Salmon. 2. Salmon fisheries. 3. Salmon
fishing. I. Title.
QL638.S2N49   333.9'5   72-9022
ISBN 0-395-14013-7

Printed in the United States of America

To
the memory of the late
W. J. M. MENZIES
and to
JOHN M. OLIN and PETER LIDDELL,
for their efforts to save
the Atlantic salmon,
DR. L. E. PERRY and LEON VERHOEVEN,
who have toiled diligently to save
the Columbia River salmon,
and
ROY F. BESSEY,
who has devoted his life to
the service of river development
for human needs,
and
my wife ELIZABETH

Acknowledgments

THIS BOOK has been made possible by the assistance of many individuals and organizations on three continents. A grant from the International Atlantic Salmon Foundation permitted me to visit Alaska and Japan to obtain essential information. The Centennial Award Lectureship bestowed by the Atlantic Salmon Association in 1969 offered incidentally an opportunity to see some of the salmon rivers of Maine and New Brunswick, and a grant from the Conservation Foundation in 1963 enabled me to visit the salmon-producing countries of Europe.

To mention all the persons and organizations who contributed information and made their facilities available would be impossible, but I would like to single out the following:

In Europe: The International Council for the Exploration of the Sea, Charlottenlund, Denmark; the Ministry of Agriculture, Food and Fisheries, London; the Department of Agriculture and Fisheries, Dublin; the Freshwater Biological Laboratory, Pitlochry, Scotland; the Swedish Power Board, Stockholm; the Electricity Supply Board, Dublin; and the Centre Scientifique, Biarritz.

I am especially indebted to Peter Liddell, Dr. A. E. Went, K. A. Pyefinch, Dr. Arne Lindroth, Dr. Leslie Stewart, Ian Allan, Pierre Phelipot, Seppe Hurme, and the late F. T. K. Pentelow and W. J. M. Menzies for taking the time and making the effort to show me salmon rivers, reading drafts of the manuscript, and supplying a great deal of material at different times.

In North America: The Atlantic Salmon Association, Miramichi Salmon Association, Maine Sea-Run Salmon Commission, California Fish and Game Department, Bureau of Sport Fisheries and Wildlife of the Department of the Interior, National Marine Fisheries Service, Oregon Fish and Game Commissions, Washington Department of

Fisheries, Alaska Fish and Game Department, Pacific Marine Fisheries Commission, International Pacific Salmon Fisheries Commission, International North Pacific Fisheries Commission, and Fisheries Research Institute of the University of Washington. All gave unremitting help and supplied materials.

In Asia: I deeply appreciate the courtesies shown me by members of the Fishery Agency of Japan, particularly Dr. Tomonari Matsushita, Director of Research; Dr. A. Furukawa, Director of the Japan Sea Regional Fisheries Research Laboratory, Niigata; the staff of the Far Seas Fisheries Research Laboratory, Shizuoka; Professor Tokimi Tsujita, Hokkaido University; and officials of the Nichiro Fishing Company who gave me an opportunity to visit their mother ships in Hakodate. Aliaky Nagasawa, of the Hokkaido Hatchery system, was extremely helpful not only in Japan but afterward, and I owe him and his colleagues a special debt for supplying reports and photographs.

Drafts of this book were read by many people who are experts in salmon biology and management. Although I list their names below, they are not responsible for the opinions expressed, nor for errors that may have crept into the text. Some of them, in fact, disagree with my views on controversial aspects of the work.

Chapter I, Dr. Ferris Neave and Dr. R. E. Foerster; Chapter II, Dr. R. E. Foerster; Chapter IV, Peter Liddell, Dr. Leslie Stewart, and R. D. Parker; Chapter V, Dr. David Piggins; Chapter VI, Pierre Phelipot; Chapter VIII, Magnus Berg; Chapter IX, Dr. Arne Lindroth; Chapter XI, Dr. Wilfred Carter; Chapter XIV, Paul T. Jensen and Donald H. Fry, Jr.; Chapters XV and XVI, Ivan Donaldson, Robert Schoning, Dr. L. Edward Perry, Dr. Fred Cleaver, Dr. Clark Spurlock, members of the staff of the Oregon Fish Commission, and Francis Seufert; Chapter XVII, members of the staff of the Oregon Fish Commission; Chapter XVIII, Robert Gonsalus and Dr. L. Edward Perry; Chapter XIX, members of the Staff of the Oregon Fish Commission and Environmental Protection Agency; Chapter XX, Harry O. Wendler; Chapter XXI, Roderick Haig-Brown and Lloyd Royal; Chapter XXIII, Wallace Noerenberg, John Wiese, and Dr. Allan Hartt; Chapters XXIV and XXV, Dr. I. I. Lagunov, Pacific Fisheries Institute, Petropavlovsk, Kamchatka; Chapter XXVII, Leon Verhoeven, Jim Chapralis, and Ian Wood.

Leon Verhoeven, formerly director of the Pacific Marine Fisheries Commission, read most of the manuscript and galleys and gave me the benefit of his immense erudition and keen critical eye. Roy F. Bessey, former director of the Pacific Northwest Field Committee of the Department of the Interior, read the chapters on the Columbia River.

Clinton E. Atkinson, fishery attaché at the American Embassy in Tokyo, was kind enough to make all the arrangements for my tour of Japanese salmon facilities and in addition was a marvelous host and companion.

The unfailing assistance and cooperation of my wife Elizabeth during our visits to foreign countries enormously facilitated my task. In fact, without her this book could not have been written.

Portions of this work appeared in *Natural History, American Forests, Sea Frontiers, Cascade, Pacific Discovery, Westways, Atlantic Salmon Journal, Alaska Industry, The Flyfisher,* and *Salmon and Trout Magazine* (London).

I am glad to acknowledge the contribution of my old friend, Frank Walser, who suggested the need for a book on the relations of man and the salmon and thus put me to work on the project.

Mrs. Lora Kelts, fisheries, forestry, and agriculture librarian at Oregon State University, made it possible for me to gain access to much valuable material and was always helpful in facilitating my research. Similar privileges at the library of the College of Fisheries of the University of Washington are gratefully acknowledged.

I deeply appreciate the work that my indefatigable editors, Mrs. Ruth K. Hapgood and Jeffrey C. Smith, have put into the editing of this book and its preparation for the press.

ANTHONY NETBOY

Jacksonville, Oregon

Preface

IT WAS IN 1953, on a warm September afternoon, that I made my first visit to Bonneville dam on the Columbia River and became acquainted with that noble fish — the salmon. Having lived up to that time in the East, I had never seen a live salmon, nor eaten it fresh.

At Bonneville, the mighty river, gathering the flow of hundreds of tributaries issuing from six states and British Columbia, has cut a channel that is straight as an arrow and flows to the sea past palisaded cliffs thickly mantled with Douglas fir and other evergreens. In places the cliffs are pierced by waterfalls, some as delicate as a bridal veil and others descending hundreds of feet in thick sprays from hanging valleys before they are dissipated, almost imperceptibly, into little pools that flow directly into the river.

I watched the salmon patiently climb the steeplechase that man has placed in its path at the dam, a series of curving, stepped-up pools down which powerful jets of water create an artificial attraction current. Accustomed to climbing waterfalls and cascades, the fish seemed to know they were in an unnatural environment. Cautiously they swam back and forth as they reached the face of the dam until they discovered the entrance to the ladders and, impelled by instinct to reach their spawning grounds, pressed ahead. I saw the large chinook and smaller silvers, a motley group of lampreys, shad, and other fish, push on until they reached the white counting board. As the keeper lifted the gate that permits them to dash upstream into the reservoir, she ticked off their number and species on a hand counter, then closed the gate.

Many people lined the fenced-in fish ladders, their eyes glued to the unique spectacle. Only when the sun was setting and the passageway was closed for the night did the spectators disperse.

From that day on the salmon have mesmerized me. I wondered

where the torpedo-shaped fishes with silver bellies and dark backs had come from. I knew they were born somewhere in the vast Columbia–Snake River watershed, perhaps in a creek so narrow a tall man could step across it or in a cold rushing mountain stream fed by the milk of melting glaciers, and that they were trying to return to that very place to spawn.

I learned that after leaving the river as tiny fingerlings Pacific salmon spend one to four years in the ocean, in fathomless seas, driven like Ulysses over a predetermined course, in foul and good weather, feeding voraciously. The fish I watched that day had probably visited the Queen Charlotte Islands; some of them may have wandered up to the Gulf of Alaska. What tales these adventurers would relate if they could communicate with us, what tricks they used to elude the sharks and sea lions, seals, and other predators, including fishermen. Although they had neither maps nor compass they were able to find their way around half the ocean with ease and return invariably to the home river.

As I delved into the life history and biology of the salmon, those who made the Atlantic and Pacific Oceans their homes, I wondered what directional clues they used. Was it true, as some scientists averred, that they can take measurements from the sun, as birds do, and perhaps from the moon? How did they find the Columbia River, the entrance to which is often shrouded in fog and mist, so that many great mariners like Captain Cook and Captain Vancouver failed to discover it? Do the salmon have a sixth sense, denied to man, which enables them to scent the waters of their home stream far out at sea?

The questions multiplied as I began my research. Some of the answers could be found in books, scientific papers, and government reports — the volume of literature on the salmon is staggering and probably equals that on Shakespeare. Reading was not enough. Over the years I visited salmon rivers in the Pacific Northwest, Alaska, western Europe, and eastern North America. I went to Japan to see the streams designed as "salmon culture" rivers. I talked to numerous biologists, fishery managers, and scientists in their laboratories. I sailed with gill netters on the Columbia, fished with trollers off the coasts of Oregon and Washington, and flew on aerial surveys with biologists of the Alaska Fish and Game Department in the Bristol Bay and Kodiak Island areas.

These journeys were always fascinating, revealing landscapes of immeasurable beauty, for the salmon (and steelhead trout) have the good taste to choose spectacular habitats and often regions rich in historic lore. I stood on the banks of little rivers in Spain where the Atlantic salmon (*Salmo salar*) were caught by cave dwellers in the Aurignacian period some 20,000 years ago and at the very same place by the legionnaires of the Roman emperors. I watched the lithe, silvery fishes return from their Baltic feeding grounds to the mouth of the Umea River in northern Sweden, where the Vikings had embarked for their conquest of Russia. I saw hordes of green-liveried sockeye pour into the Bristol Bay rivers, like armies on the march, from their long sojourn in western seas, some of them bearing on their bodies marks of the Japanese nets from which they had escaped. At Hakodate I visited the mother ships and with dignitaries of the Nichiro Fishing Company drank a toast to the captains and shouted "Banzai!" loud and clear, wishing them luck on their seventy-day trek in search of salmon on the high seas.

A persistent desire throughout my travels was to learn how man has treated the wondrous animals, in the distant past as well as in our own times. Was he always as solicitous of their welfare as on the Columbia, where he has provided ingenious ladders at the dams to enable them to reach their spawning grounds? Which people have been the wisest in handling the salmon, and which the most wasteful?

Many of the answers to my questions inspired other queries that often could not be answered, even though no species of fish has aroused such intensive curiosity among mankind and led to such exhaustive (and expensive) research. In North America, Asia, and Europe armies of scientists are engaged in probing the minutest aspects of the salmon's life and wanderings. Their movements are being tracked in the rivers and oceans, their blood is studied for keys to their inherited characteristics so that better races might be bred, and their leaping and swimming ability is carefully probed.

Around the world I met many people who spent a lifetime working with or studying the salmon. I also met many men and women who make a living as fishermen and others who are bewitched anglers. These are invariably a happy breed, and I am delighted to acknowledge their kindness and cooperation, for I learned much from them as well as enjoyed their fellowship and in many cases their hospitality.

If I have succeeded in imparting to my readers some of the pleasures I have had in chasing the salmon halfway around the world, over a period of many years, as well as in delineating the problems we face in conserving what is left of the resource, and perhaps in the case of the Atlantic salmon preventing its extinction, my task will be well rewarded.

We are beginning to realize that man is no longer the kingpin of the animal world. He has driven salmon and other fishes from numerous rivers and seas, barred them from areas where they dwelt long before man came into their ken. Yet we must recognize that man and the animals surrounding him have equal rights to existence. A world in which fish cannot live will soon be a world in which man cannot live either.

Contents

Acknowledgments   vii

Preface   xi

PART ONE
Evolution, Life History, and Migrations

i. Evolution and Distribution of the Salmon   3

ii. Life History and Migrations   11

PART TWO
Fate of the Atlantic Salmon

iii. Primitive Man and the Atlantic Salmon   35

iv. Salmon in Great Britain   45

v. Salmon in Ireland   91

vi. Iberian and French Salmon   111

vii. Demise of the Meuse and Rhine Rivers   133

viii. Norwegian Successes and Setbacks   141

ix. Baltic and Arctic Salmon   155

x. The American Experience   169

xi. The Canadian Experience   191

xii. The Greenland Fishery — Final Catastrophe?   213

PART THREE
Fate of the Pacific Salmon in North America

xiii. Discovery of the Pacific Salmon   225

xiv. The Destruction of California and Its Salmon   235

xv. The Dammed Columbia and Unlucky Salmon — Part 1   263
xvi. The Dammed Columbia and Unlucky Salmon — Part 2   292
xvii. Death and Revival of the Willamette River   311
xviii. Oregon's Coastal Streams   323
xix. Breakthrough in Salmon Culture   334
xx. The Puget Sound Fishery   347
xxi. Vicissitudes of the British Columbia Fisheries   367
xxii. Indians and Salmon in British Columbia   391
xxiii. Vicissitudes of the Alaska Salmon Fisheries   401

PART FOUR

The Asian Resource

xxiv. Asian Salmon Resource   437
xxv. Russia's Salmon Wealth and Its Exploitation   447
xxvi. Salmon Farming in Japan   473

PART FIVE

Salmon for Sport and Food

xxvii. Sport Fishing for Salmon and Steelhead Trout   487
xxviii. Salmon — Our Earliest Gourmet Food   521

Epilogue: Man and the Salmon: A Problem in
    Coexistence   530

Appendix Tables   539
Notes   561
Bibliography   575
Index   595

Illustrations

PHOTOGRAPHS

The Atlantic Salmon (following page 202)

Stages of the Atlantic salmon
Salmon leaping (U.S. Dept. of the Interior)
Craig Brook Hatchery
Salmon scale
Salmon fishing on Chaleur Bay, eastern Canada (NFB, D. Bancroft)
The River Aulne (Joseph Le Doaré)
Fishermen on the River Aulne, Brittany (Joseph Le Doaré)
Fishing on the Little Trinity, Quebec (Atlantic Salmon Assn.)
Salmon caught at the Malangsoss Pool, Norway (Norwegian National Travel Office)
The Malangsoss Pool (Norwegian National Travel Office)
A panoramic view of the Driva River, Norway (Norwegian National Travel Office)

The Pacific Salmon (following page 426)

Pacific salmon (Fisheries Research Board of Canada and Clemens and Wilby, *Fishes of the Pacific Coast of Canada*)
Celilo Falls (Gladys Seufert)
Salmon suffering from bubble disease
Taking a sampling of adult sockeye salmon (Fisheries Research Institute, University of Washington)
An Indian fish wheel in Alaska (Elmer W. Shaw)
The salmon fleet at Fishermen's Wharf, Seattle (Bureau of Commercial Fisheries, Bob Williams)

The crew of a seiner brailing salmon
The Fraser River, British Columbia
The fishways at Hell's Gate
Landing a salmon, Vancouver Island (Ray Atkeson)
The lower Columbia River (Washington State Dept. of Commerce)
Famous salmon brands of the nineteenth century (Elsam, Mann & Cooper Ltd.)
A fish wheel on the Columbia River (Oregon Historical Society)
The "iron chink" (Oregon Historical Society, Seufert Collection)
Fish ladders at Bonneville dam (Corps of Engineers)
Egg-taking at salmon hatchery (Idaho Power Company)

Drawings

A long liner   150
The first salmon cannery in North America, the Sacramento River   248
Trolling   249
A gill netter   279
A purse seiner   352

Maps

Migration Pattern of British Columbia and Southeastern Alaska Pink Salmon   18
Migration Pattern of Sockeye Salmon from Bristol Bay, Alaska   19
Oceanic Migrations of the Atlantic Salmon of Europe and North America   22
Salmon Rivers of the British Isles   44
Salmon Rivers of Ireland   93
Salmon Rivers in the Iberian Peninsula and Southwestern France   110
Salmon Rivers of France   119
River Systems of the Rhine and Meuse   135
Major Salmon Rivers of Norway   140
Salmon Rivers in the Baltic Area   154
Atlantic Salmon Rivers in the U.S.S.R.   164
New England Salmon Rivers   175

Atlantic Salmon Rivers in Canada: Quebec and Newfoundland   190
Atlantic Salmon Rivers in Canada: New Brunswick, Nova Scotia,
    and Quebec   198
Atlantic Salmon Rivers in Canada: Newfoundland   205
Distribution of West Greenland Salmon Fishery, 1969   212
Central and Northern California Salmon Spawning Streams and
    Ports Where Troll-Caught Salmon Are Landed   237
Central Valley Projects in Operation in 1969   253
Columbia River Water Resource Developments   286
Oregon's Coastal Rivers   326
Commercial Salmon Fishing Areas in Puget Sound and Adja-
    cent Waters   353
Salmon River Systems in British Columbia   366
Migrations of Major Species of British Columbia Salmon   371
Fraser River Watershed   377
North Pacific Coast Indians — Linguistic Divisions   392
Alaska   403
Distribution and Migration of Mature Chum Salmon in the Pa-
    cific Ocean   441
Distribution and Migration of Pink Salmon in the Pacific Ocean   443
Soviet Far Eastern Region   450
Areas of Japanese High Seas Fishery   456
Principal Kamchatka Sockeye Salmon Rivers   466
Major Salmon Rivers in Japan   472
Sport Fishing Centers on Pacific Coast   510

The Salmon World   endpapers

Tables and Charts

Range of Pacific Salmon and Steelhead Trout   5

Biological Stages of the Salmon   14

Biological Data for Pacific Salmon (*Oncorhynchus* species)   28

Salmon Catches in Norway, 1875–1969   152

Scientific and Local Names of Pacific Salmon (*Oncorhynchus* species)   231

Life Histories of Salmon and Steelhead Trout in the Columbia River   266

Columbia River Coho Landings, 1938–1970   306

Pack of Canned Salmon in Alaska, 1878–1971   409

World Pacific Salmon Landings, 1952–1967   457

Soviet Salmon Catches Along the Far East Coast, 1940–1969   465

Appearance of the Salmon and Steelhead Trout in the Rivers   506

Some of the Major Salmon Rivers for Sport Fishing in Pacific Coast States   509

Ocean Sport Fishing Regulations in California, Oregon, Washington, British Columbia, and Alaska   512

Nutritional Value of Salmon   527

Tables in Appendix

1. Landings of Atlantic Salmon, 1964–1970   539
2. Catches of Atlantic Salmon in Home Waters, 1960–1971   540
3. Landings of Pacific Salmon, 1952–1970   541
4. Landings of Pacific Salmon, 1964–1970, by Species   541
5. California Commercial Salmon Landings, 1916–1970   542
6. Landings of Salmon and Steelhead Trout from the Columbia River, 1866–1970, by Species   544

7. Columbia River Canned Salmon Pack, 1940–1971, Number of Canneries and 48 1-lb. Cases   547
8. Salmon Counted at Bonneville Dam, 1938–1970   548
9. Catches of Salmon on Puget Sound, 1913–1966, Numbers of Fish   549
10. Puget Sound Salmon Pack, 1940–1971, Number of Canneries   551
11. British Columbia Salmon Pack, 1940–1971, in 48 1-lb. Cases   552
12. Alaska Commercial Salmon Catches, 1906–1970   554
13. Pack of Alaska Canned Salmon by Species, 1940–1971   556
14. Salmon Catches by Japanese and Russians from Coastal Areas of the Soviet Far East, 1909–1944   557
15. Japanese Commercial Salmon Catches, 1957–1969, by Species   558
16. Salmon Catches by Japanese Mother-ship Fishery in the Pacific Ocean, 1952–1968   559

Part One

Evolution, Life History, and Migrations

I ∾

Evolution and Distribution
of the Salmon

RELATIVELY SPEAKING, the fishes are latecomers to our planet. The
first fishlike creatures — ostracoderms — appeared in Ordovician
times about 400 million years ago, when the earth was already probably 3 billion years old. In the Devonian period, often called the Age
of Fishes, some 100 million years later, true fishes of many kinds
evolved.

With the slow passage of geologic time, land and water masses imperceptibly rose and fell. The protocontinent Gondwanaland split up
into segments through continental drift. By the Paleocene epoch or
beginning of the Tertiary period (about 60 million years ago) the continents of Asia, Europe, and America were clearly defined, and fishes
in the sea, with few exceptions, were very much the same as those
now living.

After many millions of years the fishes became adapted, by a mysterious process of evolution, to life in all the strata of the aquatic
world: in the depths of the sea where light is available only from lu-
minous animals, in surface layers driven by winds and tides, and in
placid rivers and lakes. The end results are about 20,000 species of
bewilderingly varied shapes, sizes, and biological characteristics.

Salmon belong to the large group of teleost fishes that dominated
the aquatic scene in the Cretaceous period starting about 135 million
years ago, when the dinosaurs and other clumsy gargantuan animals
ruled the land and not even the remotest ancestor of man had yet appeared. In the span of some 60 million years the teleosts spread
around the world and were differentiated by trial and error adaptation into numerous families including the Salmonidae, which preferred cold, oxygen-rich waters and became habituated to the
Northern Hemisphere.

It is believed that the Salmonidae probably originated in the Arctic

Ocean as migratory fish. When the ice came down across the Northern Hemisphere they came with it. As the ice retreated and the northern seas grew warmer, colonies of these fishes that had become freshwater dwellers were trapped in the cool streams they had entered, some as far as the Atlas Mountains of North Africa, and have remained there ever since.

Origin of the Salmon: Freshwater or Marine?

There are six species of Pacific salmon belonging to the genus *Oncorhynchus* and one Atlantic species belonging to the genus *Salmo.* The steelhead trout (*Salmo gairdneri*) is also a member of the family, found only in the Pacific streams. They are all anadromous fishes: that is, they are born in freshwater, spend their adult lives in the sea, and return to the rivers or lakes where they were born when they are ready to spawn. All Pacific salmon die after spawning, but many Atlantic salmon and the steelhead trout recover from this ordeal, wander back to the ocean, and return to the river or lake to spawn again. Very few make three or more round trips; the record is seven spawnings for an Atlantic salmon.

The origin of the anadromous life of the salmonids has baffled and intrigued scientists since this phenomenon was first accurately described by Konrad von Gesner in the sixteenth century. Were they originally freshwater fishes or did they issue from a marine environment?

In 1861 the German ichthyologist A. Gunther, author of the monumental *Catalogue of Fishes,* asserted that salmon are freshwater fishes who acquired the habit of going to sea. In 1867 the British ichthyologist Francis Day expressed a contrary view: namely, that they originated as marine fishes. Nowadays scientists lean toward the first theory.

Thus Professor J. M. Macfarlane in his book *The Evolution and Distribution of Fishes* says: "Against a possible marine ancestry for Salmonidae many grave objections can be urged . . . It is difficult to imagine genera like *Salmo, Coregonus* (white fishes) and *Thymallus* (graylings) . . . which show few or no truly marine species, becoming dispersed as they are over land areas of the northern hemisphere, if they were marine — or even coastal — derivatives. A considerable number, further, show the anadromous or 'homing instinct', in that though often migrating seaward to feed, they return to rivers or lakes to spawn . . . The swim-bladder also is highly developed in primitive

RANGE OF PACIFIC SALMON AND STEELHEAD TROUT		
	North America	*Asia*
Chinook, king, spring, etc. *Oncorhynchus tshawytscha*	From Monterey Bay, California, to Yukon River, Alaska, and Point Barrow. Abundant in Columbia and Sacramento Rivers.	From Anadyr River to southern Kamchatka. Also reported in northern Hokkaido.
Coho, silver *O. kisutch*	From Monterey Bay, California, to Norton Sound, Alaska.	Does not enter Arctic Ocean but occurs in rivers along the Pacific coast as far north as the Anadyr. Abundant in Kamchatka.
Sockeye, red, blueback *O. nerka*	From Klamath River in California to Alaska. Greatest concentrations from southern British Columbia north to Bristol Bay, Alaska. Sparse above Bristol Bay; rare in Bering Strait. Does not enter Arctic Ocean.	Found in coastal rivers as far north as the Anadyr and as far south as southern Kamchatka and northern Kuriles.
Pink, humpbacked *O. gorbuscha*	From Klamath River to northern Alaska, but scarce below Puget Sound. Abundant in British Columbia and Alaskan rivers. Found in Mackenzie River emptying into Arctic.	From Bering Strait along the coast of Asia as far south as Korea.
Chum, dog *O. keta*	From San Francisco Bay to Bering Strait but not plentiful south of Puget Sound. Plentiful on Arctic coast of Alaska, east to the Mackenzie.	Abundant in the rivers of Siberia, west to the Lena, and especially in the Amur. South to Japan and Korea.
Cherry *O. masu*	Nonexistent.	From the mouth of the Amur to Pusan (Korea). Abundant in Japanese rivers.
Steelhead trout *Salmo gairdneri*	Numerous rivers from Alaska to northern California. Fairly abundant in the Columbia-Snake system.	

and freshwater types, but gradually becomes small and even absorbed in marine species. These with other strong reasons compel the writer to accept a freshwater origin for the family to which salmon and trout belong." [1]

More recent authorities like the Russian ichthyologist G. V. Nikolsky agree with Macfarlane. According to Nikolsky, the change from a freshwater to migratory life was made easy by the dilution of the seas that occurred about a million years ago in the Northern Hemisphere. Enormous masses of freshwater then significantly lowered the salinity of parts of the ocean in areas adjacent to glaciated lands. [2]

If we accept the freshwater origin of anadromous fishes we must still explain why they left their home rivers to make long feeding journeys in the perilous seas.

The Russian ichthyologist Dr. V. Tchernavin, writing in *Salmon and Trout Magazine* (1939), offers a possible explanation: Ancestors of the migratory salmonids were small, brightly colored fishes dwelling in cool streams and lakes as far back as the Eocene. Much later, during the Pleistocene, which began about 1 million years ago, when long periods of glaciation alternated with milder or interglacial epochs, they evolved into anadromous species.

At the height of the most recent Ice Age, continuous ice caps covered northern Europe as far south as 50° latitude down to a line running from London to Leipzig, Kiev, and the Ural Mountains, and in North America to a line stretching from Vancouver, British Columbia, to New York City. This immense part of the globe looked like the interior of Greenland today: a panorama of glaciers and mountains buried in densely packed ice with occasional granitic and scantily vegetated domes called "nunataks" jutting through the white mass. Animal life was scarce in this bleak land, for ice and snow were everywhere.

Inland waters were no longer ice-free even in summer, when temperatures rose. Perhaps a flock of long-tailed ducks now and then came down to rest on the open waters in their migrations across the hemispheres; cormorants, puffins, and other sea birds soared over the purple horizon on their way to milder climates. The slender, black-headed Arctic tern, flying from pole to pole, may have nested on the glistening ice sheet in such areas as the Low Countries and Denmark. But on the whole there were probably very few birds. In fact, it is believed that at the height of the glaciation in the deeply frozen regions the only signs of life came mostly from the spiders and other insects that found sustenance in the nunataks. Man probably survived at the fringe of the ice belt and in milder latitudes to the south where fauna and flora were available as a food supply.

It is conceivable that under these conditions food became scarce in the Northern Hemisphere for freshwater fishes like the Salmonidae. Many species died off, along with other animals and plants. But some salmonids probably managed to push out of the rivers into the sea in search of food and in time acquired the biological mechanisms that enabled them to be transformed early in life into saltwater fishes.

In contrast to the frozen rivers, the oceans were relatively rich in food. There fishes prospered. Some of the Salmonidae began to migrate long distances in the ocean and put on flesh rapidly, but invariably they returned to their home streams, larger and heavier than the fishes that did not go to sea. In freshwater they spawned and died. These mutations, which separated the anadromous from resident species of salmonids, occurred over a long period of time.

Evolution of Pacific Species

Actually we know little about speciation of fishes. Biological evolution is still largely a mystery, despite the revelations of Darwin and his numerous successors. It occurs on a time scale difficult for us to comprehend, where centuries, so to speak, are like years in our own lives. Mutations in nature are normally invisible to any single generation of men unless we alter the environment radically, create a new species by hybridization, or indulge in artificial breeding or crossbreeding.

If we can reasonably account for the origin of salmon as a family of fishes we must still try to explain the relationship of the Atlantic to the Pacific species. Which came first?

The predominant view now is that the Pacific salmon are (geologically speaking) relatively recent offshoots of *Salmo salar*. Thus Dr. Ferris Neave in a paper published in 1958 argues that millions of years ago some Atlantic salmon may have wandered from the Atlantic into the Pacific Ocean by either a fresh- or saltwater route, at a time when there was no Bering land bridge connecting North America and Asia, and no climatic barrier like solid ice to prevent such migration.[3] This supposition is inferentially supported by the Swedish zoographer Sven Ekman who says, "We must suppose that the present Arctic seas had formerly a milder climate which made it possible for boreal and sub-Arctic species to migrate between the northern regions of the Atlantic and Pacific [Oceans] along a route north of the Asian or American continents." [4]

Accepting Neave's theory, we can assume further that individual Atlantic salmon became isolated in the North Pacific and by a process of evolution — that is, by adapting themselves to new environments — acquired differentiating characteristics and thus evolved into the Pacific salmon belonging to the genus *Oncorhynchus*. All this took place over an immense span of time and is probably still going on.

Species in isolation, though basically alike, may acquire unique biological characteristics. For example, the thirteen species of finches Darwin found on the Galapagos Islands, 650 miles from the nearest land mass, probably had a common ancestor, but evolution resulted in substantial mutations. One group became primarily insect eaters while another subsisted chiefly on seeds, which they learned to crack open. One finch developed the ability to use a cactus spine, as a woodpecker does its beak, for chipping into the bark of trees in order to extract insects. Similarly the Pacific salmon may have evolved into six distinct species whose chief difference from the original stock is that they all die after spawning, while many of the Atlantic salmon survive and spawn again after returning to the sea.

According to Ekman the North Pacific in distant epochs seems to have been the center for the creation of new species of fishes. Among many genera common to both the Pacific and Atlantic the Pacific usually has more species (as the salmon does). The earliest offshoot of *Salmo salar*, according to Neave, may have been *Oncorhynchus masu*, the cherry salmon found only in Asia, for it is closer biologically, especially in blood composition, to the prototype Atlantic salmon than to the other Pacific species.

The exact sequence of Pacific salmon evolution can only be conjectured. During the four Ice Ages and interglacial periods that comprised the Pleistocene, radical changes occurred in the oceans and land masses of the Northern Hemisphere. During one of the early interglacials, when the Pacific was opened up to the area behind the Arctic land barrier, one of the primitive forms of *Oncorhynchus* may have broken out and broadly extended its range. "Subsequently," says Dr. R. E. Foerster, "as the land areas now occupied by the Sea of Okhotsk and Bering Sea became, in turn, elevated and submerged, with periods of geographic isolation extending over 50,000 to 150,000 years, further evolution of the genus may have occurred and the various species split off." [5]

Neave thinks that *Oncorhynchus* may have become geographically isolated from the parent stock (*Salmo salar*) between 500,000 and 1,000,000 years ago, and some of the present species may have a total evolutionary history of half this length of time or less. Most likely, by the end of the Pleistocene, 15,000 to 25,000 years ago, the six Pacific species had assumed their present biological characteristics and were distributed among the rivers of northeastern Asia and northwestern North America where they are found today. Presumably they had already marked out the routes of their oceanic migrations, which they follow with almost clocklike regularity from generation to generation.

Range of the Salmon

In the boreal and subboreal climates of the Ice Age the Atlantic salmon coexisted with the woolly rhinoceros and other subarctic creatures as far south as northern Spain. Climatic changes caused the fur bearers to disappear from these latitudes, or rather pushed them northward, but the salmon persisted. By the time of the cave dwellers in France and Spain — 20,000 to 15,000 years ago — *Salmo salar* was probably established in its present range in Europe in rivers located between 40° and 70° north latitude, and in North America from latitudes 40° to 60° north. There is evidence that during one of the warmer interglacial periods salmon frequented not only European rivers that flow into the Atlantic but others like the Ebro, Rhône, and Po that enter the Mediterranean Sea. When the climate warmed up and the Mediterranean became too warm for such cold-blooded species they retreated northward. Only "unwary fishes," as Edouard Le Danois says, "which had ventured into this sea at the end of the great glacial period have left some descendants in the lakes of Italy, Albania and even Algeria," and these are landlocked.[6] Other dwarf-size landlocked Atlantic salmon are found in various lakes in Russia, Sweden, Norway, and eastern North America, while some landlocked Pacific salmon (kokanee) dwell in lakes in Kamchatka, Japan, Canada, and the United States.

Thousands of rivers flowing into the Pacific from Kotzebue Sound, Alaska, to the Monterey Peninsula supported regular runs of salmon when the earliest aborigines colonized North America perhaps 30,000 years ago. In Asia they are found in Arctic watersheds like those of the Kolyma, Indigirka, Yana, and Lena Rivers and in numerous Pacific streams from latitude 35° to 65° north. On both continents some races venture far into the interior: for example, chinook spawn almost at the headwaters of the Yukon, 1800 miles from the sea, and chum go over 700 miles up the Amur River into Manchuria.

Among Pacific salmon pinks are more numerous in Asia than all other species combined, while in North America pinks and sockeye are the most plentiful. The steelhead trout is found only in western North America and cherry salmon only in Asia. Primarily because of the much greater human densities dwelling within its range, the numbers of Atlantic salmon have been severely reduced because of overfishing and destruction of habitat and its territory much restricted in both Europe and North America. Pacific salmon have fared much better because there are still large stocks in regions of primeval wilderness and untrammeled rivers in areas such as Alaska and the Soviet Far East. In the years 1964–1970 catches of Atlantic salmon averaged 13,000 metric tons annually compared with 400,000 metric tons of Pacific salmon (see Appendix Tables 1 and 4).

Life History and Migrations

BIOLOGICALLY the Pacific and Atlantic salmon have similar characteristics, especially torpedo-shaped bodies, and look more or less alike as adults except for size and coloration. Among the Pacific salmon only one species, chinook (*Oncorhynchus tshawytscha*), attains weights comparable to that of the Atlantic salmon's maximum (100 pounds or more); the rest of the genus are smaller. The two families of salmon also vary considerably in the extent of their river and ocean lives. All species have three well-defined stages: first, their stay in the river as juveniles, followed by a feeding period in the ocean of varying length, and finally the dramatic return to the river where they no longer feed but seek out their mates, spawn, and die. Some Atlantic salmon and steelhead trout survive the mating ordeal, return to the sea, and come back for a second marital journey in the river. A few spawn three or even four times, always returning to the ocean.

Life in the River

Every naturally spawned salmon that reaches the sea starts life as a pink ball about as large as a buckshot buried in the gravel of a cold, swift-running stream or in a lake. Sockeye (*Oncorhynchus nerka*) is the species most prone to spawn in lakes. Salmon are cold-water fishes, native only to the Northern Hemisphere, and cannot normally tolerate temperatures above 65° to 68°.

The eggs are deposited in the redds or nests and hatch out in late winter or early spring as tiny translucent fishes with black eyes and (with some exceptions) spotted backs. Their yolk sacs are still attached to their bellies, in which condition they are called "alevins," remaining in the gravel until the yolk sacs are absorbed.

The incubation period is greatly affected by water temperatures but normally lasts for about 110 days for Atlantic salmon in Canada and 50 days for Pacific salmon in the Columbia River.

The yolk sac, which provides nourishment to the alevins, is gradually absorbed over a period of several weeks; then the "fry," about an inch long, emerge from the gravel and begin to forage for food. They are extremely light-conscious: during the day they remain at the bottom of the stream, hiding under stones or in shaded places. At dusk they move about more freely but at night disperse vertically into the shallower water. An abundance of microscopic life awaits them, planktonic crustacea such as copepods and cladocerans, insect larvae, and nymphs clinging to rocks.

During the fry stage the fish grow very slowly and when they begin to approach a length of about two inches are referred to as "fingerlings" or "parr." Atlantic salmon parr have brownish backs with black spots running down the sides and a few red spots in the vicinity of the lateral line. Their bellies are light gray, creamy, or silvery, depending on the habitat. Nine to thirteen dark bars, called parr marks, are clearly visible on each side.

Young Pacific salmon in the fingerling stage (except pinks) have a similar appearance. Pinks and chum also usually migrate to the sea as fry, and their parr marks are either obscure or faint.

Growth is quickest in summer when the insect populations are most abundant and is greater in warmer than colder climates. The first year of life is the most precarious. Fry are devoured by other fish, including larger juvenile salmon, water birds, snakes, and other predators. For example, gill netting of lakes in British Columbia revealed that the major enemies of juvenile sockeye were Dolly Varden char and squawfish, but cutthroat trout, coho salmon, and prickly sculpins also made frequent feasts off them. The Columbia River reservoirs created by the hydroelectric dams have been favorable to an explosion of squawfish and other predator fish, and as a consequence they have become a major menace to juvenile salmon.

In European rivers trout and eel are notorious predators of juvenile salmon; pike, perch, chub, and roach also prey on them.

Among water birds the American merganser and belted kingfisher are particularly addicted to salmon and are known to have decimated large numbers on some eastern Canadian rivers. Removing the birds sharply increased survival of juvenile salmon.

Young parr feed mainly on the larvae of small aquatic insects, older parr on larger insect larvae such as mayflies, stoneflies, and the like, as well as on annelids (worms) and mollusks (mussels and snails).

After the parr stage comes the "smolt" stage when the fish are ready to go to sea. Physiological changes presage this crucial development. In the Atlantic salmon the parr marks disappear, tails lengthen and become more deeply forked, and bodies acquire a silvery hue possibly caused by the deposition of a substance called guanine in the skin. Pacific salmon except for pinks and chum usually undergo the smolt phase as fingerlings, while steelhead trout — a seagoing rainbow trout — conform to Atlantic salmon development.

The length of time juveniles stay in freshwater varies with the species. Pinks and chum salmon go to sea as fry while other species usually remain one to two years. Among Atlantic salmon the freshwater phase averages two years in the southern part of their range and up to four and five years in subarctic regions like northern Scandinavia, Iceland, and Greenland. Steelhead trout commonly spend two years in the river.

The proportion of each year's crop that reaches the smolt stage is quite small. Dr. R. E. Foerster, who spent a lifetime studying the sockeye, estimates that of 2 million eggs borne by 500 females that become fertilized 950,000 fry will be produced, of which only 19,000 will reach the smolt stage and go to sea.[1]

Many external as well as internal changes prepare the fish for the rigors of marine life. "Scales develop, the large blotchy body markings which were their protective coloration during stream life disappear," says Lynwood S. Smith, "and silvery deposits accumulate in skin and scales . . . The changeover in physiological functions begins a month or more before actual seaward migration and lasts from one to ten days after entry into sea water."[2]

In the headwaters of the great salmon rivers of the world there is an enormous stirring in April and May as the new breeds, alerted by the spring spates, start their downstream journeys. They are usually invisible to spectators, for they like to travel at night. "They go in schools of varying size," says Foerster. "Each school seems to have a leader usually a bit larger than the others, who acts as a guide, as it were, and who, when the school is milling around above a riffle or obstruction, seems to size up the situation, after a careful investigation back and forth, and leads the rest through or around the spot that impedes them and has held them up."[3]

Some of the rivers in North America and Asia send 30 to 40 million smolts down to sea every year. These are mighty and massive migrations, fraught with extreme hazards. Mortality is heavy and possibly in some proportion to the length of the journey. In the Columbia

River watershed, for example, the downstream travelers coming from the upper parts of the watershed in Idaho, eastern Oregon, or eastern Washington must run the gauntlet of foaming waterfalls and cascades and evade treacherous irrigation ditches that can divert and lure them to their death. Since the mighty river is now studded with a network of dams they must go through the swiftly revolving turbines in the power stations or over the spillways. At some of these barriers, efforts have been made to keep the fish out of the turbine intakes and shepherd them safely down special inclined-plane passages, sluice-

BIOLOGICAL STAGES OF THE SALMON	
Alevin	Newly hatched young with unabsorbed yolk sac.
Fry	Salmon that have absorbed their yolk sacs, emerged from the gravel, and are ready to feed. Pinks and chum usually descend to sea.
Parr	Older juveniles with prominent parr marks; Pacific salmon at this stage are usually referred to as fingerlings.
Smolt	Young Atlantic and Pacific salmon ready to go to sea.
Grilse	Atlantic salmon who spent one winter in the sea and have returned to the river to spawn.
Jack	Sexually precocious Pacific salmon, usually males, who spent one winter or less in the sea.
Salmon	Mature fish returned to the river; the female is called a "hen" fish and the male a "cock" fish.
Kelt	Spawned-out Atlantic salmon or steelhead trout; a "mended kelt" has recuperated from spawning, returned to the ocean, and may survive to spawn again.

ways, or pipes at one side of the spillway. Nevertheless many are killed at each dam or emerge in a dazed condition and become easy victims of predators. In recent years an excess of nitrogen in the river, due to entrainment of dissolved gas in water spilling over the dams, has killed millions of juveniles on the Columbia and Snake Rivers and an alarming proportion of upstream migrating adults as well.

Some rivers also present obstacles to seagoing fish in the form of moving walls of undissolved sewage, wastes from pulp mills, chemical plants, and other lethal phenomena, particularly water depleted of dissolved oxygen. On certain European and Siberian waterways the tiny travelers have to contend with enormous amounts of sawdust or bark dust left by log rafts, or sludge dumped by barges. Similar situations occur in many North American rivers. In contrast, on the still largely undammed Fraser River in British Columbia the fingerlings' passage to the sea is relatively unobstructed.

To watch the descent of juvenile salmon is a wondrous experience. "It is possible to go down to a river's edge in May and catch 40 fry in a minute or two," says Roderick Haig-Brown. "For the most part they are pinks, already silver and on their way to the sea, or the slender greenish chums," but more often they are "orange colored cohos and heavily barred, pale-finned king salmon as well." [4]

In small, clear streams the smolts ordinarily leave the spawning or rearing areas at dusk and continue the exodus until daybreak. Where the ocean is only a short distance away, the course may be covered in a single night or less, but where, as on the Skeena River in British Columbia, a journey of a few hundred miles is involved, they remain in the stream bed during the day and resume their movements at night. However, some daylight movements have been observed near the spawning areas under conditions of high turbidity or flood and also in the lower reaches of large rivers.[5]

Sockeye spawn in streams flowing from or into lakes or in lakes themselves, and the smolts quickly move out of an intricate lake system with uncanny precision. Often two species occupying the same watershed move together. It was observed in Hooknose Creek, British Columbia, where chum and pinks spawn in the same vicinity, that the main nocturnal migration of the chum began and ended about an hour later than that of the pinks.

Oceanic Odysseys

One of the most critical periods of existence occurs as the fish reach the ocean. "Since several freshwater functions are contrary to their marine counterparts," says Lynwood S. Smith, "optimum adjustment is impossible . . . during this period. Any additional stress such as high temperature, low oxygen level in the water, pollutants, or dams further complicates the situation and can lead to fatal consequences. And finally, in sea water there are a number of other changes — new food to recognize and catch, different predators to avoid, and unknown large bodies of water to traverse. It's a rough transition." [6] The salmon (and steelhead trout) feed voraciously and grow rapidly in size and weight.

Pacific Salmon

Until fairly recently we knew very little about salmon migrations in the Pacific. The great increase in fishing on the high seas by the Japanese, which created serious conflicts and resulted in the tripartite treaty between Japan, Canada, and the United States in 1952 and the bilateral convention between Japan and Russia in 1956, has led to tremendous research programs designed to trace the fishes' movements. Immense numbers of young fish were tagged or marked in coastal rivers in both Asia and North America, and larger fish were caught and tagged at sea. Recaptures of these marked individuals have given us a fairly clear picture of their romantic migrations.

The fishes start ocean life as zooplankton feeders, following the dense masses of small animals drifting with the currents. In time they develop strong jaws and sharp teeth and can hold their own in the jungle that is the sea. They devour crustaceans, such as tiny shrimp that are believed to give salmon flesh its red color, as well as anchovies, pilchards, and herring. Chinook and coho especially dote on herring, thus making them vulnerable to fishermen using herring as bait. For example, in the Gulf of Georgia, British Columbia, herring habitually spawn on certain island beaches: the herring come in droves and behind them are the hungry salmon. Many a morning I have seen stately herons standing in shallow pools spot a school of juvenile salmon, drive their bills below the surface, and take their daily meal.

Typical of the food found in the stomachs of salmon in the ocean are euphausiids, shrimps, amphipods, copepods, pteropods, and squid. Predators are numerous — the remains of salmon have been found in the stomachs of pollock, tuna, swordfish, and seals. Close to the estuaries, and even in tidal portions of streams, salmon are heavily preyed upon by seals. The Fish Commission of Oregon hires a seal hunter to reduce the population of these animals in the Columbia River.

In the estuary the young fish, only a few inches long, swim back and forth for quite some time, gradually getting accustomed to more saline waters. "While confined in these waters," says Foerster, "they must be subjected to heavy mortality from predators [especially birds], and from poor-quality water due to increased concentration of pollutants when the tide is coming in and backing up the water, thus concentrating the [noxious] chemical ingredients."

How big a toll do predators exact from the salmon when they return to spawn? Relatively little information on this subject is available, but a valuable contribution is made by George W. Frame of the Bureau of Commercial Fisheries who studied eighteen black bears, mostly juveniles and adults, as they fished for eight weeks on a salmon-spawning stream in Prince William Sound, Alaska. The bears usually fished the streams at dawn (3 to 5 A.M.) and dusk (5 to 10 P.M.). Frame calculated that 8 percent of the annual spawning run fell prey to the bears, but this, he says, is a small price to pay: "Most salmon caught by bears had already completed spawning, and a significant number of spawned-out fish that had died naturally were also eaten. Removing these thousands of expended fish from the stream probably prevents stream pollution from that source and may greatly assist survival of the salmon eggs by leaving a greater supply of oxygen and less chance of fungal infection" (*Outdoor Life*, February 1973).

Despite intensive investigations the ocean remains as it was for the ancient Greeks: a mysterious part of the planet. In its depths dwell multifarious creatures with shapes and bodies and biological characteristics that puzzle and fascinate us. When the salmon plunges into the sea it becomes part of that mystery, but gradually man has been able to unveil some of its secrets.

Dispersed over thousands of miles of the Pacific are vast schools of Asian and North American salmon, sometimes traveling together. Similarly, in Davis Strait, and off the west coast of Greenland, the Atlantic salmon of Europe and North America hobnob together, feed, and mature.

The general direction of North American salmon movements in the Pacific is now fairly clear. The juveniles usually linger in the bays or estuaries for a short time, then are really on the move. Since the major inshore currents along the North American coast are northerly, most of them go that way. Thus the Columbia and Fraser River fish may wander beyond the Queen Charlotte Islands and into the Gulf of Alaska before they turn back to commence their spawning migration to the respective rivers of their birth. Others, however, head southward. Columbia River coho and chinook have been caught by trollers as far north as Baranof Island, Alaska, and as far south as the coast of northern California. The general movements of fish from the coast of North America are in a counterclockwise direction until they are ready to come home, while those from Asian rivers are in a clockwise direction.

Young Puget Sound migrants may spend a month or two in adjacent waters, paying calls on the San Juan Islands or loitering in Ta-

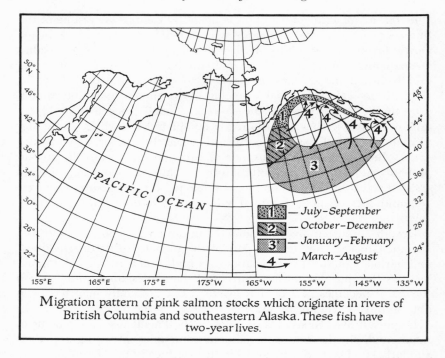

Migration pattern of pink salmon stocks which originate in rivers of British Columbia and southeastern Alaska. These fish have two-year lives.

coma Narrows. For instance, smolts marked in the Duwamish River within the Seattle metropolitan area were found traveling along the coast of Puget Sound at the rate of fifteen miles a day. They eventually circled westward and headed for the Gulf of Alaska.

Dr. William F. Royce and his colleagues of the Fisheries Research Institute of the University of Washington tracked large numbers of pinks (who have a lifetime of only two years) emanating from rivers in southeastern Alaska and British Columbia. After spending three to five months in estuaries, inner bays, and channels, these adventurers reached the ocean proper in July and headed rapidly northward and westward along the coast, following the Alaskan Gyre. The size of the migratory band at its peak was estimated from sample catches with purse seines as 750,000 fish passing daily, for thirty to sixty days, across any given line of latitude in southeast Alaska. The fish averaged ten to twelve miles per day for months on end. In late fall and midwinter the schools of pinks reversed direction and moved south, and in January and February they were spread widely over the Pacific, between latitudes 41° and 51° north and longitudes 130° and

160° west, still hitting a speed of ten miles per day and gaining rapidly in size and weight. By the spring and summer of the second and final year of their lives, they left the midocean and raced northward toward their home rivers, some individuals averaging forty-five miles per day. They had little time to spare to reach their spawning grounds at nature's appointed season.

The pinks, with but a two-year life span, most of it spent in the ocean, make only one of these elliptical 2000-mile journeys, but chum and sockeye, who may spend two or three and even four years in the sea, may complete two or even three circuits and tally 10,000 miles before they return to their home rivers. At times the different species swim together, forming bands stretching in discontinuous ranks for perhaps a hundred miles. In 1964 it was estimated that 500,000 salmon that had been at sea one year passed daily in a westward direction south of Adak Island, from late June to late August, a total of 30 million.

Some Asian species make similar long-distance treks and feed in areas frequented by North American salmon. For example, salmon from East Kamchatka follow the East Kamchatka current southwestward along the coast and then head eastward into the Bering Sea and

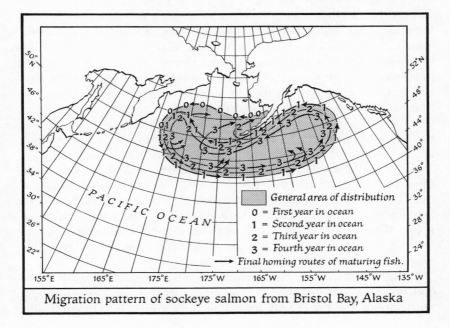

Migration pattern of sockeye salmon from Bristol Bay, Alaska

North Pacific, sometimes going as far as the western part of the Gulf of Alaska. Scarcely eighteen inches long, they cannily pick their way through the maze of Aleutian passes and islands in the foulest weather. Although shoals of North American and Asian fish feed and travel together, when the spawning urge strikes each bids the other adieu (so to speak) and returns to its own continent and home river. It is unknown, says Foerster, whether American fish ever stray into an Asian river or vice versa. According to Royce, the long journeys are accomplished by the fishes' following the currents on their return migration but swimming ahead of them.[7] The migration, says Leon Verhoeven, former director of the Pacific Marine Fisheries Commission, "is not direct; it involves crossing from one ocean current to another and frequent adjustments (due to overshooting) of the course occur."

The presence of millions of salmon over vast areas of the North Pacific has given rise to a large-scale, lucrative Japanese fishery and generated intense international conflicts, as will be seen in later chapters.

Steelhead Trout

Until fairly recently the ocean life of the steelhead trout was quite obscure. Some light has been shed by tagging fish in the rivers and learning about their movements from the recovery of the tags by fishermen. It is now known that these large silvery trout are driven by the same kind of wanderlust as the salmon. Many of them travel thousands of miles from their native rivers, while others do not venture into the open sea but merely swim to and fro with the estuarial tides and rather quickly return to freshwater to spawn. Steelhead have been tracked on journeys lasting two or three years. The size of the adult, as with salmon, is in some proportion to its stay in saltwater, but steelhead rarely go over twenty-five to thirty pounds.

For example, a smolt was tagged in Oregon's coastal Alsea River in April 1958; five months later it was recaptured and released near Kodiak Island, Alaska; finally it was recovered as a mature fish in its home stream in early 1960. A tagged steelhead from the Wynooche River, Washington, was caught south of Kiska Island by a Japanese research vessel in September 1970 some 2000 miles in a direct line from home waters.[8]

A study of hatchery-reared steelhead returning to Oregon's Alsea and Wilson Rivers revealed that about 90 percent spent two summers in the ocean and the remainder one or three summers. Oregon Game

Commission biologists believe that hatchery stock return to the rivers at an earlier age than wild fish.

The three major types of food most frequently found in the stomachs of steelhead are squid, greenling, and amphipods.[9]

Atlantic Salmon

The oceanic life of the Atlantic salmon was a mystery to us until some ten to twelve years ago. The late W. J. M. Menzies three decades ago postulated a theory, after studying the results of many tagging experiments in Canada, Britain, Norway, and elsewhere, that salmon from North America and Europe had common feeding grounds in the North Atlantic. He identified Port-aux-Basques on the Gulf of Saint Lawrence as a possible rendezvous where fishes of different countries meet and thence journey to the communal feeding grounds. This theory became a fact when schools of salmon were seen off the southwest coast of Greenland in the late 1950s, thus attracting commercial fishermen who soon not only worked along the shores but went out to the high seas to harvest these valuable fishes and took hundreds of thousands annually.

Recovery of tagged fish in the Greenland catches made it evident that they emanated primarily from Canada and the British Isles, with some contributions by the United States, Norway, Sweden, France, and Iceland. All the fish had spent one winter or more in the ocean as evidenced by their scales, which, like the rings on a tree, record their life history. No grilse have yet been found in the Greenland fishery, which means that during their first winter in the sea the salmon feed elsewhere. Recently evidence has appeared that grilse from the British Isles feed in the vicinity of the Faeroe Islands, which lie between Scotland and Iceland.

It is known that many Atlantic salmon wander over immense areas in the sea. The longest journey recorded is that of a smolt tagged in the Gulf of Bothnia, an arm of the Baltic, which was recaptured on the west coast of Greenland, 3300 miles from its starting point.

As in the North Pacific, the high seas fishery in the Atlantic Ocean has benefited a small number of fishermen, mainly Danes, and precipitated a fierce international conflict.

Guidance Mechanisms

How do the salmon, who are said to have the stamina of racehorses, accomplish their herculean odysseys? This question has long in-

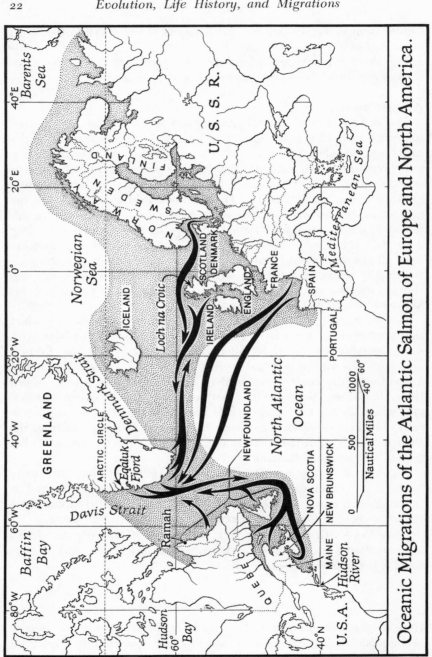

Oceanic Migrations of the Atlantic Salmon of Europe and North America.

trigued mankind. Dr. Royce and his colleagues in their study of ocean migrations suggest that their navigational ability is an inherited response to environmental stimuli. They infer that the circuits are imprinted on their chromosomes.

On the high seas they swim fairly near the surface so that it is easy for fishermen to take them. In coastal waters coho are caught by trollers in thirty- to sixty-foot depths and chinook in sixty to ninety feet. Although they follow the currents, they do not drift and their schedule is fairly consistent. "It is common," say Royce and his colleagues, "for a single interbreeding population to keep a schedule that varies from date of return of previous generations to their spawning grounds by only a few days." Their arrival in the river, as in Bristol Bay waters, may therefore be predicted with uncanny accuracy, almost like that of a scheduled airline.

The salmon seem to be masters of oceanic navigation without man's sophisticated navigational equipment. How do they do it?

Various investigators have spun theories to account for these feats. The Canadian M. C. Healey studied the migration of pink salmon fry from the Bella Coola River in British Columbia and concluded that celestial clues aid them in finding their way to the sea. The juvenile fishes were better oriented, he says, on clear than on cloudy days. This finding is corroborated by other Canadian studies.

In his book *Underwater Guideposts: The Homing of Salmon,* Dr. Arthur D. Hasler brings together evidence to suggest that the fishes are able to navigate around the globe by using the sun as a beacon, as birds do, but he admits they rely on other cues as well. However, we must remember that on the north Pacific routes there is little clear weather from one year's end to the next. Around the Aleutian Islands the skies are persistently overcast; gales and storms roil the waters in fall and winter. Black clouds often scud across the sky; the ocean is a sunless sea, and even stout human mariners find navigation difficult.

In the outer parts of Bristol Bay, for example, the average weather in June, when the salmon are homeward bound, is fog, mist, or haze 44 percent of the time, and the mean cloud cover is 80 percent. In the Central Gulf of Alaska, thronged with salmon, the average June weather is 25 percent fog, mist, or haze, and the cloud cover is even more persistent. Not many scientists put much stock in Hasler's theory, although it may partly explain the salmon's navigation in closed bodies of water.

In a study of the ocean migrations of pink salmon, Neave concluded that "the ability to set a compass course, using a celestial feature, is insufficient to account for the indicated (homing) preference." [10]

The fish seem to have a built-in compass or "searching-recognition" mechanism not related to celestial clues or physical landmarks. Salmon from Asia or North America when tagged and released at widely different points in the North Pacific seem to know how to get to their home stream thousands of miles away without difficulty, just as pigeons who have been crated and taken from Britain to Canada (or vice versa) and then released fly across the ocean to their dovecotes.

Scientists believe on the basis of such experiments as clogging the fishes' noses that the salmon use their olfactory sense as a navigational aid when nearing their home streams. Since each body of water has a unique chemical composition it is possible that the fish, remembering the smell, follows its scent as a dog follows his master's scent. This perhaps explains how salmon return to the little hatchery maintained by the College of Fisheries on the busy campus of the University of Washington in Seattle. To reach their destination they must chart a course through an intricate network of Puget Sound waters, crowded with ferries and other craft, and find the pond in a maze of still watercourses, for its water supply is Lake Union and adjacent springs.

Dr. Royce and his colleagues lean to the belief that salmon navigate with the help of infinitely small electrical voltages generated by the ocean currents as they travel through the earth's magnetic field. "The salmon migration," they conclude, "cannot be performed if they migrate or drift at random, or if they depend on any memorized visual or olfactory cues at any time during the final location of the home estuary and stream . . . They may depend on electromagnetic cues from ocean currents . . . [and] their response to all migratory cues is inherited, not memorized." Some species of fish are known to have electric organs as well as electro-receptors, but "no investigations are known concerning the electrical sensitivity of adult salmon or of the presence of receptor organs in the lateral line of salmon which might be electrically sensitive." [11]

Other biologists infer that the fish depend upon detection of the varying salinities in the ocean or perhaps take measurements from the moon. All we know for certain is that their delicate perceptiveness, which is beyond our comprehension, not only enables them to find their home river after a long absence but it also leads them to the exact tributary or subtributary of an extensive river system such as the Columbia or the Amur. The home stream may be no more than a slender creek or lake whence they emerged as fry. To reach their destination they will have passed and ignored many other streams.

The Marital Journey

Once they return to freshwater, salmon no longer feed but live off the fat stored up in the ocean. Defying every conceivable obstacle, they strive to return to the river or lake where they were born, or if incubated in a hatchery, to the stream where they were released — and no other. This is the crucial fact of their existence. Knowledge that the fry or fingerlings will definitely return as adults to the river or hatchery, no matter how difficult it is to reach, is the key to scientific management of the fisheries. Innumerable experiments have proven that this incredible instinct can rarely if ever be modified.

Ascent of the River

Ocean life takes a heavy toll of every generation of fishes, especially in the earliest period when they must adjust to the saltwater environment and to new and ferocious predators. Dr. Foerster estimates that of the 19,000 young sockeye who go to sea as the result of a spawning population of 1000 adults (500 males and 500 females), 90 percent die and 10 percent eventually return to the river. These figures, he reminds us, are hypothetical, a composite derived from many areas, and the returns assumed may well be too high in many instances. Returns, for example, of salmon bred in hatcheries in Japan are in the neighborhood of 1 to 2 percent; in Sweden it is 1 to 17 percent. The important fact is that if a run is to be maintained at least two adults must return and successfully spawn for every pair that spawned in the previous generation. On many of the important rivers of the world adequate escapement — that is, the number that are permitted to escape from man's nets, lures, and traps — is becoming difficult to maintain, and as civilization alters the pristine environment the difficulty is compounded.

Races of the same species return at different times of the year with unerring regularity. Thus in the Columbia River there are spring, summer, and fall runs of chinook, in the Amur River in Siberia summer and autumn runs of chum, and in North American rivers winter and summer runs of steelhead.

The length of time a fish requires to reach its spawning ground varies in general with the distance it has to go. The time that elapses between entry into the river and actual spawning also is dependent upon the degree of ripeness or maturity of the fish when it leaves salt-water. Some races spawn almost immediately upon arrival in fresh-water. Others arrive in the vicinity of the spawning area months be-fore they are ready to mate. Fish that spawn near saltwater, such as pinks and chum, usually are sexually mature before they enter the river, while those ascending long distances like some chinook and chum races become mature en route. The color of the fish changes with maturation and migration.

Physiological Changes

As the jaunty salmon reach the estuary they may rest for a while in order to adjust from a saline to a freshwater environment. Their bodies undergo perceptible changes. In the sea the different species look superficially alike, ranging in size from the occasional 100-pound chinook to the five- or six-pound sockeye or chum, the two-pound steelhead or Atlantic salmon grilse, graceful creatures with gleaming silvery sides, sea lice clinging to their bodies. With sexual maturity each species acquires distinct coloration, shades of yellow or red, and to some extent unique or greatly distorted shapes. The bodies of both males and females become markedly compressed, their skin thickens, and scales are absorbed. The parasitic sea lice are shed in fresh-water; the male develops an elongated, hooked jaw, and the female's sides are distended with roe. Male pink salmon acquire a promi-nent hump and hence are called "humpies."

While it is difficult to generalize about color changes as the salmon head for the spawning grounds because there are great variations within a single species, certain prominent phenomena may be noted. Atlantic salmon acquire a coppery color; steelhead trout the color of rainbow trout (in fact, they are referred to as sea-run rainbow trout). Sockeye are the most remarkable, for their bodies turn fiery red and heads olive green.

A heavy rain or spate is generally required to drive the salmon up-stream. At this time they are in prime condition, their bodies fat and oily, muscles taut, eyes keen. As they ascend their stomachs gradually shrink and the fat diminishes. Generally entry into the river and as-cent are timed by one of those exquisite correlations of nature to ena-ble the fish to take advantage of the most favorable environmental conditions: the proper flow of water, temperature, and oxygen con-tent.

In their upstream migration no obstacle deters them. Persistent, weary wanderers, they swim or climb over rocks and waterfalls, or hurtle themselves in great leaps. Dr. T. A. Stuart of the Freshwater Laboratory at Pitlochry, Scotland, has shown that the fish can make a running jump of ten to twelve feet and land precisely where it wishes if waterflow or depth is adequate.[12] It is the dissolved oxygen in the water that sustains them and allows them to forge ahead. If the oxygen level drops too low they are immobilized and may even die from asphyxiation. If the water is overheated they may fall victims to furunculosis or some other deadly disease; and if there is an excessive amount of nitrogen gas in the water, as on the dammed Columbia and Snake Rivers, they may develop bubble disease, resembling the bends that afflict human divers, and die.

In the estuaries and coastal waters salmon move both day and night, but in the river they migrate mostly by day, especially in the early morning and again in the late afternoon or evening when the light is dim, resting in pools and riffles after sunset. To follow a school of salmon upstream is an exciting experience. Their movements consist of a staccato series of stops and starts, overcoming one obstacle after another, swimming against the current. They are fast swimmers (as anglers know) and if their speed slackens the current will carry them back down unless they find a resting place. They push forward relentlessly until, exhausted, they seek a quiet pool where they can rest behind rocks or other obstructions. Then they try again.

I watched sockeye trying to ascend a waterfall on the Frazer River on Kodiak Island, remote from any human habitation, in an attempt to reach their spawning ground in the lake above. They had been traveling at the rate of thirty miles a day on this short wilderness stream. They assembled at the base of the roaring rapids, which consist of tier upon tier of forbidding rocks, sixty feet in a vertical direction, down which a powerful current of water was flowing. One could see individuals, their heads turning olive green and bodies red, survey the awesome scene and then make up their minds, as it were, to hurdle the wall of water. Some of them leaped six or seven feet in a running broad jump again and again but failed to clear the rapids; thrown back repeatedly by the current, they refused to give up.

At the foot of the falls the Alaska Fish and Game Department had installed a ladder to enable them to surmount the rapids but many overshot or could not find its entrance and were lost. Many others negotiated the cascade via the ladder and swam up to the lake beyond. It would be a few weeks before the majority would be ready

BIOLOGICAL DATA FOR PACIFIC SALMON (*Oncorhynchus* species) IN NORTH AMERICA AND ASIA

	Chinook O. tshawytscha	Pink O. gorbuscha	Sockeye O. nerka	Coho O. kisutch	Chum O. keta	Cherry O. masu
Length of time young stay in freshwater	few days to 2 years	few days	few days to 3 years	1 to 2 years	few days	1 year
Length of ocean life	1 to 5 years	1⅓ years	½ to 4 years	½ to 1½	½ to 4 years	1 to 2 years
Life at maturity, years	2 to 8	2	3 to 7	2 to 4	2 to 5	
Length, average inches, at maturity	36	20	25	24	25	
Length, range, inches, at maturity	16 to 60	14 to 30	15 to 33	17 to 36	17 to 38	
Weight, average pounds, at maturity	22	4	6	10	9	9
Weight, range, pounds, at maturity	2½ to 125	1½ to 12	1½ to 15	1½ to 30	3 to 45	8 to 20
Principal spawning months	Aug.–Sept.	July–Sept.	July–Sept.	Sept.–Dec.	Sept.–Nov.	
Fecundity — number of eggs	5000	2000	4000	3500	3000	

to spawn, but their safety was now assured as long as they could elude their predators, the brown bears who kept a respectful distance but were ready at any moment to pounce upon them.

Some salmon are known to make fantastic upstream journeys. The salmon of the Yukon now probably set the world's record, although the chinook and sockeye that went up the Columbia to its headwaters in Canada were close seconds before Grand Coulee dam, built without fishways in the 1930s, cut off about 1100 lineal miles of river and spawning grounds. Almost as soon as the Yukon is clear of ice late in May or early June, the chinook appear at the mouth of the river and move upstream steadily. A study by Charles H. Gilbert of the U.S. Bureau of Fisheries showed that when they reached Whiskey Creek, 622 miles from the sea, they had averaged 52 miles per day; at Tanana (804 miles) 60 miles per day; at Fish Creek above Rampart Rapids (851 miles) 47 miles per day; at Circle (1227 miles) 47 miles per day; and at Eagle (1402 miles) 50 miles per day. When they arrived at Dawson City, 1500 miles from the sea, they had been moving against a consistently rapid current for twenty-nine days at the rate of 52 miles per day — and had not eaten a morsel. "They contain no more oil than is needed to furnish satisfactory dog food," said Gilbert. In contrast, when the fishes came into the river they were too oily to be canned.

Chum entered the Yukon a week later than chinook and their movements were almost as rapid. Gilbert found that at Tanana they were but ten days behind and at Dawson City only fourteen days behind the larger species. Chum covered the lower 800 miles at an average speed of 90 miles per day and the next 700 miles, between Tanana and Dawson, at 55 miles per day.[13] These migratory feats in a fast-flowing river are probably unmatched among the freshwater fishes of the world.

Reproduction and Death

When they finally reach their destination the salmon prepare for the supreme ordeal of their lives. Every phase of their adventurous existence has led to this climax. In the swift waters of some rushing river the fish pair off. Shunting the male aside, the female starts to build the nest (or redd) in the gravel bed of the stream. Turning on her side and poised at an angle of 45 degrees to the current, head facing upstream, she violently flexes her tail and diligently scoops out the gravel, stones, and silt, which the boiling current then carries downstream. She repeats this performance, frequently alternating or turning her opposite side while the male stands by, driving off intruding males; sometimes the female assists in defending their territory by driving away other females. From time to time she drops down into the hollow and tests it with her anal fin. After much travail the redd assumes a saucer-like shape many inches deep and about twice the length of the fish. To accommodate a large chinook salmon, a single nest may occupy several square yards of stream bottom. Several fish may dig redds in the same riffle.

Now the nest is ready for the eggs. "All loose and fine material have been removed from the pot, or center of the redd . . . Usually there remain in the pot large stones too heavy for the fish to move far, and the crevices between these rocks provide excellent lodgement for the eggs." [14]

As with other animals, courtship precedes mating. One may observe the male swimming back and forth over the female as she rests near the bottom of the redd, often touching her dorsal fin with his body and fins, or nudging her with his snout. He may even pretend to dig, as if to say to her, "This is how it is done."

Then the male gently approaches the female, who assumes a rigid position over the center of the nest and, quiveringly, curves his body against hers. The bright pink eggs and clouds of milt are deposited simultaneously to accomplish the miracle of fertilization. Otherwise, as Leonard P. Schultz, who with his students made an exhaustive study of salmonid spawning, says, "the eggs would probably not be fertilized at all because the sperm would be carried by the current away from the nest."

Sperm is viable in water only a very short time, and the eggs only for about one and a half minutes. After an egg has been in the water four minutes its shell has changed so much that it is almost impossible for the sperm to enter the minute pore called the micropyle. If the sperm does not penetrate this opening the egg may become infertile.

A few moments after the eggs are laid and fertilized the female moves slightly upstream, turns on her side, and repeats the digging so that the current will sweep the disturbed material over the just deposited eggs to cover them. This task may take an hour or two, or until about two inches or more of gravel and sand are deposited, and in such a way that oxygen can reach the incubating ova. Some salmon bury their eggs to a depth of sixteen to eighteen inches.

The female continues nest building with one or more mates anywhere from a day to a week, or until all her eggs are deposited. The average salmon or steelhead produces only 2000 to 5000 eggs, or somewhat more (compared with millions by cod); the number depends on the species and size of the fish but generally is in proportion to the weight of the fish. Sometimes more than one male may be seen mating with a female, especially in a fast current where a large part of the sperm is carried downstream and perishes. Among the cherry salmon and Atlantic salmon, tiny, sexually mature male parr who have never gone to sea may participate in the spawning act with full-grown, sea-run females.[15]

Only a tiny percentage of the fertilized eggs deposited in the streams are destined to hatch out. The rest are eaten by fish or birds, attacked by fungi and die, washed downstream by freshets, left high and dry by receding water levels, or simply fail to develop normally.

After spawning both males and females live but a few days — none survives. Their spent, discolored, and rotting carcasses line the river or lake banks and are gnawed by wild animals and birds, drift downstream, or disintegrate where they perished, providing nutrients for the aquatic life the hatched-out fish will need to sustain their existence.

Many Atlantic salmon and steelhead trout survive the spawning act and after a respite of several months, during which they lie inertly in shallow water and do not feed, they return to the ocean. On their descent they are sometimes hooked by anglers; in fact, fishing is permitted for "black salmon," as these kelts are called, in the Miramichi River in Canada, and as many as 5000 are taken during the spring season.

In some European countries the kelts are regarded as valuable fish — in earlier centuries they were fed to indentured apprentices even though the fish are tasteless — and efforts are made to facilitate their return to the ocean. In some Scottish and Irish rivers by-passes are provided to enable them to get around hydroelectric dams. Sometimes, in periods of high water, kelts will safely descend over the spillways. In the Columbia River system, however, where there is a network of high dams, no attempts are being made (so far as I know) to facilitate descent of the steelhead kelts to the Pacific. However, many rivers are closed entirely, or in most of their upper reaches, at the end of February to protect spent and spawning steelhead.

How many salmon or steelhead recover from their mating and reach the ocean is difficult to say but the kelt population varies with the river. For example, J. A. Hutton examined 36,000 salmon on the River Wye over a period of years and found that out of every 1000 the scales of fifty-five indicated that they had mated once before and only two had spawned thrice; the rest were "maiden fish." [16] Dr. Arthur Went found a much higher percentage of kelts on some Irish rivers.

Kelts have the same unerring ability to return to the home river as unspawned salmon do. Attempts to relocate these fish by putting them into an alien stream and sending them off to the ocean invariably resulted in their returning to their home river not to the relocated one.

How long do salmon live? Among the Pacific species chinook usually seem to have the greatest longevity, while Atlantic salmon because of their ability to reach the kelt stage and survive outlive all other species. The record is held by a fish caught in Loch Maree, Scotland, which was thirteen years old (as depicted on its scales) when it spawned for the fourth time.[17] Two- and three-time spawners are much more common among steelhead.

Thus we have sketched the life cycle of the salmon. Of the hordes that return to the river, a large proportion are taken by commercial and sport fishermen and so have fulfilled their destiny of providing man with food and sport. Others fail to arrive at their spawning grounds for various reasons — they become exhausted by the need to hurdle natural or man-made obstacles, die of pollution, are killed by predators, etc. Survival of the fish depends mainly on man — on his providing them with clean and oxygenated waters and spawning and nursery grounds conducive to nest building, incubation of the eggs, rearing of the young, and restraint in harvesting them as well. The records of the nations on this score in Europe, North America, and Asia will be the subject of the rest of this book.

Part Two

Fate of
the
Atlantic
Salmon

III ∼

Primitive Man
and the Atlantic Salmon

From the Paleolithic to the Neolithic

IT IS QUITE LIKELY that *Salmo salar,* ancestor of all the salmons, if Neave's theory is correct, preceded on earth the creature we know as man. At least we know that *Salmo* was a distinct genus over a million years ago when the advanced anthropoid apes were on their way to evolving into humanoids.

The earliest traces of early man are his crude stone implements made 500,000 years ago that were found in Pleistocene deposits of the warmer parts of Europe and Africa. Toward the final stage of the Pleistocene, man began to spread over the continent of Europe. At the dawn of cultural development he was primarily a hunter and to some extent a fisherman and food gatherer. His weapons were stones and sharp pieces of wood used for cutting purposes.

The oldest known species of European man was the Neanderthal, short, squat, heavy people who lived in caves in southwestern Europe 70,000 to 40,000 years ago under severe climatic conditions resembling Lapland or Labrador today. They had no tools, though were able to kindle fire, and hunted game with wooden spears and balls of stone or hardened clay used as missiles.[1]

The Neanderthalers were replaced by *Homo sapiens,* a species that probably originated in southwest Asia, who also relied on hunting, fishing, and food gathering for subsistence. The earliest known type was Cro-Magnon, named after the rock shelter of Cro-Magnon near the village of Les Eyzies in the Dordogne Valley, then replete with bubbling streams harboring salmon, trout, and other fishes. In contast to the Neanderthalers, the Cro-Magnons were tall, muscular, well-built, the men sometimes exceeding six feet, with high-domed skulls and refined features. They developed a superior Old Stone Age culture and were skilled hunters and successful exploiters of an environment that was not as severe as that which the Neanderthalers had to endure. The four main cultures associated with the Cro-Magnon, Aurignacian, Gravettian, Solutrean, and Magdalenian, are dated 32,000 to 9000 years ago; the names are taken from the French localities where the caves and cultural and other remains of these peoples have been discovered. From the Gravettian period onward there was an explosion of nonmaterial culture, as the extraordinary cave art attests. Big game still abounded in southwestern Europe, although the climate had ameliorated; reindeer ranged the tundra of southern France and northern Spain; mammoth were plentiful; and wild horses grazed the grassy plains.

In the Dordogne Valley and on the slopes of the Pyrenees and Cantabrian Mountains, the limestone caves afforded shelter in a climate which, in winter at least, resembled that of northern Norway at the present time. With the final retreat of the ice from this region, European man entered the Mesolithic (Middle Stone) Age when the climate was generally temperate and damp. Britain remained part of the continent until rising waters from melting glaciers flooded the southern part of the North Sea bed, about 6000 B.C., and separated it from the mainland. As the glaciers melted or moved up the mountains, the tundra zone retreated and the reindeer, mammoth, bison, and wild horses died out or migrated northward. Forests replaced the tundra and covered the steppes, and small groups of human beings were scattered about in open glades or lived on the shores of the sea or lakes, and along river banks. As big game became scarce they hunted and snared small game and wildfowl and fished more intensively than their Old Stone Age (Paleolithic) ancestors did.

In the Neolithic (New Stone) Age technology advanced by leaps and bounds. Agriculture and animal husbandry were invented, enabling man to live in settled communities; hunting and fishing became less important as food supplies were more assured through farming. Men learned to make pottery and storage vessels; spin and weave, chop down large trees with stone axes, and fashion lumber. Better types of hunting and fishing gear appeared and new devices, such as canoes, nets, and traps, enabled them to expand the harvests from rivers and lakes as well as the sea.

Evolution of Fishing Gear

Even the most primitive humans know that fish can be clubbed in a stream or taken with bare hands, as bears take them with their paws.

When not actively feeding, fish tend to lie in secure places, usually under rocks or in hollows, or beneath tree roots by a stream bank. A hand is carefully immersed in the water and is then moved very slowly and cautiously until it suddenly seizes the fish, whose head is toward the current, a technique called "tickling." Patience, concentration, and some skill are needed, and these qualities the earliest humans certainly possessed.[2]

The spear is believed to be the earliest fishing device. At first it was a sharp stick, and later a sharp stone attached to a wooden handle. Eventually the harpoon was invented; it was really a javelin made of wood and commonly used in the Old Stone Age for hunting and occasionally for fishing. Harpoons had holes for the attachment of lines made of animal or vegetable fiber. Practically every Paleolithic culture uncovered by archaeologists has revealed the use of the harpoon.

With the harpoon large fish could be caught and men were able to depend less on the more dangerous pursuit of big game. It was constantly improved with single and double rows of barbs and has remained one of the basic fishing implements among primitive (and even more sophisticated) people down to the present time. In Ireland the harpoon was used as late as the Elizabethan era to spear salmon from the bridge at Galway.

A major fishing invention during the Paleolithic Age was the double-ended gorge or bait holder. It consisted of small bone rods fashioned by chipping, with a groove or notch in the center, to which a line was attached. The fish would swallow the gorge and a sudden tug on the line caused the points to pierce its gullet. Numerous barbed spearheads as well as gorges were found in Aurignacian cave shelters.

The earliest fishing hooks, apparently introduced in the Mesolithic period, were made of flint shaped like a lozenge or crescent with a notch in the middle for attaching a line. Early fishhooks were barbless. Barbed bronze hooks appeared in Swiss lake villages of the Neolithic Age and iron hooks in later sites in Ireland and elsewhere (one of these is on display in the Natural History Museum in Dublin, dated about 1000 B.C.). They may have been used in catching salmon.

Mesolithic people such as the clever Maglemosians of Denmark, says Grahame Clark, "went in for fresh-water fishing on a considerable scale, using, in addition to fish-spears or leisters, lines with barbless bone-hooks . . . and nets made from the inner surface of lime-bark and provided with sink-stones and floats of tree-bark." That the Maglemosians crossed into England is suggested by the finding of their fish-spear prongs some twenty-five miles from the Norfolk coast.[3]

In time it occurred to some men that while smaller fish may be caught in shallow water with bare hands, or with spears, gorges, and hooks, nets are far more effective. Thus the idea arose of "a seine-net worked from the bank or shore, and back again, by wading or by boat, to enclose a volume of water and 'strain' out of it any fish unable to slip through the mesh as it is drawn ashore."[4]

Some scrawls on cave drawings from Mesolithic habitations may represent nets, but no fabrics have survived. The oldest fish nets found anywhere were in a Danish bog associated with the Maglemosian culture dating from about 6250 B.C. These people lived on pine rafts moored to the shore and fished for eel and pike and ate elk, stag, pig or boar, ducks, geese, and other waterfowl. They were adept at weaving nets of lime-bast to which were attached pine-bark floats. Their wooden spears or leisters would have been appreciated by modern poachers. Grahame Clark in his book *The Mesolithic Settlements of Northern Europe* presents twenty-four designs of nets from Maglemosian sites.

Localities in Switzerland occupied by Neolithic lake dwellers, who built shelters on planks set in the water (as in a dried-up lake near Glastonbury, England), have yielded fragments of flax nets, with bits of wood that served as floats and stones or pebbles for weights. These lacustrine folk also made wooden pirogues well adapted to freshwater fishing.

Practically all the nets in use today, such as dip nets, purse seines, drift nets, trammels, and casting nets, were developed in one way or another by primitive folk on various continents. In fact, there are few modern fishing devices except those operated mechanically or in the open sea that are not basically Stone Age inventions.

Weirs set in the paths of migrating fish may be as ancient as the hook and line. On tidal streams they were originally made of osiers, brush, or even rocks, running diagonally upstream into the current, thus diverting the migrants at ebb tide and making it easy to catch them. Weirs are presumed to have existed in Europe during the Neolithic Age but no traces of them have been found because they were made of perishable materials and in time were washed out.

However, primitive fish traps have been recovered from archeological diggings. Most of them worked on the lobster-pot principle, "being made of wicker, the inturned withies at the entrance allowing a fish to enter with ease, but to find the hole and escape only with difficulty. Bait, or the mere obstruction by the trap-entrance of a habitual channel or passage, causes the fish to enter. Once in, and especially when alarmed and confused, they seldom succeed in finding the way out." [5] Traps have been effectively used to harvest salmon on the Columbia River, in Alaskan rivers, and elsewhere. An example of one of the most ancient fish traps is the osier weel, a conical basket that was set in a narrow river channel to intercept migrating fish, known to have been used in Sweden some 8000 years ago. This device was similar to the putts and putchers still employed on some English rivers.

With the introduction of metal, fishhooks became sturdier and more lethal. The Iron Age also introduced the trident, which became the indispensable weapon of the ubiquitous salmon poacher.

Salmo Salar and the Cave Men

The earliest documented association of *Salmo salar* and man goes back to the folk who dwelt in the caves of southwestern France and northwestern Spain in the Upper Paleolithic period. In caves near the Vézère River, a tributary of the Dordogne, bones have been found (usually a vertebrae column) of fish common in the streams at that time, salmon, pike, bream, carp, chub, and dace, indicating that these species were part of the troglodytes' diet, at least in the Magdalenian Age. It is interesting to note that the salmon no longer come up the Dordogne River as far as the Vézère. A short distance below the confluence of the two streams a bank of rocks, forming a rapid at high water and a cascade at low, blocks fish migration. The bed of the Dordogne has dropped considerably since Magdalenian times, when the river was narrow enough to enable the primitive anglers to harpoon or spear large fish from its banks.

People residing far from salmon and trout streams most likely ventured out in spring or summer to set up stations at natural obstacles where the migrating fish could be taken with relative ease. Traces of such a seasonal Stone Age fishery have been discovered not only in France but at New Ferry on the River Bann in northern Ireland. At the latter site archeologists found polished stone axes and sharp flints that might have been used to rip open the fish before drying and perhaps smoking them.

The high esteem in which primitive men held their food animals is shown in their artistic presentations on cavern walls and floors and

their artifacts and adornments. Fish are not represented on the famous frescoes of big game animals and horses painted on the walls of
Lascaux, Altamira, El Castillo, or other caves, but piscatorial en-
gravings on pieces of reindeer antler are fairly common. Only in a
few instances, however, are the drawings realistic enough to be identified by species: salmon and trout are the most numerous, pike and
eel next, and some members of the carp family can be discerned.

Were the graceful creatures depicted with loving care on limestone
walls, sometimes one on top of the other like a palimpsest, created as
decoration or esthetic expression, or were they inspired by a belief in
sympathetic magic? "The two views are not contradictory, or mu-
tually exclusive, but really complementary," say the renowned Henri
Breuil and his collaborator Raymond Lantier. A man painted or en-
graved or sculpted in those distant ages, as today, for sheer pleasure
and "the society in which he lived attached some importance to his
productions and guaranteed him a living more or less free from daily
cares, because his works had a bearing on the satisfaction of needs
his fellows considered vital for their existence." But the artists may
also have been magicians, "creating for love of art, [and] to increase
and multiply the game they wanted, to make the hunt [and fishing]
fruitful, and to destroy harmful beasts." [6]

The best-known depiction of salmon in cave art is a sculpture in
low relief on the floor of the Grotte du Poisson (Fish Grotto), about
two kilometers from Les Eyzies; the figure is over three feet long; its
head, mouth and gills, the dorsal line, and curving belly are drawn
with great fidelity. There is also a carving of a salmonid on the floor
of the cave at Niaux, near Tarascon-sur-Ariège, in the foothills of the
Pyrenees. The most remarkable perhaps of all salmon items is an antler baton found in the cave of Lortet in France. It depicts four me-
ticulously drawn fish swimming in a river between the antlers and
legs of a pair of stately reindeer. "The reindeer are calm and unhurried," says the anthropologist I. W. Cornwall, "the fish swimming and
leaping at a fall. It is an idyllic scene from life that the artist has por-
trayed, not the mind-picture of a hungry hunter, visualizing the pursuit and death of the quarry." [7] One feels that the untutored engraver
had observed the sleek, finely molded body of the salmon closely in
the water, and perhaps knew its secret — that it leaves its natal river
as a juvenile, wanders for years in the distant sea, and unerringly returns to its home stream to spawn. One can only surmise that primitive man, lacking written communication and using plastic art as his
medium of expression, was already a first-rate naturalist.

A Visit to Altamira

Northwestern Spain, green and lush, with a rugged coast framed by the Picos de Europa mountains towering up to 9000 feet above sea level and numerous swift rivers, abounded with salmon in the Old Stone Age. Overhanging rock faces and deep caverns, such as are often found near watercourses in limestone country, provided excellent shelters. The most famous caves are Altamira and El Castillo because of their superb wall paintings. Recently, a richly decorated cave was discovered at Ribadasella, near the mouth of the Sella, one of the few excellent salmon streams left in Spain; it was occupied perhaps as early as 17,000 B.C.[8]

Altamira was the first cave shelter of primitive man to be discovered in Spain. In 1866 a hunter, who followed his dog who had run into a thicket and fallen between two boulders, managed to remove the stones and free the dog and found he had opened the mouth of a cavern that had been sealed for perhaps 10,000 years. The incident was forgotten until in 1875 the amateur archeologist Don Marcellino de Suatuola made excavations and discovered bones of unknown animals and a few flints. He returned four years later with his young daughter who, while her father was digging in the forechamber, crept into the interior and by the faint light discovered numerous animal paintings on the walls. In 1880 Don Marcellino published his astonishing findings only to be branded a fraud.

But archeologists beat a path to Altamira and after considerable dispute the paintings' authenticity was accepted. Subsequently bones of the very animals depicted were found in the cave. Excavations in the vicinity of neighboring villages, Puente de Viesgo, Torrelavega, and others, laid bare a network of underground shelters occupied during the late Old Stone Age.

Altamira can be reached from Santillana del Mar, a medieval town preserved in amber, as it were. A Benedictine monastery was founded here in the early Middle Ages, and when the body of Juliana the Martyr was transferred to Italy a modest church was built and later replaced with a magnificent Romanesque cathedral. A village grew up around the monastery, and the name of the patron saint was corrupted to Santillana. Only a few hundred persons dwell in this quaint settlement today, but it has a magnificent *parador* and is close to one of the world's most renowned homes of Paleolithic man.

A short walk from Santillana takes you to the entrance of Altamira, situated on a grassy knoll overlooking green and fertile country through which the River Pas flows. As you approach the cavern there is nothing to suggest that you are in a place more historic than Pompeii or Herculaneum. The walls are covered with a multitude of polychrome animal paintings drawn with great fidelity and representing a steppe-tundra biotic community reminiscent of subarctic Alaska before its wildlife was depleted by man and his guns. Bison is the most common animal, lying down, walking, crouching, and in other positions. There are also paintings and drawings of cave bear, horses, deer, and mountain goats. Occasionally human beings appear, drawn merely as stick figures. Many frescoes are in deep recesses of the cavern, which may have been used as a chapel for the performance of magical rites. Radio-carbon dating suggests that the paintings were executed 10,000 to 20,000 years ago.[9]

Such were the details poured out by our guide on a visit to Altamira, leading us from one room to the next dimly lit by electricity. We turned the clock back in our imagination. The people around us disappeared and we saw instead Stone Age folk, men and women dressed in animal skins.

Outside it was bitterly cold, and the landscape was strangely different from the pastoral scene we had seen as we drove from Santander to Santillana the day before. There were then no settlements above ground, no pastures, green fields, cattle, donkeys, dogs, wheeled vehicles, or roads. In the Magdalenian period perpetual snow covered the mountains down to 4000 feet; in winter huge snow drifts piled up around the cave entrances. People stayed close to their snug shelters, and survival was always precarious. Since they had no pottery or other storage vessels, food might become scarce when big game hibernated in the mountains and fish were not running in the streams. Vigilance was necessary in order to keep out the wild animals seeking shelter from the cold.

Inside the cave, spaces were assigned to families for private quarters. One could picture the chambers filled with people; some men were preparing bows and arrows, others carving spears and barbed harpoons; women were making clothing from animal hides with bone awls and bone needles.

During the day, light filtered into the forechambers, but the inhabitants had to sit around the communal fire to keep warm. Women were suckling babies while older children played with their toys. Men were telling stories, perhaps of hunts and fishing expeditions. In a far corner a man was drawing the massive form of a bull on the wall, while a child held a conch-shell lamp filled with animal fat into which a moss wick had been inserted. As water dripping from the ceiling extinguished the lamp the boy quickly relit it. In another gallery a man was modeling a fish in clay, and in a third a crouching figure was grinding a substance, probably ocher, with a pestle in a kind of cup and then transferring it to a hollow bone, which served as a saucer. This was his paint pot.

In the pit meat was roasting, dried salmon and other fish hung from ceiling rafters, and bits of shellfish were strewn around . . .

At last our tour ended. Before we left the cave we passed a little museum at the entrance, which contains a collection of Stone Age artifacts. Here were stone axes, wedges, arrow points, awls, and a considerable collection of sea shells, some of which contained bits of dried-out paints used by the primitive artists, yellow, brown, black, gray, red, and white. They were still usable, we were told, if ground and mixed with oil. In one showcase there was a piece of reindeer bone on which the outline of a salmon could be clearly discerned.

At the foot of the mountain, the River Pas, which nourished the Magdalenians, flowed serenely. Over the centuries its bed had been lowered by about 200 feet, its course has shifted a great deal, and its salmon runs have been greatly depleted as in nearly all Spanish rivers.

R.THURSO

R. OYKUL

R.SPEY

R.DON

R. DEE

Aberdeen

SCOTLAND

R.TAY

R. FORTH

R. CLYDE

Edinburgh

North

Sea

R.TWEED

R. NITH

R. ESK

R. COQUET

NORTHERN
IRELAND

R.TYNE

R. DERWENT

R. TEES

R. EDEN

R. ESK

R. SWALE

URE

R.RIBBLE

R. LUNE

R. AIRE

Dublin

Liverpool

R. MERSEY

IRELAND

R. DEE

R. TRENT

R. WITHAM

W A L E S

R. SEVERN

Birmingham

R. TEME

R. WELLAND

R. NENE

R. YARE

R.TOWY

R. WYE

R. AVON

R. OUSE

R. USK

ENGLAND

R. PARRET

R. AVON

London

R.TORRIDGE

R. EXE

R. THAMES

R. TAW

R. STOUR

R.TEST

R. FROME

R. ITCHEN

R. TAMAR

R. DART

R. TEIGN

Salmon Rivers
of the British Isles

0   25   100

Miles

IV ∼◇

Salmon in Great Britain

HISTORICAL RECORDS dealing with man's use of the salmon and other freshwater fishes in Europe go back further perhaps in Great Britain (including Ireland) than in any other country. *Domesday Book,* the exhaustive survey made by William the Conqueror's agents in 1085–1086 to determine the wealth of his feudatories and their vassals, gives us the first full account. It lists a number of salmon fisheries along with numerous eel fisheries on the coasts and in the river valleys and fenland districts — the people then (as now) were fond of eel, a delicacy that has never found much favor in the United States. Some of the salmon fisheries were on a large scale: for example, a thousand fishes were rendered yearly to the lord of the manor at Gloucester, indicating a considerable run. Lesser salmon fisheries were reported in the counties of Devon, Hertford, and Cheshire. Many of these lucrative fisheries belonged to the monastic orders.

The medieval historians often refer to the plethora of fish in Albion's waters. Thus the Venerable Bede in his *Ecclesiastical History* (eighth century) remarked that the island "has the greatest plenty of salmon and eels." Giraldus Cambrensis (Gerald the Welshman) in his *Description of Wales* (twelfth century) describes salmon fishing in Welsh rivers with coracles (little boats made of skin stretched on wooden frames) that were carried on men's shoulders — Julius Caesar observed such craft when he invaded Britain in 55 B.C. Ranulf Higden, a monk of St. Werburg's in Chester, in his encyclopedic tome *Polychronicon* (fourteenth century) reiterates that England was "rich in noble rivers with plenty of fish; there is great plenty of small fish, of salmon and eels. So that the churls in some places feed fish [probably kelts] to sows." Often these churls, as on the Thames, were brought to court for poaching young salmon and using them as fodder, but they pleaded that they were too poor to obtain any other feed for their pigs, and usually the justice of the peace forgave them since the rivers teemed with salmon young and old.

The Rivers

The majority of rivers in England and Wales are slender bucolic streams, flowing lazily through green meadows, woodlands, and fields, or narrow mountain passes, to the sea. They pass through many an ancient village with a venerable stone church and slender steeple marking its presence in the skyline and with houses in the Tudor, Elizabethan, or Georgian style, hardly altered over the centuries. Or, in another stretch, they flow past a busy market town or a teeming city. They have a special music, sometimes a murmur, or near a rapids a kind of muted roar. Unlike the United States, where vast areas of lovely countryside are being usurped for sprawling suburbs, freeways, industrial parks, and other unesthetic uses, the English countryside retains much of its original beauty despite the growth of population, motor traffic, and industrialization. Many English rivers form a silvery thread that binds towns, villages, meadows, fields, hills, and woodlands together. They rarely run to a hundred miles, and the longest, the Thames, is 210 miles.

Let us visit some of the salmon streams. The sixty-five-mile Eden is partly a border river, dividing England from Scotland; here the antagonism between Scotsmen and Englishmen in past centuries frequently erupted into bloody battles. The scenery is quietly splendid. The Eden rises high up on the moors of the Pennine hills at a point where the counties of Westmorland and Yorkshire meet, near the source of two other prominent salmon rivers, the Ribble and Lune. When it comes into Cumberland, it is a quiet and somnolent stream, though it may plunge occasionally into a gorge, as at Armathwaite, and then pass on by Corby and Wetheral, through parklands or manorial estates where life is not too much changed, with the exception of the motorcar, from what it was two or three centuries ago. Salmon still come up to Corby and are trapped in ingenious "coops" built by the monks in the Middle Ages, but their numbers are greatly reduced and the proprietor of the waters laments their decline.

The eighty-mile Ribble is a much-abused northwest river. It flows past Lancashire cotton towns like Clitheroe and Preston (which helped to ruin the fisheries) and also stretches of exquisite beauty before reaching the trumpet-shaped estuary and dropping into the Irish Sea. Its neighbor, the Lune, is fifty-four miles long and empties into

Morecambe Bay through a seven-mile estuary. Less debilitated than the Ribble, it encompasses some of the most idyllic as well as the most ruined landscapes in England. At Kirkby Lonsdale in Westmorland it passes through "sporting" country where anglers, deer stalkers, and other hunters congregate.

Standing on an old stone bridge on the Lune on a cloudy autumn morning, I watched the late-running salmon move upstream. One could see their tails above the slatey waters as they plowed onward. Occasionally a fish would jump out of the water and display his splendid form. There were no people around except the river keeper casually puffing his pipe, geese wheeled overhead, horses nibbled on the scanty grass by the water meadows, and in the distance one heard the rhythmic sound of a woodsman's ax.

Moving into the Midlands we meet the Trent, which once was heavily populated with salmon. It rises in north Staffordshire, thirty miles from the Irish Sea, and "curls like a whiplash laid across the backbone of England . . . at first southward through the Potteries, then eastward in a great half circle round the southern ramparts of the Peak District, and finally turns due north at Nottingham to run nearly a hundred miles to the Humber Estuary and the North Sea." [1] Trent's waters were once so pure they engendered a brewing industry at Newark, Nottingham, and Burton. Many pleasant little tributaries flow into the Trent, which was connected by a network of canals with all the industrial and shipping centers of the Midlands and thus became a "working river" in which, as in the Rhine, anadromous fish can not live.

The Wye, part Welsh and part English, evokes pleasant thoughts in every salmon angler for it still has more salmon than any river south of the Scottish border. The white, foaming Wye, said Augustus Grimble, historian of the salmon rivers of the British Isles, "races between the hills and hanging woods of the Welsh border. Its banks are hemmed with vivid lines of flowers, and great salmon leap suddenly from dark swift channels." After the Wye emerges from the hills of Plynlimmon near the Welsh border, it corkscrews through the county of Hertfordshire, a rural area with many dairy farms. Much history has been recorded along the Wye by the wild Welsh and their English neighbors, as the ruins of Tintern Abbey, which Wordsworth immortalized in his famous ode, attest:

> Five years have passed; five summers, with the length
> Of five long winters! and again I hear
> These waters, rolling from their mountain-springs

With a sweet inland murmur. — Once again
Do I behold these steep and lofty cliffs,
Which on a wild secluded scene impress
Thoughts of more deep seclusion; and connect
The landscape with the quiet of the sky.

Wordsworth was not a fisherman, but the river and its surroundings must seep into every angler's pores, so to speak. Not too much has changed along parts of the Wye — especially along the classic stretch from Hertford to the Bristol Channel — since these lines were written in 1798.

The 200-mile Severn, second longest river in England, runs down the spine of the industrialized and heavily scarred Midlands, acquiring the flow of many smaller streams like the Teme, Stour, and Warwickshire Avon (which Shakespeare probably fished as a boy). Salmon make one of their longest journeys in Britain in battling their way to its headwaters to spawn. "Times are gone," says Brian Waters, "since [the townsmen] enjoyed the savage festival of poaching the spawning fish, when hooligans with torches and blackened faces speared and gaffed the helpless spent fish." Although considerably reduced in numbers, "salmon still run in pairs in the autumn . . . [and] a spring fish is the talk of the river along the Severn in Wales, for they are the only travellers of consequence." [2]

I know the Severn mainly around Shrewsbury, situated on a peninsula of rising ground and encircled by the river on all three sides. The slow-paced city is replete with timbered houses, many dating from the Tudor era, and is veined by narrow crooked streets, but the supreme interest (to a visitor at least) is the Severn. I have seen it run full and clear at times, reflecting the gray sky on cloudy days and blue sky on sunny days. Part of the Severn was usurped in the later eighteenth century by the ironmongers and bridge builders and later by the porcelain makers. The river now exhibits its best "face" below Gloucester, whence it races fifteen miles to its wide estuary. The Severn and the Wye are two of the score of salmon rivers (each with many tributaries) left in England south of the Scottish border; most of them are in the western part of the island.

A superb little stream in the south of England is the Frome, which Roderick Haig-Brown, the well-known British Columbia angler, fished as a boy. He reminisces: "At that time the Frome, like several other fine salmon rivers . . . was slowly and painfully recovering after bad days. Early in the 19th century it had been a great river with a magnificent run of fish. Uncontrolled netting and some pollution had made it almost worthless, but evidently the run of fish was not quite killed out . . . In the early 1920s there was a good run in the spring months . . . over 20 pounds as often as not and 30-pounders were common." [3]

Haig-Brown remembers fishing to a gallery of ravens and big hawks, ducks, wading birds, and numerous songbirds (for which England is famous). But the river itself was always the chief spectacle. Pike as well as salmon could be caught by skillful anglers.

Typical of the southwest's streams are the Exe and Dart. The former gives its name to Exeter, the impressive cathedral city, gateway to Devon and Cornwall. It rises in Exmoor Forest in Somerset and flows across the two counties, past ancient villages and larger settlements, to Exmouth in Devon, where it enters a seven-mile estuary.

The Dart is half the length of the Exe. I sailed up this delightful stream on a cloudy summer day from Torquay. Gulls nested in the rocky ramparts along the banks; golden wheat waved in the neatly hedged fields; cows dotted the meadows. Dartmouth, mentioned by Chaucer as a famous seaport in the fourteenth century, is now somnolent and far from the sea, with many gabled houses reminiscent of Holland, with which it once carried on a flourishing trade. Some of the villages sit on the banks of the Dart; Kingswear, for example, is a community of steep and winding streets with a tiny waterfront. We saw only one net in the river at Totnes, once a major salmon fishing center described by Daniel Defoe in his *Tour Thro' the Whole Island of Great Britain*, published in 1724–1726.

The largest producers of salmon in England and Wales now are the Wye, Severn, Lune, Dart, Tamar and Plym, Taw and Torridge, Dee, Hampshire Avon, Conway, Yorkshire Esk, Teifi, Teign, Exe, and Ribble.

Salmon enter British rivers at all seasons of the year. For the most part the short west-coast streams have summer and autumn runs only, while east-coast rivers may have spring and winter runs as well. These population patterns tend to change, for unknown reasons.

In the south of England young salmon grow rapidly and tend to migrate at one year of age, while the vast majority of smolts in English and Welsh rivers are two years old when they go to sea. Many rivers have large proportions of grilse.

Scottish Rivers

Scotland on the whole has a more rugged terrain than England. Here are the highest mountains in the British Isles, capped by Ben Nevis, which rises over 4000 feet above sea level. The heather-clad and often peaty Highlands form an imposing land mass that occupies the northern part of Scotland with the Great Glen, once the hideaway of fierce Scottish clans, forming a natural trench running northeast to southwest, dividing the region into two parts. To the west is a mountainous area drained by short, swift, and cold rivers, many of which flow through lochs (Scottish for "lakes") to the sea. These sea lochs, really fjords, penetrate the entire coastline of northwest Scotland and are sometimes of considerable length, like Loch Maree and Loch Torridon. The offshore islands of the Hebrides, separated from the mainland by deep sounds and kyles, are veined by numerous rivers and lochs. Salmon and sea trout are found in most of these rivers and their affluents, sometimes in great abundance.

Much of the Highlands is capable of supporting trees and therefore has been the object of a great reforestation program. Woodlands mean wildlife, and this is the area where deer, elk, and game abound. Towns are scarce, and villages are minute. Crofters and cattle (bred for market) are fairly numerous. Everywhere creeks and rills tumble down tree-lined banks, lakes are numerous, and the vista of sky, water, heather-rich hills, woodlands with their autumnal colors, and rocky summits is memorable indeed.

In contrast to the sparsely inhabited Highlands are the Lowlands, where cereals and other crops are grown and a dairy industry flourishes. Here one sees many prosperous farms, towns filled with substantial dwellings, and factories and mills line the river banks as on the Clyde and Tweed. The metropolitan cities of Edinburgh and Glasgow dominate the Lowlands.

The most important salmon rivers in Scotland are the Tweed (part of which forms the border with England), Spey, Tay, Dee, and Don; all of them flow from west to east. Each has many tributaries, including lakes, and comprises a complex river system. Several west-flowing salmon rivers rise in the high plateau west of the Tweed basin; such are the Clyde, descending from the central Lowlands, the Annan, Nith, and the Esk, which flows into the Solway Firth.

"The scenic charm of Tweed is its own," say Moray McLaren and William B. Currie in their recent book, *The Fishing Waters of Scotland*. "To call it a Lowland river would be unfair, for it passes by many hills that would in England seem considerable; yet it lacks the majestic tumble, flow, and fall of many rivers north and west of the Highland line." No Scottish river has seen more of the blood and thunder of history than this quiet stream, as its numerous towers and castles, many of them in ruins, such as red-bricked Melrose Abbey, attest.

The Spey is a classic type of Highland river, pouring down a picturesque valley, with the snow-capped Cairngorms in the distance. It is about 110 miles long, compared with 96 miles for the Tweed, 120 miles for the Tay, 90 miles for the Dee, and 62 miles for the Don. In its headwaters the Spey is quite slender, but as it flows down the valley, fed by lochs and many burns (creeks), it gathers considerable volume; the upper Spey provides plentiful spawning gravel for salmon. Below Grantown it assumes what William B. Currie calls the character of "a streamy river with a gravelly, boulder-strewn bed," flowing so swiftly that it may tumble the unwary angler and fill his waders with ice-cold water.

Unlike England, it is impossible to obtain statistics on catches in Scottish rivers (except the Tweed), owing to the fact that they are regarded as trade secrets by the proprietors. The Spey undoubtedly is one of the leading and most consistent producers of salmon.

The Tay as it issues from Loch Tay is half Lowland, half Highland river, hospitable to salmon; by volume it is said to be the largest in Great Britain. A description of part of its course and the place names associated with it reveals its Celtic history. "Below Ballinluig the Tay," says Currie, "in majestic sweeps, flows through the rich farmlands of Kinnaird and Dalguise, breaks through the Highland fault at Dunkeld House, and turns on its more easterly course under Dunkeld Bridge, down through Caputh, Delvine, and Islamouth" to the sea ten miles away. Not many towns are found along its banks. The gray city of Perth is the largest.

The Rivers Don and Dee enter the North Sea around Aberdeen, long a major fishing center and now the center of the petroleum industry, which has made rich discoveries in the North Sea. The talk is now of oil as well as fish, and Texas drawls may be heard on Aberdeen streets, a strange contrast to the Scottish burrs.

There are many other Highland and Lowland rivers prized by salmon fishers. I was on the Beauly in Inverness-shire, mostly owned by Lord Lovat, in October 1972, an unusually dry year when creeks and rivers were virtually empty of water and not many spawning fish could be seen; some of these had the white lesions of U.D.N. (ulcerative dermal necrosis), often a fatal disease. The Beauly is dammed at Kilmorack a few miles above its tidal reaches; here a Borland pass, operated hydraulically, lifts the salmon into the reservoir. As many as 10,000 are counted in a good year.

For two days my host and I toured the scenic Highland country called Wester Ross, driving through Strath Farrar, over heath and moorland, and then through Strath Glass, following the river of that name, to Glen Affric. We passed the extensive plantations of the British Forestry Commission and drove west to Loch Duich over the Sheil Bridge. There were no salmon or sea trout visible in the rivers or lochs, the deciduous trees were turning colors, and occasionally roe deer crossed the road on the way to their watering places. Highland cattle grazed the moors. The tiny villages, each with its whitewashed angler's hotel, seemed somnolent; tourists and anglers had departed, and the dining rooms echoed to but few voices. Motor traffic was scanty. The turmoil of the great world seemed far and faint. This is a hunter's and fisherman's paradise.

Every Scottish river has its seasonal run of salmon and sometimes two. The main run may be grilse, which arrives in west-coast streams from July onward; the full-grown fish come in spring on some rivers and in summer on others. Most Scottish salmon migrate to the sea when they are two years old, but many remain three years. The young feed well when insect life is abundant, but when the temperature drops below 45° F. they become less active. The migrations of smolts occur from the middle of April to early June, depending upon the spates and height of water levels. Many of them are known to feed in Greenland waters.

Scottish salmon spawn from September to January; in good seasons the Highland rivers are thick with these lovesick fish. In November, says Fraser Darling, it is common "in some of the eastern deer-forest country to find the small rivers far into the hills almost alive with spawning salmon ploughing up the gravel. The early-running fish usually spawn in the upper reaches and the later ones lower down." [4] The upriver journey against the current is perhaps more exhausting in the eastern than western streams. The number of two-time spawners is quite small.

Fishing Rights

In contrast to the United States, where the rivers are public property (but not the banks), fishing rights in British streams belong to the riparian owners. However, ownership of the bank does not subsume ownership of the water, and fishing rights are sometimes held by persons who have no property along the banks (as mineral rights are in Canada). Thus in effect you can buy the bed of a river because you are buying land that happens incidentally to be covered by water. You are not buying the flowing water although the common law gives you a right to have it in the same quality and quantity as your upstream neighbor received it (a very important right on a valuable salmon stream).

The system of private ownership of flowing water and the inhabitants thereof, residential or migratory, has had crucial effects on the conservation of fisheries in Britain, or lack of it. The monasteries and lay proprietors usually took good care of the rivers and kept fish passes open. But among the most stubborn problems through the centuries were the weirs, cruives, coops, and other obstructions built by riparian owners. Sometimes it proved feasible for a proprietor to throw a dam or weir across the entire width of the channel and thus take all the fish that came up to it, thereby depriving upstream owners of their share. Laws were passed outlawing this practice — Edward IV in the late fifteenth century fixed a stiff penalty of 100 marks for every offense — but they apparently proved difficult to enforce.

Salmon fisheries were valuable properties. Not only did many monastic establishments hold title to important salmon and eel fisheries, but annual gifts of these fish were frequently among the benefactions bestowed upon monasteries by pious donors. As an example, the religious houses of north England, like those at Wetheral, Calder, and Holme Cultram, welcomed grants that added to the supply of fish for their monks as well as providing cash for upkeep of the establishments. The rich abbey of Holme Cultram owned fisheries both in adjacent streams and on the Solway coast.

Protection of the Salmon

In the Middle Ages management of the rivers seems to have aimed generally at wise use and protection of the anadromous fisheries. The kings of England and Scotland from time to time promulgated laws forbidding the blockade of migratory routes and taking of salmon in what they believed (usually erroneously) to be the spawning season, and attempted to regulate the type of gear that was used. The earliest legislation was probably the edict issued by King Malcolm II of Scotland in 1030 that established a closed season for taking "old salmon" between Assumption Day (about the end of August by medieval reckoning) and Martinmas. Violators were to be severely punished. A statute dating from the reign of Richard the Lion-hearted declared that so much of the midstream channel of a river must be kept free of obstructions as to permit a well-fed three-year-old pig, standing sideways in the stream, not to touch either side.

The flow of conservation laws continued in the next few centuries. The statute of 1285 (Edward I) declared that in "the waters of the Humber, Ouse, Trent, Dove, Aire, Derwent, Wharfe, Nid, Swale, Tees, Tyne, Eden, and other waters wherein salmon be taken, shall be in defence [forbidden] for taking salmon from the Nativity of Our Lady [September 8] until St. Martin's Day. And likewise young salmon shall not be taken, nor destroyed by net, nor by other engines, from the middle of April until the nativity of St. John the Baptist [June 24]." The reference to young salmon suggests that the practice of scooping up shoals of parr and smolts continued; these fish were sold for feed at a few pence per pound.

Succeeding English monarchs confirmed and re-enacted these laws, modifying them sometimes in the light of better biological knowledge and adding to the list of specially protected rivers. Richard II made the justices of the peace (like Shakespeare's Justice Shallow) responsible for enforcing the fishery laws by appointing local conservators who continued to exist well into the twentieth century. Local courts of admiralty were given jurisdiction over estuarial fisheries. How effective all these decrees were we do not know, but the fact that successive kings had to reaffirm them, usually with a preamble lamenting the decline of the fisheries, suggests they were perhaps more honored in the breach than the observance.

Leonard Mascall in his *Booke of Fishing* (1590) gives a general picture of the state of freshwater fisheries toward the close of the Elizabethan Age. He reports the use of "fire, handguns, cross bows, oils, ointments, powders, and pellets cast in the water to stun and poison the fish" and the indiscrimate employment of "bow nets, casting nets, small trammels, shove nets and draft nets" taking fish of all sizes in closed and open times. The water bailiffs appointed to guard the streams closed their eyes to these practices, he says, while the owners seemed to be indifferent to what the lessors of the fishings were doing. How widespread these evils were we do not know, but the salmon, being the largest and most valuable of freshwater fishes, probably suffered the greatest depredations.

The laws designed to conserve the resource continued to be reaffirmed by royal decree from time to time. Thus as late as 1714, George I listed the Severn, Dee, Wye, Teme, Wear, Tees, Ribble, Mersey, Don, Aire, Ouse, Swale, Calder, Wharfe, Ure, Derwent, and Trent as requiring special protection, and forbade the taking of fry or adult fish less than eighteen inches long, blockading the streams with dams, hedges, or nets, and fishing during closed seasons, upon penalty of being fined five pounds for every offense and having fish and nets confiscated. No salmon under six pounds from these seventeen rivers, which were then in sparsely populated sections of England, could be offered for sale in London. Justices of the peace were empowered to order obstructions in the rivers to be demolished at the owners' expense. This clause apparently was not retroactive and hence did not apply to longstanding weirs but was used to get rid of certain destructive barriers, usually only after lengthy legal proceedings.

Scottish statutes paralleled the English. A law of 1318 forbade the erection of permanently fixed engines (nets or traps) that would hinder the return of the fish to their spawning grounds. King Robert III in 1400 went so far as to decree that three convictions for slaughtering "redd fish" in the forbidden time constituted a capital offense. Acts of 1424 and 1457 outlawed cruives and weirs that blocked the movement of fishes. In 1489 the sheriffs were given authority to destroy illegal fishing engines. James III created a system of conservators for all the major rivers in Scotland with full powers to enforce the conservation laws and imprison offenders or fine them up to 200 pounds — a staggering sum.

Despite the existence of so much legislation repeatedly enacted over the centuries and the presence of bailiffs and guardians on many rivers, it is certain that illegal fishing — especially poaching — was common in many parts of the British Isles.

Use of the Resource

River fishing for salmon was pursued as far back as the Stone Ages in northwest Scotland, for campsites from this era have been found on the terraces of the River Dee near Banchory. From the twelfth century A.D. onward salmon fishing is mentioned in the grants of property by the kings to religious houses, royal burghs, and the landed nobility. After the Reformation of the sixteenth century these fisheries passed from the religious fraternities, as in Ireland and England, to laymen like the Duke of Gordon and other friends of the reigning monarch.

"All streams, down to the smallest appear to have been fished," says James R. Coull, who made an extensive historical study of the northeast-coast fisheries, but outstanding were those on the Dee and Don (owned by the burgh of Aberdeen) and the Spey (owned by the Priory of Pluscarden and afterward the Duke of Gordon). Of lesser importance were the fishings on the River Findhorn, owned mostly by the Kinless monastery and the Priory of Pluscarden and after the Reformation by the royal burgh of Forres; the Deveron, which belonged to the town of Banff; the Ness, owned by the burgh of Inverness; and the Ythan, controlled by local lairds. The fishings on the Ugie, a smaller river, belonged to the abbey of Deer, on the Nairn to the burgh of that name, on the Lessie to the Bishop of Moray and later to the town of Elgin. All these properties were featured in royal charters and exploited usually up to the headwaters, but most of the fishing occurred in the lower reaches and estuaries, for the charters often specifically convey the right to fish "in salt and fresh water." [5]

The greater part of the harvest in the medieval era was taken for local subsistence but in the thirteenth century we hear of an export trade in salmon in Aberdeen and other Scottish cities. Salmon are frequently mentioned in the Exchequer rolls from the fourteenth century on: between 1307 and 1379 they are recorded from Aberdeen, Banff, and Inverness, in 1467 from Forres and Elgin. In 1488 the Scottish government's revenue from salmon exports was £310, a huge sum, of which 40 percent came from Aberdeen. In the sixteenth century the volume increased when the laymen who obtained control of the monastic fishings worked them for the utmost profit. More and more of the catches went to England. By 1669 some £200,000 worth of Scottish salmon was exported annually, suggesting that harvests were of immense proportions. After the union of Scotland and England under the name of Great Britain in 1707 this commerce was stepped up.

Rentals for the salmon and eel fisheries provided considerable revenue to their proprietors. For example, the lower River Don alone was bringing £30,000 annually in the early eighteenth century.

The chief method of fishing in the medieval period was by net and coble (a short, flat-bottomed rowboat sometimes equipped with a sail) or coracle on the lower rivers, and with fixed "stell" nets along the beaches. Hector Boece in his *History and Chronicles of Scotland* (1527) also mentions the use of traps or creels in the sea. It was customary to build obstructions known as "yares," braes, or dikes to trap the fish or enclose them in stretches of the river. In the sixteenth century cruives or weirs with wooden traps were built across some of the streams. Lines and leisters (long-handled forks with barbed tines) were traditional fishing gear. The latter was the favorite weapon of the "sportsmen" who fished at night from boats with blazing torches. Toward the end of the eighteenth century the main effort around the coasts of Scotland was concentrated on catching salmon in bag nets as they swam along the shore toward their home rivers.

Perth, Berwick, and Glasgow shared the medieval trade in salmon, a commodity which then, as now, found ready markets on the continent as well as England. Except for Glasgow, these cities remain important fish marketing centers.

Travelers have left records of the teeming British rivers. For example, the Spanish ambassador Don Pedro de Ayala, who penetrated into the wilds of Scotland in 1498 as far as the Beauly and Spey, was astonished at the immense quantities of fish taken out of the waters. The Elizabethan "water poet" John Taylor noted the hauls from the prolific Tweed. Richard Franck, who made an angling tour of Scotland in the Cromwellian era, reported that at Stirling "the Forth relieves the country with her great plenty of salmon, where the burgomasters as in many other parts of Scotland, are compelled to reinforce an ancient statute that commands all masters and others not to force or compel any servant, or an apprentice, to feed upon salmon more than thrice a week." The statute mentioned has never been discovered, but similar tales about the overabundance of salmon (probably kelts) fed to hirelings are found in every country (including the United States) where *Salmo salar* once was plentiful.

In the seventeenth century the Rivers Dee and Don together produced about 170 tons of salmon annually. In 1712, 1270 barrels were exported from these streams, chiefly to Germany, Spain, Portugal, and Holland, and in 1713 to Venice as well.[6] Daniel Defoe in his *Tour* took note of the fisheries as well as agriculture and manufacturing wherever he went. The salmon taken at Perth, he said, "and all over the Tay, is extremely good, and the quantity prodigious. They carry it to Edinburgh, and to all the towns where they have no salmon, and they barrel up a great quantity for exportation." [7] At Aberdeen salmon landings were enormous and the profits "prodigious."

In Caithness and the north of Scotland generally there were "salmon in such plenty as is scarce credible and so cheap that, to those who have any substance to buy with, it is not worth their while to catch it themselves. This they eat fresh in the season and for other times they cure it by drying it in the sun, by which they preserve it all the year." On the other hand, at Annan and Kirkcudbright, which at one time had good salmon fisheries, the industry had fallen into desuetude.

In England Defoe, traveling on a spying mission for Robert Harley, Lord Oxford, always with an eye on mercantile life, reported the amplitude of fish in numerous rivers. Thus, the Tamar "is so full of fresh salmon, and these so exceedingly fat, and good, that they are esteemed in both counties [Cornwall and Devonshire], above the fish, of the same kind, found in other places; and the quantity is so great, as supplied the country in abundance . . . The fish have a se-cure retreat in the salt water for their harbor and shelter, and from them they shoot up into the fresh water, in such vast numbers to cast their spawn, that the country people cannot take too many." [8]

At Totnes Defoe saw scores of salmon netted daily. They sold for two pence each, much less than in London where "for such fish not at all bigger, and not so fresh, I have seen 6 shillings 6 pence each given."

Fish was an important item in the English diet from medieval times onward not only because it was obligatory to abstain from meat on Fridays and during Lent but because there was little meat, either lamb or beef, until sheep raising became common in the seventeenth and eighteenth centuries. Fish was available wherever there were fruitful rivers, fresh during the summer and salted or smoked during the winter. Powdered salmon preserved with crushed salt and smoked salmon hard and salty were widely eaten in the British Isles in the fifteenth and sixteenth centuries. Scottish people, including royalty, ate "kippered salmon," probably spawned-out fish.

When supplies were abundant, salmon was peasant's food in north England and even in Wales. Celia Fiennes found at the end of the seventeenth century that the miserable inhabitants had very little meat, poor mutton, but "very good salmon and eels and other fish."

When transportation improved and means of preserving fish in ice (which the Romans had long before perfected) was discovered, salmon could be shipped throughout the kingdom by ship or overland conveyance. Dorothy George in her book *London Life in the 18th Century* says that in 1758 there was at least one London entrepreneur who was an extensive importer of salmon: "He claimed to import 12,000 kits of pickled salmon from Scotland in a year besides great quantities of fresh salmon and from 1500 to 2000 salmon trout from Berwick in a week." He owned six fishing vessels, each with a crew of six to nine men, and for six months in the year employed 1300 to 1500 men in his various activities, which included retailing and whole-saling. [9]

In 1786 George Dempster, a Scottish merchant, began to ship sal-mon in ice from the River Tay to Billingsgate market in London, a dis-tance of 400 miles. His innovation was soon imitated by competitors in Scotland and also spread to Ireland; by 1817 over 700,000 pounds of iced salmon were reaching London annually from the Rivers Don and Dee, and by 1838 a regular boat service was taking fish from Edinburgh to London. If the iced fish arrived in prime condition they could be kept fresh for ten days in cool weather and a week in summer.

Impact of the Industrial Revolution

The turning point in the history of the salmon was the development and spread of the Industrial Revolution in the period from 1750 to 1850. The invention of the steam engine, spinning jenny, and other textile machines; the growth of the iron, steel, and other metallurgical industries, and of coke and coal production; and new chemical and related works, usually situated on once sparkling rivers, helped to seal the fate of the anadromous fishes.

Cotton mills, potteries, and other plants mushroomed and blighted the verdant Midland counties; steel mills scarred the green Welsh valleys. Population grew by leaps and bounds in the slum cities. One by one some of the noblest rivers were poisoned, polluted, canalized, or blockaded, and rendered incapable of supporting migrating fish. Manchester usurped the River Irwell, Liverpool the Mersey estuary, Leeds the Aire, Sheffield the confluence of the Sheaf and Yorkshire Don, Newcastle the Tyne, and the pottery towns of Staffordshire sprawled along the valley of the Trent. Birmingham was situated on the Tame, a tributary of the Trent, and Glasgow on the Clyde.

South Wales became the nation's metallurgical center at the end of the eighteenth century. Swansea, on the River Taw, and its environs had a copper smelter and tin-plating works; Merthyr Tydfil boasted thirteen blast furnaces. In Scotland industrial development and urban growth — the major forces that destroy rivers — centered around the Clyde, Forth, and sections of the Tweed.

Pollution was a major cause of river destruction, but waterways were also dammed to provide power for cotton mills, corn mills, woodworking plants, and other operations, without regard to the needs of the fish. Until the twentieth century there was virtually no effective antipollution legislation or control on water abstraction. Cities ran their liquid wastes into pipes or ditches connected with a flowing stream, while solid wastes were flushed into sewers where they could be carried off into the river by liquid wastes. Excessive abstraction dried up streams at crucial times for the salmon.

Early Victorian capitalists brutally exploited the labor of little children and grownups and brooked no interference with their money-making activities. It was hardly likely that many of them gave any thought to the fishes. They trusted to the beneficent properties of flowing water to dilute and carry out to sea the washings from their mines, the dyes from their bleaching plants, the sludge from their metallurgical works, and the garbage from their towns and cities. This was long before the government of Great Britain dared to interfere and attempt to institute controls that would at least reduce the hazards to human health. It took much longer to pass laws to curb pollution, partly at least, for the sake of the fishes. In fact, this effort still continues without too much success.

We may take the Trent as a classic example of a despoiled river. The headwaters are a network of streams draining the towns where Wedgwood, Spode, Minton, and others established their potteries, the great industrial district of Birmingham, and the manufacturing area around Leicester. Salmon were still numerous in the Trent in the early nineteenth century. In his book *A Natural History of Tutbury* Sir Oswald Mosely says that many salmon were then taken at Kings Mill near Dennington, and that they were certainly numerous on the Dove, Izaak Walton's favorite stream, where anglers awaited them at this point. Some of the fish ascended the falls and went as far as Rochester. Unscrupulous locals "shot them, speared them from accessible points in the weirs, and nabbed them in shallow water out of season. They travelled at the rate of 25 miles a day and often made perpendicular leaps of up to 12 feet." But as the pollution load and number of weirs increased fewer salmon were seen in the main stem or in the tributaries.

The year 1905 was probably the last in which these fishes appeared in great quantity in the Trent, said Kenneth Seaman in an article in *Trout and Salmon* (March 1969). Three heavily polluted tributaries ruined the main river: the Churnet, which runs into the Dove; the Foulea Brook (aptly named), which comes in at Stoke on Trent; and the Tame, which enters at Alrewas. The result was a kind of nightmarish landscape.

Peter Lord describes the Trent at Stoke as it looks today:

[The river] seems almost to be in hiding, ashamed of what it has become, a receptacle for the sewage effluent of teeming Hanley and the waste from dozens of gruesome outfalls. It is as though only darkness could blot out the memory of an upstream landscape so grotesque it could not be imagined: a place where the flow becomes mingled with a series of menacing subsidence ponds, lapping at the base of a gigantic slag heap which smokes sulphurously from the red hot materials tipped at frequent intervals down its obscene flank . . . The flora of Stokes does not extend much beyond the indescribable rush, nor the fauna beyond the brown rat . . . When [the Trent] emerges from its confused passage through the center of Stoke, it has the look about it of a major river in the making, and the smell of a bad dream . . . Foulea Brook alone has more than doubled its pollution level; after wandering for half-a-dozen miles through Tunstall, Burslem and the Etruria district, this tributary deposits into the Trent what can only by stretching the imagination be called water, for its fifteen million gallons a day are an unsavory soup containing among other noxious ingredients roughly a ton of ammoniacal nitrogen.

Beyond the pottery towns, however, the river undergoes a vast improvement. Its banks are "carpeted with greenery and flowers instead of caked with sterile black mud, the fragrance of spring-spurred blossoms or autumn-blown leaves instead of the stench of smoke and sewer, the silver song of black birds. instead of the ranting roar of blast furnaces." [10] The fact remains, however, that for the first twenty miles of its 170-mile course the Trent is today a dead river — fish cannot live in it.

In the early Victorian period 200,000 persons jammed the hideous slums of Manchester. There was not a single public park, and sewage from homes and factories was flushed into the River Irwell so that in time little or no natural water normally entered from the source of the stream in the moors to its grave in Manchester Ship Canal. There was no aquatic life whatever. An unknown bard penned the famous lines in 1901:

> If with a stick you stir well
> The poor old river Irwell
> Very sick of the amusement
> You will very soon become
> For fetid bubbles rise and burst.
> But that is not the worst,
> For little birds can hop about
> Dry-footed in the scum.

In 1877 Archibald Young, Commissioner of Salmon Fisheries for England and Wales, published the following list of rivers affected by pollution, thus giving a comprehensive picture of the impact of the Industrial Revolution on the aquatic environment:

River	Kind of Pollution
Axe	Sewerage
Camel	China clay, mines
Dart	Chemicals, mines, paper works and washings
Dee	Oil and alkali works, petroleum, paper works and wood washings
Dovey	Mines
Eden	Sewage, tin works, mines
Exe	Sewage, paper works
Fowey	China clay works, mines
Kent	Manufactures
Ogmore	Coal, tin, sewage
Ribble	Sewage, factories, chemicals
Stour	Sewage
Tamar and Plym	Mines and clay works
Taw and Torridge	Sewage
Tees	Mines, sewage
Teifi	Debris from slate quarries, mines
Teign	Mines
Towy	Mines, chemicals
Trent	Sewage, factories
Tyne	Chemicals, mines, coal washings

Scottish rivers in the industrial regions were also despoiled and ruined by pollution. Whiskey distilleries poured into the Spey and its tributaries enormous quantities of organic wastes inimical to aquatic life. In 1850 there were eleven distilleries on this river using 2270 barrels of malt a week; by 1900 the number of distilleries had risen to twenty-seven and the weekly consumption of malt to 50,000 barrels. A peculiarly toxic effluent was the result: the residue of the first distillation, called "pot ale" or "burnt ale," killed many fish in the Spey and its tributary the Fiddich before it was brought under control.

The waters of the Gala and Teviot, affluents of the Tweed, were "blae" with the dyes and wastes of woolen mills, though much of the stuff was nontoxic. Fish in the Nith were killed by coal washings, while on the River Doon discharges from collieries and ammonia works poisoned fish on numerous occasions and in 1870 virtually exterminated them for a distance of fifteen miles from the sea. On the Tay the effluents of bleaching works left the lades white with dead smolts.

Raw sewage also contaminated some large Scottish streams. In the Forth many dead salmon were picked up below Stirling at times of low water and more probably were washed away by the tides. On the Clyde and Irvine, pollution practically killed off the anadromous fish runs. A pollution blockade at the mouth of a river, held up for a long distance by the tide, frequently locks out hordes of fish waiting to enter and accomplish their spawning journey.

The destructive effects of industrialization and urbanization were specially noticeable in the Forth, which acquired the sewage and miscellaneous effluvia of Stirling, Alloa, Kincardine, Grangemouth, Queensferry, and later the town and naval station of Rosyth. It was heavily fished by hang nets and sweep nets when the estuarial waters were reasonably clean. "But the deposition of sewage and rubbish, of coke and cinders from the increasing shipping on its waters, and from the gas works and coal pits along its shores, have played havoc with the fauna," said James Ritchie, writing shortly after World War I. "The large members of the fauna [including salmon] have departed, the oyster beds are ruined, the cockles and mussels are not what they once were; but the most rapid change has taken place amongst the shore animals, for in many places the old fine stretches of sand and rocks whereon the people of the towns once spent happy hours are buried beneath many inches of filthy cinders which have altered the courses of the streams and blotted out all traces of life." [11]

It was not only pollution that helped to empty the rivers. Rising prices induced by growing demand and declining supplies generated increased fishing activity. In many rivers the maximum amount of floating and fixed gear was employed, often in defiance of the laws. Highly efficient Scottish-type stake nets were introduced in the early part of the nineteenth century in the north of England, at the mouth of the Tyne (then probably England's richest salmon river), around Morecambe Bay, the mouth of the Trent, and in the Lune estuary. Putts and putchers were traditionally fished in the Severn estuary — in 1860 over 11,000 of these contraptions were in operation. Easily erected and removed, they were catching fish without regard to closed seasons, evidence of the failure to execute the salmon laws.

Poachers worked with impunity, especially in Scotland where so-called sportsmen like the novelist Sir Walter Scott used to treat his guests to the nocturnal spectacle of "burning the waters" on his estate at Abbotsford on the Tweed. It was the custom for Scottish country people everywhere to snatch a few salmon for the pot, but streams like the Tweed were looted by poachers operating singly or in gangs, usually near the spawning grounds, armed with tridents and using dynamite or chlorides to stun and take the fish.

To many respectable people, however, poaching was not a sin or criminal act but a sport. William Scrope in *Days and Nights of Salmon Fishing in the Tweed* (1898) and Thomas Tod Stoddard in the *Art of Angling* (1836) and *Angler's Companion* (1853) glorified the practice for which the Tweed and other streams flowing out of the Highlands were ideally suited. They were "clear and rapid rivers — torrents black with mosses, or pellucid as diamonds — lakes large, and gleaming tarns deep, still and terrible, some stored with prime, subtle trout, and others are frequented by the active salmon." Stoddard admitted that with the leister "vast numbers of salmon loaded with spawn are annually slaughtered, at a time when they can be turned to very little profit, but we are by no means prepared, seemingly, to condemn a practice permitted by immemorial usage, and which obtains the character of a manly and vigorous sport." And it cannot be suppressed, he added, as long as there exists "the old spirit of the Border." [12] It was said on the Tweed that for every salmon caught legally two were taken by poachers until the Tweed Acts of 1857 and 1859 prohibited this kind of fishing and the very possession of a leister made a person liable to prosecution.

Remedial Legislation

By 1860 it had become apparent that many salmon rivers in England, Wales, and Scotland had lost an appreciable portion of their stocks and some were in danger of becoming totally derelict. The old fishery laws promulgated in an agricultural age were poorly enforced and generally ignored and had in fact become obsolete in the industrial era with its growing population, spread of cities, and usurpation of rivers by factories and mills. There was widespread demand by river proprietors, anglers, netters, and publicists, among others, for action to save the salmon.

Charles Dickens in his weekly magazine, *All the Year Round,* of July 20, 1861, issued the cry "Salmon In Danger!" now so familiar to us over a century later. "A few years, a little more over-population, a few more tons of factory poisons, a few fresh poaching devices . . .

and the salmon will be gone — he will become extinct." Parliament must step in, "like a policeman into a riot," he said, citing many examples of wanton fishing and arrogant defiance of the laws.

Parliament had already stepped in before Dickens issued his pronunciamento by appointing a Royal Commission of Inquiry. The commission reported in 1861 that "the considerable diminution of salmon in the rivers of England and Wales was fully substantiated. In some rivers the fact was patent and notorious . . . The instances of extinction were but few; diminution, in a greater or less degree, existed in every river visited. Weirs, fixed nets and fish traps, insufficient close time, pollution, destruction of unseasonable or of immature fish, the want of an organized system of protection, and confusion and uncertainty of the law, were the chief causes of the decrease of the salmon fishery." [13]

The commission recommended the appointment of permanent inspectors of salmon fisheries assisted in their duties by local boards of conservators, the establishment of more uniform regulations for harvesting the fish both seasonally and weekly, and the regulation or suppression of fixed nets and other harmful methods of fishing. These suggestions were enacted into law in the Salmon Fisheries Act of 1861. Additional legislation in 1865 gave the boards of conservators jurisdiction over entire rivers or groups of rivers and introduced a licensing system for both net and rod fishing. Similar legislation was later provided for Scotland.

Appointment of energetic Inspectors of Salmon Fisheries was an important move. Frank Buckland, who held the post from 1867 to his death in 1880, was an ideal choice for the position. He was an enthusiastic fish culturist, a man with a strong sense of humor, and utterly devoted to conservation. His primary duty was to sell the new fishery law to the river owners as well as fishermen and to mill owners and others who were usurping the rivers. Usually, says his most recent biographer G. H. O. Burgess, these people "resented Government interference in what they regarded as their rights. Here Buckland's diplomatic and entertaining manner was of considerable value . . . [He had] a capacity for managing men. He had the happiest way of conciliating opposition and of carrying an even hostile audience with him." [14]

In his first report (1867) Buckland summed up the results of six years of the new fishery act. In eleven of the rivers he inspected some improvement had occurred, in seven little or none, and in five there had not been enough time to show definite results. Pollution and impassable weirs were the most formidable obstacles to migratory fish. For example, on the Severn and its tributaries there were seventy-three weirs, on the Taw and Torridge seventy blocking forty miles of spawning grounds, on the Derwent eight, on the main Dee (in Wales) five, on the Swale six, etc. Many of these weirs had fish passes, but they were not effective. On the Coquet, for example, there was Acklington dam, eleven feet high, a curving wall built right across the river that completely stopped the fish. Buckland saw salmon jumping like "arrows out of a bow, as much as nine feet in the air, again and again, but not one got over." Many gave up and swam back and forth in the boiling water. The Duke of Northumberland, a kindly man who owned the water, was planning to provide a ladder for them, and his plans were nearly completed. So Buckland pinned up a large piece of paper on the weir that read

NOTICE TO SALMON AND BULL TROUT

No road at present over this weir. Go down stream and take the first turn to the right, and you will find good travelling water upstream, and no jumping required. — F.T.B.

Year after year the indefatigable inspector roamed the English and Welsh rivers, noting their condition. He recommended additional legislation, especially the adjustment of seasonal harvests. "Salmon," he said, "will not ascend rivers according to Act of Parliament, but will come up when it pleases them to do so." His recommendation was finally enacted, and the new law, he reported, "takes cognizance of the habits of the fish; and for the future it will be unlawful, without the sanction of the Home Office, for the netsmen in late rivers to catch salmon during certain days in September, and the rods will be allowed to fish during certain days in November."

The indefatigable inspector wore himself out in the post, carrying on a variety of official and unofficial duties, writing endless magazine articles and books, lecturing on fisheries across the land, and engaging in cultural experiments in the hope of reviving derelict rivers such as the Thames. He died in 1880 at the age of fifty-four.

Despite the work of Frank Buckland and other inspectors, it is doubtful if the new laws helped to slow down the decline of the salmon runs. They focused attention on the crucial problems but were easily circumvented for lack of an adequate system of enforcement and failed to tackle one of the most serious evils — pollution.

The state of the rivers was statistically assessed by the Inspectors of Salmon Fisheries for England and Wales in their report for the year 1869: "Out of 36,000 square miles [of water] which ought to be productive of this most valuable fish only one-fourth, or little over 9,000 square miles, produces salmon at all." They concluded that "it is the existence of weirs [mostly used for manufacturing and milling] which has operated against the improvement of other rivers, by preventing the cultivation of the 27,000 square miles of country which I have shown to be inaccessible to salmon." [15]

The Tyne, then the most prolific of English rivers, may be taken as an example of the failure of nineteenth-century legislation. In 1870 the nets, working night and day, took 129,000 salmon out of the river, and the next year almost as many. According to the Inspectors for Salmon Fisheries in their report for 1869, at the mouth of the Tyne one could see, as night approached,

> Hundreds of lights glimmering in every direction from literally hundreds of boats engaged in fishing . . . Nets tied together floating along with the tide barred the passage of the harbor in every direction; it was impossible to reach the harbor without steaming through the nets. I found the more distant nets usually anchored in defiance of the law, and the same men constantly fishing with three or even four nets but with one license.

Deposition of industrial wastes and raw sewage combined with overfishing eventually decimated the runs. By 1900 the average Tyne catch had fallen to 12,000 fish; by World War II, when Tyneside had become the center of a vast industrial complex and the city of Newcastle and neighboring communities poured their sewage untreated into the river, there were very few anadromous fish left.

The Tees, which produced almost 10,000 salmon as late as 1905, was derelict by the mid-1930s, when filth and lack of oxygen made it impossible for salmon to live there. The Severn and Ribble were similarly poisoned and overfished.

Many years earlier Frank Buckland had summed up the plight of the salmon with his inimitable wit in *Land and Water:*

> Perhaps the most unfortunate thing in the world is the salmon. Everybody and everything, from the otter to the fisherman, persecutes him. He is naturally an inhabitant of the sea. He runs up the rivers, and would almost jump into

the pot on the kitchen fire if allowed, but every effort is put forth to keep him at a distance. He gets fat in the sea, though what his food is nobody quite knows. He is in the habit, however, of going up the rivers to his country quarters in the mountains, along with his wife and family. Then almost at the outset, he is caught by a seal lying in wait for him, as in the Tay, for instance. Then comes a net, then a weir, and next a steamer frightens him back; then the refuse from the towns forces him to choose between returning and being poisoned. The weirs across rivers are the main cause why our fisheries have fallen off; yet all that is wanted is a fish-ladder, a series of steps or boxes extending up over the weir. If the salmon succeeds in leaping the weir, he next meets with an angler, who may however fail to hook him; then on arriving at his proposed destination, he encounters the poacher, who tries to spear him with a trident. Escaping him, the salmon at last reach their breeding place, where Mistress Salmon begins stirring the gravel with her tail, and making a hollow nest to lay her eggs . . . The trout then comes to eat the eggs; next a whole swarm of flies and insects; then the water-ouzel, who goes to eat the flies, is shot by ourselves, under the idea that the bird is after the eggs, and not after the flies. Other enemies come; the jack, and the otter who follows the little salmon on their way to the sea, where the angler-fish lies in wait for them. The result is that not one egg in ten thousand becomes food for man.

Destruction of the Thames

The Thames, the longest river in England, is a notable but not unique example of the total destruction of a renowned salmon producer, a fate it has shared with the Seine, Rhine, Connecticut, and many other major waterways in Europe and North America.

Rising on the dip slope of the Cotswold Hills, the Thames acquires the flow of thirteen sizable streams before finishing its 210-mile run to the sea. Much of the landscape of the upper Thames Valley is rural England in its most attractive guise: slow-moving, willow-fringed waters sliding through broad meadows, and a succession of picture postcard hamlets with musical names such as Cricklade, Kempsford, Lechlade, and the like. The lower Thames, like the upper, is a narrow river until it reaches the outskirts of London, having cut through the chalk escarpment in the Goring Gap and entered the London basin. Some of the towns along its banks like Henley, Marlow, and Maidenhead still possess some of their original charms. The river changes its character at Teddington Weir, which is the upstream limit of tidal influence. Around Windsor and Hampton Court it passes willow-bordered banks lined with trim suburban houses and then gives way to the docks, mills, warehouses, power stations, oil depots, and other accouterments of an industrial age that have polluted its waters and ruined fish life. At Gravesend the river is 700 yards wide and gradually broadens until it reaches the main estuary. Nore Lightship, sixty miles below London, is the official terminus of the Thames. Here it drops into the North Sea.

As you stand on London Bridge gazing at the murky Thames, it is difficult to imagine that once it was a pure and limpid stream. Edmund Spenser, the Elizabethan poet, called it "silver-streaming Thames," and fat and noble salmon thrived in it. Underneath this very bridge the fish could then be seen leaping in the waters; fishing stations where netsmen and their boats were ensconced were found at Billingsgate, Chelsea, Wandsworth, and further upstream.

For at least 1500 years the Thames provided sport for anglers. "It is on record," says A. Courtney Williams in his *Angling Diversions,* "that Roman soldiers, set to guard the fort at Laleham, near Staines, saw many big salmon leaping the ford on their way to their spawning beds." The fish originally were found as far up as Lechlade in Gloucestershire. We know that in the reign of Edward III a petition (written in French) was presented to the King requesting him to stop the practice of taking salmon parr (used to feed pigs) from the river between Gravesend and Henley. At the bottom of this document, preserved in the archives of Parliament, there is a note, presumably ordered written by the King: "Let the statute be made held and kept, and on this let Commissions of Enquiry be made and duly punish the defaulters found therein."

In Elizabethan times salmon were caught in commercial quantities at various places on the lower Thames. An entry in the Wandsworth's churchwarden's book of 1580 notes that "the fishers of Wandsworth took between Monday and Saturday seven score salmon in the same fishings, to the great honor of God." [16] Netters operated at Chelsea as late as the reign of Charles II, using horses to draw up their boats. In 1664 Sir Walter St. John yielded his rights to this fishery to local fishermen. The village of Fulham (which lies between Chelsea and Hammersmith) also had a fishery at a rental of three salmon a year, and as late as 1813 an occasional fish was caught there, although by then the species had begun to abandon this stretch of the Thames.

Among eulogists of Thames salmon was Izaak Walton, a London ironmonger, who in *The Compleat Angler* (1653) said that "though some of our northern counties have as fat and as large [fish] as the river Thames, yet none are of so excellent a taste." There were then salmon and plenty of trout in the delightful tributary, the Lea.

What records we have of the fishery in the eighteenth century suggest that the runs were fairly good. On June 7, 1749, forty-seven salmon were taken in one day below Richmond Bridge, in 1754 the haul at London was so great that the price fell to sixpence a pound, and in 1766 some 130 salmon were sent in a single day to Billingsgate. A few years earlier Roger Griffiths, a city water-bailiff, in his book *A Description of the River Thames* complained that the fishery was being ruined by illegal methods of netting and by destruction of spawn and begged "the Lord Mayor, the Conservator of this profitable river, to do all in his power to preserve, and save from destruction the fishery thereof."

Yet the fishing must have remained lucrative, for in 1798 over 400 netsmen were working the river, taking many species, but salmon was always the most valuable. As late as 1810 the nets accounted for 3000 salmon and it was not unusual to take ten in a single haul. But there was trouble ahead, for as the diary of the holder of the fishings at Boulter's Landing (Maidenhead) noted, a steady decline set in: in 1794 he caught fifteen fish averaging 16½ pounds for a total of 248 pounds; 1797, thirty-seven fish weighing 670 pounds; 1806, sixty-six fish, 1124 pounds; 1804, seventy-two fish, 943 pounds; 1812, only eighteen fish, 224 pounds; and 1821, two fish. This was probably the last year he made any effort to catch salmon. The last salmon was taken out of the river in 1833.

Hard as it may be to believe, the Thames used to breed gigantic fishes, comparable to those taken on some Norwegian rivers. Dr. W. Wright in his book *Fishes and Fishing* mentions a seventy-pounder killed in 1798 at Laleham, where the river narrowed and formed what the local people called a "salmon pass." Richard Coxon as an old man told the fish-culturist Francis Francis that he netted a seventy-two-and-a-half-pound salmon in 1820 at Twickenham.

By the middle of the nineteenth century Salmonidae could no longer live in the polluted river. The Reverend Benjamin Armstrong noted in his diary for July 10, 1855:

Took the children by boat from Vauxhall bridge to show
them the great buildings. Fortunately the Queen and Royal
Princes drove by. The ride on the water was refreshing except for the stench. What a pity that this noble river should
be made a common sewer.

The conclusion of a commission of inquiry that looked into the condition of the Thames listed the major causes of the ruin of the fishery
as: (1) deposition of sewage, (2) discharges from gas works, (3) non-
observance of closed seasons by netters, (4) poisonous drainage from
mines, (5) obstructions to fish migration by weirs and stake nets, and
(6) navigation by steamers.

Optimists like Frank Buckland and his friends from time to time
tried to restock the river, laboring under the delusion that all that
was necessary was to release salmon ova or fry, as they did at Moul-
sey and Sunbury in 1860, when an occasional salmon still strayed into
the mouth of the Thames and was taken in a net. Nothing came of
this endeavor.

In 1898, after a report was released that the river had been in some
measure purified, a Thames Salmon Association was formed that in
the next ten years planted about 100,000 fry, but not a single mature
fish was ever recovered.

In recent years pollution has been considerably abated, but only
coarse fish such as chub and dace can live in the Thames, not salmon.

Dr. Carleton B. Chapman, Dean of the Dartmouth Medical School,
in an article in *The Pharos,* published by the Alpha Omega Alpha
honor society in July 1972, points out that the condition of the
Thames is still far from perfect even though the river now receives little or no organic wastes of human origin. Measurement of dissolved
oxygen showed considerable deterioration between 1893 and
1950–1959, and this did not bode well for the reintroduction of
salmon, but in the last decade conditions have improved markedly.
The problem today is that the river is used not only for dumping industrial and organic wastes, but it also receives the discharges of
heated water from power plants. It is unlikely that salmon can live
in the Thames until it is much more fully cleaned up.

The effects of dumping several million tons of sludge annually into
the North Sea has aroused Scandinavian countries; an international
control mechanism is sorely needed. The best remedy, of course, is to
keep organic nutrients and other pollutions out of the river; the organic substances should be spread on farmlands where they will be

useful in building soil fertility and the industrial wastes should be recycled, as many environmentalists are urging.

Resuscitation of the Wye

To resuscitate a major river after it has been ruined as a habitat for
anadromous fishes is difficult and expensive. In the case of the
Thames, a great artery of commerce, it has proven impossible, but the
Wye, a smaller and more bucolic stream, has had a happier fate. The
upper Wye is a magnificent stream, with the water cascading from
pool to pool; lower down it is wide and fast-flowing. Until the late
nineteenth century the Wye was netted all the way to Whitney, ninety
miles from the sea, and illegal fishing was common. Parr were taken
by the bushels, while adult fish were speared in low water or gaffed
on the spawning beds. Even kelts were freely nabbed, for there
seems to have been no enforcement of the Salmon Acts.

H. A. Herbert, historian of the Wye, said the closed season varied
from one county to another, and where the river was the boundary
"fishermen could operate on one side during the closed period and
laugh at their neighbors while doing so." [17] In 1862 the landed proprietors organized the Wye Preservation Society and thus began the
long struggle to revive the salmon runs. In 1875 the Wye Fisheries
Association was formed with the avowed purpose of obtaining control
of the net fishing and protecting the spawning beds. At first the association met with stubborn opposition, but by systematically leasing
netting rights as they came on the market it eventually controlled almost the entire river. In fact, net fishing had so heavily depleted the
runs that the rights had become almost worthless. The association
then began to sublease the fishings to anglers, and in 1901 the Duke
of Beaufort sold his rights on the lower river to the Crown and the
fisheries were taken over by the association.

Wye salmon runs declined gradually until about 1890, then precipitously. In the years 1902 to 1904 all the nets were removed from tidal
waters and commercial fishing was reduced to a minimum. A spring
run was re-established in 1904 and 1905, and in 1909 all netting
above Brockweir Bridge was banned. Twenty years later the Wye
Board of Conservators purchased the remaining netting rights and
then limited commercial fishing to the wide and turbulent tideway.

In a relatively short time the Wye was converted into a premier
sportsmen's river, bringing far more income to the proprietors than
when it was fished mainly by netsmen. By 1931 rod catches were ex-

ceeding net catches and this trend has continued. In the years 1965 to 1969 the nets took 750 salmon per year compared with 5520 by the rods. Now the Wye is the leading salmon angling river in England and Wales and one of the three or four best in the United Kingdom.

A sidelight is cast on the Wye's potential by the record of Robert Pashley, who took 9800 salmon with the fly from this river in a lifetime of angling, 1906 to 1951, averaging over a hundred for forty-one years; in 1936 he killed 678 fish; in 1926, 535; in 1933, 461; and in 1946, 379. These records probably cannot be matched in the entire annals of flyfishing for salmon in the British Isles.

Decline of Scottish Rivers

In Scotland salmon had by the 1860s become a costly food, for here too the supply was declining, although not as rapidly as in England. "Except for the Tay," said Alex Russel, "the decline was universal and alarming, extending over almost every river and district, from the southwestern Doon to the northeastern Dee; although in one or two cases, such as the Spey and the rivers of Sutherland, where the fisheries are in the hands of one proprietor who had resorted to wise moderation, a great difference for the better was discernible." The greatest evil was the excessive number of stake nets, bag nets, and other fixed gear that intercepted the fish as they nosed their way along the shores in search of their home streams. From Buchan-shire to Fortrose the coast was "draped with salmon nets with very little regard to the neighborhood or distance of a river." [18]

As in England, the decay of the resource as reflected in diminishing rentals was manifest enough to prompt Parliament to take action. First came the Tweed Acts of the 1850s that outlawed the deadly stell nets as well as the spear and the leister, reduced the fishing seasons, prohibited dumping of poisonous substances into the waterways, and attempted to remove dikes and dams that hindered fish migration. In 1858 a similar act was passed for the Tay and in 1862 and 1868 came comprehensive legislation for the other Scottish rivers. These laws, it was later recognized, were as weak as or weaker than their English counterparts.

The initiative for better conservation laws in Scotland generally came from the proprietors and especially anglers who repaired to Highland streams for their holidays. In some instances proprietors banded together, as on the Tweed, Spey, Nith, and the Wye, to reduce netting, restock the waters, eliminate migratory barriers, and effect other improvements. Antipoaching legislation with stiff penalties formed part of the conservation program in both Scotland and England.

Despite the Scottish Salmon Fishery Acts of 1862 and 1868, said Commissioner Archibald Young in 1877, overfishing at the mouths of the rivers was still prevalent. "No definition of what constitutes a fixed engine [supposedly barred] is given in the acts . . . The upper proprietors complain that they — in whose waters the salmon are bred — have too little power; and that they have no interest to preserve the fish and prevent poaching, as only a miserable remnant of salmon is permitted to reach their waters during the fishing season and that, until the nets are off, the lower proprietors have a practical monopoly of the fishing.

"Although a majority of Highland streams are uncontaminated by pollutions," he added, "the lowland rivers, and several in Perthshire, Forfarshire and Aberdeenshire are much polluted." [19] The Tweed was a notorious example: there were ninety-three mills and factories in the four counties through which it flowed and most of them discharged refuse of a more or less injurious nature into the waters. Tweed catches of adult salmon (who had been at sea two years or more) dropped from an average of 40,000 in the years 1811 to 1815 to 7400 in 1895 to 1899 and grilse from 68,000 to about 8500. Between 1879 and 1892 some 95,000 dead salmon, grilse, and sea trout were found in this river, probably killed by a disease similar to that which has recently affected British and Irish rivers.

While adequate statistics for Scotland as a whole are not available, it appears that there was a sizable reduction of the stocks during the nineteenth century. For example, the average number of boxes of Scottish salmon sent to Billingsgate market fell from over 30,000 in 1834–1838 to about 19,000 in 1895–1899. Mill dams and pollution in the industrial areas (like the Clyde) put some rivers entirely out of production. There was no strong antipollution law applicable to Scotland until 1961!

Growth of Sport Fishing

While the commercial fishing industry in England and Wales, and to a lesser degree in Scotland, was declining, there was a simultaneous growth in sport fishing, for salmon is widely regarded as the premier game fish, a battler who challenges the stamina and skill of anglers. Salmon and trout fishing is an ancient British sport, but only in re-

cent centuries has it become the delight of kings and queens, aristocrats and commoners. From the time of Dame Juliana Berners (or
Barnes), whose *Treatise on Fishing with an Angle* was published in
1486, after it had circulated in manuscript form for many decades,
the tradition of fly-fishing had been growing in the British Isles.

The industrial era inspired many well-to-do people, including merchants, bankers, politicians, diplomats, writers, and scholars to take
up the sport, to dance a fly on a quiet stream, far from the hectic
counting house, board room, laboratory, or lecture hall. Izaak Walton's *Compleat Angler* was often reprinted and became the *vade
mecum* of fishermen, not so much for its practical knowledge as for
the mood it inspired. The Victorian poet and scholar Andrew Lang,
a devotee of salmon fishing, aptly apostrophized Walton:

> Old Izaak, in this angry age of ours,
> This hungry, angry age — how oft of thee
> We dream, and thy tranquility:
> And all thy pleasures in the dewy flowers,
> The meads enamelled and the singing showers,
> The shelter of the silvery willow-tree,
> By quiet waters by the river Lea!
> Ah, happy hours, we cry, ah, halcyon hours!

Queen Victoria owned six miles of the River Dee in Scotland and
leased fifteen miles more, Prime Minister Gladstone sought respite
from the cares of office on purling Scottish streams, and lesser lumi-
naries filled their notebooks and diaries with tales of adventures in
pursuing *Salmo salar* and sometimes published them.

Lord Grey of Fallodon, Foreign Secretary in the difficult years immediately preceding World War I, expressed the delight busy men
found in fishing: [20]

> It is a great moment when, for the first time of the season,
> one stands by the side of a salmon river in early spring. The
> heart is full with the prospect of a whole season's sport. It is
> the beginning of a new angling year, and the feel of the rod,
> the sound of the reel, the perpetual sight of moving water
> are all with one again after months of longing and absence.
> Every stream looks as if it must hold a salmon, and as if the
> salmon must rise, and one begins to cast trembling with ex-
> citement and eagerness.

Realizing the growing value of salmon water, riparian owners formed associations to protect their interests and to work with the boards of conservators to improve their fishings. Many of them established regulations designed to conserve the stocks; some leased their holdings, while others fished themselves. For example, Colonel Fife Cookson of Lee Hall, who owned two miles of both banks of the Tyne when that river was still productive, never permitted strangers to fish his waters, employed nets and not gaffs to land the catches until the kelts had departed, and limited angling to fly-fishing and only to the least deadly of flies.

In the halcyon Victorian days anglers traveled to their beats in pony-drawn wagonettes or carts. Few or no rod-caught fish were sold — they were given to friends or dependents — and a gentlemanly code of behavior prevailed. The size of the bag might be only a secondary consideration, although many people in their fashion were determined to set records like that of Robert Pashley. Magazines like *The Field* chronicled their feats and catered to their interests, and the number of books devoted to the sport were legion.

In the twentieth century spreading wealth brought salmon and trout fishing into the ken of increasing numbers of people, although it always remained, in contrast to the United States, a prestigious sport and became more expensive as runs declined and stocks became scarcer, especially in England and Wales. Desirable stretches of salmon water fetched higher and higher prices when they came on the market, and the number of clubs and syndicates devoted to salmon and trout fishing multiplied.

New Conservation Laws

Britain sailed along with ineffective fishery laws for three quarters of a century after the 1860s, while many of the rivers continued to deteriorate. It was not till 1923 that the problem was tackled again by Parliament. The Salmon and Freshwater Fisheries Act of that year consolidated all the earlier laws and added important new features. Dams or weirs on fish-migration routes were now required to have ladders or passes approved by the Minister of Agriculture and Fisheries. It became "an offense to pollute waters so as to make them harmful to fish," but practices in use or employed by "prescriptive right" were excepted, "provided that the best practical means within reasonable cost were used to prevent such discharges doing injury to fisheries."

A more important piece of legislation was the River Boards Act of 1948, which for the first time placed nearly every river system in England and Wales under a board responsible for the control of the fisheries, land drainage, and prevention of water pollution. Thirty boards were created, each authorized to tax their counties or county borough councils for funds to carry out needed conservation works, thus adding considerably to revenues obtained from fishing licenses. For the first time these local bodies could obtain the means to hire adequate protective personnel and undertake capital improvements such as building fish passes and hatcheries, do research, etc.

The Rivers (Prevention of Pollution) Act of 1951 empowered the boards to issue regulations (called bylaws in England) that set standards for effluent discharges. It now became an offense to cause, or knowingly permit, poisonous matter to enter a nontidal stream (although previous polluters were not affected). Sewage outfalls created after the enactment of the law required the approval of river boards before they could be licensed. Additional legislation in 1960 and 1961 strengthened the boards' powers to prevent noxious matter from entering tidal as well as estuarial waters — a major step forward in the battle against pollution. In fact, any discharge into a watercourse now required government consent, and the consent had rigorous conditions attached to it; breach of these conditions constituted a prosecutable offense. Whereas the 1951 act referred to new discharges only, the 1961 act covered all existing discharges.

The Water Resources Act of 1963 transferred all the functions of the boards to river authorities, including jurisdiction over freshwater fisheries, pollution control, land drainage, and use of water for agriculture. The act created twenty-nine authorities and added to their function water conservation, which included the protection and proper use of inland waters and water in underground strata, the augmentation and redistribution of water resources, and where necessary the transferring of water resources from one area to another — including the creation of reservoirs, estuarial storage, and recharging of underground aquifers. Over half the members of the new authorities were appointed by local governments and the rest by the Minister for Agriculture, Fisheries and Food and the Minister of Housing and Local Government to represent specifically the interests of land drainage, fisheries, agriculture, nonagricultural industry, and water supply industry.

The river boards have been consolidated into ten regional all-purpose water authorities. Each will have a small membership and the chairman and probably a majority of the members will be appointed directly by the Ministers and the rest by local authorities. The basis for each Regional Water Authority (RWA) is management of each watershed in an integrated manner, somewhat like the United States' Tennessee Valley Authority.

Scotland was slated to have fourteen area boards to manage its salmon fisheries, the first reorganization in over a century, financially supported from license fees that will be required of anglers for the first time in Scottish history.

How effective have all these laws been in saving the salmon resource?

The work of the river authorities has certainly been beneficial in the unending fight for clean waters (and by implication enhanced fisheries). "Each annual report," said the late F. T. K. Pentelow, writing in *Nature* in 1958, "includes an impressive list of new works installed for the better purification of waste waters, and wherever the effluent from these works discharges to non-tidal streams the river board imposes conditions designed to insure that the discharge does not cause pollution." However, there were still in 1958 many streams in the Midlands, South Lancashire, the West Riding of Yorkshire, and the Forth and Clyde areas in Scotland where, Pentelow said, "no fish can live, the water is black, brown, grey or even strikingly colored, where the consistency may be that of thin mud and the odor likely to be a public nuisance."

Yet despite the stronger legislation and greater public awareness, water pollution generally increased in England after 1958, while the Scottish salmon rivers destroyed by the Industrial Revolution have not shown much improvement. Increasing use of pesticides and chemical detergents has complicated the problem because their residues are difficult or impossible to dilute. "The net rate of passage to the sea of polluting matter discharged to an estuary," said B. A. Southgate in his address to the Salmon and Trout Association at its annual meeting in 1965, "may be so slow that a very high concentration accumulates in the central reaches. Also — what was not known before — the rate of supply of oxygen from the surface of the water is surprisingly small," to the detriment of such fishes as salmon, which need well-oxygenated waters to accomplish their migration. Other causes of pollution are sewage from towns and cities, drains from farm feeding lots, etc.

The pollution of English rivers has received considerable newspaper attention in recent years. Anthony Pearson reported in *The*

Guardian of July 14, 1969: "Little notice has been paid to the [Rivers Prevention of Pollution] Act by those responsible for pollution. Moreover, penalties are ludicrously small, the maximum for conviction being £20, mere pin pricks to large industrial concerns . . . It is more than worth their while to pay an occasional £20 for the use of a convenient and otherwise free means of waste disposal."

Brian Silcock in the *Sunday Times* of October 21, 1969, concluded that "after more than 15 years of steady progress in cleaning up Britain's rivers, the process has now come almost to a standstill. Pollution of some rivers is actually increasing again . . . the result of decisions by the Minister of Housing and Local Government not to back river authorities which attempt to improve their rivers except in exceptional circumstances." The nearer the sea the weaker the law: "The Clean Rivers [Estuaries and Tidal Waters] Act only governs discharges which began after it was passed in 1960; and since most estuary towns were tipping raw sewage into their rivers long before then, they can cheerfully continue."

How serious the situation is was further revealed in a series of articles in the London *Times* in March 1970. Yet it seems that the English are at last waking up fully to the extent of water pollution and its menace. Many industries have begun to install, or are planning to install, recycling and other facilities to keep their muck out of the streams. Municipalities are making greater efforts to build sewage treatment plants. For example, Bristol has spent many millions of pounds to clean up its beautiful river, the Avon, and the Thames Conservancy has done yeoman work to cleanse the upper sections of England's prime waterway. The Bristol Avon River Authority is installing fish passes at various weirs on the Avon so that the salmon (which have dwindled away) will be able to reach their spawning grounds some day — now few of these fishes reach the estuary and they are certainly strays.

The Department of Environment's "River Pollution Survey of England and Wales," updated to 1972, shows that "as might be expected, the principal improvements (between 1970 and 1972) have been achieved in non-tidal rivers."

Streams in the industrial and heavily populated belts remain grossly defiled: 57.7 percent of the nontidal Trent is polluted, 62.5 percent of the Mersey and Weaver, 36.8 percent of Hampshire streams, 36.7 percent of Lancashire rivers, 57.1 percent of the waters under the jurisdiction of the Port of London Authority (excluding the London area), and 39.8 percent of Essex rivers. The purest streams are in Lincolnshire; Devon; Cornwall; Wales, including the Wye; and in the upper Thames.

Backing up the war on pollution is a militant nonpolitical and non-profit organization, the Anglers' Cooperative Association, founded in 1948 by a London barrister and angler, the late John F. Eastwood, with the assistance of the Fly Fishers Club. They were determined to fight polluters by asserting common law rights, which say that a riparian owner is entitled to have the water passing his property in its natural state, unaltered in quality, volume, or temperature. Any material change amounts to pollution and hence is an infringement of his property rights. The A.C.A. began to sue on behalf of individual and club clients and forced the courts to rule that anyone, whether an industry, local government, or farmer, who uses the rivers as the cheapest way of getting rid of wastes is breaking the law and must pay damages.

Since 1952 the A.C.A. has prosecuted about 700 cases and scored many spectacular successes. For example, in one case it obtained damages of over £100,000 for fishermen who had their sport killed by factory and other effluent discharges that poisoned the waters they leased. It helped to clean up the River Derwent by forcing the city of Derby to improve its sewage disposal system and successfully fought such industrial giants as English Electric, Monsanto Chemicals, Imperial Chemical Industries (the "Dupont" of Britain), and British Celanese, as well as nationalized industries and small companies.

The A.C.A. has over 13,000 members and member clubs, with a central office at 53 New Oxford Street in London.

Scotland also has polluted rivers and estuaries. "There can be no denying," says William B. Currie, "that this lovely river, the Teith [which flows into the Firth of Forth] is suffering from the effects of the Alloa and Grangemouth pollutions of the Forth estuary. That such foul discharges should be allowed to continue, when there is an Act to prevent it and to provide a remedy, is disgraceful." Not only have salmon catches dwindled in the Teith but sometimes fishermen haul out of the water salmon that are inedible because of contamination by oil. "Further," says Currie, "I know of at least one case where an estuary netting station on the Forth has become uneconomic because of oil-tainted fish."

Other "black" spots are the Rivers Ayr and Lugar, which flow with the slurry from washing plants at the coal pits nearby; here the work of the local Purification Board and the efforts of the A.C.A. have in recent years effected some improvements, but much still needs to be done. The lower Clyde remains a disgraceful stream, although it once had as many salmon as any river in Scotland. It has been a half century since the last salmon, a grilse, was taken out of its polluted tributary, the Kelvin, and was for many years kept on display in a glass tank in a fish shop in Glasgow. The middle and upper reaches of the Clyde, above Bothwell, are still clean and productive and support a large number of trout fishermen.

A factor of some consequence in reducing Scotland's salmon stocks, though unmeasurable, has been the damming of streams to generate electricity. The earliest hydro schemes were developed at the Falls of Foyers on the east side of Loch Ness in 1895, at Kinlochleven in 1906, and at Lochaber in 1921. These were followed by harnessing the falls of the Clyde in 1924 and the falls of the Conon in Ross-shire in 1926 and the Grampian and Galloway projects in the 1930s. After World War II the hydroelectric era really went into high gear with nationalization of Britain's power industry, including generation and distribution, and creation of the North of Scotland Hydro-Electric Board and South of Scotland Electricity Board. In 1968 a total of 2,730,000 kilowatts of capacity was installed in the south and 1,750,000 kilowatts in the north of Scotland (where salmon rivers were mostly affected).

In harnessing rivers such as the Tummel-Garry in the Tay watershed, the engineers attempted to devise, in collaboration with fishery experts, the best facilities as required under the enabling legislation for passing both juvenile and adult fish over the impoundments. W. J. M. Menzies, consultant to the North of Scotland Hydro-Electric Board, said that they tried to satisfy all the interested parties so there would be fish and power too. Among the facilities provided at the dams are fish ladders (at Pitlochry) like those on the Columbia River and fish locks, a unique invention of the Scottish engineer Joseph Borland, which trap the migrants and lift them in a hydraulically-operated chamber up to the reservoir. To offset the drowning out of spawning grounds, the North of Scotland Hydro-Electric Board has opened up many waterfalls to fish migration, thus creating new salmon habitat on stretches of rivers like the Lochay and Braan. Hatcheries have been built to supply stock for planting in Scottish streams. Extensive research on the biology and migratory behavior of salmon is conducted at the Freshwater Fisheries Laboratory at Pitlochry, which provides data for improved facilities for fish migration and other aspects of salmon conservation.

What are the results? Anglers have ruefully watched their favorite rivers drowned out by the dams. They have voiced their grievances in the press and to local and national government officials. They saw favorite beats flooded out, and while owners of the rivers that were inundated, like Lord Lovat who holds title to over 180,000 acres in the Highlands (quite overshadowed by the Countess of Seafield's 305,000 acres and the Countess of Sutherland's 1,400,000 acres), were amply compensated, they were much the poorer, at least in sport. Looking at one of his favorite haunts, now a placid reservoir, the well-known angler Arthur Oglesby probably spoke for many fishers: "This is a very high price to pay for the doubtful benefits of increased electricity."

Speaking of the Tummel-Garry project, William B. Currie remarks in *Fishing Waters in Scotland:*

> The hydro scheme has changed the Garry considerably. The water abstracted from the raised Loch Garry is fed down through the turbines at Invergarry, thus short-circuiting the river for the whole of its course, save for the last, long pool where the river enters the loch. This has had two effects. First, fish that would normally have waited in numbers in the Garry itself do not now do so, and the actual river pools have fallen back in yield, but the effect on the long pool where the river joins the loch has been beneficial . . . [Nevertheless] the feeling among anglers who knew this river well before the coming of the Hydro Board is that things are but a pale shadow of their former selves.

The worst fears of opponents of Scottish hydroelectric schemes have not been realized, although there have been fish losses of some magnitude. One of the most pressing problems is to safeguard the smolts and kelts on their downstream journeys. Fish ladders and lifts are provided for upstream migrants, but smolts are usually allowed to go through the turbines; the kelts are too large to take this route and have to be bypassed around the dams by means of grids or screens.

At some projects, like the Galloway in South Scotland, there was at first a progressive falling off in the runs, then a revival. At most of the installations in North Scotland the stocks have been fairly well maintained with some help from hatcheries, at least until very recent years when the spread of U.D.N. and netting of salmon on the high seas around Greenland began to be felt.

*

The Summing Up

The life of the salmon depends basically on two factors: (1) the condition of the rivers in which they are born and spend their juvenile and spawning phases and (2) freedom to forage in the ocean without hindrance by man, their chief predator. In primitive ages the fishes enjoyed optimum conditions. Human population was scarce and fishing pressures light. The rivers were pure and undamaged except by natural catastrophes like earth slides and other upheavals.

With the coming of civilization, using the term in a euphemistic sense, the anadromous fishes were subjected to new and difficult conditions. Many rivers were occupied by cities, towns, and factories and were soiled, poisoned, and obstructed. Fishing pressure increased relentlessly as the salmon's value rose and the supply decreased.

England and Wales

In England and Wales the stocks declined sharply in the nineteenth and through the twentieth centuries. In the 1870s six rivers, the Tyne, Severn, Tees, Usk, Ribble, and Dart, produced a total of 185,000 fish annually in good years. A century later the total production in these streams was only about 15,000, the Tyne and Tees being totally derelict! Destruction of the Tyne, probably in its natural state the most prolific salmon river in the British Isles, is a disaster comparable to the demise of the Rhine, described in Chapter VII.

In the last three decades total rod and net catches in the rivers of England and Wales have rarely exceeded 50,000; no substantial efforts have been made to augment the runs. The largest producers are now rivers lying mainly outside the industrial centers.

Of the 143,000 salmon and grilse taken by commercial fishermen in 1970, about 90,000 were caught around the coast of Northumberland, mainly fish headed for Scottish rivers. The rods took almost 19,000 salmon and grilse.

Despite the low level of abundance, considerable netting is permitted in the estuaries and along the coasts. In 1971 there were approximately 298 drift nets in operation in England and Wales, plus 224 draft or seine nets, 317 stop, lave, and haaf nets, 8400 putts and putchers (conical baskets set to catch the fish on incoming tides), 32 coastal fixed nets, and 8 traps.

Because of the boom in sport fishing and scarcity of salmon the value of salmon water has risen to astronomical heights. For exam-

ple, the right to fish five eighths of a mile of one bank of the Wye sold
for about $64,000 in 1969. The London *Times* reported on February
20, 1970, that "in spite of salmon disease and other alarms, salmon
fishing continues to attract good prices when it comes on the market."
The Stanley Fishings on one of the best stretches of the Tay in Perthshire, covering about a mile and three quarters of one bank and producing rod catches of over 500 fish annually, had just been sold for
$288,000. In Scotland, salmon water was then valued at between
$600 to $700 per fish caught, based on the average of the previous five
years. Prices have generally trebled in the last decade.

Speaking from the point of view of the angling public, Mr. Charles
Wade, Director of the Anglers' Co-operative association, summed up
the condition of the salmon rivers of Britain at the end of 1972 as follows:

> The rivers in Britain have never been monitored with the
> same interest as they are getting now. And the basic exer-
> cise is to find out how much water, and where, is available
> for the national need for industry and domestic usage.
> Clean water in the right place, and plenty of it, say the hy-
> drologists, is a prime need.
>
> And in all this the fish come a very poor second.
>
> The Department of the Environment asked the regional
> authorities for a detailed record of every river and stream.
> When that record was delivered we could see in black the
> stretches of water that are grossly polluted and in the main
> fish-less. For every 1,000 square miles of territory, we have
> in England and Wales a 43 mile length of water which
> comes into this category.
>
> We also have a vast programme of water abstraction
> planned, which will mean less dilution and more pollution.
>
> The economic value of a river is always weighed against
> the amenity value, and until the two can be linked, the fish-
> ing in British waters, particularly for salmon, cannot give
> cause for content.
>
> Gravel abstraction is also going on apace, which of course
> means the loss of valuable spawning areas.
>
> On the river Coquet in Northumberland which is the only
> purely game fishing river on the East coast, and where there
> is a counting station at the mouth of the river, only one third
> of the 1971 run (barely 500 salmon) passed through in 1972.
> And 1971 was itself anything but a good year.

The Coquet does have some pollution, but it is one of England's purest rivers. It has been hit by water abstraction to the extent that this Autumn on several occasions just over 10 million gallons of water per day went into the North Sea.

Not one game fish river in Britain has substantially improved. They can all be said to have deteriorated.

The Government is anxious to keep in mind the needs of the anglers, but they have in mind some legislation which has made every angler suspicious.

Scotland

Scottish salmon stocks have fared much better than the English, owing chiefly to the slower pace of industrialization and urbanization and the vast extent of relatively pristine habitat, especially in the Highlands. In the period 1960 to 1970 the nets took an average of 393,525 salmon annually and the rods 67,175. Scotland produces about as many Atlantic salmon as any other country, including Canada, as Appendix Tables 1 and 2 show.

As Alick Buchanan-Smith, Parliamentary Under-Secretary of State for Home Affairs and Agriculture, told the annual meeting of the Salmon and Trout Association in November 1971, "Our rivers have a fortunate advantage over many English and even Welsh rivers in that they are, for the most part, free of pollution. Even the Clyde, although it has no salmon except in its lower estuary, provides good trout fishing. The large east coast rivers, ranging from the Tweed in the south, through the Tay, the North and South Esk and the Aberdeenshire Dee, to the Spey, are all relatively free of pollution — amazingly so in this day and age. There is virtually no pollution in the salmon rivers along the north and west coasts and in the islands both Hebridean and Northern."

All the evidence points to the fact, however, that while Scotland remains one of the leading producers of Atlantic salmon, its stocks have measurably diminished since the eighteenth century, although much less than those of England and Wales. For example, average annual catches of salmon and grilse in the Tweed fell from about 110,000 in the years 1811 to 1815 to only 16,000 in the last decade of the century. Since then, according to Colonel R. M. Ryan, superintendent to the River Tweed Commissioners, they have bounded back to about 40,000 annually, but grilse catches are only a small fraction of those reported in the early 1800s.

Reliable statistics for Scotland as a whole are available only since

1952, and they indicate a fairly consistent production. A very large proportion of commercial catches, amounting to over half in recent years, are small fishes (grilse). The Tweed, Tay, North Esk, Dee, and Spey accounted for over half the harvests in the 1960s. The most serious adverse factors have been Greenland's netting and U.D.N. disease. Fish badly infected with this disease have large patches of the fungus *Saprolegnia,* which is ulcerative and often lethal.

Commercial fishing is subject to stringent controls in Scotland. Drift netters took to the open sea in 1960 and returned to port with large numbers of salmon; this situation was permitted to exist until the government in September 1962 issued an order under the Sea Fishery Industry Acts of 1959 and 1962 prohibiting the landing of drift-netted salmon in any port of the United Kingdom.

Nets or traps are used along the Scottish and English coasts, while in the lower sections of the rivers the old-fashioned net and coble (now propelled by an outboard motor) is often employed. The most intense fishing is on the rugged coast facing the North Sea from Montrose to the Moray Firth, and in Northumberland.

As the schools of salmon return from the ocean, they are faced with a breastwork of stationary nets. Bag nets are anchored off the Scottish coast 70 to 100 yards apart, constituting a wall of netting with a leader 30 to 100 yards long designed to lure the fish into the head or trap. Men come out from time to time to inspect the nets and collect the catches, which may consist of a few fish or none, or a hundred in a tide. Fly nets are set between tidal high and low water on sandy shores so that a man can clamber out along the ropes to the head in low water. The collections are taken to netting stations, boxed and iced, and sent on their long journey to market, usually Billingsgate. Some of the inlets along the Scottish coast are so steep that the boxes have to be hoisted up from the beach by winches or carried by sturdy-shanked ponies to the top of the cliff. The nets work day and night with the exception of the forty-two-hour closed period during the weekend, when the leaders of the bag nets are brought ashore to dry, checked, and mended, while the heads of the fly nets are tied up on the poles. On the west coast of Scotland the bag nets are 50 to 100 yards from shore on prominent points like Rhu Stoer, Rhu Coigach, Gailleach Point, Greenstone Point, and Ardnamurchan. The number of nets is limited in order to permit as many fish as possible to escape, but the right to set up these contrivances may be quite lucrative and is zealously guarded by the fishing companies.

Tom Weir in *Scotland's Magazine* of August 1965 describes a morning with the fishermen in the Moray Firth. Leaving Gardenstown about seven, they headed for the coast in a white mist that reduced visibility to a few yards. The screaming of gulls and kittiwakes nesting in the cliffs guided them to their destination — "bird radar," the fishermen called it. When they reached the net the crew of five gathered in the edges and eased it out of the water. The fish are lured by the lead and enter the "poke," where they follow their noses around and around but cannot get out because they use their tails and not their noses as guides. This morning the net held ten glittering silvery salmon, worth 8s. to 10s. a pound at Billingsgate, and an assortment of other species that were discarded as of no value. For every 100 salmon caught the men are paid a bonus in addition to their regular wages.

From the Solway Firth to the Outer Hebrides, and along the northwest coast, this is the rhythm of the salmon fishermen's life, not as romantic or exciting as the quest for herring or cod in the deep-sea trawlers, but the Gardenstown men prefer it because "it is a nice change to be able to sleep at home and do the job of mending nets, etc. ashore." Twice a day and once on Saturday the cobles go out to collect the fish and inspect the nets.

Fishing in the rivers may be less spectacular. The crew moves the coble slowly across the stream, shooting the net as they go, roughly in a semicircle, and finishing at the landing, where the crew is joined by the man with the rope. The ends are then hauled in and the trapped fish, flapping crazily in their endeavor to escape, are removed. If the tide is high and water turbulent the fishermen may use a power winch to pull the rope. The net must remain stationary or drift with the tide. The netting season in Scotland usually begins in February and ends in August.

The Future?

On October 21, 1972 the following letter from a reader appeared in the London *Daily Telegraph:*

I recently attended a symposium arranged by the International Atlantic Salmon Foundation and Atlantic Salmon Research Trust held in New Brunswick, Canada.

All countries interested in preserving the Atlantic salmon were represented in one way or another except Denmark, who pulled out at the last moment, and Spain. Those nations who had most at stake had Government representation except Britain.

The British felt that this was not only an embarrassment to ourselves but also a slight to our host country Canada. The Americans were there in force, including their Ambassador in Canada . . .

If the British Government are really interested in preserving a species which is in great danger of extinction, not least from the Greenland fishery, this really is not good enough.

The salmon of the British Isles is an enormous national resource both commercially and recreationally, and one which we have taken for granted far too long. One has only to look to the Continent to see all too clearly what can happen.

The salmon runs in England and Wales are now at an all-time low. There is need for the English to reorient their thinking about how this resource, which has great historical, recreational, and economic value, should be managed.

The first need is for much more research on the salmon and on the potentials of the rivers that now support the runs and others that may have the capabilities to produce these fishes. There is no up-to-date river survey and little knowledge generally of escapements and size of stocks.

In a report issued in February 1972, the National Environmental Council said there is need for long-term fundamental research on the salmon based on both observation and experiment, on waters under experimental control. It suggested that a river system be studied from source to mouth, including tributaries. The requirements for such a river would be that it is under a single ownership, has an average run of 500 salmon, is uncomplicated by sea trout if possible, has reasonable accessibility, has conditions as natural as possible, and is likely to be representative of a number of rivers.

Second, if the salmon runs are to be augmented, a large-scale program of artificial propagation should be launched; this is now regarded by biologists as a basic tool of management.

What evidence I have been able to find suggests that the economics of such a program would be as feasible in England as it has been in Sweden (whose hatcheries now supply one out of every four salmon caught in the Baltic Sea). M. J. Bulleid, writing in *Salmon and Trout* (July 1972), says that an establishment turning out 100,000 smolts per year could bring the cost down to ten pence (about twenty-five cents) per fish. If a return of 3 percent of the adults were obtainable, the cost of producing one adult for the River Usk, for example, would be $7.50, which by our standards in the United States is not excessive.

Dr. David Piggins of the Irish Salmon Research Trust reports returns of 5 to 10 percent of hatchery fish, and Dr. Carlin in Sweden noted returns of 1 to 17 percent. Higher returns would of course reduce the cost of producing adults. Bulleid concludes, "I am sure that development of the artificial propagation of salmon within the framework suggested above can make this an economically viable concern within the next decade."

Third, experience in other countries indicates that when a resource has reached such a low point as in England, where 40,000 to 50,000 salmon and grilse are taken annually compared to five or six times that number a century ago, curtailment of commercial fishing is clearly called for. A concomitant step would be the expansion of the inadequate research program, which should include an extensive survey of the rivers still capable of harboring anadromous fishes and their spawning and rearing capacities. Britain also desperately needs a school of fisheries — there is none in the British Isles.

As will be evident in later chapters, the program sketched here to augment England's salmon supply is feasible, but it can only be realized if there is a national willingness to save the resource. There are of course many people working toward this goal, as evidenced by the activities of the Salmon and Trout Association, the Atlantic Salmon Research Trust, the Anglers' Cooperative Association, and others, but progress is slow. Sacrifices will be necessary: those who make their living fishing commercially may lose their livelihood, but they would be properly compensated. Anglers would benefit by having more fish to catch. Most important of all, the national government must open its purse, for little can be accomplished without its help. As one biologist put it to me, "It is just as important for the nation to subsidize the salmon fishery, which provides food and sport, as to subsidize a Shakespearean theatre."

As for the Scottish fishery, on the whole it seems to be relatively well managed. Alick Buchanan-Smith, in his address to the Salmon and Trout Association in 1971, said: "It is clear that there are current problems which will continue to affect catches in Scotland for some considerable time. We must, I fear, accept that there is little likelihood of anyone finding a solution to U.D.N. and, as with similar outbreaks of disease in the past, we must simply wait until it runs its course . . . Nor is there any immediate prospect in relation to the Greenland fishery (which takes many Scottish fish) of obtaining a solution which would be entirely to the satisfaction of the interests in this country; but the Government will continue to work with the international fisheries commissions for adequate safeguards for United Kingdom stocks and catches."

In November 1971, the Department of Agriculture and Fisheries for Scotland issued a white paper containing proposals for implementing reports of the Hunter Committee, which made an exhaustive study of Scotland's salmon fishery. The committee's recommendation that all commercial fisheries for salmon should be scrapped and replaced by a single trap in every river that would count the runs and take an agreed and reasonable proportion was rejected, chiefly on the ground of excessive cost. Recommendations dealing with administration of the fishery were accepted: Scotland will have about fourteen area boards, comparable to England's water authorities, which will be responsible for salmon and trout and also coarse fisheries. They will have wider powers than the existing district salmon fishery boards and will be financially supported by license fees (at present no license is required to fish for salmon in Scotland). The government also accepted the Hunter Committee's recommendation that the ban on drift-net fishing for salmon off the coast of Scotland and the Tweed "should be made permanent and steps will be taken to implement this." [21]

V

Salmon in Ireland

"IN TIMES LONG PRIOR to history the coast inhabitants of Ireland utilized the products of the sea for subsistence," says Alfred Moore in his historical study of the Irish salmon industry. "That is proved by the so-called kitchen middens, or shell mounds, frequently found close to where oysters, clams, mussels, and cockles are about." [1] Remains of fish are not as well preserved as shells, but it is certain that the Neolithic (and perhaps Paleolithic) inhabitants of Ireland were attracted by shoals of fish that came up the rivers and learned to catch them, using metal hooks like the one preserved in Dublin's Natural History Museum and making fishing lines and nets out of flax.

We have little information on the early Gaelic inhabitants of Ireland and their food sources, but the Christian hermits who descended upon the island in the fifth century A.D. must have reckoned with the fishing possibilities of their locations so as to have a food supply. Later, when the numerous abbeys were built, the monks usually selected sites close to a stream like the River Cong in County Mayo, where fish, and especially salmon and eels, abounded.

The inland fisheries were valuable assets to the ecclesiastical establishments, supplying food for the monks, of which there were often many (3000 in Cong Abbey alone), as well as revenue from leases. At Cong, incidentally, the monks set a fish trap attached to a bell in the refectory and when salmon entered the stream, the bell was activated and the fish retrieved. Cong Abbey was long ago torn down and replaced with the pseudo-Gothic Ashford Castle, but the fish trap is still there.

Some houses had the right to keep a fishing boat on the river, and frequently they were granted tithes of fisheries in distant waters. According to Dr. Arthur Went, who has made the study of early fisheries his hobby, the bulk of the weirs, elaborate stone structures for trapping fish, belonged to the monasteries at one time or another before their dissolution during the Protestant Reformation. After that they fell into the hands of favorites of the Crown such as Sir Walter Raleigh, who obtained the valuable Lismore fishery on the Blackwater River but had to sell it, for a princely sum to be sure, to the adventurer Richard Boyle, who became the Earl of Cork. This property remained in the family until it came into the hands of the Dukes of Devonshire by marriage in 1758. It remains there.

The Danes, who invaded Ireland from the beginning of the ninth century and established the principal coastal towns, probably conducted an overseas trade in fish using their long, high-prowed black boats (one of which may be seen in the Oslo Museum) as carriers. We know little about this activity, but the Danes gave the names to two prominent localities where many salmon were caught: Lax Weir ("lax" is the Danish name for salmon) on the River Shannon, which had fifty-one stone piers and was fished for about a thousand years before it was demolished, and Leixlip on the River Liffey above Dublin. Giraldus Cambrensis (Gerald the Welshman) in his *Topography of Ireland* (1187) describes salmon jumping over this cataract:

> They bend their tails backwards towards their mouths, and sometimes in order to gain more power for their leap, firmly compress their tails in their mouths. Then suddenly releasing themselves from the sort of circle thus formed, with a particular jerk, like the sudden reaction of a bent rod, they spring from the bottom to the top of the leap, to the great astonishment of the beholders.

Salmon Rivers

Ireland has over 600,000 acres of lakes and some 9000 miles of fish-bearing rivers, many of which are accessible to salmon. The rivers mostly run southward, carving out long valleys and often spreading into lakes that are merely flooded portions of the plain. They cut through the mountain ranges, says the geographer Grenville Cole, "as if they climbed them, and had worked out their valleys like a saw." [2]

Salmon run into nearly every stream flowing out to the indented coast. Many are short and drain lakes of varying size, such as the two-mile-long Sligo, which serves as an outlet for Lough Gill into Sligo Harbour, and the five-and-a half-mile Corrib, which drains three

Ireland

Showing locations of salmon
weirs in former times. Those weirs shown as circles
were described as, or known to be, salmon weirs and
those shown as squares were described as "fishing
weirs," but they were almost certainly salmon weirs.

large lakes. There are also many full-bodied, lengthy rivers populated with salmon and often with eels. These flow serenely under
azure but more often leaden skies, across the purplish surface of treeless bogs or the verdant farmland of the central plain. Thanks to
abundant rainfall, the rivers usually maintain a constant flow that
provides the fishes with plenty of water for their migration. Often the
land is bathed in melancholy mist. The numerous mountains do not
rise much above 3000 feet, and since their mantle of forest has usually
been destroyed — Ireland is probably the most deforested land in
western Europe — they present bare, heather-clad summits and sometimes fairly steep gradients to the wind and the rain. From the air
Ireland seems to have an emerald-green sheen, but on the ground the
landscape is more often brown or rust, yellow or gray like the ruined
medieval stone churches that dot the landscape.

The 190-mile Shannon is Ireland's longest and most majestic river,
rising in the high moors of Cuilcagh, nearly 2000 feet above sea level,
and dropping 1800 feet as it crosses the heart of Ireland to Lough
Allen, among gloomy hills. A slow and deep river, it swallows up, as
it were, a half-dozen lakes.

The Cork Blackwater issues from the uplands a few miles east of
Killarney and its fairy lakes and runs eastward for ninety miles to
Cappoquin, past Fermoy and Lismore (site of a famous and ancient
salmon fishery) and other towns planted on wooded banks that rise
steeply toward the moors. It is a stream beloved of anglers, as the
writer-fisherman Stephen Gwynn said: "a river proper, not the prolon-
gation of a lake system."

The Barrow, considerably longer than the Blackwater, starts at the
northwest end of the Slieve Bloom mountain range in Tipperary at a
height of 1500 feet, maintains a southerly course, and flows through
good farming country. At New Ross it is joined by the Nore and at
Waterford by the Suir, one of the largest of its tributaries. The Nore,
Barrow, and Suir are called "The Sisters," and together they have
produced enormous quantities of salmon. Dr. A. E. J. Went tells us
that in the twelfth century the nunnery of Kilculliheen was endowed
by one Milo Fitzdavid with the right to net the waters of the Clone, a
tributary of the Nore, and by the time of the dissolution this establishment had a number of salmon properties.[3] The priory of Inistioge,
founded in the days of the Celts, also had a fishery on the River Nore,
which in the sixteenth century came into private hands and eventually passed by marriage to the first Duke of Ormond in 1613.

An important river in the north of Ireland is the Erne, about seventy-two miles long, which links a series of lakes in County Cavan and County Fermanagh and reaches the sea in Donegal. This is the region the Irish poet William Butler Yeats made famous. At Belleek, where exquisite eggshell pottery is made, the Erne plunges in a series of rapids toward Ballyshannon, three miles away, now dammed for the generation of electricity and provided with a fish ladder.

An interesting river in southern Ireland is the sixty-mile Lee, coming out of the brow of a deep valley through a series of cascades and eventually reaching the city of Cork (which means "a marshy place"). Its fishes were greatly appreciated as far back as the days of Saint Finbar, a seventh-century monk who founded the city of Cork. William B. Daniel, in *Rural Sports* (1807), noted that "the river produces excellent fish, particularly trout and salmon, the latter are always in season, like those of the River Wye in England." [4]

In eastern Ireland the major salmon rivers are the Boyne, Liffey, and Slaney. The Boyne flows through County Meath from its southwest corner to the sea below Drogheda, while the Liffey, Dublin's river, rises in the Wicklow Mountains, only a dozen miles from the capital, and runs a corkscrew course of eighty-two miles to Dublin Bay. Salmon go up as far as Barrymore Eustace. The Slaney is a moorland stream that comes out of the Wicklow Mountains and flows through counties Carlow and Wexford to reach Saint George's Channel at Wexford. The best fishing is between Bunclody and Tullow.

The six counties of Ulster in Northern Ireland that form part of the United Kingdom are major producers of salmon. The Foyle, Bann, and Erne are the most important rivers. The Foyle is only twenty-four miles long and amazingly productive. It forms part of an extensive river system that drains much of County Tyrone and County Donegal, emptying into Lough Foyle after passing the city of Londonderry. The Bann is a picturesque river coming out of the Mourne Mountains and running for a distance of forty miles past Coleraine into Lough Neagh, the largest lake in the British Isles. I have seen the famous salmon fishery at Coleraine, five miles from the sea, which is privately owned, like most fisheries in Ireland. The eel fisheries on the Bann are also substantial and highly prized by their owners. I watched the eel traps being emptied in October, the end of the season, when there were few salmon left in the river, for the spawning season was at hand and they were in the gravels of the headwaters. The river ran placidly through the green and neat countryside, oblivious so to speak of the civil war that was raging in Northern Ireland, a haven of tranquillity for troubled spirits.

There is a great range of abundance in Irish rivers: in some an occasional salmon enters after an autumnal rain, while in others there are consistently large runs. As in Scotland, grilse (here called "peal") weighing six to seven pounds form up to 80 to 90 percent of the stocks in some rivers. Full-grown salmon may reach seventy pounds in some Scottish streams like the Tay, but the largest known Irish salmon was a fifty-eight-pounder caught on the Shannon in 1872.

The great majority of juveniles leave the Irish rivers at the age of two; their migrations, as reported by Dr. Went on the basis of exhaustive studies, extend from fairly close to the coast to far out in the ocean to Greenland or the west coast of Sweden.

There is usually one predominant age group in each river. Grilse normally come up from the beginning of May until September; small "spring fish," which have been two years at sea, appear at the end of the year and are seen until April; small "summer fish," with over two years in the ocean, arrive about mid-April and are abundant until mid-June, and large "summer fish," weighing from fifteen to twenty pounds, run from December to May. Went reported that on the basis of identification of almost 3000 kelts entering Irish rivers 3.5 percent had spawned twice and 0.2 percent thrice.

Use of the Salmon

The wants of the medieval monks were simple, says Helen Landseth: "a little hut in the wilderness . . . a clear pool to wash away sins, a beautiful, enfolding word . . . Twelve brethren to be in the houses . . . salmon to feed them, and trout, and leeks, and the bees' bland honey. Silence and fervour." [5] In contrast, the peasants were not accustomed to eating fish or dainty meats; they lived in thatched huts with earthen floors (as many still do in the remote parts of Ireland), without ovens or chimneys. In the sixteenth century Fynes Moryson, Secretary to the Viceroy of England, found that the Irish lords and their retainers likewise seldom ate "fish or fowl, though they have great plenty of both, because they will not take pains in catching them, and so leave them all for the English. They gladly eat raw herbs, as water-cresses and shamrock, and most commonly eat flesh, many times raw; and if it be roasted or sodd, they seldom eat bread with it . . . [and] keep most of their corn for their horses." [6]

Irish fish resources were developed mainly by foreigners. Philip II paid a large sum for permission to send Spanish fishermen to Irish waters. Sir Humphrey Gilbert in a report to Queen Elizabeth said that 600 Spanish vessels were fishing off the Irish coast and in the rivers. After the defeat of the Spanish Armada in 1588 these vessels ceased their visits, but in some parts of western Ireland there are still legends of Spanish fishermen and a few jetties are called Spanish piers. During the Cromwellian regime Sweden obtained the right to net the herring and other fishes, and in the reign of Charles II the Dutch were granted the right to exploit the fisheries. Later in the seventeenth century the French became the chief fishers on the coast and in tidal waters. They established themselves at Portrush in the north near two famous salmon rivers, the Bush and the Bann. It seemed difficult to interest the Irish in commercial fishing, although poachers, called "pecharooms," infested a number of rivers. "The want of business capacity, so often bemoaned in Ireland, was then far greater than in our time," says Alfred Moore in *The Irish Salmon Industry* (unpublished).

Until Ireland achieved its independence after World War I, the wealth of the rivers (as of the land) was mostly shipped out of the country. "The Irishman," noted Alexis de Tocqueville during his travels in Ireland in the 1830s, "cultivates beautiful crops and takes his harvest to the nearest port, and puts it on an English ship; then he goes home and eats potatoes. He rears cattle, sends them to London, and never eats meat." This situation had existed for centuries.

Fish was not a staple of the people's diet even when it was cheap and plentiful. After the Restoration of Charles II in 1660 a large fresh salmon sold for only three pence in Dublin and at the beginning of the eighteenth century no more than eight pence. In the year 1689 some 900 tons of salmon were exported from Ireland. Rivers were often jammed with fish, "always fat and never out of season," as an English traveler remarked on visiting the Boyne in the seventeenth century, and this, he added, "is a rarity not to be met with in England." Later travelers echo his words, down to the Great Hunger of the 1840s. The red-flaked fish, dressed in a gallant panoply of sauces, graced the tables of the well-to-do Englishmen, but the common people seldom ate it. In fact, as Cecil Woodham-Smith says in her book *The Great Hunger,* there was scarcely a peasant woman "who could do more than boil a potato. Bread was rarely eaten and ovens were unknown among the lower classes." [7]

Fishing Methods

Salmon were caught in Ireland in the earliest times by fixed engines in tidal waters or the sea (that is, weirs or fixed nets), drift nets, snap nets, spears, hooks, snares, and the like. The most effective of primitive impoundments were the head weirs, V-shaped contrivances originally made of wattles and stakes to set on the seashore or extended across a river channel; they could trap large numbers of fish dropping downstream with the falling tide.[8] These weirs took advantage of the salmon's habit of moving up and down the estuary with the tide, upstream on the flood and downstream when it turned. The funnel of the head weir guided the fish toward the gap where they were taken in the net. In ancient times weirs were quite common on Irish rivers, as at Clontarf, site of the battle in which King Brian Boru finally defeated the Danish invaders on Good Friday, 1014. The head weir near Duncannon Fort on Waterford Harbour was known to have been in place from the thirteenth century to the 1860s.

Since heavy floods would damage or destroy the brushwood weirs they were eventually converted into stone structures like those at Galway and Leixlip. Legislation was passed in 1783 requiring owners to provide a gap, called "the King's gap," so that a proportion of the run would pass upstream to provide brood stock. All but two of the numerous head weirs that were in existence when the Salmon Fisheries Act of 1863 came into effect were declared illegal on the ground that they obstructed navigation.

At the beginning of the nineteenth century some head weirs were superseded by more efficient bag nets or stake nets, introduced from Scotland. In 1863 there were 163 stake nets in operation, of which 97 were on the Shannon, 33 at the mouth of the Blackwater River in Munster, 14 in Waterford Harbour, and 12 on the Foyle. The 1863 act reduced their number to 62, with 48 left on the Shannon. The stake net was a simple affair: it consisted of two parts, a leader and a head or trap. A salmon moving along an estuary or small bay meets the leader and finding its passage blocked swims along into the trap, from which, theoretically, it could escape but once inside the inner pocket seldom does.

Bag nets of similar design were set close inshore along the coasts where the stake nets were useless. There were about 250 bag nets in operation until 1863 when their number was reduced to about one-fifth. Another type of fixed engine that effectively fished the salmon was the riverine weir — their number was legion, and sometimes they remained in place for centuries. There were salmon weirs on the River Boyne as early as 1203. Lismore Weir, built in 1575, was washed away in 1944, after a profitable existence of three and a half centuries. Sometimes weirs were associated with mill dams.[9]

Salmon were also caught with draft seines or haul nets fished from small boats in bays, estuaries, and rivers; they accounted for a large proportion of the catches from at least the second half of the twelfth century.

The Salmon Fisheries Act of 1863, a counterpart of the 1861 legislation for England and Wales, sharply reduced the number of fixed engines so as to lighten the pressure on the stocks. Use of spears, leisters, and similar instruments for killing salmon, as well as night fishing, were declared illegal. A weekend closure was set for the first time, Ireland was divided into seventeen districts with Boards of Conservators appointed for each, and this system remains in operation today, although it has long been obsolete.

While the amount of fixed gear was sharply curtailed by legislation, a drift-net fishery off the Irish coast arose in the later nineteenth century that has since grown to large proportions. Drifters are now up to sixty feet long and carry crews of four to six men. They use nets six feet deep suspended from a cork head rope and weighted very lightly or not at all; every boat is in effect working up to 880 yards of net or about a half mile, the legal limit. At first the drifters fished only at night, but later it was found that good catches could be made in daylight by intercepting the shoals of salmon heading for home as far as ten miles offshore. In recent years drifters have taken about a third of the Irish catch; draft nets (or seines) fished from the banks take 40 percent, stake nets and other minor devices 13 percent, and rod and line 14 percent.

The right to fish appurtenant waters originally went with ownership of the land, as in Britain. Owners of the manors therefore had the fishing rights, but with the passage of time many of the fisheries were sold separate from the land — the same as in England.

Trends in Abundance

Ireland escaped the ravages of the Industrial Revolution by remaining basically an agricultural country and thus a pleasant land to visit. The rivers were usually free of pollution and barricades that destroyed pristine English streams for salmon production. The major evil in the nineteenth century, so far as anadromous fish were concerned, was overnetting. In his book *Salmon Fisheries* (1877), Archibald Young listed fifty-six major rivers in Ireland, of which the best were the Shannon, Erne, Nore, Suir and Barrow, Moy, Ballisodare, Galway, Sligo, Lee, Bush, Bann, Foyle, and Cork Blackwater. The Moy yielded an average of 32,550 salmon annually from 1882 to 1893;

from the Barrow 420 tons of salmon were shipped to England in 1872; and Lax Weir on the Shannon alone took 15,000 fish annually. Young estimated that the rivers he listed produced aggregate catches valued at £400,000, a tremendous sum a century ago.

The first comprehensive survey of the Irish rivers was published by the aristocratic angler Augustus Grimble in the first decade of the twentieth century. He noted that the Irish Inland Fishery Commission of 1903 reported that the coast was lined with miles of fixed nets, many of them working illegally, without regard to closed periods, under the very eyes of the coast guard. Some of the estuaries, like the Garavogue in County Sligo, were "ceaselessly netted by small mesh nets under the pretense of catching small sea fish and flounders, and these nets take myriads of salmon." [10] The drift nets used in coastal fishing were supplied by the fish companies in London, which, "under the cloak of helping poverty-stricken Irish fishermen, only gave them a very small percentage of the profits while pocketing the bulk of it themselves." These nets took the lion's share of the catches, said Grimble, so that every season fewer salmon went up the rivers.

Ticking off the rivers one by one, he found that the Moy, controlled by the Moy Fishery Company, had too many nets in freshwater. The Ballisodare in County Mayo, which flows into Ballisodare Bay, had lost much of its stock. Here in 1853 the proprietor by act of Parliament had erected a fish pass over the shelving rocks and also laddered the tributary, the Owenmore River; he planted salmon stock and eventually built up a run that produced annual catches of 5000 to 10,000. Now, Grimble reported, only some 3000 salmon were being taken. When I visited the Ballisodare in 1963 it was not much improved, though the site was picturesque and especially interesting, for here the poet Yeats had spent many summers as a boy. His uncle George Pollexfen was part owner of the Middleton and Pollexfen flour mill, which took its power from the Ballisodare. The mill was still humming, but the old man who tended the ancient fish ladder did not remember Yeats, though he knew that the poet was buried outside Drumcliff, five miles from Sligo, in sight of the mountains he loved and the island of Innisfree he eulogized.

In his tour of County Sligo and other parts of Ireland Grimble found evidence of much illegal fishing and poaching on the lakes and their short feeder streams. Keepers were scandalously underpaid and hence often connived with poachers to share the loot. Justices rarely convicted offenders — many of them were relatives, and anyhow they were poor people and needed whatever they obtained from selling a filched salmon or two. Likewise the coast guard blinked at the "miles of drift and fixed nets illegally working" under their very eyes, in the estuary of the Garovogue and elsewhere.

Many rivers like the Moy were being overfished in Grimble's opinion but none as much as the Bann, that pristine stream that flows through the soft green landscape of Northern Ireland. "Poor Bann!" apostrophized Grimble. "Never was there a river more suited to give large returns to legitimate fishermen, or to provide the best of sport for the rod. In all our experience we have never come across any river so unfortunate as this one. Others suffer from one or two, or perhaps even several, of the evils already enumerated, but for the unhappy Bann there exists in their strongest form every conceivable evil that is deadly to salmon life." [11]

Grimble found too many nets almost everywhere — "rivers of twine," he called them — working night and day when the salmon were running. On the famous Cork Blackwater, largely owned by the Duke of Devonshire, there were three stake weirs, eighteen draft nets, eighty-nine drift nets, and twenty-seven snap nets in a twenty-mile stretch, or one for every 250 yards. Still it was one of the best salmon waters in Ireland and as an angling river had no peer, especially below Fermoy.

The bulk of the catches continued to be exported; London and Liverpool received most of the shipments. Profits from the fishing industry went to the proprietors, who were usually Englishmen, and the lessors, who were also English. Before the coming of the railroads inland markets for fish caught along the coasts did not exist so that a widespread taste for it did not develop. Men who owned a curragh (coracle) fished for their families or for neighbors and traded their surpluses for potatoes.

Fish vs. Dams

With the establishment of the Irish Republic (Eire) in 1922 the nation launched a program of natural resource development designed to raise the people's standard of living. High on the list was the harnessing of rivers to generate electricity needed to ameliorate the drudgery of farm life and provide energy for manufacturing and illumination for homes and shops. The Shannon River scheme, completed in 1927, was the first and largest hydroelectric project and was followed by the harnessing of the Lee above Cork, the Liffey at Leixlip, the Pollaphuca, the Erne at Ballyshannon, and the Clody.

The Shannon project involved the construction of a dam provided with a fish pass and generating station at Ardnacrusha three and a half miles above Limerick City and a dam at Parteen below Killaloe. Power is transmitted as far as Dublin by the nationalized Electricity Supply Board. The ESB purchased all the private fishings on the Shannon above Limerick and took "statutory responsibility for development of the fisheries, subject and without prejudice to its primary function of supplying electricity." After an initial period of difficulty, during which the fishery could only be maintained at a relatively low level of production, the board launched an expansion program designed to reopen a major area above the dams to salmon rearing and migration. A hatchery built at Parteen produced smolts and younger fish that were released into the Rivers Shannon, Lee, Erne, and sometimes the Liffey to compensate for losses caused by the dams.

Despite the salmon disease U.D.N. and Greenland's netting of Irish fish, the average run in the Shannon in the 1960s was about 45,000 compared with 20,000 in the previous ten years. The count through Ardnacrusha fish pass jumped from 1130 in 1959 to 7180 in 1965. A decline in 1966 coincided with the advent of U.D.N. in the river, but the escapement crept up steadily to almost 7000 in 1969. The hatchery and rearing station at Parteen was producing 200,000 smolts per annum in 1970.[12]

The dam at Ballyshannon on the River Erne is also provided with a fish pass. As one watches the fish arrive from nearby Donegal Bay, enter the long ladder, and slowly climb it to reach the placid reservoir (which drowned out a famous salmon leap), one marvels at the strength and determination of these creatures, trying to cope with man's blockades and rarely giving up. Yet there have been losses here, as at other hydroelectric projects in the British Isles. Commercial fishing has had to be sharply curtailed on the Erne and is now permitted only after the escapement reaches a stipulated level; thus the season may last only a few days or a couple of weeks, depending on the size of the run.

A hatchery and rearing station has been built on the Lee designed to produce 150,000 smolts annually to restock the river, which has two dams, at Carrigadrohid and Iniscarra above the city of Cork, which flooded out a beautiful valley. Natural runs in this stream dropped precipitously, owing to difficulties of migration past the dams and the serious inroads of U.D.N.

On the Liffey, dammed at Leixlip, an ingenious pass that resembles a canal lock was built to permit the salmon to move upstream to their spawning grounds stretching almost as far as Golden Falls dam. However, no longer do anglers try to hook a salmon in Dublin itself, where the Liffey is polluted.

The Irish Resource Today

Ireland, including Ulster (which is part of the United Kingdom), has probably produced as much salmon as any other country in recent years (Appendix Tables 1 and 2). It is one of the few lands where the resource has increased rather than decreased in the twentieth century. This good fortune is due partly to the drastic reduction of fixed gear after 1863 and partly to the relative absence of industrial development and concomitant pollution.

Some 3 million people live in the Republic and 1.5 million in Ulster. Both segments of the island are primarily devoted to agriculture and small manufacturing and are marked by the absence of belching smokestacks and mining activities. There is an extensive cattle industry; along the roads in the interior one may see more cows than cars and men wearing long khaki coats and caps driving them to the weekly market at the nearest town or village. Dairying is widespread and among the pleasantest memories of a visit to Ireland are pony carts taking cans of milk to the creameries, sometimes accompanied by a little dog who trots ahead. Wheat, oats, barley, and sugar beets along with potatoes are the chief crops. The standard of living is still fairly low, especially in the western part of the Republic.

Northern Ireland is a better organized, more prosperous land, with the harried metropolis of Belfast as its chief manufacturing center. The six counties are also delightfully rural, with numerous cattle grazing on the deep green pastures, spruce farmhouses and good roads, and much hog and sheep raising. The rivers are generally crystalline and pure.

Of prime significance in the improvement of Ireland's salmon stocks has been the increase of runs in the Foyle system, which came under the management of the Foyle Fisheries Commission created by the Parliaments of Eire and Northern Ireland in 1952. Purchase by the commission of the valuable fishing rights in the Foyle, and the creation of a licensing system and uniform regulations on both sides of the border, as well as sanctuary areas to conserve fish stocks, have shown remarkable results. Catches in the Foyle District (which account for about 90 percent of the total in Northern Ireland) rose from 45,000 salmon in 1952 to an average of over 100,000 in 1965–1970.

Total catches in Ireland and Northern Ireland were between 1500 and 2000 metric tons annually in the second half of the 1960s — the bulk is exported, although there is an increase of consumption in the Republic's home market.[13]

According to Dr. Went, Inspector of Fisheries and Scientific Adviser to the Department of Agriculture and Fisheries, the Republic's inland fisheries employ some 6000 persons part or full time, of which 3850 are engaged in netting under Common Law rights, 700 in protection of the fisheries during the open and closed seasons, and 750 in netting in the Foyle area, as gillies, or on protection work.

Irish stocks have benefited from the extensive research undertaken by the Department of Agriculture and Fisheries in recent years, which principally concentrated on learning about the biology and migrations of races that frequent the various rivers. Tagging of thousands of salmon and kelts to determine their movements in the ocean has added considerably to the knowledge of *Salmo salar* in the British Isles, including information on growth characteristics of fish, size and age of salmon returning from the sea, and especially migration routes after they leave the rivers. Development of rivers for hydroelectric purposes has necessitated a great deal of research on the problems of passing anadromous fish over dams, both upstream and downstream. Significant advances have been made in the design of fish passes to accord with the peculiar needs of the Irish rivers. For example, Irish engineers adapted the Borland lift, a Scottish invention, and the Denil fish pass, a Belgian scheme, to their streams with considerable success. They improved the technology of passing smolts and kelts around dams.

In 1955 a research program was initiated by the Salmon Research Trust of Ireland, sponsored by the Guinness Brewing Company and Department of Agriculture and Fisheries, centered at Newport, County Mayo, under the direction of Dr. David Piggins. It operates a hatchery that produces about 10,000 smolts per year bred from selected stock for the purpose of studying survival characteristics as a means of developing economical rearing techniques. Returns from these releases reached 5 percent in 1969 and around 3 percent in 1970, much above the general level. The Trust's smolt-producing station is one of the few in Ireland; there is a hatchery on the River Cong that produces 150,000 yearlings per year and another at Parteen, as already mentioned.

Irish stocks have been affected, like the British, by U.D.N., which first appeared in the Cummeragh River, County Kerry, in 1964 and spread rapidly, reaching epidemic proportions in some waters. In 1969 the Department of Agriculture and Fisheries released a report saying that the scourge is probably due to a virus, and the secondary fungus infection that causes the discoloration can be controlled, at least in hatcheries, by the use of malachite green, thus enabling the infected individuals to be artificially spawned and produce healthy offspring. We visited a hatchery in Northern Ireland where this treatment was being given, and the results were quite satisfactory. Treatment of natural waters, however, would be prohibitively expensive and impracticable. By 1972 the disease had tapered off somewhat in both Irish and English waters.

Commercial netting in Ireland accounts for 90 to 95 percent of the total salmon catch.

Let us go to Killary Harbour in Connemara on the west coast of Ireland to see how the fishermen wrest a living from the sea. Flanked by walls of mountains, the harbor winds in from the ocean for eleven miles to its head at Leenane. Two large streams empty here — the Erriff and Bundarogha. On a little inlet to the south of Killary's mouth there is a quay, and among the rocks is the tiny settlement of Rosare, sheltering hardly more than a half-dozen families. Here live the brothers John and Festy Mortimer and their families. They keep a few cows and sheep and do odd jobs when they are not fishing. This includes the building of curraghs, those small wooden boats covered with tarred cloth used by fishermen on the west coast. Curraghs are propelled by oars and manned by two persons who can lift them ashore and carry them above the high tide. In the spring and summer the Mortimers are salmon fishermen.

For generations the local people have gone up the rivers to await the arrival of the spring salmon, due April 20. These are usually heavy fish; later come the lighter and more numerous summer salmon.

"It will be a long time before I forget where I was on April 20, 1964," said John Reader in *Ireland of the Welcomes*. "I merely stood and sat and talked with the Mortimers on the shores of Killary, they had no hauls, nor even saw a fish." Their curragh, moored to a boulder, sat on the beach between the two rivers — the law forbids them to fish within one-half mile from the defined mouth of the river; the net (eighty yards long) was piled ready in the stern; the oars were in the thole pins, swaying with the movement of the sea. The men spaced themselves along the shore. "John had his collar up and Festy whistled through his teeth. They moved about, sitting on the rocks, or on the grassy bank above the beach or sheltering behind the wall of slate, built by the fishermen during the previous season, during the more severe showers."

It was a cold day with intermittent rain, typical spring weather. "You could see the showers coming down the Killary from the west. Leenane was a clump of grey and white a mile or two across the water." When the wind blew, the waterfalls in the mountains looked like white smears. "The new ferns were growing up through the dead bracken — the beginning of Connemara's change from winter rust . . . to summer green."

All day the men kept their eyes on the water. In the summer, when the rivers are low, the salmon congregate here, waiting for the flood to take them up. Now the fish were scarce, but if the fishermen spied a silver flash out of the water they could be in their curragh in thirty seconds; the net would be laid out and the salmon swiftly encircled. When the fish were running, a single haul might bring fifty; indeed, a few years earlier virtually every crew around the coast took thousands during the season, although they only fetched two shillings a pound.

"With talk, showers and some sun, tea, Festy's singing, mostly rebel songs, and waiting, the day passed," said Reader. "Six-thirty came and it ended — no fish. They put the net out on the steep bank and left the Killary. If they had been catching fish they would have waited until dark . . .

"They would be back the next day and the next; as the summer came their days would become longer, from 7 or 8 A.M. until 10 at night, catching salmon and waiting for them. 'I've been on the Killary 35 years,' says Festy. 'Often waited three weeks, and more, without a fish. It's better we're here waiting for him than him waiting for us. He has to come sometime.' " [14]

Angler's Paradise?

Anglers took an average of 36,300 salmon from 1960 to 1969 in Ireland. Sport fishing is an important producer of foreign exchange and at the same time creates employment for persons catering to fishermen in hotels and inns, gillies, and the like. The number of rod licenses issued jumped from 5100 in 1950 to around 10,000 in the late 1960s. Dr. Went has estimated that every visiting angler spends not less than £30 ($78) to hook a salmon, and since many bring their wives and children, additional revenue accrues.

Ireland is becoming known as an anglers' paradise. The pristine rivers, the slow, lazy tempo of life, the sparse population and empty roads away from the capital are potent attractions. The courtesy and hospitality of the people, and not least the relative abundance of freshwater fishes, lure increasing numbers from abroad. In Ireland it is perhaps truer than in other countries that as Viscount Grey of Fallodon said in his classic *Fly Fishing*, "every stream looks as if it must hold a salmon, and as if the salmon must rise, and one begins to cast trembling with excitement and eagerness."

The best salmon water is privately owned and strictly preserved, but beats can be hired from proprietors or inns, often at moderate prices. Recognizing the great demand for fishing, the Irish Tourist Board has advertised Ireland's angling potentials widely. About 15 percent of the annual salmon and grilse catch is taken by rods.

In 1970 the Irish Tourist Board invited Peter Liddell, a member of the English Sports Council, to survey the Republic's salmon rivers and recommend improvements in their management. His report, released in February 1971, covered visits to about fifty rivers and was the first comprehensive survey since Augustus Grimble published his book *The Salmon Rivers of Ireland* in 1903.

Liddell found many things to criticize. He thought that the division of the Republic into seventeen districts with Boards of Conservators supervising them was out of date. The boards seemed to be incapable of carrying out their responsibilities:

> I found widespread frustration, amounting in many cases to despair, among members and staffs of Boards at their inability to do almost any of the work which they clearly see to be necessary. They have inadequate powers, inadequate resources and inadequate staffs; the structure of membership is quite unsuited for the task and none of them feels that it is properly backed by the Department of Fisheries.[15]

Boards have no power to alter licenses duties, no power to refuse a net license, no power to regulate the number of nets, no money to employ patrol boats or vehicles for their staffs, and in most districts there is widespread resentment at the lack of support given to the boards by the courts.

From ancient times poaching has been a great evil. The maximum penalty, rarely imposed, is £25 (compared with £100 fine and two years' imprisonment in England plus forfeiture of any boat or vehicle used for taking or destroying fish by poison). In Ireland, said Liddell, the first offense usually brings a one- or two-pound fine, imprisonment never, and there have been cases where the fine was but a few pence. In contrast to poor management by the Boards of Conservators was the excellent management of the Rivers Lee, Shannon, Erne, and Clody by the Electricity Supply Board.

Liddell concluded that "the salmon rivers are in decline, and unless legislative and administrative remedial action is taken with the utmost urgency, this decline will continue to a stage when the rivers will cease to be attractive to tourists." His major recommendations are that the present system of district boards be abolished and instead six regional boards established, financed by grants from the government, license fees, taxes, etc., to carry out the functions of fishery management, pollution prevention, and land drainage; a national policy for the uses of rivers be formulated; "the commercial salmon fishing should be regulated so as to allow for attractive and successful angling"; and a nationwide system of river monitoring be instituted. Most important of all is the need for better regulation of closed seasons and fishing gear, and reduction of drift netting in the ocean which takes an excessive toll of the stocks.

In 1973 the government took effective steps to reduce drift netting, which in 1972 reached a record high when every available boat went to sea off the southwest coast to cash in on the salmon boom. Licenses were limited to 649, the approximate average from 1969 to 1971, or about half the number issued in 1972.

In recent years the rights of foreign owners of salmon rivers have been challenged by an organization called the National Waters Restoration League. It claims to have nineteen branches and is dedicated to the purpose of converting all rivers owned by foreigners to public ownership and management by the local community for the benefit of the community. Expropriation of titles to rivers without compensation is their goal, although "gratuities" might be considered in hardship cases.

To advance their program the league has staged destructive "fish-ins" on private waters, defying the authorities by taking salmon from private preserves, and in the common parlance "raising hell" wherever they could. Their main argument is, says Liddell, "with some justification, that under the present system many rivers are neglected or being allowed to deteriorate; therefore, this system is no good and must be replaced by national ownership." The league's activities seem to have begun to prod the government into a more realistic consideration of the problems of freshwater fisheries, including their ownership. According to Dr. Piggins, the league "has already ruined much of the fishing on the River Moyne." [16]

Summing up the Irish salmon situation, one might say that while this "undeveloped land" has so far escaped the great evils of water pollution and river destruction, it has perhaps been complacent and lackadaisical about its freshwater fisheries. The troubles in Northern Ireland have greatly reduced the visits of foreign anglers to the Republic. Now the time has come, as Liddell suggests, for the government to take a hard look at this valuable asset, to reorganize the system of management, and to allocate more funds for the conservation and augmentation of the resource.

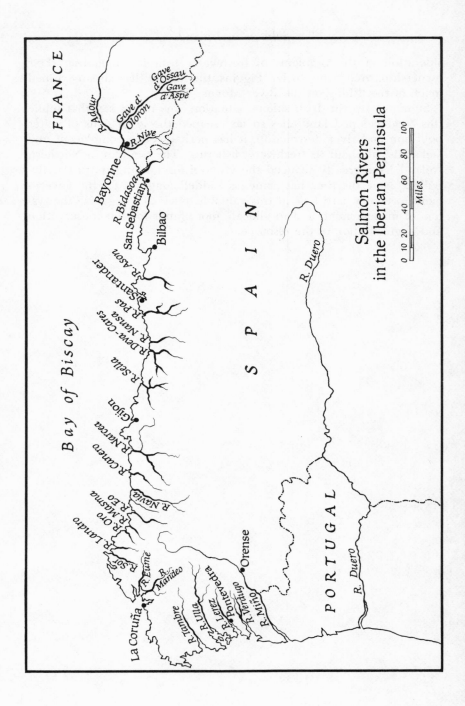

FRANCE

R. Adour

Gave d'Ossau
Gave d' Oloron
Gave d'Aspe

R. Nive

Bayonne

R. Bidasoa

San Sebastián

Bilbao

R. Ason

Santander

R. Pas

R. Nansa

R. Deva-Cares

R. Sella

Gijón

R. Narcea

R. Canero

R. Navia

R. Eo

R. Masma

R. Oro

R. Sor

R. Landro

R. Eume

R. Mandeo

La Coruña

R. Tambre

R. Ulla

R. Lerez

R. Pontevedra

R. Verdugo

R. Miño

Orense

R. Duero

R. Duero

Bay of Biscay

S P A I N

PORTUGAL

Salmon Rivers
in the Iberian Peninsula

0 10 20   40   60   80   100
Miles

VI ∽

Iberian and French Salmon

THE FATE OF *Salmo salar* on the continent of Europe has to a large extent paralleled its history in the British Isles. Some of the nations — notably Holland, Portugal, Denmark, Switzerland, Belgium, and Germany — drove these noble fishes from the rivers, while others reduced them to a token resource. A few countries have made strenuous efforts to conserve the stocks.

Portugal and Spain

The Iberian peninsula is well favored with rivers that crisscross the land, and most of those emptying into the Atlantic Ocean were originally populated with anadromous fishes. The northern and northwestern portion of the peninsula bounded by the massif of Galicia and the Cantabrian Mountains is marked by ample rainfall well distributed throughout the year, deciduous forests, and humid types of agriculture, in sharp contrast to the rest of Iberia, which is mainly bathed in sunshine, sparsely forested, and noted for its olive and orange groves, vineyards, sheep, and goats.

The salmon rivers that flow out of the Picos de Europa mountains, which rise to 9000 feet above sea level, are swift and cold and strewn with rocky ledges and cascades the salmon have to climb. They flow down steep, narrow valleys, past forests of chestnut, oak, and poplar, into rias of the Bay of Biscay. In this part of western Europe the earliest members of the species *Homo sapiens* lived for uncountable centuries in limestone caves, and much of the area outside busy cities still has a quiet splendor and pastoral quality, with villages not much changed since the Middle Ages.

There are at least fifty salmon rivers in the peninsula, although many of them have long since seen the last of these fishes. Two famous rivers are the Douro, about 490 miles long, which traverses the historic provinces of Castile and León, and drops into the Atlantic Ocean at Oporto, and the Tagus, longest in Iberia, which rises in Teruel province in northeastern Spain and flows for over 600 miles through ancient cities like Toledo and Alcántara and thence to Lisbon. If you visit Lisbon today you will probably not find anybody, including the oldest inhabitant, who ever heard of salmon in the Tagus, yet Tirso de Molina, the seventeenth-century author of *The Trickster of Seville* (the original play about Don Juan), tells us that here

> You spy
> All kinds of vessels, among which
> Those of the Conquest tower so high
> That, looked at from the ground below,
> Their mastheads seem to touch the sky . . .
> Citizens, while they're at table
> Can buy great loads of fish
> And most from their own doors are able
> To catch as many as they wish.
> And from the nets where salmon flounder
> It's scarce a stone's throw to the dish.

There is little information about the history of the salmon in Portugal, for there are none left. In Sweden I met a biologist who had been invited by the Salazar government to investigate the possibilities of restoring the fishes to some of the streams, but his verdict was that it was unfeasible.

The salmon rivers of Spain are mostly short, twenty to forty miles long in the province of Galicia, with a few like the Ulla and Tambre extending to seventy miles; in Asturias they are from fifteen to eighty-five miles, while in the provinces of Santander and Guipuzcoa (in the Basque country) they are usually shorter. Next to the Douro and Tagus in length is the Miño, a 200-mile Galician river that flows from the Sierra de Meira Mountains to the sea near the Portuguese frontier. These streams nurtured the men of the Old Stone Age, the prehistoric Iberians about whom we know little, and later the Celts, Greeks, Phoenicians, and Romans who conquered the peninsula. In the salmon-producing areas there are still arched stone bridges built by Roman legionnaires, and men still fish from them as the Romans did.

Salmon thrived in the pastoral and agricultural ages in Iberia because the rivers were uncontaminated and unblockaded except by rocks and waterfalls, which the athletic fish could hurdle. Protection of the fisheries was a royal tradition: in 1258 Alfonso el Sabio established what is the first known closed season, and Juan II in 1435 issued an edict directed against poachers, subjecting them to an enormous fine if caught throwing quicklime, henbane, daphne, mullein, or other poisonous matter into the waters. Specific gear regulations seem to have originated in the reign of Philip II at the end of the sixteenth century: he forbade fishing with "cloths of straw, or linen, or sheets, or with hand baskets [when] little salmon are running or when fish are spawning" and permitted each province to issue its own regulations for nets so that "fish would not be wasted."

There is plenty of evidence that the Spanish rivers produced bountiful harvests in past centuries. Fishing rights were the patrimony of the abbeys and other ecclesiastical houses as well as the feudal nobility and the Crown. The best fishing sites were intensively exploited, usually by means of weirs called *postas* or *apostales*, remains of which could still be seen in some streams (like the Pas) in the present century.

Sañez Reguart in his *Historical Dictionary of the National Fishing Arts*, published in 1791–1795, estimated the daily catch in the province of Asturias alone at 2000 and in all of Spain at 8000 to 10,000 fish. Projected on a three-month season of about sixty fishing days, this suggests an annual catch of 600,000 to 900,000 salmon. Income from certain fisheries is known to have been substantial. The municipality of Pravia obtained 100,000 reals annually in the decade 1780 to 1790, but a half century later the return had dwindled to 8000 reals, indicating that the runs had declined considerably.

In Spain, as in other countries, legends were handed down about indentured servants on the great estates in Asturias and Santander provinces who petitioned their masters to reduce their salmon ration because they were heartily sick of it. Max Borrell, Sports Consultant to the Bureau of Tourism, suggests that the fish were emaciated kelts found on the riverbanks or spawners who were easily netted — in any case, tasteless fish. Borrell vainly attempted to document these tales but only found indentured contracts stipulating that if tenants could not meet their rental obligations in wheat they could make up the difference in fresh salmon at the current market price, or in poultry.[1]

Amid the political and economic upheavals of the nineteenth century the Spanish fishery was dissipated. Mill dams that diverted the flow of streams or blockaded fish migration were built, ignoring the

1795 decree of Carlos IV that channels must be kept open at all times to permit migratory fish to reach their spawning grounds. Later came hydroelectric projects of small capacity built without fish ladders, or with inefficient ones; in fact, sometimes the ladders were dry and hence useless. Streams also were littered with dams without ladders and cataracts fish could not climb. I saw a few of these on my visit to Spain, the salmon hurling themselves against the cataract time and again, then, exhausted, drifting back downstream to regain their strength and make another assault, or die. Borrell, the fishing companion and mentor of General Franco, told me that El Caudillo (an aficionado of *Salmo salar*) sometimes becomes frustrated when he witnesses such scenes and vows to dynamite the dams — but he never does.

After Franco had suppressed the Loyalists in the civil war of 1936–1939 and restored order in Spain, he issued a decree on February 20, 1942, banning nets from the rivers and estuaries and turned the salmon resource over to the sportsmen. By then the total catches had fallen to 2000 to 3000 fish per year.

In the troubled years before the civil war, and especially during the war, many of the streams were looted. Peasants living on the edge of poverty took the valuable fish to eke out a livelihood or add to their meager food supply. Gangs operated in organized fashion, using motorcycles for quick getaways, hiding their fishes in the caves that are numerous in the vicinity of some rivers, retrieving them in the morning and selling them in Bilbao, or the city of Santander, and other places. Wardens were not only scarce, they were usually ineffectual. Violators of poaching laws were rarely apprehended and municipal judges had a lenient attitude.

"The major weakness of the fishery legislation," said the Marques de Marzales writing in the 1920s, "consists in the leniency of its enforcement. There are not so many mechanical defects [in the laws] as there are weaknesses in their application, and this increases their inefficiency even more." [2] Divided administration of the fisheries, as in France, worked against conservation. Fishing in the estuaries was controlled by the Ministry of Marine and in the rivers by the Ministry of Development (Fomento). The former permitted netting throughout the week and opened the season on February 15, which was a month too early according to Marzales; also, it permitted nets to be spaced much too closely.

For example, some fifty netsmen fished the Eo estuary, working day and night, seven days a week. Those salmon which managed to escape the barrage were faced by a series of three low dams, of which the first was passable, but the second had no fish pass and could be only negotiated in spates, and the third, a hydroelectric impoundment about ten feet high, had a defective fish ladder. Despite these handicaps the Eo in Marzales' time still produced about 2000 salmon annually; its potential was 50,000. Similarly, the catch on the Sella was down to 3000 or one tenth of its capacity, and the Narcea, with seventy excellent pools, yielded barely a thousand fish when it was capable of producing 50,000. By 1930 Spain produced some 20,000 salmon a year, a far cry from the bountiful harvests of the eighteenth century. Reform of the fishing regulations was urgently needed, and a commission was actually working on this project when the fall of the Bourbon dynasty and ensuing civil war made its task impossible.

Pollution was not a serious factor in the decay of the resource except on a few rivers like the Narcea, a tributary of the Nalón, which flows through a region with heavy coal deposits. "For at least 75 to 100 years," says Borrell, "its waters flowed completely black, full of coal washings and all sorts of impurities. Not one single salmon has been seen in the Nalón for many years. The Narcea runs into the Nalón about twenty-five kilometers from the estuary and the junction of both waters keeps on being black right down to the sea. Do the salmon know, by taking the risk of going through the black tunnel, that the Narcea many miles above is clean? And what about the smolts going out to the sea?" [3] The Narcea remains a reasonably good salmon river, although it has been seriously affected by hydroelectric developments.

Sportsmen's Rivers

Spain is the only European nation that has eliminated netting and turned the rivers over entirely to anglers. Many Spanish country folk welcomed this move, which permitted them to fish legally by purchasing a professional's license for a small sum. In fact, most of the rod and reel fishermen became professionals; in 1966, for example, according to Borrell, at least 80 percent of the total catches were made by them.

The Spanish rivers are divided into restricted zones called *cotos* and free waters. In the free area anybody who has a license may fish during the season, usually April through June, while on the *cotos* a special permit is needed. Three rivers, the Narcea (Asturias), Deva-Cares (Asturias), and the Eo (Galicia) are national fishing preserves:

to fish them it is necessary to have not only a license but a permit from the State Tourist Department. Sections of each preserve are divided into beats, and each is large enough for a day's fishing: beats are allotted in rotation so as to give anglers an opportunity to fish a complete section during the day. For the convenience of anglers the government has built *refugios* (chalets) furnished with necessary conveniences, including kitchens, washrooms, and lounges. There are cement walks along the banks, suspension bridges, and other amenities for the comfort and convenience of fishermen.

On the other salmon rivers the farmers who have riparian rights retain the right to half the fishing licenses issued for reserved sections of that stream; the remaining half goes to sportsmen. Every salmon caught must be registered with a warden and only those taken in the free zones may be sold. The *Guardia civil,* the national constabulary one sees everywhere in Spain wearing spruce gray uniforms and tricornered patent-leather hats, guards the rivers, and severe punishment awaits the poacher or other illegal fisher.

The results of Spain's experiment in permitting only rod and reel fishermen to take salmon has been only moderately successful. Catches rose from 2000 to 3000 in the 1940s to an average of almost 7000 fish annually in the 1960s. There are only a small number of rivers left: the Narcea, Deva-Cares, Eo, Sella, Ason, Ulla, Bidasoa, Navia, and a few others. In 1971 the total catch dropped to 2700, the lowest in over thirty years, due partly to extremely poor water conditions and the presence of considerable numbers of fish affected by U.D.N. type of disease.

It is also worthy of note that a salmon tagged as an adult in the Disko Bay area of Greenland was subsequently recaptured in the Ason. This may suggest that the feeding grounds of Iberian fish beyond the grilse stage are in the same waters as those emanating from France and the British Isles.

There is naturally great competition in the Spanish rivers. "Rod and reel fishermen from dawn to dusk, every day of the season, with all kinds of barbs and lures, such as flies, spoons, devons, prawns, worms, and what have you" are trying to catch salmon, says Borrell. They send their fish to Madrid, where they are auctioned at fantastic prices during the height of the season. The best beats are crowded and "even children queue up, not to fish, but to sell their turn to a professional." [4] A fair-sized salmon caught by a countryman may fetch more money than he can earn in a factory or on a farm in a fortnight, or even a month.

Little has been done by the Spanish government to improve the rivers or to restock them. The salmon hatcheries I visited were archaic and concentrated on producing fry. Budgets for salmon conservation were hard to determine but little was being done in the way of laddering dams, removal of stream obstructions, and the like.

Meanwhile pressure on the resource is mounting. The number of national fishing licenses sold jumped from about 10,000 in 1950 to 150,000 in 1966. "On a good fishing day, in the River Sella, one is likely to see from 300 to 500 professionals fishing with everything. Once upon a time nets almost exterminated the salmon; now, unless drastic steps are taken, the runs will be very much depleted by a multitude of hooks," concludes Borrell, himself an international angler of note. "Professionals are only allowed to fish in the best pools for 30 minutes if others are waiting to do so, but I have seen a dozen waiting their turn."

So precious and scarce is salmon that a salmon bank, of which General Franco is a customer, has been established in Madrid. Any member can borrow from it providing he agrees to pay back in kind at the earliest opportunity. Since the price of fresh and smoked salmon has soared to $20 a pound early in the season only the very rich can afford it. Ironically, as Philip K. Crowe, American Ambassador to Norway, wrote after a fishing trip to Spain in April 1971, "the high price raises the incentive for poaching and despite the severe penalties some still goes on. The River Ulla has only four guards who patrol the public beats. Farmers have access to it far inland and illegal catching of salmon, sometimes even with dynamite, is occasionally reported." [5]

The fate of *Salmo salar* in Spain is indeed melancholy. The list of defunct rivers that once hosted these lively fishes is long. It includes the Miño, Eume, Sor, Oro, Landro, Jallas, Mandeo, Masma, Allones, Mero, El Puerto, Tambre, and Verdugo in Galicia; the Barcia, Canedo, and Nalón in Asturias; the Saja and Miera in Santander. Galicia, once rich in salmon, may be written off except for the River Eo; and there is but one substantial river left in the Basque province of Guipuzcoa, the Bidasoa.

Like France, Spain is a nation where there is seemingly little interest in saving the salmon. A minimum of funds goes into fishery conservation. There is no fishery management as we understand it in the United States; the Spanish equivalent of our Fish and Wildlife Service acts as a kind of custodian of the resource but does little to enhance it.

In 1972, however, salmon runs in Spain took an upward leap when anglers caught over 7000 fish.

French Rivers and Their Stocks

"In the Rivers of Aquitaine," said Pliny the Elder in his *Natural History,* published in the first century A.D., "the Salmon surpasses all others [in taste]." This is the first mention of *Salmo salar* in historical records.

The fourth-century Roman poet Ausonius, a native of Bordeaux, in his famous *Idyll of the Moselle,* the result of a trip on that delightful river, also eulogizes the salmon among other freshwater fishes. When the Romans colonized Gaul they found the inhabitants to be fish-eating people, and the most esteemed species were salmon in the west and mullet in the Midi. We can be certain that Roman gourmets soon heard of these savory fishes and imported them for their Lucullan feasts. By the time of Pliny there was already a trade in Gallic fish, for the Romans had learned the art of transporting them in salt.

Most of the great French river systems flowing into the Atlantic, from the Pyrenees to the Belgian frontier, harbored anadromous fishes, especially salmon. Probably no nation on the continent of Europe was so richly endowed — and none dissipated its wealth more completely.

French rivers are but lacy threads that bind together the variegated landscapes: mountains, forests, valleys, marshes and dunes, rocky coasts and sandy shores. They flow across verdant fields, rich with crops of wheat or corn, neatly terraced vineyards, grassy meadows, and sometimes pine or oak forests plunging down flower-strewn narrow defiles. Even with the upsurge of population and growth of cities, the landscape of France still seems on the whole peaceful and beautiful, for here, it is said, no work of man is permitted to destroy natural beauty. The total absence of freestanding billboards, neon signs, honky-tonk developments, and other horrors of the American countryside deeply engrave the esthetic qualities of the French land on the minds of visitors.

In their wilderness state the rivers and many of their tributaries had lengthy stretches that were ideal for spawning and rearing of salmon. The Moselle, for example, rises in the Vosges Mountains of northeastern France, forms the boundary between Germany and Luxembourg, and passes the cities of Nancy, Metz, and Thionville before entering the Rhine at Koblenz, running a course of 320 miles.

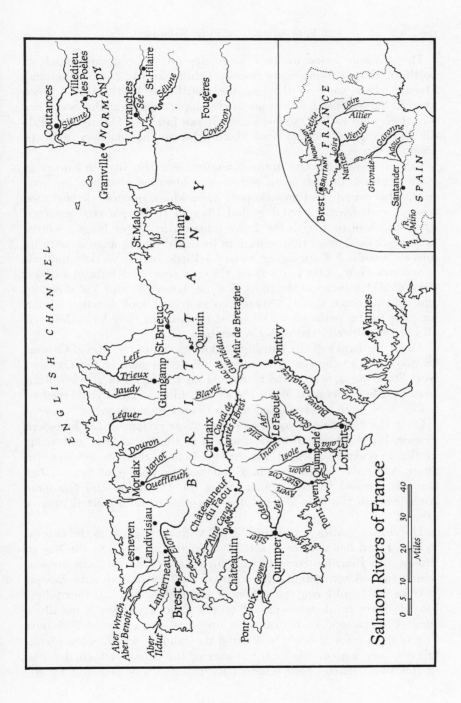

Salmon Rivers of France

The 470-mile Seine drains a large depression occupying much of northern France, with many bucolic tributaries like the Somme and Marne, where some of the bloodiest battles of World War I were fought. Salmon used to ascend to the upper waters of the Seine before they were locked out by dams without ladders. During the Middle Ages anglers used to hook these fishes in the shadows of Notre Dame in Paris.

Salmon were abundant in the 625-mile Loire. No river in Europe is more pleasant to visit even today; its numerous chateaux are museums that recall the romantic past when kings, queens, elegant mistresses, and courtiers lived gilded lives in their spacious quarters. Over much of its length the Loire remains, in Victor Hugo's words, "a tranquil oval sheet that reflects in its liquid depths a castle with its turrets, woods and springing waters." Little of the world's hubbub penetrates here. The Loire flows through several delightful valleys, the Val d'Orleans, Val de Blois, Val de Touraine, and Val d'Anjou, and as you drive through them you stop and look for the salmon jumping in the pellucid waters — but in vain, for they have deserted all but the Allier in the upper watershed.

Along the banks of the Dordogne, flowing out of the Massif Central for 300 miles to the sea at Bordeaux, dwelt the men of the Old and New Stone Ages, who were nourished on the fishes of the bountiful river. Little is recorded about the salmon in this extensive watershed before they were exterminated in the twentieth century.

Once the Garonne, a more extensive river system in southwestern France, lured salmon to its headwaters in the Val d'Aran and as far as the Pyrenean valley of the Ariège (where there is evidence of Stone Age cave dwellers), which touches the border of Spain. The Gironde, formed by the confluence of the Dordogne and Garonne, flows through the Médoc wine district; once it too attracted runs of salmon.

The Adour gushes out of the Pic du Midi de Bigorre in the central Pyrenees and flows for over 200 miles north and south to the Bay of Biscay near Biarritz. Some of its affluents are cold mountain streams, which meander through rather narrow valleys dotted with Basque villages with moldering stone houses and little shops and inns where lusty farmers drink wine out of quaint flagons. There is usually a small Romanesque cathedral, and one may see old men and boys fishing from ancient bridges, seeking the salmon, which, once plentiful, are now scarce. Major tributaries of the Adour, which rise east of the Roncesvalles area where Charlemagne was defeated by the

Basques (an incident romanticized in the medieval French poem, *Song of Roland*), are the Gave d'Oloron, the Nive, and the Saison.

The biological characteristics of the French salmon are similar to those of the Spanish or British. The larger fish enter the rivers, such as the Loire or Adour, from November to March and may take a year to reach their spawning grounds. In Breton streams they usually spawn during the first fortnight of December.

In the Gave d'Oloron one-year smolts predominate; in northern rivers smoltification takes longer. In Brittany the smolts descend to the sea from March to the end of April.

Smaller fish called *Madeleineaux* (grilse) enter the rivers usually before the main runs. Very few grilse are now found in the Adour or Loire but they are almost the only salmon left in Breton and Norman streams. In Brittany they come up the year round except in dry periods. Some inkling of where the French salmon feed in the ocean was obtained when twelve smolts tagged in the Gave d'Oloron in April 1969 were recaptured as adults in Greenland waters in the autumn of 1970.

Age of Abundance

In the Middle Ages the freshwater fishes were cherished by the people of France, for they were not only dependable sources of nutriment but in time of grain failures meant the difference between famine and sustenance. The fisherman was an important person in the community. "I never go to Oloron," said the late L. de Boisset, "without gazing with renewed pleasure at the admirable portal of the Romanesque cathedral of Sainte-Marie on which is sculpted, besides the old men of the Apocalypse, the basic occupations of mankind, of which one is a fisherman with a salmon on his shoulder." [6]

Statutes designed to protect the inland fisheries date from the reign of Charlemagne in the early ninth century and are probably the prototype of such legislation in Europe. A spate of similar laws dealing with nets, meshes, closed seasons, and minimum size of fish that could be sold followed in succeeding reigns. Until the eleventh century only fishing for salmon and eels was regulated. By the reign of Henri IV violation of these laws must have become alarming, for an edict of 1597 declares that "with an excessive number of engines, fishermen are depopulating the rivers, streams and brooks. [Therefore] they are forbidden to fish with any gear, even legal ones, which have not been authorized by our officers." The nobility and monasteries who owned the fisheries were required to abide by royal edicts designed to conserve the runs and allow the fish to move to their mating grounds with a minimum of delay. On the whole, it is believed that the rivers and the fisheries were well protected down to the Revolution of 1789. In Brittany, Limousin, Auvergne, and the lower Pyrenees districts the supply was usually abundant.

There was probably little abusive fishing. "The Seigneurs," says R. Bachelier, "took good care to assure the return of at least a certain proportion of the salmon to the spawning grounds."[7] Thus the watergates of the mills were closed every night and on Sunday so that the entire flow of the stream passed over the channel; likewise when the flow was heavy arrangements were made to permit the simultaneous floating of timber and ascent of the fish.

In the happy agricultural age, before the advent of the Industrial Revolution, which has played havoc with the environment in every country where it has spread, French rivers were usually limpid and pure; poaching was not, as it later became, a widespread menace. The peasantry tended to be law-abiding out of fear or respect for the laws that protected property; punishments were speedily inflicted on violators.

The fisheries of Brittany, Normandy, the Loire basin, and elsewhere produced considerable revenues for proprietors as well as food for the populace. For example, in 1090 Alain, Count of Brittany, wishing to have the blessings of heaven, donated to the monks of Landevennec the fishery in the River Aulne, which brought 4500 livres annual revenue. The fish were sold not only in this province but as far as Paris. Until the Revolution in 1789 the yield was at least 4000 salmon annually in the Aulne, or more than are now caught in all of France. According to Louis Roule, Brittany produced as much as 9 million pounds of salmon in the eighteenth century in good years (around 900,000 fish), bringing an aggregate income to fishermen of some 200,000 livres (equal to £200,000).[8]

Salmon as Food

Because they were plentiful, salmon and other freshwater fishes became dietary staples. In the castles they dined on wild boar, venison, game birds, ducks and geese, chickens, and other food, but when available, salmon and other fishes from nearby rivers or lakes were added to the menu. In the lower Auvergne and lower Loire regions, we are told by the chroniclers, knights celebrating a jousting victory would call for a dish of salmon among the dozen courses they were accustomed to devour at a sitting, eating without forks or knives and only rarely with spoons. The fish, in its silvery coat, head and eyes intact, was brought by pages on a pewter platter to the sound of trumpets. Servants handed round whatever sauces or spices were available, and the repast was washed down with draughts of wine made in local vineyards.

Many religious houses depended on the salmon, trout, and eels for a considerable portion of their food supply. It was the custom in some French establishments to dress up the fish for notable feasts. The menu of a banquet given by the canons of Brioude (on the Allier River) to an ecclesiastical potentate in 1719, for example, included among sixteen courses salmon cooked à la hollandaise and served with white wine with pomegranates.[9] The fish was held in high repute. Abraham de la Framboisière, French court physician in the sixteenth century, echoed the sentiments of many people when he extolled "the tender flesh of the salmon, oily, sweet, very appetizing and excellent to the taste, preferable as a delicacy to all other fish."

Louis XIV was indifferent to good cooking though he was a glutton, but Louis XV was more fastidious and fond of freshwater fish, such as Lake Geneva trout and Loire salmon, which were sent to Versailles every fast day. This was a hint that the burghers who gave state banquets for the King and his entourage took seriously.

French cooking reached its apogee in the eighteenth century when the rich competed with each other in giving banquets and creating new dishes served on rare china with fine silver. "A new system of cookery [was created]," says Paul Lacroix, emphasizing "smaller dishes, containing all the essence and aroma of the larger ones." In this age appeared such famous dishes as *Saumon à la Royale, Saumon à la Chambord,* and *Saumon Impériale,* worthy of standing beside regional masterpieces like *Sole Normande, Bouillabaisse Marseillaise, Pic Anjou,* and *Turbot Franche-Comtois.*

Age of Scarcity

The Age of Abundance passed with the Revolution of 1789. The Legislative Assembly and Convention at first deprived the nobility who owned the rivers of their rights in the streams, thus opening the floodgates that led to looting of the stocks. Under the consulate, fishing rights on navigable waters were restored to the state but public fishing was also permitted. At the same time riparian owners recovered their properties on nonnavigable waters.

The ordinance of April 25, 1829, which remained the basic fishery code of France until 1941, stipulated that

> Proprietors have the right to fish up to the middle of the stream, without prejudice to contrary rights established by possession of title. The soil and bed of the river belong to them but not the river itself. The fish become their property only at the moment when they are taken out of the water by legal means.
>
> Nobody is allowed to fish on privately owned rivers or ponds without a valid certificate of authorization . . . The free movement of water and fish must be assured.

This was a wise law but, like many others dealing with fisheries, rarely enforced.

Free access by citizens started the depletion of the rivers. For example, a retired army surgeon living at Brioude on the upper Allier noted in his diary in 1830 that the river "is no longer as populated with fish as it used to be." Barbel, eel, lamprey, and dace were commonly taken, "but salmon is scarce and dear. It sells for three and four francs the pounds and old men have seen it sell for 40 and 50 centimes and even 25 centimes the pound." [10]

During the nineteenth century, rivers were increasingly encroached upon by canals, weirs, and dams, and some fell victims to pollution. Men of property argued they had a God-given right to use the waters as they pleased and ignored the laws that should have saved the migratory fishes. Supine governments did not hinder them. For example, a law of 1865 required owners of mill dams and weirs to provide fish ladders for which the state would reimburse them. However, it did not stipulate that adequate streamflow had to be provided, nor did it apply to barriers already in existence. This law did little, says Bachelier, to prevent the eventual lockout of the fishes from some of their immemorial haunts, as on the Seine.

Numerous streams became impassable because they were studded with mill dams or were canalized. Canalization of the Aulne "brought in its train numerous barrages which proved to be obstacles to the ascent of salmon," says Yves Gestin. So on this river and others along the Breton coast they became scarce by the 1850s.[11]

Failure to enforce the 1865 law is regarded by Bachelier as the prime reason for the drastic diminution of salmon in the Loire watershed. Hydroelectric dams without fish ladders stopped fish migration; most of these structures were no more than six meters high, until Grangent dam was constructed on the upper Loire with a height of fifty meters. Fish ladders were not installed despite the urging of the Bureau of Waters and Forests, which was endeavoring to revive the runs by laddering some dams and cataracts and planting salmon eggs in suitable waters.

The status of the salmon rivers in 1881 is recorded by Émile Moreau in his *Natural History of French Fishes*. The species was then already scarce in the Moselle and quite reduced in numbers in the Meuse and its affluents, the Semoy and Chiers. It was still found in the Somme but was scarce in the parent stream, the Seine, above Quillebeuf; arriving at Montereau, the fish abandoned the main river and went up the Yonne or the Cure. Some of the Breton runs, as in the Odet, Ellé, and Sienne as well as the Sée and Sélune in Normandy, were still in good condition, while in the bay of Mont-Saint-Michel, crowned by the spectacular abbey, netters made handsome catches. Moreau reported that runs were slim in the Charente, which empties into the Bay of Biscay, and diminishing in the Garonne and Dordogne Rivers, but abundant in a few tributaries of the Adour. Even the Bidasoa then had a fair stock of salmon.

Overfishing also played a crucial role in depopulation of the rivers. In the estuaries and tidal zones veterans of the merchant marine, called *Inscrits maritimes*, have enjoyed a monopoly of commercial fishing since the days of Jean Baptiste Colbert, Louis XIV's minister. Thanks to ministerial protection they were able to disregard conservation laws and fish as and when they pleased. For example, a law of December 19, 1863, established a closed season in both freshwater and saltwater in the Loire from October 20 to January 31, but it was blithely ignored by the *Inscrits*. Moreover, they were permitted to lay their nets as far as Thouars, eleven kilometers above Nantes (where the tidal zone ends). How rewarding their operations were may be surmised from the fact that they sent some eighty tons of salmon annually to the market Les Halles in Paris in the years 1884–1887. But in time the catches dropped off. By 1901 they were sending only thirty tons. Extra privileges were granted them to compensate for the loss of income. Thus a ministerial order of September 31, 1934, strongly protested by the Bureau of Waters and Forests, authorized the *Inscrits* to fish with drag nets as well as hoop nets of any suitable length. They continued to exploit the Loire and other rivers up and down the Atlantic coast until World War II called many of them back to the sea.

Richard Vibert and L. de Boisset summed up the general situation on French rivers in 1944:

> The causes of the impoverishment of our waters are many and well known. They are first of all abusive fishing practiced in the estuaries thanks to obsolete regulations which accord to the *Inscrits maritimes* privileges that should be modified. Then, certain rivers have been polluted by industrial and urban wastes. There is also poaching by scoundrels who, for lack of surveillance, rarely fall into the hands of judges and when they do are often treated with regrettable indulgence . . . Particularly reprehensible is inexcusable poaching practiced daily by ignorant or dishonest trout fishermen who do not return to the water the juvenile salmon they hook and thus destroy . . . the seed stock of future generations. Finally, and most important, there are the impoundments badly designed and without a thought for the passage of migratory fish. A single impassable barrage on a watercourse is sufficient to make the salmon disappear . . . The struggle lasts four or five years, the time it takes for the last alevin born on the spawning grounds to return to the river. Then the river becomes sterile, definitely and totally, upstream as well as downstream.
>
> All these causes of the ruin of our salmon rivers are the consequence of 150 years of democracy. Government elected through the power of money spares the salmon no more than [other resources]. The result is that France, which should be in the front rank of salmon producers in Europe, imports annually 20,000 quintals (2 million pounds) of salmon of which the greatest portion are mediocre tinned salmon which America distributes in the two hemispheres as proof of its superior civilization.[12]

Current Status of the Salmon

In the thirty years since this passage was written French stocks have continued to decline with but small efforts to reverse the trend. Conservation programs, usually instigated by sportsmen or government bureaus, were poorly funded. In addition, growing pollution and damming of rivers militated against restoration of the runs.

Reading French fishery magazines one gets the impression that little or nothing is being done to keep poisons out of the rivers. For example, a news item in *Saumons & Truites,* published by the Society for the Preservation of Salmon in Brittany and Lower Normandy (1971), reports that millions of fish were seen drifting belly up in the River Odet after an accidental release of ammonia; the Blavet, Aulne, Läita, and Steir, all pleasant little streams, are polluted by sewage from the towns and effluents from abattoirs, dairies, distilleries, etc. Sewage purification plants are badly designed, poorly operated, or nonexistent, and little is being done to abate these evils despite the clangorous demands of angling clubs and other people. Local government seems to be impotent, for it is difficult to isolate the source of any given form of pollution; the laws are weak and the will to enforce them is feeble.

An important factor in the deterioration of the fisheries has been the divided authority of government agencies, each jealous of its power and unwilling to share it. The Ministry of Marine has jurisdiction over the estuaries and tidal waters, the Bureau of Bridges and Roads (*Ponts et Chausées*) controls canals, the Bureau of Waters and Forests (*Eaux et Forêts*), within the Ministry of Agriculture, is charged with regulating freshwater fishing beyond tidal waters. They rarely agree on measures to safeguard the fisheries. The national power agency, *Électricité de France* (EDF) is indifferent to fish conservation and ignores the requests of land and water agencies to protect the runs. As a nation France seems to be unwilling to invest in salmon restoration programs and has virtually given up hope of saving what is left of the species.

Vibert and de Boisset in *La Pêche Fluviale en France,* published in 1944, estimated the annual salmon catch at that time as 5000 to 6000 in the Loire, 10,000 to 18,000 in the Adour basin, and 6000 to 7000 in Brittany and Normandy. This was a tremendous drop from the levels of a century before; since then the runs have further tobogganed and are now at an all-time low. Bachelier estimated that salmon spawning areas in the Loire watershed declined from 2200 hectares (4935 acres) in 1789 to 295 hectares (729 acres) in 1918 and 195 hectares (482 acres) in 1962. Only small segments of the Loire basin, chiefly the Allier, possess salmon. The river made a notable comeback a few years ago due to a fry-planting program, but improvement in the runs quickly brought out the wheel-type fish traps, laid aside for thirty years, which had been responsible for depletion of the runs in the first place!

According to the International Atlantic Salmon Foundation, reports received from the National Association for Protection of Salmon Rivers (ANDRS) show that approximately 2900 salmon were taken by sport fishermen and 1800 by commercial fishermen (*Inscrits maritimes*) in 1971 in all of France.

Most of the salmon rivers of any consequence are now in Brittany: the Élorn, Aulne, Guer, Odet, Steir, and Jet produce the best catches. "A notable exception in other regions was the Gave d'Oloron where 220 salmon were reported by anglers [in 1971] and a further 600 never made it that far upstream and were recorded in catches of estuarial net fishermen." [13]

Brittany is a peninsula crisscrossed by numerous rivers and blessed with a jagged coast and many small bays. It is an old settled land, where the Celtic heritage is still strong; place names are usually Celtic, and in remote areas one may meet old people who speak Breton, a language akin to Cornish, which is spoken across the Channel. At every turn of the road there may be an ancient village with a quaint name, a prehistoric ruin (such as a menhir or dolmen), a Celtic cross, or a farm lined with hedgerows in the English fashion. Many British anglers used to cross the Channel to fish for salmon or trout in the Breton rivers, but their numbers have dwindled.

As Pierre Phelipot, former secretary of the Association for the Protection of the Salmon in South Brittany and Lower Normandy, says in an article in *Plaisirs de la Pêche* (summer, 1968), between the netsmen fishing in tidal waters and the poachers plying their nefarious trade, it is a wonder that so many fish escape to give anglers a modest harvest and breed new generations.

> Six or eight *Inscrits* [he reports] take 3,000 salmon and grilse annually and almost all the large sea trout in the estuary of the Scorff while 150 anglers take only 400 to 800 . . . I know several of these otherwise worthy fellows who profit handsomely from their privileges considering the price of salmon per kilogram. They are quite reticent about their exploits, and listening to them you would think they scarcely eke out a livelihood. However, those who like us have taken the trouble to watch them for any length of time, either in the Laïta or the Scorff, can affirm that they make considerable inroads on the salmon runs as they scour the estuary with their nets. Their best catches are made when the water is

low in the river and the salmon are not ascending. At the beginning of the season (February–March), their catches are often poor but starting in April it is otherwise. Having the right to fish in the estuaries up to August 1, while rodsmen must cease June 15, they make their best hauls in June and July when, along with the salmon, the grilse and sea trout arrive . . .

On the Laïta the *Inscrits* use immense seines which theoretically ought not to exceed 120 meters. The management of these nets is difficult but quite effective. Before seining, the fishermen observe the salmons' presence by their leaping in the water. When discovered, few fish escape. Thus, last July one net took 27 salmon in a single drift, and this was certainly not a record for the season. Actually the *Inscrits* on the Laïta are forbidden to drag their seines close to the shore but they easily avoid this regulation by running the boat aground on one of the many sand banks which are uncovered at low tide. I don't know how many salmon are caught in the vicinity of the town of Pouldu but I know a fishmonger in that area who obtains 1,000 to 1,500 fish from them annually. This means they catch many more, for the hotels and other fish dealers take as many.

One must be blind not to see that net fishing in the estuaries is the principal — I do not say the only — cause for the scarcity of anadromous fish in the streams.

In 1969 a fresh salmon weighing ten pounds or more was selling for 100 to 350 francs ($18 to $63).

Poaching remains a lucrative way of life for some people, as illustrated by an interview, published in a Breton paper in 1968, with an old woman reputed to have pilfered thousands of salmon out of the Laïta during her long career:

> Small, with gray, well-combed hair, bright laughing eyes, exuding humor and gaiety despite her 87 years, Marianne is always lucid.
>
> Never having attended school (it is not necessary to one who masters the art of poaching), she speaks only Breton.
>
> At the word salmon, small eyes sparkle with malice, for the royal fish of our rivers has no secrets from her.
>
> "I have been a poacher for 30 years, taking every year more than a hundred salmon."

Marianne, born in the town of Guilligomarch, settled after her marriage at the opening of the century at Locmaria, in Guidel. A seamstress by trade, she resided in a small cottage several hundred meters from the Laïta. Times were difficult. She had to go from house to house to make aprons and skirts. There were no family allowances and in the small house six mouths had to be fed daily.

Then, towards her twentieth year, Marianne began, like her husband, to cast nets into the Laïta at night.

At this time, fish were plentiful. Sometimes she used up to 20 nets of various dimensions, the longest measuring 17–18 meters and the smallest 6–7 meters.

She tracked down the salmon (the fish which brought the highest prices), but also fished for trout and set eel-baskets.

Marianne rarely ate salmon, which she preferred to dispose of at Quimperlé, but smoked eels for personal consumption. She operated mostly during the fishing season . . . Once the nets were cast in a level place they had to be watched for other poachers were apt to steal their contents.

"Have you had difficulties with the police?"

Marianne, to whom we offered a bonbon, did not evade this question.

Laughing, she said, "Every year the police who at that time were on horseback reported me."

"But that cost you a great deal?"

"No . . . I never paid . . . I preferred to go to prison."

" — Prison — "

"Yes, in prison, prison," Marianne repeated. "Besides," she added, "it is not too bad there. The food is decent."

" — Did you stay long?"

"Oh no. Eight days, fifteen days more or less, but always outside the fishing season so as not to lose any earnings."

Marianne is a character . . . She has been in prison a dozen times. She feels no shame.

Never having stolen nor killed anyone, she does not believe she ever committed a crime.

Very courageous, she repaired the nets herself and worked hard to raise her six children. Three of them are alive.

Kenavo, Marianno. The fish wardens can sleep in peace. There are no more poachers of her type.

She still does not like salmon, preferring trout. If the way of life in her time forced her to operate outside the law, we must not be too harsh with her.

What hope there is to save the French salmon lies principally with a few aggressive sportsmen's groups. They hold conferences, pester ministers, issue newsletters and bulletins, and try to arouse a lethargic nation to the crisis in anadromous fisheries. Their program is summed up by René Richard, president of one of the largest organizations:

1. Curtailment of net fishing in the estuaries.
2. Modification of water regimen to permit the free migration of fish; this would involve the removal of abandoned dams and suppression of privileges granted to mill owners to impound waters.
3. Control of catches.
4. Precise definition of permissible methods of fishing for salmon.
5. Creation of a single agency for managing the rivers, somewhat like the river authorities of England.

For every step forward in France there seem to be two backward. Just as the Breton runs were apparently improving, U.D.N. disease hit the rivers and now they are threatened by the upsurge of rainbow trout hatcheries — this food fish is being produced at the rate of 10,000 tons a year in France. "The hatcheries," says Pierre Phelipot, "have the right to dam our small rivers. In many places the greater part of the river flow is deflected to the hatchery, so salmon and sea trout cannot run . . . These hatcheries are rudimentary. They do not recirculate the water, so they pollute our streams.

"Our organization is seeking to obtain special laws to protect our salmon rivers; without them the streams will be ruined. We also seek to curb the *plaisanciers,* men who because they have a boat may fish with a net at the mouth of the river. In the Bay of Mont-Saint-Michel about 2000 salmon are netted every year." [14]

As the years pass, however, conservationists seem to lose hope, for the fact is that France's stocks are now at a nadir and the nation is doing little to prevent them from vanishing.

National and departmental governments scarcely pay lip service to freshwater fishery conservation. *Salmo salar* is an endangered species.

The savory fish is known to the French people now usually as an imported luxury, from England, Denmark, Canada, or the United States. In fact, France is the second best customer for American salmon: In 1970 the United States exported 5.6 million pounds worth almost $5 million and in 1971 7 million pounds worth $5.1 million. However, one rarely sees this fish on French restaurant menus except in high-priced establishments. In fish markets it fetches astronomical prices.

VII 〰

Demise of the Meuse
and Rhine Rivers

THE MEUSE is an international river that originates in southern Lorraine and runs a zigzag course of 580 miles, mostly northward, passing varied and impressive scenery, including the Forest of Ardennes, then watering the vinelands and hop gardens of Belgium and finally the lowlands of Holland (where it is called the Maas) before joining the Schelde and Rhine to empty into Europe's busiest estuary.[1]

We do not know the size of the original salmon runs in this huge basin, but their fate is worth recording. In this area the fishes managed to find their way through a heavily populated estuary, but they could not surmount the high weirs or dams not provided with fish passes nor cope with the wastes of coal mines and steel mills encountered in the industrialized section of the Meuse.

In the Dutch section of the Meuse the first weirs were constructed around 1925. Their fish passes were apparently so inefficient that the number of salmon reaching the spawning grounds was almost negligible and completely insufficient for the conservation of the population. The adults were held up so long downstream trying to hurdle the weirs that the fishermen could obtain a much higher percentage of the run than when the river flowed freely. Although the Meuse remained virtually the only unpolluted waterway in the Netherlands, in contrast to its Belgian section, and was eminently suitable for a profitable fishery, the runs ultimately vanished. In 1914 21 companies were operating seines and 218 companies were working dip nets on the river, employing a total of 1100 men; by 1936 only 8 companies were working seines and 45 were operating drift nets with a total of 330 persons. Later figures are not available, but salmon have almost vanished from the Meuse. The annual statistical bulletin of the International Council for the Exploration of the Sea occasionally reports a ton or two landed in Holland but none in Belgium.

The 820-mile Rhine, the longest river in western Europe, originates in the Swiss Alps and passes through France, Austria, Lichtenstein, Germany, and Holland. As it comes out of the Swiss mountains the river is a pure and invigorating stream from which one may drink safely. As it enters Lake Constance, however, it is thick with mud, then emerges emerald green. At Schaffhausen it explodes into the cataracts of the Rheinfall, the limit of salmon fishing, after which it becomes a swift and sometimes turbulent river with many branches. It then flows for 160 miles across a plain framed by the Vosges Mountains on the west and the Black Forest on the east, passing cattle-studded landscapes rich in knightly lore, and less romantic scenery after entering France. In the Netherlands it again divides into two branches — the wide sweep of the delta embraces the great ports of Rotterdam and Antwerp, connected by a canal to the Schelde. At the Hook of Holland the once crystalline Rhine, now slimy and yellowed with the muck of factories, mines, villages, towns, and barges, sinks into the North Sea as if it were tired and ashamed of its life and seeks only annihilation. Salmon in large numbers used to come up as far as the Rheinfall at Schaffhausen.

The Rhine is navigable for large-scale barge traffic as far as Strasbourg and at certain seasons of the year as far as Basel.

The history of the river mirrors that of western Europe. Stone Age men dwelt along its banks, as around Lake Constance. The Romans built fifty forts on the river in the centuries after Julius Caesar and his legions crossed it; Celts, Huns, and Franks swarmed over the Rhine.

Then came the age of industry. The river was canalized, sails gave way to steam and later to the diesel engine, factories arose on the banks, towns siphoned their sewage into the river, and the waters that once were so pure one could drink from them almost anywhere became savagely polluted. They were also harnessed to turn the wheels of machines that manufactured Krupp's cannons and Thyssen's steel. In the Alsace region French potassium works alone now dump 7 million tons of salts into the Rhine annually, and when the river crosses into Holland it brings along this cargo as well as sewage from numerous towns and wastes from 16,000 barges that move coal, oil, iron ore, automobiles, cheese, wheat, and other products up and down the Rhine. For much of its navigable length the bed of the stream is now coated with a thick layer of petroleum sludge, and the bacteria count in the estuary is 1,500,000 per cubic centimeter. At times large stretches of the Rhine are completely deoxygenated — fishes cannot live in them.

Thus the Rhine is now only a working river, carrying Europe's freight in a humdrum fashion, living so to speak on memories of the

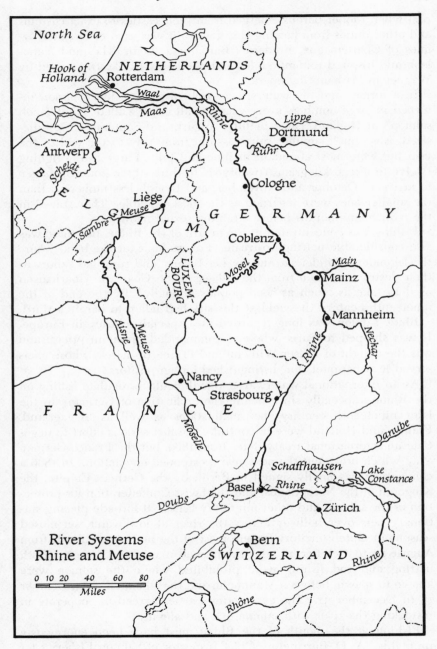

River Systems
Rhine and Meuse

0 10 20   40   60   80
Miles

past when robber barons emerged from their castles to exact customs and other duties from passing ships, when it was used to ferry the armies of Charlemagne, Frederick Barbarossa, Louis XIV, and Napoleon and inspired romantic tales and poetic myths like those used by Wagner in his haunting operas.

In a former age the waters were rich in aquatic life. Salmon returned in large numbers every year. Small grilse, called "Saint Jacob salmon" in Holland, came in July, August, and September. Middle-sized fish — small summer salmon — ran from May to the end of the year but were most abundant in June and July. Large fish, weighing twelve to fifteen kilograms (twenty-six to thirty-three pounds), began to arrive in October and November, and though less numerous than the smaller ones were regarded as the most valuable. They stayed in the river many months before attaining sexual maturity.

Fishing was concentrated at the mouth of the Rhine, but there was also considerable netting upstream. For example, at the bend where the legendary Lorelei sat and by her beauty and song led sailors to their destruction, men from the villages of St. Goar and Goarhausen used to take as much as 5000 pounds annually.[2] By the end of the nineteenth century the yield at this site had fallen to barely a third.

Rhine salmon was long regarded as a special delicacy in Europe. It was shipped to Paris, where it commanded premium prices, and was the delight of Kaiser Wilhelm and Prince Bismarck, whose chefs served it at banquets for distinguished foreign visitors.

As an international waterway it was difficult to regulate fishing on the Rhine, especially since before the unification of Germany in the later nineteenth century the small states as well as Switzerland, France, and Holland were in control. The first serious effort to negotiate an international treaty dates from 1869, but the Franco-German War, which broke out the next year, postponed any action. In 1886 a convention was finally signed in Berlin by the German Empire, the Kingdom of the Netherlands, and the Swiss Confederation for protection of the salmon and other migratory fishes. It forbade placing stationary nets over halfway across the river at low water, set closed seasons in Dutch territory (where most of the netting occurred) from August 27 to October 26, and established a weekend closure. Both netting and rod fishing were prohibited where the salmon were known to spawn, between Mannheim and the Rheinfall, from October 15 to December 31. The contracting parties agreed to cooperate in restocking the river with salmon ova and alevins.[3]

Fishing at the mouth of the Rhine must have been enormously profitable. A. D. Barrington, Chief Inspector of Salmon Fisheries for

England and Wales, said in his annual report for the year 1886 that "the great draft nets at Kralingen [near Rotterdam] dwarf anything seen in England and Wales." [4] In 1885 they caught 69,500 salmon averaging 17.1 pounds, a total of 1,200,000 pounds; those at Amerstol took 6500 and at Gorinchen 6000 fish, for a grand total of 82,000.

According to Dr. P. P. C. Hoek, scientific fishery adviser to the Dutch Government, in a paper read to the fourth International Fishery Congress held in Washington, D.C., in September 1908, the international convention was working well, at least in Dutch waters. The big seines had ceased operations on Sundays and closed down a fortnight earlier than before the convention was signed. "These changes are quite in accordance with the general idea of the treaty," he said. "Those who fish in the lower parts of the river are to spare a considerable part of the ascending salmon, so that those higher up may profit . . . and also that part of these fish may reach the upper regions, there to spawn. The fishermen of the middle and higher regions, on their part, must also take into consideration the interests of the whole river. They are to spare a part of the ascending fish for natural propagation."

How well this plan worked out may be seen from the fact that catches declined drastically. The number of salmon auctioned at Kralingen dropped from an average of 59,600 annually in the years 1871 to 1889 to 38,300 in 1890 to 1907. In 1907 65,000 were caught in the entire river, and some of the productivity was due, said Hoek, to artificial propagation.

Worse was to come. The runs tobogganed around World War I. C. L. Deelder and D. E. Van Drimmelen described the debacle in a paper read at the seventh annual meeting of the International Union for the Protection of Nature held in Brussels in 1960. Radical alteration of the water regimen was disastrous: "Continuous improvement of the navigability of the rivers became a necessity; measures were also taken to ensure a better control of water drainage. At a later phase, hydroelectric plants were constructed on the upper rivers . . . Regulation of the river beds and construction of weirs brought about a complete change in the character of these rivers . . . More and more weirs appeared in the upper sections . . . and in most of the tributaries . . . [making] it in many cases completely impossible for [migrating fish] to reach their natural spawning grounds."

Ironically, World War II proved to be a boon to the fishery, for destruction of the weir near Kembs by Allied bombers facilitated fish migration to the upper reaches, resulting in a noteworthy revival of the runs four and a half years later. But eventually they petered out.

Even before the rapid growth of industry along the banks of the Rhine and some of its tributaries had befouled the once crystalline river, hydroelectric projects made migration of fish to the headwaters difficult or impossible. By 1930 there was a series of dams ten to forty feet high on the upper waters, tapping the flow for the generation of electricity. Some had poor fishways, others none. The upper Rhine became inaccessible to the salmon while the lower and middle Rhine were increasingly polluted. According to Deelder and Van Drimmelen, "Several spawning grounds in the tributaries became so badly polluted that they could no longer serve as such . . . Local pollution in the main river created migration blocks and made the reaches above the affected areas no longer accessible for spawners." Fewer and fewer salmon appeared at the auctions and in the 1950s they vanished.

Some feeble attempts have been made to clean up the Rhine in recent times. In 1950, the International Commission for the Protection of the Rhine Against Pollution was set up by Germany, Switzerland, the Netherlands, France, and Luxembourg, although its establishment was not ratified until 1963 and Austria never joined. "This organization, however, has no powers whatsoever," writes Jon Tinker in the *New Scientist* of October 26, 1972. "It can only recommend action on its member governments, and even its recommendations are often hamstrung by the need for international unanimity."

Some idea of the status of this river is given by Tinker after an extensive journey from Switzerland to the mouth: "In Switzerland, the Rhine is very much a secondary problem so far as water pollution is concerned: a river can be relied upon to cleanse itself eventually . . . In cantons whose effluents drain into lakes, many sewage works are now using tertiary (chemical) treatment, to remove the phosphates which are the main cause of eutrophication." The situation worsens as you go downstream.

In December 1970 the West German government made what seems like the first serious move to curb pollution of the Rhine when Dr. Jurgen Bernhold, head of a shipping firm whose barges were dumping 20,000 tons of detergent straight into the stream instead of transporting it to Rotterdam as regulations required, was sentenced to a year in jail and fined almost $30,000. Eleven other members of the company were given seven- to twelve-month sentences and small fines. The defense claimed that what the Hamburg firm did was universal among those operating Rhine barges, and *they* were getting away with it!

In 1970 between the Aar-Rhine confluence and the German-Dutch border there were nineteen major nuclear and conventional power stations; by 1975 the number will be tripled. To reduce thermal pollution the German states (*länder*) have required all nuclear plants to have cooling towers and no conventional station may heat up the river by more than 3° C. But Bavaria shows every sign of ignoring these requirements and France refuses to join the agreement.

France too permits potash mines to pollute the river with mountainous deposits of brine, thus seriously reducing the Rhine's capacity to break down sewage and other organic residues. There are of course other sources of pollution than heat and brine: sludge from the thousands of barges that navigate the river, untreated or partially treated sewage from German and French territories where standards for pollution control vary with the states or departments, and so on.

Rhine salmon are now but a memory. As one journeys along the river he can no longer see any fish jumping in the water as if they were glad to be home again after a long absence in the ocean — in fact, there are apparently few or no salmon left in the rivers of West Germany, Switzerland, or Holland. Today in the Rhine only eels and whitefish can be caught, and they are often so tainted with oil as to be inedible.

In 1963 I heard some talk of planting salmon eggs in "Vibert boxes" on the French side of the Rhine in Alsace, where promising nursery grounds existed. But it is hard to believe that even if the eggs were incubated salmon could live again in what has been called the longest sewer in Europe.[5]

There is a little museum on the German side of the river at the Rheinfall, much frequented by tourists. Here one may see photographs of salmon fishing in former times. At Stein-am-Rhein, a Renaissance Swiss village preserved in amber, as it were, there are restaurants called "Salmon Steubli" with brass signs of the fish swinging in the doorway. But not often is the fish served there, and when it is, one may assume it came from Canada or the Pacific Northwest in the United States.

As we contemplate the fiasco of the Rhine, we might recall the words of Louis de Boisset and Richard Vibert in their remarkable book *La Pêche Fluviale en France,* published during World War II: "Woe to the guardians of the public wealth who, through ignorance or the crime of carelessness, have permitted the property of which they were the keepers to slip through their hands, since they can be sure that God on the Day of Judgment will make them pass on the left side."

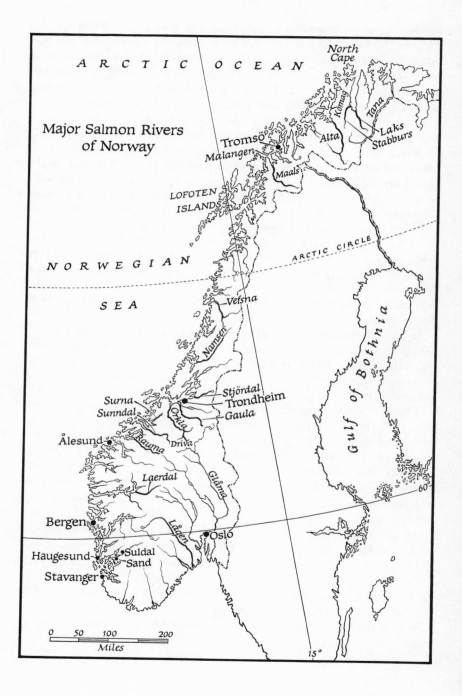

ARCTIC OCEAN

North Cape

Major Salmon Rivers of Norway

Tromsö
Malangen

Komag

Tana

Alta

Laks
Stabburs

Maals

LOFOTEN
ISLANDS

NORWEGIAN

ARCTIC CIRCLE

SEA

Vefsna

Namsen

Gulf of Bothnia

Stjördal
Trondheim

Surna
Sunndal

Orkla

Gaula

Ålesund

Rauma

Driva

Laerdal

Glåma

60

Bergen

Låven

Haugesund

Oslo

Suldal
Sand

Stavanger

0   50   100   200
        Miles

15°

VIII ~~

Norwegian Successes
and Setbacks

As WE MOVE northward on the map of Europe we may tick off great
rivers once renowned for their anadromous fishes but which are now
sterile. Leaving the Low Countries we note that the turbulent North
Sea used to feed the Weser and Elbe with a plentitude of salmon before man overfished them and civilization destroyed their habitats.
The Weser, flowing northward, is formed by the confluence of the
Fulda and Werra Rivers in Hanover and follows a gentle course of
280 miles across Germany to Bremerhaven. How far salmon used to
ascend this waterway I have been unable to learn.

The Elbe comes out of the Riesen Gebirge in Czechoslovakia; entering Germany, it becomes the country's second most important
river, a workhorse like the Rhine, with a total length of 700 miles. It
drops into the North Sea at Cuxhaven. In ancient times *Salmo salar*
went up this waterway as far as the borders of Czechoslovakia, but
there are now, I believe, no salmon in the Elbe, nor in the Weser, nor
many in any stream in Czechoslovakia, and few in East Germany.
In the Scandinavian peninsula, which comprises Norway, Sweden,
and part of Finland, there are still considerable stocks of salmon,
chiefly in Norway. Iceland, also a Scandinavian country, has a very
small supply. Denmark has driven the salmon out of its rivers.

Nowhere in Europe have these fishes chosen more sublime scenery
for their habitation than in Norway. The coastline is 1250 miles long
as the crow flies and extends over twelve degrees of latitude, curving
around the north of Sweden beyond the North Cape and to the Barents Sea. The northern counties are still in the Ice Age, although
there remain but few and scattered ice caps.

Rivers and Their Fishes

Norway is veined by numerous fjords of incredible beauty, many of
which serve as highways for fishes migrating to and from their rivers.

Some of the fjords, like Sogne Fjord, run inland for many score miles and are up to two and a half miles wide and two thirds of a mile deep. Offshore there is a belt of skerries, from a few feet to over a thousand in elevation, which have been stripped of rock by ice and water erosion. Most of the salmon rivers are short and often furious and are found in the central and northern counties, including Finnmark, which borders the Arctic Ocean. Many exhibit radical changes in flow. During the winter, when the earth is frozen, they are at an ebb, but when the thaw comes they swell enormously and become full-bodied streams — salmon usually ascend on the spring flood. In late summer the streams may run dry and then flood again in autumn. The best fishing is during the last part of the spring flood, from early to middle June in south Norway and from the last part of June to early July in north Norway. But the season varies from river to river, starting in late March and ending the last of August. About 200 Norwegian rivers and their affluents attract regular runs.

I have seen creeks in northern Norway so narrow a tall man could step across them, yet they contained spawning salmon. Troms and Finnmark provinces have the most northerly salmon streams in the world.

In the cold waters of the north salmon mature slowly. In the Finnmark and Tröndelag districts most of the parr remain three or four years in freshwater and occasional specimens five years. Once they have left the river they tend to move rapidly out to the open sea. Magnus Berg of the Norwegian Directorate of Fish and Wildlife reports that of 659 fish caught in Tana Fjord, a northern river, 48 percent had spent two winters in the ocean, 32 percent three winters, and 18 percent four winters. The larger rivers tend to produce heavy salmon, while in small rivers large fish are seldom seen. Moreover, because "spawning can hardly be as great a hardship in short and slow rivers as in long and rapid ones," says Berg, "in northern Norway . . . much of the salmon population spawns twice and conditions are therefore different from those in the south." [1]

Migrations

Where do the Norwegian salmon feed? Knut Dahl and Sven Sømme spent many years beginning in 1935 seeking to discover migratory circuits by tagging smolts at coastal stations. They learned that the fish went mostly in a northerly direction. However, at Rong, near Bergen, an appreciable movement was in a southerly direction to east Norway and west Sweden, although many salmon also went north. At the Melvaer marking station there was also a southerly movement, and several of the fish crossed the blustery North Sea and were captured as adults in the Moray Firth and the Forth and Tweed Rivers in Scotland. British salmon are sometimes caught in the Norwegian Sea. Smolts tagged at Titran, 220 miles north of Melvaer, generally moved toward the North Cape; one was recovered at a distance of 350 miles and another 500 miles, while a third went around the Cape and was captured at the mouth of the River Wyg in the White Sea, 1500 miles from the marking station.[2] A few individuals went south from Titran and were taken in the Skagerrak, but none seemingly crossed the sounds into the Baltic Sea. Later, some fish tagged in Norway turned up in the Greenland fishery.

Salmon from the west coast of Norway reveal a marked northerly migration pattern and do not move into the Baltic Sea.

The larger salmon who have been in the ocean two or more years arrive first and go up the rivers, while the grilse do not come until the middle of June. From then on the smaller fishes are most numerous in the catch until the very end of the season, when there is usually another influx of large fish. A peculiarity of the Norwegian fishes, according to Leiv Rosseland, Director of Freshwater Fisheries Research, is that salmon from different rivers grow at different rates. It was found that fish from the Tovdal River on the average weighed only 1.1 kilograms (2.2 pounds) after one year in the ocean, while corresponding salmon from the Arøy were almost twice as heavy. A Tovdal fish that had been two years in the ocean weighed on the average 3.7 kilograms (8.1 pounds), but an Arøy fish of the same age was almost twice as heavy.

The Fishery

The association of man with salmon in Scandinavia dates at least from the Neolithic and Bronze Ages. Inhabitants of the Arctic regions as far back as 1000 B.C. showed their appreciation of the animals that sustained them by carving their images on rocks, as the earlier cave dwellers did in France and Spain. Most of the pictures represent elk, red deer, reindeer, and bear and occasionally fishes such as whales, halibut, flatfish, and salmon. Rarely are human figures depicted.[3] A number of primitive fishing implements made of bone or antler have been discovered on ancient sites around Varanger Fjord. The nomadic Lapps of the far north used traps made of osier to catch salmon at the mouths of rivers and sometimes also fashioned crude seines.

In southern Scandinavia, especially Denmark, where the Maglemosian people lived on the banks of rivers or margins of lakes, numerous excavations show they fished on a considerable scale. There is a runic inscription from the early historic period on the Sele farm in Norway that refers to seine fishing at the mouth of the Figgen River, an excellent salmon stream today.

The oldest Scandinavian legislation on conservation goes back to about the year 900. It laid down the principle that "the salmon shall go from the beach to the mountains, if it wish to go." "This means that no man was allowed to close the salmon rivers and take all the fish for himself," says Magnus Berg. "But as the centuries passed and population increased many rivers were closed by traps or other gear, or by dams, and in some of them, especially in southeast Norway, the salmon almost disappeared." [4] A comprehensive fishery code was not enacted until 1848 and has since been revised many times.

Fishing rights in the rivers belong to the owner of the nearest shore. Hence a good salmon fishery is valuable to farmers and helps them to make ends meet.

In 1855 the government made an investigation of the status of the salmon and other freshwater fisheries and as a result inaugurated a conservation program that included hatcheries, salmon ladders, opening of rivers closed by dams, and other measures to protect the stocks. The new regulations restricted fishing to four days of the week or less for all gear except the rods, prohibited net fishing in estuaries, and the like. "Fortunately the river owners did cooperate as they understood these measures would benefit them, for they were induced to protect and restore the salmon stocks," says Berg.[5] The principal gear was the bag net, whose numbers jumped from 1700 in 1875 to around 9200 during World War II. It is a self-fishing device, set along the shore, which traps the fish seeking their home waters. No watchman is needed; the nets are emptied from time to time. In some districts, as in Finnmark, salmon are caught in spring by trolling from a motorboat in the river, but this gear has never been commercially feasible on a large scale. During the past century Norwegian netters have tended to move out of the rivers to the outer coasts and the high sea.

Until very recent years total catches have remained more or less stationary in the rivers, but after 1950 a long-line and drift-net fishery developed on a large scale in the sea and caused depletion of brood stocks. The result is that Norway's salmon resource is now seriously jeopardized.

Conservation

Because of the trichotomized life of the species, which spends its youth in freshwater, middle life in the ocean, and maturity and old age in the river, management of a salmon fishery is most successful in territorial waters and especially in the river. The basic aim is to obtain the maximum yields yet permit adequate numbers of fish to escape the fishermen and breed another generation. This goal may be pursued by:

1. Protecting the runs through biologically sound regulations that are well enforced.

2. Safeguarding the river or lake environment by preventing pollution and other deleterious changes in the water regimen, especially keeping up the flow and the dissolved oxygen content at levels fish need (salmon cannot survive if dissolved oxygen falls below five parts per million).

3. Keeping the rivers free from manmade obstructions or providing efficient passage over or around them.

4. Building ladders at difficult natural obstructions, clearing logjams and other barriers, and generally improving the pathways to the spawning grounds.

5. Restocking depleted streams with young fish that will return to the place of their release.

Norway has successfully applied nearly all these principles. About 150 waterfalls have been laddered since World War II, mainly in the northern counties, thereby opening up some 600 additional miles of water for spawning and rearing of young. Netting has been eliminated in most rivers, in order to give the stocks an opportunity to build back, and long-line fishing for salmon is prohibited in the twelve-mile coastal zone. Beyond this line, however, long lines are used and drift nets are also common.

Sport Fishing — The "Lords Rivers"

For many centuries the Norwegian rivers sustained the local people with fish and also in some areas provided them with income. After the Napoleonic Wars, when political conditions were stabilized and travel in Europe was again unrestricted, a few wealthy Britons invaded the continent seeking opportunities for their favorite pastimes. Some of them went to Switzerland and France to climb the Alps, then a novel adventure, while others, carrying fishing rods instead of pitons, pushed their way up the northern fjords to cast for salmon. The unlettered farmers, astonished at the arrivals' willingness to pay for the privilege of fishing their waters, welcomed them with a warmth that contrasted with their native taciturnity. Sir Hyde Parker, eighth baronet, and William Belton were among the earliest invaders. They fished the Alta and Namsen Rivers in the 1830s and sent back roseate reports, which inspired an hegira of British anglers. Belton's book *Two Summers in Norway* (1840) was apparently read by many of the bankers, diplomats, industrialists, and other wealthy persons who liked to fish for salmon. Sir Henry Pottinger discovered the possibilities of the Tana River in 1857 and gave considerable information about it in his book *Flood, Fell and Forest.* In those days a journey to the Tana involved a steamer from England, 200 miles away, and many days of travel by pony and cart and then canoe.

The Britons purchased or leased fishing rights not only on the Tana but the Namsen, Rauma, Stjørdal, Driva, Laerdal, Alta, and other streams that became known to the local people as "lords rivers." Among the aristocrats who frequented them were the Dukes of Roxburgh and Westminster, Lord William Beresford, the Earl of Leicester, Lord Arbuthnot, and many others. They usually brought hickory rods that were as much as twenty-four feet long, suitable tackle and other gear, and even provisions unobtainable in rural Norway. "I find it saves a deal of trouble," advised Fraser Sandeman in his *Angling Travels in Norway,* "to obtain supplies in Bergen or Trondheim, and the only provisions which I take from England are ham or bacon, and lime-juice cordial, which I find wholesome to take now and again where vegetables are scarce, which is generally the case in the country." It is also a good plan, he added, to send lettuce seeds ahead by post, so that by the time the fisher arrives on his river they "may be fit to pull, and he can sow a second crop. Green food of this description is a great comfort, especially if the summer be one of continuous heat." [6]

The visitors literally lived like lords. They built comfortable lodges and stocked them with sturdy furniture, books, gaming tables, etc. Many brought their wives and children, for the women were sometimes as ardent anglers as the men. An American traveler described the arrival of an English family at Kristiansand in the 1870s set for a summer campaign against the salmon. It took a lighter to carry all their baggage and supplies, "among which were many baskets of champagne, with a great abundance of provisions of nearly all kinds which good living could suggest . . . Off they went, with the good wishes of their friends left behind, with a journey of 30 or 40 miles before them to reach the river they had rented." [7]

British anglers left a tradition of gentility and courtesy that still lingers. They were rich, generous, and good sports. They fished night and day, and some set mighty records, like the Duke of Roxburgh, who in 1860 took thirty-nine salmon and grilse in one night on the Alta, and the Duke of Westminster, who seventy-five years later landed thirty-six salmon weighing 792 pounds in one night on the same stream. Since the sun never sets in summer in the far north men sometimes fished around the clock, hiring gillies in shifts.

As two world wars and socialist governments reduced the ranks of aristocrats in Europe as well as their wealth, many of the lords rivers were acquired by native and foreign plutocrats, American and British tycoons (like Sir Thomas Lipton), angling clubs, travel agencies, airlines, and shipping companies. Princes, also reduced in numbers, still fished the Laerdal, Alta, and other streams. For instance, Nicholas II's finance minister Nicholas Denisoff, who died in 1970, held the Arøy for fifty years and leased it to wealthy clients. Incidentally he holds the world's record for a fly-caught Atlantic salmon, sixty-eight and a half pounds.

Typical of the lords rivers is the Namsen, flowing into Namsenfjord in Trøndelag, a typical lords river that holds salmon in its deep pools over a stretch of thirty miles. In 1952 the Copenhagen newspaper *Berlingske Tidende* leased the Vibstad stretch and permitted twelve rods to fish simultaneously for two weeks in the summer. This proved to be so successful that hundreds of readers clamored for the privilege. Other sections of the Namsen were leased by a Swedish newspaper.

The Namsen lies in an idyllic and secluded part of northern Norway. It rushes through a deep and often rocky valley. From his boat the fisherman may see elk pause in the forest clearing, remain visible for an instant, and then turn away. The water is cold and blue, reflecting the cerulean sky. Patches of snow lie on the shoulders of the mountains toward the west. Overhead curlews cry hauntingly and the wind soughs through the pine woods that cling to the slopes. Since the nights are very short in summer the birds begin to sing at midnight when pink rays illumine the mountaintops.

The Namsen usually runs low and clear between its banks, but in spate it turns brown and may rise three feet above the normal level, making fishing impossible. After several days the flood thins out, fresh water from the sea rolls in, and with it come the husky salmon who move from pool to pool toward their spawning beds, occasionally jumping out of the water to show their magnificent silvery forms. The fish are taken by spinning or with a fly, or by harling from a boat, a form of trolling that allows the angler to use three rods simultaneously. Numerous giants have been caught on the Namsen since William Benton and Sir Hyde Parker discovered the river in the 1830s, but Parker's sixty-pounder is still the record.

There are other glorious waters in the northern counties of Trøndelag, Troms, Nordland, and Finnmark. The Alta is one of the most expensive rivers in the world to fish. Salmon congregate over a distance of more than twenty miles, reposing in beds strewn with large pebbles and gravel; the current is too swift for rowing, and the long narrow boats are punted by two men over and around the pools and rapids. Alta has only five beats, each for two rods, and skilled anglers who sleep through the day and fish during the eight-hour twilight have been known to kill as many as ten salmon averaging twenty-seven pounds each in a night.

Mals, 250 miles above the Arctic Circle, is a long and broad river, containing the renowned Malangfoss beat, which lies below the Malang waterfall. Here the river churns through 500 yards of broken boulders and mossy ledges before dropping seventy-five feet into the pool. The thundering falls blocks the entire spawning run and holds it up for almost one month. Thousands of silvery-pink salmon lie waiting in the tumbling currents until the water level drops and permits them to move up the ladder to reach their spawning haunts in the tributaries. The pool itself has been likened to "a water-filled stadium, 300 yards in diameter, shaped like a gargantuan bottle with the waterfall in the narrow throat." There is ample room for two or three boats at the edge of the pool where record catches have been made. The Earl of Dudley hooked a sixty-pounder in 1951, and fifty-pounders are not uncommon.

The Laerdal, flowing through a lovely valley into Sogne Fjord, has probably hosted more bluebloods, kings, princes, and titled personages than any river in the world. Some of its pools are named after British anglers. The largest fish taken on the Laerdal was a fifty-four-pounder gaffed by Bjarne Nolde.

Suldal River lies in Rogaland, 200 miles southwest of Oslo. Salmon run for about fifteen miles between Suldalsvatn Lake and its mouth.

The valley is wedged between narrow gorges, and the river tumbles in white water chutes down to timbered basins, past charming farmsteads and small villages. Fished by British anglers since 1884, the Suldal's extensive runs were eventually decimated by netsmen. Sport fishermen took control of the river around 1925, banned netting and trapping, and succeeded in nursing back the stock. The average salmon now caught weighs about twenty-five pounds, and a record specimen of sixty-four pounds was killed in recent years.

As demand for salmon angling has increased in recent decades the value of Norway's rivers grew rapidly. In the first decade of the twentieth century eighty rivers brought a total of 300,000 kroner in annual rentals to the farmers; in 1951, the total jumped to 450,000 kroner and in 1969 to over 3,100,000 kroner (about $530,000). In 1969 the Laerdal was rented for the record sum of $83,000; next came the Driva $63,750, followed by the Alta (formerly the top earner) $47,600, Namsen $24,800, and Vefsna $20,300. The largest catches were made in the Tana, Namsen, Gaula, Driva, Rauma, Laerdal, Komag, and Stjørdal Rivers.[8]

High Seas Fishery

Norway has been one of the top producers of Atlantic salmon for about two decades.

With the exception of Ireland, Norway has been the only country in Europe that has managed to increase its stocks. But now a dark cloud hovers over the horizon as a growing onslaught is being made on its stocks by drift netters and long liners operating in saltwater.

A peculiar drift-net fishery existed in a few fjords early in the twentieth century. Two men in an open sailboat operated a net 150 feet long and 20 feet deep, with a mesh of five knots to the foot. As many as ten nets were joined together and allowed to drift through the night in inshore waters. There were about 200 such drifters in operation in 1908, but their catches were usually small and eventually their numbers declined sharply. Now the boats are larger and their nets longer and they pursue salmon far offshore, from Bergen to Finnmark, beyond territorial waters. In the old days nobody really knew where the Norwegian salmon went to feed, although the general direction of their migrations was outlined by Dahl and Sømme in the 1930s. Now their movements are known, unfortunately, and the fishermen pursue them relentlessly, as off Greenland.

Modern drifters are large, gasoline-powered vessels; their nets are

shot as they steam slowly downwind, then the engines are stopped
and they swing around to face upwind. They drift through the night,
regardless of weather. When fish strike the nets they are fatally
coiled in the mesh. After each drift the nets are hauled aboard and
the fish are removed; when an ample cargo is accumulated it is
rushed to port. Magnus Berg reports that the nets not only catch
clean fish but kelts, which are practically worthless, and immature
salmon, with years of growth ahead of them. Besides decimating the
breeding stock, the nets inflict serious injuries on fish that manage to
escape, and this prevents them from spawning when they finally
reach their home rivers.

Long-lining in international waters in the Norwegian Sea began on
a very small scale in 1966 when ten boats participated; the next year
almost three times as many were competing, and the total catch was
about seventy-seven tons; in 1968 there were forty-six vessels that
took 408 tons and in 1969 fifty-one boats, including forty Danish, an
undetermined number of Norwegian, and a few German, Swedish,
and Faroese vessels, that caught a grand total of 918 tons. In 1969
the alarmed Norwegian government proclaimed a ban on drift-net
fishing inside a basic line drawn between the outermost skerries
along the Norwegian coast. However, no limitation was placed on
fishing beyond territorial limits. An agreement negotiated among
the various nations in 1970 preserved the status quo in the Norwegian
Sea — that year the long-line and drift-net fishery landed a record
of 958 tons of salmon.

Long-lining occurs from 30 to 300 nautical miles west of the north

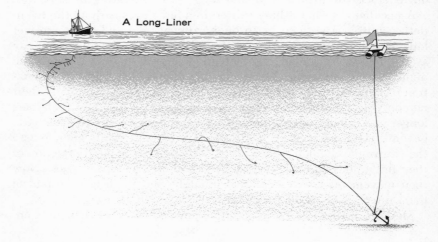

A Long-Liner

Norwegian coast, taking salmon as far as the eastern side of North Cape and Bearen Island. The most lucrative area is from the Lofoten Islands north to Troms. In the southern sector of operations even Swedish and British salmon are caught, while in the northern area Russian fish are interrupted on their homeward journeys, but the high-seas fishery mostly exploits Norwegian fish, as tagged specimens prove. The fleets are most active from April to the end of June, but some boats prowl the sea in February and others in the autumn. With the high price that salmon fetches, these catches are quite lucrative.

The effects of drift netting and long-lining in the sea have reduced home water catches from 1692 tons in 1967 to only 1034 tons in 1971 and escapement into the rivers, thus jeopardizing the livelihood of many fishermen and returns to farmers who own the rivers. No longer is Norway regarded by sportsmen as the best country to catch large salmon.

Appendix Tables 1 and 2 show the precipitous decline of Norwegian catches.

Catches on the Driva, for example, fell from 23,172 kilograms in 1965 to 13,055 kilograms in 1971. The increased number of nets at the mouth of this river, from 28 in 1963 to 1540 in 1969, was a contributing factor. There was no netting inside the river, but five salmon traps were still operating in 1969.

Catches on the Alta also fell drastically as indicated by the official figures, from 1250 salmon weighing 5785 kilograms in 1964 and 1448 weighing 10,828 kilograms in 1965 to 598 weighing 2658 kilograms in 1968. What is equally disturbing is that trophy-size fish are becoming increasingly scarce. Similar trends were reported on other prestigious streams.

In 1971 the twenty best rivers and their catches, including small amounts of sea trout and migratory char, were as follows (in kilograms):

River	Catch	River	Catch
Namsen	13,454	Surna	5,309
Driva	13,055	Komag	5,020
Ørsta	12,870	Mals	4,447
Lagen	10,371	Rauma	3,913
Gaula	8,998	Orkla	3,661
Bondal	7,887	Aurland	3,570
Tana	7,865	Etne	3,538
Laerdal	7,733	Verdal	3,270
Stjørdal	7,260	Alta	3,205
Neiden	7,007	Vefsna	3,200

Much of the salmon caught by rod and reel in northern Norway are now sold to local fish markets at high prices. "These prices tend to encourage a kind of professional fisherman whose objective is more to make money than it is to enjoy the sport," says Ambassador Philip K. Crowe, an ardent angler. "By ruling that only flies can be used and keeping the cost of fishing well above any reward for the salmon caught, some rivers in Norway have preserved good fishing for the few who can afford it." [9] Only fly-fishing is permitted on the Alta and on sections of the Laerdal.

There are other threats to the Norwegian resource besides high seas fishing. Increased development of hydroelectric power to satisfy the voracious demands of the aluminum, forest products, and chemical industries threatens some races of salmon. For example, the Norwegian government has a plan under consideration to dam the upper part of the Gaula, Norway's fifth largest salmon producer, and even to build a power plant on the great fosse, where there is now an ancient ladder. Catches have been dropping on the Gaula since 1965;

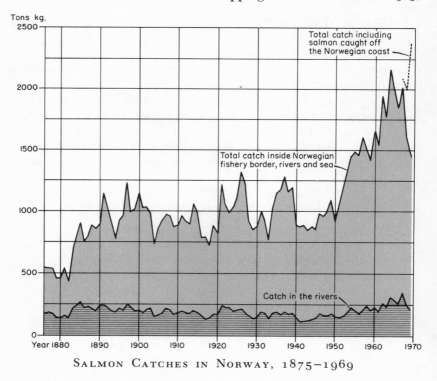

SALMON CATCHES IN NORWAY, 1875–1969

the giant fish of yesteryear are rarely seen, and the record forty-eight-pounder caught by Rolf Olsen on July 6, 1930, will probably never be surpassed.

In southeastern Norway some rivers are menaced by drifting atmospheric pollution from foreign countries, especially from the British Isles. According to Brynjulf Ottar, head of the Norwegian Institute for Air Research, as quoted in the Manchester *Guardian* of January 8, 1970, southern Norway's forests and freshwater fisheries could be eventually destroyed unless steps are taken internationally to curb air pollution.

To counter these adverse trends the government continues to build salmon hatcheries, install ladders at waterfalls, and maintain some control over the rivers. According to the Food and Agriculture Organization's *Aquaculture Bulletin* (October 1972) there are now 25 holding stations for spawning salmon, 160 hatcheries, 30 rearing stations for fingerlings and 4 for smolt, and a number of small natural ponds for fingerlings. All these facilities are used for sustaining wild stocks. In addition, there is a burgeoning salmon mariculture industry, described in Chapter XIX.

But if offshore fishing continues on a large scale, the conservation program may be abandoned. "River owners or the salmon fishermen in Norway would not like to see the same conditions as in the Baltic," says Magnus Berg, "where the Swedes produce most of the salmon and the Danes take the lion's share of the catch." If such a development occurs, "the rivers will probably be used for other purposes than the raising of salmon and the production will be so reduced that the fishery in international waters will stop because there will be no fish to catch. And that will be the end of the giant salmon of Norway." [10]

It would seem that Norway could effectively curb the harmful high seas fishery not only by international agreement, similar to the phase-out of the Greenland salmon fishery negotiated by the nations in 1972, but by forbidding its nationals to engage in long-lining and drift netting in offshore waters, as the British government stopped the ocean fishery off the Scottish coast. At the time of writing there are no signs that Norway is moving in that direction.

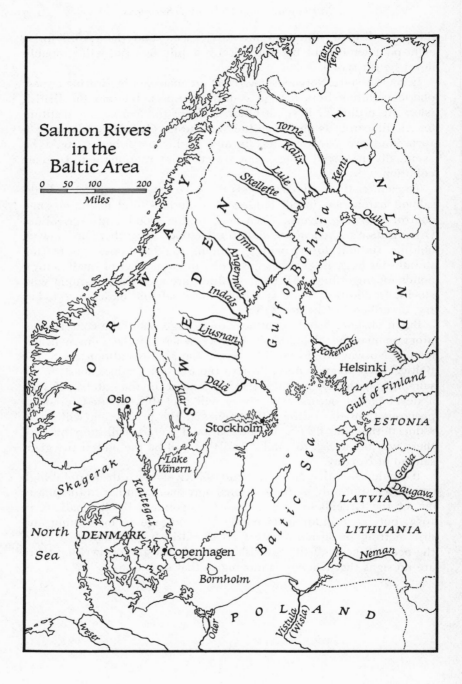

Salmon Rivers
in the
Baltic Area

0   50   100   200
Miles

NORWAY

SWEDEN

FINLAND

Tana
Teno

Torne

Kalix

Lule

Skellefte

Kemi

Oulu

Ume

Angerman

Gulf of Bothnia

Indals

Kokemaki

Kymi

Ljusnan

Helsinki

Dalä

Gulf of Finland

Klara

ESTONIA

Stockholm

Oslo

Gauja

Lake
Vänern

Daugava

Skagerak

LATVIA

Kattegat

LITHUANIA

Baltic Sea

North
Sea

DENMARK

Neman

Copenhagen

Bornholm

Weser

Oder

POLAND

Vistula
(Wisla)

Baltic and Arctic Salmon

The Baltic Sea and Its Fishes

FISHERMEN of a half-dozen countries ply the waters of the Baltic, a great and deep inland sea, 1050 miles long, encompassing 157,000 square miles, and plentifully stocked with cod, herring, sprat, and to a small extent salmon. Its greatest depth is about 1200 feet between the island of Gotland and the Swedish mainland. The northern reaches in the Gulf of Finland and Gulf of Bothnia are ice-bound for three to five months of the year, depending on the severity of the winter, and in some years the sounds connecting the North Sea and the brackish waters of the Baltic freeze over.

Denmark, Sweden, Finland, Russia, Poland, and Germany, all originally large producers of salmon, border the Baltic Sea. Of these, Denmark has driven the fishes from its rivers, Poland has reduced them to a token resource, and in Germany they are a vanishing species (it is difficult to obtain information on the subject).

Salmon find the southern Baltic waters a favorable habitat; here they feed and grow rapidly and are eagerly sought by fishermen from Denmark, Sweden, Finland, Poland, and Germany. During the first year in this protected body of water the salmon feed mainly on insects floating on the surface of the water; later they go on a fish diet. The smolts move rapidly from their northern rivers to the south, swimming close to shore. Dr. Borje Carlin reported that smolts released near the mouth of the Indal River in northern Sweden at the end of May reached the main basin of the Baltic by September and October. After more than a year, some of the fish left their rich pastures and started their homeward journey. These one-winter fish, all males, were caught in Swedish rivers and along the coast in July, August, and September of the year following smolt migration.

During the second winter the remaining fish of a given year-class are spread throughout the main basin of the Baltic proper and are subjected to a very intense fishery. Salmon from the various Baltic lands commingle, feeling safer from nonhuman predators as they grow larger.

In the spring of the second year a considerable proportion of the stock leaves the feeding grounds and heads for natal waters, where they are exposed to an intensive fishery in the estuaries and rivers. Few salmon appear to venture through the sounds into the North Sea, although fish from rivers on the west coast of Sweden have been found in the Greenland fishery.[1] Some Swedish salmon stay in the pleasant Baltic waters three or four winters; upon their return they weigh ten to fifteen kilograms (twenty-two to thirty-three pounds). After four winters few members of any year-class remain.

Not all the salmon from northern rivers migrate as far as the southern Baltic, where the heaviest fishing occurs. A small and varying percentage stay in the Gulf of Bothnia and mature there.

Carlin's extensive studies show that the Baltic salmon have an uncanny ability to find their native rivers after an absence of several years. "It is evident," he says, "that the homeward migration is divided into two different stages, one being the return voyage . . . to the coast in the vicinity of the river mouth, and the second the final orientation into the river. From the works of Hasler and his collaborators we have reason to believe that the first one could be a rather complicated navigation, guided by the position of the sun, and that the second one is connected with a memory of the smell of the home river."

Carlin found that smolts reared in one stream and planted in another, sometimes very far away and under such conditions that they would go to sea promptly, always returned to the river where they were released, not to the parental stream. "This indicates that the memory of the smell of the water of the home river is not imprinted during the two years or more of their parr stage, but during a few days, at most a couple of weeks, immediately before entering the sea."[2]

Fish and Power, Too

Where do the Baltic salmon come from? Finland has small stocks, Poland even less; Sweden is the largest contributor and Soviet Russia next. Sweden has made an enormous effort to preserve its salmon in the face of increasing usurpation of the rivers by hydroelectric developments. It is one of the most highly electrified countries in the world, with a per capita consumption exceeded only by that of Norway, Canada, and the United States. Eighty percent of the hydroelectric potential is in the north, where the bulk of the salmon rivers are located — the Dal, Ljungan, Indal, Angerman, Ume, Skellefte, and Lule.

The voracious demand for electricity (chiefly for manufacturing) after World War II brought the nation face to face with the question, as in other European countries and the United States, of whether it is possible to have fish and power, too. Unlike France, Spain, and Finland, to cite but a few examples, Sweden undertook to answer this question in the affirmative — as Ireland and Scotland have. It was determined to save the fisheries and add the expense to consumers' electric bills.

In the early phases of hydroelectric development Sweden followed the conventional procedure of installing fishways at the dams. But it became clear as more projects were built that every barrier, even with fish passes, was diminishing the stocks. Moreover the Swedish Water Courts, acting under a special water law, would not approve licenses for power dams unless the farmers who owned the rivers were compensated and loss of wild fish was replaced by artificial production.

Carlin tells how the challenge was met:

> The salmon stocks in our rivers have been suffering from damages caused by logging operations and dam building for a considerable time. Pollution has not been a major problem in the northern rivers, since most of the polluting industries are situated near the river mouths or on the coast. As long as the power plants were utilizing single steep falls, their main influence on the salmon was to prevent the spawners from reaching the spawning grounds. This could to a certain extent be compensated for by building fishways. Also, at least theoretically, the lost spawning could be replaced by planting salmon fry from hatcheries, although it has never been proved that the hundreds of millions of fry that have been planted in the rivers during many years has had any effect at all in improving the salmon stocks.
>
> In rivers with several dams the salmon could be collected at the lowest dam and transported past the dams to be released above the obstructions, and this has been done in some Swedish rivers quite successfully.[3]

As the spawning areas were destroyed by hydroelectric schemes, fewer fishways were constructed and many old ones were removed. Reliance was increasingly placed on sustaining the runs by artificial production on a scale never before attempted in Europe. The salmon were reared at considerable expense to the smolt stage and liberated at the mouths of the rivers below the dams. Financed by the electric power industry, which is partly government and partly privately owned, the program was started in 1951, said Carlin, "with more hope than actual knowledge about how it would work."

If you visit the Bergeforsen dam on the Indal River in northern Sweden, the lowermost in a series of thirteen generating stations stretching from Lake Størsjon to the Gulf of Bothnia, you will see logs hurtling down the 425-foot chute at the rate of 21,000 per hour, heading for the mill downstream, but no fish are using this bypass. At the rearing plant below the dam the salmon are trapped as they return from the Baltic Sea and stripped of their eggs and milt. A plaque informs the visitors that:

> The station is built to produce fry and young migratory fish who, before the erection of the power plant, could reproduce freely in the river. Through the river they reached the sea, maintaining rich populations of salmon, sea-trout and river spawning whitefish. Now, instead, the fry and young are liberated from the rearing station.

From modest beginnings in 1951 the hatchery program expanded until it now comprises seventeen "fish factories" producing about 2 million smolts annually for release in the Ljusnan, Ljungan, Indal, Angerman, Ume, Skellefte, Lule, and other rivers where natural production has been eliminated or reduced to token levels. Since two years are required to rear the fish to the smolt stage, "it could never be expected," said Carlin, "to be a very good business from a purely fishery point of view because its costs would be very high."

The Swedish rearing plants are models of efficient and antiseptic operations. In nature only one egg out of a hundred eventuates into a smolt, according to Carlin, but in artificial rearing, in Sweden, at least 50 percent survive to the smolt stage and go to sea.

The Baltic Fishery

Salmon are relentlessly pursued in the Baltic for eleven months of the year by gill netters and long liners issuing from the island of Bornholm, from Swedish and Finnish fishing villages, from Kiel in Germany, and from Danzig in Poland. They operate mainly around Bornholm (which belongs to Denmark), where the sea seems to be particularly rich in food the salmon like, and farther north between the Swedish islands of Öland and Gotland. They also fish off Memelland down to Brüster Ort and in the Bay of Danzig. Despite a convention signed in 1966 by Denmark, West Germany, and Sweden setting a minimum size of sixty centimeters (23.6 inches) for fish that can be taken, the bulk of the catches, at least those made by the Danes, seems to consist of small and immature fish. For example, of the 500,000 salmon landed by Danish vessels in the east Baltic in the 1967–1968 season, 278,000 weighed only one to three kilograms (2.2–6.6 pounds), 116,000 three to four kilograms (6.6–8.8 pounds), and 106,000 over four kilograms. These figures suggest that the minimum net size is too small and the fishery would gain by permitting more salmon to remain in the sea another winter or two, harvesting them preferably when they return to the rivers.

Total Baltic catches fluctuated in the 1950s and 1960s between 2000 and 4000 metric tons. In the years 1964 through 1967 Danish fishermen took 54 percent, Swedish 16 percent, Finnish 12 percent, West German 7 percent, Polish 6 percent, and Russian 5 percent. Sweden contributes about half of the salmon in the Baltic Sea, Finland 10 to 15 percent, and Russia and Poland most of the remainder.

The Danish fishery has grown rapidly in the past two decades. Before World War II only a few Danish vessels fished for salmon with drift nets in a zone twenty to twenty-five kilometers (twelve to fifteen miles) from Bornholm from February to May, and with long lines from October to January. Within one kilometer of the Bornholm coast fixed nets were used. In those days twenty-five to fifty metric tons were landed annually compared with an average of over 1100 tons from 1961 to 1968. Profits are high: in 1969 the price paid to fishermen was around twenty Danish kroner per kilogram or $1.20 a pound.

A typical forty-ton cutter operating in the Baltic carries a crew of four men. Fishing is a ceaseless task of laying out nets or lines and hauling them in, often in cold and even subzero weather or in the teeth of a gale. The waters are frozen one winter out of five and the sea is a thin sheet of ice. Catches must be cleaned and packed in narrow quarters. In the night, when most of the fishing is done, passing ships may foul the lines and sometimes collisions occur. Each night's catch must be landed at the nearest port and the gear readied for another drift.

Copenhagen, where fishermen from the Baltic and Greenland and Norwegian waters land their catches, now vies with London as the major European marketplace for Atlantic salmon. About 50 percent of the volume sold there is smoked for the luxury trade.

Sweden is the only country in Europe, except possibly Russia, which has been interested enough in its salmon to invest heavily in hatcheries. Although an expensive undertaking, it has returned most of the investment and maintenance costs.

To obtain information on the fate of the smolts released into the Baltic rivers the Swedish Salmon Research Institute through 1963 tagged 800,000 fishes before they were sent off to sea. The average return to the home stream was extraordinarily high, about 12 percent for the Bothnian rivers, or fifty kilograms (110 pounds) of adult fish for every hundred smolts — a record that cannot be matched anywhere in Europe. These returns suggest that the stocks have been maintained at levels roughly equal to those that existed before the rivers were blockaded and the number of fish available to the commercial fishery had not suffered. In addition, the hatchery program provides at least a fourth of all the salmon caught in the Baltic Sea, the Danes being the largest benefactors of Swedish largess.

River Fisheries

Swedish river fisheries were quite extensive at one time — of the fifty streams known to have held salmon, three-quarters empty into the Baltic. The central and northern Baltic rivers flow through a region of soft, undulating, and sparsely settled landscapes covered with forests of spruce, birch, and pine. The villages are filled with wooden houses painted in gay colors, each with its white church surmounted by a black steeple. Railway bridges are of vast dimensions and the rivers are full of log rafts being floated to the sawmills and pulp mills. In the winter heavy snows blanket the earth and the waters are frozen solid. Then the white-barked birches stand as sentinels against the bleak skies, while the pines and spruce form symmetrical green patterns to enliven the scene. There is little daylight. Young salmon are hibernating in the deep water, waiting for spring and the insect world to call them back to life.

Originally the far northern rivers were fished by the reindeer-keeping Lapps, who built barrier traps across the narrows and took many salmon. The Scandinavians in the Middle Ages fished with seines, and one imagines that the Vikings who sailed their long ships across the Baltic and out to the North Sea stored plenty of fishes for these journeys, including those which took them to Iceland and North America.

I visited the mouth of the Ume River with a Swedish biologist who was showing me the eel traps and salmon weir. "Here," he said, "the Vikings embarked across the Baltic for the conquest of Russia. Did you know that the name Russia is Scandinavian?" I answered that I did not.

As we walked along the bank, flanked by a forest of white birch, no human habitations could be seen. In the fading twilight coppery fishes occasionally jumped out of the water in swift, arclike movements. It was too early to see the eels, who move at night.

Here populations of anadromous and catadromous fishes live side by side, a not uncommon occurrence in Europe. The salmon come back to their native river after a long journey in the sea to spawn and breed another generation; the eels, born in the distant Sargasso Sea, come as tiny elvers, feed and grow, and after many years in the rivers return eventually to the Sargasso Sea to spawn and die. Not many salmon survive the mating; all the eels perish and the eggs incubate at the bottom of the ocean.

Until fairly recently the fishing industry had flourished in Norrland rivers, providing the farmers with a food supply and extra income. Most of the catches were sold at a central marketing center whence they were shipped to Stockholm and other large cities. The peasants generally prepared the salmon in simple ways, baked or partly steamed on top of potatoes in a boiling pot, just as the Vikings used to do. Nowadays salmon is prepared in a more sophisticated manner: At breakfast one is served smoked salmon, really the mild-cured "lox" sold in American delicatessen stores, and at dinner salmon may be poached or grilled.

The usual arrangement in the nineteenth century was for several farmers to own a weir or seine jointly and divide the harvest from the river according to the number of people in each household. Abundance fluctuated and one year's catches was no index for the next. On the whole, according to studies by Dr. Arne Lindroth, the swings were due chiefly to "changes in the biological balance induced by climatic factors." Cyclical fluctuations in population of fish and birds that prey on salmon, and insects and fishes that constitute their food supply, may be influential, but there are no real clues, says Lindroth, for the quality of the northern Swedish rivers remained fairly stable until they were harnessed for power production.[4]

One by one the power industry has usurped most of the streams. The energy goes chiefly to industry, and the demand, as in the United States, is voracious. River fishing has fallen to a very low level and farmers now must usually purchase their salmon, for not many are left in all but two or three northern rivers.

In the years 1964–1970 an average of 600 metric tons of salmon were landed annually in Sweden (Appendix Table 1). In 1970 1370 tons of salmon were imported from the United States alone.

Finland's Salmon

Finland is a heavily forested land dissected by thousands of rivers and lakes. Practically the entire country lies north of latitude 60° N. Finland stretches from the Gulf of Finland to well within the Arctic Circle; some of the rivers flow into the Arctic Ocean and the others into the Baltic. About 70 percent of the land is covered with trees; pine, Scots fir, Norway spruce, and birch mixed with aspen predominate. Some of these species are excellent pulping trees — pulp, paper, and other forest products account for about 60 percent of exports.

"The presence of [50,000] lakes," says the geographer Andrew C. O'Dell, "besides adding to the charms of the landscape, has permitted the opening up of the forests by providing waterways as well as by stabilizing runoff, and so encouraging the development of hydroelectricity." [5] As in other Scandinavian countries that have very high standards of living, the Finns are massive consumers of electricity, most of which is used by industry. Power production tripled between 1950 and 1965; "hydroelectric development is moving at such a rapid pace," says the biologist Seppo Hurme in *The Anadromous Fishes in the Baltic-side Rivers of Finland*. "[that] all of our rivers will be full of dams in the next twenty or thirty years." Unlike Sweden, however, Finland has harnessed its rivers with little or no consideration for the anadromous fishes — in fact, the bulk of the stocks have been destroyed.

For example, the 300-mile Kemi, which flows through the Lapland fells and tundra to the Gulf of Bothnia, a region inhabited by few human beings but large herds of reindeer, lynx, and elk, has the largest power potential of any Finnish river. The Kaakama salmon weir at the mouth of the Kemi was fished for several hundred years. In the period 1923 to 1948 the annual catch here fluctuated between 800 and 2500 kilograms of salmon and 250 to 2800 kilograms of trout, providing the farmers not only with food but with income as well.

South of the Kemi flows the Oulo, also a northern stream, only sixty-five miles long, passing a series of waterfalls from Lake Oulo to the Gulf of Bothnia. Before hydroelectric plants were built, salmon used to ascend to Lake Oulujärvi and its feeder streams and spawned in both the lake and river. Now there are few salmon in the Oulo and none in the Kemi.

A similar fate befell the two great salmon rivers of southern Finland, the Kymi and Kokemaki. In 1948 the biologist T. H. Jarvi wrote: "These rivers almost completely lost their original conditions and simultaneously their importance as salmon rivers. Dams now block the ascent of salmon and consequently have done away with feeding areas for parr. Several fishing stations where my material was formerly collected have had to cease operations. This occurred in the western arm of the Kymi River at Ahvenkoski Rapids in 1931 and in its eastern arm, the Langinkoski Rapids and Kanninkoski Rapids in 1938 . . . This is also the case in the Kokemaki River. The construction of a power station at Pirila Rapids in Harjavalta in 1940 has stopped the ascent of salmon to the upper part of the Kokemaki River." [6]

In 1966 Seppo Hurme published his survey of Finland's rivers, a project undertaken at the behest of the International Council for the Exploration of the Sea. "Each salmon and trout river," he says, "has been investigated particularly as fishery production units, taking into consideration nature, usage, care and conservation." The forty-seven waterways were divided into four classes: (1) six large rivers, (2) twenty medium-sized streams, (3) seventeen small rivers, and (4) four uncertain. Hurme found that "natural salmon and trout stocks have now died in 15 rivers due to cultural effects. This includes 4 large and 6 medium-sized rivers, so that the loss of salmon and trout is notably large." Destruction of habitat was also apparent in other streams, "so that the preservation of salmon and trout stocks is now fully threatened." [7] Hurme listed the following reasons for the disappearance of the fishes: damming of rivers, pollution, regulation for drainage and flood control, drying of swamps and bogs, timber floating, silting of river mouths, overfishing at river mouths, and catches of small salmon in the southern part of the Baltic Sea.

Among major Finnish rivers only the Torne, which forms the boundary between Sweden and Finland, and the Ii have not yet been completely dammed and continue to contribute substantial numbers of smolts to the Baltic.

Hurme has projected an ambitious scheme for repopulating the riv-

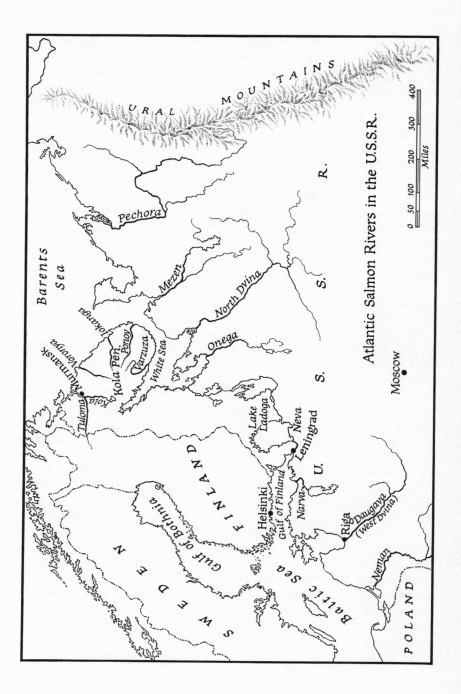

Atlantic Salmon Rivers in the U.S.S.R.

MOUNTAINS

URAL

Barents Sea

Pechora

Mezen

North Dvina

Onega

Iokanga

Ponoy

Varzuga

Voronya

Kola Pen.

Kola

White Sea

Murmansk

Tuloma

FINLAND

SWEDEN

Gulf of Bothnia

Helsinki

Gulf of Finland

Lake Ladoga

Neva

Leningrad

Narva

Baltic Sea

Riga

Daugava (West Dvina)

Neman

POLAND

Moscow

R.

S.

S.

U.

0 50 100   200   300   400
Miles

ers by means of large-scale artificial production; the fishes would be released, as in Sweden, below the lowermost dams. They would thus augment the Baltic supply and a certain percentage would return to provide a perpetual breeding stock. He estimated that the six large rivers could support plantings of 3,425,000 smolts annually and all the other suitable waters an additional 1,075,000 fish, or about as much together as the potential of all Baltic rivers on the Swedish side. But he cautioned that "the state machinery works very slowly in handling such matters," and the huge amounts of capital involved could probably not be found in Finland. However, the new Finnish Water Law, like its prototype the Swedish Water Law, imposes an obligation on power agencies to compensate for losses of natural runs. Under this program the first modern salmon hatchery in Finland, at Monatta, was completed to produce 200,000 smolts annually for release in the Oulu River.

Hurme has also studied the possibility of rehabilitating some of the small salmon and trout rivers in southwestern Finland that flow into the Baltic. "The old belief that southwestern Finland is poor salmon territory is not altogether correct," he says. "The fact is that the southern part, from Hangö to Turku, is a noteworthy salmon-fishing area, due to these rivers, and particularly the open sea, near Paimio." Obstructions and pollution have ruined them. He selected five streams where about 100,000 smolts could be planted yearly, but "there are other small rivers, streams and drains which flow into the open sea, and could well be included in the [salmonid] program," in accordance with the Water Law and its obligations.[8]

The increasing pollution of the Baltic Sea does not bode well for the fisheries, especially species like salmon requiring considerable amounts of dissolved oxygen. The Club of Rome's study, *Limits of Growth,* published in 1972, notes that the accumulation of organic wastes in the Baltic, where water circulation is minimal, has resulted in steadily decreasing oxygen concentration. In some areas, especially in deeper waters, the oxygen concentration is zero and almost no forms of aquatic life can be supported. In time the salmon populations will certainly be affected if this trend continues.

Denmark, Poland, and Russia

North of the Elbe, the most important salmon river was the 100-mile Guden, the longest river in Denmark, which issues from north central Jutland and flows into Randersfjord, an inlet of the Kattegat. Now there are no salmon in the Guden. Having driven these fishes out of their country, the Danes are taking the salmon of other nations in large numbers in the Baltic Sea, Norwegian Sea, and Greenland waters.

Poland still contributes to the Baltic melting pot. Salmon have apparently disappeared from the Oder River, which has its source in the mountains of Moravia and is fed by many tributaries over a 500-mile course that terminates in the Bay of Pomerania. Only a remnant of the once prolific runs are still found in the Vistula River, which flows from the Carpathian Mountains for almost 700 miles, passing Warsaw, to the Gulf of Danzig. They spawn in at least two of the tributaries, the Sota and Skawa above Cracow. No figures are available on the size of the Vistula runs, but Lindroth estimates that about 100,000 smolts are being produced in Poland annually.

Like Germany, Poland, beset by complex economic and political problems since the last world war, seems to be disinterested in conserving its salmon stocks. Sea trout have replaced salmon as a favorite freshwater fish. This species is receiving a big play by sport fishermen, and its eggs are exported to many countries, especially France, where it is being used to create a substitute recreational fishery for the vanishing salmon.

Soviet Russia's Atlantic salmon stocks are believed to be considerable, for there are many productive rivers flowing into the Baltic Sea and Arctic Ocean. The Baltic rivers include the two major Lithuanian waterways, the Niemen and Venta, and the Latvian Daugava (West Dvina), which issues from the swampy area of the Valday Hills, only a few miles from the sources of the Dnieper and Volga, and drops into the Gulf of Riga 635 miles away.

Arctic rivers are more numerous and impressive. They include the Onega, the North Dvina, 455 miles long, with many tributaries (of which one, the Vychegda, is 655 miles long), and the 550-mile Mezen, all emptying into the White Sea. The longest Arctic Atlantic salmon river is the Pechora, which rises in the northern Ural Mountains and follows a course of 1100 miles to the Barents Sea. It is said to be the easternmost limit of Atlantic salmon's range, although the species has been reported in the Kara River to the east. Salmon push their way far up the Pechora to mate in the foothills of the Urals.

In a paper published in the *Journal du Conseil* (Vol. XXIII), issued by the International Council for the Exploration of the Sea, N. M. Vladimiriskaya claims that only large fish reach the upper waters of the Pechora, a journey of perhaps a thousand miles (which must be a record for *Salmo salar*), yet she found that 11 percent of the specimens examined were two-time spawners and 2 percent three-timers. Females in this group outnumbered males by two to one. Pechora smolts usually have been in the river over three years, by which time they are five inches long and weigh nine ounces.

There are also salmon stocks in the shorter Ponoy, Chavanga, Pislica, Chaloma, Kola, and Tuloma Rivers flowing into the Barents Sea. In these waters the fishes enter the rivers in the spring, whereas those in the White Sea tend to return in the fall. Spawning in the Arctic region occurs from September to November; the eggs usually take six months to hatch in this frigid climate. The young fish stay in freshwater of the Kola Peninsula one to five years, and catches in this area comprise salmon four to seven years old. Some of them may be five feet long and weigh up to forty-five kilograms (almost 100 pounds).[9]

The feeding grounds of the salmon native to Arctic rivers are believed to be in the southern part of the Barents Sea and northern part of the Norwegian Sea as far as Spitsbergen. They are harvested in the coastal zone and at the river mouths with set seines and drift nets. Inside the rivers they are taken with lines or spinning gear. No salmon are fished in the ocean in Russia. Fishing lasts from the time the ice retreats in the spring until it reappears in the autumn.

The Russians say they have instituted measures to conserve the Atlantic salmon, as they do the much more numerous Pacific salmon. Fishing is prohibited on the spawning grounds and adjacent to dams, gear and seasons are closely regulated, and a limit on catches is established. It is not permitted to obstruct more than two thirds of a river channel, and the migratory routes must be kept clear. How well these measures are enforced we do not know.

There are fish ladders at some of the dams; for example, a ladder twenty meters high (sixty-six feet) at Tuloma dam on the Tuloma River (on which the ice-free Arctic port of Murmansk is situated) consists of a series of stepped-up pools; 7300 salmon were reported to have been counted here in 1958. There is a fishway at Kegum dam on the Daugava River that utilizes 8.25 cubic feet of water per second as attraction current. These installations suggest that the Russians safeguard the fishes when power is generated.

There are hatcheries producing smolts to replenish the streams. The magnitude of their output is not disclosed, but the Soviets claim they can rear seagoing smolts in eight months (compared with two years in Sweden) through the use of specially prepared feeds.[10]

The status of Russia's Atlantic salmon stocks is difficult to ascertain owing to the lack of information available in non-Russian literature — few Russian papers on this subject have so far been translated into English.

Kazimierz and Rutkowicz in their book on the Barents Sea claim that the Russians harvested some 1800 tons of Atlantic salmon per year in the period 1920 to 1939. Data published by the International Council for the Exploration of the Sea show that catches averaged about 1000 metric tons in the years 1955 to 1966. Eighty to 90 percent of the total probably came from stocks originating in Arctic rivers and the remainder from Baltic streams. Dr. Arne Lindroth estimates that the Russian Baltic rivers send about 2 million smolts to the sea each year, a drop from the original 3-million level, indicating that there has been a substantial loss of original stocks.[11]

On a recent journey to Murmansk, Ambassador Philip K. Crowe discussed the status of the Atlantic salmon with scientists of the Polar Institute. He says: "Dr. Sergei S. Surkon, the salmon specialist, told me that the Kola Peninsula catch, which was 600 tons in 1960, will not be more than 250 tons in 1972. He laid the decline mainly to deep-sea fishing off the Lofotens. The Kola salmon, like those of Norway, are caught on this feeding ground by the long baited lines of Norwegian and Danish commercial fishermen. He was pleased at our success in persuading the Danes to stop salmon fishing off Greenland and hoped that a similar agreement could be worked out for the Lofoten feeding grounds."

So rare has salmon become in Murmansk Oblast that sport fishing has been prohibited until this year when one river, the Titovka, was opened to the public on a special license with a limit of one fish per day, but only one angler in twenty actually caught a fish. Rivers are still netted by the state, but "only fifty percent of the salmon are caught and the rest are allowed to go up the river to breed."[12]

X ~~⌒~~

The American Experience

In the Beginning

L'ANSE AUX MEADOWS is a tiny fishing village on the Newfoundland coast. Here the Norwegian scientist Helge Ingstad, after searching many years for traces of the Vikings along the Atlantic shoreline, from Rhode Island to Hudson Bay, heard reports from fishermen of old ruins beneath the sod. In the early 1960s he began to dig carefully along the wide meadowland at the edge of a brook. The stripped cover revealed a Viking homesite, and beside the brook were an old smithy with anvil and charcoal, slag from melted iron, and nearby rusty nodules of bog iron. Radiocarbon readings dated these finds from the Middle Ages. Later a soapstone whorl of Norse design from around 1000 A.D. was found. Further excavations uncovered sites of additional habitations. Here, it is believed, Leif Ericson and his followers, sailing from Greenland, established the Vinland colony, probably in the year 995. At least many people are so convinced.

The old Norse saga of Eric the Red which described Leif's adventure says:

> We found that there were quite a few salmon in the river, especially in the autumn, and sometimes we even caught one with our bare hands. The fishermen also from time to time made excellent catches of salmon out at sea and the fish were, on the average, larger than their relatives that we knew from Greenland.

This is the first documented record of man and the Atlantic salmon in North America.

Long before the Vinlanders came, the Newfoundland coast was inhabited by Indians who made full use of the rich animal and fish populations; they fashioned fishing boats out of the tall trees that surrounded them but were ignorant of agriculture or the art of pottery making. At Port au Choix, a fishing village on the northwest coast of Newfoundland, archeologists have uncovered the burial ground of these people and sketched a picture of their way of life about 4000 years ago.

"They followed a more or less fixed seasonal round in exploiting the region's food resources," says James A. Tuck, leader of the team that excavated the site. "In the late fall each year, when the caribou congregated after the first snow to move from summer to winter grazing, the migrating herds were a prime target . . . A few days of caribou hunting might furnish enough meat for the winter months, and this basic winter ration could be supplemented with fresh kills of beaver, hare or larger mammals."

During the winter the Indians probably stayed close to the inland sites, but in the spring they moved to the coast to hunt the harp seals as they drifted southward with the ice pack. After that there might be another caribou hunt when the animals moved to summer pasture. Then the Indians would return to the coast to spend the summer fishing in the rivers; in the autumn they would prey on the multifarious ducks and other nesting birds and gather the wild berries. When the first snow fell the bands went inland again for the caribou hunt.

These archaic Indians had excellent hunting and fishing weapons, including toggling harpoon heads and leisters with finely carved bone barbs. They used stone, bone, antler, and ivory for making ornamental as well as utilitarian items and could work wood, bark, and skin with considerable skill.[1]

According to Erhard Rostlund in his exhaustive study *Freshwater Fish and Fishing in Native North America*, "there is theoretical reason for thinking that Atlantic salmon, per unit area, was at least as plentiful as Pacific salmon" before the white man came. *Salmo salar* "was only one of several anadromous species on the east coast, but the other fishes — shad, alewife, eel, sturgeon, or striped bass — did not compete with the salmon for spawning grounds.

"Hence, if the eastern rivers were proportionately as well provided with suitable spawning grounds as the western rivers . . . and utilized by salmon to about the same extent in both regions, then the salmon population could have been as large in the East as in the West."

✿

The Colonial Era

Five hundred years after the Vinland people disappeared, the North American continent was discovered anew. In 1497 the Italians John and Sebastian Cabot, sailing under the British flag, explored the Newfoundland coast and corroborated Leif Ericson's report of the plenitude of sturgeon, shad, and salmon in the rivers. A few years later the Portuguese brothers Corte-Real followed in their wake and in their report noted the prevalence of cod, herring, shad, and salmon, among others. In fact, these mariners had found a bank or shallow area in the ocean, the sunken remnants of the northern Appalachian highlands and coastal plain. Here the waters were extraordinarily rich in plankton and insect life that nurtured pullulating fishes, which in turn attracted masses of sea birds, gannets, gulls, murres, and others.

The salmon roved far inland in Labrador and Quebec and populated the rivers emptying into the St. Lawrence almost as far as Niagara Falls. They were plentiful in the Maritime Provinces and ran up over two score rivers in New England. Thus they went up the Penobscot to Grand Falls near Millinocket, the Kennebec above Caratunk Falls, the Androscoggin to Rumford Falls, the Saco to Hiram Falls, and the Connecticut to Beecher Falls (372 miles from the ocean).

Many lakes in the Maritime Provinces, Quebec, and Maine, and a few in the Adirondack Mountains, harbored the small landlocked version of *Salmo salar* called Ouananiche by the Montagnais Indians. Originally these were anadromous fishes, survivors of very ancient races trapped by ice or earth movements that prevented them from going to sea. There were landlocked salmon that attained large size in Lake Ontario and its feeder streams, and seagoing salmon in Lake Champlain and its effluents.

It was the Indians who taught the white men how to fish for salmon in eastern (as in western) North America. Salmon were caught usually at the falls of the rivers or at outlets to the lakes where temporary villages were set up when the fishes were running. Usually they built weirs of stone and saplings, and the fish were taken with nets made of hemp, tree bark, or deer sinew. They were also caught with spears, hook and line, and even with baskets.

There were fishing stations at many of the falls, such as Amoskeag Falls on the Merrimack, where the river dropped eighty feet in a half mile over granite ledges, and at Bellows Falls on the Connecticut, where the flow descended in a roaring cataract over steep rocks. At the Salmon Hole, where the Ammonoosuc River, after dropping several thousand feet from Mount Washington, enters the Connecticut River, the Indians were known to take huge quantities of salmon, including specimens weighing up to twenty-five pounds.[2] Thoreau, in *A Week on the Concord and Merrimack Rivers,* describes the vestiges of an Indian weir near the confluence of the two streams where salmon, shad, eel, sturgeon, lampreys, and bass were caught in Colonial times. In this area wrote Daniel Gooking in 1674, "at the beginning of May, the English magistrate keeps his court, accompanied by Mr. Eliot, the minister . . . This place being an ancient and capital seat of Indians, they come to fish, and this good man takes the opportunity to spread the net of the gospel, to fish for their souls." [3]

Each year a group of aristocratic sportsmen met at Amoskeag Falls to fish for salmon. The Reverend Joseph Seccombe, graduate of Harvard, was customarily invited to deliver the sermon without which any such outing was regarded as incomplete. His *Discourse Utter'd in Part at Ammauskeeg Falls in the Fishing-Season: 1739* has recently been reprinted.

By the end of the seventeenth century many families in the Connecticut Valley were smoking or salting salmon for their own use, or buying it for one or two cents a pound. Alewives and shad, being far more plentiful, cost much less, but these were regarded by the gentry as poor people's food, on a par with lowly pork. So abundant was salmon in the eighteenth century, noted Dr. Samuel Latham Mitchill in *The Fishes of New York* (1814), that "when [people] went to the river to buy shad the fisherman used to stipulate that they should also buy a specified number of salmon."

The diary of Dr. William Bentley, pastor of East Church in Salem, Massachusetts, contains numerous reference to the delicious fish that he, like other epicures, preferred to the more abundant and popular shad. For example, in April, 1793, he noted:

> This morning we rose and rode 3 miles towards the [Merrimack] river . . . Here we saw the people on each side seining for salmon and other fish. We saw 1,000 alewives caught in one draft. They had taken one salmon of 20 lb. wt.

July, 1799:

> Haggett has seen 3 salmon caught through the ice by a hook in February at Pentucket Falls and they are known to be in the river till September with their spawn.

On May 20, 1800, salmon were selling for nine pence apiece in the Salem market. On May 28, 1805, Dr. Bentley saw men fishing for salmon, shad, and other migratory fish at the falls of the Merrimack. Four years later, on May 11, 1809, he "enjoyed a salmon of 16 pounds sent me by some friends in Salisbury."

An export trade in salmon can be traced to 1628, when the fishes were packed for shipment abroad by Thomas Purchase in the Merry-meeting Bay area of Maine. There he

> . . . pitched his habitation near the foot of Pejepscot Falls
> . . . It is said that he was a trader in furs and peltry, catch-
> ing, curing, and packing salmon and sturgeon for a foreign
> market . . . Records show that during a three week period
> about 39 bbls. of salmon besides what they spoiled for lack
> of salt, and about 90 kegs and many bbls. of sturgeon, and
> that if they had been fitted with salt, and apt and skillful
> men, they might have taken abundance more.

Purchase's employee Christopher Lawson was the first commercial fisherman on the Kennebec. As settlement of the Maine coast expanded, the fishery was more fully exploited, but the salmon pack did not reach an impressive volume until trap weirs were used, first on the Kennebec in 1808 and the Penobscot in 1815, followed by the Union, Machias, and St. Croix Rivers. Documents indicate that on the St. Croix daily catches of as much as 100 barrels were reported in the early nineteenth century, and a single individual could occasionally obtain 50 to 100 fish.

Profile of the American Salmon

The premigratory life of *Salmo salar* in North America resembles that of its European cousin. Smoltification takes longer in northern waters than in the southern parts of the range. The vast majority of salmon in New England rivers (now virtually depopulated) went to sea at two years of age, but in New Brunswick streams about two-thirds tarried three years, while in Newfoundland, including Labrador, the bulk remained in freshwater three and four years.

Oceanic migrations have been well established in recent years by tagging studies. About 800 kelts were tagged by the Atlantic Sea-Run Salmon Commission in Maine from 1962 to 1966, of which thirty were eventually recovered. Leaving the rivers about May 1, these fish apparently took fifty days to reach the Halifax area on the southwest

Nova Scotia coast and after ten to twenty more days were found along the Newfoundland coast. Then they rounded Cape Race and from late summer until well into autumn dropped from sight. Late autumn found them in the vicinity of southern Greenland, where they hobnobbed with European salmon and where many were taken in Danish nets. By early winter some of the American fish turned homeward, weighing fifteen to twenty pounds. Many were netted along the northeastern Newfoundland coast, but a few managed to reach their home rivers after completing a journey of 2000 to 3000 miles.

Atlantic salmon return to home waters in the United States usually in the spring, when the ice has broken up in the rivers, the ground has thawed, and flowers poke their heads above the ground. In the Connecticut River, most of the fish arrived in April and May, a few in July and later; sometimes stragglers appeared in winter. If they could surmount the natural obstacles, and this depended upon the amount of water available, they moved steadily toward their mating grounds. Usually they spawned in the fall.

Depopulation of American Rivers

New England rivers continued to produce a plenitude of anadromous fishes as long as they were in a relatively wild state. "Shad, bass and salmon more than half sustain the province," wrote Peters in his *History of Connecticut* (1783). "From the number of seines employed to catch fish passing up the locks one might be led to suppose that the whole must be stopped, yet in six months' time they return to the sea in such multitudes of young ones as to fill the Connecticut River for many days, and no finite being can number them."[4] Salmon and shad were taken together in sweep nets worked from the wharves, or by scoop nets in the deep basin at the foot of South Hadley Falls. Netsmen were known to catch 3700 in a single drift of a seine in Old Saybrook's South Cove.

The Merrimack, issuing from Lake Winnipesaukee and Lake Pemigewasset in the White Mountains of New Hampshire, was a pastoral river flowing through the verdant lower valley to meet the sea at Newburyport. Hordes of shad and salmon came up its sparkling waters and were fished for centuries by the Indians. Salmon spawned in the upper tributaries, especially the Pemigewasset. In the lower river as late as 1790, 60 to 100 fish were caught in a day with a ninety-yard seine near the river's mouth at Amesbury.

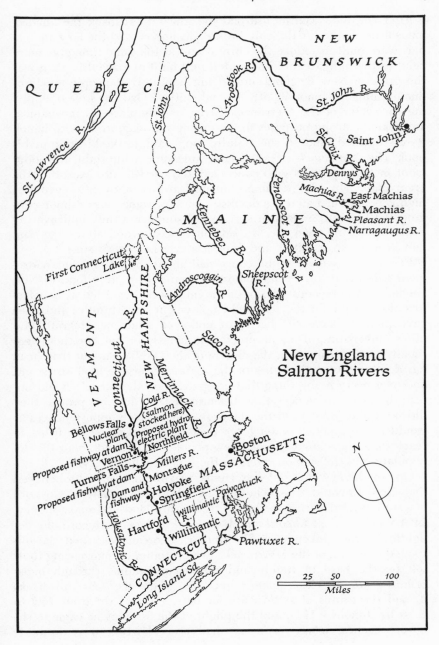

New England
Salmon Rivers

After the industrialists usurped the lower Merrimack the anadromous fishes found life difficult. Mill dams impounded the flow and canals were built to reduce the current and at the same time give more head to the mill stream. The cotton mill built at Lowell in 1822 was the pride of New England, employing hundreds of people and producing immense amounts of yarn and cloth. "That the idea of applying the water of the Merrimack River, at this place, to mechanical and manufacturing purposes to the extent and magnitude with which it was applied, and so successfully too," said J. W. Meader in his book *The Merrimack* (1869), "shows uncommon foresight and judgment in those persons who conceived and carried into execution the great plan." In 1847 an imposing mill and dam twenty-seven feet high was built at Lawrence downstream. For some years salmon congregated below this dam in spring and summer, vainly endeavoring to hurdle it. By 1860 the last salmon that spawned above the dam had lived its span of life, and none has ever been seen since.[5]

Few people seemed to be concerned about the fate of the anadromous fishes that formed an important source of protein food in New England. The tycoons who built the mills were regarded as benefactors of mankind, for they created employment opportunities and often gave plentiful sums to charity or endowed chairs at Harvard and other universities. They accepted, consciously or not, for they were usually God-fearing men, the dictum of the Old Testament that "man has dominion over the fishes of the sea and over the fowl of the air, and over every living thing that creepeth upon the earth." It did not disturb their consciences that, because of their lust for profits, they did not build fishways at the dams or provide such appurtenances as would permit enough water to go over them and allow the fishes to reach their spawning grounds. Few people complained about the depopulation of the salmon rivers in the nineteenth century.

One of the few that did was Henry David Thoreau, who believed that New Englanders — including his fellow townsmen in Concord — were obsessed with two things: to worship God and make money. In *A Week on the Concord and Merrimack Rivers*, the record of a delightful journey taken with his brother, Thoreau described the unspoiled stretches of the Merrimack, "which comes on murmuring to itself by the base of stately and retired mountains, through moist primitive woods whose juices it receives, where the bear still drinks it, and the cabins of settlers are far between, and there are few to cross its streams." He noted the plight of the fishes as he came to the lower reaches, where "salmon, shad and alewives were formerly abundant . . . and taken in weirs by the Indians, who taught this method to the whites, by whom they were used as food and manure, until the dam and afterward the canal at Billerica, and the factories at Lowell, put an end to their migration hitherward; though it is thought that a few more enterprising shad may still be seen."

"Perchance after a thousand years," he added with wry humor, "if the fishes will be patient, and pass their summers elsewhere, meanwhile nature will have levelled the Billerica dam, and the Lowell factories, and the Grass-ground [Concord] River run clear again, to be explored by new migrating shoals." [6]

The Merrimack is now one of America's most polluted streams. "Were the philosopher of Walden to look upon today's Merrimack he would likely weep for the river and the children of this nation's tomorrow," says Senator Frank Moss in *The Water Crisis* (1967). "If the Merrimack of today represents the future of American water courses, the time may yet come when nature will indeed have levelled the dams, the factories, and the towns of America. Its long history of pollution makes the famed river an instructive example of how this water sickness spreads."

The fate of the Connecticut River illustrates the process by which Americans, in their prodigal exploitation of natural resources and lack of a conservation conscience, deprived themselves of a substantial source of food. As late as 1790 salmon and other migratory fishes ascended the river to its farthest reach. But less than a decade later a corporation known as the Upper Locks and Canal Company built a sixteen-foot dam across the Connecticut at Hadley Falls — there was no state law requiring the installation of a fish ladder. Later, other dams were built, without fish passes, downstream. By 1814, according to Dr. Samuel Latham Mitchill in *The Fishes of New York*, New York City was no longer able to get its salmon supply from the Connecticut. Yet about this time the peripatetic Reverend Timothy Dwight, President of Yale University, noted that "the waters [of the Connecticut] . . . are remarkably pure and light . . . The tributary streams, almost without exception, issue from hills, formed by stone, covered with gravelly soil." Salmon had almost entirely deserted the river, and shad, formerly taken from as far away as Bellows Falls, were stopped by a dam at Montague. Instead of shad and salmon, which the people liked to eat, the river was crowded with bass.[7]

In 1872, when a solitary salmon strayed into a fisherman's net at Old Saybrook, nobody in the vicinity could identify it, for even the memory of the species had faded. Dams without fishways also effectively locked out the salmon from the upper waters in New Hampshire and Vermont, while industrial wastes from the textile mills and sewage from the towns completed the rout. Today, says Philip K. Crowe, "when one crosses the Connecticut on the bridge at Lebanon, N.H., one can see the ruin of a river: oily-looking water and at times the faint, rank smell of fermenting sewage." [8] Nevertheless an attempt is being made — at great expense — by the federal and state governments to restore salmon to the Connecticut.

By 1860 salmon fishing was profitable only in a few Maine streams — there were no longer any of these fishes left in other New England states.

It was in Maine that the lumber industry in virtually all its modern facets was born, that the basic techniques of logging and driving logs from forest to sawmill were evolved, and that the typical nineteenth-century cycle of cutting, burning, and liquidating the virgin stands was perfected. The white pine that grew in abundance, often reaching 150 feet in height and occasionally 250 feet, straight as a candle; the shorter Norway pine, also remarkable for its tall trunk; and the spruces growing beneath the pines were all logged with religious zeal. They were regarded as "green gold" to be rapidly converted into boards and boards into profits. The lumber barons grew rich and, like the textile manufacturers, founded potent dynasties, many members of which became leaders of our nation. But the forests and the watersheds, and the fish life they harbored, were greatly impoverished.

Maine lumbermen set the classic stamp on the American land. They usually removed all the trees that were tall, straight, and well-formed and could be easily rafted and milled. If in the process they left few or no seed trees, damaged soils and cover by dragging logs over them, jammed the rivers for miles, and dumped mountains of sawdust into river beds — what matter? Free enterprise ruled in the nineteenth century, and men could do as they pleased with the land to which they gained title (often fraudulently) and the stumpage they purchased (or purloined). Ecology was unknown, and relatively few people gave any thought to the future of our natural resources.

Originally there were about twenty major rivers in Maine that supported regular runs of salmon: the Piscataqua, Mousam, Saco, Presumpscot, Royal, Androscoggin, Kennebec, Sheepscot, Medomak, Saint George, Penobscot, Union, Narraguagus, Wescongus or Pleasant River, Machias and East Machias, Orange, Dennys, Saint John, and Saint Croix. By 1870 only seven were left with any salmon. Occasionally anadromous fishes appeared in a half-dozen other streams, but in all the rest "the ancient brood of salmon," said Charles G. Atkins, "was long ago extinguished, and the rare specimens occasionally observed must be regarded either as strays from some of the better preserved rivers, or as early returning members of the new broods established by artificial culture in several rivers."

Atkins succinctly described the causes of these losses: "The fishermen's nets and spears and pounds would hardly have sufficed to extinguish the brood of salmon in a single river. Commonly these two classes of destructive agents cooperated. The dams held the fish in check while the fishermen caught them out. In some rivers the dams alone would have sufficed to exterminate them." [9] Maine rivers, like those in other New England states, were literally forested with small dams that impounded water for cotton mills, shoe factories, tanneries, firearm and clock manufacture, ironworks, paper mills, and the like. Very few had efficient fishways, and many of them had none, as Maine Fisheries Commissioner E. M. Stilwell found in his 1872 survey made at the request of the United States Commissioner of Fisheries.

In navigable rivers the riparian proprietors owned the soil from the high-water to the low-water mark, and this title carried the right to erect "fixtures for fishing or other purposes, or even to make a net fast to the shore or bottom within the 100-rod limit," but it did not include ownership of the fish. In nonnavigable waters the riparian owner held the land under the water from each shore to the middle of the stream and had the exclusive right to fish by any method in the water covering his land. The public right extended only to boats or timber passing up or down.

Using these rights, the proprietors blockaded the streams as they wished, even though there were in Maine, according to Atkins, 433 fishery laws passed by the legislature between 1820 and 1880, of which 161 related to anadromous species. The aims of this legislation were "first, the preservation of the supply of fish; second, the harmonizing of conflicting interests; and third, the prevention of fraud in the sale of fish products." The first goal "was attained by provisions compelling the removal or abatement of obstructions, especially by the construction of fishways, and by a great variety of provisions touching the time, mode and extent of fishing." [10]

The courts, Atkins said, rendered repeated decisions upholding the principle that "every owner of a mill or dam built it under the condition that a sufficient passageway be allowed for the fish, and the limitation, being for the public benefit, is not extinguished by any neglect to compel compliances." Relatively heavy penalties were specified for breaches of these laws. As far back as 1741 a general act was passed by the Colonial legislature providing for the appointment of courts of justice or committees to inspect dams and decide on questions involving the adequacy of fishways. In 1786 this function was assigned to committees chosen by the towns. Early in the nineteenth century the county commissioners acquired this duty "in cases not governed by special acts, of which, however, there were very many, covering the majority of the rivers and giving fishway questions into the hands of the local officers." In 1868 the state commissioner of fisheries acquired jurisdiction, with the power to order fishways built or repairs made at his discretion. However, little or nothing was ever done to implement this legislation — mill dams and weirs multipled and the fish were locked out in one river after another.

The Penobscot and Other Rivers

By 1889 the catch of Atlantic salmon had dropped to 150,000 pounds a year, of which 70 to 90 percent came from the Penobscot River and the rest from a few other Maine streams. Fortunately the upper basin of the Penobscot was still covered by virgin forest, noted Atkins, "with neither tilled fields nor manufactories to foul its waters, nor lofty dams to limit the range of the salmon." This was an ideal breeding area, abounding "in gravelly beds, alternating with quiet rapids and deep pools, in which the salmon may bide their time, and to which they may retreat after spawning." [11]

In contrast, the lower stretches of the Penobscot were much abused, for they served as a highway for rafting logs to the mills. In 1840 Maine had about 1380 sawmills clustered around tidewater, of which 250 were along the shores of the Penobscot and its major tributaries. Each spring the logs tumbled down from lakes and streams, forming the grand drives, poled by nimble-footed men, heading for the booms at Bangor, Veazie, Brewer, Old Town, and Orono. When Thoreau canoed along the east branch of the Penobscot in 1857 he saw much forest denudation, areas where only straggly and unsound trees had been left, and he divined, not unreasonably, that the aim of the lumbermen was "to drive the forest all out of the country, from every solitary beaver-swamp and mountain-side, as soon as possible." Bangor was then the nation's leading lumber mart and its harbor was so thick with ships "that on many days small boys would walk across . . . to Brewer on their decks." [12]

The river accumulated beds of sawdust and bark, log booms stretched for miles, sand bars were created, channels were constricted. The fish found their oxygen supply depleted and their migration routes difficult or impassable. More deadly pollution came with the advent of pulp mills and other manufacturing using large quantities of water and chemicals. The first pulp mill was built at Great Works in Old Town; the industry spread upstream, dumping cooking liquors, chips, and bark dust into the waters to the point where they "exceeded the capacity of the river to absorb the load," [13] thus making life ever more hazardous for the fishes.

Salmon were fished at the mouth of the Penobscot and in the river by weirs, traps (called pound nets), and gill nets. In 1887 Atkins reported the existence of 165 weirs, 65 traps, and 36 gill nets taking a total of about 10,000 fish annually. Thereafter the catches fell steadily despite the planting of young salmon from the federal hatchery at Craig Brook near Orland, Maine, the first in the United States. Only 6400 salmon were landed in 1896; then the harvests plummeted to 1200 in 1928 and a mere 40 in 1947, when the river had deteriorated so much that the Penobscot was placed by the state in the "nuisance or Class D (waste-carrying) condition." A survey by the Maine Water Improvement Commission discovered that the worst stretches were around the confluence of the east and west branches and in the estuary, where in summer there was a veritable oxygen block, the filth floating back and forth with the tide and preventing fishes from moving from saltwater to freshwater. Thus died the best salmon stream in Maine and one of the richest in eastern North America.

I visited the Penobscot a few years ago. There were none of the booms or sawmills that Thoreau had seen and no merchant ships in the harbor. Mounds of sawdust were still lying at the bottom of the river, and it was sometimes found in suspension in fishermen's nets. Like neighboring river towns, Bangor seemed to be unaware of its romantic past. The acrid and obnoxious smell of a paper mill drifting downwind assailed the nostrils. The river flowed in lonely splendor, deserted alike by salmon and by men, for its waters were too polluted to be safe for swimming. According to the Federal Water Quality Administration, now the Environmental Protection Agency, 70 percent of the Kennebec River is polluted, 60 percent of the Merrimack, 40 percent of the Penobscot, and 35 percent of the Connecticut.

Next to the Penobscot the Kennebec was the best salmon producer in Maine. It had famous Indian fishing stations. Originally the supply of salmon was plentiful; about the time of the Revolution dip-net and drift-net fisheries sprang up at Skowhegan and Caratunk (where it was said two men could take a boatload in a day). A weir fishery also existed at the mouth of the river, and at least forty dugout canoes used to fish each year with drift nets at Taconic Falls, catching up to 120 fish apiece as late as the early nineteenth century.[14] After the demise of the Connecticut and Merrimack Rivers the people of Boston looked to the Kennebec to supply them with salmon.

In 1837–1838 a dam was built at Augusta in defiance of state law, thus preventing fish from moving into the upper waters. Thereafter the runs fell off rapidly, for the only breeding grounds remaining were the gravel beds in the first half mile of the stream. Atkins estimated the catch at about 1500 fish in 1873, of which 900 were taken below Bath and 600 above it. In 1880 only 270 salmon were caught, and eventually the species disappeared from the Kennebec.

The same melancholy fate befell the Saco River, which flows down from the White Mountains in New Hampshire and across Maine for about a hundred miles. Salmon used to come up in goodly numbers as far as Hiram Falls and into the Great and Little Ossipee Rivers. In 1872 there were thirteen impassable dams on the Saco. *Salmo salar* became extinct in this river around 1860.

Sport Fishing

There is very little sport fishing for Atlantic salmon in the United States now, and it is difficult to believe that once this game fish was pursued by many Americans. In the Colonial period, gentlemen of means, like their compeers in England, used to dance a fly on many a pleasant river like the Connecticut, Kennebec, or Merrimack. But sport fishing on a sizable scale was really a nineteenth-century development. "The streams of Maine and those of northern and western New York in which salmon were formerly abundant were, before the era of railroads, too distant to be frequented by anglers from populous districts of the east," says Charles E. Goodspeed in his history of salmon angling in the United States. Yet fly-fishing was known to have been practiced in the Penobscot and Dennys Rivers in the 1830s and in the Aroostook and Union Rivers around the Civil War. This sport was confined to the men of leisure or of liberal cast of mind, for oddly enough there was a widespread feeling that fishing was a wanton and sinful pastime. "Hunting and fishing, for mere sport," said the *Housekeeper's Manual*, a popular book published in 1873, "can never be justified." However, in 1886 Henry P. Wells in *The American Salmon Fisherman* declared that the number of fly-fishermen was then ten times as large as a decade earlier. His work deals chiefly with Canadian rivers; it lists only three rivers, the St. Croix, Dennys, and Penobscot, where angling might be profitable in New England. Of these only the Penobscot offered good sport, for it was being stocked with fish from the Craig Brook hatchery.

Wells reported that over fifty salmon were hooked at Calais, Milltown, and Baring on the St. Croix in 1885: "Dennys is a fine natural stream, but much obstructed with nets, drift trash from sawmills, and other abominations . . . These abuses will doubtless soon be brought to an end. Then this river will be well worthy the attention of the angler." [15] On the Penobscot there was some good angling at Medway, seventy-five miles above tidewater at the junction of the east and west branches, and also at Quissaticook, a cold stream issuing from Mount Katahdin, and at the pool below Bangor dam.

From 1885 onward the history of salmon angling in the eastern United States was confined almost entirely to Bangor pool. Wealthy Americans betook themselves to the wilds of Canada to pursue *Salmo salar*, where there were many rivers abounding with the species. Less well-to-do fishermen, from Boston, New York, and other places, flocked to Bangor, and until 1905, they had reasonable success. Then the decline set in as pollution from pulp mills, poaching, insufficient restocking, and uncontrolled weir fishing in Penobscot Bay emptied the river. In 1904 Dean Sage in his book *Salmon and Trout* declared that the Penobscot "is fast going under" and the St. Croix, which still accommodated a few anglers, was gradually fading out. The Dennys had already been listed as a futile place to angle for salmon. By 1940 the Penobscot was also a dead river, and fly-fishing ceased in Bangor pool, a sorry epitaph for a glorious stream.

Decimation of Lake Ontario and Lake Champlain Salmon

The American penchant for destroying wildlife encompassed lake as well as river inhabitants. The unspoiled wilderness around Lakes Ontario and Champlain once teemed with anadromous fishes. The Jesuit Fathers Le Moyne and Le Mercier on their diplomatic mission in 1654 for the French government to the Onondaga Indians were surprised to see canoes coming down the Oswego River filled with salmon. There were so many of these fishes in the streams that they could be easily killed with paddles. At least fifty rivers on both the Canadian and American sides of Lake Ontario originally supported salmon runs. Records of the original settlers amply attest to their abundance.

It was once assumed that the Lake Ontario fish were a seagoing variety of *Salmo salar,* but an examination of scales from two specimens in a museum, all that is left of the stocks, by the Canadian biologist A. A. Blair showed they were denizens of the lake, which they used for feeding, and the tributary streams, which they used for spawning. Salmon used to go up to the Finger Lakes and were so numerous in that vicinity that in some rivers they could be pitchforked by the wagonload in the early nineteenth century. They passed the town of Oswego, New York, in April and returned as kelts to the lake in September. The Salmon River in New York provided good fishing as late as the 1830s and was still somewhat productive in the 1870s.

The Genesee, which flows through the city of Rochester, New York, attracted prodigious numbers of salmon, which migrated as far as the falls. But in 1817 one Elisha Clark built a dam for a mill at Rochester and blockaded the river without apparently eliciting any protests. For several years the fish returned to the Genesee and futilely attempted to reach their spawning grounds. It was reported that some 10,000 were clubbed, speared, and pitchforked below the impoundment.

On the Canadian side of Lake Ontario salmon ceased to appear in the streams from Toronto westward by the 1860s but were still seen in rivers east of that city. Restocking with salmon bred in the hatchery on Wilmot Creek brought a temporary revival in the 1870s. The last specimen seen on any stream feeding the lake was observed on Wilmot Creek in 1896. That ended the history of *Salmo salar* in Lake Ontario. The causes, according to Samuel Wilmot, fish culturist, were (1) "murder on the fishing grounds," that is, unrestrained trap-net fishing along the lake shores and at the mouths of the rivers, and (2) settlement and clearance of the land that stripped vegetative cover and, allied with poor agricultural practices, induced erosion and siltation of waterways. Repeated attempts to restock the rivers with Atlantic salmon eggs and fry were unsuccessful.

Now, seventy-five years later, the state of New York in cooperation with the province of Ontario has announced plans to stock Lake Ontario not with *Salmo salar* but with coho, chinook, and steelhead trout. Success of the program, however, depends upon control of the sea lamprey, which has multiplied in explosive fashion since the Saint Lawrence Seaway connecting the Atlantic Ocean and Great Lakes was built. Control of this predator will be accomplished by killing its larvae with a chemical in every stream system on the New York side of the lake, along the Saint Lawrence River, and in the estuaries. "If all goes as scheduled, New York anglers," says the announcement, "can expect a salmonid fishery in Lake Ontario that will rival the other Great Lakes' sport fisheries." [16]

Lake Champlain divides the Adirondack and Green Mountains and is connected with the Saint Lawrence through the Richelieu River at Sorel. Salmon found the waters of the lake congenial and were fairly copious in many tributary streams, such as the Big and Little Chazy, Salmon, Saranac, Little Ausable, Bouquet, Otter Creek, Winooski, Lamoille, and Missisquoi Rivers. The fish are believed to have been a sea-run variety of *Salmo salar,* which, like Lake Ontario salmon, attained fairly large size. Few details, however, are known about their biological characteristics or migrations, as no published studies are available.

Tales of salmon gluts in upper New York state are recorded in local histories. Thus Winslow C. Watson, historian of Essex County, said that as late as 1813 1500 pounds were taken in a single drift of a seine near Port Kendall, and old settlers told him that in their youth "the fish so crowded the streams at spawning season that it was unsafe to ride a spirited horse through the ford owing to the powerful strokes delivered by the salmon." [17] By 1842, when Daniel P. Thompson published his *History of Vermont,* the salmon had become exceedingly rare in that state. The last run in the Ausable River was said to have occurred in 1838 and in the Saranac River in 1824. Attempts were made to restock Lake Champlain with Atlantic salmon in the 1870s, but they were without success.

One wonders if renewed attempts will be made to adapt Atlantic or Pacific salmon to Lake Champlain. If so, there will have to be a cleanup. In the village of Ticonderoga, situated on the lake, a pulp mill was built by the International Paper Company a half century ago, superseding a plant erected in 1877. It operated until a few years ago and in its long history left as its heritage a 300-acre mound of sludge, which is twenty feet thick in places. Tourists used to come to this lovely town and, smelling the pulp mill and stinking sludge, quickly take the ferry for Vermont shores, saying, "Never again."

Today the black ooze has stopped coming from the mill, but gas bubbles rise from the decomposing sludge and bits of decaying matter occasionally float to the surface. The air and water at the foot of the Adirondack Mountains are purer than when the mill was in operation, but aquatic life is virtually nonexistent. The state of Vermont is threatening to sue the state of New York if it does not remove the offensive muck in the lake, a project that would cost $2 million, and even then the results would not be guaranteed, for stirring up the sludge (which reduces oxygen levels to zero) might spread it and cause untold damage. The International Paper Company, having abandoned the Ticonderoga mill, apparently feels it has no obligation to the community or the states to clean up its mess.

Can New England Rivers Be Revived?

Although sporadic efforts were made in the last century, interest in cleaning up and restocking New England salmon rivers is a relatively recent phenomenon, inspired chiefly by anglers who wish to renew acquaintance with *Salmo salar*. Alfred L. Meister, biologist of the Atlantic Sea-Run Salmon Commission of Maine, says, "In a land where fishing and hunting is accepted as a God-given-right, it was inevitable that a public clamor would arise for Atlantic salmon fishing." This clamor culminated in the creation of the commission by the Maine legislature in 1947. Although never endowed by the state with more than a token appropriation, it undertook to survey the once teeming Maine rivers and with the help of federal agencies, supplemented by contributions from power companies and sportsmen's groups, made plans for restoring eight streams: the Dennys, Sheepscot, Machias and East Machias, Narraguagus, Pleasant, Aroostook, and Penobscot.

Most of the commission's efforts have dealt with the Penobscot, which admittedly is in a parlous state, "victimized by a citizenry unwilling to accept responsibility for waste treatment as an essential of civilized progress." [18] For many years the commission was frustrated by the presence of both pollution and migration blocks in some of the rivers it undertook to revive. "Polluters dragged their feet," says David O. Locke, a member of the commission, "saying it would do no good to clean up the rivers if there were obstacles the fish could not pass. Owners of dams without fishways took the position that fishways would be of no avail if the unclean conditions of the rivers continued. No one wanted to be first." [19] At length legal obstacles were removed by the state legislature and some progress was made.

Fishways were built at Veazie, Bangor, and West Enfield on the main stem of the Penobscot; others are planned on some of the tributaries.

Pollution abatement has proceeded at a slower pace. The Maine legislature finally classified the river as a Class C stream, meaning it must be rendered suitable for fish life (an ironic decision for it was once supremely endowed with fish). The deadline for attaining this goal, however, was pushed ahead to October 1, 1976!

The ultimate aim is to eventually establish a run of 1200 to 3000 salmon on the Penobscot, providing a harvest of 180 to 750 fish for sportsmen. Whether this target — negligible compared to the runs of a century ago — is attained depends upon several factors: purifying and cleaning up the river, removing obstructions, and ample stocking. It is hard to believe that such problems can be readily solved, for a great river once dirtied, sullied, and hacked to pieces by dams, power plants, and pulp mills is difficult to restore to anything like its pristine purity, and unless the salmon have clean water, they will not go up the rivers to spawn.

Under the Dingell-Johnson Anadromous Fish Act and the Accelerated Public Works Act the federal government had spent $1.4 million up to 1972 in salmon conservation programs in Maine, with the state contributing $1.1 million. Two thirds of the money has been invested in the Penobscot and the remainder in the Machias, Dennys, Piscataqua, and Narraguagus Rivers.

The Greenland fishery has had a deleterious impact on the Maine runs; also many fish returning to their home rivers in Maine have been taken in the nets festooned around the Newfoundland coast.

Latest reports are that only three small Maine rivers provide anglers with the opportunity to catch salmon: the Narraguagus, where 137 fish were taken in 1972, the Dennys with 50, and the Machias with 65.[20] These are pitiful returns for the enormous amounts of state and federal funds spent in the past fifteen years on Maine's salmon restoration program. A note of promise was the return of 333 salmon to the Bangor fishway in 1972, and their ascent of the main stream to spawn. Salmon were nonexistent in this once prolific river only five years ago; however, the goals of planners of the restoration program are still far in the future.

Attempts began a few years ago to restore salmon to the Connecticut River when federal funds, to be matched by state funds, became available, despite the fact that pollution, power dams, and a nuclear generating plant posed tremendous obstacles. In May 1970 ten truckloads of smolts purchased in Quebec were released below Holyoke dam (now provided with a fishway); 14,000 smolts from the federal trout hatchery at Berlin, New Hampshire, and the state trout hatchery at Palmer, Massachusetts, joined these Canadian fish, some of which, it was hoped, would return to the river after two or three years in the ocean.

The latest report on the Connecticut River Program is that "fish passage has been provided on two of the six dams on the main stem that will be passable to salmon. Negotiations for fish passage are in progress on the upper four dams." The cleanup has been accelerated, but formidable difficulties remain. In 1972 Congress appropriated $125,000 for advance planning and land acquisition for a salmon hatchery at Bethel, Vermont, to breed smolts for stocking the river. To some observers the attempt seems unfeasible, for no Atlantic salmon river the size of the Connecticut, nor one so wickedly abused, has ever been successfully restored.

The Bureau of Sport Fisheries and Wildlife reports that "preliminary stocking of Atlantic salmon has been made on the White River in Vermont and the Cold River in New Hampshire. While the stocking of smolts has been limited because of high cost, it is hoped that returns in 1972 and 1973 will demonstrate the feasibility of upstream stocking. Paralleling this effort, there will be additional stocking in the Salmon River in Connecticut." [21] However, the bureau admits that pollution in "many of the former salmon streams may partly deter the restoration efforts," although "with the return of the salmon, the cleanup efforts have been accelerated."

"At this point in time," admits the bureau, "we have successfully restored salmon [only] in the Narraguagus and Machias Rivers." [22] Meanwhile two new Atlantic salmon hatcheries are being built, one near Ellsworth, Maine, and another on the White River near Bethel, Vermont.

In the spring of 1973 a new organization was formed by well-known anglers, Restoration of Atlantic Salmon in America, Inc., with headquarters in Hancock, New Hampshire. Its aim is to restore the Atlantic salmon to its former abundance in the rivers of New England. RASA was organized by the principals of the Committee on the Atlantic Salmon (CASE), under the leadership of Richard A. Buck. CASE spearheaded the movement to get the Danes, Norwegians, and other fishermen to phase out their high seas netting of salmon — including runs emanating from Canadian and United States rivers — as described in Chapter XII. RASA believes that the major problems in reaching their goal, pollution, nuclear plant discharges, inefficient fish ladders, and the general apathy and indifference of politicians as well as businessmen and industrialists, can be overcome. They plan to launch an educational campaign to convince the people of New England that they must work together to restore a resource to their rivers that once was a source of much food and sport.

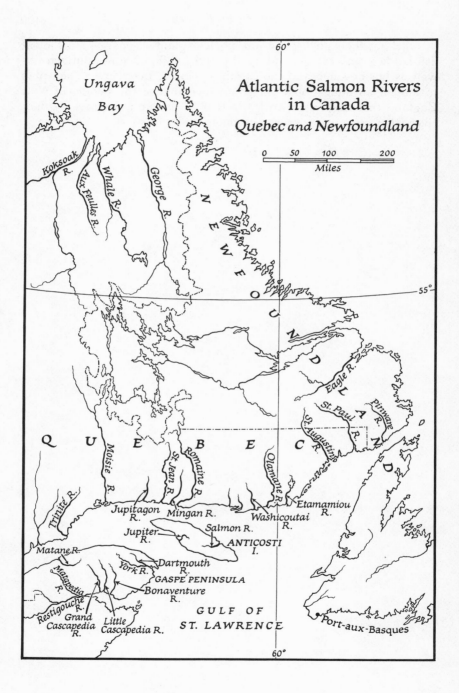

Ungava
Bay

Atlantic Salmon Rivers
in Canada
Quebec and *Newfoundland*

0   50   100   200
Miles

Koksoak R.

Aux Feuilles R.

Whale R.

George R.

N E W F O U N D L A N D

60°

55°

Eagle R.

St. Paul R.

Pinware R.

St. Augustin R.

Q U E   B   E   C

Moisie R.

St. Jean R.

Romaine R.

Olamane R.

Trinité R.

Jupitagon R.

Mingan R.

Washicoutai R.

Etamamiou R.

Matane R.

Jupiter R.

Salmon R.

ANTICOSTI I.

Dartmouth R.

York R.

GASPE PENINSULA

Matapedia R.

Bonaventure R.

Restigouche R.

Grand Cascapedia R.

Little Cascapedia R.

GULF OF
ST. LAWRENCE

Port-aux-Basques

60°

XI ∼◊

The Canadian Experience

Salmo salar has fared much better in Canada than in the United States. Although pursued by fishermen as relentlessly as in our country, the slower pace of industrialization and settlement, sparser population, and maintenance of many rivers in their natural wild state, particularly in northern Quebec, Newfoundland, and Labrador, have saved a substantial proportion of the original resource. Canada now produces probably as much Atlantic salmon as any other country (Appendix Tables 1 and 2).

Atlantic Salmon Rivers

In the vast area comprising the provinces of Quebec, New Brunswick, Nova Scotia, and Newfoundland-Labrador there are hundreds of salmon rivers of various dimensions from latitude 40° to 65° north and far into the interior, flowing through the eastern half of the Canadian Shield and to Ungava Bay. Until the advent of air transportation only the rivers in the southern portion of the area were intensely exploited by net and rod fishermen, but now the frontiers, so to speak, have been pushed back into the most remote wilderness.

Canada's Atlantic salmon streams include rivers of incomparable beauty, rugged and gentle, flowing with amazing speed to their destination or dawdling across the plain as if they were in no hurry to reach the ocean. The plenitude of fishes some of them harbored, as found in the accounts of old settlers and explorers, is a familiar story.

"There are," says Wilfred Carter, Executive Director of the International Atlantic Salmon Foundation, "almost incredible tales of the hordes of sleek salmon which filled the rivers of eastern Canada . . . in diaries and historical records. We are told of streams choked so thickly with ascending salmon that one could almost literally walk from shore to shore on their backs. There are numerous and frequent references to the great abundance in some areas which enabled their capture by cartloads, and the handiest fishing instrument was the pitchfork. Some of these were destined for shipment by schooner to the British market, presumably salted. The greater proportion saw their destiny fulfilled as fertilizer on the cleared plots where the early settlers planted their precious seed for the autumn harvest." [1]

Salmon in eastern Canada thrive in a wide variety of climates and terrain. In Labrador much of the land is bleak and frozen the largest part of the year; the scouring action of the ice sheet and subsequent erosion by frost, wind, and water have removed most of the topsoil from the uplands. Mosses and lichens carpet the boulder-strewn land; in the southern half of the peninsula the slopes are covered with forests of black spruce, interspersed with scattered larch, birch, white spruce, and balsam fir. As one moves north the woods gradually thin out and the trees become stunted and straggling, confined to sheltered ravines and hollows. Part of Labrador is included in the province of Quebec and part in Newfoundland.

There are extensive mineral deposits in Newfoundland and considerable runs of fish in its rivers and along its shores. South of Newfoundland are the shallow seas, or banks, sunken remnants of the northern Appalachian Highlands and the Atlantic coastal plain, which in the remote geologic past had extended past Nova Scotia and Newfoundland. In these waters, the immense shoals of cod shed their eggs, and their larvae feed on the plankton and their fry on the tiny crustaceans. As the cod grow to maturity they follow their food supply, mainly herring, capelin, and squid. In the wake of the cod come the far less abundant anadromous fishes, salmon, shad, and others, from their feeding grounds, in the case of the salmon cold Greenland waters; they head for their spawning rivers through the Gulf of Saint Lawrence or along the coasts of Labrador and Newfoundland, Nova Scotia, New Brunswick, or Maine.

Because of the multitudinous fishes, the Grand Banks attracts enormous numbers of sea birds, who are eager, so to speak, to join the feast. There are kittiwakes, terns, razorbills, murres, gulls, and puffins constantly wheeling and plunging into the often icy waters, filling the air with their mewings and squawkings, sometimes bewilderingly to the trawler men searching for the fish through the fog.

Quebec is the largest of the eastern "salmon" provinces. The Canadian Shield occupies much of the area north of the Saint Lawrence River, while the Appalachian Mountains extend through the area south of the Saint Lawrence. Southern Quebec has a warm and humid climate in summer, while much of northern Quebec has a very short but pleasant summer. Numerous rivers flow through a plateau wall to the Saint Lawrence, and most of them from the Ontario border to the Strait of Belle Isle originally harbored good runs of salmon. In contrast to Newfoundland, Quebec is mountainous and heavily forested; forests drop down to the water's edge in the Gulf of Saint Lawrence, and numerous villages dot the landscape with their trim white-frame houses and little churches.

The topography of New Brunswick generally resembles that of Maine, especially along the extensive coast. Some of the world's highest tides occur in the Bay of Fundy, which anadromous fishes must traverse to reach their natal streams. Agriculture, forestry, and fisheries are the mainstays of this province's economy. The major salmon rivers include the Saint John, which empties into the Bay of Fundy, the Miramichi, which drops into Miramichi Bay, and the Ristigouche. These waterways, along with the Saint Croix, an international river, have rich historical associations: here were seen the conflicts of whites and Indians and later the strife between loyalists and the rebels who took up arms against George III.

Nova Scotia is the smallest of the Maritime Provinces, a picturesque peninsula of 21,100 square miles (compared with 28,000 square miles for New Brunswick, 524,000 square miles for Quebec, and 153,-000 square miles for Newfoundland-Labrador). With many excellent harbors and numerous rivers, Nova Scotia became a major fishing center during the Colonial period and was the gateway from British North America to the homeland.

The earliest settlers found the rivers so full of salmon and other fishes that they established town sites like Liverpool and Medway near the mouths of the streams partly to take advantage of the fishery. In this area salmon seem to have been heavily fished for export in the later eighteenth century.

In New Brunswick William Davidson and the English firm of Robin, Piper and Company held fisheries on the Miramichi and Ristigouche (now among the choicest angling rivers) in the 1760s. During and after the American Revolution the fishing industry of the Maritime colonies expanded rapidly, with cod as a mainstay, but herring, mackerel, and salmon were also fished heavily and sent to England and the West Indies. John Cartwright, brother of Edmund Cartwright, inventor of the power loom, was the first to organize the salmon trade in Labrador and made a fortune.

The salmon fishery in Labrador, Newfoundland, and parts of Quebec came to be monopolized by the Hudson's Bay Company until it surrendered its lands to the Dominion of Canada in 1869. The main difficulty confronting the company in exploring and exploiting the resources of the interior was the harsh physical environment.

Exploitation of the Quebec Fishery

Although the Hudson's Bay Company was primarily interested in furs, it conducted an extensive fish business in the nineteenth century. In 1831 the Mingan district, in charge of Chief Trader Joseph Felix La Rocque, consisted of four trading posts and nine salmon fisheries in lower Quebec. It was also the largest buyer of salmon on the Labrador coast, where it owned the nets and fishing houses or "posts" situated in the long inlets. The native fishermen gave the company half the catch as rent and obtained commodities from its store for the rest. Donald A. Smith (later Lord Strathcona), chief factor in Labrador from 1847 to 1860, distinguished himself among other things in expanding the salmon trade.

In their lust for profits, which amounted to as much as 12 percent of the capital annually in the period 1840 to 1857, the company often overfished the rivers as it overkilled the beaver, otter, marten, and other fur bearers. There is little or no evidence of a conservation conscience among its directors dwelling in London or its men in the field. Genio Scott in *Fishing in American Waters* (1875) reported discussions during an angling excursion in Canada with government agents who had formerly been employed by the company: "All agreed that the company had greatly depleted the rivers of salmon, and necessitated the exercise of wisdom and care on the part of the Government to restock them with a supply as ample as would be required for rendering them profitable, besides supplying the needs of the growing population." [2] Scott saw fishing huts and stations belonging to the company standing idle and going to ruin.

The Saint Lawrence was the most valuable salmon river in eastern North America, an 800-mile waterway flowing from the northeastern end of Lake Ontario to the Gulf of Saint Lawrence along a belt of lowland. En route to the ocean it passes the enchanted Thousand Islands and innumerable falls and rapids and is joined by many pleasant and sometimes turbulent streams issuing from the north and south. At its mouth, where the river becomes the Gulf of Saint Lawrence, it is ninety miles wide and before the construction of the Seaway was navigable for 400 miles. Now ocean ships have direct access to the cities on the Great Lakes.

Richard Nettle in his book *Salmon Fisheries of the St. Lawrence,* published in 1857, gives a comprehensive picture of the resources in the principal streams from Anse au Sablon to the Saguenay River, including the island of Anticosti, whose inlets, bays, and creeks, he said, "swarm with large quantities of salmon," where an afternoon's tide churned up 500 to 600 fish for the Hudson's Bay Company nets. But that happened, he said, many years before. Now the fishery was much depleted because the company's men, "not content with netting and spearing in the bay, ascend the rivers and fish both by day and by night, not only during the fishing seasons but also spearing the fish on their spawning beds. In fact, so few have been taken lately by the Hudson's Bay fishermen, that they are becoming careless of the fisheries . . . and indeed, they themselves have even tended to destroy them, from the use of what I would call illegal nets." [3]

Protection of the rivers and estuaries was incredibly lax. Quoting Reverend William Agar Adamson, "one of the best authorities in the province," Nettle said that American schooners used to arrive in the Bay of Seven Islands with armed crews and set their nets in the Moisie River "in despite of the Hudson's Bay Company." The Bersimis River was boldly usurped by an American company that in 1856 speared large numbers of fish "and after glutting the Boston and New York markets . . . brought some boxes to Toronto in September, when they were out of season and unfit for use."

"Such," he said, "is the present state of the fisheries of the River St. Lawrence — for the same mode of destruction is practiced in every river where they are wont to congregate — only that in the lower part of the district mill dams have not yet been built, and it is to be hoped that, when it becomes necessary to build dams therein, every precaution will be taken by the erection of chutes or slides, so that the fisheries of these rivers may not be destroyed, as one within this district has been, the Escoumains." [4]

Nettle surveyed all the Saint Lawrence streams west from Anse au Sablon. On the Escoumains the nets used to take 150 to 200 fish on a tide and the angler was sure of sport. That was before a mill dam was built on the river, "the right of way stopped, and that splendid and valuable stream (which yielded its proprietors £6000 to £8000 per annum) utterly destroyed."

The 110-mile Saguenay is the chief tributary of the Saint Lawrence. Its source is Lake Saint John, whence it issues from two outlets, the

Grand and Petite Decharge, drops 300 feet in thirty-five miles, and is
swollen by powerful subtributaries, the Shipsaw and Balin from the
north and the Au Sable and Chicoutimi from the south. The lower
seventy miles or so courses through a deep, broad, fjord-like channel
scoured by ice and rock during the Pleistocene epoch. "As a nursery
for the salmon few rivers can equal it," said Nettle.[5] There were also
originally ample populations of sturgeon, pike, white fish, trout, pick-
erel, cod, herring, and smelts. Log jams had damaged many tributaries, but some of the principal ones were still well endowed with
fish.

The Murray used to be called by the inhabitants "the Salmon
River" because of the immense quantities of fish it contained. Then a
mill dam erected by an American lessee blocked the stream and
drove out the salmon; this structure was eventually torn down and
the fish began to return. Now the poachers were active night after
night, principally at the Chute, despite the lately passed act forbidding the taking of salmon with the spear.

The Jacques Cartier is sixty miles long and the favorite, said Nettle,
of fly-fishers from Montreal and elsewhere. There used to be splendid
salmon runs as far as Dery's bridge, some dozen miles from the
mouth. First the large fish made their appearance; then came the
grilse. But Louis Dery, the lessee, scooped up large numbers in the
narrow gorge at the bottom of a waterfall and sent them to market.
"Once they were counted by the thousands; a few years ago by the
hundreds; and now they can scarcely be numbered by the dozen." [6]
Only after a new proprietor purchased the fishing rights and ended
netting at the pool were large numbers of salmon able to reach the
higher waters.

South shore rivers were also subjected to ruinous exploitation. The
Rimouski, Great and Little Métis, Tartigo, Blanche, Matane, and
Chatte all still had considerable stocks but were not producing at capacity. If protected during the spawning season, and if fishways were
erected at the rapids, dams and wherever necessary, this district, said
Nettle, "would soon become a mine of wealth and a source of great
profit to both fishermen and purchaser." [7]

In the Gaspé and Saint Bonaventure regions there were magnificent
streams, "richer than the diamond mines of the East." From the Ristigouche alone 2000 to 3000 salmon used to be taken daily, but the
volume had fallen to a tenth of that by the middle of the nineteenth
century. The annual export of 2000 barrels of fish to Britain and the
United States from Campbellton had dwindled to 300. This decline

was attributed by one exporter "to the spearing and netting of the fish on the spawning grounds by the Indians and the 'barbarians' who are driven to this nefarious practice by the white man who purchases the fish." [8]

Salmon were still abundant in such Gaspé rivers as the Saint Anne, Magdalene, York, Saint John, Malbaie, Grand, and Great and Little Pabos and in the Bay of Chaleur. However, lack of protection and impassable obstructions were here as elsewhere depopulating the streams.

Fifty years after Nettle published his survey, E. D. T. Chambers in *Game Fishes of Quebec* affirmed that there was little salmon water left west of the Saguenay. Some fish still went up the Murray, but mill refuse choked the Grant River and the Jacques Cartier was severely impaired. Streams east and west of Quebec City could be successfully revived, he said, if the dominion regulations concerning the location and mesh of salmon nets were properly enforced, pollution abated, fishways installed at all dams below the spawning grounds, and poaching stopped. Chambers noted that while many of the rivers were deteriorating, their value for recreation was growing enormously due to the upsurge in salmon angling.

Exploitation of Maritime Fisheries

As in Quebec, the New Brunswick laws were not well enforced. Parley in his book *The Fisheries of New Brunswick*, quoted by Nettle, painted a dreary picture of nets constantly set during the season, Sundays, and weekdays; drift nets stretched across the streams, which prevented escapements, and fish were speared on the spawning beds.[9] Parley urged prompt action by the authorities. Fisheries belonging to the Crown in rivers whose banks were ungranted should be leased, he said, on condition that they would be fished only at the proper season and protected at all other times.

Parley revealed the deplorable condition of some New Bunswick rivers, particularly the Saint John, longest in the province, in part forming the border between the United States and Canada. On this stream Indians and settlers ceaselessly pursued the fish, while mill or splash dams locked them out. Occasionally a dam fell into disrepair or loggers destroyed it, and the fish had an opportunity to return to their ancestral homes. Old settlers spoke wistfully about the good old days before dams were built in the Kenebecasis (then known as the Salmon River); when the fishing was excellent, a man could take £90

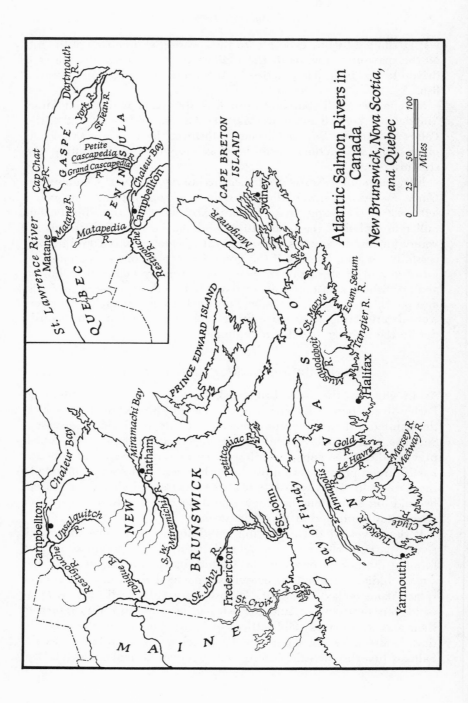

Atlantic Salmon Rivers in
Canada
*New Brunswick, Nova Scotia,
and Quebec*

Miles
0 25 50 100

worth of salmon (an enormous sum) in a season, and a team of two persons could haul out forty barrels in a couple of days.

It is evident from the testimony of Nettle, Parley, and others that some of the freshwater fisheries were as abused in Canada as in the United States during the nineteenth century, but the resource was considerably greater. However, systematic exploitation was carried on under the illusion that renewable natural resources were illimitable and, as Wilfred Carter says, "the country [was] so sparsely settled that they would have mocked anyone . . . so presumptuous as to suggest that many of those same rivers would be barren of salmon before their very eyes." [10]

In some areas the provincial government was engaged in restocking programs, yet no efforts were made to limit netting at the river mouths. On the Ristigouche, American angler Henry P. Wells observed in 1885, "the casual observer would think any escape impossible from the labyrinths of nets which, for miles below the head of the tide and in close proximity to one another, bar the ascent of salmon to the spawning grounds." Of the fish taken with the fly hardly more than one in ten was free from net wounds.[11]

Sir Wilfred Grenfell saw similar scenes in Labrador later in the century.

The provincial and national governments were unable to patrol the enormous number of streams effectively. They had neither the manpower nor the funds.

A survey by F. H. D. Vieth of Nova Scotia rivers in 1881 and 1882 revealed the loss of salmon fisheries due to causes similar to those in other provinces. Extensive logging had caused quick runoff on many streams, higher water temperatures in summer than salmon can tolerate, and silting of stream beds by the deposition of eroded material — a combination of familiar circumstances.

Almost every river in Nova Scotia, said Vieth, had one or more dams without fishways. "The only exceptions on the mainland . . . were the Mersey and Medway with good fishways, a portion of the St. Mary's, and several smaller rivers such as Nine Mile and Pennant unobstructed." Heavy freshets on Cape Breton Island made construction of dams on the large rivers unfeasible, but all the tributary brooks were barricaded. And sawmills dumped their sawdust and other wastes into the waters and ruined spawning areas below the dams.

In 1897 the Nova Scotia Department of Fisheries reported that of twenty-seven salmon rivers emptying into Northumberland Strait only four were unobstructed and all the others were blocked by mill dams without fishways — the same general situation as existed in Maine. One inspector revealed that in his district 90 percent of the fishways were not even operable.

The only reason that the Nova Scotia fishery did not disappear was that many of the dams permitted the fish to pass at certain times of the year. Some were low structures with a spillway or sluice gate and impounded very little water. Operations were confined to a few months of the year, and the rest of the time the gates were opened; also, during freshets water flowed over the low-head obstructions and the salmon managed to reach their spawning grounds. Although salmon catches had increased at the end of the 1880s, the potential of the Nova Scotia rivers was hardly exploited.[12]

Rise of Sport Fishing

Sport fishing for Atlantic salmon goes back to Colonial days in both Canada and the United States. In the second half of the nineteenth century it began to attain wide popularity at a time when the prince of game fishes had disappeared from most of Maine's rivers, forcing American sportsmen to seek them in the wilds of Canada. To reach their destination the fishers had to take a long train ride or venture by ship along the Atlantic coast or the Saint Lawrence River and then go by stage and canoe to a fishing camp. Three weeks or a month were needed for a Bostonian or New Yorker to have a minimum of sport and much longer for a really good holiday. But the rewards were munificent.

"To spend a summer month on one of the great rivers which empty into the Gulf of St. Lawrence is to rest the mind by the most absolute exclusion from the world," said Genio Scott. "When I assayed the ascent of one of the great rivers . . . north of the island of Anticosti, the world was tranquil. For a month I admired the grandeur of the mountains, the majesty of the broad and rapid river, the elegant play of salmon, and the dexterity of the seals; and at night the brilliancy of the northern horizon and gorgeousness of the lunar bow enraptured me." [13]

For example, to reach the Miramichi River the angler had to go by way of Saint John, New Brunswick, take a boat for Fredericton to buy provisions and stores, and there embark on a stage coach for Boiestown to engage guides or canoe men. To reach the Matapedia River he went by way of Saint John and Bathurst, then to Dalhousie, and thence to Campbellton, where he hired such guides as he could find, usually half-breed Indians who were generally neither sober nor honest and not even good canoe men. Those who headed for the Cascapedia or the Bonaventure River on the northern shore of the Bay of Chaleur were advised by Thad. Norris in *The American Angler's Book* (1864) to hire a boat and guides and purchase stores at Bathurst and cross the bay in a sailing craft.

Norris advised his readers: "All the stores that are really necessary . . . and many of those that may be called luxuries, including good brandy and fine Scotch ale and whiskey may be had of Messrs. Ferguson, Rankin and Co. at Bathurst. Desiccated vegetables and meat, solidified milk, essence of coffee (if the angler wants them), smoking tobacco, and claret, he had better take from home." [14]

Many of the Canadian rivers were owned by the Crown, while others were held by individual proprietors who leased them to anglers. The sport was marvelous on the unsullied streams. On the Nipisiguit, three miles above Bathurst, there were a number of pools that could be fished without interference by the locals and where the isolation and wildness added enormous zest to the sport. The water was so clear that salmon could be seen quite plainly and the angler could play his fly above their very noses. The silence was awesome. "If the birds sing high above the shrubbery and stunted timber, they are not heard by the fisher down in the deep ravine through which the river flows; but a voice of ordinary pitch, a thump of the canoe, or the splash of a salmon when it falls, after leaping above the water, is heard a long distance off, and the sound is prolonged and reflected from the almost perpendicular rock that walls in the stream on either side. Thus you frequently know when another angler, though he is not visible, has a fish on." [15]

Moisie, Ristigouche, and Miramichi were names that thrilled salmon anglers, connoting the best sport of its kind in North America if not the world.

The Moisie, whose headwaters are in the high tableland of Labrador, is one of the longest salmon rivers in eastern North America and, says Edward Weeks, "surely one of the most powerful. It is a river of unpredictable mood, wild beauty and deception. The wide, fast flow of June water in the lower pools, ruffled as they are generally by a northwest wind, sharp from the Arctic, seems of intimidating depth . . . To anyone who has stood beside the tumult of white water where the McDonald River slams into the Chutes or has heard and seen the uproar at the Basin after the ice goes out, the untamed power of the Moisie is overwhelming, and one wonders how any fish could survive in it." [16] Here the Montagnais Indians used to spear as many as 900 large fish by torchlight of an evening.

There was an elite fishing club on the Moisie as early as 1902, but in 1925 the famous Moisie Salmon Club was formed by a group of American millionaires. In the forty-seven years of its existence the club, one of the most exclusive of its kind in North America, has had only thirty-five members, of whom ten are still active.

In the 1890s gentlemen who could afford to fish the Ristigouche River, which forms the border of the provinces of Quebec and New Brunswick, took the train from Montreal to Matapedia and then embarked on a horse yacht, which consisted of a barge on which was mounted a cottage pulled by three strong horses. The driver sat on the middle horse and steered his charges through the shallower water. On the afterdeck or back porch there was a cow to provide milk; the interior had a sleeping cabin, kitchen, and saloon. The barge towed a couple of canoes. The best fishing was in the sixty-mile stretch above tidewater. The Ristigouche Salmon Club was the peer of the Moisie Club in the wealth and corporate eminence of its members.

Nowadays superhighways and airlines have brought the Canadian rivers within relatively easy reach of almost any part of the continent, and only the remotest streams, like those flowing into Ungava Bay, are still difficult to reach.

Attempts to Halt Depletion

Commercial salmon fishing has been concentrated at or near the mouth of almost every river from South New Brunswick to the Ungava in the north. The gear includes gill nets, drift nets from motorboats, trap nets, pound sets, and weirs. Federal regulations prescribe the maximum size of the nets and minimum mesh size as well as the weekly closure and fishing seasons.

Concern for the future of the resource led to the formation in 1949 of a Federal-Provincial Coordinating Committee on Atlantic Salmon, which resulted in stepped-up conservation efforts and expanded research by both the federal and provincial governments.

In 1951 Scottish expert W. J. M. Menzies was invited by the Atlantic Salmon Association, one of the leading salmon conservation organizations in Canada, to make a comprehensive study of the resource. Analyzing the catch figures and taking account of normal fluctuation

Stages of the Atlantic Salmon: Parr; parr to smolt, now ready for sea; a female salmon in its prime; a male spawner with the long head and hooked lower jaw.

Salmon have an indomitable urge to reach their spawning grounds. If there is ample flow they can hurdle obstacles up to 10 or 11 feet high.

Craig Brook Hatchery, operated by the federal government at Orland, Maine, is the first salmon hatchery built in North America. It has recently been modernized.

A scale, like the rings on a tree, tells us the salmon's age and how long it has been in saltwater.

Salmon are caught with trap nets around the coast of eastern Canada, as on Chaleur Bay.

Salmon angling on Breton
streams like the Aulne was a
popular pastime until pollution
poisoned the waters. Excessive
netting at the mouth of the
river and in the tidal zone
also helped to deplete
the fishes.

The Little Trinity is a typical Quebec
salmon river beloved of anglers.

The Malangsfoss Pool in Norway holds many large salmon like this 27-pounder. It is an angler's dream.

The Driva in Norway offers salmon anglers an opportunity to indulge in their famous pastime amid sublime scenery.

in numbers, "peak years being followed by depressed periods, which, again, are followed by peaks," he concluded that there had been a serious decline in the stock in the previous two decades. The trend was general throughout the area, although Quebec had not lost as much ground as New Brunswick and Nova Scotia, perhaps because of "better protection, and possibly the more remote situation of most of the north shore rivers."

Out of his long experience Menzies offered recommendations for bolstering the stocks, of which the most important were:

1. Licenses for shore nets should be reduced.
2. The number of drift netters operating in Miramichi Bay should be curtailed and the maximum length of net dropped to 400 fathoms.
3. Licenses for the Port-aux-Basques drift-net fishery should be restricted to the current holders.
4. Regulation of fishing on the Labrador coast should be investigated and a commission appointed to examine the limits to which netting at each river mouth should be kept.[17]

He also suggested that the weekly closed time should be reexamined, shore and drift nets reduced, and the Nova Scotia commercial season be closed down for a fortnight at the end of June. He said that a patrol service should be provided to enforce the weekend closures on all coasts and a regular permanent warden service established for the rivers instead of the existing political-patronage guardians. He believed that protection of the rivers should be the responsibility of the government and penalties for poaching increased substantially. Menzies also recommended that fish passes be built where necessary, a code of regulations for power dams drawn up, and a comprehensive research program vigorously pursued. A few of these recommendations were later implemented; others were not.

Deteriorating Environments

In 1957, J. L. Kask, Chairman of the Fisheries Research Board of Canada, summarized the status of the Atlantic salmon rivers:

Most of the rivers that formerly supported salmon runs and no longer do have lost their runs more from adverse changes in the very restricted and demanding fresh water environment in which they are born and spend the first half of their life, than from overfishing . . . Agricultural, urban and industrial pollution (including spraying forests and waters with DDT) contribute substantially. Removal of adjacent forest cover with attendant fast run-offs and exposure of critical river areas to increases in light and temperature can have deleterious effects. Multiple water uses for irrigation, power, navigation, etc. and physical interference with the river itself such as often accompanies logging, mining, or road building all can, and do, affect the river as an environment for living organisms.

Examples of how salmon have been affected by industrial and agricultural pollution are numerous. For instance, some of the rivers on the island of Newfoundland, usually regarded as a secure haven for freshwater fishes, have been damaged by deposition of poisons that smother plant and invertebrate life, reduce light penetration and general food production, and rob the fishes of oxygen. At Buchans, for example, some 360,000 tons of ore-producing lead, zinc, and copper concentrates were processed annually; 260,000 tons of wastes were tossed into Buchans brook whence they flowed into Red Indian Lake and downstream to the Exploits River, an excellent salmon stream. Studies showed that below the point where the material entered the brook, no life existed, and in the lake there were lethal deposits at the bottom, while in the lower river dissolved zinc and copper concentrations were present in amounts that had adverse effects on migratory salmon populations.

A copper deposit near Gull Pond, a major lake on South Brook, Halls Bay, was causing fears for the salmon and trout in the adjacent stream, which provided about the only sport fishery for salmon between the Exploits and Humber Rivers.

In 1965 two large newsprint mills in Newfoundland, at Corner Brook on the west coast and Grand Falls on the Exploits River, were polluting prime salmon water. During low flows the oxygen content, reduced by the algae produced by the waste liquor dumped into the stream, was too low for fish to survive. The addition of town sewage compounded the evil.

Deleterious effects from copper and zinc mining were visible in the Northwest Miramichi River in New Brunswick. In this province enormous damage to the fishes had been inflicted in the 1950s and 1960s by the spraying of DDT on extensive areas of forest in an attempt to

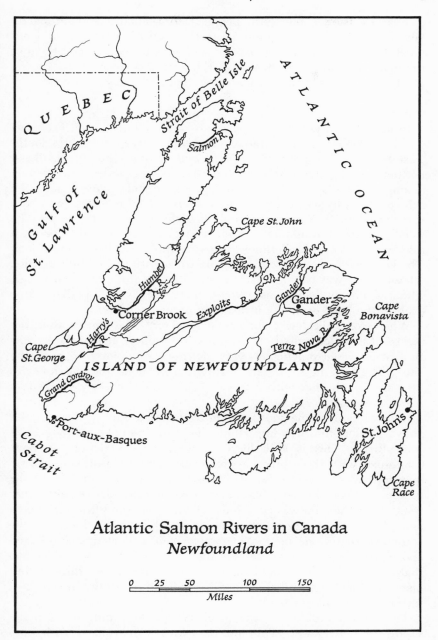

Atlantic Salmon Rivers in Canada
Newfoundland

```
0     25    50        100        150
|_____|_____|_____|_____|
              Miles
```

combat the spruce budworm plague that defoliates and ultimately kills the trees. Here the foresters treating government land did not touch base with the fishery experts who might have warned them of the dangers they ran, even though the serious consequences of using DDT were then not as well known as they are today.

Other Problems

In addition to pollution some rivers were suffering from extensive poaching. On the Great Miramichi and especially on the Little Southwest branch, said a writer in *Field and Stream* (July 1970), illegal netting and jigging was common: "There is a widespread feeling among . . . Indians and whites alike that a certain percentage of the fish are theirs to get by any means available. Children learn at a very early age how to 'sweep the pool' at night with ½ inch mesh. The usual price for the midnight catch is $1.75 per grilse and $5.00 for a salmon . . . As with all things, a good supply can lower the price." The year before he had seen a pickup truck with its bed full of grilse, whose owner was having a hard time selling them for fifty cents each. These same bootlegged fish would have been worth perhaps $100 each to the local economy if taken on an angler's fly.

Where were the law enforcement officers? "The conservation department is under-staffed . . . The Fisheries officer at Red Bank, New Brunswick, is out practically every night of the salmon run, gathering nets. 'The law,' he says, 'requires us to apprehend the violator with his hand on the net with a fish in it . . . It's not likely we'll make many arrests.'"

Construction of the $110 million Mactaquac dam, a dozen miles above Fredericton, was imperiling stocks on the once teeming Saint John River. This is a flashy river with wide variations in flow. Combined with three other hydroelectric projects upstream, Mactaquac provides power to farms, factories, and homes throughout the province. About 11,000 salmon and grilse used to pass the site every year. After the dam was completed about a thousand fish were taken annually for propagation at the new salmon hatchery. The rest of the adult fish that came up to Mactaquac were collected and released above the barrier, where they became available to anglers. The fish that escaped the rods would spawn naturally if they got through, but many smolts would probably be killed going through the three sets of turbines in the power plant.

The critical problem of the hatchery was to obtain an adequate supply of pure water. Polluted river water was mixed with pure ground water and then chemically treated, but if the purity level dropped below a certain point juvenile fish died in the ponds. The superintendent was a worried man when I visited him in 1969.

Impact of the Greenland Fishery

The decline of the Atlantic salmon resource in Canada has been accelerated, as in the British Isles, by the growth of the Greenland fishery in the early 1960s. Operating off the west coast of the subpolar island and in Davis Strait, catches jumped from sixty metric tons in 1960 to 1539 tons in 1964, fluctuated between 1965 and 1968, and averaged 2260 tons in 1969–1971 — about 17 percent of the world catch. On the basis of tagged fish recovered in the fishery, it has been estimated that Canada supplies well over half the total harvests.

What this means in terms of Canadian stocks is suggested in a paper by Bertrand Tetreault and Wilfred Carter, who studied the fate of 20,456 smolts tagged in 1968 in Quebec. They postulated that 27 percent of the fish that had survived to enter the commercial fishery were taken in the inshore Greenland nets, 29 percent by the offshore Greenland fishermen and 32 percent by the Newfoundland nets. Only 9 percent were taken by the Quebec commercial fishery and 3 percent by anglers. No estimates were made of the proportion of the run that managed to escape and reach the spawning grounds. Only salmon who have been at sea more than one winter are taken in Greenland.

If this has been the typical fate of Canadian smolts feeding in waters around Greenland, it may well account for much of the drastic decreases in Canadian catches of adult salmon in recent years, down from 2859 metric tons in 1967 to 1837 metric tons in 1971 (Appendix Table 2).

T. B. Fraser, late manager of the Atlantic Salmon Association, pointed out in *The Atlantic Salmon Journal* (1971, No. 2) the complex factors that militate against the Canadian migrants. Those fish which escape from the Greenland nets and Newfoundland fisheries, he said, mostly pass south of the island, "then take their respective routes to New Brunswick and Baie des Chaleurs, to the Gaspé coast and north shore [of the Saint Lawrence]. Part of the returning migration to Quebec rivers is intermingled with the New Brunswick fish and is exploited by the Miramichi drift nets. The fish escaping this large drift-net fleet then run the gauntlet of the New Brunswick and Quebec shore nets as they approach home waters." In 1971 377 fishermen were licensed by the Quebec government to operate a total of 44,745 fathoms (about fifty-seven miles) of shore nets on the shores of the Saint Lawrence River. Fraser pointed out that drift nets off the Maritime Provinces take only large salmon, like those which migrate to Greenland — Quebec does not permit drift netting off its coast.

"Being at the tail end of the migration, Quebec's total catch is quite low considering the number and size of its rivers. A very large proportion of the large female fish produced in Quebec rivers are exploited in Newfoundland and the Maritimes as well as in the Northern [Davis Strait–Greenland] fishery."

An essential fact suggested by Fraser is that there is very little scientific management of Atlantic salmon rivers in Canada. The successful techniques applied on the Fraser and Columbia seem to be ignored on the Atlantic side. There is relatively little knowledge of the size of the stocks in the various river systems. Spawning counts are made on only a few rivers in the entire range of *Salmo salar* in Canada.

It was clear after the disastrous 1970 and 1971 fishing seasons that the Canadian resource was in a critical state. The 1971 commercial catch was much lower than in 1970, and anglers fared no better. In 1971 anglers took 65,000 salmon and grilse, compared with 92,000 in 1970 and 105,750 in 1967.

"In Nova Scotia, New Brunswick, and that part of Quebec south of the Saint Lawrence River," said Wilfred Carter, "my crystal ball indicates that salmon are fighting a losing battle to retain their foothold."

Drastic Emergency Action

For many years Canadian fishery conservation organizations had been pressuring the provincial and national governments to curtail commercial fishing on the declining runs of *Salmo salar*.

Steps in this direction were taken in 1969 by the Quebec provincial government, which announced on March 20 that, in order "to conserve the stocks . . . no new applications would be accepted for commercial netting at sea and fishermen who did not use their nets in the previous two years would not be able to renew their licenses since the Department of Tourism, Fish and Game considers that there was sufficient gear in operation during the last two seasons to handle the catch which the species can support." Also, all commercial fishing would be suspended for five years on an experimental basis in the immediate area of the Matane, Cap-Chat, and Saint Anne Rivers in the Gaspé, in hope of converting these streams into top recreational attractions, with emphasis on sports fishing, since this mode of taking salmon is less taxing to the resource than netting.

After the 1971 season, more drastic action seemed necessary. The newly formed North American Atlantic Salmon Council, sponsored by the International Atlantic Salmon Foundation, with headquarters in New Brunswick, embracing many of the leading conservation groups in North America, proclaimed that "within North America . . . there has been an unfortunate tardiness in recognizing that some of the ills afflicting the salmon are rooted in outdated concepts of what constitutes progressive management. Another inimical factor is the exploitation privileges inherited from an era when the abundance of salmon may have justified such an obvious luxury . . . Today's programs of renewable resource management implies rational planning for future development." In short, the council urged that in addition to working for curtailment of the Greenland fishery the Canadian government and all those concerned with the fishery should take cognizance of the excessive commercial exploitation of the runs on the return to their homeland and also that they should step up "the rehabilitation of the Atlantic salmon's habitat," a task that will require "massive (government) assistance."

In February 1972 Denmark, a chief exploiter of the Greenland fishery, sent a delegation to Washington to negotiate an agreement leading to curtailment of high seas fishing, a step it reluctantly took in response to passage by Congress of a bill authorizing the President to prohibit the importation of fish and fishery products from any nation that does not practice fishery conservation on the high seas. This was the first break in the Danish attitude of intransigence about high seas salmon fishing and resulted in a bilateral agreement between the United States and Greenland promising a gradual phaseout, within a period of five years, of offshore fishing around Greenland. By 1976 the fishery would be confined to inshore netting at a level of about 1100 tons annually, compared with a total of 2600 tons taken in 1971. This agreement was approved in June 1972 at the annual meeting of the International Commission for the Northwest Atlantic Fisheries. In December 1972 the Danish parliament ratified the agreement, thus assuring its enforcement.

In April 1972 Jack Davis, Minister of the Environment, announced an immediate and total ban on commercial salmon fishing in the following areas: the New Brunswick drift-net fishery (floating nets in the

Saint John and Miramichi estuaries), New Brunswick inshore fishery (nets attached to the shore), and the Newfoundland drift-net fishery (floating nets off Port-aux-Basques).

On May 26, 1972, the Province of Quebec announced the total prohibition of commercial salmon fishing in the entire Gaspé Peninsula. Areas excluded from the ban were the Newfoundland and Labrador inshore fishery, which accounts for a large proportion of all the salmon taken commercially; the inshore fishery on the north shore of the Saint Lawrence to the eastern limit of the province of Quebec; and the entire province of Nova Scotia. Altogether about 40 percent of the Atlantic salmon commercial fishery was eliminated, covering about 900 fishermen who would be compensated to the extent of $2.3 million in 1972 and lesser amounts in the following years.

The ban was expected to be in effect at least five years and might be extended to cover additional areas. The official reasons for exclusion of the Newfoundland and Labrador inshore fisheries was that they had not been seriously depleted by the Greenland catches, while the Nova Scotia catch was considered too small for inclusion. "In the light of available catch data," commented Wilfred Carter, "these reasons leave us somewhat skeptical and unconvinced."

As the 1970 commercial catches show, the great bulk of the netting occurs around Newfoundland:

	Salmon	*Grilse*
	(number of fish)	
New Brunswick	65,000	
Nova Scotia	17,400	
Quebec	35,400	
Newfoundland-Labrador	270,000	500,000
Total	387,800	500,000

The steps taken to reduce the commercial fishing in Canada and on the high seas not only bode well for recuperation of the resource but have lifted the hopes of anglers who experienced increasing disappointments in recent years. While to some observers the recent measures seem rather belated, they reflect the real concern for survival of the precious Atlantic salmon in North America, a much smaller and far less valuable resource than the Pacific salmon, which hitherto seems to have occupied most of the Canadian government's attention.

The Quebec sport fishery showed dramatic improvement in 1972. On the three major rivers the catches were as follows:

	1970	1971	1972
Grand Cascapedia	279	121	442
Matapedia	452	370	1087
Ristigouche	429	215	790

Other rivers showed similar results, while the Quebec commercial catch dropped, by design, in order to give the runs a chance to build back.

Excellent water conditions and a ban on commercial fishing made for a very good year for New Brunswick anglers: over 32,000 salmon were taken compared with 19,295 in 1971, and the average weight was the highest in a decade. On the Miramichi system the catch was double the previous year's.

Angling catches were down noticeably in Newfoundland-Labrador, from 37,000 in 1970, 33,000 in 1971, to 27,000 in 1972. The commercial catch also declined somewhat due to closure of the important Port-aux-Basques drift-net fishery and a reduction of several hundred licences in the Newfoundland set-net fishery.

The 1972 commercial harvest, with far fewer fishermen, was about one-third larger than in 1971.

There is, at last, hope that enough money and technical skill will become available for restoration and restocking of rivers, further curtailment of netting, and expansion of artificial propagation, now recognized as an essential tool of fishery management by salmon biologists. The best use of the resource, as demonstrated by the American and Canadian ban on ocean fishing [18] for Pacific salmon except by trolling, is to harvest the runs as they return to the rivers and not before, thus permitting effective control of catches and escapements to provide a perpetual crop.

There is a hopeful new outlook for restoration of the depleted stocks in eastern Canada, as both the government and nongovernment interests such as the International Atlantic Salmon Foundation launch research, build new research plants like the Huntsman Laboratory in Saint Andrews, New Brunswick, and conduct educational programs to awaken national interest in *Salmo salar*.

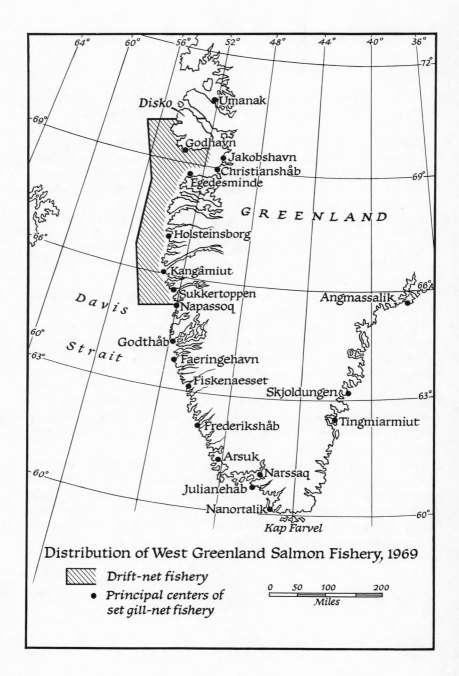

Distribution of West Greenland Salmon Fishery, 1969

⧄ Drift-net fishery
● Principal centers of
   set gill-net fishery

0   50   100   200
Miles

XII ∽

The Greenland Fishery —
Final Catastrophe?

THE WORLD'S STOCKS of *Salmo salar* were at their lowest level in history when a new and perhaps the most burdensome of evils appeared: discovery of the feeding grounds of fishes from both North America and some European countries. For centuries fishermen had searched the ocean in vain for salmon. In his book *The Open Sea: Its National History* (1959), Sir Alister Hardy reported that little was then known about the salmon's wanderings in the sea, since very few of these fishes had ever been found in the nets of fishermen. Menzies in *The Stock of Salmon* (1949) postulated the theory, based on his extensive study of tagged fish recaptured and recorded in various countries, that perhaps the salmon utilized one-direction staging areas, established probably as far back as the Pleistocene era. In these areas shoals of fishes assembled, like armies ready for the march, and dispersed in a given direction to the lush pastures of the sea. Menzies identified Port-aux-Basques in the Gulf of Saint Lawrence as one of these rendezvous. He suggested that their destination was the North Atlantic and there, joined by salmon from the continent of Europe, they moved and fed together in cousinly fashion, so to speak.

Menzies' theory came true with startling suddenness when Jørgen Nielsen, chief of the Greenland Fisheries Investigations for the Danish government, examined many salmon caught with the jig in the cod fishery and found that their parr life, as evidenced from the scales, was much shorter than the four or five years needed for smoltification in the cold Kapisigdlit River, the only one in Greenland known to harbor the species. This could only mean that an invasion of foreign fish had occurred and the feeding grounds of salmon from various countries had unfortunately been discovered. Nielsen's findings were not published until 1961 but gill netting for salmon along the west coast of Greenland, near Napassok, where a freezing plant had been built, began in 1959.

The Salmon Fishery

Greenland is the world's largest island, extending from 60° to 82° north latitude. The topography suggests that it is still in the Ice Age, a panorama of glaciers and mountains buried in deeply packed snow and ice, rising in places to 10,000 feet elevation, with occasional granite domes projecting above the white mass. Some 48,000 persons, chiefly Eskimos, live in this area of 840,000 square miles — three times the size of Texas — where trees grow only to dwarf size. The willow birch reaches ten feet and the alder only three feet. Most of Greenland is a lofty plateau, and only in the coastal rim and along some of the deep fjords does the soil support vegetation. In the valleys away from the coast luxuriant flowers make a brief appearance in summer. The adjoining seas breed cathedral-like icebergs in profusion.

Settlements dot the fringe of both the east and west coasts and even here human existence may be precarious, with temperatures in the north falling to 94° below zero and wind gales occurring frequently in the south during the six months of winter. Historically the Eskimos lived by hunting seals and other marine animals, but as the seas off the west coast became warmer in the 1920s great shoals of cod appeared, while the seal herds left for "greener" pastures. The natives then turned to cod fishing and also exploited the shrimp, halibut, and capelin. When salmon appeared around the shores they turned to this species.

As colonists of Denmark, the Greenlanders are heavily subsidized by the mother country — to the tune of $100 million a year since 1970. The Royal Greenland Trading Company is charged with developing the island's meager natural resources, maintaining supplies, and carrying out plans to improve living conditions and lessen the drain on the Danish treasury. The company virtually monopolizes the economy, including production and distribution of goods and services as well as transportation.

Spurred on by the Greenland Trading Company, which loaned the natives money to buy nets and obtain boats, the assault on the salmon accelerated swiftly. In 1960 and 1961 the fishery spread to Holsteinsborg, Godthaab, and Frederikshaab on the west coast, and nets were strung along the shore in an area of about 600 miles between 60° and 69° north latitude. By 1964 some 2600 Greenlanders were engaged in the fishery as the company doubled the price paid for salmon. Inshore harvests jumped from sixty tons in 1960 to 1539 tons in 1964. "Reports of such enormous catches," said Peter Liddell, "came as a severe blow to those of us who were trying to improve the stocks in our home rivers because evidence from tagged fish recovered in the nets showed that they virtually all had migrated as smolts or kelts from the rivers of the British Isles, eastern Canada or Maine."

In 1965 the fishery assumed a more fearful aspect as offshore fishing by drift netters began. Two boats from the Faeroe Islands, a dependency of Denmark, turned up in Davis Strait, which divides Greenland from Canada, and made good catches. A larger flotilla fished the next year, and in 1967 the "real experts," as Nicholas Evans of the London *Sunday Times* calls them, "arrived, tough Danish fishermen who brought their tiny 30-ton boats all the way from Bornholm in the Baltic where they had been fishing for salmon." In 1968 they were joined by Swedish and Norwegian vessels, and a total of 548 metric tons was cargoed offshore and 579 tons inshore. The real breakthrough came in 1969 as the ocean fleet swelled to sixty-seven boats, some of which were of 100- to 350-ton burden, which took 850 tons of salmon.

The 294-ton cutter *Polarlaks,* hailing from Bornholm, was one of the largest drifters in Davis Strait. It carried a crew of twelve to fourteen men and boys and was equipped with new and amazingly effective gear. *Polarlaks* began fishing on August 15, 1969, west of Greenland by setting 400 100-foot nets at the Hellefiske bank on level with Sukkertoppen, at a distance of thirty nautical miles from the coast. Drifting occurred at night, with the temperature around 40° F.

During the next month Captain Ole Martensen scoured a large area, thirty to ninety miles from shore, in the same general latitude, making catches of 200 to 300 salmon per night and once an incredible 1425. Then suddenly the fish disappeared and the *Polarlaks* went north to Disko Bay, where the nets were set at distances of ten to fifty miles from shore on a level with Christianshaab, in waters with floating icebergs, the temperature sometimes falling below freezing. Fishing continued until the end of October; then the vessel headed for Copenhagen with a cargo of 21,000 salmon worth $160,000. Every adult member of the crew received $8000 for the season's work and the boys $3600. On board was also the Danish Fishery biologist Ole Christensen, who took scale samples and recorded any tagged fish that were recovered.

Interviewed by a Copenhagen newspaper, Martensen exulted in his success and said he planned to go to Japan to learn the techniques of fishing on the high seas from Japanese fishermen. He promised to return in the spring of 1970 with a new 135-ton cutter equipped with the most modern Japanese gear.[1] Other cutters made catches comparable to that of the *Polarlaks* in 1969. In 1970 the offshore salmon fishery landed 1244 tons and in 1971 a whopping 1240 tons, including 340 tons by Norwegians, 255 tons by Faroese colonists of Denmark, and 645 tons by the Danes, 510 taken by gill net and 135 by drift net. Inshore catches in 1971 were 1375 tons, making a record high of 2615 tons.

Greenland "is a country which the Danes subsidize at an annual rate of £1000 ($2500) per year per head of population," said Nicholas Evans in the London *Sunday Times* (December 14, 1969). "Looking down into the maze of waterways, you see, like strings of pearls, the white floats of the nets that are killing the salmon. It is conceivable that they are there because of the determination of the Danes to make their chilly empire into a commercial proposition. To that end, it seems, they are willing to sacrifice the most valuable fish in the world."

Accelerating Conflict

Despite the outcries of anglers and other conservationists in the producing countries, the United States, Canada, and Great Britain, the Danish government made no attempt to impose restrictions on the lucrative fishery. Salmon of any size could be taken and operations continued night and day during the three-month season, September through November. An analysis of the 1964 harvest, for example, revealed that almost half of the catch consisted of fishes weighing from one to three kilograms (2.2-7.7 pounds), and nearly all were spending their second winter in the ocean. No grilse (one-winter sojourners) were found, suggesting that the salmon foraged elsewhere during their first year in the sea. All the specimens examined had food in their stomachs and most of them were sexually immature.

In 1965 the Greenland crisis was aired at the annual meeting of International Commission for North Atlantic Fisheries (ICNAF) in Halifax, Nova Scotia, and a group of international scientists was appointed to sample the catches, study the recovered tags, and assess the impact on the stocks of producing countries. On this basis they estimated that the 1964 landings deprived Canada of 480 tons of large salmon, equivalent to 28 percent of the large fish taken in Canada that year; Great Britain, sixty-six tons, or 6 percent of its nongrilse catch; and Ireland sixty-six tons, 22 percent of its large salmon landings. In the years 1963 to 1969 over 800 tagged fish were found in

West Greenland nets, of which 73 percent came from Canada, 19 percent from the United Kingdom, 5 percent from the United States, and the remaining 3 percent from Norway, Ireland, Iceland, Sweden, and Denmark.[2] These figures proved that a severe and unrelenting burden was being placed on the stocks of *Salmo salar* in Canada and Great Britain and to a much smaller extent those of other countries.

As the fishery accelerated, said Wilfred Carter in 1970, there was the real possibility that the producing nations might abandon their stream preservation and improvement programs and perhaps their hatcheries, "thus preparing the way for the extinction of the species which can only reproduce naturally in those streams." He estimated that $2,675,000 had been invested in Atlantic salmon preservation in North America in 1969–1970, projected to rise to $5,375,000 within five years. These figures do not include accumulated capital and operating expenditures on research, river management, protection, fish ladders, hatcheries, etc. The landed value of the 1969 commercial catch in North America was reported at $2.3 million, and although no reliable data are available for the angling catch, "it has at various times been estimated to be worth 10–15 times the commercial catch."

How much this value would be increased if the Greenland fishery did not exist is a matter of conjecture. "Two important points remain, however, after all the extrapolation of figures . . . has ended. A salmon captured by a fisherman of any country in the sea is a dead salmon and cannot subsequently become available to the fisherman in the home country that produced it. There is an exploitation saturation point for every renewable resource including Atlantic salmon. After that limiting point has been passed the way is prepared for the extinction of the species." [3]

The Counterattack

Although income from salmon fishing represents only about 5 percent of its total income from fisheries, Denmark until 1972 opposed any meaningful curtailment of this activity in the face of hostile world opinion. In the earlier years the Danish government did not attempt to rationalize the operation, but as opposition spread, chiefly fanned by sportsmen's groups, the Danish government launched a propaganda campaign, using specious arguments to convince the opposition that there was no proof the enormous hauls on the high seas were adversely affecting runs in the producing countries. Denmark even posed as a friend of *Salmo salar* and talked vaguely of undertaking a conservation program in Danish waters, where salmon was extinct.

The American Committee for the Atlantic Salmon Emergency (CASE), directed by Richard H. Buck and organized in 1970, became the most effective spokesman for the groups attempting to curtail or eliminate the slaughter of *Salmo salar*. It sponsored a public relations program using well-known personalities in show business and athletics to bring the message, "Save the Atlantic Salmon!" to millions of Americans via television and other media. People who were neither interested in the Atlantic salmon, nor had seen or eaten it, began to tell their friends, "Don't buy Danish goods — The Danes are killing off the Atlantic salmon!"

CASE, which went out of business in 1973 after doing a splendid job, succeeded in getting a bill through Congress (Public Law 92-2191) signed by President Nixon in December 1971 that authorizes him to prohibit the importation of fish or fish products from any country, upon determination of the Secretary of Commerce, which does not conduct an acceptable "international fishery conservation program." Since Denmark had been exporting some $10.5 million worth of fish products to the United States annually, this measure quickly brought results, as noted in the previous chapter. Norway, too, is covered by the prohibition.

As a result of this agreement, endorsed by ICNAF, the take of Atlantic salmon on the high seas will be as follows (in metric tons):

	1972	1973	1974	1975
Danish and Faroese vessels	800	600	550	500
Norwegian vessels	285	215	200	185
Other	10	10	5	5
Total	1095	825	755	690

By 1976 the fishery should be phased out and perhaps sooner if public pressure in the producing countries is effective. As for fishing for salmon by local Greenland fishermen around their shores, the ICNAF nations agreed to limit average catches to 1964–1971 levels of 1100 metric tons. In 1972 only 726 tons were taken on the high seas and 1306 tons inshore, for a total of 2032 tons, more than in any other country.

The phaseout should measurably help to reduce the toll on migrating Atlantic salmon. Unlike the comparable Pacific treaty that sets quotas on Japanese fishing in the mid-Pacific and is monitored by Soviet inspectors, no monitoring arrangements seem to be established in the Atlantic Ocean.

British conservationists expressing their views in such organizations as the Salmon and Trout Association, and Canadians through the Atlantic Salmon Association and Miramichi Salmon Association, have been less aggressive than the Americans and less willing to use the weapon of economic sanctions, which proved to be the key to phasing out of the high seas fishery. Ironically, much of the salmon caught in Greenland is marketed in England, so that the British are buying back their own fish while their runs are declining!

Who Owns the Salmon?

The basic question is: who owns the fish in the sea and who is entitled to catch them? Unlike such purely marine species as cod and herring, which spend their entire lives in the ocean, the salmon have a home country and bear a postmark on their bodies, so to speak. They are produced in a given nation and are but transient residents of international waters. Often their production involves heavy expenditures in hatcheries and in stream improvement and other conservation programs.

Their temporary presence in the ocean has generated bitter conflicts first in the Pacific and then the Atlantic. In the Pacific Japan operates a vast mother-ship fishery, described in Chapter XXV, which dwarfs salmon operations in the Atlantic.

It is generally assumed that a nation has exclusive rights to the fishes in its territorial waters, although it may lease fishing privileges to other countries, as before World War II Russia permitted Japan to harvest salmon on a large scale on and around the coasts of Siberia. On the high seas, however, property rights in fisheries are vague and ill defined. "A basic characteristic of all fisheries is that they are common property natural resources," say Francis T. Christy, Jr., and Anthony Scott in their book *The Common Wealth in Ocean Fisheries*. "No single user has exclusive rights to the resource nor can he prevent others from sharing in its exploitation. An increase in the number of users affects each user's enjoyment of the resource."

The difficulty is that the ocean's resources cannot be readily apportioned among rival claimants. The doctrine of freedom of the seas, first enunciated in 1608 by the Dutchman Hugo Grotius, has acquired a kind of biblical sanctity. Grotius argued that "property cannot exist on the oceans because the usual conditions for the holding of property rights do not apply. These conditions he took to be two: first, the power of occupation, which may be interpreted as the power of a navy to hold a body of water, but may more generally be interpreted as the ability to enclose and appropriate a body of water, and secondly, the inexhaustibility of the resource. . . . The seas are inappropriable and inexhaustible, therefore they are not property and may be used inoffensively by everybody." [4]

Although various nations, especially Great Britain, rejected Grotius' doctrine and claimed sovereignty over certain seas, freedom to exploit the fisheries without let or hindrance has come down as a basic tenet of international cooperation. Only in very recent times have territorial enclaves, ranging from twelve miles in most countries in North America and Europe to 200 miles for Peru, been erected. The aim is to keep out alien vessels, thus in effect making the fishes that can be caught in these areas the private property of each nation.

The Greenland fishery became the subject of discussion and negotiation in the only available international meeting place, ICNAF. In 1972 Denmark and other nations capitulated to what might be called *force majeure* and agreed to phase out salmon fishing on the high seas.

In the Pacific Japan was forced in the 1950s by Russia and the United States, the producing countries, to agree to similar treaties circumscribing freedom of the seas for her fishermen, at least in taking salmon. Japan knew that if her fleets crossed the abstention lines set by the treaties, sanctions would be imposed by the producing countries.

There is no question about the right of Greenlanders to fish for salmon in inshore waters, although they are thus helping to reduce stocks of a vanishing species.

The Summing Up

When man first entered Europe in sizable numbers at the end of the last Ice Age, the Atlantic salmon proliferated in numerous European and North American rivers. Today its range is greatly constricted. It has been driven out of some of the most renowned rivers: to mention but a few, the Seine and Rhine in France, the Guden in Denmark, the Thames in England, the Douro in the Iberian Peninsula, the Elbe and Weser in Germany, the Kemi and Ii in Finland, and the Connecticut and Penobscot in the United States. The species has in fact vanished utterly from Portugal, Switzerland, Denmark, and the Low Countries and is quite scarce in Spain, France, Poland, East Germany, and the United States. No people destroyed their Atlantic salmon more ruthlessly than the Americans.

John M. Olin, a sportsman who has fished for the prince of game fishes for decades and contributed a goodly part of his fortune to save the species, says:

"Even though the agreement has been reached with the Danes to phase out the high seas fishery, it is my considered opinion the stock of Atlantic salmon has been so severely hurt that even though the phase-out is accomplished, the west Greenlanders will still be taking an unwarranted number of fish in their nets off the west coast of Greenland. Even if the high seas fishing were stopped and the Canadian efforts are effective, the life cycle of the salmon indicates that it would be six or seven years before there is any appreciable indication of restoration of the stocks returning to the rivers." [5]

Part Three

Fate of
the
Pacific Salmon
in
North America

XIII

Discovery of the Pacific Salmon

Bering's Expedition

IN early January 1725, as Peter the Great was nearing the end of his hectic and fruitful life, he drew up instructions for an ambitious expedition to the Far East to determine where the lands of the czars ended; to find out whether it was true, as travelers reported, that the continents of Asia and America were not united; and, if possible, to discover a passage to China and India through the Arctic Sea. Peter himself drew up the instructions, signed them on January 26, and selected Vitus Bering, a Dane in the service of the Russian navy, as captain-commander to carry out the project. A month later the Czar was dead, but the first contingents of Bering's convoy had already left Saint Petersburg, heading for the Urals and the steppes and that remote no man's land, Kamchatka.

Bering explored Siberia and Kamchatka and returned after five years convinced he had sailed around the northeastern corner of Asia and demonstrated that the two continents were not connected. But he did not find the northeast passage, for the sea that separated Asia and America, which is forty miles wide at its narrowest point, was continually obscured by fog.

Arctic exploration had a bewitching influence on the Russian court, like space exploration today, and before long Bering proposed another expedition, grander in scope than the first, which would head for Kamchatka and then chart the western coast of America and establish commercial relations with the inhabitants. It would also explore the Amur River, chart the Arctic coast from the Ob to the Lena River, and possibly visit Japan.

When the second Bering expedition left Saint Petersburg in 1733 it was encumbered with commissions that went far beyond the captain-commander's proposals. Among other tasks he was instructed by the Academy of Sciences to bring back an account of the geography, resources, and natural history of Siberia and Kamchatka. At its peak the party comprised well over one thousand men and two thousand carriers, porters, and others. There was a large contingent of scientists, including an astronomer, geographer, physicist, and naturalist, and their assistants and servants. Their baggage included several hundred scientific volumes, seventy reams of writing paper, and an enormous supply of drafting materials, scientific apparatus, and artists' paraphernalia. The scientists, in fact, comprised a kind of itinerant Academy, luxuriously accoutered, who traveled at a leisurely pace across the Siberian wastes.

Most of the scientists were Germans, attracted to the court of Saint Petersburg by generous emoluments offered by a country that was just emerging into the modern world. Among them was Georg Wilhelm Steller, a young man who had served as lecturer at the Saint Petersburg Academy of Sciences. Appointed adjunct in natural history, Steller was ordered to join Bering in the last months of 1737. Traveling alone, he crossed the Ural Mountains, pushed on to Irkutsk and Yakutsk, and finally reached Okhotsk, where he took a ship for Kamchatka and landed at Bolsheretsk. Ostensibly he went as assistant to the German scientists Georg Gmelin and G. F. Muller, but "as these gentlemen found it altogether too uncomfortable to travel any further than Yakutsk, he took upon himself the exploration of Kamchatka." [1] In March 1741, after a difficult journey of 5000 miles, Steller joined Bering at Avacha Bay on the east coast of Kamchatka and accompanied him on the packet *St. Peter* across the misty Bering Sea to Alaska — the first white men to reach the peninsula.

After sighting Mount Saint Elias, the expedition landed on Kayak Island, thus laying the basis for Russia's claim to Alaska. On the return journey the *St. Peter* was wrecked off the coast of Bering Island in the Commander group. An epidemic of scurvy took the life of the weakened and disheartened captain as well as many of his crew in December 1741. Steller's remarkable ingenuity and cheerfulness helped the famished survivors through the dreadful winter. In the spring the salmon returned to the rivers and along with the meat of sea lions, sea cows, and other mammals provided the men with substantial nourishment. A new packet was built and the curtailed expedition returned to Kamchatka.

✿

Steller's Explorations and Discoveries

For the next three years Steller continued his scientific explorations under difficult conditions, collecting specimens of animals and plants, making copious notes, and drafting papers on natural history. In 1744 he was ordered by the Academy of Sciences to return to Saint Petersburg but died en route, mainly from exhaustion, aged thirty-seven.

No man before Steller, whose peregrinations covered almost half of northern Asia and who was the first scientist to visit Alaska, had had such opportunities to study the natural history of the Arctic world, and no one at that time was better equipped to take the fullest advantage of them. "He was blessed with a retentive memory, a keen power of observation, and an ability to generalize and interpret his data," says F. A. Golder. "He was strong, tireless and devoted to his work . . . His wants were few and easily satisfied. His fellow scientists had cooks, servants, supply wagons, and camping outfits, but Steller was his own cook and servant and lived off the country. One plate, one cup, one pocket knife, and his blankets constituted his personal baggage. Traveling light, he covered much ground and went to places where his more dignified and unencumbered colleagues could not follow, and in the end he achieved more than they." [2]

Among other achievements Steller was the first scientist to discover and identify the various species of Pacific salmon. He observed them in the great Siberian rivers like the Lena, in rushing streams emptying into the Sea of Okhotsk, and in the torrential rivers of the Kamchatka Peninsula. He saw the bronze fishes leaping in the Bering Sea, watched them pound into the estuaries, clog the channels of streams and cause the banks to overflow.

Let us glance at the Kamchatka River, one of the major waterways of the almond-shaped, fog-beset, windswept peninsula. Here the salmon runs begin in the middle of May. The chinook come first and within a few days are followed by the sockeye in massed formation. It is a long river, 335 miles from its source near Ust-Bolsheretsk to its outlet in the Pacific at Ust-Kamchatsk. The chum appear early in July; in August the coho are abundant. At times the fishes pour into the Kamchatka rivers in such volume that their entry is heralded by a thunderous noise, "somewhat similar to the noise of boiling water splashing in a gigantic cauldron," says I. F. Pravdin, a Soviet scientist who in 1926 observed a run of pinks over a verst long (two thirds of a mile) and 100 meters (330 feet) wide, comprising millions of individuals, densely packed, pushing upstream with such irresistible force that the astonished fishermen let them pass unimpeded.[3] In 1925, 10,750,000 pinks were taken in the Bolsheretsk region alone. Steller must have witnessed similar runs.

In his lengthy wanderings spaced over a period of nine years, Steller discovered thirty new species of fishes in addition to the fur seal, sea lion, sea cow, and sea otter. He seems to have accumulated enough information on the various species of Siberian salmon to have pieced together their curious life histories. He knew that the fingerlings depart on schedule from their natal rivers and after one or more years at sea return home wearing strange liveries, flaming red, copper, green, or blueblack; lice-ridden; ready to spawn when they reached suitable gravels of rivers or lakes, sometimes in the very localities where they were born. He watched their courtship and mating and saw the hordes of spawned-out fish floating down the rivers . . .

Steller did not live to publish his findings. His papers and specimens were deposited with the Academy of Sciences in Saint Petersburg, which turned them over to other members of the Bering expedition such as Stepan P. Krashnennikov. Like Steller an adjunct in natural science, he was commissioned to write a report on the natural history of Kamchatka and thus received much of the credit that belonged to Steller.

In Steller's journals, published long after his death, there are only glimpses of the salmon. For example, he reports finding in an underground habitation of the Kamchadales — the natives of Kamchatka — "lukoshes, or utensils made of bark filled with smoked fish of a species of Kamchatka salmon . . . called 'nerka' [sockeye] in the Tungus language but in Kamchatka known as 'krasnaya ryba' [red fish]. It was so cleanly and well prepared that I have never seen it as good." [4] He relays Krashnennikov's report of a journey over the terrible mountains into the central valley through which flowed the Kamchatka River, describes the cold waters, fierce erupting volcanoes, and terrifying earthquakes, and tells of the fantastic numbers of fish clogging the streams. He tells how the natives fished for the ubiquitous salmon with nets spread out from boats and also by means of weirs.

Additional details about Kamchatka's natural history are given by Sven Waxell, the Swede who took command of the *St. Peter* after Bering's death, in his book *The American Expedition* (which unaccountably was not published for two hundred years). He describes fishing for salmon under the ice in the Urak and Okhota Rivers: the inhabitants were accustomed to search for pools and deep holes, "and should they find one, they can be fairly confident of getting fish. All that is necessary is to hack an opening in the ice and the fish come along of themselves, in such a way that they can be seized in the hand and thrown upon the ice. Each fish usually weighs six to seven pounds." [5] But in winter, Waxell adds, the salmon are very dull and weak and taste poorly.

Many of the water courses "freeze in winter, others do not; and in the spawning season into one and all fish throng in such numbers that a short, sudden spate will leave the banks littered with large salmon-like fish, there to gasp, die and pollute the air. Fish! Even the lumbering Kamchatka bear wades out into the water with his hind legs and with his front paws scoops them up on the bank." [6] The Kamchadales lived almost exclusively on fish, and "smelled accordingly," noted Waxell.

Natural History of Kamchatka

The first extensive account of the Pacific salmon was given to the world by Krashnennikov in his *Natural History of Kamchatka and the Kurilski Islands,* published in Russia in 1755. This report, based partly on Steller's materials as well as his own findings, was remarkably accurate. All the salmon species, he says, "are brought forth and die in the same river, come to their full growth in the sea, and spawn only once during their whole lives: for which purpose they swim up the rivers, and having found a proper place in smooth water, they make a hole with the fins that are under their gills, and there deposit their roe . . . Those fish which are bred in a great river continue near to its mouth, feed upon things brought down by the stream, and when the time of spawning approaches they will enter no river but that which produced them."

Each species "always ascends the rivers at the same time . . . In the month of August sometimes two, three and nay even four species come up at once; but each keeps separate from the others," observing the same order, returning like the seasons with clocklike regularity. "The largest and best of these fish, and which comes first out of the sea are called 'chavitcha' [chinook]; it resembles the common salmon, though it is a great deal broader; is about three and a half feet long . . . [has] white flesh, weighs 70 to 80 pounds, and has a rich delicate taste." [7] *Chavitcha* was not as plentiful as the other species of salmon except in the Kamchatka River, and even there the natives ate it only on feast days or holidays. The Kamchadales, noted Krashnennikov, were particularly fond of *chavitcha*, especially the belly, back, and head. In fact, they esteemed it so highly that they refused to permit the Russians, for whom they were fishing, to take the first fish. "However impatient the master may be to taste the new fish . . . the fishermen will have the first, looking upon it as a great sin if they do not eat it themselves, and with all due ceremonies." Fishing for *chavitcha* began the middle of May and lasted six weeks.

After the *chavitcha* the *nerka* (sockeye) came into the rivers. "It is about 21 inches long; its flesh is extremely red, its back bluish with black spots, belly white and tail forked, weighing about 15 pounds." *Nerka* inhabited every river that ran either into the Penchinska or Eastern Sea, coming up in great shoals about the middle of June. It is more plentiful, noted Krashnennikov, "in such rivers as run out of lakes than others; nor does it live long in the former, but hastens directly into the latter; in the depths of which it lies till the beginning of August, at which time it comes near the shore, and tries to get into these other lakes." Here the Kamchadales caught them with nets, by means of weirs or other methods.[8]

Waxell added that while the natives liked to eat *nerka,* it seemed to disagree with the Russians. A kind of local bread called *eukol* was made from it, and the fat was boiled to make a butter and sometimes a glue.

Somewhat resembling nerka was the salmon called *keta* or *kaeko,* which had paler flesh and was found in all the streams emptying into the Eastern Sea. A peculiarity of this species was that its snout was bent and its teeth, after it had been some time in the river, resembled a dog's. We call it chum or dog salmon.

Most plentiful of all species was *gorbuscha* or crooked-back fish (known to us as pink or humpy), "about 18 inches long and flattish; its flesh is white; its head small; its snout sharp, and considerably crooked . . . though this fish is not bad, yet the inhabitants have such plenty of what they esteem better, that they use this only for their dogs." [9]

Knowledge of the newly discovered fishes spread slowly in the scientific world. An English translation of Krashnennikov's book appeared in 1764. Thomas Pennant incorporated an account of the salmon in his famous *Arctic Zoology* published in 1784, based on materials provided by Dr. Peter Simon Pallas, a member of the second Bering expedition. Since Pennant's nomenclature did not follow Linnaeus' binomial system, Pennant gave only the vernacular (Russian) names to the species. When the German Johann Julius Walbaum in 1792 brought up to date Peter Artedi's standard *Encyclopedia of Fishes,* originally published in 1738, he Latinized Steller's names and thus we have *Oncorhynchus tshawytscha, O. nerka, O. keta, O. gorbuscha,* and *O. kisutch.* The genus *Oncorhynchus,* meaning snout-nosed, was attached to the group by the American ichthyologist George Suckley in 1861 to distinguish it from *Salmo salar.*

SCIENTIFIC AND LOCAL NAMES OF PACIFIC SALMON *(Oncorhynchus* species)					
Region	*O. tshawytscha*	*O. kisutch*	*O. nerka*	*O. gorbuscha*	*O. keta*
Alaska	King	Coho	Red Sockeye	Pink Humpback	Chum Dog
British Columbia	Chinook Spring Tyee °	Coho Blueback	Red Sockeye	Pink	Chum
Washington State	King Chinook	Coho Silver	Sockeye Blueback	Pink Humpback	Chum
Columbia River and Oregon coastal streams	Chinook Spring	Coho Silver Silversides	Sockeye Blueback	Humpback Humpy Pink	Chum
Sacramento River	King Quinnat	Coho Silver			
Asia	Chinook	Coho	Red Sockeye	Pink	Chum

° Over 25 pounds.

Captain Cook's Discoveries

After Vitus Bering it was Captain James Cook, on his third voyage around the world in the little square-riggers *Resolution* and *Discovery,* who explored the vast North Pacific world. Cook had read James Grieve's translation of Krashnennikov's *Natural History of Kamchatka* as well as the account by Jacob Van Stahlin, Secretary of the Russian Academy of Sciences, of *The New Archipelago, Lately Discovered by the Russians in the Seas of Kamchatka and Anadir.* The maps he had of the Asiatic coast were tolerably accurate, but for North America there were many blanks, some of which he admirably filled in.

Cook reached the Oregon coast, "a great and beautiful land with distant snowcapped mountains," in March 1778 after being at sea almost two years. Anchoring offshore for a few days, he headed northward against prevailing westerly winds in fog, gales, and squalls. He failed to discover either the salmon-rich Columbia or Fraser River and anchored in Nootka Sound on the western side of Vancouver Island.

Here he traded for fish and fur and noted in his diary the mode of life, habitations, and manners of these red-skinned people who offered him human skulls and dismembered parts of human bodies as presents. The Nootka, he observed, migrated to the outer coast of Vancouver Island between March and August, where they fished for halibut and cod, hunted whales, and gathered shellfish. In September they moved to the mouths of the rivers to trap the hordes of incoming salmon. Cook was fascinated by their fishing gear, "nets, hooks and lines, harpoons, gigs . . . The hooks are made of bone and wood together and rather unartificially but the harpoon is ingenious enough." He noted that their canoes, hollowed out of trees, were forty feet long, seven feet broad, and three feet deep, and were navigated with exquisite skill; their long wooden houses, occupied only during the rainy season in fall and winter, were built with considerable art. Like all the North Coast Indians, the Nootka were primarily fish eaters, practiced no agriculture, hunted very little, and collected berries and roots to vary their diet. They venerated the salmon and created an elaborate mythology and system of rituals around it.

From Vancouver Island Cook sailed along the sheltered coastal waters of northwestern British Columbia and southeastern Alaska, threading through bays, sounds, channels, and arms of the sea. After discovering and naming Prince William Sound, he found that the mainland turned southward. Searching through fog and haze, with continual rainfall and fresh wind, he came "to a headland around which the sea swept again to the north-northeast in a broad gulf which stretched away as far as he could see." [10] Here rivers tumbled down from a chain of snow-capped mountains that stood tier upon tier on each side of the shore, golden in the midafternoon sun. This was Cook Inlet.

During his stay here the friendly Indians brought sea otter pelts and a large quantity of fish, mostly halibut and "very fine salmon," to trade for old clothes, knives, beads, and whatever baubles they could get. Now the men had all the protein food they badly needed, for their supply of cattle and sheep taken aboard in England had long vanished.

Leaving Cook Inlet, the expedition passed down the Alaska Peninsula "in almost constant misty weather with drizzling rain so that we seldom had a sight of the coast," said Cook.[11] At length they found a channel through the Aleutian Islands, amid strong and cold currents, beset by fog, with rugged barren mountains always as a backdrop — and shipwreck imminent. The next protracted landing was at Dutch Harbor in Unalaska. As elsewhere, the Englishmen received a cordial welcome; the natives were eager to trade their fresh fish for commodities they fancied, particularly tobacco, the "supply of which was not half sufficient to answer their demands."

From Unalaska the vessels nosed their way eastward along the north shore of the Alaska Peninsula until they came into an arm of Bristol Bay, into which a river flowed that was about a mile broad issuing out of a chain of mountains to the southeast. "It must abound with salmon," Cook noted, "as we saw many leaping in the sea and some were found in the maw of cod we caught."

From Bristol Bay the expedition followed the indented coast of Norton Sound and made a landfall at Cape Denbigh. Here was the outflow of two great salmon rivers, the Yukon, longest in Alaska, and the Kuskokwim. Cook did not explore them, for "always somewhere behind was an impressive wall of vast rolling mountains."

Although he could not have imagined it, the Eskimos who greeted Cook had probably occupied the Denbigh beaches as long ago as 3500 B.C., when the ground was covered with sod and the climate was milder;'they pursued the seals and walruses with toggle harpoons and snagged fish in the sea with hook and line. The natives came aboard singing and carrying animal skins, berries, and dried fish for sale "at a very easy rate," commented Captain Charles Clerke, commander of the *Resolution*, in his journal. "I overheard one of the people damning his eyes very heartily because they gave him only a salmon for a small yellow bead." [12]

From Norton Sound Cook moved out into the Bering Sea and, passing Bering Strait, reached the Chuckchee Sea and then the Arctic Ocean late in summer, charting the coasts until impenetrable ice blocked his journey. This was the climax of his third (and last) voyage, a heroic passage of leaking ships in ice-jammed waters "noisy with the sea's surge; great floes ground together in the swell, lifting and smashing with a sort of malevolence which was frightening to watch and hear, as if the ice was grinding its massive teeth to get at the ships." [13]

Cook then turned back toward Unalaska, which he reached in December 1778, but he did not tarry here. With winter coming on he set sail for the warmer climate of Hawaii, where earlier, on the way north, he had been welcomed as a kind of god. He planned to go to Petropavlovsk, Bering's base in Kamchatka, in the spring, but was murdered in February 1779 by frenzied Hawaiians at Kealakekua Bay. Captain Clerke succeeded to the command and took the *Resolution* and *Discovery* to Avacha Bay late in April.

The diaries of Clerke and other members of the expedition give us a full account of their stay in Kamchatka. Food for the long voyage home was, of course, one of their primary concerns. "The ground beginning to be clear of snow," noted Lieutenant James Burney, brother of novelist Fanny Burney, "sent a party on shore to cut wood, found nettle tops and onions in every clear spot. We likewise tapped the birch trees, which gave a good quantity of a sweet juice; with this the ships companies' allowance of brandy was mixed every day. The ice having in some places broke off from the shore, caught with our seine plenty of salmon, cod and flat fish." [14] A bullock was butchered to provide the first taste of beef since they left the Cape of Good Hope in December 1776. The Kamchadales taught the sailors how to seine for herring, of which they took aboard almost ten tons. Some of the men constructed a float of logs and seined a large quantity of salmon that was stocked for the homeward trek.

The *Resolution* and *Discovery* returned to England in October 1780. Cook's voluminous diaries, which appeared in 1784–1785, and previous journalistic accounts of his third voyage, gave the world its first comprehensive picture of the scenery, strange inhabitants, extraordinary climate, and natural resources of North America from Oregon to the Arctic Ocean, an enormous region of land and sea masses, islands, archipelagoes, bays, and sounds; waterways running northward into the ice-locked Arctic and others westward to the open Pacific; and rivers issuing from glacier-covered mountains and flowing through broad valleys and tundra to the turbulent sea. Here dwelt savage and semisavage tribes and also innumerable species of birds, fishes, and marine and land animals.

Unlike the fabled El Dorado whose gold enticed the Spanish conquistadors to America, it was mainly the fur-bearing animals that brought explorers and trappers to the North Pacific in the wake of Captain Cook, for their peltries could be bartered from the Indians and Eskimos for baubles and sold in China or Russia for enormous sums. Not for over a century after Cook's death did men realize that there was also enormous wealth in the sea and rivers and that the salmon was the most valuable of all the North Pacific's wildlife resources, from the Sacramento River to the Yukon.

XIV ∽⃝

The Destruction of California and Its Salmon

PACIFIC SALMON were first exploited in large numbers in California, a state that can boast it pioneered the art of salmon canning, an industry that was destined to spread throughout the world wherever these fishes were found in colossal quantities and which at the same time often destroyed the resource.

In California the delectable chinook and steelhead trout thronged the rivers of the Central Valley, and in addition those of the north coast, flowing through the cathedral-like redwood groves, in the wild, cold mountain streams of the north, and in the semiarid areas of the central part of the state. In the 1880s, for example, a traveler on the narrow-gauge North Pacific Coast Railroad, which ran for eighty miles from San Francisco to Duncan's Mills, could see salmon speared by the hundreds in the Russian River. If he went north from there by stage, he traversed scenery of incredible beauty around the headwaters of Sacramento River and could stop, said the *Pacific Tourist,* a railroad guide published in 1884, to indulge in "the best fishing and hunting in the world." He would be surrounded by lofty peaks and "the countless volcanic buttes of Shasta Valley, the bare rocks, the dark forests, the bright moss, the bracing atmosphere, the frequent storms playing around the white cap of Shasta," and often be in sight of streams rich with jumping anadromous fishes.

Except for the northwestern section, California is not now renowned as salmon country. Stocks declined in the richly endowed Sacramento River long ago, the canneries are closed, and commercial fishing for salmon is permitted only in the ocean.

The fate of California's salmon mirrors the state's use and misuse of many of its natural resources. In the last half century a serene land of infinitely varied landscapes, endowed with an abundance of fertile soils, immense forests and grasslands, mountains, and deserts — a demiparadise — was invaded by hordes of people from the ends of America and abroad seeking riches or a better life in a clement climate. In the process rivers and watersheds were turned topsy-turvy; farmlands and orchards were bulldozed and covered with towns, cities, and Cyclopean highways; forests were reduced to lumber or pulp; grasslands were trampled into dust; and the foothills and lowlands were planted with endless tracts of dismal houses. Like other forms of aquatic life, most of the salmon became victims of this unparalleled destruction.

The Prodigal Fishes

Only two species, chinook and coho, here called king and silver, are native to California, along with steelhead trout. They were originally found in numerous rivers from the Oregon border to Monterey Bay. The largest salmon stocks were in the Sacramento and San Joaquin watersheds, which are tributary to San Francisco Bay. These rivers are 450 miles long in a north to south direction, fertilizing the great Central Valley, which lies between the coast ranges on the west and the snow-topped Sierra Nevada on the east. This great trough, filled in during countless ages with alluvium from eroding mountains, forms the present valley floor. The soils are among the most fertile in the world providing they are adequately watered. The Sacramento and San Joaquin, with their numerous tributaries, are the lifeblood of California, as the Nile is to Egypt.

Before an explosive human population descended upon the state, chinook migrated long distances to spawn in the main stem of the Sacramento and in tributaries like the McCloud, Pit, Feather, American, and Yuba Rivers. They thronged the San Joaquin and its tributaries — the Cosumnes, Mokelumne, Calaveras, Stanislaus, Tuolumne, and Merced. The two rivers empty into a vast swampy area, now largely drained and cultivated, forming a confusion of channels from which they turn westward, passing Suisun Bay, Carquinez Strait, and San Pablo Bay before dashing through the Golden Gate to the Pacific.

Originally the Sacramento was one of the world's richest chinook rivers, exceeded only by the Columbia. Most of the fishes migrate to the ocean in the first months of their lives when they are but a few inches long. In rivers that are cool all summer, a small percentage of juveniles remain till they are over a year old (and are sometimes

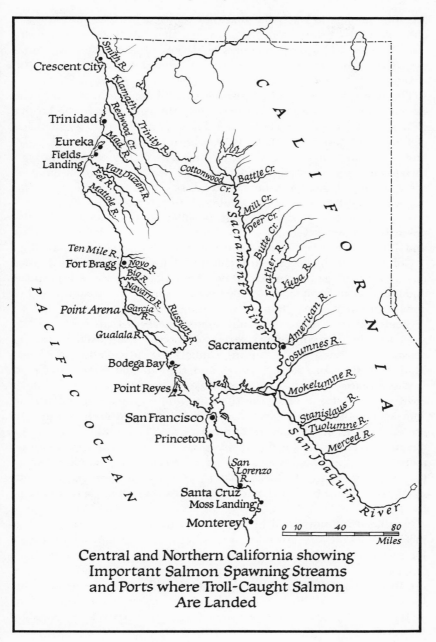

Central and Northern California showing Important Salmon Spawning Streams and Ports where Troll-Caught Salmon Are Landed

taken by anglers in the belief that they are trout). In California adult chinook mostly return from the sea when they are three or four years old. There are also large numbers of "jacks," usually males, weighing only three pounds or less, who return after only two years in the ocean.

Through the sagacity of nature the chinook generally return to the warmer parts of California late enough in the year to have the benefit of a suitable supply of cool water for spawning — that is, between October and January. There is also a run of spring chinook, who find a cool area in the upper watershed where they remain through the summer and spawn in the fall. Rivers that are too warm have no spring runs, but there may be a good fall run. For successful spawning the water must be below 58°, while 50° to 52° is ideal.

There is a winter run of kings peculiar to the Sacramento who reach the upper waters about Christmas and mate primarily in May and June when other streams are too warm for successful spawning.

Coho is a minor species in California, found chiefly in the coastal rivers north of San Francisco Bay. After hatching these fish spend about a year in freshwater, so they cannot survive in streams that become extremely low or too warm in summer.

Steelhead trout were originally more numerous than coho and almost as abundant in some rivers as chinook. They used to throng coastal rivers such as the Smith, Klamath, Trinity, Redwood Creek, Mad, Eel, Russian, Napa, Carmel, and Big Sur and were also found in the Sacramento and some of its major tributaries. Along the north coast most steelhead enter the rivers in winter and spring, but in the Sacramento the principal run comes in the fall and early winter. In the Eel and Klamath they enter almost the year round.

Since juvenile steelhead remain in the river one or two years or more, they cannot live in waters that are too warm or too low during the summer. Most steelhead mature at three or four years of age when they return to their home streams to spawn; some stay longer in the sea.

Steelhead are now (and have been) far more numerous than cohos in California. There are many rivers with good steelhead runs that have no cohos. Water developments have ruined or eliminated steelhead runs in many California streams. Runs in the north-coast rivers are in fairly good shape, although considerable damage has been inflicted upon them. Because of a planting program in the Sacramento system, its steelhead stocks are now larger than they have been for decades.

*

The Indians

The Indians who inhabited the Sacramento–San Joaquin watersheds and the north coast were isolated from other aboriginal cultures by mountain barriers and deserts and hence developed relatively homogeneous folkways centering around food gathering and fishing. The dog was their only domesticated animal until the Spanish invaders introduced the horse.

Many of these people subsisted mainly on fish and on the acorns that were plentiful in the oak stands; they supplemented this diet with other nuts, berries, birds, and even insects and rodents. The acorns were hulled, parched, and pulverized, and the tannic acid was leached out. Acorn meal was boiled and sometimes roasted and could be stored for winter consumption.

We know a great deal about the California aborigines (who had no written language) from the extensive anthropological investigations made by the University of California under the leadership of Professor A. L. Kroeber, thanks to bequests by Mrs. Phoebe Apperson Hearst and other wealthy people. Much of the material was collected from surviving tribesmen.

The aboriginal population from the Oregon to Mexican border has been estimated by anthropologists as high as 250,000. Of the numerous bands the riverine Indians engage our special attention, as they lived along the north-coast streams and parts of the Sacramento River (where salmon fishing was not as important as in the north). These "salmon people" are identified by the languages they spoke: Hupa, Tolowa, Yurok, Karok, Shasta, Pomo, Yokuts, etc. They were rather sedentary folk, dwelling in villages along the rivers, lagoons, or the nearby valley bottoms. The climate of northern California is mild, food was abundant and easily obtained, and hence they had much leisure for producing a high order of artistic work as well as a rich body of imaginative oral literature. Little clothing was needed — the whites who first came upon them, as in Trinidad Bay near the Klamath River, were astonished to find the men going naked in summer, while in winter they wore only wraps of tanned dog or doe leather on their shoulders. Women were also scantily clad.[1]

Much of the food supply of the northern tribes consisted of fish, of which salmon, caught in the streams, was the most important. When Juan Bautista de Anza discovered Carquinez Strait in 1776, he saw Indians netting salmon from rafts. In the sloughs and interior streams they relied on crude weirs or spears or simply clubbed the fish and took them with bare hands.[2]

The social structure of these people was highly developed, and their religion was rich in ceremonials and mythology. They were well adjusted to their environment and also to their restricted universe.

The Yurok

The Yurok, said Professor Kroeber, who made an extensive study of this tribe, "love a small, snug, known and unchanging world, and in imagination often contract their universe, even short of bounds of their actual knowledge. They are incurious and really antipathetic toward what may be beyond . . . They want their world stable; they dread its tilting and slipping, its shaking by earthquake, its flooding, its invasion by famine or by epidemics advancing like clouds. It is the warding off of these threats that is the formal motivation of their greatest rituals, 'the world renewals.' " [3]

One of the vital "world renewals" was associated with the annual return of the salmon, a ceremony comparable to the rites of spring in ancient Greece and other agricultural or viticultural societies out of which sprung the belief in the resurrection of Christ and the Christian celebration of Easter.

The Yurok lived along the Klamath River in villages of wooden houses, usually around lagoons or the mouths of small streams, in a forty-mile area from Trinidad Bay to Wilson Creek and on ancient river terraces for about thirty-six miles upstream. The river was their highway — they were adept canoe makers. They probably never numbered more than a few thousand persons and "never ventured into the interior of the country nor on the ocean . . . They concentrated much of their technical and spiritual faculties on the annual salmon runs (the periodical gift of food sent to them from a mysterious source 'across the ocean'), which to them meant not only sportive massacre but also supply for winter storage, fraternization of the tribe as a nation, and spiritual rebirth." [4]

First Salmon Ceremony

There were many strict taboos associated with the return of the salmon, and only specially selected persons could manage the elaborate rituals, of which the first salmon ceremony was the most important. On the Klamath the runs started in late June or early July. Stray fishes who came before the regular run might be eaten only by the aged — all others were forbidden to touch them.

"My father," said the Yurok who related the story of the first salmon ceremony to Professor Kroeber and his associate Robert Spott, "was the last man who assisted the formulist [or shaman, an old man who obtained his position because he possessed the necessary medicine imparted by supernatural powers] and ate the first salmon. He was notified about a month in advance of the event that he had been chosen for the honor. At first he refused to serve but he was persuaded to do so. From that time on he was under severe restrictions and kept himself clean. He had to eat apart from all other people, use his own special food baskets, and from a separate stack of acorns, or at least specially cooked ones. He drank no water during this month."

A week before the spearing of the first salmon, said the Indian, the shaman "had my father come across the river from the village of Rekwei to Welkwau. He was asked to bring a blanket made from a five-pointed deer, his pipe, and a basket of tobacco. He was to leave behind all his white man's clothes. Each day he was to get sweat-house wood, and he was to eat only what the formulist's niece, who had been chosen to prepare the first salmon, would cook for him."

On the sixth day before the expected coming of the fish the shaman said to his young assistant: "This is the last day you will eat freely. Beginning with tomorrow you will not eat until evening, so eat freely today."

Three days later the two men began to clear a path from the village north along the sand spit to where it touched the Klamath River, removing every pebble and bit of weed. Women were forbidden to tread this path, and men going to fish along the bank were asked to circumvent it.

The old man instructed his assistant carefully: "I will spear the salmon, but you will carry it to the house. While you are carrying it you must not step across any stick of wood. That is why we are clearing the path. And you must watch for the spot from where you can see Te'golol [a notch or low divide in Big Rattlesnake Mountain]. Up to that point you must carry the salmon on your right shoulder. There you must be sure to throw it onto your left shoulder, and you must change nowhere else."

The night before the spearing the shaman and his helper stayed in the sweathouse. The old man spent much time talking to and petting his pipe. He made a fire in the pit with angelica root and allowed it to burn until its strong smell suffused the house. And he "prayed on behalf of the whole world, asking that everywhere there be money, fish, and berries, and food, and no sickness."

In the dim light of the morning the two men went outside to cool off, and then they bathed. When they saw the sun illumine the hill to the east, they knew that the time had come to go to the river and watch for the salmon. The shaman then returned to the sweathouse to change his raiment, a deerskin blanket he wore around his shoulders, and tie his long hair with a strip of otter skin about two inches wide. The young man also put on a new blanket, while in the "living house" the girl assistant donned a new dress.

"Now follow me," said the shaman to his assistant. "The harpoon is lying ready. Carry it on your right shoulder. Take a good grip on it but not too hard . . . because you may not change your hold until we come to the end of the spit." Then he picked up his basket and walked slowly toward the river, being careful not to touch the harpoon the other man was carrying.

Along the bank men were lined up fishing. One of them came up to the shaman and said they were catching lampreys and sturgeon. "Continue to take lampreys but not sturgeon," said the old man, "and when you see the first salmon, shout. When I come with the harpoon, all of you stop fishing, and start for home without crossing our trail. Tell this to each man."

Then the old man prayed silently, facing the swift-running river. Afterward he smoked his pipe and blew the smoke in all directions, east, west, north, and south. It was not till afternoon, when their shadows were in front of them, that the two ritualists heard the cry "Salmon!" reverberating along the river. Thereupon the shaman picked up his harpoon and moved toward the water's edge, looking for the oncoming fish. When the salmon was abreast of him, its fin sticking out of the water, he said to it, "Stop running!" The fish seemed to hear him and obeyed. The old man took two steps backward and said, "Now run again!" The salmon moved on but stopped when the shaman asked it to do so.

This performance was repeated five times before the old man grasped the pole of the harpoon with both hands, swung it twice, and cried, "You will stop running. As you pass every fishing place you will leave your scales, to the head of the river, ending there. Now run on." The fish listened and then disappeared. The first salmon actually was never speared.

Along the bank the men resumed fishing for lampreys until another salmon was spotted. Again a shout went up; the harpoonist spoke to the fish, then gripped his pole, made four feints, and on the fifth try speared it. Across the river at Rekwei, to which many of the Welkwau inhabitants had retired some days before, wailing and crying was heard, as if a human death had occurred.

The shaman now put down the harpoon shaft and took the toggle head out of the fish, which was laid in the sand with its head upstream. Untying his hair, he placed the otter skin across the fish's belly. As the salmon flapped its tail, he picked up a stone and struck it on the head, then threw the stone into the river.

Now the shaman addressed the fish in moving words: "I am glad I caught you. You will bring many salmon into the river. Rich people and poor people will be happy. And you will bring it about that on the land there will be everything growing that there is to eat." At the end of each sentence, said the narrator, the salmon responded by flapping its tail.

Blowing tobacco smoke in all directions, the old man told his assistant to take the fish and carry it on his shoulder, as previously directed, and not to look back or around him. As the two trotted back to the village, "all the people called out the names of the kinds of food [they liked] from the sea and the land, and dentalia shells and woodpecker scalps [which passed for money among them] and everything else they wanted. The shouting sounded as if the sky were coming down."

The first salmon was taken into the "living house," which had been swept as clean as the river path, and put on two wooden trays that were stood up at the far end of the pit. Two women sitting near the notched ladder by the pit were crying. The girl assistant undid her hair tie and laid it across the fish, just as the shaman had laid his otter skin band, and then she cut up the fish according to the older woman's instructions. The formulist arose, took angelica from a wooden trunk, threw it on the fire in the pit, and prayed. When the angelica was burned to glowing coals the girl placed the fish's belly on it; when it was cooked she cut it into four pieces with a sharp stick and laid them on the flat basket. The two men swallowed a few pieces.

Afterward they went into the sweathouse, where they stayed all day and until the next morning but did not sleep. From time to time the shaman prayed for a bounteous harvest.

What remained of the first salmon, the guts, back, head, and tail, was not eaten but was thrown back into the river. It was believed that if the sea gulls and crows fought for these morsels the run would be poor, but if the birds sat around and ignored them the run would be good. "That year," said the narrator, "the birds did not fight for the remnants of the fish and plenty of salmon came in."

With the completion of the first salmon ceremony the path down to the river was no longer taboo and could be used by anybody. All meals had to be taken by the people indoors and they could drink only at the spring, but on the sixth day these taboos were lifted.

"It seemed to my father," said the narrator, "as if no time at all had passed before the twenty days of his service were up. In fact, he stayed twenty-eight days before he returned to Rekwei. And after that he carried sweathouse wood and kept himself clean for a month at home." [5]

The Kepel Dam

Close to the junction of the Trinity and Klamath Rivers were the Yurok settlements of Kepel and Sa. Here each year as the salmon returned from the ocean the Indians constructed a communal weir or dam that consisted of a tight fence of poles and stakes driven into the bed of the stream, strengthened and shored up against the force of the current and so carefully built that fish could not escape. There were openings at regular intervals along the weir leading into small enclosures or pens that trapped the fish crowding against the lower part of the barrier as they tried to move upstream. Although erection of the weir was technically simple, it became the grand project of the year, attended by minutely detailed ceremonials and taboos.

Ten days were required to build the Kepel weir, and after ten days of fishing it was demolished. The schedule never varied, although there was no real justification for it. "The Yurok had such primitive ideas of structural engineering," says the ethnologist T. T. Waterman, "and the current of the Klamath River increases so greatly in volume in the rainy season, that they could never succeed in harnessing the stream permanently. The salmon run, however, extends over a number of weeks, and the dam would certainly have stood for two or three times the length of the period for which it was utilized." [6] Some of the upriver people who also depended on the salmon for their food supply would probably have come downstream and destroyed the weir if it had remained in place.

Construction was directed by a shaman. Although in later times the Yurok had plenty of the white man's axes they continued to use Neolithic tools in building the weir: sharp stones, mauls, and elkhorn wedges. When the time came for the salmon to reappear the shaman came down to Kepel, established himself in a temporary shelter, and sent messengers to announce to the river folk that work on the structure would soon begin. But first he had to go through time-honored rituals. Standing on the roof of the sweathouse, he began the medicine, while his underlings hid in their houses where the sacred fires were burning. After a day or more, the shaman and his helper went to the river to select a site for the weir and cut young fir trees for stakes. Every step of the procedure was accompanied by rituals suggesting imitative magic.

One morning at daybreak, at a given signal, several hundred people in a number of villages began cutting stakes in the woods. The hills resounded with their chopping. All the stake cutters were also under ceremonial restrictions. "They slept in the sweathouse the night before," said the Indian who narrated the event. "They had to go without breakfast and did the work while fasting."

The dam chief and his assistant now left their camping place and went to the top of a hill to cut three special tan-oak stakes, one for each flank of the barrier and another for the center. They were not allowed to eat while working. For the next four days the two men remained in the sweathouse while a constant stream of materials was brought to the site by canoe. On the fifth day the workmen assembled, as many as seventy at times, while others were cutting stakes, carrying messages, and doing other chores.

Before the first stake was implanted in the river the shaman stood and talked to it, "shaking it at intervals as one shakes a man when he wishes to rouse him. He told the stake he wanted good luck and plenty of salmon. Then he split it. Then with a shout everybody began to split stakes on the site and the work on the river began." Throughout the construction period the medicine man, wearing a deerskin blanket around his shoulder, sat on an eminence above the river keeping an eye on the work and sending out orders for supplies. Only material for each day's work could be brought to the site — no more. In effect the shaman was not so much a superintendent of construction as a priest exerting influence with the supernatural powers to ensure its success.

After sundown each day the shaman and his assistant were permitted to eat their lone meal of the day, but it had to be consumed away from the site, on the sandbars or in the village. Anyone who came within sight of the dam had to shade his eyes so as not to look at the unfinished structure. "Looking at it would spoil it," said the narrator. Women were forbidden to come near.

It was extremely important that ten days — no less, no more — be occupied in building the weir, for ten, like five, was to the Yurok a mystical number. There had to be ten gates or openings, each enclosed with a framework of stakes hinged at the top. When salmon entered the trap the fishermen lowered the door and pulled them out with a hand net. All the men who participated in the operation, including the stake cutters, shared in the harvest.

"Every night when work was finished people went home in their boats," said the narrator. "On this trip they danced in the canoes. One man stood in the bow holding an oar upright. The other men, except the rower, stood in a row, holding on lock-step fashion, and danced. The songs they sang were called 'songs of the dam.' They did not dance as hard as they did on shore, but just so that the boat bounced in the water."

When the weir was finished the shaman himself was paddled down the river and his canoe was deliberately capsized. When he swam to shore he received a drubbing with poles carried by the workers. The meaning of this brutal ritual, says Waterman, is not clear.

Indians from distant places came to celebrate the construction of the Kepel dam, Tolowa from Crescent City, Karok from Orleans and beyond, Hupa from the Trinity River, and Yurok from Trinidad Bay. That day there was a deerskin dance after supper, part of the "world renewal" ceremony in which both men and women participated, the men wearing woodpecker-scalp headbands and white deerskin blankets and carrying long flint and obsidian blades. They danced with a slow step to plaintive, wordless tunes sung by a few men in the middle of the line. Next day there was an even more elaborate deerskin dance, repeated several times by different groups.

"After the exertions in erecting the dam," said the narrator, "everybody laid over for several days," mixing jollity with the task of getting the annual supply of salmon. Ten days after the dam was erected it was demolished.

The aboriginal world we described was destroyed by the white man. The Indians were driven off their lands and placed on reservations. There is an 87,500-acre Hoopa Valley Reservation twenty miles upriver on the Klamath; the bulk of it borders the Trinity River but there is frontage on both banks of the Klamath. The present population is estimated at about 5000 Yurok and Hupa. No longer do they concentrate their lives on fishing for salmon, sturgeon, lampreys, and candlefish (eulachon), though they are permitted to engage in subsistence fishing. They have fought to maintain their sense of identity, but this is difficult. They operate fishing resorts, sawmills, and other businesses, and on the whole they are no better off than other reservation tribes up and down the Pacific coast. Unemployment is common.

Tribal traditions like the first salmon ceremony have decayed. If they still exist they are but a pale reflection of the colorful rituals of aboriginal times. Commercial fishing on the Klamath was banned in 1934, but the Indians are allowed to work tribal fishing holes. However, the river is now a sportsman's paradise; from midsummer through autumn the lower Klamath is crowded with anglers, and the villages of Requa, Camp Klamath, and Klamath Glen are jammed with campers, trailers, boat owners, etc. Part of the area is in the Redwood National Park.

An annual salmon festival is held at the new Klamath City townsite late in June. According to the travel writer Mike Hayden, it "is a blend of country fair, Indian culture and Chamber of Commerce hokum." A princess is crowned dressed in ancient finery. Songs and dances are featured, including the Yurok world renewal dance, the brush dance, and the deer skin dance. Only the men dance but at times the women sing. A salmon barbecue is featured and even the rough Indian stick games are played. Sometimes there are not enough local Indians to participate so Indians from Oregon are brought in.

Commercial Fishing

The rich stocks of salmon began to be fished commercially about the time of the gold rush of 1849, when gill nets and seines were already operating on the Sacramento and San Joaquin Rivers and in Suisun and San Pablo Bays. John Sutter, on whose property gold was first discovered in 1848, was engaged in commercial salmon fishing, among many other activities.

In 1864 a new era was opened in the history of the salmon industry in North America when G. W. and William Hume and Andrew Hapgood, all of whom came from Maine, decided to attempt canning the salmon for which they had been fishing in the Sacramento River. They purchased a large scow and added an extension to their cabin, which they used as a can-making shop. The scow was moored in the Sacramento River opposite K Street in the city of Sacramento.

With their crude machinery they packed 4000 cases of forty-eight one-pound cans the first year, but only half the pack was merchantable; the rest had spoiled and even the good cans were hard to sell, for Americans were at first skeptical about eating canned fish. In fact, the early products of Hapgood, Hume and Company were sold mainly in Australia and South America. However, the industry prospered and by 1883 there were twenty-one canneries in California,

THE FIRST SALMON CANNERY IN NORTH AMERICA

This sketch of the first salmon cannery in North America, operated
on the Sacramento River, California, in 1864, was made for
Pacific Fisherman in 1903, the artist working under the personal
direction of G. W. Hume who, with his brother William and
A. S. Hapgood, established the industry in this primitive plant.

most of them in the San Francisco Bay area (where not a trace is
left), utilizing the large chinook that populated the rivers.[7]

With a prodigal disregard for the future and in the absence of any
effective regulation, millions of salmon were taken in the next two decades from the California rivers; the bulk of the catches went into
cans. In the 1870s, when the Columbia River and Alaska fisheries
were just beginning to be tapped, San Francisco was the marketing
center of the industry, a place where fishing boats were outfitted, cannery workers recruited, mainly from the Chinese colony, and ships
came to take the products to Valparaiso, the Sandwich Isles, Liverpool, New York, and elsewhere.

Sacramento salmon was known around the world until the resource
was depleted, and then the Columbia, Fraser, and Alaskan salmon
took over the markets. The California production reached a peak of
200,000 cases in 1882, when about 12 million pounds of fish were
caught. In 1883 the California Fish Commission estimated there were
1200 sailboats and rowboats engaged in salmon fishing in the rivers.
During the next decade the catch fell to around 6 million pounds annually and thereafter declined until a nadir of 2 million pounds was
recorded in 1891, when only three canneries were left. In 1919 the
last cannery closed its doors.

Landings picked up, however, with the introduction of powerboats and the advent of trolling off the coast, stimulated by the demand for mild-cured fish (a light salting process). The first trollers were small boats rigged with leg-of-mutton sails; toward the end of the century many shifted to powerboats. By 1914 the troll fishery had spread north to Point Reyes, and later as far as Eureka and Crescent City. Landings by trollers, chiefly at San Francisco and Eureka, steadily eclipsed catches in the rivers where the gill netters operated. Trollers took mature and immature fishes, mostly chinook and coho, many of which came from the Columbia and Oregon's coastal streams.

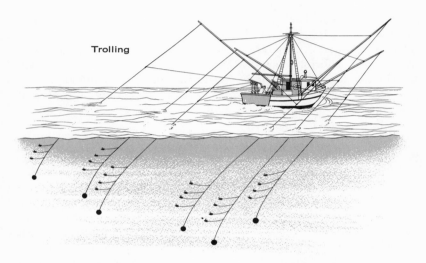

Trolling

The salmon canning industry, suffering from dwindling supplies, was abolished by act of the California Legislature in 1919. The annual catch in the Sacramento dropped to less than a million pounds in 1920, with a value to fishermen of some $60,000. Two forces that became a familiar pattern in the history of Pacific salmon wherever they are found were responsible for the decline in abundance: over-fishing and/or destruction of the environment.

Environmental Destruction

Addressing the American Fishery Society in 1892, Livingston Stone, who had established the Pacific Coast's first salmon hatchery, on the McCloud River in northern California, said:

Not only is every contrivance employed that human ingenuity can devise to destroy the salmon of our west coast rivers, but more surely destructive, more fatal than all is the slow but inexorable march of these destroying agencies of human progress, before which the salmon must surely disappear as did the buffalo of the plains and the Indian of California. The helpless salmon's life is gripped between these two forces — the murderous greed of the fishermen and the white man's advancing civilization — and what hope is there for the salmon in the end?

This refrain has been heard again and again ever since, not only in North America but in Asia as well.

Environmental destruction began long before the tumultuous development of California started. Dr. Joel Hedgpeth, who made a study of the early days of salmon fishing in California, concluded that "the intensive fishery between 1864 and 1882 had less effect on the salmon runs than the hydraulic mining which damaged hundreds of miles of rivers during these same years."

Mining

Hydraulic mining for gold was originated by two men, Joe Wood and John Payne, near Marysville in 1852. From this simple beginning the pace of hydraulic mining, with improved machinery, intensified — and its disastrous effects spread over the Sacramento and other salmon rivers. The muck left behind by the miners filled the Feather and Yuba and American Rivers, building up channel beds that made navigation impossible and suffocating large numbers of migrating fish. Huge mounds of silt were created that flowed over valley lands when the rains came, periodically inundating some of the cities through which the rivers flowed. It was a wonder that any salmon could get through some of these horrendous obstacles until in 1883 the courts outlawed hydraulic mining in the Sacramento–San Joaquin Valley.

Water Developments

There were other forces inimical to the fishery. As irrigation agriculture spread in the Central Valley, especially in the San Joaquin River system, survival of fishes became increasingly difficult. Dams, both high and low, were built without fish ladders; some of those that had ladders were so constructed that they were useless from the start, while others on diversion dams (used for irrigation) were effective at first, but the gravelly river bottoms were scoured away through the years and the fish could no longer use areas below the dams to dig their redds. Many young fish died in unscreened diversion ditches.

For example, on the Merced River there were about twelve miles of stream bed with gravels suitable for salmon spawning, but there were also obstructions. The fifteen-foot irrigation diversion dam near Snelling, built in 1918, had a good working fishway in high water, and there were some screens over the ditches to prevent fingerlings from getting trapped in them. At Merced Falls a twenty-foot dam was built in 1913 to form a mill pond and generate power for a sawmill. It had screens over the powerhouse intake, but the fishway was out of order for a number of years. About twenty miles above the falls there was Exchequer dam, 120 feet high and impassable to fish. Other rivers were beset with similar hazards to migratory salmon.

The result of such difficulties became obvious with the passage of time — the runs diminished. In 1928 residents along the Merced River reported that salmon were becoming so scarce they hardly saw any. Yet not many years before they were so numerous that it looked as if one could walk across the stream on their backs. A great deal of the water in the Merced was used for irrigation in the spring, summer, and early fall, the dry season in that part of California; hence the fish found it difficult to ascend until after the rains came. As a result, the spring and summer runs were virtually killed off and only fall chinook came up to spawn.

This situation became common in the San Joaquin watershed. Usually plenty of snow melted in the spring, but the high temperatures in the rivers below the dams killed off the spring runs. The small flows remaining after diversion for agricultural use reached 80° F. or more in summer and were lethal to fish attempting to reach their spawning grounds.

Some of the major dams like Folsom, 340 feet high, on the American River were equipped with faulty fish ladders. Uncounted numbers of juveniles met their end going through the turbines at Folsom and other power plants. Fortunately the great overflow basins that used to flood the Sacramento Valley for miles during the rainy season and trap and kill the fish had by 1929 been reclaimed, and bypasses were constructed so that very little harm was done to the fish runs. However, pollution from the drainage of rice fields in this area killed many adult fish and poachers speared hordes of them.

The Central Valley Project

In 1929 the California Fish and Game Department estimated that only 510 linear miles of the original 6000 miles of spawning grounds were left in the Sacramento–San Joaquin watershed. In the 1930s California entered a new era with the launching of the Central Valley Project by the Bureau of Reclamation. "Before the project was built," says the bureau's brochure, "the valley's fickle rivers had been the hope and despair of farmers and city folks alike. Too often during winter and spring the river roared through the land and spilled mountain rain and melting snow in floods over the flat valley. Too often during the hot summers the same rivers dwindled to a trickle or less."

Continuing in lyrical prose, the brochure says: "Men piling sandbags on Sacramento River levees and men digging wells deeper and deeper into the San Joaquin Valley dreamed of a day when winter floods could be held back and the water saved for the use on the land during the growing season. As more millions of people flocked into the valley, the need for making that dream come true became more apparent. A controlled source of water was essential to support such continuing and expanding growth."

The brochure says nothing about the side effects of the great Central Valley Project, designed to convey water from the north-central part of the state, where it is abundant, to the southern areas, where it is scarce. The project stimulated the growth of population and polluting industries and the spread of cities in cancer-like fashion, making much of California a nightmarish land of superhighways, polluted air and fouled waters. For a long time its planners gave scant attention to the anadromous fishes and other wildlife of which Californians once were proud.

"When Shasta dam, the first great unit of the CVP was started in 1938," says Joel Hedgpeth, "it was generally believed, even among biologists, that the chinook salmon were almost extinct in the rivers of central California, and that little would be lost by the construction of a few more dams. No one seemed to know or remember about the salmon that had to be burned at Bullard's Bar on the Yuba River from 1921 to 1924 when a dam was being built there, and the value of the market and sport fishery was minimized." [8] There was no way known to get adult fish over such a high structure as Shasta dam or juveniles downstream through its lengthy reservoir. Almost at the last minute, as it were, the Bureau of Reclamation, which had built the project, ordered a survey to be made of spawning grounds that would

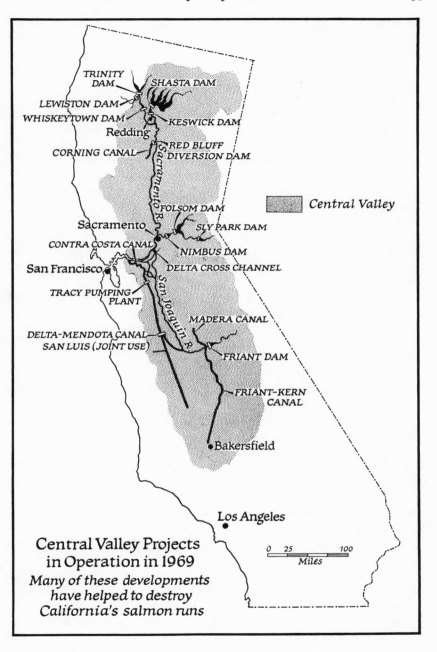

TRINITY DAM
SHASTA DAM
LEWISTON DAM
WHISKEYTOWN DAM
KESWICK DAM
Redding
CORNING CANAL
RED BLUFF DIVERSION DAM
Sacramento R.
FOLSOM DAM
Central Valley
Sacramento
SLY PARK DAM
CONTRA COSTA CANAL
NIMBUS DAM
San Francisco
DELTA CROSS CHANNEL
TRACY PUMPING PLANT
San Joaquin R.
MADERA CANAL
DELTA-MENDOTA CANAL
SAN LUIS (JOINT USE)
FRIANT DAM
FRIANT-KERN CANAL
Bakersfield

Los Angeles

Central Valley Projects in Operation in 1969

Many of these developments have helped to destroy California's salmon runs

0   25   100
Miles

be flooded out by the reservoir. The first season's work by the biologists revealed an unexpectedly large run of salmon passing the site, and later counts indicated the run was increasing — some 27,000 chinook were finally counted. The question was: how could these fish be saved?

Every remaining river in northern California was surveyed in the hope of finding a home for the displaced chinook; however, there was "nothing left but a few streams hardly large enough to accommodate their own depleted runs." [9] Incidentally, while combing nearly a thousand miles of salmon water in the Sacramento River basin, the biologists found not one effective fish screen on diversions used for power or irrigation; many of the ladders were inoperable at times of low flows. A few dams had no fishways. Numerous laws on the books dating from 1870, when the California Fish and Game Commission was established, called for protection of the runs, but actually the streams could be legally dried up by water users, thus making ladder laws unenforceable. Salmon and steelhead trout disappeared from many rivers.

Since there was no hope of transporting the fish above Shasta dam, there being no place to put them, they were collected over a period of a few years below the barricade, transferred to a newly built hatchery, and there propagated artificially. The offspring were planted in suitable downstream rivers. After Shasta dam went into operation there was actually an upsurge in the runs, because the steady flow of cool water, free from silt, improved the quality of the Sacramento River downstream from the dam. The fall run of chinook in the Sacramento has been sustained and is now larger than before the dam was built, but the spring run decreased, while the winter run has grown from a few hundred to about 60,000 fish.

Overall, however, the CVP has been quite deleterious to the salmon runs. By the 1950s all the essential elements of the initial phase were built, and by 1969 the project was virtually completed as shown on the map (page 253). Shasta dam has blocked off the upper segment of the Sacramento River. It catches and stores flood waters, which are released into the reservoir of Keswick dam. Between Redding and Sacramento some of the water from Keswick is diverted to irrigate half a million acres of land. Near the city of Sacramento the flows are augmented by water from the American River, which is detained behind Folsom dam.

Below Sacramento the Delta Cross Channel carries water from the Sacramento into natural channels leading to the Contra Costa and

Tracy pumping plants; from the former the water is delivered into the Contra Costa Canal and various pumping plants in the San Francisco Bay area for municipal, agricultural, and other uses. At Tracy there are lifts that raise the water a few hundred feet to the Delta-Mendota Canal, whence it is diverted far to the south to Friant dam on the San Joaquin River to be used chiefly for irrigating farmlands, some of which produce crops that are in surplus supply and are heavily subsidized by the federal government. The Trinity River, an excellent chinook and steelhead stream, has also been dammed and its water goes through a tunnel to augment the Sacramento River flow.

The "Chinese maze" and diverted flows created by the CVP has confused and killed untold numbers of salmon.[10]

Irrigators or power companies hold a first lien on the water, and fish, so to speak, must stand in line. Often there is not enough water left for them to complete their spawning migrations. To compensate at least in part for these considerable losses hatcheries were built.

For example, Nimbus hatchery was built in 1955 to produce chinook salmon and steelhead trout to compensate for the loss of 85 percent of the ancestral spawning grounds of these fishes in the American River. Irongate hatchery on the Klamath River, built by a private power company to compensate for the loss of spawning grounds upstream, has the capacity to incubate 16.5 million chinook eggs, 1.5 million coho eggs, and 2 million steelhead eggs. There are other salmon and steelhead hatcheries in the state, including the Feather River plant, now under construction, which will replace spawning grounds cut off by the Oroville dam.

The Central Valley Project (and others) was designed to meet the needs of a surging population, its industrial dependencies, towns and cities, and most of all the highly remunerative croplands thirsty for water — California produces more agricultural products, in terms of value, than any other state. To critics of the state's water plans like Ralph Nader and his group of researchers, who recently published a two-volume study, *Power and Land in California*, the CVP is primarily a scheme to enrich big landowners and industrialists.

The fact remains that California is crisscrossed with dams, canals, diversion ditches, pumping stations, and other engineering facilities that have done immense damage not only to natural beauty but to aquatic and other forms of wildlife. "Today," wrote the ecologist Raymond Dasmann in 1964, "dams stand on most of the major rivers draining into the Central Valley, and are proposed or are under construction on all the others. Two major operations under way include the Feather River project, being carried forth by the state, and the San Luis project of the federal government. The state project will pen up the largest remaining free river in the Sierra Nevada, and transfer Feather River water southward. The San Luis project will make possible the transfer of water from the Feather and other northern rivers southward along the west side of the San Joaquin valley to irrigate lands across the way and ultimately, to supply the needs of southern California communities as far south as San Diego." [11]

Nor is this all. In 1969 the Bureau of Reclamation announced that "other developments within the near future are necessary if the Central Valley project is to meet the needs of a growing economy." It casts its eyes on the still wild north-coast rivers for which it proposed "a comprehensive, multiple-purpose plan which would provide for both immediate and long-term needs in northwestern California and would also make available millions of acre-feet of surplus water for use in the Central Valley." The bureau promised the smog-ridden, city-jammed people of southern California that if its plans were carried out there would be added "hundreds of miles of shoreline and thousands of acres of sparkling-clear water to attract tourists from all over the United States." [12] The Army Corps of Engineers' plan to dam the free-flowing north-coast rivers has been temporarily stopped by the California legislature.

The Balance Sheet

With the help of hatcheries, there was a brief upsurge in salmon populations in California from 1944 to 1947, after which both ocean and river catches dropped steadily until 1957, when the Sacramento River was closed to commercial fishing. In 1958 only 3,657,000 pounds were landed, the lowest in the twentieth century. After that catches recovered to 6,000,000 to 9,000,000 pounds thanks to an improvement in chinook runs in California and coho in Oregon and Washington: these fish are taken by trollers in the ocean and landed in California ports. There was also a great increase in sport fishing for steelhead and salmon, centering around coastal ports where party boats enjoy a lucrative business, and in the north-coast rivers.

In July 1970 the California legislature passed Resolution Number 64, which said:

> Whereas, the salmon and steelhead trout resources are a priceless and irreplaceable resource of this state, and

Whereas, the survival of these resources is now threatened; now, therefore, be it

Resolved by the Assembly of the state of California, the Senate thereof concurring, As follows:

The Director of the Department of Fish and Game shall appoint an Advisory Committee on Salmon and Steelhead Trout which shall ascertain, study and analyze all facts relating to the preservation, protection, restoration and enhancement of salmon and steelhead trout resources of this state, including, but not limited to, the operation, effect, administration, enforcement and needed revision of any and all laws in any way bearing upon or relating to the subject of this resolution, and to report thereon to the director, who shall submit such report to the Legislature, including in the report its recommendations for appropriate legislation.

On March 15, 1971, the committee, consisting of sportsmen, commercial fishermen, biologists, charter boat operators, and others, issued its findings under the title *An Environmental Tragedy.*

Said the committee: "Man, unfortunately, in his headlong rush to develop California and produce goods and services, has paid little heed to environmental quality and the uniqueness and irreplaceability of the salmon and steelhead resources. These resources are now seriously threatened and once lost, may be gone forever. Only resolute action will prevent such a disaster . . . Analysis of Department of Fish and Game records on the status of salmon and steelhead populations provides startling evidence of declining trends headed toward ultimate disaster." The lowest point in salmon catches, said the committee, was reached in 1939, when 2.7 million pounds were landed compared with 13 million pounds in the years 1919, 1945, and 1946. There were eighteen consecutive years, from 1926 through 1943, when the commercial catch never reached 7 million pounds (Appendix Table 5).

The committee found that in streams of the north coast steelhead trout runs dropped from an average of 290,000 in the decade 1940–1949 to 100,000 in 1960–1969, an 80 percent loss; silver salmon runs fell from 147,000 to 57,000 or 65 percent; and king salmon runs from 255,000 to 91,000, 64 percent. North-coast rivers harbored at least four fifths of California's remaining steelhead trout. The heaviest losses occurred in the Sacramento and San Joaquin watersheds.

The committee laid the blame for these catastrophes on extensive damage to watersheds and spawning streams from logging, mining, road construction, gravel extraction, grazing, pollution, and most of all damming of the rivers. In the Central Valley the remaining area of spawning streams was only about 300 miles, a small fraction of the original.

"Damage to spawning streams through degradation of the watershed continues at an alarming rate . . . This results from both government and private industry each carrying out its own special purpose objective without sufficient consideration of its activities on the resources." Two examples out of many were cited by the committee: on the Garcia River in Mendocino County thirty-seven out of 105 miles of salmon territory were severely damaged, fifteen miles moderately and thirty-seven lightly damaged, leaving but sixteen miles in good condition for fish spawning and rearing. On eighty-four-mile Redwood Creek in Humboldt County sixty-four miles were severely damaged, four miles moderately and six miles lightly damaged, so that only ten miles were in a condition favorable for production of anadromous fishes.

The committee warned that California would lose its valuable salmon and steelhead before the end of the century unless "prompt aggressive action is taken to halt the destruction." All efforts to reverse the declining trend by the Department of Fish and Game have failed because it has been prevented from obtaining sufficient legal authority to protect the rivers from encroachment by other governmental agencies such as the state water agencies, the Bureau of Reclamation, and Corps of Engineers, or by private developers. (The Corps and the Bureau through manipulation of the rivers of the Pacific Northwest and California have killed off more salmon and steelhead than all other federal agencies combined.) Nor has the California Department of Fish and Game been given sufficient funds or authority to correct past destruction or assure future protection of the anadromous fisheries. With population growth continuing relentlessly, demand for water in central and southern California becomes overwhelming.

Hence, concluded the committee, "an all-out effort is now needed to correct past damage and restore the potential of these spawning streams, to prevent damage from future developments, and to expand salmon and steelhead programs for priority protection and enhancement work." [13]

The report was welcomed by many people, particularly anglers who had formed the Committee of Two Million dedicated to preserving the remaining wild rivers of the north — the Eel, Klamath, Trinity, and Smith — where salmon and steelhead still flourish in large numbers.

The Committee of Two Million has published a "Box Score of Proposed Devastation," tabulating the best available information on what would happen to the northern rivers if proposed projects are constructed, the data obtained from the State Department of Water Resources, Department of Fish and Game, the Corps of Engineers, Bureau of Reclamation, and other sources. Four proposed dams on the Klamath River would block runs of about 930,000 fish of which two-thirds are steelhead and the remainder mostly kings; four projects on the Trinity would destroy spawning grounds for almost 700,000 fish, of which 60 percent are steelhead and the remainder almost entirely kings; and seven dams on the Eel would affect runs of 350,000 salmonids of which kings comprise 60 percent and steelhead 40 percent.[14] Citizen revolts in the north-coast counties against further development of their valleys combined with the growing willingness of many California state legislators to create wilderness sanctuaries resulted in the Behr bill, signed by Governor Reagan on December 21, 1972. This establishes a "California Wild and Scenic Rivers System" on the Eel, Klamath, Trinity, and Smith Rivers and on the American River north fork. Dam building will be prohibited on the Eel for twelve years and on the other rivers indefinitely. This measure will give the north-coast salmon and steelhead rivers a strong measure of safety. The state Resources Agency will have to submit a rivers management plan to the legislature so as to begin the long step upward for most of what is left of California's decimated salmon runs.

The Merced River

In the generally dark picture of environmental destruction it is refreshing to report an instance in which the pendulum is starting to swing in the other direction. This is the case of the Merced River, whose runs of king salmon had dwindled to less than two-dozen fish in the early 1960s. In the earlier years salmon ran great distances up the San Joaquin, as we have noted, and also entered three main tributaries, the Stanislaus, Tuolomne, and Merced. Friant dam, built by the Reclamation Bureau, eliminated the fisheries from the upper part of the watershed, and since 1948 the Merced has been the southernmost spawning stream in the Central Valley.

Unfavorable water conditions in the lower San Joaquin, coupled with irrigation diversions in all three tributaries, ruined the fish runs.

Reversal of the trend has been due to a rehabilitation program undertaken by the Reclamation Bureau, the California Department of Water Resources, and a local irrigation district. In years of low flow the department places a partial barrier at the head of Old River, forcing more of the water to flow down the San Joaquin past Stockton. If necessary, the bureau agrees to release up to 60,000 acre-feet from its Delta-Mendota Canal in any year to keep dissolved oxygen from dropping below the critical level for upstream migration of adult salmon.

The Merced Irrigation District has obtained a grant from the state of California for salmon enhancement work on the Merced below Crocker-Huffman dam, the uppermost limit of salmon migration. It calls for four enhancement features: increased stream flows, installation of six fish screens at irrigation diversions, a pond for rearing salmon to yearling size, and the release of a minimum flow of 180 to 220 cubic feet per second from McClure reservoir behind the enlarged Exchequer dam from October through March each year.

Virtually all the physical enhancement features of the MID were completed in early 1971 — yearlings had been released into the river since 1967. As a result of all this work, the runs of king salmon have been slowly increasing: in the fall of 1970 a total of 4700 adults spawned in the Merced. The Stanislaus and Tuolomne have shown similar trends, and improvements are expected to continue.[15]

The Citizens Advisory Committee issued a supplementary report entitled *A Conservation Opportunity* on May 15, 1972. Taking stock of the resources, it noted that 40,000 salmon spawned in the San Joaquin River tributaries in the fall of 1971 as a result of timely action by the Departments of Fish and Game and Water Resources and the U.S. Bureau of Reclamation, compared to 1963 when the river tributaries supported only 320 spawners, and it appeared that the runs were threatened with extinction. However, while the restoration program is paying dividends, the runs are still well below the historic level of over 200,000 fish.

"The yearling king salmon rearing program at Feather River hatchery is making an outstanding contribution to the ocean sport and commercial fisheries," the committee reported. "Ten percent of the 100,000 marked yearlings released in the 1968 brood year have been taken in the ocean as three- and four-year-old fish.

"There was a substantial increase in the numbers of king salmon arriving at Trinity River Hatchery during 1971. Unfortunately, the steelhead count was little better than the dismal runs of recent years."

The committee outlined a basic plan for the future.

At the Federal level

1. Protect and improve water quality, the condition of spawning gravel, and flows at the proper times in salmon and steelhead streams throughout the state.
2. Add to this a well-planned program of stocking young salmon and steelhead from hatcheries and spawning channels.
3. Maintain and enforce scientifically sound and equitable regulations on catch — the final product.

Many specific examples of how these goals could be attained were listed:

1. Amend the Federal Water Project Recreation Act to provide that all project and operational costs for anadromous fish enhancement programs in conjunction with federal water projects shall be borne by the federal government.
2. Amend the Anadromous Fisheries Act to increase the federal grant from 50 to 75 percent of project costs and to increase the annual expenditure authorization from $5 million to $20 million.
3. Amend the Federal Power Act to subject federal agencies to its licensing provisions in order to assure adequate, continuing project responsibility to fisheries protection. (This would be an enormous help in fish restoration programs.)
4. Obtain congressional approval for a Central Valley fishery rehabilitation program granting the Secretary of Interior specific authority to undertake projects for the restoration of salmon and steelhead resources heretofore damaged through the development of Central Valley water projects under the control of the Secretary.

At the State level

1. Amend the Forest Practice Act to require the preparation of detailed logging plans to be approved by the Department of Fish and Game.
2. Amend the Water Code to provide that stream flows required for the preservation of fisheries are not subject to further appropriation.

3. Amend the Fish and Game Code to extend the Department's authority over critical streambed spawning areas to key North Coast and Central Valley streams where such authority is now lacking.
4. Direct the Federal Power Commission and Department of Water Resources to seek conditions in all future power licenses, water permits and similar grants of public authority to require project agencies to be responsible for fish and wildlife throughout the life of the project.
5. Legislation should be passed to clearly establish a general fund responsibility for the protection, restoration and enhancement of the salmon resources related to commercial fisheries. Such a contribution should be viewed as an investment to the present and future economy of the state.

The committee issued what in effect is a war cry and a challenge: "The history of fish and wildlife resources in the country leads us to one universal principle. Attempts to maintain the status quo result in gradual attrition and eventual loss of the resource. Federal and state mitigation policies have been a failure and are no longer acceptable to meet society's needs . . . Those responsible for management of the resource, for its harvest and for the environmental changes that threaten it must cooperate in a positive effort not only to protect, but to *maximize* the salmon and steelhead fishery!"

XV ∼◯

The Dammed Columbia
and Unlucky Salmon: Part 1

The Pristine River

STARTING AS A RIVULET on the silty formation called Canal Flats, which leads to Windermere Lake, a gemlike body of water nestling in the great trench between the Selkirks and the Rockies in British Columbia, the Columbia emerges as a full-blown river heading northwest. After a northwest course of about 150 miles it abruptly reverses direction, leaving the trench, and turns southward, entering the United States near the northeast corner of Washington state. Between the Canadian border and its confluence with the Snake, the Columbia forms another big bend and then turns southward, after which it heads west for the Pacific Ocean. At its mouth around Astoria the river is two and a half miles wide and although it has now been mostly converted into a series of lakes, it still flows to the sea with considerable vehemence.

In its 1250-mile course the mighty Columbia cleaves the Cascade and coastal ranges and acquires the flow of at least 150 tributaries, many of which are extensive and complex river systems. The river passes through Rocky Mountain trenches and valleys, long, semiarid stretches, and then through areas of heavy rainfall west of the Cascades and finally through the coastal mountains. On the average it pours more water into the ocean than any river system in North America except the Saint Lawrence, Mississippi, and Mackenzie. The 259,000 square miles of watershed embraces large parts of British Columbia, Washington, Oregon, and Idaho and small segments of Montana, Wyoming, Utah, and Nevada.

The Snake, largest of the tributaries, is itself over 1000 miles long. Issuing from the Rocky Mountains in Yellowstone Park, Wyoming, it sweeps westward across southern Idaho, then heads north to form the border between Idaho and Oregon and between Idaho and Washington, and finally turns west again and joins the Columbia around Pasco, Washington.

Between its headwaters and the sea the Columbia drops 2400 feet, creating a tremendous power potential, which has now been almost entirely harnessed. Its lower reaches pour through deeply cut stream beds, where the flow is swollen by many streams and creeks that tumble down steep and narrow gorges. The Snake drains a somewhat drier region, including the Snake River plain, rugged and inaccessible mountains, and deep, lengthy canyons.

In its pristine state the Columbia's flow fluctuated widely, being heaviest in spring and early summer when the snow melts in the mountains and lightest in late summer and autumn when the rugged slopes are mostly bare. Before it was tamed by a network of dams, the river periodically burst its banks, obliterated its dikes over long stretches, and wrought ruin and disaster. In May 1948, when the last major flood occurred, precipitated by unusually warm weather that caused rapid snow melt, the Columbia went on a wild rampage that wrecked homes, farms, bridges, roads, factories; wiped out completely the community of Vanport City, then the second largest city in Oregon; and inundated large sections of adjacent Portland. Many lives were lost, and property damage was estimated at over $200 million.

It is hard to picture the Columbia River before the watershed was settled by white men, before cutting began in the lush evergreen forests, the sod was broken for agriculture, irrigation was introduced, cattle and sheep were stocked on the plains, and towns and cities arose. The landscape unfolded in an undulating sea of trees. The air was sweet and clean, and the waterways, teeming with fish, ran pure and clear except after heavy rains. Men traveled along the game and Indian trails in the silent forests on foot or horseback or paddled their canoes on the streams. On the west slopes of the Cascades the forests comprise mainly Douglas fir towering up to 250 to 300 feet, clothing the mountains to the 5000- and 6000-foot elevations. On the east side of the Cascades red-barked ponderosa pine predominate, standing in parklike formations. Alpine lakes and limpid streams dot the mountain wilderness.

When the river was undammed myriad wildfowl came in the spring to the lower and mid-Columbia and returned in the autumn to rest on the ponds, lakes, marshes, and sloughs: honking geese and quacking ducks, swans and pelicans, herons and cranes, gulls and smaller birds like terns and plover. Golden and bald eagles, ospreys and hawks roosted in the trees. Coyotes and other predators were numerous.

Big game was plentiful. There were elk, deer, and bear, and in the eastern part of the basin antelope and mountain lion. Quail, ptarmigan, and grouse were plentiful. The rivers teemed with salmon, sturgeon, eulachon (smelt), and many other varieties of fish.

Salmon Runs

Salmon and the Columbia River are synonymous. Originally there were more chinook, coho (here called silvers), and steelhead trout in this watershed than in any other river system in the world. There were also large populations of sockeye (here called blueback) and smaller numbers of chum and pinks. Hundreds of streams harbored these fishes, as did creeks, brooks, even rivulets, from close to the ocean to the far interior. For example, there were runs in the uppermost reaches of the Owyhee, a tributary of the Snake that flows in Oregon, Idaho and Nevada. Mr. C. G. Fairchild, an old-time resident of this area, says that "until dams were built early in the twentieth century in the lower reaches of the south fork, all the streams flowing into the Owyhee were spawning grounds for salmon. From Tuscarora, from Mountain City, and from the farthest reaches, the people gathered along the streams to spear salmon for winter menus. Although there was always trout to catch, in spring salmon spearing was the favorite sport." [1]

Mature salmon are found in the Columbia the year round, and they appear at well-defined seasons: there are spring, summer, and fall chinook runs; summer and winter steelhead runs; coho come mostly in late summer, sockeye in spring through summer. Normally the fish pass rapidly to their spawning grounds, some of which are close to the sea and others far upriver. Chinook and sockeye ascended to the headwaters in British Columbia, a thousand miles or more from the ocean, until Grand Coulee dam, built without fish ladders, locked them out.

Columbia River salmon usually make extensive journeys in the Pacific. Many of the coho go south, while others head north and spend their first winter in the Gulf of Alaska, come east in early summer of their second year, then go north, then south in a zigzag direction for several months before heading homeward. Coho spend two or three years in the sea and are caught by trollers from southeastern Alaska to northern California.

THE LIFE HISTORIES OF SALMON AND STEELHEAD TROUT IN THE COLUMBIA RIVER					
Species	*Time spent in freshwater*	*Age at maturity*	*Time of entry into river*	*Main spawning areas*	*Time of spawning*
Chinook					
spring	1 year	3–5 years	Feb.–May	Mountain streams in Idaho, eastern Oregon and Washington and the Willamette River in Oregon	Aug.–Sept.
summer	3–12 months	3–5 years	June–July	Salmon River and streams of eastern Washington	Sept.
fall	3 months	2–5 years	Aug.–Sept.	Main Columbia and lower Columbia tributaries	Sept.–Dec.
Coho	1 year	2–3 years	Aug.–Dec.	Lower Columbia River tributaries	Oct.–Dec.
Sockeye	1 year	3–5 years	June	Okanogan, Wenatchee rivers in Washington	Oct.
Chum	0	3–4 years	Nov.–Dec.	Below Bonneville	Nov.–Dec.
Pink	0	2 years	Sept.		Oct.
Steelhead					
winter	1–3 yrs.	3–6 yrs.	Dec.–March	Below Bonneville	Dec.–March
summer	1–3 yrs.		June–Sept.	Above Bonneville	Dec.–March

Chinook travel more extensively, as a rule. After leaving the Columbia they go north as far as the Queen Charlotte Islands and beyond. Some adventurers have been tracked all the way to Adak in the Aleutian chain. They may stay in saltwater as much as four winters and even five. They too are trolled offshore from southeastern Alaska to northern California.

The Indian Fishery

The lower Columbia area, from about The Dalles to the sea, was inhabited by a group of people, divided into various bands, called by the anthropologists Chinook. Salmon for protein and eulachon for edible oil were the major fishes taken by them. Eulachon came up from the sea in mountainous numbers each spring and were easily caught, while salmon required well-organized fishing. We know a great deal about the Indian fishery from the diaries and reports of early explorers such as Lewis and Clark (1803–1806); David Thompson, geographer of the Northwest Company, who explored the Columbia from its source to the mouth in 1807–1811; David Douglas, the Scottish botanist for whom Douglas fir is named, who collected plants for the London Horticultural Society in the 1820s; and many others.

On August 3, 1805, when the expedition was in the vicinity of the Lemhi River in Idaho, a tributary of the Salmon River, and not far from the summits of the Rocky Mountains, Meriwether Lewis recorded in his diary: "An Indian gave me a piece of fresh salmon roasted, which I ate with relish. This was the first salmon I had seen and convinced me we were in the waters of the Pacific Ocean." Lewis knew that by following the salmon's track for hundreds of miles, the expedition would eventually reach the sea.

Some weeks later, on October 24, when the party had reached Celilo Falls, Captain Clark wrote in his diary: "This village lay in the prosperous area of the jumping salmon where life was good and where the red men had time to .contemplate on Life and God." [2] Radiocarbon dating of artifacts found in the vicinity by Professor L. S. Cressman indicates that Indians were living here probably as long ago as 11,000 B.C. [3]

Lewis and Clark were fascinated by the fishery and collected much valuable information about it. On a rough sketch map of the Columbia, from below the entrance of the Snake River to a considerable distance above the Wenatchee River, Clark delineated about a hundred fishing stations or groups of lodges where the natives were engaged in catching, drying, or pulverizing salmon. In one day's journey of twenty-one miles the party passed twenty-nine lodges, each housing five or six families whose inhabitants were thus occupied. Large quantities of split and drying fish hung on scaffolds outside and sometimes inside the wooden huts.

"The multitude of this fish," noted Clark, "is almost inconceivable. The water is so clear that they can readily be seen at the depth of fifteen or twenty feet, but at this season they float in such quantities down the stream, and are drifted ashore, that the Indians have only to collect, split and dry them on the scaffolds." [4]

In some areas the main village, situated at a river mouth or shoreline of a bay where the tidal flats were exposed, was occupied only in winter when fishing ceased. In the spring or summer the band moved to its fishing grounds.

At various places along the Columbia Lewis and Clark observed the red men engaged in making pemmican: "The manner of doing this is by first opening the fish and exposing it to the sun on their scaffolds. When it is sufficiently dried it is pounded between two stones until it is pulverized, and is then placed in a basket about two feet long and one in diameter, neatly made of grass and rushes, and lined with the skin of a salmon stretched and dried for the purpose. Here they are pressed down as hard as possible and the top is covered with skins of fish, which are secured by cords through the holes of the basket . . . The whole is then wrapped up in mats, and made fast by cords, over which mats are thrown again." [5] Each basket weighed 90 to 100 pounds and twelve made a stack. At one village Clark counted 107 stacks totaling at least 10,000 pounds. Much of the pack was bartered with members of distant tribes who came from as far as British Columbia and beyond the Rocky Mountains.

The aborigines employed a variety of gear to take salmon. In smaller tributaries like the Walla Walla River, they built weirs across the channel that stopped ascending fish. Lewis and Clark drew sketches of these contraptions that consisted of trees supported by willow stakes to which cylindrical baskets, eighteen to twenty feet long, were attached. On shallower streams, or where the fish exposed themselves by jumping or climbing over rocks, they were usually speared or harpooned. When a harpoon is lodged in a fish the detachable point or blade has a shock-absorber effect that lets it thrash about without coming free. It can then be taken in the net.

Salmon were also caught with dip nets and long nets of the seine and gill-net type made from the fiber of wild hemp, wild flax, or grass. Nets were drifted where the river bottom was fairly smooth and the bank sloped gently. One end of the seine was kept on shore and the other taken out in a canoe and circled around the area where the fish were believed to pass. When the salmon were in the net both ends were pulled, the lead (actually stone) line being carefully kept on the bottom and slightly ahead of the "cork" line. Some of these Indian nets were eight feet deep and 300 feet long.[6]

The natives also trolled for salmon from canoes, using fiber lines and bone .hooks to which pieces of smelt or herring were attached; stones were used as sinkers. (Numerous bone hooks and sinkers have been found in sites of aboriginal settlements along the Columbia such as Sauvie Island, adjacent to Portland.) Basket traps were probably employed in tidal bays. They were set before high tide and checked at the ebb, and fish that strayed into them were then collected.

Ownership of fishing sites was strictly controlled among the Indians. Around Celilo Falls the south or Oregon side belonged to the Wasco band and the opposite or Washington side to the Wishrams. Sometimes Indians from distant places were invited to share fishing stations.

Through marriage, inheritance, payment for wives, and occasional purchases, ownerships became scattered and an individual might have a share in a productive eddy or lagoon far from his native village. There were, of course, communal fishing places, at weirs and elsewhere, and reciprocal rights, by which individuals traded fishing privileges.

On the basis of available evidence Craig and Hacker in their historic study of the Columbia River fisheries estimated that before the white man invaded the watershed the Indian population was about 50,000, and each person consumed on the average about one pound of salmon daily throughout the year. On this basis they placed the annual salmon catch at 18 million pounds — more than is taken today by commercial and sport fishermen — testimony to the plentitude of fishes and the red men's skill. (See Appendix Table 6.)

In addition to Celilo Falls, there were important Indian fisheries at the falls of the Willamette River (now Oregon City), at the junction of the Snake and Columbia, at the confluence of the Columbia and Methow Rivers, at Kettle Falls on the upper Columbia (drowned out by Grand Coulee dam), and at Salmon Falls on the Snake. In British Columbia salmon nurtured the tribes dwelling on or near the Columbia; some of their traditional fishing places were drowned out by the reservoir behind Grand Coulee dam and others by subsequent hydroelectric projects.

The Celilo Fishery

To visualize the aboriginal fishery in its most dramatic form we must try to recreate the scene at turbulent Celilo Falls when the salmon were running. Here the mighty river flowed over the edge of a massive geologic formation and dropped into a long, narrow, and steep chasm. The flow was broken into narrow channels by protruding rocks, small islands, and rugged waterfalls, providing ideal if treacherous fishing grounds.

Upstream migrants could only traverse this eight-mile area in slow stages. Strong currents and turbulent flows forced them to seek eddies and sheltered pools along the banks, where they rested between assaults on the rapids. When they came up to the barriers, the natives awaited them, fishing from dangerous scaffolds at the edge of the rocks with dip nets or spears. It was a thrilling performance. A man would stand motionless for a long time, peering into the boiling waters, then suddenly lunge with his implement and bring up a hefty chinook or smaller coho (and sometimes a gigantic sturgeon). He had to be alert and agile to accomplish this feat. Sometimes a man would slip from the platform when spray clouded his vision, or cascading waters hurled him to the cauldron below, and he drowned.

Fishing stands on the rocks and islands were a family inheritance. One man caught all his family could clean and prepare in a day and then another took his place. Ten or twelve persons might fish from one stand in the course of twenty-four hours. Fishing started at dawn, when the sun rose over the horizon and the salmon began to move, and continued through the day and sometimes, when the moon was full, into the night. In later times, when the Indians were confined to reservations, families would drive over from distant places. Many stayed for weeks in the rickety houses of Celilo village.

Around Celilo Falls salmon could be caught nine months of the year, but the heaviest runs came in spring and early autumn. Groups from the interior who had no fishing grounds, or whose fishing grounds were poor, came here to trade for dried salmon. It is interesting to note that because Shoshoni-speaking people from Idaho were in contact with the Chinook of the lower Columbia, Lewis and Clark engaged Sacajawea, "the Shoshoni woman," as official interpreter for their expedition.

At Celilo Falls there developed in prehistoric times a great trade from which the "mercantile Chinook" (as Philip Drucker calls them) profited handsomely. In addition to fish they bartered slaves brought by the Klamath and Modoc tribes from northern California, furs from the cold country in the interior, dentalia shells, baskets, and woven rabbit skin robes from the Fraser River in British Columbia. All these polyglot folk eventually developed a kind of language called "chinook" with which they could communicate; it was later used by American and European traders.

Celilo Falls was inundated by The Dalles dam in 1956.

Chinook Lore

The imaginative Chinook had an elaborate mythology in which the salmon played an important role along with the wolf, bear, fox, eagle, raven, and especially the coyote. In their minds these animals were semihuman and lived exactly like themselves. Sometimes they assumed human shapes and mingled with the mundane folk on earth as the Homeric gods did.

Coyote was the greatest of the animal people, a kind of folk hero wielding supernatural power that he often used for the benefit of the human as well as lesser animals. He was cunning, vain, handsome, greedy, and cruel, as well as beneficent. He had a paramount influence in the supernatural world and therefore loomed large in Chinook folklore.

William K. Peery, in his charming book *And There Were Salmon*, tells how Coyote created the Columbia River and peopled it with salmon:

> Speelyi, the Coyote god, felt sorrow in his heart for the Indian people. They lived along the great Wauna, or river which we call the Columbia. They lived too on the bays and small streams along the coast, as well as the inland plains. Coyote was sorry for the Indian people because they spent so much time being hungry . . . The Wauna had a stream bed but no water. Coyote had asked Neahcanie (who built the world) if he could put water in the dry channel. Neahcanie told him it was perfectly all right. Coyote put the water in the river. But this did not satisfy Coyote. Still the people did not have food. They had no way of saving their food. They could kill game, but the game spoiled. Coyote thought of these things. Then he thought of salmon. There was the answer. Salmon could be dried. It would keep. The Indians in the hot interior through which flowed the Wauna could make pemmican on the hot rocks. Yes, salmon was needed by the people. So Coyote put salmon in the river. They swam to all the other rivers and out to the sea and to other bays along the coast. So everywhere there was salmon.

In a collection of legends related by Chinook tribesmen, Ella E. Clark tells how Coyote taught the Indians to catch and prepare salmon. In his journey up the Columbia Coyote stopped at the Little

White Salmon River and showed the people how to make a fish trap. "He twisted young twigs of hazel brush and hung the trap in the river."

When he came to the larger White Salmon River he fashioned a spear from a white fir tree and showed the people how to catch salmon with it. Wherever he tarried he instructed them to cook fish in a pothole — previously they had always eaten it raw — and to broil it by holding it over the fire on sticks. He put the salmon in the hole, poured a little water over it, dropped hot stones into the hole, and covered it with green grass to hold the steam. Thus the fish steamed until it was tender.

It was Coyote who told the Indians that every spring they must have a big feast to celebrate the return of the salmon: "Then you will give thanks to the salmon spirits for guiding the fish up the streams to you, and your Salmon Chief will pray to these spirits to fill your fish traps. During the five days of the feast, you must not cut the salmon with a knife and you must cook it only by roasting over a fire. If you do as I tell you, you will always have plenty of salmon to eat and to dry for winter."

Everywhere Coyote sent the fish into the tributary streams if he was treated kindly and in some places narrowed the course of the river to make fishing easier. But at the Chelan River, where the inhabitants refused to give the old man a nice young girl for a wife, Coyote angrily blocked up the canyon with huge rocks and formed Lake Chelan — and to this day there are no salmon in the lake. On the Okanogan River he created a waterfall because the girls there refused to marry him; he did likewise on the Spokane River. "I will make falls," he said, "so that the salmon cannot get past them to your people farther up the river."

Coyote planted trees, as well as huckleberries, strawberries, and serviceberries, and camas and other roots so that food would be ample for the Indians. Like Jove, he showed humans how to make fire by twirling sticks between their hands. He taught them to make dip nets from maple and willow and to catch salmon with them. He showed the people living near the big falls how to make platforms and spear fish from these places and also how to fashion basket traps for catching fish as they tried to leap over the cascades.

Coyote admonished the Indians that salmon must always be kept clean, for if they were not clean they would be affronted and would not return to the river. He urged them to be restrained in the use of the fish: "You must never cook any more than you can eat. If you cook three salmon when you are able to eat only half of one, the salmon will be ashamed and will refuse to enter your river." [7]

First Salmon Ceremonies

The Chinook, like other Pacific Coast tribes, had a rather vague idea of the cosmos and the supreme being, but they believed in the immortality of the animals, who were very important to them, and around this belief they wove taboos and rituals.

The phenomenon of the salmon played a large role in their religion. The fish thronged the streams and returned with astonishing regularity every year to the bay or cove with which they were familiar. After a brief rest they moved upstream and headed for their natal (and often distant) waters. After spawning they died, and their lean and discolored bodies lined the river banks, disintegrated, and drifted back to sea. The next year the very same fishes appeared.

"What was more logical," says Philip Drucker, "than the concept that the salmon ascended the streams to benefit mankind, died, and then returned to life?" Thus the belief arose "that the salmon were a race of supernatural beings who dwelt in a great home under the sea. There they went about in human form, feasting and dancing like people. When the time came for the 'run,' the Salmon-people dressed in garments of salmon flesh, that is, assumed the form of fish to sacrifice themselves. Once dead, the spirit of each fish returned to the house beneath the sea. If the bones returned to the water, the being resumed his [human-like] form with no discomfort and could repeat the trip next season." [8]

It was evident that the fishes' migration was purely a voluntary act: therefore it behooved human beings to be extremely careful not to offend them, for they could at will refuse to come back, and that would be a calamity. To return the salmon bones to the water after the fish was eaten was consequently essential. The Indians assumed that if some bones were not returned, the salmon being at resurrection would be minus an arm, leg, or other organ and refuse to come again to the stream where he had been so cruelly treated. In line with these fancies, every Indian group, like the Yurok, developed extensive regulations and prohibitions in handling the fish in order to maintain good relations with them. None was more important than the rituals associated with the taking of the first fish.

These new arrivals were greeted with prayers and incantations to show the tribe's gratitude, joy, and relief. Sometimes the first-caught salmon was treated as though it were a visiting chief of high renown and was accorded due honors.

Enter the Settlers and Commercial Fishermen

Although the Oregon country was first explored by white men searching for furs that could be sold in European and Chinese markets at a fabulous profit, the commercial possibilities of the fisheries were not entirely overlooked. The Hudson's Bay Company, primarily engaged in the fur business, supplemented the food supply at its trading posts with salmon purchased from the natives. In 1823 the men at Fort George (Astoria) began to pack salmon for export. However, Fort Langley on the Fraser River was regarded as a more suitable locality for this business and here a saltery was established.

American traders endeavoring to break into the Columbia fish business at first met with little success. In 1829 Captain John Dominis of Massachusetts, commanding the brig *Owyhee*, entered the river to pick up a cargo of salmon, spent two summers in the area, and packed only about fifty barrels. He purchased the fish from the Indians chiefly in exchange for tobacco and delivered the pack in Boston, on a journey around Cape Horn, where it sold for ten cents a pound.

Captain Nathaniel Wyeth of Cambridge, Massachusetts, made a fruitless overland trip to the Columbia River in 1832, returned two years later on a combined fur trading and salmon fishing venture, and established a trading post at the mouth of the Willamette on Sauvie Island, which was long inhabited by Indians. This venture too was a failure.

Other easterners were more successful. Captain John Couch of Newburyport, Massachusetts, one of the founders of Portland, reached the Columbia in 1840, packed a cargo of fish, and returned home. He returned in 1842 and established a saltery at Willamette falls (now Oregon City).

After the boundary dispute with England was settled in 1846 Americans were able to make greater headway in the salmon trade and the British faded out of the picture in the Oregon country. By 1854 large quantities of fish were being salted around Astoria at the mouth of the river and at Cascade Falls 150 miles upstream; these were shipped to the east coast, Hawaii (then known as the Sandwich Islands), and South America. By then immigrants began to flood the Oregon country: in 1859 Oregon had become a state with 60,000 settlers and Washington Territory harbored 12,000 persons.

These settlers demanded wagon roads and railroads through the mountains and removal of the Indians, who had massacred the zealous missionaries Dr. Marcus Whitman and his wife at Walla Walla in 1847 and conducted the bloody Cayuse War in 1847–1850. Major Isaac Ingalls Stevens, a tough West Pointer and governor of Washington Territory, was determined to oblige them. After inducing some of the Puget Sound Tribes to cede their lands to the United States, he called a council in 1855 of the Yakima, Umatilla, Nez Percé, Cayuse, and other tribes in the Columbia valley to meet with him in council at Walla Walla. With a mixture of suavity and force he persuaded the chiefs to accept removal to reservations in return for payment of about a million dollars. Like previous agreements negotiated by Stevens, the treaty guaranteed the Indians "the right to fish at their usual and accustomed grounds and stations as long as the river flowed," a right that was to have enormous consequences in the struggle to exploit the valuable fishes of the Pacific Northwest.

As the lands filled up with settlers, conflicts arose about the Indians' right to fish at their accustomed places. Again and again the issue was taken to the courts until finally the United States Supreme Court in 1905, in the words of Justice Joseph McKenna, ruled that "the right to resort to the fishing places in controversy was part of the larger rights possessed by the Indians, upon the exercise of which there was not a shadow of impediment, and which were not less necessary to the existence of the Indians than the atmosphere they breathed."

After they had been moved to reservations the Indians continued to fish at Celilo Falls and other traditional places as well as on their reservations.

In contrast to the white man, the Indians did not waste their natural resources; they were instinctive conservationists. Andrew P. Johnson, descendant of Tlingit chiefs, told me: "We were taught by our parents never to waste fish, especially salmon; to take no more out of the water than we needed, or could eat. If we deliberately killed fish that exceeded our wants my father would chastise us severely — and we never repeated the offense." [9]

Indians did not regard salmon or other animals as commodities for sale. They would barter fish, as the Chinook people did, with other tribes, but no pecuniary value was placed on them. Without the impetus of a commercial fishery, the natives could scarcely have overfished the salmon, which seemed to be an inexhaustible resource. When the Indian and white man's culture collided later in the nineteenth century, many Indians, in order to survive, had to fish for money and therefore adopted the white man's exploitative attitude toward the animal world. Their sense of conservation, along with their awe of the wondrous animals, withered away.

Enter the Canneries

After the Civil War commercial fishing was rapidly stepped up to accommodate a new industry destined to exploit the bounties of the rivers to the full and ruin many of them — salmon packing.

Preservation of food by canning, one of the great inventions of mankind, is attributed to François Appert, a Parisian confectioner and distiller who in 1809 won the prize of 12,000 francs offered by Napoleon for a new method of food preservation to feed his huge armies. In 1810 a patent was granted in England to Peter Durand for preserving fruits, meats, and vegetables in tin canisters (hence the word "can"). The first successful preservation of fish is attributed to Ezra Daggett, who, using Appert's methods, began canning cod and oysters in New York City in 1819. In 1825 John Moir was canning salmon on a small scale in Aberdeen, Scotland.

In 1866 the Humes and their partner Andrew Hapgood moved their operations from the Sacramento River to the Columbia. They chose a heavily wooded cliff in Wahkiakum County, Washington, known since then by the name George Hume gave it, Eagle Cliff, as site of their cannery. That year they packed 4000 cases of forty-eight one-pound cans, doing all the work by hand, and the next year 18,000 cases. The fish were caught in two small gill nets and fishermen were paid fifteen cents apiece, while the canned product fetched $16 a case. Competitors soon moved in, for a "river of gold" had been discovered.

In 1873 there were eight canneries on the Columbia; ten years later a peak of fifty-five was reached, with Astoria, then a colorful town inhabited mainly by Chinese cannery workers, as the center of the industry. There were also plants at Ilwaco and Westport on the lower Columbia, on the Willamette around Portland, at The Dalles, and as far upriver as the mouth of the Deschutes. Nearly every sizable coastal stream in Oregon also had one or more fish canneries.

The Columbia River pack increased swiftly, from 100,000 cases in 1869 to 630,000 cases in 1883, when about 43 million pounds of salmon were caught — only chinook, the largest species, was then taken. (Not for thirty years would this level be reached again, and only because all species were then being utilized.) In the late 1880s salmon canning was getting under way in Alaska, which had the largest treasure trove of anadromous fishes in North America; the Sacramento River was declining, and the Fraser and Puget Sound runs were beginning to be heavily exploited.

About 4000 persons were employed in Columbia River canneries at their height, of whom about 90 percent were Chinese working for pitiful wages under exploitative Chinese contractors.

Astoria

When Mont Hawthorne, a cannery foreman, started his career in 1883 at Astoria, the town was mostly a city on pilings. "The streets were made like wooden bridges," he said in his memoirs. Canneries lined the waterfront, and close to them were the bunkhouses for the Chinese. There were saloons aplenty, several dance halls, a honky-tonk theater, a gambling and red-light district. "Chinatown was right next to 'Swill Town.' During a Chinese holiday Chinatown was festooned with colorful lanterns and bright red streamers and looked like a miniature Hong Kong. On Chinese holidays the workers, accustomed to laboring from dawn to dusk, had a day off."

When the canneries were in operation Astoria exuded the sickly odor of fish; offal was tossed into the river and there were no sewers. When the tide changed the dead fish would drift back to the beach and the bears came out of the surrounding woods to eat them. In a banner year like 1883 the runs were enormous and tons of fish were thrown overboard — the canneries could not handle them.[10]

Like most cannery towns, most of the plants in time disappeared due to exhaustion of supplies, to mechanization of the industry, and to consolidation of companies. Today Astoria is a drab town — only two canneries are left and they process tuna as well as salmon. Of the colorful Chinese and their Oriental trappings and habitations there is scarcely a trace. Therefore it was interesting to read in the Portland *Oregonian* of August 2, 1970, an interview with the last of the Chinese labor contractors, Kee Brown, who came to Astoria in 1902 as a baby strapped to his mother's back. "I learned the canning business from the ground up," he reminisced. "Give me tin, acid, and a soldering iron and I can still make a salmon can. In those days the season began in April, when the Chinese arrived from Canton, Seattle, Portland, or San Francisco. We had as many as 125 men in a crew. There was never any written agreement between the contractor and the laborers, only with the cannery. We got forty-eight cents for each case of salmon canned and ready for shipment. Salmon was selling for four dollars a case. We paid the men fifteen dollars a month during the four-month season." They were fed and lodged at the company's expense.

The men worked nineteen hours a day but later labor laws kept them down to a maximum of twelve hours. "The canneries guaranteed the contractors so many cases a season," said Brown, "and in good fishing years we made money."

At the age of 69 Brown was still somehow associated with a cannery. "The past sixty years in Astoria have been good to Kee," said the reporter. "He fathered six sons and two daughters who grew up to become good American citizens." His father, who brought him to the United States from Canton, lies buried in a cemetery west of Astoria beside the wife whose bound feet did not prevent her from following her husband across the Pacific to make his fortune by exploiting his fellow countrymen under a system of contract labor.

The early canneries were typically a shed built on pilings at the river's edge. Fish were received on the docks direct from the boats, cleaned, washed, slimed, and cut to fit a one-pound can that included a piece of the fish's back and belly. Cans were filled, salted, placed in a retort, and cooked under ten pounds of steam pressure for an hour; they were then cooled, washed, labeled, and boxed. Altogether the fish went through thirty processes and over fifty hands. The basic procedure has not changed to this day, except that much of the work is automated, the number of hands reduced, and the premises greatly improved in sanitation.

Machines introduced around the turn of the century produced double-seamed cans called sanitary cans, thus eliminating the old method of sealing the tops with acid and solder. A contraption called the "Iron Chink," which automatically dressed the fish by decapitating its head and removing the entrails, tails, and fins and preparing it for cutting into sections and placing in cans, was invented around the turn of the century and revolutionized the industry. Later came automatic filling, vacuum sealing, and labeling machines. By 1910 canneries were able to pack 2000 cases in ten hours for less than what 800 cases had formerly cost. Today the process has been greatly speeded up.

Fishing Gear and Fishermen

In the earliest days of the industry catches were made almost entirely in the river, from Astoria upstream, with gill nets or seines paid out from sailboats twenty-two to twenty-four feet long. In 1889 about 2000 of these craft were in operation on the Columbia. When gasoline motors came along, power replaced sail; by 1910 almost the entire fleet was motorized.

About 60 percent of the catch was then taken with drift gill nets and the rest mostly with seines, which tended to become larger and more efficient, extending sometimes to over 2400 feet. Some of them were pulled by teams of horses, two double teams on the tail end on the beach and as many as five teams on the lead or offshore end. Some of the horses, according to the late Stewart Holbrook, were tired relics of the Portland street-car system. Horse seining was confined to the lower seventy miles of the river.

Some fishermen used set nets, which consisted of gill-net webbing placed in a fixed position close inshore, at a slough or eddy, thus intercepting the salmon as they rested before continuing their ascent. In 1936 set nets were banned by the state of Washington, and some years later all fixed gear as well as seines were outlawed on the Oregon side of the river. Later both states harmonized their regulations. Now only the Indians fish for salmon in the Columbia with set nets, while white fishermen are allowed to employ only gill nets.

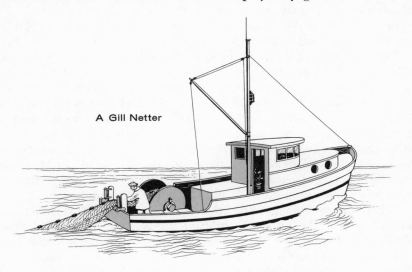

A Gill Netter

One of the most ingenious contraptions was the fish wheel. S. W. Williams, who built the first one in 1879, claimed that it could take 14,000 fish a day. It was most effective in narrow channels where there was swift-running water to rotate the wheel, as at the Cascades above Bonneville and around Celilo Falls. The salmon were guided into the revolving dippers and down a chute into a large bin within the structure of the framework supporting the rotor. Some wheels had long leads of piling running out into the river, directing the fish into dips or scoops. In 1899 there were seventy-six wheels on both sides of the Columbia. The Seufert Company, which had a cannery at The Dalles, at one time owned or leased twenty-seven wheels operating on both sides of the river.

Their best wheel, number five, caught 417,855 pounds of salmon in 1906 and the next best, "the Tumwater," took 290,365 pounds in 1923. In contrast, an average catch by an Astorian gill netter was ten tons or 20,000 pounds per year. By 1926 the company was operating only twelve wheels, three on the Washington side and nine in Oregon.[11]

At their peak the wheels took 5 percent of the total catch on the river, but there was much opposition to them from the gill netters and the Oregon legislature finally outlawed them in 1926 and the Washington legislature in 1934.

Traps modeled on east-coast or European weirs were used to catch salmon as they approached from a downstream direction. Essentially the trap was a pile and web structure with leads reaching to the shore and a pot and spiller out in the river. Traps accounted for about one fifth of the annual catch until they were banned in Washington in 1935 and in Oregon a few years later.

The efficiency of much of the gear depended on water conditions. Gill nets and set nets work best during periods of rather murky water and in darkness. On the other hand, seines and traps that operate in such a way as to enclose a school of fish and impound them in a small space, from which they may be readily removed into the hold of a vessel setting the net, work best during periods of low, clear water since the fish must actually see the web and follow along it in order to be taken. Since the Columbia River was usually muddy in May and June, gill nets and set nets tended to be most effective at this time of year when the spring chinook and bluebacks were running.

When dependable gasoline motors came along many fishermen moved out to the open sea to troll for salmon, as in California. Trolling is a hook and line technique that has become a major form of salmon fishing for both commercials and sportsmen. A commercial troller may fish up to eight steel lines, run out by means of a power winch called a "gurdy" through leads attached to poles, with as many as ten hooks on each line.

Trolling off the Columbia bar was started about 1912 by Norwegian immigrants who discovered that at certain times of the year they could take more fish in this manner than by netting in the river. Often they would set their nets at night and troll during the day. By 1920 the fleet of motorized trollers off the Oregon and Washington coasts had swelled to over a thousand.

In the later nineteenth century the fishermen were mostly Finns, Norwegians, Danes, and their American-born sons. Usually they lived along the river and worked part of the year as loggers. Astoria became a Scandinavian town, with Finnish names on the shops and Finnish culture predominating, as reflected, for example, in the numerous sauna baths. These foreigners "were literate people," says Stewart Holbrook. "It wasn't long before they could support newspapers in their own language . . . and almost from the first they had a fishermen's protective union." They also organized their own packing cooperatives. Like fishermen everywhere, they refused to be pushed around by the canners and demanded a fair return for their labor. Periodically they would go on strike because the packers would not pay them enough for the fish. For example, in 1896 fishing ceased for several weeks during the height of the runs and the National Guard had to be called out to keep the peace.

Sometimes the fishermen resorted to sabotage to protect their interests. Lucille McDonald in her *History of Southwest Washington* describes the assault of the gill netters in 1884 on the fish traps strung out along the Washington shore between Fort Canby and Point Ellice. Raids were made at night; mooring lines of the pile drivers were cut, setting them adrift and damaging the traps. Terrorized watchmen were helpless. These fish wars lasted into the early 1900s when the number of traps had grown to over 500 alone on this relatively small stretch of river and did not end until all stationary gear was declared illegal.

Regulating the Fishery

At the height of the fishery the main river was crowded with armadas of small vessels, while the trollers worked offshore. There was a universal belief, common in the United States, that the fisheries, like the forests, were inexhaustible. Did not nearly every creek, brook, and rivulet, as well as larger bodies of water in the 259,000 square miles of the Columbia River watershed, teem with salmon and/or steelhead? It was impossible to believe that the supply would ever seriously diminish.

But some people thought otherwise and timid efforts were made by state legislatures to restrain the fishermen's greed. Regulation began in 1877 when the Washington territorial legislature ordered closure of the Columbia River fishery during the months of March, April, August, and September, with additional weekend closures in May, June, and July. Oregon followed suit in 1878 but omitted the April closure. Over the next few decades this pattern of regulation prevailed, based on the theory of giving the fishes an opportunity for thirty-six to forty-eight hours each week, and weeks at a time, to reach their spawning grounds without running the gauntlet of nets and traps.

Actually these laws were of little consequence, for the stingy legislatures failed to provide staffs to enforce them. The earliest regulatory body in Oregon dates from 1887, a board of three persons designated to supervise the fishing industry. It was replaced with a Game and Fish Protector who in 1905 was superseded by a Master Fish Warden and ultimately by the Oregon Fish Commission. In Washington a Fish Commission was established in 1890 by the first state legislature; it was replaced in 1929 by a Department of Fisheries and Game, which was later separated into two bureaus, as in Oregon. None of these agencies until recent times had much money to properly enforce the laws.

The first report of the Oregon Game and Fish Protector, issued in 1894, had an important message. It said:

> It does not require a study of statistics to convince one that the salmon industry has suffered a great decline during the past decade, and that it is only a matter of a few years under present conditions when the chinook of the Columbia will be as scarce as the beaver that once was so plentiful in our streams. Common observance is amply able to apprehend a fact so plain. For a third of a century Oregon has drawn wealth from her streams, but now, by reason of her wastefulness and lack of intelligent provision for the future, the source of that wealth is disappearing and is threatened with annihilation.

He pointed out that in the five years 1880–1884 the peak of salmon production had been reached and in 1885 the runs started to drop; despite "more close and persistent fishing" the pack fell from 630,000 cases in 1883 to 310,000 cases in 1889. "Salmon that ten years ago the canners would not touch now constitute 30 to 40 percent of the pack." [12]

Appendix Table 6 shows salmon and steelhead trout landings from the Columbia River from 1866 to 1970 and Table 7 the pack from 1970 to 1971.

From 1895 to 1917 the output of canned fish (where the bulk of the catch went) fluctuated considerably, but the trend was downward. In the years 1915–1920 there was a considerable revival, but about 30 percent of the catch now consisted of smaller species, sockeye, coho, chum, and steelhead trout, which did not command the prices of the more savory and larger chinook. "Man is undoubtedly the greatest menace to the perpetuation of the great salmon fisheries of the Pacific Coast," said John N. Cobb of the U.S. Bureau of Fisheries in 1917. "When the enormous numbers of fishermen engaged and the immense quantity of gear employed is considered, one sometimes wonders how any of the fish, in certain streams at least, escape." The records show that landings held up fairly well until about 1930; after that they began to toboggan, due partly to decreased demand during the Depression and partly to depleted stocks.

In analyzing the 1938 Columbia River runs Willis H. Rich, Director of Research of the Oregon Fish Commission, attributed the decline to an escapement — that is, the number of fish that managed to elude the fishermen and reach their spawning grounds — "well below the level that would provide the maximum sustained yield." He pointed out that "such regulations and restrictions as have been imposed upon the Columbia River salmon fisheries apparently have very little effect insofar as they may act to reduce the intensity of fishing and provide a greater escapement." He regarded the weekend closure as of little value from the standpoint of conservation, while the beneficial effects of the closed season on the lower river (August 25 to September 20) were largely offset by intensive fishing during September and October above Bonneville. He concluded that "on the whole, it would appear the chinook salmon runs [which constituted about two thirds of the total catches] are subjected to an exceedingly intense fishery without any effective protection whatsoever, except such as has been afforded by the elimination of certain forms of gear and artificial propagation." [13]

Development of the Watershed

No matter how many fish escape the fishermen and their gear, sustainment of the runs depends on preservation of freshwater habitat and free access to the streams and lakes where adults will spawn, for the homing instinct cannot be denied. In short, the rivers must be unobstructed or, if dammed, provided with efficient fishways. There must be adequate water flow, the water must have the proper temperature, and above all the stream must be clean and rich in dissolved oxygen. In the nursery streams food must be ample for growth of the fry, and the smolts must be able to reach the sea. Development of the Columbia River watershed in the twentieth century profoundly altered the ecology of numerous streams and lakes and contributed to the decline of the once fabulous resource.

Any profound disturbance of the watershed influences the quality and supply of water in which fish live and propagate. Under pristine conditions the surface of the land is to a large extent a sponge that absorbs rain and snow. Part of the precipitation is used by surface vegetation, but much of it flows into subsurface storage. The advent of agriculture, which began about a century ago on a fairly large scale in the Columbia River basin, initiated ecological changes that in many areas adversely affected the quality and sometimes the quantity of water needed to support fish life. As the land was cleared and put to the plow, or stripped of timber in the type of clear cutting that prevailed, it began to contribute silt loads to the streams. In the semi-arid part of the basin where irrigation is needed to grow crops, continually greater amounts of water were abstracted from the streams in summer, leaving inadequate flows for fish.

Grazing of cattle and sheep, which reached a peak in the Pacific Northwest around the turn of the twentieth century, led in many areas to a diminution of ground cover and capacity of the soil to hold water.

Frequent and devastating forest fires, like the Tillamook burn in western Oregon that devastated 230,000 acres in 1933, not only denuded the cover but ruined many salmon streams by choking them with silt. Added to the impact of clear cutting, the forested part of the watershed, where the lands were often butchered, became increasingly unable to support migratory fish. Moreover, sawmills, plywood mills, and pulp mills were permitted to recklessly dump their noxious wastes into the rivers; logjams on the small and larger bodies of water often prevented fish migration; gravel beds were scoured by dredging operations, especially in the estuaries, which are the vital transition zones for fishes who live in both freshwater and saltwater; highway and road construction resulted in erosion and upset the water regimen; and sometimes gravel was scooped up from the river banks by sand and gravel operators, with the permission of the states,

thus depriving the salmon of redd material. It was not uncommon
for the gravel to be full of incubating salmon eggs as it was removed
from the rivers!

More detrimental to the fish populations than watershed development was the construction of dams for multiple purposes. Where
no ladders were provided these dams usually locked out the fish altogether. Many small fish were lured to their deaths in the irrigation
ditches that honeycombed the semiarid areas, and sometimes the
larger salmon missed their direction and met a similar fate.

The U.S. Corps of Engineers' comprehensive "308 Report" on the
Columbia River, published in 1948, said: "Over 300 dams have been
built in the Columbia Basin up to the present time, these structures
varying in size from splash and irrigation dams to . . . Bonneville
and Grand Coulee. Yet in only a few instances has any thought been
paid to the effect these developments might have had on fish and
wildlife." 14 The worst offenders were the private utility companies,
which, with the consent of the states, erected hydroelectric dams
without ladders or with inefficient ones, like those above Swan Falls
on the Snake River above Lewiston, on the Clearwater in Idaho, and
on the Clackomas, a tributary of the Willamette in Oregon.

Nobody knows how large the toll inflicted on the anadromous fisheries by all these forces. Soon a much greater menace arose
with the advent of megalithic dams on the main stem of the Columbia and Snake Rivers, the highways to the sea of millions of adult and
juvenile salmon and steelhead.

The Megalithic Dams

The first version of the Corps of Engineers' 308 Report was released
in finished form in 1932; it outlined a ten-dam plan, with Bonneville
as the lowermost project on the Columbia and Grand Coulee at the
upper end. Long promoted by local people, these two megalith dams
were started late in 1933 by President Franklin D. Roosevelt as a political payoff to the Pacific Northwest region, without congressional
approval, as a Public Works Administration project. Grand Coulee,
597 miles from the sea, is a power and irrigation project built by the
Bureau of Reclamation, the largest of its kind in North America at
that time, with a reservoir of 150 miles from which water would be
released to irrigate eventually a million acres of dry land in eastern
Washington. It was decided that no fish could be passed over such a
barrier rising 350 feet above the mean level of the river.

Bonneville dam, 145 miles from the ocean, is a power and naviga-

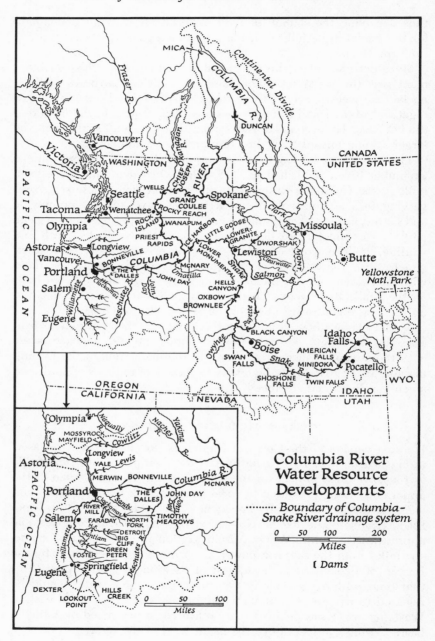

Columbia River
Water Resource
Developments

.... Boundary of Columbia-
Snake River drainage system

0   50   100   200
Miles

(Dams

tion project built by the Corps of Engineers. The Engineers' original plans did not include fish ladders. When this oversight was brought to his attention the Chief of the Corps is reputed to have said, "We do not intend to play nursemaid to the fish!" [15] Had his view prevailed the entire salmon population that spawned above Bonneville dam would have been wiped out! Public agitation forced the Corps to change its mind.

When Bonneville dam, seventy feet high, was authorized, Frank Bell, U.S. Commissioner of Fisheries, was requested to find some way of getting anadromous fish over the barrier. "I wrote to every civilized country in the world," he said, "and at no place could we find where they had passed fish over as high a dam as Bonneville would be." A team of biologists and engineers, including Harlan B. Holmes, Milo Bell, and Henry Blood, was appointed to design the fishways.

One of the key problems was how to lure the upstream migrants, accustomed to unobstructed passage in the river, into the fish ladders. "If the entrance is not readily available," says Canadian engineer C. H. Clay in his book *Design of Fishways and Other Fish Facilities,* "the migrating fish will be delayed for varying lengths of time and in the extreme case may never enter the fishway." The Columbia River at Bonneville dam is a half mile wide, so Clay's point was particularly germane. Furthermore, any dam that forms a barrier "imposes an entirely new stress on the fish which normally migrated upstream past the site . . . This stress is not limited to the effects of enforced delay, but includes the effects of all of the other physical changes in the environment (temperature, velocity and quantity of flow, etc.) resulting from construction of the dam."

An arrangement that became known as the powerhouse collection system was introduced. This is a flume with multiple entrances, attached to the downstream face of the powerhouse, which the fish can enter at a number of locations across the breadth of the tailrace channel and thus be enticed into the ladders down which powerful jets of water produce an artificial current. Faith in shepherding the adult salmon upstream was pinned basically on the fish ladders, one on the Washington shore, another on Bradford Island in the river, and a third on the Oregon side, with its entrance at the mouth of Tanner Creek. Each ladder consists of a series of curling, stepped-up pools, forty feet wide and twenty feet long, with a vertical drop of one foot between each pool.

In addition to the ladders six locks capable of accommodating 30,-000 fish per day were built. They are a combination of old-fashioned elevators with tilted floors and ship locks, but have been rarely used for salmon although often employed to lift shad and sturgeon (whose numbers have dwindled since the damming of the Columbia).

There was equal concern about getting the tiny fingerlings downstream past the dam so they could make their way to the sea. "Little was known," says Milo Bell, "of the numbers of fish that we might be expected to handle at the dam and only limited knowledge of the downstream migration that might be expected. It was assumed that the fingerlings would go over the spillway if their migration coincided with the period of high water that would be in excess of power needs and thus be allowed to spill; otherwise they would have to pass through the turbine blades in the powerhouse. Passage through turbines was almost completely an unknown subject and we had many anxious moments . . . Research was conducted as best as possible on certain of these items and that gave us faith that our approach would produce a satisfactory set of conditions. But if you were a gambling man you could have found some odds that the whole facility would not have been completely functional." [16]

Not only was the entire fishing industry apprehensive while Bonneville dam was being built, but conservationists throughout the country felt obliged to voice their fears. In an article in the *Saturday Evening Post* in November 1937, before the dam was completed, journalist Richard L. Neuberger wrote: "Prevalent throughout the principal salmon producing regions of the world is the almost unshakable opinion that within a few years the fighting fish with the flaky flesh will be one and the same with the dodo — extinct." According to Neuberger, George Red Hawk, aged chief of the Cayuse tribe, "looked grimly at the surging river. 'White man's dam,' he said, 'means no more salmon.' "

The entire fishing industry had their eyes on Bonneville in the spring of 1938 when the dam was completed. Much depended on the success of the ingenious ladders, traps, fish locks, and bypasses, for if they did not succeed in passing the hundreds of thousands of adults who came up the river and millions of juveniles who went downstream, the salmon and steelhead resources of the Columbia River would be in mortal peril. But the cunning fish did not disappoint them, although many adults certainly failed to find the ladders and died without spawning, while others were delayed two or three days or longer. Most of the salmon readily found the swirling collection troughs, moved into the channels leading to the fish ladders, gradually swam or flipped themselves from pool to pool, and arrived at the gate, where they were counted and permitted to enter the reservoir and proceed to their spawning grounds, wherever they might be. Before the 1938 runs had ceased, 470,000 salmon and steelhead along with over 600,000 miscellaneous fish (of little or no commercial value) passed the dam (Appendix Table 8).

Thousands of spectators came to watch the fish climbing the ladders, thus creating a new tourist attraction. Since it was not previously known how many salmon and steelhead inhabited the watershed extreme care was taken to keep accurate score. With this data scientific management of the Columbia River was possible.

The fingerlings who went through the revolving turbines at the powerhouse or, when water was high, had to go over the spillway, suffered heavy mortality.

The thousands of salmon that came up to Grand Coulee, the first phase of which was completed in 1938, were not entirely abandoned, although they could no longer reach their spawning grounds. Their homing instinct induced biologists to try a large-scale experiment, costing $5 million, to relocate the runs, which consisted of about 17,000 chinook, 8000 blueback, and 3000 steelhead trout. They were trapped at Rock Island dam, 120 miles downstream, and removed to holding ponds and later incubated in three new hatcheries in Washington. This program was not a great success. The spring chinook run that used to spawn above Grand Coulee suffered most; these included fish running to forty to seventy pounds, "June hogs," which vanished utterly. Bluebacks in the Grand Coulee salvage program initially showed a large increase and steelhead somewhat less.

The success of Bonneville fish ladders gave engineers confidence that the Pacific Northwest could have fish and power, too. After the Second World War the federal construction agencies, including the Corps of Engineers, Bureau of Reclamation, and Bonneville Power Administration, joined by many economic and political groups, lobbied intensively to get congressional approval for the balance of the Corps of Engineers' ten-dam plan. Fishery interests, however, did not join in this campaign because they were convinced that more high dams would injure the fishery.

From 1938 to 1949 the U.S. Fish and Wildlife Service was engaged in a series of complicated experiments to determine the effect of Bonneville dam on downstream fish migration. The results indicated a loss of seaward migrants in the neighborhood of 15 percent. This figure gained wide currency and was substantiated by later studies, at least to the satisfaction of biologists, and further convinced many people that the Corps of Engineers' scheme, combined with plans of private and publicly owned utilities to build hydroelectric projects on the Columbia and Snake Rivers, would eventually kill off most of the salmon and steelhead.

In the 1940s and 1950s little was known about the effects on migratory fish of supersaturated nitrogen gas created in the reservoirs by heavy spills of water over the dams, a phenomenon that is now regarded as the most lethal of all concomitants of dam building.

In the 1950s the fishing industry urged Congress to go slow in authorizing additional barriers on the rivers. Nevertheless The Dalles, John Day, and McNary dams were authorized by Congress, mainly for power development, with some navigational benefits. Excavations were started at The Dalles site in June 1951. The Indians who had fished at Celilo Falls from time immemorial were paid $27.2 million for the loss of their fishing rights and property. The Seufert Canning Company received $700,000 for its property and fishing rights. In reality commercial fishing interests offered little opposition to this project because it was thought that it would eliminate the heavy Indian fishery that reduced the upriver escapement.

Last First Salmon Rites

On April 20, 1956, when The Dalles dam was about to form its reservoir and the colorful and ancient fishing site at Celilo Falls would be drowned out forever, the last of the First Salmon rites were held at Celilo village. It was a warm, sunny day. Hundreds of Indians gathered in the village, women wearing multicolored flowing garments and scarves and men in conventional store clothes. Emissaries of Tommy Thompson, the aged chief of the host tribe, the Wyams, had to seek elsewhere than the Columbia for the fish needed at this feast. They bought 400 pounds of salmon in Portland, and members of the Warm Springs tribe helped out with donations of venison. From Warm Springs reservation also came the roots needed for the rituals.

The stolid, bronze-colored chief, said to be a hundred years old, sat at the head table in the longhouse at Celilo surrounded by silent and respectful tribesmen. Some people ate on mats laid on the earthen floor, while others sat at wooden tables. On benches in the rear sat the white visitors, quiet and absorbed. Outside the longhouse salmon were smoking on spits over log fires tended by women, just as they had been when Lewis and Clark camped at Celilo Falls in 1805.

The chief blessed the first salmon caught the week before and made a speech in Indian language surcharged with emotion. Before it was over the vigorous old man was weeping. He could so well remember the immense changes that had occurred during the long lifetime the gods had given him. One wondered how many of the younger people, now more or less assimilated to the white man's culture, understood this sentimental attachment to the river and the way of life in which the salmon played so large a part. They sat sad and mute.

After the First Salmon ceremony the chief permitted newsmen to take his picture, seated in front of the tepee erected near the longhouse with his much younger wife Flora.

Usually the salmon festival continued for several days, but this year it was largely confined to one day, Sunday. There were bone games, played for high stakes, in the afternoon and evening, and tribal dances at midnight.

The destruction of Celilo Falls, like that of Kettle Falls and other places where the Indians had fished for centuries, marked the end of an era. The aboriginal way of life was shattered.

"When the dam is finished," said Henry Thompson, son of the Wyam chief, "and there are no more fish at Celilo, my father will still live here, and will die here. I, too, will die here. Both of us were born at Celilo, and here," pointing to the Indian cemetery on a bluff above the village amid the rimrock, "we will be buried."

Tommy Thompson died in 1959, and without him, without the falls, and with salmon caught elsewhere, the First Salmon ceremony, held in the new village of Celilo, which the government built, lost much of its flavor and significance and was eventually abandoned.

XVI ∽

The Dammed Columbia and Unlucky Salmon: Part 2

Fish versus Dams

DESPITE THE LOBBYING of power, industrial, and navigation interests, supported by local chambers of commerce, port districts (every town along the Columbia seemingly has a port district), utility companies, and newspapers, Congress balked at appropriating money to start construction of new multipurpose projects after work was begun at The Dalles dam. This reluctance was due mainly to the well-founded fear that the increase of such barriers would multiply the fish kills, perhaps in geometric ratio. The issue reached a climax during hearings of the subcommittee of the House Appropriations Committee on the army's Civil Works Bill in the spring of 1952, held after the Senate had appropriated money to start construction on Ice Harbor dam on the Snake River.

General Chorpening, Chief of the Corps of Engineers, assured the subcommittee "that with the experience gained in operation of Bonneville dam, there will be no difficulty at this project in the proper handling of the fish problem."

Congressman Rabaut disagreed. "I notice," he said, "that the total height of the dams on the Columbia and lower Snake River is 760 feet. The highest existing fish ladder in the world today is at Bonneville, which is 65 feet and the downstream loss is 15 percent. As we progress up this river and gain this height of 760 feet—up the Columbia and lower Snake—we get these different elevations: Bonneville, which has been completed, 65 feet; The Dalles, 88 feet; John Day, 132 feet; McNary, 100 feet; Ice Harbor, 100 feet; Lower Monumental, 93 feet; Little Goose, 100 feet; and Lower Granite, 82 feet . . . There must be a tiring effect upon the fish going up the river, in the vicinity of The Dalles or McNary or Ice Harbor or any of these other places . . . The fish loss is going to be something which should be determined."

General Chorpening did not accept the alleged 15 percent loss of downstream migrants at Bonneville dam, but he recognized the magnitude of the problem of passing fish up and down so many barriers. "We have made some progress in getting salmon over dams," he said, "but there is the killing of the little fry going downstream; we have not been able to solve that."

After listening to testimony pro and con, the subcommittee decided that Ice Harbor dam should be denied construction funds. In a memorable peroration, Representative Clarence Cannon of Missouri, Chairman of the Appropriations Committee, said: "The construction of this dam means eventually the complete extinction of a species of salmon which thereafter can never be resuscitated or recreated. Only God in His infinite power and wisdom can create a new species of animal life, and when that is once destroyed there is no power on earth that will reproduce it. We accomplish miracles in our laboratories but we have never yet been able to create in our test tubes the celestial spark of life. The total extinction of life for all time to come is something we cannot even contemplate, regardless of the need for power for the few years that will be required to develop some method of avoiding this permanent restriction of an important food supply." [1]

Opponents of Ice Harbor cheered, while the advocates of the project resolved to continue their fight. They directed at Congress a stream of petitions, resolutions, and requests from local interests, even though in 1953 they had lost the support of the Republican administration, which, oriented against public power, refused to budget funds for any new federal starts in the Pacific Northwest.

When the Democrats recaptured Congress in 1955 Senators Warren Magnuson of Washington and Wayne Morse of Oregon were determined to secure funds for ground breaking at Ice Harbor. Rather than wage a committee or floor fight, where they would run full tilt into Republican opposition, they persuaded the Joint Senate-House conference committee handling the army's Civil Works appropriation for the fiscal year 1956 to add $1 million to start the project. Despite last-minute protests of the fishing industry, caught napping by this parliamentary maneuver, both houses permitted the small appropriation to stand. Even Congressman Cannon apparently was now convinced (mistakenly as it turned out) that anadromous fish could be passed over a 100-foot dam. Once Ice Harbor was built, it was certain that the rest of the lower Snake River complex of federal dams would be constructed. And so it happened — see map page 286.

By 1957 the center of the fish versus dam controversy had shifted, although it was by no means confined to the middle section of the Snake. When Secretary of the Interior Douglas McKay in 1953 refused to intervene against the application of the Idaho Power Company for a license to build three power projects on the Snake, he reversed a policy followed by Democratic administrations and wrecked, at least in part, the Corps of Engineers' 308 Plan. The result was a scramble by private and local public utilities to usurp valuable dam sites. This turn of events merely compounded the problems and jeopardized the fish runs on the Snake, which in 1952 produced about a third of all the salmon and steelhead that used the Columbia as a highway to the sea.

Death at the Dams

The Columbia in 1973 was almost completely harnessed from Bonneville to Grand Coulee except for the stretch between McNary and Priest Rapids dams, while the lower Snake River is also dammed. Besides eliminating a large portion of the breeding grounds of the anadromous fishes, these projects have created a steeplechase that the intrepid fish must hurdle both in their ascent and descent of the river.

"It must be made clear," says C. H. Clay, "that the mere provision of fishways or fish-passage facilities at a dam does not insure the continued existence of their original level of abundance of the migratory fish for which the facilities were designed. The construction of a dam in a stream can have many diverse effects on the physical characteristics of the river. Water temperatures can be changed both above and below the dam. The normal pattern of seasonal flow in the river can be altered, with floods occurring later than normal or not at all. Silt may be settled out in the reservoir above the dam. All of these physical changes can greatly affect, either directly or indirectly, any fish required to pass upstream or down through the altered portion of the river." [2]

All these consequences of damming a mighty river have occurred on the Columbia. Nowhere in the world have salmon been asked to cope with so many man-made difficulties, and the wonder is that they continue to exist in respectable numbers. Consider, for example, the fish who spawn in the upper reaches of the Columbia (and will spawn nowhere else), such as the Okanogan in Washington. They have to negotiate Bonneville, The Dalles, John Day, McNary, Priest Rapids, Wanapum, Rock Island, Rocky Reach, and Wells dams, a grand total of nine, with accumulated elevations of 612 feet in a stretch of about 400 miles. At each obstruction they must find the entrances to the fish ladders, adjust themselves to the currents and other new conditions in the reservoirs, and have enough stamina to reach their home stream and spawn. Many upstream travelers are lost in the long and arduous voyage; many adults and much of the progeny of successful spawners are killed, chiefly from bubble disease induced by supersaturated nitrogen gas.

Fish heading for Snake River tributaries in Idaho, such as the Clearwater, Grand Ronde, or Salmon Rivers, must pass Bonneville, The Dalles, John Day, and McNary dams on the Columbia and after entering the Snake, the Ice Harbor, Lower Monumental, and Little Goose dams, each of which is equipped with fish ladders, for a total climb of over 800 feet in a stretch of about 500 miles. Young fishes must make the same journey, going through the blades of the turbines in the powerhouse or over the spillways. In either case the perils are great: many are decimated, others succumb in the still waters to bubble disease, which resemble the bends in human divers. Young salmon are also eaten in large numbers by predators, which have increased since the rivers were converted into slack-water pools.

"Extensive effort has been made to improve fish passage ever since Bonneville dam was built," says William E. Pitney, of the Oregon Game Commission. "The U.S. Fish and Wildlife Service, Corps of Engineers, private and public utilities, and the resource management agencies of the several states have struggled with the many problems. Improvements have been made, but for each gain an almost unending host of other problems has been recognized. Once it had been determined that adult fish could be passed above high dams it was quickly discovered that their young were ineffective in finding their way downstream through the many miles of slack water. This resulted largely from the water being impounded at the time of year the migrants should have been carried by the freshets to the sea. Some of those which do leave the reservoirs find only the turbine systems as outlets and are killed by the pressure changes or spinning blades." [3]

Speaking at a seminar on reservoirs at Oregon State University in October 1968, Lawrence Korn of the Oregon Fish Commission said, "We have presently little idea how efficiently fish pass the impoundments on the Columbia River. We know more about passage efficiency at dams on tributaries such as the Willamette and the Deschutes Rivers. Water currents have been markedly changed in the reservoirs, or even eliminated, thus confusing juvenile salmon and in many instances preventing them from going downstream. Reservoirs also encourage the upsurge of predators like scrap fish which feed on salmonids. Finally the water levels and amounts discharged at the dams are determined not by needs of fish but demand for power, irrigation water, and flood control." As a consequence, the "flow may be too high at times or too warm for fish passage, or so low and polluted that the oxygen content is inadequate for fish life."

The increase of squawfish and other coarse fish in the reservoirs behind the dams has taken an enormous toll of salmonids. High temperatures in summer inspired by the slack water in these pools — the Columbia above Bonneville is no longer a river but a series of lakes — have at times generated outbreaks of columnaris disease fatal to salmon.

Often the downstream travelers are delayed in their migration because their built-in time clocks become disoriented. Howard L. Raymond of the Bureau of Commercial Fisheries (now the National Marine Fisheries Service) found that before John Day reservoir was formed young chinook traveled from Ice Harbor to The Dalles dam in 14 days on the average at the rate of eighteen kilometers (10.8 miles) per day; after the reservoir was filled they were slowed down to eleven kilometers (6.6 miles) per day, and it took twenty-two days to cover the same distance.[4]

Not only does the changing flow pattern seem to slacken fish movements but according to Donald L. Park of the Seattle Biological Laboratory of the NMFS, the season of downstream migration is also changing. "Historically," he says, "most juvenile chinook salmon have migrated down the Columbia River in the spring when the environmental factors were most favorable for their survival. Flows were generally high, water temperatures were within optimal ranges for salmon, the river was sufficiently turbid to protect them from predators, and no impoundments delayed their migration to the sea . . . [Now] the juveniles have to migrate down an almost totally impounded river during July and August, when environmental conditions . . . are far from optimum. By mid-July the spring runoff is usually completed, flows are reduced, water temperatures begin to rise, and the water clears up and thus affords little protection from predators."[5]

Much work is being done in an attempt to solve the downstream migration problem. At the 1968 meeting of the Pacific Marine Fisheries Commission Dr. L. E. Perry of the Bureau of Sport Fisheries and Wildlife said that the Corps of Engineers, in cooperation with the Bureau of Commercial Fisheries, had achieved a breakthrough in research on such migration. They learned that most of the young salmon stay close to the surface of the water near the ceiling of the draft tubes that enter the turbines. Also, it had been found that these fish will escape through any opening in the ceiling of the draft tubes, such as slots provided at the closure gates. "A fair percentage of the fish at the present time migrate into these gate slots but find no way to escape. Plans are being made to provide outlets from these slots so the fish can be released below the dam."

John Day dam has such features built into it, and the Corps of Engineers later installed similar outlets at other projects. But conditions worsened rather than improved.

Perry pointed out in 1968 that losses of downstream migrants are 10 to 15 percent at each dam. "If these are accumulated between the Salmon River and lower Columbia, the downstream population of little fish ends up being 43 percent of the original number in Idaho. In other words, 3 out of 5 never reach the Pacific Ocean!"

According to the Washington Department of Fisheries, nitrogen supersaturation alone killed more than 5 million fish in the Columbia and Snake Rivers in 1971, including over 90 percent of the downstream chinook salmon and steelhead travelers. All the agencies involved in operation of the dams, including the Corps of Engineers, which has charge of federal installations; the Bonneville Power Administration, which markets the power; and the state and federal fishery agencies, which supervise the fisheries, have worked feverishly to solve the nitrogen problem by some adjustment of generation schedules to minimize spillage, by installing slotted gates at turbine intakes, and by trucking large numbers of juveniles around the dams. Yet a team of scientists from the U.S. Environmental Protection Agency reported on July 18, 1972, that "the incidence of bubble disease in sockeye salmon may have increased significantly this year as compared with observations in past years." [6] Supersaturated nitrogen has been found in the Columbia all the way to its mouth.

Fishery Development Programs

As the effects of the dams on the fish runs became apparent, Congress was asked to supply funds for compensating programs. As far back as

1938 it had appropriated $500,000 for surveys and improvements for the benefit of anadromous fishes in the Pacific Northwest. This money was used by the Bureau of Fisheries to survey some of the streams tributary to the Columbia and develop a rehabilitation program. It was merely a beginning. In 1946 Congress broadened the program by authorizing the Secretary of the Interior to utilize the services and facilities of the state agencies in developing and enhancing the resource. The objective was to maximize fish runs in the tributaries below McNary dam; in 1957 the program was extended to the upper Columbia River basin.

The Fishery Development program has five major facets: (1) expansion of artifical propagation of salmon and steelhead trout, (2) removal of stream obstructions such as logjams, waterfalls, small abandoned dams, etc., to permit fish to pass up to their spawning grounds, (3) screening of water diversions and construction of fishways at waterfalls, (4) transplantation of upriver races to downstream areas, and (5) establishment of fish refuges.

The results of these extensive efforts have been manifest throughout the watershed. Many waterfalls that used to be difficult for salmon to climb have been laddered; splash dams and logjams were removed on many creeks, brooks, and little rivers, thus opening up hundreds of miles of spawning and rearing areas; defective fish ladders were repaired or replaced. Over 800 screens have been installed in irrigation ditches — 400 in Oregon's John Day River system alone — to safeguard the fishes' passage in the river. At one of these screens on the main stem of the Salmon River, for example, 15,000 young salmon were counted in a thirty-day period. The Lemhi River in Idaho had only a meager stock of salmon before eighty-five irrigation diversions were screened in the 1950s — by 1961 the run had increased to over 4000 spawners.

The major accomplishment of the program, however, has been the financial stimulus and technical aid given to artificial propagation of salmon and steelhead as described in Chapter XIX.

The Tamed Columbia

The once turbulent Columbia River is now fairly tame. Lewis and Clark, could they return, would hardly recognize much of it. The Indians and their villages along the banks, the lodges and racks of drying fish, the little canoes have all disappeared. The waters seldom rage in the spring but flow quietly to the sea. A network of huge concrete dams with their powerhouses, spillways, and spidery webs of electric wire, speeding power to towns and cities throughout the Pacific Northwest, greets the eye.

In fact, the Columbia is no longer a river but a series of quiet, slack-water pools. The deep chasms and canyons and the rocks over which the river beat itself endlessly as the torrent came down from the mountains have been drowned out. There is only a fifty-mile stretch of free-flowing water. Much of the wildlife is gone, and there has not been a major flood since 1948.

In the tidal portion of the river there are many towns and cities on both banks, and bridges, airports, docks, warehouses, and factories and mills spew wastes into the river and poisonous gases into the air. Around Portland, all the spoils and detritus of an industrial and affluent society plague the river. Here warehouses, oil depots, grain elevators, packing plants, and other factories pour voluminous wastes into the channels and sloughs.

The nontidal stretches appear to be less damaged. The brooding cliffs and rimrock are relatively unmarred. From the bluff at Crown Point, thirty miles above Portland, one can see the sun set in a golden haze over the Pacific on a warm summer day. The river is opalescent in the twilight. Cars and trucks roll along the highway below, and occasionally the screech of a freight train is heard. Passenger trains have been abandoned. The sharp pinnacles of rocky summits in the east are etched against the sky with its mackerel clouds. The hills are still clothed with Douglas fir and interspersed with plowed fields on the Washington side.

Above Bonneville the river is strangely empty. Despite the federal expenditure of hundreds of millions of dollars in dredging a barge channel and providing navigation locks at every dam, barge traffic is meager; grain is mainly carried downriver and petroleum upriver. Side-wheelers and stern-wheelers, which once were numerous, long ago left the river. There is but one excursion boat, which runs from Portland to Bonneville dam in summer. Most of the small craft one sees racing along the channel are used for recreation and fishing. Below Bonneville hundreds of gill netters ply the river when fishing is permitted.

Fifty years ago the river was crowded with netsmen. Scows went up and down collecting their catches from Astoria to Celilo Falls. There were fishing stations on both banks. Cozy inns provided warm meals and drinks. Watchmen sitting beside lantern-lit fish wheels were ready to drive away the fish pirates. In the canneries the machines clicked all day and, when the runs were unusually heavy, into the night.

Now at each dam the transmission towers hum with the music of electricity moving at phenomenal speed to its destinations. At night strobe lights warn aircraft away from these battlements. At Troutdale and The Dalles and near Maryhill (on the Washington side) the chimneys of aluminum smelters vomit poisonous white smoke into the air; eastward the towns are far between, and automotive traffic speeds along the highways. The little railway stations are shuttered. In brief, the Columbia is now a sleeping giant, its surface only occasionally ruffled by the strong winds that blow through the gorge.

"If we had left the river in a natural state — kept the dams off the main stem — the salmon resource would have perpetuated itself," says Francis Seufert wistfully. Seufert's grandfather came from San Francisco in 1884 to establish a cannery at Seufert, Oregon, three miles east of The Dalles. The company bought most of the salmon caught around Celilo Falls and had one of the largest fish and fruit canning operations above Cascade Locks. But after Grand Coulee dam cut off headwater runs of spring chinook and much of the blue-back the fish business began to taper off. Some 2 million pounds of fish were canned annually in the 1940s, but the 1950s brought a decline. The doors were closed in 1957 after the federal government purchased its fishing rights and property. All that now remains of the great days in this historic locality are excellent photographs taken by Mrs. Seufert that may be seen in the small museum on the bluff above The Dalles.

The Tormented Snake River

The Snake River in its pristine state was hardly less mighty than the Columbia, and it has suffered similar changes. Long before the Bureau of Reclamation and the private power companies began to barricade the river, the irrigationists built low-head dams on the tributaries that impounded water to irrigate farmland and generate small amounts of power.

The Reclamation Bureau had its eyes on the Snake almost at its birth in 1904 and in fact claimed it as a kind of fief. After the Second World War the bureau devised a multiple dam scheme, chiefly to generate power on the lower and middle Snake, but the Republican administration in 1953, closely linked to the privately owned utility companies, killed all chances of its implementation. Instead Idaho Power Company was granted licenses to build Hell's Canyon, Oxbow, and Brownlee dams, which have virtually destroyed the fish runs above these impoundments. The company has provided funds for construction of hatcheries to compensate for fish losses.

While the company was vainly struggling to save the salmon in the stretch of the river it had usurped, other utilities were attempting to grab power sites on the middle Snake, which includes the Hell's Canyon, an area that consists

> of a series of swift white-water rapids flowing into deep pools in one of the deepest canyons in the United States. The immediate shore is principally a series of rock faces dropping almost vertically into the river, or stretches lined with great boulders interspersed by occasional sand bars and back eddies. There is no doubt that [it] represents one of the last of this country's great rivers that has been little changed by man and still challenges his best efforts to tame . . . a scene of primitive ruggedness probably not equaled anywhere in the United States today.[7]

Various schemes were proposed, but all of them threatened in some degree the continued existence of the anadromous fishes in the Salmon, Grande Ronde, and Imnaha Rivers and main stem of the Snake. In 1964 the Federal Power Commission after lengthy hearings awarded a license to a combine of private and publicly owned utilities to build High Mountain Sheep dam, but four years later the United States Supreme Court invalidated the grant chiefly on the grounds that the project would not protect and would probably seriously damage the fish runs. This was one of the few High Court decisions declaring that salmon are more valuable, inferentially, than electricity.

In January 1968 another combine, including the rejected applicant for High Mountain Sheep, applied for a license to build a high dam at a new location above the Salmon River (which produces a large portion of what is left of the Snake River runs), giving the FPC the choice of two alternative schemes. Their claims were based on the alleged urgent need for power in the Pacific Northwest. They assured the commission that their designs "would provide adequate protection for other uses of the water resources [in addition to power], including fish and wildlife, recreation and flood control and navigation." Like all previous schemes, this application was vigorously opposed by conservationists, who, in the words of Wade B. Hall of the United States Forest Service, wished to prevent the conversion of the river "from a vibrant stream, with quiet pools, long stretches of swiftly flowing water and many thrilling rapids, into a placid pond where water movement appears to be only vertical as its elevation rises and falls to reveal the ever-changing amount of reservoir bottom." In 1968 an estimated 150,000 and in 1969 186,000 salmon and steelhead spawners used the areas that would be destroyed by the newest proposal.

On October 22, 1970, the FPC staff counsel recommended against granting a license to any of the applicants, denying that the power is urgently required, since other sources of generation are available, and affirming that the need to preserve the fish and wildlife and prevent the demise of the free-flowing river are paramount considerations. Early in 1971, however, the FPC examiner who conducted the lengthy hearings and had been responsible for awarding the license that was later nullified by the United States Supreme Court recommended that the application for twin dams in the Middle Snake be granted but that they should not be built before 1974. Meanwhile United State senators from Idaho and Oregon, with the support of numerous conservation groups, are attempting to get a bill through Congress declaring the Middle Snake a sanctuary river, not to be molested by dam builders.

Resurgence of the Indian Fishery

Before 1957, when The Dalles dam eliminated the ancient Indian fishery at Celilo Falls, the Oregon and Washington Fish Commissions formulated regulations for commercial fishing on the Columbia above Bonneville that were applicable to both Indians and non-Indians. After 1957 the area above Bonneville was closed to net fishing, but the tribes were permitted to take salmon for subsistence and ceremonial purposes. For a few years they abided by the regulations and then they began to fish with nets above Bonneville and sell their catches. Only the Warm Springs Indians among the four tribes who were supposedly paid off for their fishery rights remained faithful to the 1957 agreement.

Efforts by the states to negotiate reasonable settlements were unsuccessful, although limited voluntary restraints were adopted by some of the tribes. The issue reached a climax in the summer of 1964 when the Indians defied the order of the Washington and Oregon Fish Commissions forbidding fishing for summer chinook, a run that had fallen to critical levels.

From 1960 to 1965 harvests by Indian nets in areas closed to commercial fishing jumped from 45,000 to nearly 1 million pounds. As a consequence, the Oregon Fish Commission in the spring of 1966 announced its intention to order the state police to strictly enforce the law prohibiting commercial fishing. Indians were arrested, but usually they were not found guilty by the courts. In 1968 the Indians and their lawyers petitioned the United States District Court for an injunction to prevent enforcement of state regulations.

The brief filed by George Dysart, Assistant Regional Solicitor of the Department of the Interior, cleverly argued that money paid to the Indians was not for their fishing rights but for "essentially a flowage easement over these areas." In other words, the Indians could not only catch all the fish needed for their subsistence on reservations but they had "the right to go to the usual and accustomed fishing places to take fish free from interference by the state or others." The only restraints they recognized were those necessary to prevent destruction of the runs. And then, only the tribes themselves could prescribe the regulations, not the state.[8]

Judge Robert C. Belloni of the United States District Court accepted Dysart's arguments and ruled that the state of Oregon "must so regulate the taking of fish that, except for unforeseen circumstances beyond its control, the treaty tribes and their members will be accorded an opportunity to take, at their usual and accustomed fishing places by reasonable means feasible to them, a fair and equitable share of all fish which it permits to be taken from any given runs."

Thanks to the Belloni decision, a kind of private and lucrative fishing preserve has been acquired by the Indians in the 130 miles of the Columbia stretching from the Bridge of the Gods near Cascade Locks to the Umatilla River. They now take about as many fish here as before Celilo Falls was flooded, and in fact their proportion of the total salmon harvest in the Columbia is greater than it was in 1957.

Commercial versus Sport Fishermen

Management of the Columbia River fishery is in the hands of the fish and game agencies of Oregon and Washington. Their job is to regulate both sport and commercial fishing with the aim of maximizing the runs on a perpetual basis yet give both groups an opportunity to take the maximum number of salmon and steelhead. To this end some two score or more biologists study every phase of the fishery, make continual forecasts, and carefully monitor the river. With the steady decline of the runs commercial fishing seasons were curtailed from 272 days in 1938 to 77 days in 1971 so as to give the stocks an opportunity to build back. Also the type of gear that may be used is minutely regulated.

Paralleling the drop in commercial fishing has been an enormous growth of sport fishing. One cannot live in the Pacific Northwest very long before becoming aware that salmon and steelhead support a recreational industry of considerable magnitude and economic importance. The number of licensed anglers on the Columbia River jumped from 40,000 in 1946 to 200,000 in 1970, and their catch of chinook and coho zoomed from 26,000 to 265,000. These men and women troll for salmon from boats of every description, inside the river and offshore. On a warm summer day one may see 5000 craft with an assemblage of 20,000 persons off the mouth of the Columbia. Salmon are also fished from the banks, as are steelhead trout.

Angling clubs and federations wield considerable political influence and engage in bitter struggles with commercial fishermen for a larger share of the fish supply. Thus in the early 1960s sportsmen's groups spearheaded by the Izaak Walton League launched a drive to have all nets banned from the Columbia. They succeeded in putting a measure on the Oregon ballot but were beaten by the well-organized and well-financed campaign of the commercial salmon industry. Subsequently the sharp increase in runs of silvers (coho) in the Columbia, due to the breakthrough in artificial production, abated the sport versus commercials conflict.

Status of the Columbia River Fishery

Salmon and steelhead stocks in the Columbia River watershed have suffered great losses in the past century. About two thirds of the area where the fishes originally spawned have been rendered inaccessible to them.

Appendix Table 6 tells the dramatic story. The great decline began about the time Bonneville and Grand Coulee dams became operative. From a peak of 31.6 million pounds in 1941, landings fell steadily for a decade, then in the 1950s cataclysmically. Chinook runs, which were the mainstay of the fishery from its beginnings, reached low levels, while coho, the next most important species, almost disappeared by 1960. Sockeye were virtually eliminated because their spawning and rearing habitats, in the upper Washington watershed, had been blocked by dams or drowned out, while chum, once providing as much as several million pounds of food a year, disappeared from the Columbia River. Catches in the 1960s, trending upward, were in the neighborhood of 5,000,000 to 9,000,000 pounds per annum, of which chinook provided more than half and coho nearly all the rest. Successful hatchery breeding of coho and to a lesser extent chinook (and steelhead), accounts basically for somewhat improved runs in the 1960s.

In 1970 the Oregon Fish Commission published a status report on the various stocks:

> *Spring chinook* remain primarily a wild run. Landings fell from a high of 3,400,000 pounds in 1955 to 750,000 pounds in 1970. The heyday of this run occurred long before Bonneville dam was built, and the recent slight improvement is due to production of hatchery fish. Spring chinook suffered a serious blow in 1971 however, when about 50 percent of the juveniles issuing from Snake River tributaries were destroyed by nitrogen disease before they reached the Columbia.
>
> *Summer chinook* catches reached an all-time low of only 18,000 pounds in 1966 compared with 3,400,000 pounds in 1939, due chiefly to loss of spawning areas and adults and juveniles at dams. These fish are so scarce that netting is rarely permitted. (A slight improvement in the run resulted in modest fishing in 1971.) The stock has been stabilized, says the Oregon Fish Commission, at about 75,000 fish, a tiny fraction of their 19th century abundance. The run consists almost entirely of wild fish, for little success has been attained in breeding them in hatcheries.
>
> *Fall chinook*, though greatly diminished from pre-Bonneville dam days, have fared better than the other chinook runs in recent years because of success in artificial production. About 5,000,000 pounds were landed in 1970, a fourth of the 1940 level. The Oregon Fish Commission estimated the run at 300,000; much of it is harvested in the ocean off British Columbia and Washington state.
>
> *Coho* stocks reached a nadir around 1960, after which they

exhibited a remarkable comeback as millions of hatchery-bred fingerlings were released every year in numerous streams and eventually a large proportion became available to fishermen. The run is now estimated at about 1,000,000 and the harvest is mainly in the ocean by trollers. In 1970 over 500,000 coho were taken by fishermen.

Sockeye, once counted in the millions in the Columbia River, have been reduced to some 100,000, while *chum* salmon, never too plentiful, have almost disappeared. *Pink* salmon were also never abundant in the Columbia; they are caught in the ocean off the Oregon coast while en route to northern streams.

The fleet of gill netters in the river has fallen greatly. In 1971 some 650 gill-net licenses were issued in Oregon and 709 in Washington, and many of these were used by part-timers or "moonlighters." There are only eight salmon canneries left, processing commercial and sport catches (Appendix Table 7).

The summer runs of steelhead trout have sharply diminished because of the loss of rearing areas, particularly in the upper Snake

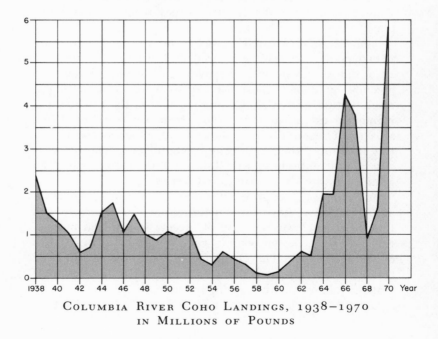

COLUMBIA RIVER COHO LANDINGS, 1938–1970
IN MILLIONS OF POUNDS

River basin, while winter steelhead that spawn in the lower part of the watershed, such as the Cowlitz River, are holding their own. Commercial landings fell from a high of 2.7 million pounds in 1941 to an average of 437,000 pounds in the years 1965–1971. The sport catch, however, is substantial. Hatchery success in producing steelhead is increasing.

Does the Fishery Have A Future?

Despite efforts to save the Columbia River fishery in the past thirty-five years at a cost of $300 million in conservation programs, mainly federal, its future is threatened by many forces: accelerated development of the watershed for power generation, flood control, industrial and consumptive uses of water, adverse logging practices, road building, spraying of forests with poisonous chemicals, and other activities that impair the regimen of streams. The Corps of Engineers, for example, seems bent on damming every feasible river tributary to the Columbia and along with the Bureau of Reclamation is intent on destroying wilderness and natural beauty.

A potential threat is the nuclear power industry. Despite tremendous public protests, Portland General Electric Company, in partnership with other utilities, secured a license from the Atomic Energy Commission to build the Trojan plant on the south side of the Columbia River at Rainier, Oregon, thirty miles below Portland. No nation except France has up to now been foolish enough to build a nuclear plant on a river containing substantial salmon populations. Although Trojan will be equipped with cooling towers, potential damage to the fishes (and human life) from any malfunctioning of the machinery, and especially failure of safety devices, cannot be discounted.

The National Marine Fisheries Service, which has monitored the fish runs at the Trojan site, reports that well over 1,000,000 adult salmonids pass the Trojan site each year in addition to American shad, Columbia River smelt, cut-throat trout, and white sturgeon.[9]

Trojan will not be in operation until 1975. A disaster at the plant might kill a substantial proportion of the Columbia River fishery. This is not a mere fantasy, for "the history of nuclear fission is studded with accidents, each due to the mechanical failure of safety devices or human error, or a combination of both," says Gordon Rattray Taylor in his remarkable work *The Doomsday Book.*

It would be more rational to keep nuclear generation out of the Columbia or any other river that harbors considerable fish populations, but the power promoters take no heed of this. Leaders in the industry such as H. Russell Richmond, Administrator of the Bonneville Power Administration, and their industrial, political, and journalistic allies continue to beat the drums for more hydroelectric projects and nuclear plants, warning that gargantuan amounts of additional generating capacity are needed to meet public demand, else the region will suffer dire consequences. They predict brownouts and blackouts if these so-called requirements are not met, resulting (they say) in curtailment of industrial operations and possibly rationing of power for household use. In their most hysterical moments they suggest that children and adults will be unable to watch television during the hours of peak electricity use, and there may not be enough juice to heat homes, run air conditioners, etc. At the same time that the BPA administrator issues such lugubrious warnings the agency strives to lure new aluminum mills, an industry that takes about 40 percent of all the federally generated power in the Pacific Northwest. The only reason for the existence of an aluminum industry in the region is the availability of low-cost power subsidized by the federal government, for the raw material, alumina, has to be brought halfway around the world.

The industries that consume much of the power generated at the dams provide relatively few jobs and at the same time pollute the waters and foul the air. "The list of BPA industrial customers reads like a who's who of polluters," says Professor William G. Rogers, Jr., of the University of Washington Law School.

Many people are awakening to the fact that while electricity is a great boon to mankind, there is a price to pay in destruction of valuable food fishes and their habitats. Thus the city council of Astoria, Oregon, has refused to grant a construction permit to a company that has a power contract from BPA to build an aluminum smelter on Youngs Bay in the Columbia River estuary.

The council was moved by a letter sent to Governor Tom McCall, an ardent supporter of the project, by a young fisherman, Jim Roberts. Answering the governor's claim that the proposed smelter "would have the best technology available," Roberts said:

> The best technology available is not good enough, and I will
> tell you why. The Youngs Bay estuary . . . is now every fall
> teeming with silverside salmon (coho). Thanks to the Ore-
> gon pellet . . . the Klaskanine hatchery each year hatches
> and raises two million silverside fingerlings. It is estimated

that these fingerlings consume three metric tons of plankton
per day during their growth period . . .

All fluorides settling in an area over 100 square miles will be
washed into the Youngs and Lewis and Clarks Rivers.
Biologists have expressed concern about possible fluoride
damage to this fish life-cycle.

We are told we must trust our regulatory agencies, but . . .
AMAX and other aluminum companies have built smelters
that have seriously damaged the environment. (One killed
50 square miles of ponderosa pine.) None of these other aluminum plants sat at the apex of a great and sensitive salmon
run (at the mouth of the Columbia River).

Look at the lawsuit fact sheet I have enclosed. None of the
regulatory agencies protected these people . . . Fortunately
these incidents concerned only a few isolated individuals,
but what is possibly at stake now is our whole Youngs Bay
salmon run . . .

If this plant is built without a thorough estuary study or if
this plant is built with only the "best-technology-can-give"
pollution controls, and something happens to this great
salmon run of ours . . . the wrath of the people . . . will fall
on those officials who, without proper foresight or research,
and against the advice of trained biologists, let this smelter
be built and our salmon life-cycle destroyed.[10]

Summing up, we may conclude that the Columbia River fishery has
been the victim basically of our straining after economic progress
without paying adequate attention to the effects of hydroelectric projects, nuclear plants, irrigation works, timber cutting, and especially
the ecological changes that follow in their train. The low-cost power
generated at the dams has certainly been a great economic boon to
the region, but the people were lulled by the belief that they could
have all the electricity they desired and fish, too. They were willing
to tax themselves heavily to build fish ladders and invest in other
conservation programs. The best scientific and technical knowledge
was mobilized to enable the intrepid salmon to get over the dams and
reach their spawning grounds, but apparently nature is conspiring to
halt man's efforts. The nitrogen disease is but one (and a major
one) of the many problems involved in getting salmon and steelhead safely upstream and downstream.

Thus it is conceivable that if watersheds continue to be developed, a time may come when relatively few salmonids will be seen climbing the curling ladders at Bonneville or any other dam and that the runs perhaps may be confined to rivers below that locality where there are no high dams and few if any fish problems. The rest of the watershed may by then be almost entirely deserted. Such an eventuality, however, is too awful to contemplate.

The great bulk of the original fishery has already been lost, and only the spurt in hatchery propagation has to some extent arrested the tide. If we are to stave off worse consequences certain steps should be taken.

We should first of all reach a decision among water users to give fish a much higher status than they now have. Power managers and irrigationists must be convinced that the fish also have high priorities and rights to the river flows. Not only must management of the rivers give a much higher priority to needs of the fish, but the undammed sections of the Columbia and Snake should be given sanctuary status. By that I mean we should build no more dams or nuclear plants on these rivers, or pulp mills on tributaries harboring large stocks of salmon and steelhead, nor should we impinge any further on the migratory routes of the fishes. Perhaps it is not quixotic to suggest that we should destroy (paying due compensation to the owners) some of the power dams like Pelton and Round Butte that ruined a marvelous fishery on the Deschutes River and the three Idaho Power Company dams that bar the upper Snake River to anadromous fishes. If society in its wisdom some day decides that food and game fishes are more valuable to the nation than electricity (which can be generated elsewhere), some of the territory once inhabited by the salmon and steelhead will be returned to them. This is a most important desideratum.

XVII ∼

Death and Revival
of the Willamette River

THE WILLAMETTE, 185 miles long, flows northward entirely in the
state of Oregon, emptying into the Columbia near Portland. It is
a complex river system formed by the confluence of the Coast Fork
and the Middle Fork. As it flows northward it receives many tributaries that drain the Cascade and Coast ranges, such as the McKenzie, Santiam, Molalla, Yamhill, Tualatin, and Clackamas Rivers, each
a fairly extensive system in itself. Snow-fed creeks and rivers pour
off the forested mountains to swell the Willamette, which in winter
or spring often rises to levels that overflow the banks, while in summer there may be scarcely enough water to sail a shallow-draft
boat. Because of wide fluctuations in flow some of the upper tributaries have been dammed by the Corps of Engineers to keep the
river in check and also produce small amounts of power. The Corps
seems to have taken control of the Willamette and in addition to
many projects already built has many more on its drawing boards,
some of rather dubious feasibility.

Settlement of the Valley

Settlement of the Oregon country actually began in the fertile Willamette Valley, with its deep rich soils and stands of grass so high
they sometimes hid the emigrant trains. A provisional government
was formed on the river's bank at Champoeg in 1843, and this gave
support to the United States' claim for a large portion of the Pacific
Northwest in the Oregon Boundary Treaty with Britain in 1846.
Abundance of fish in the rivers and game in the surrounding prairies
and woods as well as rich soils were a profound attraction to settlers.
There were salmon and steelhead in the main river below and
above the great falls of the Willamette (at Oregon City), a series of

cascades about a half mile wide down which the white waters pour in fury, creating a veil of spray that gives an eerie cast to the scene. To the Indians the falls, called in Chinook language "Hyas Tyee Tumwa-ter," was not a natural formation but a creation of the god Talipas to permit them to catch plenty of fish — it was easy to net or spear the jumping salmon here, as at Celilo Falls, or Kettle Falls, or Spokane Falls. Here the Clackamas, Klamath, Multnomah, and Molalla tribes kept a rendezvous each spring.

At the falls the Hudson's Bay Company factor, Dr. John McLough-lin, built a sawmill and an outpost for trade in fur and salmon and when he retired took up residence in a huge house on the escarpment above the river. The first seat of organized American government in the Oregon country was at Oregon City.

There is little information about salmon fishing on the Willamette during the nineteenth century. The falls were laddered in 1890 by a crude masonry fishway that was destroyed by the first surge of high water and was not rebuilt until 1904, and then inadequately. The principal runs above Oregon City were spring chinook and steelhead, but a small number of fall chinook managed to negotiate the turbulent cascades, usually along the left bank, at a time of relatively low water.

In the nineteenth century settlement spread along the river. Portland replaced Oregon City as the chief metropolis and the capital was moved to Salem upriver. The river was the principal means of transportation and scores of communities dotted the banks, served by a system of riverboats. In 1899 a tiny powerhouse was built at the falls and electricity was transmitted thirteen miles to light up fifty-five street lamps in Portland. This was the first long-distance transmission of power in the United States.[1]

Death of a River

In 1905 a paper mill was constructed at Oregon City using electricity generated at the falls. At first it was a small operation, producing only sixty tons of newsprint and twenty tons of wrapping paper daily, but it was destined to expand greatly to meet the demands of a paper-devouring civilization. By 1950 a huge complex of mills straddled both sides of the river, their machines running night and day, drowning out the music of the falls with their cacophony, pouring enormous quantities of chips, sugars, and spent pulping liquors into the river, and emitting noxious smells into the air. Here were manufactured newsprint, coated stock for printing *Life* and *Time* and other magazines, paper toweling, toilet paper, wrapping paper, and even mulch paper for Hawaiian pineapple fields.

Pulp mills also arose at Newberg (originally a Quaker settlement where Herbert Hoover lived as a boy), Salem, Albany, Lebanon, and Springfield on the McKenzie River. The Springfield plant was part of a forest-products complex so that here the river was used not only for flushing the wastes of pulp and paper manufacture but also those of veneer, plywood, and particle board plants.

Pulp is made by cooking wood chips under intense pressure with chemicals and reducing them to tiny fibers. The liquors may be disposed of in various ways: (1) by discharging them into the rivers or lagoons without treatment, (2) by burning without recovering either heat or chemicals, (3) by burning with recovery of heat and chemicals, and (4) by conversion of wastes into marketable products. Until prodded in recent years by federal and state governments, the mills generally chose the least expensive method of disposing of their wastes: they were discharged into the nearest body of flowing water and in time washed out to sea. However, if there was inadequate flow to dilute the materials, sludge and slime were formed, thus impairing the stream's purity and forming layers of muck on its bed.

Older mills were usually the groundwood or calcium-based sulfite types; the newer ones were mainly kraft (sulfite) mills, which, in addition to the usual wastes, emitted sulfides and mercaptans into the air whose presence in only one part in a billion can be detected by the human nostril. When the wind is right a kraft mill makes its presence known for many miles around.

To the refuse discharged by pulp mills into the Willamette were added the wastes of fruit canneries around Salem, a metallurgical plant at Albany, and the untreated sewage of most riverside communities, including the metropolis of Portland. Thus the pristine river became grossly polluted. At times in summer when the natural flow dropped to a very low level there was not enough oxygen to support fish life; even crawfish crawled out of the water to get some air. No one knows how many anadromous fishes, trying to make their way upstream, suffocated and died each summer.

The so-called Refuse Act of 1899 required a permit from the Corps of Engineers for every waste discharge of a certain type into a navigable stream, but the Corps made no effort until 1970 to implement this law, either on the Willamette or any other waterway in the United States. As a result, many rivers died a slow death or, like the

Willamette, became moribund, dangerous to fish as well as to humans who came in contact with it.

Nor was the state of Oregon, like most states, interested in controlling water pollution, until in 1938 the voters by means of an initiative — not by act of the legislature — put on the ballot a measure that created the Oregon Sanitary Authority. But for several years the Authority was inert. It came to life in 1948 and adopted standards for water purity and waste disposal and began to nudge municipalities, including the recalcitrant city of Portland, to build sewage treatment plants and reduce the load of organic poisons flushed into the rivers. In Oregon the public was awakening slowly to the menace of water pollution as people died from disease acquired while swimming in the river.

However, progress was meager since the Sanitary Authority had only a small staff and budget; violations of its regulations were numerous and generally ignored. In 1952 the Willamette mills were asked to reduce their discharges of sulfite effluents and a few complied by storing them in reservoirs prior to barging them downstream to the Columbia with its greater flow, while others installed facilities to recover some of the strong pulping liquors. As the number of pulp mills increased, the pollution load, augmented by sewage and other discharges, made survival difficult for anadromous fishes.

Effects on the Fishery

The effects of pollution may be understood from a study conducted by the Washington Department of Fisheries. Its biologists submitted salmonids in the laboratory to the kind of polluted waters they face in streams and estuaries. Thus when young chinook were put in a one to twenty solution of synthesized kraft waste effluent in seawater, 70 percent died after twenty-three days and a large portion succumbed after only eighteen days. "The dead fish fed well and reacted normally until shortly before death, when they became sluggish and settled to the bottom."

In another experiment chinook averaging 176 millimeters (about seven inches) were exposed for seven days to relatively high concentrations of synthesized kraft mill effluent in a stagnant and aereated medium. The dissolved oxygen content was reduced and the pH increased in the higher concentrations. "Almost immediately after introduction of the dilutions, from 1 to 8.5 and 1 to 3.1, the fish were aware of the presence of the effluent. In the 1 to 3.1 dilution the fish respired slowly and irregularly and were very sluggish, as though partially anesthetized, before loss of equilibrium occurred within 30 minutes."[2] In less than twenty hours all were dead!

Pink salmon were as helpless as chinook in the presence of kraft mill poisons. When 190-day-old pinks, averaging thirty grams in weight, were exposed to condensate, the main waste component of kraft mill discharges, it took only six minutes to kill them off in a one to one dilution, twenty-five minutes in a one to three, six and a half hours in a one to seven, and twenty and a half hours in a one to fifteen dilution.

In addition to kraft mill wastes the biologists endeavored to determine the tolerance levels of young salmon to sulfite waste liquor and by-product wastes as well as to detergents, fungicides, germicides, insecticides, organic glues (used in plywood plants), and other by-products of chemical plants. They also studied the effects on young fish of inorganic pollutants like ammonia and various metal compounds, which are more toxic than most organic compounds. The biologists found unmistakable evidence, despite industry denials, that "pulp mill wastes are a major source of industrial pollution . . . Organic wastes contain carbon compounds and are generally oxidizable so that they reduce the oxygen content of the water. The volume of inorganic wastes discharged in this state [Washington] is smaller than that of organic wastes, but comparable amounts are generally more toxic to fish." They concluded that "the increasing discharge of industrial wastes into the waters . . . has become of special concern to agencies responsible for the protection and conservation of natural resources . . . Pollution has been a contributing factor to the decline of the salmon industry and has also affected the trout fishery."[3]

In January 1967 the Federal Water Pollution Control Administration (now the Environmental Protection Agency) issued a report on the Willamette River's condition that galvanized public attention and angered the pulp and paper industry. It said: "One of the most serious conditions of water occurs in the lower reaches . . . Marked pollution also exists in two major tributaries, the South Santiam River and Tualatin River [which obtains the sewage from a large suburban area around Portland]. In each case pollution's effects on water uses are severe and persistent, recurring with varying intensity each summer." Salmon can migrate in water that has dissolved oxygen concentration of at least five parts per million, but unfortunately in Portland harbor the level in summer often fell below three parts per million and sometimes to absolute zero!

"While no upstream migration of salmon presently occurs during the summer," said the report, "untimely low flows and consequent deficiency sometimes result in an 'oxygen block' that prevents the later stages of the spring migration upstream, or delays the fall migration." [4]

The FWPCA charged that over 90 percent of the pollution load came from pulp and paper mills and the remainder mainly from municipal sewage. The seven mills were dumping effluents equal to the sewage of communities with four million people, or twice as many as lived in all of Oregon.

"The state of Oregon," said the FWPCA, "has required a high level of waste treatment for municipalities of the basin; and for the most part they have responded to the state's demands . . . [but] the pulp and paper industry has largely resisted efforts to enforce effective pollution abatement procedures." [5] Some mills were discharging into the streams zinc hydrogen sulfite, which is used as a bleach and also as a "slimicide," as well as mercuric compounds, which poison human beings and animals and have a tremendous longevity, get into the beds of streams, and through the food chain are ingested by various fishes and birds in high concentrations.

A View of the River

In the spring of 1967 Herbert E. Simison, Regional Information Officer for the FWPCA, took a boat trip up the Willamette to see its condition. He reported:

> Moving upstream into the Portland harbor area, the river banks are lined with industrial establishments. No outfalls are visible. But a February report by the Oregon State Sanitary Authority listed 20 industries on the Willamette in the Portland reach with wastes described as grain wash water, oily water, acetylene lime wastes, caustic wastes, heavy oil and asphalt, salt waste in cooling water, carbide wastes, and glue wastes . . . A look straight down into the water showed it to be inky black and bubbles were observed rising to the surface. The bed of the river was paved with decomposing sludge which sucked the oxygen from the water . . . Several miles upstream there were many houseboats, all of them dumping untreated sewage and other liquid wastes into the river. In the vicinity of Lake Oswego, an area of suburban homes, the river was not black. But under the surface large

globs of stringy bacterial slime were everywhere in the water. This slime grows in wild profusion because it can feed on the nutrients coming from pulp mill discharges, principally the wood sugars. The situation was so bad that one fisherman, in a letter to the editor, wrote that the river was "the slimiest I've seen it in 45 years. I've never seen it so polluted as last Friday, and I've been fishing since 1920. We couldn't troll 50 feet without stopping to clean our lines." In this same reach of the river huge rafts of putrid sludge were always seen in late summer when the river was lowest. The river bottom is covered with a thick layer of sludge. As summer river temperatures rise, the gases beneath the sludge cause mats of decaying sludge to rise as rafts up to six feet long and float down the river until they disintegrate and drop to the river bed again.

All of this — the sludge, the wood sugars, the toxic sulfite waste liquors — damaging to the fish but not visible in the water — and the resulting low dissolved oxygen levels, came mainly from the mills on the Willamette River.

In the Columbia the combined rafts of muck from the Willamette River and paper mills at Camas, Washington, above Portland and St. Helens and Longview below Portland at times had palpable effects on the fish. Fingerlings were forced to rise to the surface for air and many were killed by seagulls, while others died from lack of oxygen. Gill netters found their nets shrouded with slime. "The normal life span of nylon gill nets in reasonably unpolluted water should be three to five years," said Kenneth Backman, spokesman for the Columbia River gill netters, "but now the working life of such nets is only a year, and it costs $1500 to replace each one." This factor alone drove some fishermen out of business.

In the summer of 1967 the governor's Willamette Greenway Committee made a trip downstream from the river's confluence with the McKenzie. They found that the upper Willamette was still mainly a wild river, lovely and unspoiled. Its banks were lined with slender, drooping willows and clusters of cottonwood and maple. Blue and white lupines added dashes of color to the landscape. They did not see a house or human being for the first fifteen miles of the journey. Hawks, ospreys, and mergansers flew overhead; buzzards calmly watched from the banks or the gravel bars as the flotilla passed; great blue herons, standing in the marshes, took flight as they approached. An occasional angler, in the water up to his thighs, waved to them.

Except for the marks of the gravel diggers, banks torn up, and piles of rubble that clogged the channel, the upper stretches were untrammeled much as in the days when the Hudson's Bay Company men roamed its banks looking for beaver.

The first bridge was encountered eighteen miles below the McKenzie and the first tributary, Long Tom River, at thirty-eight miles. Cliff swallows built their nests under the bridges and were diving merrily over the water. Few riverside communities could be seen in the long stretch from Eugene to Corvallis, for many of those that had arisen in the nineteeth century ceased to exist when river transportation ended.

At Corvallis, a university town, came the first visible sign of water pollution: a sewer disgorging foul wastes. Here riversides were used to dump abandoned automobiles and other junk; a factory poured its muck into the water despite a Corvallis ordinance forbidding the practice. No salmon could be seen, but the side channels as well as the main stream were populated with largemouth bass, crappie, catfish, and bluegill. Remains of beaver dams were observed. Below Corvallis the water quality and rate of flow deteriorated. In places the river was so low that the Greenway Committee was almost stranded, even though arrangements had been made with the Corps of Engineers to release extra water from its storage reservoirs on the upper tributaries. It did not seem possible that anadromous fishes could live in the deoxygenated river.

Signs of human activity increased as the flotilla moved downstream: houses and barns, hay drying in the sun, an occasional village, a mill sucking its water supply from the river and putting back discolored sickly wastes. Occasionally a log raft passed, or a pleasure boat.

Between Salem, the state capital, and the purlieus of Portland, the river traffic increased. Towns became more frequent as did evidence of pollution: fishes with bellies up, dead pigs, slime rafts, white foam, open sewers. Below Willamette Falls the river, in the words of a spokesman for the Izaak Walton League, was "a stinking, slimy mess, a menace to public health and a biological cesspool."

Rehabilitation of the River

In 1965 Congress passed the Clean Water Act, which was designed to prevent the further deterioration and degradation of the nation's rivers and lakes by requiring the states to formulate water quality standards and enforce them. Oregon was one of the first to develop standards satisfactory to the federal government. This event coincided with the passage of legislation requiring waste discharge permits from the state by industries using public waters. At the same time the State Sanitary Authority (now the Department of Environmental Quality) adopted a much tougher attitude toward polluters, private and public. Cleanup of the Willamette, the most abused large waterway in Oregon, was therefore accelerated. By 1969 all municipalities in the lower river basin were operating both primary and secondary sewage treatment plants that remove up to 90 percent of the organic matter and were disinfecting effluents, although this does not mean that the waters are safe for what is called "contact sports." In the spring of 1971 the federal Environmental Quality Commission issued a national report that listed the Willamette in Portland harbor as still a contaminated stream. A few persons who tried to swim in waters of Portland Harbor in recent years caught meningitis and died.

By 1968 primary treatment — removal of settleable solids — was in effect at all Willamette pulp and paper mills, and by 1970 all but two had chemical recovery systems in operation, and these were given two years to eliminate their sulfite wastes. One sulfite mill, at West Linn, was closed in 1969, but a new one appeared at Halsey, reputed to be the *dernier cri* in effluent control. Four mills still did not provide secondary treatment for their wastes and they too had two years to meet this requirement. According to the Northwest Pulp and Paper Association, investment in water pollution controls by the pulp and paper industry on the Willamette totaled about $25 million at the end of 1970.

All this work has had beneficial effects on the fishery, especially the steelhead runs above Willamette Falls. Dissolved oxygen levels no longer drop in summer to the critical lows, partly because water is released from upstream storage reservoirs. The annual plague of offensive sludge rafts has ceased to appear in the outskirts of Portland. Moreover, in 1970 the rate of bottom sludge decay at long last exceeded the accumulation rate. But there was still excessive bacterial slime and only the promised diminution of sulfite liquor discharges by 1972 could "bring continued inhibition of slime growth," said the federal Environmental Protection Agency.[6] No progress has been made, however, in keeping offensive pulp mill odors out of the air.

Anticipating the cleanup, the Oregon Fish Commission in the early 1960s began to breed coho and chinook for release in the river and contracted to have new fishways built at the falls so that salmon and steelhead could more easily negotiate these obstacles and reach their upstream spawning grounds. State and federal agencies made massive plantings of fall chinook, coho, and steelhead in the watershed. By 1968 partial rehabilitation of the river was noticeable as more salmon returned. That summer the lowest monthly average of dissolved oxygen had risen to 5.2 parts per million for the first time in many years — this is the lowest DO level salmon can tolerate. As a result, over 4000 fall chinook were counted at the falls. In 1969 and 1970 the DO count stayed above 5 ppm, and in 1970 18,000 adult coho salmon, 8000 fall chinook, and 26,000 steelhead were counted at the partially completed ladder at the falls. In 1972 18,000 fall chinook passed the falls as the ladder was finally completed and DO levels stayed well above the danger zone. Hatchery releases accounted for much of the success of the rehabilitation program.

Downstream Fish Migration Problems

While the upstream migration problem seemed to be on its way to solution in the Willamette, there remained serious difficulties in getting the juvenile fish past the huge industrial complex and maelstrom at the falls. Young salmon and steelhead are often sucked into the hydroturbine intakes at the mills and under certain water conditions are decimated or stunned so that when they come out into the open the gulls make Lucullan feasts of them. John McKean, Director of the Oregon Game Commission, declared: "It is believed that the turbine mortality is a major factor in keeping salmon and steelhead runs in the Willamette system from reaching full potential."

In October 1970 the Oregon Game and Fish Commissions approved a plan to protect downstream migrants as the paper company on the east side of the river agreed to shut down its turbines during the spring months, March to June, when the fingerlings head for the sea, and to install acceptable fish screens at the water intakes. The company was advised that further modifications or changes might be required in the future to safeguard the increasing number of fall and winter migrating fish.

The paper mill and public utility that operate small power plants on the west side of the river were not as agreeable about shutting down their turbines. They continued to operate on a business as usual basis until District Attorney Roger Rook of Clackamas County on September 30, 1971, filed a court action against the two firms claiming $28.5 million compensation to the people of the state for the loss of more than 5 million fish. This action astounded the companies as well as the nonmilitant state agencies. Governor Tom McCall stepped into the breach to negotiate a settlement. Although the district attorney's suit was thrown out of court, it had the desired effect. Early in November the governor announced that seventeen out of twenty-nine of the fish-killing turbines would be shut down for nine months each year and the state agencies were endeavoring to work out a scheme to mitigate the effects of the remaining twelve turbines. The power company would be allowed to operate those blades in its generating plant that had enough flexibility to permit the smolts to pass with minimum losses while studying the feasibility of a new battery of modern turbines at another location. Moreover the two companies, now in a benign mood, agreed to contribute $165,000 or 25 percent of the state's share of a new salmon hatchery to be built on the McKenzie River system to compensate for fish losses.

To the thousands of anglers who congregate in their small boats at the foot of the falls or further downstream trying to catch a few salmon, District Attorney Rook's stratagem was the outstanding event of the year. Too long had they watched the fish carcasses float past them down the river and the gulls merrily scoop up smolts in the cul-de-sac around the paper mills. Now the salmon would have safer and easier passage on their journey to the sea, although not all the downstream migration problems had been solved, and would return to their spawning streams in increasing numbers.

Future Outlook

As the outlook brightens for cleaner water and better flows, more adequate fishways and fewer lethal turbine blades, the restocking program moves ahead full steam to exploit the potential of the Willamette watershed for producing salmonids. The Oregon Fish and Game Commissions declared in 1970 that "the opportunity exists at this time to provide the sport and commercial fisheries of the Pacific coast with an additional harvest of 800,000 naturally-produced chinook and coho salmon and summer and winter steelhead." In September 1972 the Oregon Fish Commission announced that "the Willamette system's full development could result in an annual Pacific Coast sports and commercial harvest of 640,000 fall chinook [alone] and a Willamette Falls escapement of 105,000." [7]

The areas staked out for fish breeding extend over most of the valley, including many small as well as larger streams. In addition to the restocking program, improvements are planned to open up additional spawning and nursery areas. Tributaries originating at low altitudes are occasionally subject to extremely low summer and fall flows; here more dams and storage reservoirs, appropriately placed and operated, will be beneficial to the fishery as well as in curtailing floods. But it is of the utmost importance that the water used by migrating fish be maintained as far as possible in relative purity, especially in the lower valley where about two thirds of Oregon's population dwells and where urban and suburban sprawl and freeways are swallowing up much farmland and adding to the problem of maintaining high water standards for both human and fish life. While the Willamette is a much cleaner river than it was a few decades ago, and much less hostile to anadromous fishes, it is far from the purity of the nineteenth century, at least in the lower reaches. Then it was everywhere a pellucid, bucolic stream, flanked by green fields and majestic mountains, reminiscent of lovely Welsh rivers like the Wye. Nevertheless, the Willamette represents a major example of success in cleaning up an important river and rehabilitating and expanding its stock of salmonids.

XVIII ∽

Oregon's Coastal Streams

As you drive along the Oregon coast the landscape unfolds in a kind of misty grandeur; bold mountain spurs and rugged headlands stand guard between the long, curving sandy beaches. There are numerous little coves and bays piled high with driftwood. Rocks stand out to sea and the waves beat relentlessly against them; rivers, each forded by a cantilever steel bridge, flow out of the mountains. Slender white lighthouses with red roofs are spaced at intervals of twenty-five miles or so, and their rotating beacons illuminate the beaches.

In Oregon the Coast Range is an irregular series of maturely dissected hills and ridges, once densely covered with conifers and now considerably denuded by clear cutting. The main range extends somewhat brokenly across the state from the Rogue River Range to the Columbia. The coastal mountains are relatively low, from 2000 to 4300 feet, cut by many rivers that glide westward through the shoestring valleys and narrow passes to the Pacific. The rivers bear names associated with Indian bands who lived along their banks: Rogue, Coquille, Coos, Umpqua, Siuslaw, Alsea, Yaquina, Siletz, Nestucca, and Nehalem. Each is fed by rills, brooks, and creeks that drain the steep hillsides.

This is a region of heavy rainfall; mist often hides the promontories and fog rolls in from Cathay nearly every afternoon. The climate is mild, but the rainfall averages about 72 inches annually and in some localities well over 100 inches. This is a green and fertile land, producing timber on a luxurious scale, interspersed with meadows that cows graze almost the year round. Only in summer does the sun shine abundantly.

Fish and shellfish were plentiful in the coastal streams in aboriginal times: chinook, silvers (coho), chum salmon, and steelhead trout surged up the rivers. Archeologists have found numerous kitchen middens containing shell heaps, bone and stone fragments, and miscellaneous refuse indicating the existence of prehistoric settlements along the rivers from the Columbia in the north to the Klamath in the south, often at successive levels or strata.

Aborigines

When the first white men came, the Clatsops, a branch of the Chinook tribe, lived along the Columbia and on the coast as far south as Tillamook Head; the Klaskanine, an Athabascan people, occupied the Nehalem River area; further south dwelt other Athabascan-speaking people, the Coquilles, Chetcos, Siuslaw, and Umpquas. Members of the Salishan group occupied Yaquina Bay and Alsea Bay; on Coos Bay and the lower Coquille River there were three tribes of the small Kusan family.

The river and coastal Indians were skilled fishermen and woodcarvers, who made war canoes that could carry up to sixty men out to sea, excellent bows and arrows, and household utensils of cedar root fiber or tough grasses. They depended heavily on shellfish and fish for food and venerated the Salmon Spirit. In the later nineteenth century the Indians were removed from their native lands and herded into the Siletz and Grand Ronde Reservations on the coast; sometimes they did not accept this fate without a bloody war and massacres. A chief of the Rogue River Indians expressed the feelings of all the tribes during peace negotiations that ended the terrible wars of the 1850s:

> This is my country; I was in it when these trees were very little higher than my head. My heart is sick fighting the whites, but I want to live in my own country. I will, if the whites are willing, go back to the Deer Creek country and live as I used to among the whites; they can visit my camp and I will visit theirs; but I will not lay down my arms and go to the reserve. I will fight.[1]

Assault on the Fishery

After the Indians had been expelled from their lands the whites took over. One of the first rivers to be exploited for its fisheries was the Rogue, where gold had been discovered, at Jacksonville, in 1851, and where the salmon and steelhead ran in huge numbers. The river rises in the Cascade Range northwest of Crater Lake and flows through the Klamath Mountains in a northwest-west course to the ocean at Gold Beach, a distance of about 200 miles.

In 1876 R. D. Hume, who with his brothers had pioneered salmon canning on the Sacramento and Columbia Rivers, came to the Rogue looking for a new fishery to exploit. Seeing that the river was amply stocked with spring and fall chinook, he purchased an existing saltery and the lumber mill that went with it and began to buy land on both banks. Eventually he owned a stretch of twelve miles from the mouth of the river upstream, thus acquiring a virtual monopoly on the fishery. Besides a stationary trap, he used set nets in the spring and a 750-foot seine in the fall to harvest the salmon.

In 1877 Hume built a small hatchery that was later enlarged and improved. He was in fact the first private individual to undertake artificial propagation of salmon on the Pacific coast. From 1880 to 1900 he packed an average of 16,000 cases annually. He also operated a saltery that packed over 500 barrels yearly, each weighing 200 pounds. Hume was probably the first Oregon canner to break into the English market. At the turn of the century the Liverpool firm of Pelling and Stanley was importing 250,000 cans of Oregon salmon yearly, mainly from Hume.

Hume dabbled in mining, saw milling, and other ventures and by the end of the century, when he was elected to the state legislature, was probably a millionaire. Called the "Salmon King of Oregon," he was arrogant, combative, and litigious, defying the law and the courts when they interfered with his strong moneymaking proclivities. He must be credited, however, with some foresight, because he realized that the Rogue River could not indefinitely support his intensive kind of fishing. He was convinced that restocking the river with fish from his hatchery was partly responsible for his large packs (a doubtful assumption) and maintained that the catches fell off when no hatchery work was done. In 1893 he published a treatise on artificial propagation that described his methods, rather crude by modern standards. This, however, was a pioneer effort.

Hume castigated the packers for their failure to support salmon culture and fishery conservation (which of course he did not practice). He predicted that "unless such steps are taken, in less than ten years the packing of salmon on the Columbia River will have become impossible as a business proposition." [2] His forecast was only off by a few decades, for in the 1950s the salmon canning business ended on the Oregon coast and had not long to go on the Columbia.

In general, salmon stocks on the coastal streams were as hard-fished as on the Columbia, there being little or no restraint imposed

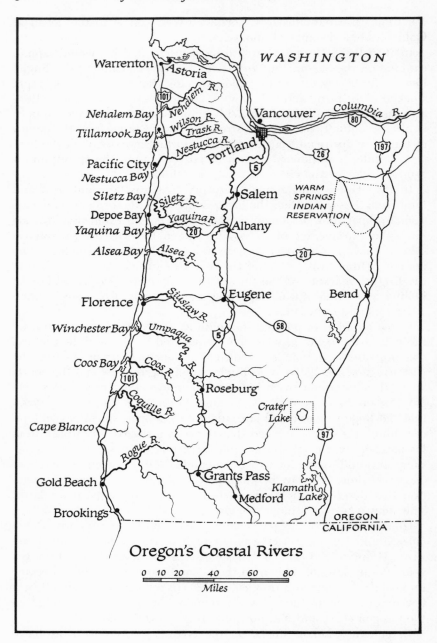

Oregon's Coastal Rivers

0   10   20   40   60   80

Miles

by the state. The 1889 report of the Board of Fish Commissioners listed seventeen rivers that supported extensive commercial fisheries. The Nehalem had one cannery; the Tillamook Bay area, where three mountain streams debouched, had three that packed 37,000 cases of forty-eight one-pound cans in 1887. South of Tillamook is the Nestucca, a slender but beautiful river that flows past lush meadows on its way to the ocean; in the 1880s it supported a cannery that processed about 6000 cases annually.

Virtually everywhere the fishermen plied their nets without restraint. The Yaquina River, said the Board of Fish Commissioners, "is so narrow that nets and traps can be extended nearly, and in some instances, entirely across the stream, thus virtually preventing all the salmon from reaching their spawning grounds." About 60,000 fish were taken each year out of this small river.

South of the Yaquina flows the Alsea, which was fished from its falls to within two miles of the sea, a distance of twelve miles. The catch in 1887 was about 50,000 salmon, but, the board noted, in the previous three years fishing had been curtailed, presumably because the runs had fallen off. The Siuslaw, emptying into the sea at Florence, had three canneries, but only one was in operation in 1888; here, as on other coastal streams, "the fish are caught with gillnets and seines, the most of which are handled by residents living along its banks, thus giving employment for a few months at fair wages."[3]

South of the Siuslaw flows the Umpqua, a major river, with its head in Diamond Lake under the lee of Mount Thielsen. The north fork plunges down to Lemolo Lake, the impoundment of Lemolo Falls, then picks up several tributaries until it is joined by the south fork above Calapooya Creek. The south fork also rises in the Cascade Mountains, not far from Diamond Lake, and winds through forested valleys to what is now Roseburg and its confluence with the north fork. Then the river snakes its way through the coastal mountains, past Scottsburg, and rushes over the tidal waters coming in from the ocean to Reedsport and Winchester Bay. There were two canneries on the Umpqua in the 1890s and annual catches of up to 600,000 pounds of silvers and chinook were recorded.

The Coos River empties into Coos Bay with its numerous arms and sloughs, which for the most part are short and narrow, permitting nets to be laid across the entire width of the channels. The board's 1889 report recommended that fishing be prohibited in all these little streams where salmon spawned.

Some conception of the magnitude of the coastal fishery was given by the report of the United States Commissioner for Fish and Fisheries for the year ending June 30, 1896. A total of 5,730,000 pounds of salmon was harvested in nine watersheds, of which the Rogue, Tillamook, and Siuslaw Rivers provided almost half, as follows:

Nehalem	483,000	pounds
Tillamook	932,000	"
Yaquina	152,000	"
Alsea	414,000	"
Siuslaw	836,000	"
Umpqua	602,000	"
Coos River and Bay	665,000	"
Coquille	640,000	"
Rogue	1,006,000	"
Total	5,730,000	pounds

The coastal fishery employed 1200 persons and the pack totaled 87,360 cases in 1895–1896.

Closure of the Rivers

It was clear that the streams could not long tolerate such heavy exploitation. Consequently the state gradually established limits beyond which the nets could not go; fishing seasons were shortened, and gear restrictions were imposed. But these measures came too late to arrest the tide of depletion. Spring chinook practically disappeared, while fall chinook catches on the coast dropped from 2,-000,000 to 3,000,000 pounds per year in 1923–1927 to 500,000 pounds in the late 1940s. Silvers also decreased. The number of canneries dwindled and their output, which reached a peak of 197,000 cases in 1906, and lesser peaks in 1910 (104,000 cases), 1911 (154,000 cases), and 1914 (116,000 cases), fell rapidly after World War I. It was clear that drastic steps were necessary to prevent depopulation of the rivers. Accordingly Oregon banned commercial fishing on the Nestucca after the 1926 season, on the Rogue after 1934, and on the Coos, Salmon, and Umpqua Rivers after 1946. Netting of steelhead trout, a favorite of fly fishermen, was curtailed on many coastal streams after 1928 and virtually abolished after 1946 as the result of pressure by sportsmen. The last cannery on the Oregon coast south of the Columbia closed down around 1953. In 1956 commercial fishing for salmonids was banned on all coastal rivers except for chum fishing in Tillamook Bay.

John T. Gharrett and John I. Hodges, biologists of the Oregon Fish Commission who published the results of their extensive survey of the coastal streams in 1950, pinpointed the causes of the fisheries' collapse as (1) overfishing, (2) careless logging, especially stripping the forest cover in the mountains, which ruined watersheds during the era of cut-out-and-get-out lumbering, (3) forest fires that resulted in siltation of streams, such as the Tillamook fire of 1933, which was started by a careless logger on a dry summer day and destroyed 300,000 acres of prime virgin timber, one of the greatest forest disasters in American history, (4) sluicing logs down the rivers, which blocked fish runs, (5) power and irrigation dams without fish ladders, and (6) dredging of stream bottoms and banks that removed gravel needed for spawning (efforts by conservationists to have this activity stopped by state law were blocked by the state Department of Geology and Mineral Industries).

Gharrett and Hodges concluded that "the coastal rivers and their salmon populations are not beyond redemption, and that under proper management can be made to yield annually several times their present production." [4]

Little evidence remains of the once flourishing packing industry on the coast. At Reedsport, Kernville, and other places one may see the rotting timbers of long-abandoned canneries. Old-timers reminisce about the days when netsmen worked the streams in spring and summer and into the mellow days of autumn, when cannery lines manned by black-robed Chinese clicked incessantly, and when steamers came up to the docks (now mostly vanished) to take on board cases of salmon and unloaded them at Portland or San Francisco, where they were sold in local markets or put on freight cars for shipment east or ships destined for the Atlantic Ocean.

After commercial fishing was outlawed in the rivers fishermen turned to trolling off the coast — the only form of commercial fishing that is legal off the Oregon and Washington coasts. The ocean troll fishery for chinook and silvers expanded rapidly after 1956 (chum and steelhead are rarely caught in the sea).

Meanwhile the watersheds were put under the joint management of the Oregon Fish and Oregon Game Commissions, which began to make extensive surveys of available spawning and rearing areas and to institute conservation programs, including not only removal of logjams and other impedimenta but installation of fish ladders and screens where necessary and large plantings of hatchery stocks.

Sportsmen's Rivers

The coastal rivers and hatcheries now produce fish for both the sportsmen and commercial trollers and are managed with this dual purpose in mind. In 1970, for example, the Oregon Game Commission released about 2,000,000 steelhead smolts in some twenty rivers and 2,500,000 chinook smolts in seven watersheds. Such massive plantings and other conservation measures have helped to build back the stocks of some rivers, but others show relatively little improvement. The annual spawning survey of the Oregon Fish Commission in 1969 indicated that "stocks of spring chinook and chum salmon remain at critically low levels. At present they represent only 33 and 36 percent of their long-term averages, respectively." Fall chinook numbers were the lowest since 1953–1956, about 66 percent of their long-term average, and coho counts were next to the lowest, only 44 percent of the long-term average.[5] While there is no close correlation of these findings with the number of fish caught, they suggest that recovery of the stocks has been generally slow. Without massive plantings of hatchery fish most of the rivers would have probably become relative deserts so far as salmonids are concerned.

The booming sport fishery on the Oregon coast now creates more wealth than the commercial netters ever brought to the region. On any summer morning in such towns as Warrenton, Depoe Bay, or Newport there is a stir and bustle soon after the sun rises. The slippery docks are crowded with charter boats and private cruisers. The screech of sea gulls mingles with the rattle of tackle boxes, the sound of motors, and the buzzing of excited fishermen.

Innumerable little boats are out on the ocean every day unless there is a storm, from the Columbia River to Winchester Bay and farther south; fishermen are dangling their lines from the afterdecks, keenly eyeing the water, the bows rising and falling with the swells. Over their radios skippers are talking to each other, telling where the fish are being caught, and where they are not. Thousands of people use the charter boats every summer, and thousands more take their own craft into the churning sea except on days when the Coast Guard hoists storm warning flags. Coho and chinook are the prime catches.

Stream fishing is for steelhead and to a lesser extent chinook and coho, which climb the long rivers, of which the Umpqua and Rogue are most famous. The Umpqua has been restored to something like its former glory since the nets were removed. Counts of chinook at Winchester dam jumped from an average of 2745 in the years 1946–

1950 to 11,585 in 1966–1969 and summer steelhead from 3150 to almost 8000. The 1969 runs of chinook and summer steelhead were the highest on record, and the hatcheries contributed as much as one out of three fish. That year anglers took 15,000 steelhead and 21,600 chinook out of the Umpqua.

The Rogue is a fast, mad river in its lower stretches, the kind that attracts keen anglers. It is sometimes called "Zane Grey's River," for this dentist who wrote popular Western fiction was a fanatic fisherman and made the river famous in his stories and angling feats. His cabin still stands at Winkle Bar; he was one of the first to run the turbulent river from Grants Pass to the sea. Grey discovered the Rogue in 1920 and fished there every summer until his allegiance shifted to the neighboring Umpqua.

The Rogue has not fully recovered from the abusive fishing of Hume's day, from denudation of the coastal mountains, and from the shortage of water and impediments of irrigation dams in the upper reaches. The Corps of Engineers in its empire-building mania has fastened on the upper Rogue and is blockading the main stem at Lost Creek and impounding the tributary Elk Creek. It also plans to dam the Applegate River, a bucolic tributary of the Rogue. These projects, which will cost the American taxpayer $200 million, are of doubtful value, though sold to the Congress mainly as flood control, recreation, and fishery enhancement undertakings. They have been promoted primarily by land speculators and politicians eager for "pork barrel" benefits. The new hatchery that was used to gain approval of the dams from such organizations as the Izaak Walton League, National Wildlife Federation, and anglers generally will produce salmon to restock the river. Thus another whitewater river will be lost to posterity.

The Estuary Problem

A severe handicap in preservation of fisheries is defilement of the estuaries. The Oregon coast has fourteen bays totaling 41,000 acres, all inhabited by anadromous fishes. South of the Columbia the largest is Coos Bay, while the smallest is the Salmon River estuary.

We are just beginning to appreciate the crucial value of estuaries to marine life. "They are a remarkable system of the containment and efficient utilization of organic matter, water, minerals, and sunlight," says Rollie Rousseau, Oregon Game Commission biologist. "The salt water wedge pushed along the estuary bottom by the incoming tide brings in nutrients from the ocean. Currents and tides circulate and recirculate fresh in salt water, thus distributing these rich foods throughout the sloughs, inlets, and lagoons.

"The estuary itself is also a producer of nutrients. Microscopic plants flourish in the water. Salt marsh vegetation nourished in the rich waters brought from the ocean at flood tide produces enormous yields of organic matter. In addition, mud flats and shore areas alternately covered and exposed as the tides change produce a variety of small animal life such as worms, snails, and insects upon which larger organisms feed. In turn these organisms are the foundation for the food chain that is so vital to fish and wildlife production." [6]

Some Oregon estuaries have been grossly abused, dredged, or employed as dumping grounds and sewers. They are at the mercy of real estate promoters and the Corps of Engineers, which is charged with the supervision of navigable waters, and their ecological values have sometimes been cruelly ignored. For example, the builder of a miniature Disneyland on the lovely Salmon River estuary justified his action by saying he was making economic use of wasteland!

In Oregon poor logging practices on steep slopes and mining and road construction in upstream areas induce soil erosion that results in heavy silt flows into estuarine channels and lagoons. Periodic dredging and channel widening by the Corps of Engineers produces soil deposition destructive to shellfish. Coos Bay is perhaps the worst example. Here the sloughs are lined with log booms and filled with sawmill trash deposited by firms that have twenty-year permits from the state for their activities. A paper mill that refuses to install pollution-control equipment and sends its waste out to sea further despoils this estuary. Davis Slough no longer supports any game fish and wildlife is becoming scarce. Its surface is impassable and its bottom is covered with debris.

Isthmus Slough in Coos Bay is also virtually a dead-water hole. "The fish are gone," reported Don Holm in the Portland *Oregonian* (May 2, 1971). "The bottom is covered with layers of toxic bark residues, oozy mud in which no life exists. The banks where we once [fished] . . . for chinook are cluttered with logging junk and car bodies and overgrown with brambles. Low tide reveals mud flats cluttered with garbage and dead dogs."

"Isthmus Slough is not completely hopeless," says Dr. Paul Rudy, marine biologist with Oregon State University. "It will take a long convalescence, but I think it will recover eventually — if we start treatment now."

Some of Oregon's estuaries are still relatively unspoiled, but pressure to develop them is unabated, and the compliant Corps of Engineers usually assists the land developers. Creation by Congress of the Oregon Dunes Recreational Area, which includes Winchester Bay, will save the Umpqua's estuary. George Reed, Executive Director of the Oregon Wildlife Federation, declares, "Oregon's coastal rivers are assuming greater importance as producers of salmon, steelhead and other recreational resources." In 1970, 500,000 persons in the state purchased regular angling licenses, and 350,000 bought special salmon-steelhead permits in addition. "Every mile of river," says Reed, "is extremely important from here on for the continuity of this recreation."

XIX ⁓

Breakthrough in Salmon Culture

THE ARTIFICIAL PROPAGATION of salmon may be traced to a German Lieutenant Jacobi, who was the first to obtain positive results from attempts to fecundate salmonid eggs. In 1763 he published an article in a Hanoverian scientific journal in which he announced the successful propagation of fry in a wooden box filled with gravel. He sent a memorandum of his work to the great French naturalist Georges Louis Buffon, who had it translated in 1783. Thus began the history of salmonid culture.

Early Hatcheries

The first salmon hatchery in England was built at Troutdale in Cumberland in 1868 and the first in the United States at Orland, Maine, in 1871. In 1872 the U.S. Fish Commission received a $15,000 appropriation from Congress for the propagation of food fishes. It was decided to use this money to build a salmon hatchery in California to produce fish for stocking the rapidly declining eastern streams. Livingston Stone, a retired Unitarian minister who had recently taken up trout culture, was selected to carry out the assignment. He and two companions found their way to the remote McCloud River in the hills of northern California and built a rudimentary hatchery. At that time it was not generally known that the Atlantic and Pacific salmon are separate species with radically different life cycles.

In the beginning the McCloud hatchery was merely an egg-gathering station. During the first season 50,000 eggs were taken, of which 30,000 survived to the eyed stage. "These were packed in sphagnum moss and shipped east. In March of the following year, 1873, a few hundred fingerlings were released in the Susquehanna River (which never had salmon). Thus began the unsuccessful attempt to transplant the Pacific salmon to the Atlantic." [1]

Despite the lack of success the belief that Pacific salmon could be bred with ease in hatcheries spread. In 1887 Stone built the first hatchery in the Columbia River watershed on the Clackamas River in Oregon. The number of hatcheries thereafter increased steadily under the illusion that little more was needed to restore dwindling streams than to stock them with artificially bred salmon. In 1900 the state of Washington had fifteen stations and Oregon as many, producing mainly chinook, while sockeye hatcheries were operating in British Columbia. The station at Ontario, Oregon, had a 15 million egg capacity and the central hatchery at Bonneville four times as much. It was assumed that one adult fish could be produced from nearly every egg that hatched.

This assumption failed to materialize because there was little knowledge of the biology, diseases, diet, feeding, and rearing habits of young salmon, and almost nothing was known about their life in the ocean. "Artificial propagation," said Tom Barnaby of the U.S. Fish and Wildlife Service, "was in the trial and error stage, with ample evidence that many of the trials were errors." [2]

Early hatcheries were characterized by large egg takes, early releases of the juvenile fish, and indiscriminate transplantations. Nothing was known about genetics or races of salmon. It was therefore not astonishing that relatively few of the fish reached adulthood and returned to the hatcheries. They were victims of improper diets and feeding techniques, inadequate disease control, and general ignorance of release requirements.

After the turn of the century the practice of rearing the fish for varying periods in outdoor ponds replaced releasing them as fry. This change was the result of the discovery that larger fish had a better chance of survival. But the art was still rudimentary, and few positive results could be shown in terms of contribution to the runs.

Two decades ago if you had visited a salmon hatchery like the one at Bonneville, built in the early part of the century, you would have seen a kind of butcher shop attached to the establishment. The diet fed the fish consisted largely of cannery and packing-house waste such as fillet scrap, rockfish carcasses, salmon and tuna viscera, heads, eyes, and tails of fish, along with condemned pork and beef, horse products, tripe, and hearts. "This kind of diet we now know was ineffective," says Ernest Jeffries, Director of Hatcheries for the Oregon Fish Commission. "It was often unbalanced; much of the feed leached into the water and was lost; and decomposed food particles actually robbed the little fishes in the ponds of oxygen. Also, salmon scrap in the diet was a source of virulent diseases in hatched-out fish." [3]

The Breakthrough

In the late 1950s artificial propagation entered a new and more successful phase. Discoveries in the field of fish physiology, nutrition, and above all pathology contributed to a breakthrough. Behind this achievement was intensive research, much of it financed by federal funds as compensation for fish losses at Columbia River dams; the work was done by the Fish and Wildlife Service, Oregon Fish Commission, Oregon State University, and other institutions.

Salmon culture depends to a large extent on two factors: clean water at the right temperature and proper diet. Studies of fish diet at the Willard Laboratory in Washington, operated by the Bureau of Sport Fisheries and Wildlife, showed that salmon have a rudimentary pancreas and low production of insulin. They cannot be fed food high in carbohydrates and thus require extensive amounts of protein. As more hatcheries were built the food requirements not only increased the cost of operations but at times an adequate supply was hard to obtain. Studies were therefore concentrated on developing cheaper and better foods than the traditional horsemeat and beef scraps. Out of this search came the Oregon moist pellet.

The standard formula for the pellet is now 10 percent tuna viscera, 30 percent turbot, dogfish, and pasteurized salmon viscera, and 60 percent meal and vitamins. The ingredients comprise a wet fish mix, a meal, and a vitamin package made into moist pellets that are bagged and frozen. The Oregon Fish Commission stopped using raw fish products in 1958 and in 1959 went completely on a pellet diet now universally used in salmon and steelhead hatcheries around the world. Pellets produce healthy specimens that are able to survive quite well in the ocean. Tuberculosis and other diseases that used to decimate entire populations are now rare, although accidents occur, as in a hatchery in Oregon that lost its entire stock one year when the water was supersaturated with nitrogen gas because of a faulty intake from a storage reservoir.

A major plant producing the pellet is at Hammond, on the Oregon coast, near Astoria. Production is now at the rate of 8 million pounds annually, and pellets are sold to hatcheries throughout North America and Europe.

Improvements in propagation techniques have been rapid since 1960. At the Salmon-Cultural Laboratory of the Bureau of Sport Fisheries and Wildlife on Abernathy Creek near Longview, Washington, Roger E. Burrows experimented with controlled environments to breed young salmon. He has developed a reconditioning system that makes possible at least a 90 percent reduction in the quantity of water needed for rearing the fish. "With this reduced water requirement the control of water temperature and water quality and the sterilization of the supplemental water supply to eliminate fish diseases are practicable. With this type of system, efficient salmon culture is possible at any desirable location along the migration route of the fish to be propagated." [4]

Burrows found that reconditioning and temperature control of the water system speeds up the growth of fingerlings, and since the larger fish have much better chances of survival in the ocean, the return of adults to the hatchery is increased. This also means that more fish produced under this regimen are available to the fishermen.

Cycle of Reproduction

The cycle starts when the fish return to the hatchery or to the stream where they were released. It seems that memory of natal waters is associated with the place from which the smolts departed. If they are permitted to go to sea directly from the hatchery, as is often the case, they will return to that very spot. Thus, in the early fall one may see the husky salmon crowd the gates of the hatchery at the Little White Salmon River on the Washington side of the Columbia. As the adult fish come up they are directed by means of racks at the foot of a ladder to a large pond. Here the fish mill about furiously until they are hand-spawned. The ripe female is anesthetized, an incision is made into her abdomen, and her eggs are dropped into a bucket and fertilized with the milt drawn from the male. The average female chinook carries about 5000 eggs. Unripe females whose eggs are "green" are kept in the pond until ripeness is indicated. Then she too is emptied of her salmon-pink eggs.

Sometimes the returning adults are collected in the rivers where they were released and to which their memory led them even though they were hatched in a breeding station on another river.

The fertilized eggs are placed in trays with cold water running over them.

Duration of the incubation period in the hatchery varies with the species. Fall chinook eggs take 130 days to hatch at 40° F. and only 33 days at 60° F. Hatcheries that keep the water at 52° to 53° F. permit the eggs to hatch out in about 45 days.

After hatching the alevin are left in trays for five or six weeks until the yolk sacs are absorbed. In the next or fry stage the fish are fed finely ground dry meal. As they grow they are given moist pellets. Fall chinook are reared for 30 to 120 days, coho about 12 to 14 months, and steelhead trout up to two years. Experiments are in progress at various hatcheries to shorten the rearing phase of coho and steelhead.

A modern salmon hatchery has a far different look than its forebears of a generation ago. The butcher shop is gone, and few people are seen on the premises. The place has an antiseptic look. At the Bureau of Sport Fisheries and Wildlife's $7 million Dworshak hatchery in Idaho, which produces mostly steelhead, the entire operation is automated. An IBM computer regulates not only the flow of water but its temperature and quality and also the feeding operations. A unique feature is that some of the ponds use recirculated water. There are very few persons in this plant, which has the capacity to produce 3,500,000 migrant-size steelhead, the largest in the world. Here experiments with warming water have made it possible to bring the fish to the smolt stage in about one year. They are released into the rivers in April and May and return from the ocean after eighteen to twenty-four months.

The salmon and trout hatcheries built by the city of Tacoma on the Cowlitz River in western Washington cost $9 million. As the fish arrive from the Pacific they are diverted into a collection channel and ladder leading to a resting pool. Here they leap down a small, rubber-padded "waterfall" and are guided into holding tanks or hatchery ponds where the females and males are spawned. When the fish reach the fry stage they are moved to outdoor ponds or raceways and fed every twenty minutes by automatic feeders suspended from the walls. As they grow in size they are fed less frequently. Throughout the rearing process they must be protected against diseases. Drugs are incorporated in the food to combat internal diseases, and as a precaution against external diseases the fish are given chemical baths frequently. The Cowlitz hatchery can produce 4 million spring chinook, 10 million fall chinook, 4.6 million coho, and 650,000 steelhead.

Every spring numerous "fish pullmans" may be seen on the highways leading to the salmon rivers of Oregon, Washington, and Idaho.

The juvenile fish are released by the millions and bidden godspeed. At first they are bewildered, swim aimlessly for a few minutes, but soon find the current and, swimming with it, head for the ocean, which may be fairly close or hundreds of miles away (as in Idaho). They are lost to sight for one to three or four years and then are seen again knocking, so to speak, at the gates of the hatchery, where they are spawned and the cycle begins again.

There are now some eighty anadromous salmon and steelhead trout stations in the Pacific Northwest. Many of them are subsidized by the federal government; others are operated by the states, electric power companies, municipalities, or public utility districts. In 1970 they produced over 100 million chinook and coho and 5 million steelhead smolts, which were planted in the Columbia River system.

Sometimes spawners return to the hatcheries in such large numbers that they create problems. The surplus fish are donated to state or county institutions and to the school lunch program (in Oregon) or are put out for bid and sold on the commercial market. Spawned-out carcasses are sold for fertilizer and pet food.

Dr. Lauren Donaldson of the College of Fisheries of the University of Washington has shown that selective breeding of salmonids can produce rapid growth and increased fecundity. His many experiments have contributed to improved hatchery stocks.

Results of Hatchery Operations

In recent years considerable efforts have been made to evaluate the results of artificial propagation programs, especially those financed by the federal government. The National Marine Fisheries Service reported in 1970 that between 1964 and 1968 about 35 percent of the fall chinook taken in commercial gear offshore and in the rivers below Bonneville, and some 50 percent of those caught above Bonneville, were of Columbia River hatchery origin. The Oregon Fish Commission estimated that over half of the coho landed in the troll fishery off the Oregon coast in 1969 were artificially produced. The Washington State Department of Fisheries reported similar findings.

The comeback of coho stocks in the Columbia River is closely related to enormous plantings in the watershed during the past decade. Artificial production of fall chinook on an increasing scale has served to arrest somewhat the decline of this species, while the growing success in breeding steelhead has helped to sustain the steelhead runs, especially in streams outside the Columbia River drainage. Nitrogen bubble disease in the Columbia River has wiped out some of the gains made in the hatcheries.

"Hatcheries are good, there is little doubt," says Dr. L. E. Perry. "Studies show they are economical and give a good return on the investment . . . But they do cost money to build and operate and this money must be obtained from some place, hence there is a limit . . . There are also problems of proper sites and the maintenance of various river fisheries for local use." [5]

The success of United States hatcheries has inspired the Canadians, who abandoned their stations in the 1930s, to again undertake the artificial propagation of Pacific salmon. Five hatcheries are planned in the vicinity of the Strait of Georgia and one has been completed. The aim is to provide fish mainly for anglers, whose numbers are skyrocketing. A report issued by the Department of Fisheries in Vancouver, British Columbia, late in 1971 states, "In general, coho salmon can be introduced more readily into barren river systems and produce better returns, than can fall chinook salmon . . . Hatcheries built on streams with either small or non-existent runs of cohos have been able to produce large numbers of these fish by introducing eggs or fry from other areas. Perhaps the ideal situation is to locate hatcheries on barren streams tributary to rivers with large runs so that egg-takes are sufficient, homing problems are reduced and returns of hatchery fish isolated."

Spawning Channels

Salmon are now spawned and hatched in specially created ponds and channels along the coast and in rivers and lakes. The basic purpose is to provide gravel beds and an aquatic environment that will increase the survival rate of the eggs and fry over that in natural streams. The first practical spawning channels were built in the Fraser River watershed for the propagation of pinks. Some of the impetus came from the staff at the Pacific Coast Biological Station in Nainamo, British Columbia. They demonstrated the destructive effects of silting and flooding on salmon eggs in the gravel of natural streams and suggested that natural production might be substantially augmented if water flow in streams could be controlled and the quality of gravel improved.

It was found during the experimentation which preceded the building of spawning channels that if such physical conditions as exist in nature could be reproduced and then maintained and controlled throughout the incubation period, a higher survival rate would be obtained, at least for pink and chum salmon. The Canadian biologist W. P. Wickett demonstrated that artificial propagation in this manner could double the rate of survival in the wild.[6]

If properly located the artificial channels furnish all the normal food organisms of a natural stream; they are merely controlled extensions of the stream in which the flow and depth of the water are regulated and the gravel is of an ideal size for spawning and incubation of eggs. Dangers to which natural streams are subject, such as deposition of bark and other materials that smother eggs, flash flooding, or extreme low water and prevalence of predators, are virtually eliminated. However, for species like sockeye, whose fingerlings remain in freshwater up to two years, provision must be made for rearing.

The International Pacific Salmon Fisheries Commission, which manages the Fraser River, has built a number of relatively inexpensive channels. For example, the Commission reported in 1969 that the Pitt River channel, built in 1963 with a capacity of 4 million eggs, resulted in a return of 97,000 adult sockeye from the first year of operation and 115,000 from the second year, with commercial fishermen taking the bulk of the fish. The benefit-to-cost ratio was estimated at fourteen to one. Weaver Creek channel, completed in 1965, produced 170,000 adult sockeye in 1969, the first year when results could be tallied; fishermen caught 110,000 of the sockeye, resulting in a seven to one benefit-to-cost ratio.[7]

The Pitt River installation is an incubation channel in which eyed eggs are buried, with the resulting sockeye fry descending into Pitt Lake to rear. At Weaver Creek the sockeye spawn in the channel and the resulting fry descend the creek to the Harrison River, then ascend to nearby Harrison Lake, where they remain until they are ready to go to sea.

The Washington Department of Fisheries, the Oregon Game Commission, and the Idaho Fish and Game Department also maintain spawning channels. However, as the Washington Department of Fisheries says: "In view of the large production capacity of the hatchery system in the lower Columbia, natural rearing area development in this section is of low priority except for making accommodations for hatchery surpluses that cannot be reared within the present facilities." [8]

✿

Marine Aquaculture

Considerable interest is being shown in saltwater culture of both Pacific and Atlantic salmon. The fishes are hatched in freshwater and then transferred to saltwater cages; they are not allowed to migrate to the sea. This involves control over the fish during their entire life cycle and can result in breeding them selectively, as cattle are bred, for characteristics best suited to market demands. Research on such possibilities is being conducted by the College of Fisheries of the University of Washington at four locations in Puget Sound, with grants from the National Marine Fisheries Service.

Typical is the station at Manchester, Washington. Here the fry are placed in circular steel or fiberglass tanks supplied with freshwater and saltwater, and the salinity is adjusted. When the fish are able to live in saltwater they are transferred to floating pens and fed moist pellets. Shrimp meal is added to their diet to control the redness of their flesh. This feed is supplemented by plankton and other small forms of marine life carried in with the tidal currents. It has been found that under such controlled conditions salmon grow much faster than in the wild and are ready for market as pan-sized fish in eighteen months or less.

The NMFS has begun to test the market for these products by distributing them to major suppliers, restaurants, retailers, and wholesalers in metropolitan areas. Acceptance seems to be assured if quality is controlled.

Meanwhile private companies are also engaged in saltwater salmon culture to produce fish for the market. Union Carbide Corporation has formed a subsidiary that is breeding salmon in floating sea cages to a weight of 0.7 pound after twelve to fifteen months. Some have already reached hotel tables.

The Japanese are also experimenting with saltwater culture, concentrating on chum, the most plentiful species in Asia and the easiest to propagate. The fish are reared in a hatchery for a year and then transferred to a large circular saltwater pool with a capacity of 3000 adults.

Saltwater culture of Atlantic salmon is apparently a going business in Norway, Scotland, and Canada. Sea Pool Fisheries, a private company, has opened a $4 million fish farm at Clam Bay, Nova Scotia. The company began marketing its fish in Montreal in 1971 and now has plans for exporting them to the United States.

Similar experiments are reported from Norway. A company

in Bergen has spent some 20 million kroner on salmon rearing since 1969 according to a report of the Norwegian Information Bureau of November 17, 1972. Organized in 1969, it has four plants, two for breeding fish to the smolt stage and two for fattening them to market size in saltwater. Hatching capacity is 2 million fry and smolt capacity 300,000 a year. The two saltwater plants have a combined capacity of more than 500,000 kilos (1,100,000 pounds) of salmon. The firm marketed 200 tons in 1972, sold fresh in chilled condition, and within a few years it hopes to achieve an annual output of 1500 tons. The fish weigh about three kilos when marketed.

The fish are incubated in freshwater and transferred to saltwater when they reach the smolt stage. The saltwater plant on the island of Sotra west of Bergen consists of pens that enclose the ocean waters with barriers of iron or aluminum gratings in a concrete framework. The water is recycled, as in an aquarium, and the fish are fed pelletized food fortified with vitamins. While the first or freshwater stage of the operation is very difficult because the young fish are vulnerable to disease and parasites, especially when temperature rises in summer, the second or saltwater phase presents even more problems because saltwater rearing is still a little known field, says the managing director of the firm. Sea birds are a menace, and so are "outsider fish" that feed on young salmon. There is also a certain amount of cannibalism.

"In addition to environmental problems," he says, "food wastage and fish excrement consume quantities of oxygen. At the worst, these factors can result in a shortage of oxygen and development of hydrogen sulfide, particularly at the bottom. Changes of weather can cause these lower layers of water to rise and in severe cases be toxic enough to kill the fish." [9]

On the whole, it seems that experiments with saltwater salmon culture are too early to evaluate, although considerable progress has been made and private industry as well as government agencies are showing enormous interest in the field. Magnus Berg of the Norwegian Fish and Wildlife Service wrote on January 10, 1972: "I think these experiments are promising but we need more experience." Should the breakthrough come, as it did in hatchery breeding in the 1950s, it will add enormous quantities to the world's salmon supply, although they will be not the romantic, daring ocean voyageurs who capture our imagination but tame factory products produced for the table.

Norway's pioneer achievements in saltwater culture have inspired competitors, chief among them being the Lever Brothers plant on the west coast of Scotland, which offers considerable promise of economic success.

Promoters in Brittany have launched a saltwater-salmon plant, experimenting with both Atlantic and Pacific species, on the island of Er in the estuary of the Tréguier River. Behind this scheme is the government's Oceanology Center of Brittany and a private firm. With France importing some 10,000 tons of salmon annually, principally Pacific salmon, the Breton scheme has a large market available if it proves successful.

Thus we may conclude that while the production of wild Atlantic salmon has been steadily decreasing in Europe and North America, the losses will probably be made up to a growing extent by expanding production from hatcheries and table-sized fish from marine aquaculture.

Transplantations

The breakthrough in salmon culture has accelerated the age-old efforts to transplant these fishes to barren waters and to new parts of the world. Perhaps the greatest success has been achieved in stocking the Great Lakes. Except for Lake Ontario, which originally harbored considerable stocks of landlocked Atlantic salmon, the Lakes have not been known as a habitat for salmon species.

The advent of a new salmon fishery came almost by accident. The sea lamprey, a notorious predator, invaded the twenty-seven-and-a-half-mile Welland Canal that connects Lakes Erie and Ontario, but it found few fishes to gorge on. The almost complete absence of predators set the stage for the invasion of the alewife, a small pelagic fish closely resembling shad or herring, which reached staggering proportions. This proliferation led biologists to plan the introduction of a species that would prey on the alewives and if possible create a new fishery as well. Coho salmon were chosen, and in 1966 eggs from Oregon and Washington hatcheries were introduced into upper Michigan streams and into feeders of Lake Superior. In 1967 more coho and about a million chinook eggs were planted in the Upper Great Lakes.

The results dumfounded the state fishery men. In the following years the salmon were seen in huge numbers in southern Lake Michigan (and Lake Superior) following the alewives on which they feasted. In the fall they returned to the mouths of the streams where they had been planted and a tremendous sport fishery was born. Since 1967 all the Great Lakes have been planted with species of Pacific salmon, and hatcheries have been built to produce the seed stock.

To a native Midwesterner like myself it comes as a pleasant shock to see salmon fishing in the Great Lakes states advertised in national magazines. When I lived on the shores of Lake Michigan the only salmon we saw were in cans, and angling for these princely fishes was regarded as the sport of nabobs who could afford to travel to the rivers of the Pacific Northwest or Canada. We were fortunate to catch small trout in nearby streams.

In the early days of salmon culture, when enthusiasm ran high, many efforts were made to transplant *Oncorhynchus* species in different parts of the world. C. P. Idyll in *The Sea Against Hunger* (1970) notes that Pacific or Atlantic salmon eggs, fry, or fingerlings were planted in the Hudson River, in streams in Argentina, Italy, Mexico, Nicaragua, Chile, the Hawaiian Islands, Australia, Germany, France, Ireland, Finland, and New Zealand. Nearly all were failures except in New Zealand, where chinook eggs from California were taken in 1875. It took more than a quarter of a century for runs to be established in several rivers of the South Island, where there is now a flourishing sport fishery (see Chapter XXVII).

Efforts to plant Pacific salmon in Atlantic waters have almost invariably failed, although the Russians came near to success in recent years. From 1933 to 1939 over ten million eggs of chum from rivers in Sakhalin and Kamchatka, resulting in about nine million fry, were planted in streams flowing into the White and Barents Seas. In 1937 and 1938 some adult chum were caught, but the experiment was a failure.

In 1957 a large pink salmon planting was undertaken, this time with eyed eggs, and at first showed signs of considerable success. The adults began to appear in the Barents and White Seas in 1960; some were netted by fishermen and others were allowed to enter the rivers to spawn. In fact, the adults were caught or were seen spawning in Norway, Iceland, Spitsbergen, and even in the region of Aberdeen, Scotland. Altogether about 80,000 fish were counted in 1960. Hence additional plantings were made, but there were almost no survivors from the 1960 spawn of migrants and few from the 1961 group. Thus ended perhaps the largest effort to restock Atlantic rivers with Pacific species.

In the past few years I have heard of experiments in stocking

Pacific species in the southern hemisphere, notably Chile and Argentina. The results are not known, but they attest to man's indomitable hope of extending the range of the salmon, both Atlantic and Pacific, to areas where they have never been seen, or where the runs have disappeared. No amount of failure will deter these experiments.

XX ∽

The Puget Sound Fishery

Vancouver's Discovery

ON APRIL 17, 1792, Captain George Vancouver, commanding the sloop-of-war *Discovery* and the armed tender *Chatham*, reached the coast of New Albion, the land discovered by Sir Francis Drake and explored by Captain Cook on his third voyage in 1778. At a point called Deception Bay Vancouver went ashore and afterward noted in his journal that "the country before us presented a most luxuriant landscape . . . The most interior parts were somewhat elevated, and agreeably diversified with hills, from which it gradually descended to the shore, and terminated in a sandy beach. The whole had the appearance of a continued forest extending as far north as the eye could reach." [1] This was Puget Sound, extending about eighty miles from the east end of Juan de Fuca Strait to Admiralty Inlet and having many branches, including Hood Canal. The Sound harbors one of the richest concentrations of fish and shellfish in the eastern Pacific.

This is a land of mist and mountains. The climate is extremely moist, with gray days predominating during the year and sunshine evanescent. The prevailing onshore winds bring warm, moist air from the Pacific Ocean, and as it meets the mountain barrier it is transformed into rain or snow. Thus the lowlands of western Washington obtain 35 to 50 inches of rain a year, the foothills 75 to 100 inches, and the mountain areas 100 to 200 inches, mostly in the form of snow.

Many of the numerous streams entering the Sound originate in the snow fields of the high Cascades. They are nourished in summer by melting snow; some run milkily to the sea. They vary from cold streams tumbling down rocky gorges to warmer ones meandering across the lowlands. Nearly all of these waterways breed salmon and steelhead trout. Of great importance to the anadromous fishes are the estuarine areas where the mixture of semisalt and semifresh water provides the transition zone for juvenile and adult salmon as they move from one environment to another.

When Vancouver visited Puget Sound many bands of Indians were living along the tidewater portions of the rivers and on the tangle of green and forested islands offshore and in the Strait of Juan de Fuca. These people were given mellifluous names by the explorers, usually transliterated from their incomprehensible dialects, such as Samish, Duwamish, Stillaguamish, Humptulips, Puyallup, Makah, Clallam, etc.

The aborigines, noted Vancouver in his journal, were "low and ill-made with broad faces and small eyes . . . Their foreheads appear to be deformed or out of shape. The head has something of a conical shape. They wear the hair long with quantities of red ochre inter-mixed with whale oil or some other greasy substance that has a disgusting smell." The men wore shell earrings and the women shell necklaces, armlets, and anklets. Except for a deerskin blanket over their backs, the men were naked in summer; in winter they wore buckskin shorts, belts, breechcloths, leggings, moccasins, and basketry hats of excellent workmanship. The women wore petticoats of grass or cedar bark fastened with a cord around the waist; in rainy weather they had additional garments made of natural materials.

The summer dwellings of the Puget Sound Indians, who were heavily dependent upon the prolific salmon for much of their food supply, were temporary wooden huts, usually close to the fishing grounds. Their permanent villages featured well-made cedar houses 40 to 100 feet long and 14 to 20 feet wide, with an opening along the ridgepole and a single door for an entrance. Each dwelling accommodated several families; space was allotted for bunks, and there was a fire for every family. Here they stored their winter's food. Only occasionally did the men go into the dense coniferous forest to kill a deer or elk or smaller game.

Here the Puget Sound people had lived for countless centuries when the explorers and white settlers intruded upon their picturesque land and ultimately destroyed their way of life and much of the environment as well.

Timber and Fish

American immigration into the Pacific Northwest resulted in the Oregon Boundary Treaty of 1846 with Great Britain, which gave most of the Puget Sound region to the United States. Timber and fish were and are the major natural resources. In 1847 a group of pioneers organized the Puget Sound Milling Company and established a sawmill at Tumwater near Olympia, destined to be the capital of the territory and later the state of Washington.

Here was one of the most luxuriant commercial forests in the world. On the west slopes of the Cascade Mountains and on the Olympic Peninsula Douglas fir grew abundantly, mixed with hemlock, Sitka spruce, and cedar. From the snowy pinnacles of Mount Rainier, Mount Baker, and a dozen other peaks the landscape unrolled in Alpine grandeur. Through the mountains flowed innumerable rivers and creeks where the leaping fishes spawned, undisturbed except by bears and other predators.

The mountainous Olympic Peninsula featured the unique rain forests, dominated by fir, hemlock, spruce, and cedar, with huge sword ferns, salal, huckleberry, and other plants carpeting the mossy ground. Moss dangles from the branches of the trees and ferns climb from the base to join them. On the rotting remains of fallen giants a variety of plants have taken root, feeding upon the decaying wood, lichens and mosses, and more complex organisms. Here life and death jostle each other. Sprightly young trees grow on the stems of the fallen ones.

The Puget Sound forests began to be cut about the time of the California gold rush for masts, windjammers, houses, sidewalks, corduroy roads, and the like. The Indian problem was soon tackled and disposed of in the customary fashion: in 1853 Major Isaac Ingalls Stevens was installed as governor of the territory and Indian agent as well, and he lost no time in forcing the red men to sign treaties ceding their territories to the United States. By the Treaty of Medicine Creek the Nisqually and Puyallup tribes ceded about two and three-quarter million acres of land, much of it heavily forested, in return for $32,500 and three small reservations. Article III of the treaty gave them "the right of taking fish at all usual and accustomed grounds and stations . . . in common with all citizens of the Territory, and erecting temporary houses for the purpose of curing, together with the privilege of hunting, gathering roots and berries and pasturing their horses on open and uncleared lands." This type of clause was also included in the Treaty of Point Elliott (January 1855) and the Quinault River Treaty of 1856.

Memorable are the words of Chief Seattle of the Duwamish tribe addressed to Governor Isaac Stevens before signing the Treaty of Point Elliott ceding their lands to the United States. The Chief is quoted in *Uncommon Controversy: Fishing Rights of the Muckleshoot, Puyallup and Nisqually Indians:*

Every part of this soil is sacred in the estimation of my
people. Every hillside, every valley, every plain and grove,
has been hallowed by some sad or happy event in days long
vanished . . . the very dust upon which you now stand re-
sponds more lovingly to their footsteps than to yours, because it is rich with the dust of our ancestors and our bare
feet are conscious of the sympathetic touch . . . even the
little children who lived here and rejoiced for a brief season, still love these sombre solitudes . . . And when the
last Red Man shall have perished, and the memory of my
tribe shall have become a myth among the white man,
these shores shall swarm with the invisible dead of my tribe
. . . At night when the streets of your cities and villages are
silent and you think them deserted, they will throng with
the returning hosts that once filled them and still love this
beautiful land. The White Man will never be alone.

He admonished the white man to "be just and kindly with my people, for the dead are not powerless. Dead — I say? There is no
death. Only a change of worlds." But his words went unheeded.

Settlers moved into the lands vacated by the Indians, who at times
showed their resentment by massacring them but were rapidly suppressed with great brutality. Early in the history of the white man's
relations with the red men in the West somebody coined the adage,
"The only good Indian is a dead Indian," and it swept the land. Development of the resources of Washington Territory continued at an
accelerated pace throughout the century.

Commercial salmon canning began in the Puget Sound area in
1877, a decade after the Hume brothers built their establishment at
Eagle Cliff on the Columbia River. By 1890 there were ten plants in
the Olympia area at the head of Puget Sound. By the end of the century the Puget Sound pack, profiting from the runs of Fraser River
fish in the Strait of Juan de Fuca, exceeded the Columbia River's.
Indians did most of the fishing in the early days of the industry.

As on the Columbia, signs of overfishing appeared and fears for the
resource were voiced. Traditionally the Indians stopped fishing and
removed their traps, weirs, and nets from the rivers when they had
caught their yearly supply. The white man, to whom the salmon was
a salable commodity, fished as long as the run continued, unless restrained by law. Since government control over the fisheries was
weak in Washington as elsewhere, uncontrolled fishing continued for
decades.

All five North American species of the genus *Oncorhynchus* are found in the waters of Puget Sound along with steelhead trout. Pinks and sockeye account for the bulk of the catches; most of the sockeye and many of the pinks taken by Washington fishermen are headed for the Fraser River. Pinks are found in significant quantities only in odd-numbered years for reasons that are unfathomable. Initially salmon were taken commercially in Puget Sound by every conceivable type of gear except the fish wheel; now the only commercial gear permitted are purse seines, gill nets, and reef nets. Trolling is permitted in the Strait of Juan de Fuca but not in Puget Sound proper.

In the early decades of the fishery regulations were limited to the establishment of closed seasons and banning of some types of gear from spawning rivers. But, as in the Columbia River, these regulations "indicated no particular understanding, nor even a consistent theory, of the parameters determining the life history of the Pacific salmon," say the economists J. A. Crutchfield and Giulio Pontecorvo. "As best we can determine from the dim record, most of the regulations promulgated . . . were based on an intuitive feeling that certain types of gear were excessively destructive, or were undertaken in response to the interests of one pressure group or another." [2] Seldom if ever were the eroding effects of civilization on the freshwater environment considered as factors in the decreasing abundance of fish.

Production of canned salmon, which accounted for the bulk of the catches, reached a peak of 2.5 million cases in 1913, thanks partly to the fabulous sockeye run to the Fraser River that year. After that the pack went downhill, reflecting a decline in Fraser River stocks due to the disastrous rock slide at Hell's Gate, as recounted in the next chapter, and due to overfishing of local stocks and deterioration of habitat in the state of Washington. An astute student of the fishery, John N. Cobb, wrote in *Pacific Fisherman*, the industry's trade paper, in December 1921: "When reproached with their shortsightedness [packers] clamored for the establishment of more salmon hatcheries as though the latter could accomplish the miracle of increasing the supply of fry from a steadily decreasing supply of eggs."

Effective regulation began with the creation of the Washington Department of Fisheries in 1921. As the salmon runs declined the owners of fixed gear fought bitterly with the net fishermen; each sought to obtain state regulation of the other's activities. The final result was the passage of Initiative 77 by the legislature in 1935, which outlawed fixed gear — traps and set nets — from all waters in the state. Puget Sound was divided into two areas: (1) the waters inside of a line from Angeles Point on the Olympic Peninsula to Partridge Point on Whidbey Island and intersecting 122° 40' west longitude and (2) an outer area extending north and south of these lines. Commercial fishing was originally restricted to gill nets in the inner area, but purse seines were allowed after October 5. On the other hand, all legal commercial gear was permitted to fish north and west of the "77" line. Amendments to Initiative 77 permitted purse seines to fish certain waters of inner Puget Sound in August in odd-numbered years when the pinks are running.

Initiative 77 not only had salutary effects on the stocks but stimulated settlement of the long-standing dispute between Americans and Canadians on the division of the Fraser River sockeye runs, as described in Chapter XXI.

Fishing intensity, however, increased in Puget Sound after 1935. The number of purse seines licensed jumped from 191 in 1939 to 452 in 1961 and gill netters from 450 to 856. In 1969 over a thousand gill nets, 384 purse seines, and 63 reef nets were licensed in the Sound. Usually too large a proportion of the migrant fish were being caught and too few were allowed to escape.

In addition to fishing in tidewater and along the ocean, a hook and line troll fishery for chinook and coho developed off the coast of Washington. The Pacific Marine Fisheries Commission estimated that in 1951 the trolling fleet operating in Washington waters numbered 1300 boats. In 1971 the number had increased to about 5600; most of the increase was in small boats of the type commonly used in sport fishing. About 10 million pounds of salmon, or one-fourth the total Washington commercial catch, were taken by trollers in 1971.

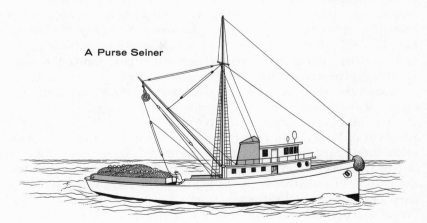

A Purse Seiner

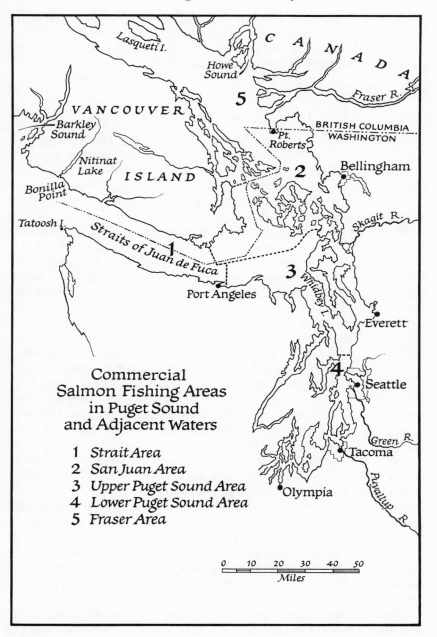

Commercial
Salmon Fishing Areas
in Puget Sound
and Adjacent Waters

1 Strait Area
2 San Juan Area
3 Upper Puget Sound Area
4 Lower Puget Sound Area
5 Fraser Area

0 10 20 30 40 50
Miles

Trollers land their fish at Neah Bay, at the entrance to the Strait of Juan de Fuca, Lapush at the mouth of the Quillayute River, Westport, and Ilwaco. Seattle, Aberdeen, and Hoquiam occasionally receive fish from some of the larger trollers.

Environmental Decay

The pristine beauty of Puget Sound that enthralled the early explorers was still intact when Washington acquired statehood in 1889. A transcontinental railroad guide published in 1884 described the Sound as "a most beautiful sheet of water — a succession of bays with enchanting shores on two and sometimes, apparently, on all sides, sloping up to hills and well-timbered mountains." [3]

The Great Northern Railroad reached Seattle in 1893, and thenceforth the city became the chief metropolis of the state and later of the Pacific Northwest as well: the disembarkation point for people and freight bound for the Orient and Alaska and the leading fish marketing center of the North Pacific coast. As settlement and industrialization expanded, much of the forest land was cut, usually on a cut-out-and-get-out basis, leaving hideous scars on the landscape. Rivers were blockaded by logjams, and many of the hills around Seattle and Tacoma were sliced and mashed to create suitable building lots.

The Weyerhaeuser combine, which had helped to devastate the white pine forests of the Northern Great Lakes states, was in the forefront of the assault on western Washington's forests. "In 1900," says the company's official history, written by Professor Allan Nevins and co-workers, "came a transaction that startled the West and heralded a new era in the lumber history of America." [4] The company announced the purchase of 900,000 acres of timberland at $6 an acre from the Northern Pacific Railroad, which had obtained a veritable duchy of 39 million acres of the public domain in return for the privilege of building a transcontinental railway. The 1900 deal was only the beginning of the Weyerhaeuser timber empire in the Far West. A survey of holdings ordered by President Theodore Roosevelt in 1908 showed that the company then owned lands containing some 96 billion board feet of high-grade timber, the second largest private timber hoard in the country. Much of the area harbored salmon and steelhead rivers.

While the lumbermen provided employment for the settlers and thus stimulated the economy, they contributed significantly through their logging methods to the obstruction and pollution of the waterways and by their pulp and paper manufacture to the fouling of the air and the waters. The official histories are silent on these matters. For example, in the 700 pages of *Timber and Men: The Weyerhaeuser Story* there is no reference to "pollution," nor is there any discusstion of the environmental effects of the company's operations. Until state and federal laws forced the Weyerhaeuser Company to install antipollution facilities in its pulp and paper mills and improve its logging practices to safeguard the watersheds, it merely followed the customary methods of the forest products and other industries by dumping wastes, often in monumental quantities, into the nearest public waterways. Weyerhaeuser was not alone in following these practices.

The lumber industry grew swiftly until the Washington annual cut reached 5 billion feet in 1962, the second highest in the nation — Oregon was first. "Before the advent of modern logging equipment and practices," say the biologists Henry O. Wendler and Gene Deschamps, "The most prevalent and economical medium for transport of logs to the mills was water. Logging and driving companies constructed a system of log dams to maintain ponds for holding logs and to create a supply of water to move their cut timber . . . Since salmon were plentiful, little or no consideration was given to their passage over these barriers. Almost all of the structures were total blocks to anadromous fish and cut off considerable areas that had been utilized for the spawning of adults and the rearing of young."

As stream driving of logs was replaced by railroads and later trucks, the dams became obsolete and "many operators abandoned the installations without attempting to remove them." There was no state law requiring the removal of these obstructions. Some operators attempted to blast or dynamite them without much benefit to the fishes. "The dams remained until they rotted away, were washed out or eventually were removed by the Washington Department of Fisheries or other agencies . . . Some have endured in the streams and remain as total blocks or hindrances to fish movement."[5]

The pulp and paper industry was probably more inimical to the anadromous fishery than the logging industry. Early mills were small and created relatively minor pollution problems in their immediate vicinity, but as the demand for paper products in the United States rose to fantastic levels, due partly to what might be called the packaging revolution, so did the production of pulp and the flow of effluent into the streams. By 1962 eight of the pulp mills situated in Puget Sound and around the Strait of Juan de Fuca were discharging over 190 million gallons of waste water daily, equal to the wastes of roughly 12,400,000 people or over four times the population of the entire state of Washington. Since 1962 the industry has grown apace. In January 1972 Washington had twelve companies operating twenty-two mills in sixteen cities; annual production of pulp varied from 3.8 million tons in 1967 to 3.7 million tons in 1972. While the number of mills has increased the installation of controls has reduced the flow of pollutants in some areas. A few mills were closed because they could not meet government water quality standards or were economically unable to install necessary facilities.

Fishermen had long complained that the mills were poisoning and killing the salmon and steelhead that came near their discharge points, but not till 1967 did anyone — in this case the Federal Water Pollution Control Administration — publish a comprehensive study of the extent of such pollution. For example, biologists introduced live boxes containing juvenile salmon into the waters of Bellingham Bay, where one mill dumps its cooking liquors, in order to test water quality and observed highly significant fish mortalities in the vicinity of the plants. Some tests were concluded in minutes. The area, they found, was lethal to juvenile salmon because of "the single or combined effects of (1) toxic sulfide waste liquors, (2) low dissolved oxygen concentrations, (3) low pH values, and (4) a combination of other deleterious materials." [6]

The Everett harbor and the Port Angeles area received several mill-waste streams. Here the waters surged with spent cooking liquors, while the bottom steadily built up with sludge. (The air near a pulp mill of course is nauseating when the wind blows in the right direction.) Juvenile test fish introduced in Everett harbor died within twenty to forty-five minutes after being placed in the polluted water. "In one experiment fish kills observed at a floating live-box were associated with detected concentrations of total sulfides, whereas observations of no-kill were associated with the absence of detectable sulfides." [7] The biologists concluded that the pulp and paper mills were not only killing off large numbers of young salmon migrating through Everett harbor but were also damaging oyster, crab, and clam larvae and eggs of English sole, cod, smelt, and herring.

Around Port Angeles sulfides and other poisons from three pulp mills were the principal causes of fish mortalities, although untreated sewage from the city of Port Angeles added to the pollution load. The mills were discharging 25.7 tons of suspended solids per day and the city was adding 1.8 tons. The Rayonier, Inc., mill contributed about 92 percent of the combined discharges, said the federal report;

because of the sluggishness of the waters inside Ediz Hook, the deadly pollutants spread throughout the harbor and for a considerable distance eastward. All the young test salmon coming into contact with this foul water became disoriented and were snatched up by the gulls or died otherwise.

The report's findings were summarily rejected by the pulp and paper industry. Roger Tollefson, their spokesman, himself a biologist, affirmed that "present levels of spent sulfite liquor in outer bays and harbors are not harmful to any other legitimate uses." He laughed off the conclusions of the $1.5 million study: "To say that the results of the juvenile salmon box experiments are of any consequence would be the same as saying that the death of some robins held captive in a sack attached to the exhaust pipe of a car would prove that exhaust fumes are doing extensive damage to our bird population." [8]

Another spokesman for the industry said, "We seriously question the validity and interpretation of the scientific studies . . . As a matter of fact, the natural abundance of Puget Sound and its recognized fertility are incompatible with the conclusion of the studies that pollution exists in this area." [9] Federal and state officials rejected these rationalizations and pressed the mills to install pollution controls required by the new federal and state laws.

After many conferences all but two of the companies, Scott Paper Company in Everett and Rayonier in Port Angeles, had agreed by 1971 to limit their discharges of sulfite waste liquors. Actually all the mills, including sawmills, were liable to prosecution under the federal 1899 Refuse Act, which made it illegal to discharge anything besides municipal sewage into navigable waters without a permit from the Army Corps of Engineers. However, these plants were not required by the Corps to request a permit until late 1971, and to date none has been issued because of pending court cases dealing with the permit program. Some of the mills have state permits. In the opinion of the United States attorney in Seattle, these companies were complying with federal law, although they had no federal permits.

Rapid population growth and spreading urbanization and industrialization have been the major causes of both the deterioration of the waters of Puget Sound and the destruction of surrounding landscapes. The scenic beauty of Seattle, Tacoma, and the Puget Sound around Olympia faded away as factories, warehouses, and the usual tracts of dreary housing, shopping centers, and freeways, highways and streets covered green fields, dried up running brooks, stilled the murmur of rills that used to flow down the hillsides, and killed off the fish. "Over the long run," said Dr. E. O. Salo at the Northwest Estuary and Coastal Zone Symposium held in October 1970 in Portland, Oregon, "the greatest threat to optimal use of the Puget Sound system is not posed by direct effects of industrial and municipal discharges on water quality, but by failure to identify and evaluate estuarine effects of land use, not only on the water front but upstream. All the important fish and shellfish resources of Puget Sound are vulnerable to this kind of careless development. Salmon, steelhead trout, and cutthroat trout require extensive systems of small feeder streams that are being systematically destroyed by improperly regulated land use far away from Puget Sound itself."

In short, "while the large problems of industrial and domestic pollution appear to be under control or can be controlled . . . the piece-meal destruction of the small estuaries continues." The principal offenders are municipalities and port districts, real estate developers, home owners that require flood control from wave action, and of course watershed misuse. "The ocean in the Pacific northwest is still a tremendous flusher and can assimilate considerable abuse, but the shoreline and the estuary are delicate and vulnerable and are being encroached upon steadily . . . by municipalities and housing developments of doubtful esthetic and social [values]."

Trends in the Fisheries

The general trend in Puget Sound catches has been downward since before the first world war. It is not easy to pinpoint the exact causes, as Crutchfield and Pontecorvo say, because "it is a complex multispecies fishery, shared by the nationals of two countries and harvesting high-value fish." The most important components of the commercial catches are pinks and sockeye, followed by coho, chum, and chinook. Catches of chinook, which have the highest market value, dropped steadily after 1914, when 426,000 fish were caught, to a low of 63,000 in 1939, rebounded somewhat in 1947 to over 100,000, but did not reach that level again until 1966.

Harvests of coho dropped from one and a quarter to one and a half million fish during World War I to about one-third that number during World War II but have since recovered somewhat. Pinks comprise up to two thirds of the total salmon catch in odd-numbered years, but this fishery too has seriously decreased and is but a small fraction of the peak recorded in 1913 when almost 16 million fish were landed. Catches of sockeye, mainly of Canadian origin, have followed the varying fortunes of the Fraser River runs. Immense plantings of hatchery coho and chinook have bolstered the commercial as well as sport catches in Washington. Appendix Table 9 shows commercial catches, net gear only, from 1913 to 1966.

In contrast to Oregon, the canning industry has retained its vigor in the state of Washington, as Appendix Table 10 shows, packing mainly pinks and sockeye. In 1971 there were eighteen canneries in operation producing over 520,000 cases, the highest output in a dozen years.

Summarizing their economic analysis of the Puget Sound fishery in 1969, Crutchfield and Pontecorvo said: "Clearly, landings are well below peak levels achieved in previous periods, and it seems unlikely that any economically feasible program regulating fishing effort can restore fully the losses attributable to growth in population, industry and other elements of human activity that impinge on successful propagation of salmon." They believe that regulation "has averted a disastrous collapse in landings, and has permitted some recovery in several important areas, notably the Fraser River sockeye." [10]

In 1970 the total salmon catch in Washington state waters, including the Columbia River, was 4,050,000 fish aggregating 37,600,000 pounds.

The Sport Fishery

Sport fishing has grown even more dramatically in Washington than in Oregon and is an important economic force that challenges the commercial fisherman. More salmon and steelhead are caught by anglers than in any other state or province. So potent politically are the sportsmen that they pushed through the Washington legislature a bill making steelhead a game fish that cannot be taken with commercial gear or sold in commercial channels in the state. A similar bill failed to pass the Oregon legislature.

In 1971 Washington anglers hooked 1,355,000 salmon, of which 1,-199,000 were taken in saltwater and 156,000 in the rivers. The sport catch in Puget Sound–Juan de Fuca Strait was 381,000 fish.

Angling for salmon goes back to Indian days. The aborigines around Cape Flattery were observed by explorers fishing with hook and line using herring as bait, as today's fishermen do. The white man's sport fishery dates from territorial days. In Puget Sound angling from a small boat is possible the year round because of sheltered waters and the presence of feeding salmon. The fishery has spread to Juan de Fuca Strait and into the ocean proper. Mature salmon may be taken in Washington rivers every month of the year, but catches are very low in January and February. The main species pursued are chinook, coho, and pinks.

Increasing population, higher incomes, more time for recreation, and an explosion of boat ownership have multiplied the number of anglers. The largest concentrations of fishermen, apart from the Columbia and Grays Harbor area, are in Elliott and Shilshole Bays around Seattle and Bremerton, the Narrows and Commencement Bay at Tacoma, and off southern Whidbey Island. Considerable numbers of fish are caught by sportsmen off the Olympic Peninsula, in the Lapush, Neah Bay, and the Sekiu–Pillar Point areas as well as around the San Juan Islands, Admiralty Inlet–Possession Point and Skagit–Deception Pass areas, and in Hood Canal.

In summer the blue waters of the Strait of Juan de Fuca are thronged with sleek cruisers and yachts, many of which venture across the international boundary to fish around the wooded Gulf Islands. So popular have southern British Columbia waters become that in 1972 the province instituted a stiff license fee for foreign boats, and their number consequently decreased.

Washington rivers are famous for steelhead trout, which are pursued by thousands of anglers in summer and winter. In 1970 165,000 of these fish were taken by sportsmen, including 116,000 of the winter run and 49,000 of the summer run. This was a 40 percent drop from 1969.

Much of the recent growth in sport fishing has been due to the successful production of coho and chinook in Washington hatcheries. At times coho have returned to rearing stations in such prodigious numbers as to swamp their facilities. For this reason laws forbidding fishing for salmon in specified areas of Washington rivers have been abrogated in order to give anglers an opportunity to hook the surplus supply. For example, 23,750 jack (immatures) and 9500 adult coho were caught by anglers in the Washougal River in a forty-day period of open fishing in the fall of 1967. The Department of Fisheries says that "the net economic value of this recreational fishery was estimated to be substantially more than the net value that would have resulted from . . . selling the fish to commercial buyers." [11] This practice is in contrast to the Japanese custom of never permitting salmon that return in numbers surplus to hatchery needs to be taken by anglers; they are always disposed of in the marketplace.

A fascinating study issued by the Washington Department of Fisheries in September 1972 discusses the problem of improving salmon angling in the Puget Sound region. Despite the encouraging sport catches of 1970 and 1971 success has declined badly in Puget Sound waters in the previous twenty years, in striking contrast to the remainder of Washington state's waters; ocean sport catches especially have risen and the state is now the top salmon angling state on the Pacific coast.

The Sound's once superb resident coho weighing four or five pounds at maturity have fallen to one fourth of their previous magnitude, while the inner Sound has entirely lost its resident pink salmon, fish that spent their entire lives in these waters and were thus available to anglers while still actively feeding. Catches of resident chinook, or "blackmouth" as they are called, are down although not to the disaster levels of the other two species. Finally, large chinook and "hooknose" coho returning from the ocean are not being caught as they once were. And the great upswing in hatchery production has not apparently helped anglers in the Sound, although it has contributed to the upsurging sport and commercial catches by Canadians. The biologists attribute the drop in sport catches not only to the disappearance of some species but to the shortage of what they call "biting salmon" — that is, those that are still feeding and available at times and places where sportsmen are fishing.

Many man-made projects and developments are believed to be killers of biting salmon because they ruined, eliminated, or impaired the streams where they used to return at times when anglers could take them. Such are Cushman dam on the north fork of the Skokomish River and the powerhouse at Potlatch through which its waters are diverted; La Grande dam on the Nisqually River; the White River dam near Buckley; the diversion dam on the Cedar River; a dam on the Elwha and the lower diversion dam on the Green. Some streams that once produced resident coho now flow through freeway culverts! The greatest single factor probably in the decline of sport fishing in the Sound is environmental degradation.

In a speech to the Northwest Steelheaders in July 1971 Fisheries Director Thor Tollefson outlined a program that his organization planned to enhance the Puget Sound sport fishery. It includes the release of "delayed" coho — fish that will enter the Sound after the period when coho normally migrate to the ocean — in an attempt to quadruple the present catch of resident coho, to increase the run of early-running coho that return in midsummer as bright fish who are more inclined to take an angler's hook than the present stocks, to introduce the rearing of spring chinook in Puget Sound hatcheries, to launch a pink salmon hatchery program, to change sport fishing regulations to promote a greater catch, to remove the gonads from surplus hatchery salmon and permit them to return to the Sound since there is evidence that such fish resume feeding, add weight, and can live for years and thus become available to anglers, and finally to adjust the times and places where commercial fisheries operate so as to minimize net catches of the stocks that sportsmen can take. By the spring of 1972 Tollefson reported that "we appear to be off to a first-rate start" on this program.

Lake Washington's Sockeye Fishery

Sockeye has not been a prominent species in Puget Sound, although it is extremely abundant across the border in the Fraser River system and northward. It is therefore astonishing to have a major sockeye run appear almost quietly and without much previous notice in the heart of a busy metropolis like Seattle.

In its pristine days Seattle was surrounded by limpid rivers and lakes teeming with fish life. Settlement began around the shores of Elliott Bay. As population increased the city spread in all directions and usurped the shores not only of the Sound but of Lake Washington and Lake Union, which once teemed with wildlife.

No sockeye except kokanee were known to exist in Lake Washington when in 1935 the federal Bureau of Fisheries planted 96,000 sea-run sockeye fingerlings in the Cedar River, a tributary of the lake, and a smaller number in adjoining Lake Sammamish. At that time the area was bucolic countryside, fields and woods interspersed with pleasant hamlets and villages, and the streams flowed through farmlands and forests.

As Seattle's population exploded the lake shores filled up with houses and other developments while the rural settlements were swallowed up by sprawling suburbs. Two floating highway bridges were built across Lake Washington. At Renton, on the south end of the lake, the Boeing Airplane Company built a huge plant in World War II to assemble its aircraft; freeways succeeded the quiet country roads that used to ramble across the countryside. Few people remembered, or cared about, the salmon planted during the Depression in the lovely Cedar River.

For more than twenty years only a small number of sockeye returned each year to the river and adjoining lakes, but by 1958 the population had jumped to 15,000 to 20,000 adults, by 1964 to 45,000, and by 1967 to 190,000. No netting had been permitted and few sportsmen fished these small salmon. As the run seemed destined to overwhelm the lake, fishery officials were confronted with a unique dilemma: how to harvest and protect a huge salmon run in the midst of a busy metropolis? Fortunately the Cedar River was part of Seattle's domestic water supply. The Seattle Water Department cooperated with the Department of Fisheries by providing a sufficient flow of water to keep the spawning beds covered. The highway engineers who designed a state road paralleling the river were considerate of the fishes and worked closely with the department in planning their construction so as not to disturb the stream.

All these measures paid off. In 1971 550,000 sockeye returned from their ocean junkets and the commercial fishermen awaited them. Special dispensation was granted by the legislature permitting both purse seiners and gill netters to operate in fresh water. The logical area for their operations was the Ship Canal that connects Lake Washington with the ocean, but this was deemed impractical because the time of the run, June 15 to about mid-July, was a busy period for canal traffic. Therefore a twenty-mile zone was established in central Puget Sound, between Seattle and the southern end of Whidbey Island, where the fish could be netted; a free corridor was created to permit the steelhead, chinook, and coho who would be heading for the Skagit, Stillaguamish, and Snohomish Rivers to reach their destination without being caught in the nets and also to enable sport fishermen and their boats to move freely in and out of Seattle harbor. Purse seiners were permitted to fish during the day and gill netters at night, three days a week for four weeks, with an extra two days in the fifth week. Sport and Indian fishermen participated in the harvest.

Altogether about 264,000 sockeye were commercially harvested, while some 183,000 fish escaped the nets and moved to their spawning grounds. To reach the Cedar River they had to run the gauntlet of metropolitan boat traffic. "Threading their way through Puget Sound," said an observer, "they turn off at Shilshole Bay, marked by a huge marina and high rise apartments and into the Ship Canal where they are confronted by the Hiram Chittenden locks . . . About 10 percent of the fish make use of the ladder provided for their convenience, the rest go through the locks with the boats." Once past the locks the salmon continued through the canal into Lake Union, in the heart of the city. "They get a fish's eye view of the University of Washington and the Seattle Yacht Club before turning into Lake Washington to spend the summer. Come fall, they will swim past the sprawling aircraft plant at Renton and directly under the Renton City Library, which spans the Cedar River. And now, at last, they are home." [12] A few will go north in Lake Washington to Sammamish Slough and Lake.

After spawning the red fish quickly expire; their bodies disintegrate and fertilize the Cedar River so there will be food for their offspring who will be transformed into gleaming smolts and go to sea, making the remarkable metropolitan journey in a reverse direction.

Indian Fishing Controversy

It is difficult now, as one visits Puget Sound or the Olympic Peninsula, to imagine oneself back in the early nineteenth century when this was Indian country and few white men could be seen: the ineffable beauty of the land, its towering forests and sparkling rivers, the shining mountains and endless parade of migrating geese and ducks on a spring day, and gulls, plovers, sandpipers, and terns along the shimmering white beaches. Settlement and land use have greatly changed the picture. There remain a few thousand Indians on various reservations who are not often seen on the streets of Seattle, Tacoma, or Olympia but feel in their blood the magnet of their ancestral land.

Clarence Pickernell, a Quinault Indian, puts it as follows:

> This is my land
> From the time of the first moon
> Till the time of the last sun.
> It was given to my people . . .
> I take good care of this land,
> For I am part of it.
> I take good care of the animals,
> For they are my brothers and sisters.
> I take care of the streams and rivers,
> For they clean my land.
> I honor Ocean as my father,
> For he gives me food and a means of travel.
> Ocean knows everything for he is everywhere . . .
> He sees much and knows more.
> He says, "Take care of my sister, Earth,
> She is young and has little wisdom, but much kindness."
> I am forever grateful for this beautiful and bountiful earth.
> God gave it to me.
> This is my land.

Love of the land has withered away among urbanized white people who now inhabit Puget Sound and the Olympic Peninsula, but to the Indians it is still a psychological and social force. They regard the rivers as their own, and many are determined to fish them in defiance of law. Three small tribes, the Muckleshoots, Puyallup, and Nisqually, have been in the forefront of the fight to exercise the rights they believe they possess to fish on off-reservation streams in whatever manner they choose, particularly on the Green, Nisqually, and Puyallup Rivers where the state forbids nets to be used and permits fishing for steelhead only with hook and line. The conflicts have been bitter as Indians put their nets in these and other rivers. Pitched battles have occurred between state police and Indian fishermen, and many cases similar to those precipitated by the Indians on the Columbia River have come to the Washington courts. Yet despite some adverse decisions, Washington state fish and game agencies have pressed their campaign to eliminate what they regard as illegal fishing harmful to the resources and have won their battles in the courts.

The Department of Fisheries provides off-reservation fisheries for several Indian tribes, often at times and in places where non-Indians are forbidden to fish. Some of the tribes use methods and gear outlawed for non-Indians such as spears, set nets, hoop nets, etc. Yet the Indians remain unsatisfied.

The decision by Judge Belloni in the Columbia River controversy, granting the Indians the right to fish at their accustomed places in contravention of the ban on net fishing above Bonneville dam, was viewed by Washington state Indians as a favorable turning point in establishing their off-reservation rights. But Washington officials have not established separate fishing seasons outside the Columbia River and continue to arrest Indians who try to fish off their reservation with nets.

The latest in a series of decisions was rendered by the United States Supreme Court on April 22, 1972: it let stand a Washington state court ruling against Muckleshoot Indians convicted of illegally taking steelhead with a gill net. The court rejected Indian claims that the state law barring such activity is an infringement of the off-reservation rights of treaty-protected Indians.

On May 4, 1972, the Washington Superior Court forbade the Puyallup Indians from catching steelhead with commercial gear in the Puyallup River. The majority opinion, written by Justice Robert Hunter, said that the Indians' rights are "subject to the reach of the state powers and regulations are not discriminatory against the Indians." He stipulated, however, that "the Game Department must provide annual regulations for a Puyallup Indian net fishery of steelhead if it is determined such a fishery would not be inconsistent with necessary conservation." In other words, he upheld the view that the Indians outside their reservations are subject to state fishery conservation laws and regulations like all other citizens.

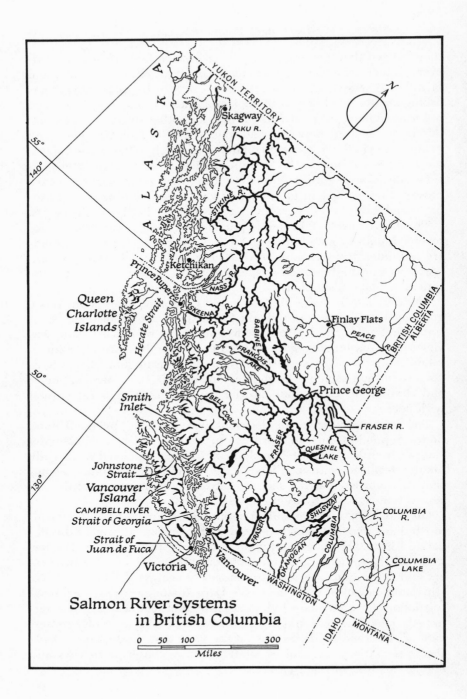

Salmon River Systems
in British Columbia

0   50   100   300
Miles

Vicissitudes of the British Columbia Fisheries

BRITISH COLUMBIA is 700 miles long as the crow flies, stretching from latitude 49° to 60° north, a land area exceeding that of Texas but with a population of only 2.2 million. Its fissured and jagged coastline totals some 16,000 miles, while offshore lie the Queen Charlotte Islands and Vancouver Island, longest in the eastern Pacific, and numerous lesser sea breaks. Rain and mist prevail a large part of the year along the coast; in the interior the landscape ranges from junglelike forests where precipitation exceeds 100 inches to arid valleys that obtain only ten inches annually.

If you take the ferry in summer from Kelsey Bay on the northeast coast of Vancouver Island through the Inside Passage to Alaska, you pass a fjordlike verdurous land. The boat winds in and out of quiet, narrow sounds. Some of the mountaintops are tinged with snow; the sea changes from golden in the afternoon to blood-red in the long twilight. Opalescent clouds move across the sky and numerous islands float by, mountainous, or low and wooded, with steep rocky banks. Many are uninhabited. A lighthouse or a Coast Guard station occasionally interrupts the wilderness. There are few settlements until you reach Prince Rupert near the mouth of the Skeena River.

Here and there a gill netter may be seen, his orange float marker bobbing in the clear water. A tug propels a heavily laden barge heading for Alaska; a timber raft passes. In the morning the water has a glassy sheen and the rockbound coast is reflected as in a mirror. This is a world of mountains, forests, rivers, lakes, rock, snow, and fish, and not much has changed since the land was first peopled by the aborigines perhaps thirty centuries ago.

✻

The Rivers

The topography of British Columbia is dominated by mountain ranges and "trenches" with long intermontane lakes and long, straight river reaches that break through the divides.

There are about 1500 rivers and lakes in British Columbia that support stocks of salmon and/or steelhead trout. Of these the Fraser, Skeena, and Nass systems are the largest and most productive. All but a few of the major rivers flow directly into the Pacific. The outlets of several drainages, including the Yukon, Taku, and Stikine, are in Alaska. The Okanagan rises in British Columbia and joins the Columbia River in the state of Washington. About 500 miles of the Columbia itself, or 40 percent of its total length, lies in Canada.

The richest salmon river in Canada is unquestionably the Fraser, notable for its sockeye and pinks but also possessing considerable populations of chinook (here called "springs" and if large enough "tyee"), coho, chum, and steelhead trout. Like the Columbia, it is an historic river, the artery for the voyageurs, trappers, miners, and farmers who came into the interior of western Canada to seek their fortunes. The Fraser watershed of 84,000 square miles — about a third the size of the Columbia — is dotted with many emerald lakes and veined with lengthy tributaries. The river follows an S-shaped course of 850 miles from its source near Mount Robson in the Canadian Rockies to its mouth near Vancouver, passing varied climatic zones and contrasting landscapes, ranging from coastal communities that may have little or no snow in some winters, with roses growing in backyards, to areas that are touched with frost every month of the year.

In its upper section the Fraser flows through the Rocky Mountain trench in a northwest direction, then swings to the south through the Cariboo Mountains, where it is joined by the Nechako from the west. In the middle section it continues to move south across the interior plateau, acquiring the flow of two major tributaries from the east, the Quesnel and Thompson Rivers, and two from the west, the Blackwater and Chilcotin. Below the Thompson the river enters a rugged seventy-mile canyon that cuts across the coast ranges via the aptly named Hell's Gate, amid spectacular scenery, then meanders across the flood plain of 900 square miles. In this stretch it is joined by the Harrison, Pitt, and Veddar Rivers before reaching the delta, where it divides into two main channels. Precipitation is lower in the delta than in the coastal mountains. From Hope upstream the valley is increasingly arid.

The Skeena, about 360 miles long, is essentially a mountain stream fed by short rivers like the Bulkley, Babine, and Sustut coming from the east and the Kispiox and Kitsumgallum from the west. Long, narrow Babine Lake, with an area of 300 square miles draining north through the Babine into the Skeena, supports the major population of Skeena River sockeye. Like all mountain streams the Skeena is sometimes erratic. Early summer heat causes rapid snow melt and then the river runs madly down the valley, topping its banks, sweeping aside all obstructions and wreaking immense damage. The Skeena reaches the Pacific at Prince Rupert.

The Nass issues from the coastal mountains and flows for about 200 miles in a south and southwest direction, dropping into the ocean at Portland Harbor, about thirty miles north of Prince Rupert. It produces principally pinks and sockeye.

There are other important salmon and steelhead rivers, including the Stikine and Taku in the north; the Bella Coola, which flows into Burke Channel, famous for its heavy runs of pinks; Rivers and Smith Inlets renowned for their sockeye; and streams on Vancouver Island that breed large numbers of sockeye, chum, and pinks, and on the Queen Charlotte Islands, which also produce pinks and chum.

The Runs

Except for Alaska, British Columbia is the chief producer of salmon in North America. In the decade of 1962–1971 the average yearly landings totaled 24.3 million fish with a value at dockside of $34 million, of which pinks constituted 12.8 million, sockeye 4.4 million, coho 4.2 million, chum 1.9 million, chinook about 1 million, and steelhead 20,000.[1]

Prized for its rich red flesh, sockeye is the mainstay of the net fisherman's catch in a good year. The Fraser, Nass, Skeena, Rivers and Smith Inlets and their tributaries produce most of these fish. In the late nineteenth and early twentieth centuries the Fraser alone provided annual catches of 20 to 30 million sockeye in the dominant cycle year. Some races of sockeye go 700 miles inland to their spawning grounds. They ascend from June to November, depending on the distance to their destination and its climate.

Pinks are found in 600 streams in British Columbia, but about 75 percent of the total emanate from fifty-seven rivers. They appear in large numbers only every other year. There are two distinct populations: those which come in even- and those which come in odd-numbered years. For reasons unknown, great disparity in abundance exists. In the Fraser River and Puget Sound areas pinks are quite plentiful in odd-numbered years and almost nonexistent in even-numbered. In some areas the reverse is true. In still other areas, such as the Skeena and Bella Coola Rivers, pink runs may occur in almost equal quantities in years of both cycles.

About 970 streams are known to support coho salmon, and 260 rivers produce chinook. Coho migrate up the rivers in September and October and spawn in late November and December. Being the largest of Pacific salmon species chinook fetch the most money to fishermen and are the trophy fish of anglers. The record commercial chinook caught in British Columbia is 120 pounds. Some of these husky fish push their way almost to the very source of the Fraser, at Rearguard Falls, 750 miles from the ocean.

Chum inhabit some 850 Canadian streams and are the last of the species to appear in the rivers, spawning usually in late fall in tributaries near the coast or in the main stems of the rivers, rarely more than 100 miles inland. However, some rivers have both summer and fall runs of chum; the latter are most abundant. Their flesh is creamy pink, excellent in flavor, but prone to lose its color during cooking and hence does not command top prices. The catches are mainly canned or smoked. In Japan, chum is rapidly gaining popularity in fresh markets; it is canned in Russia and Japan under the name "keta."

"Jacks" are common among chinook, steelhead, coho, and sockeye: these are undersized males that mature a year in advance of the normal population.

Tagging of fish has shown that most of the British Columbia salmon spend their ocean lives east of 165 ° west longitude, although an occasional individual will stray farther west and accomplish migrations totaling a few thousand miles. For instance, a sockeye tagged as a mature fish at 177 ° west longitude was recovered in the Nass River the same year, and another tagged as an immature at 177 ° east longitude was found in Rivers Inlet two years later. Canadian chum, sockeye, and steelhead make extensive odysseys through the Gulf of Alaska and sometimes as far as the mid-Aleutian islands. Pinks usually stay closer to North American shores.

A joint study by Canadian and American scientists for the period 1957–1964 revealed that salmon from the two countries hobnob in marine waters off southeast Alaska as well as off the coasts of British Columbia, Washington, Oregon, and even California and are caught by fishermen of both nations. According to Harold Godfrey of the

Pacific Biological Station at Nainamo, British Columbia, Canadian trollers take up to a third of the total harvest of chinooks bred in Columbia River hatcheries, and based on 1967 returns to the rivers of fish from the 1964 brood year, Canadians take 60 percent of the coho produced by Washington State hatcheries. Data on American catches of Canadian fish except sockeye and pinks are not available: harvests of Fraser River sockeye and pinks, under control of the International Pacific Salmon Fisheries Commission, are divided among fishermen of both nations.

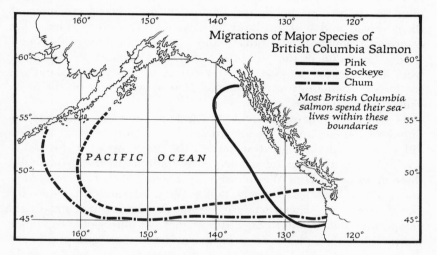

Traders and Canners

In 1827 the Hudson's Bay Company established Fort Langley, thirty-five miles above the mouth of the Fraser, as its headquarters in southern British Columbia. Fish naturally provided a large portion of the men's diet, and in fact about one third of the annual expenses in western trade went to buy salmon. Chief Factor Archibald McMillan promoted an international trade in salmon, chiefly to the Sandwich Islands (Hawaii), often amidst severe difficulties.

In lush years the sockeye were so plentiful that men were afraid to enter the river lest their boats be capsized by schools of fish rushing through the waters. It was not uncommon for the natives to bring in a thousand fish before eight in the morning, and many canoes had to be turned away for lack of facilities to salt and pack them. In time a saltery was established at Fort Langley, a cooper was brought from England, and exports of salt salmon were increased. Shipments to Hawaii were 400 barrels in 1840 and 1700 barrels in 1848.

In 1849 the company was granted sovereignty over the territory of Vancouver Island, and a few years later settlers began to arrive in sizable numbers. Local demand for fish increased, and the company attempted to meet the needs by large-scale purchases from the natives at the price of sixty fish for a $4 blanket.

Settlement was accelerated by discovery of gold in the Fraser River in 1858. At the height of the craze about 25,000 persons were panning for the yellow metal, and when deposits petered out many of them stayed and took up land for farming. Trade expanded. The company's monopoly was broken and a frontier economy developed. At the formation of the province of British Columbia in 1871 there were an estimated 90,000 settlers: Victoria on Vancouver Island was the largest community with 3600 and New Westminster on the lower Fraser next with 1650.

As white settlement expanded the Indian way of life that had endured for millennia was threatened and the salmon, as Hugh McKervill says, "faced their greatest enemy: the white man and his industry." [2] The first successful cannery was built in 1870 at Annieville, three miles below New Westminster, by a young Scots fisherman Alexander Ewan and his partners James Wise, Alexander Loggie, and David Hennessy. Ewan was to become the dominant figure in the competitive industry until his death in 1907. A supply of cheap labor, mostly Chinese, a plenitude of inexpensive raw materials, and booming markets attracted entrepreneurs from many parts of the world. Some of them, however, failed to understand the peculiarities of an industry dependent upon the vagaries of nature and lost their capital; a few became wealthy. Expansion and mergers were the rule and exploitation of the fishermen a constant objective.

Canneries spread to the Nass, Rivers Inlet, Alert Bay, and other localities on the mainland coast, and to Vancouver and Queen Charlotte Islands. Production soared from 62,000 cases (forty-eight one-pound cans) in 1880 to over 400,000 cases in 1890. It averaged 700,000 cases in the decade 1900–1910, 1,200,000 cases in 1910–1920, and 1,500,000 cases in 1920–1940, and 1,280,000 cases since then.

The number of canneries increased from twelve in 1880 to a peak of eighty in 1913. At one time there were forty on the Fraser River, concentrated at Steveston. Overfishing and the disastrous blockade at Hell's Gate in 1913 decimated the Fraser runs and forced many canneries to close. To supply this huge industry required an armada of fishing vessels. At first they were mostly rented to the Indians, who received as little as a nickel per fish, or at best $50 a month and keep.

After the gold rushes many white men turned to fishing; later came hardworking, frugal immigrants from Japan who settled chiefly around Steveston and took up truck gardening and fishing for a living. Hundreds of Americans also entered the Fraser fishery, even after licenses to fish in Canadian waters were limited in 1892 to British subjects.

Most of the net fishermen came to be controlled by the canneries. Since a boat and a linen net were expensive, a company was willing to finance a man providing he delivered his entire catch to it. This arrangement was also advantageous to the fishermen because, in the event of a heavy run, canneries might be overloaded and would prefer to take the catches of those indebted to them rather than buy from an independent. If they had to buy, they might cut the price. Thus few fishermen could risk staying independent and chose instead to go into bondage to the companies.

Eventually some of the fishermen formed cooperatives in order to be free of company control. They adopted the policy that the entire catch of every member must be accepted by the cannery providing it passed the quality test. Some of the cooperatives set up their own collection stations and even built canneries, a few of which are operated to this day on troll-caught fish.

At best, fishing is a gamble with nature. Men are willing to invest their money in a boat and gear and work hard in the hope of striking it rich. Adventure and challenge is in their blood. With luck a person may obtain a year's stake in a few weeks. Those who are skillful in handling boats and nets and knowledgeable about the fishes' movements may do well year after year. In the industry they are known as "highliners" and are eagerly sought by the canneries, but their numbers are few.

Before the Canadian Pacific Railway reached the coast in 1885, markets for Canadian fish were mainly overseas. It took a ship up to five months to deliver a cargo to England before the Panama Canal was opened in 1914. It would then be in storage for perhaps two months. Thus the packer would have to wait a considerable length of time before receiving payment. As a consequence he was usually in debt to the brokerage house, which acted as agent, for a commission, and which advanced money for supplies as well as cash to the Chinese labor contractor. The broker also handled insurance on the cannery, the pack, and the shipment while in transit and sometimes chartered the vessel that carried the cargo abroad. He also imported materials, such as tinplate and machinery, needed by the plant. When a packer showed signs of financial weakness the broker promptly foreclosed. Relatively few canners escaped the broker's clutches and many fell victims to the more ruthless ones. Market gluts, labor strife, and falling prices added to the difficulties of the business.

The Fraser with its abundant sockeye accounted for a large portion of the total salmon pack until 1913. How long the heavily fished stocks would have continued to produce bountifully without the Hell's Gate calamity that year nobody can say. Roderick Haig-Brown points out that "by the end of the century the fishery was so intense by both Canadians and Americans that it probably approached full exploitation of the runs though sheer abundance of fish often overloaded the canning facilities and excessive numbers of fish escaped to the spawning areas in some years." [3]

The rickety town of Steveston was the center of this industry. In 1901 it had twenty-nine canneries strung out along the waterfront. Plank streets and shoddy wooden structures were its landmarks; fishing boats with sails blowing in the wind crowded its wharves. Chinese in pigtails, Indians, Finns, Swedes, Americans, and Canadians jostled each other on the narrow pavements and in the numerous saloons. For two or three months of the year the town was "alive and kicking" and during the remainder it was asleep, noted a reporter for a Toronto newspaper in 1901. Since that was a dominant year, when 25.8 million sockeye were landed, the markets were glutted and much was wasted.

> It was lamentable [he said] to see the great overplus of salmon at the canneries this year. . . . If there had been anybody on hand with salt and barrels he could have sent off carload after carload of good sound salmon, which he could have purchased at five cents apiece. At present large quantities of fish have to be thrown away or used as manure. The abundant catch of this year means much to Vancouver. It is so much wealth cast up by the sea into the outstretched hands of these British Columbia workers. [4]

The industry has changed considerably since this account was written. Transportation methods and facilities have vastly improved, markets have expanded, and processing has been centralized in a few large plants that can, salt, smoke, freeze, or distribute salmon fresh and also process halibut, flatfish, cod, rockfish, herring, etc. In Steveston taverns and their jukeboxes have replaced the sawdusty saloons, and there is more of a permanent than a floating population, for diversification keeps fish processing going the year round.

Fishing and Fishermen

Commercial salmon fishing in British Columbia occurs principally along the inner coast and estuarial waters. The coast is protected from the ocean's fury by thousands of islands, reefs, and rocks. Seiners and gill netters ply the usually placid channels and inlets that sometimes cut deep into the mountainous coastline. Trollers operate in more open waters and a very large fleet of seiners and gill netters works the entrance to the Strait of Juan de Fuca.

"In early spring," says the veteran fisherman A. V. Hill, "fleets of small trolling vessels venture out into the waters off Vancouver and Queen Charlotte islands to meet the salmon schools which will later swarm into the coastal streams and the larger Fraser and Skeena Rivers." They also take salmon bound for the Columbia and other United States rivers.

"The sea may become quite rough off the Canadian coast, and even the protected waters are not always kind to the men who seek to wrest a living from them," adds Hill. Tides up to twenty-five feet roar through the narrow channels, causing "treacherous rapids and whirlpools, which even the fast passenger steamers are not able to stem." [5] Tides and winds can whip smooth waters into vicious tide-rips, and even sturdy fishing vessels may be overturned by williwaws sweeping suddenly down the mountains. However, there are innumerable inlets and coves where fishermen can find shelter and anchorage for their boats.

Fishing areas are generally chosen by the fishermen themselves, who are free to move around. Success naturally depends on being in the right place at the right time. "The thrill of pulling in the best catches of the season cannot be described," says Hill. "These are the moments that a fisherman lives for. His prestige in the fleet, no less than his pocket, depends on the gains he may make during this short period, of which he has dreamed all through the preceding winter."

The Canadian industry has had a turbulent labor history. There have been conflicts among the fishermen, seiners versus gill netters, trollers versus the rest, and especially fishermen versus processors. Each group is organized in an association fighting for its special interests. Indians and Japanese also have their protective organizations. Sometimes a man may belong to more than one group because he fishes several types of gear during the year.

Varying fortunes of the fishermen, with scarcity of fish giving way to gluts and vice versa, is partly responsible for the strife. Unions have frequently balked at accepting prices offered by the companies, and companies, pressed by bitter competition and the uncertainty of a raw material supply, refuse to be intimidated and thus many strikes have occurred. These stoppages may last a few weeks or days; meanwhile the swarms of fish ascend the rivers unharvested.

Disaster at Hell's Gate

In the year 1913 a record-breaking sockeye run occurred on the Fraser River. The waters of Juan de Fuca Strait at the southern end of Vancouver Island and Johnstone Strait at the northern end through which the fish had to pass were crowded with boats as wave upon wave of fish headed for the river. It was estimated that 38 million returned from the sea that summer and 31 million were taken in the nets (compared to an average of 9 million in the previous twenty years), leaving 7 million to make their way to the spawning grounds. But disaster lay ahead and no such escapement materialized.

Between Lytton and Yale the Fraser flows through one of the deepest canyons in North America. Here the river becomes an extraordinarily rapid and turbulent waterway, racing between rocky cliffs and steep canyon walls. On the west or right bank are the tracks of the Canadian Pacific Railroad, completed in 1885, and on the east or left bank the Canadian National Railroad (formerly the Canadian Northern).

Hell's Gate was probably always a difficult passage for fish, at least at some water levels, for here the flow may vary by a hundred feet during the year. During construction of the railroad the rubble and rock blasted from the cliff walls were dumped into the river and fish passage became difficult or impossible except at a few isolated ranges of water level. It was said that the river flowed on edge as it rushed through the narrow Hell's Gate.

In building the Canadian Northern the engineers apparently gave no thought to stream stability or the needs of migratory fish who went past the Gate. In 1913 an obstruction of rock and gravel had built up in the narrow channel below the rapids; this proved to be insurmountable. Vast numbers of salmon collected in pools and eddies, unable to advance upstream. They died without spawning.

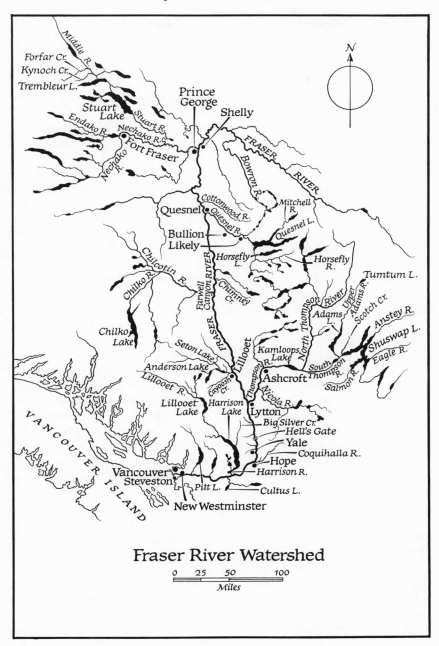

Fraser River Watershed

0   25   50   100

Miles

Already in July masses of fish were seen to be in difficulties as the river started to drop. Temporary fishways were blasted out and channels kept open, but these emergency measures could permit only a small portion of the migrants to pass. Early in August thousands of red fish were milling around in a stretch of ten miles below the Gate; many succeeded in gliding or jumping over slippery rocks, but as the flow dropped in September and October movement became extremely difficult. The river and its side channels and lagoons literally turned red with dead and dying sockeye and many upstream tributaries were quite empty of spawners that fall. The run was a disaster.

In 1914 conditions improved somewhat, at least during the early part of the sockeye run. "Until August 14," said the official report of the Canadian government, "the passage of Hell's Gate had seemingly been successfully accomplished by all the fish which attempted it . . . On this day, however, with the steady lowering of the river, a new condition presented itself." The fish could not negotiate the east side of the stream because of a great rock slide that had occurred the previous February. To facilitate their migration a flume was built around this point, and in addition dip netting was resorted to in order to get them past this obstruction. By September the river was low enough to make fish movement easier, but immense losses had already occurred.

Even though the rock slide was partially removed, for years afterward salmon continued to encounter difficulties at the Gate, especially when the water level was between twenty-five and fifty feet on the gauge. Delay in passage killed many fish before they could reach their natal waters, especially late in the season when they were near spawning and had only a limited amount of energy. Dr. W. F. Thompson in his study of the effects of Hell's Gate on the sockeye run concluded that in the twenty years 1913 to 1933 United States and Canadian fishermen were deprived of catches worth "between a quarter of a billion and a third of a billion dollars, or an average of between $12 and $15 million annually." [6]

Despite the spectacular decline in the runs it took a long time to fully repair the damage, mainly because the fish, while born in Canadian territory, had to pass through American waters to reach their destination. This in effect made them an international resource that required bilateral agreements to solve the problem. There were also other factors that prevented an agreement, especially the perennial question of who owns the fish and who is entitled to take them.

In 1908 an international commission had been created to consider uniform and common regulations in the two countries, and its recommendations were actually enacted into law in Canada. But American fishermen and packers objected to its stipulations and the treaty was sidetracked. Canada thereupon repealed its legislation.

John N. Cobb, writing in 1930, said:

> On the American side a few people, among these a few of the more intelligent canners, pleaded for the enactment of laws that would adequately protect the salmon, but these were overborne by the great bulk of the packers and fishermen who, disregarding all the warnings and teachings of experience, insisted upon going ruthlessly forward with the slaughter, and when reproached with their shortsightedness clamored for the establishment of more salmon hatcheries, as though the latter could accomplish the miracle of increasing the supply of fry from a steadily decreasing supply of eggs.[7]

There was urgent need for international action to save the Fraser's stocks from overfishing, but deliberations were marked by a quarter of a century of inaction. Moreover, many people did not believe that the Hell's Gate blockade was a serious factor in declining catches. It was not till 1937 that a bilateral treaty was ratified by both nations, creating the International Pacific Salmon Fisheries Commission headquartered in New Westminster, British Columbia, consisting of three representatives from each country with authority over convention waters on both sides of the boundary. It was authorized to investigate the status of the Fraser River salmon in both freshwater and saltwater, to establish hatcheries if these were needed, and to recommend to the respective governments such projects as seemed to be required to improve the propagation of fish in convention waters. The commission was also given full power to regulate the fishery, including mesh sizes and types of gear, but not until eight years had elapsed.

A key provision of the treaty was that harvests were to be shared equally, as far as possible, by Americans and Canadians. Each country was made responsible for the enforcement of regulations in its waters: in Canada the federal Department of Fisheries and in the United States the Washington State Department of Fisheries. Each government was to contribute equally to operation of the commission and such investments as would enhance the fishery — a unique example of international fishery cooperation.

Although all five species of salmon plus steelhead are found in the

Fraser, the commission was restricted at first to the study and regulation of the sockeye. Not till 1957 were the pinks placed under its control on the same basis as the sockeye, to be harvested equally by Canadians and Americans.

Management of the Fraser River

Restoration of the Fraser's plenitude has been a slow and laborious task, only partially successful. First, it was necessary to prove beyond a reasonable doubt that Hell's Gate was at times a block to sockeye migration. This was done by painstaking research under the supervision of the first director of the commission, the American biologist Dr. W. F. Thompson, and was reinforced by a prolonged period of blockage in the year 1941. Second, it was necessary to build adequate fishways, and third, fishing on the various runs or races had to be managed in such a manner that adequate escapements would occur.

When the commission started work in 1938, only part of the Adams River sockeye run (a major segment of the Fraser run) had come back to something like the capacity of its spawning area, mainly because these fish come through Hell's Gate when water levels are unusually favorable. One or two other races were also coming back. Fishways were finally completed at the Gate in 1946 at a cost of $1 million, a tiny fraction of the losses incurred during the years of apathy and neglect.

The fishways consist of two gigantic flumes 45 feet high from the base to the deck, 220 feet long on the right bank, and 460 feet long on the left bank, attached to the sides of the narrow, rocky canyon, whose bottom is 600 feet below the railroad and adjoining highway. The right bank fishway is twenty feet wide, and the left bank fishway is part twenty feet and part twelve feet wide. In addition to these facilities on each bank, smaller fishways were subsequently built on top of the original ones when it was found that sockeye were blocked at high water levels that submerged the bottom fishways. The operating range of the fishways is from elevation twenty-three feet to elevation fifty-four feet, or through the levels at which blocks occurred. The structures are submerged at water levels above elevations of fifty-four feet. As the fish swim below the surface the turbidity of the water does not usually permit observation of them swimming through the structures. It was not till 55,000 sockeye had been tagged and traced that the water levels at which the fish could not pass Hell's Gate and the effect of such levels on the different races of sockeye that spawn above the canyon were determined.

Fishways were also installed at Bridge River Rapids near Lillooet and at Farwell canyon on the Chilcotin River. Thanks to all these devices, salmon can ascend the many rivers and lakes in the upper watershed. Fluctuations in the Fraser, which may be as much as six or seven feet in a day and a hundred feet between high and low water, do not affect operations of the Hell's Gate fishway.

Pinks are weaker swimmers than sockeye and the abundant pre-1913 runs to the upper Fraser and its tributary, the Thompson River, were completely exterminated by the Hell's Gate blockage. When the Gate was provided with fishways some of the pinks from lower river races dispersed and spawned above the Gate, and today there are substantial numbers of these fishes in Seton Creek and the Thompson River in odd-numbered years.

Management of a river like the Fraser is a complex and difficult task, especially because of the treaty provision that the catches must be divided equally between the two nations. Basic requirements are (1) extensive knowledge of the various races (a race is a stock of fish spawning at a specific time in a given river, or in specific areas of the river system), their life cycles, habitat needs, and migrations, (2) careful monitoring of the runs and enforcement of regulations so as to provide a proper balance between catches and the escapement needed to perpetuate the crop, and (3) constant vigilance to protect the watershed (if possible) from developments that would adversely affect the aquatic environment.

In the first bulletin published by the commission Dr. Thompson showed that each race of sockeye has individual characteristics and each passes the crucial Hell's Gate at approximately the same time every year when temperature and water level are most favorable. Thus the main run going to the Chilko river arrives at the Gate from July 30 to September 11, the Nechako River fish from August 2 to September 21, and the Shuswap-Adams River fish, generally the largest contingent, from September 9 to October 27. This arrangement by nature seems designed not only to prevent undue congestion in the narrow portion of the river but is in fact an exquisite adaptation during countless centuries of each race to the environmental conditions existing on its spawning and rearing area.

Each race also has a given journey to make and a given length of time to accomplish it. Sockeye that must make a run of 700 miles to Stuart Lake in the headwaters of the Fraser enter the river early in summer, while those that head for Chilko Lake in the middle of the watershed and have a much shorter journey arrive a month or more later. By studying the scales of sockeye taken in sample catches in saltwater, biologists can tell which area they are bound for — the growth rings on the scales identify their place of origin as well as length of time they lived as juveniles in freshwater. Forecasts of the annual runs to specific areas are based on these studies plus estimates of the number of juvenile fish that went to sea from the previous brood year. The success of these predictions naturally varies considerably, for conditions in the ocean cannot be known and nature has a perverse way of upsetting scientific predictions. But the predictions are the basis for the regulations and are valuable in shaping the fishing industry's plans for the season.

Actual management during the fishing season is on a day-to-day basis. If the army of salmon heading for Stuart Lake or Adams River, for example, seems to be smaller than expected, fishing on these stocks is halted for a day or two on both sides of the boundary so as to permit a greater number to escape and insure a desired crop of spawners. Conversely, if there seem to be more Chilko River fish in the ocean than are required for projected escapement needs, an additional twenty-four or forty-eight hours of fishing time is allotted by the commission.

At the height of the season the commission's office in New Westminster is like a battlefield command post. All salmon that are taken off the coast or in the river are reported to headquarters. Men with earphones sit glued to the communications network, receiving and correlating data. Maps and charts for each tributary hang on the walls, and graphs showing the trend of the catches and their racial composition are drawn every morning so that the biologists can decide if things are going as expected or if adjustments have to be made in order to divvy up the catches and also obtain the desired escapement.

On Tuesday August 4, 1970, I had an opportunity to observe the weekly opening on the Canadian side. Precisely at 8 A.M. the fleet was lined up in Albion Box off Steveston; the Americans, based in Blaine, Washington, had begun fishing the day before. Flying over the Fraser delta one could see the boats spread out in the sea in the paths of the fish returning from their hegira in the Pacific, fat and primed for ascent of the river. The San Juan Islands were green and lustrous, while the Olympic Mountains in Washington were obscured by a veil of clouds.

In 1971, 5,930,000 Fraser River sockeye and 4,500,000 pinks were landed. The sockeye total exceeded that of any year in this cycle dating back to 1899, but of course it was much less than peak years before 1913 or the fabulous 1958 run. The sockeye run was estimated at 7,600,000 fish, of which 86.7 percent were caught commercially, 2.3 percent were taken by the Indian fishery, and 11 percent were recorded on the spawning grounds. Canadian fishermen garnered 52.5 percent of the fish caught in convention waters and Americans 47.5 percent.[8]

The average annual catch of sockeye in the period 1950 to 1971 amounted to only 36 percent of the average catch of some nine million fish in the years 1894 to 1913. Substantial increases in production of both sockeye and pink salmon are needed, if pre-1913 levels of abundance are to be reached, as the chairman of the IPSFC said at the annual meeting of the commission.

The Incredible Adams River

For purposes of management the Fraser is divided into a number of subwatersheds. Runs of sockeye and pink (the major species) vary considerably in each of them. In the years 1954, 1958, and 1966 the Adams River was by far the most prolific; in some years it produced more sockeye than all the other streams in the watershed combined. Adams River sockeye usually show up in the nets during the first two weeks of August, and by the end of the month they build up to tremendous numbers. A million fish may be taken in one day by the combined American and Canadian fishing fleets. In 1958 the run was a record 18 million, in 1970 only 3.5 million.

Spawning of such huge numbers of red fish occurs mostly on 160 acres of gravel located about 300 miles above Steveston. It takes the four to five pound salmon fifteen days to arrive at their destination traveling at the rate of twenty miles a day. Indians collect their share with dip nets as the sockeye battle the tumultuous current along the Fraser's canyon walls and with spears as they ascend Little River between Little and Big Shuswap Lakes. Two days are required for their journey from Hell's Gate to the Thompson River, thence they go through Kamloops and Little Shuswap Lakes to Big Shuswap Lake and into Adams River. They spawn about nine days after arrival and are dead within eighteen days. The fry emerge from the gravel in the spring and spend their first year of life in Big Shuswap Lake; most survivors migrate out of the lake in the following spring as yearlings three or four inches long, go down the Thompson River to the Fraser, and thence to the Pacific Ocean.

From 1 to 2 million fish may mate in the 160 acres of gravel at one time. This spectacle is open to the public, and during a single weekend 30,000 persons may witness it. The fish are well distributed throughout the area, footpaths are laid out along the river, and spectators stand goggle-eyed watching the thrashing, mating fish who seem to be oblivious to their presence. Pairs of spawners are put into viewing tanks, thus giving camera fans an opportunity to photograph them at close range. There are graphic displays of the life history of the sockeye and evils of pollution. In a huge tent home economists give salmon-cooking demonstrations.

Adams River is seven and a half miles long with a drainage of only 1600 square miles. Little River is about two and a half miles long and spawners concentrate on about 140 acres. It is estimated that every one of the combined acres of the two rivers is capable of producing a crop of sockeye valued at roughly $150,000, probably the most precious spawning grounds in the world.[9]

Dam the Fraser?

Successful protection of the teeming rivers from adverse development has been a prime reason for sustainment of British Columbia salmon stocks despite crucial setbacks on the Fraser and other rivers. "By far the most serious threat to salmon runs in the immediate future is that of hydroelectric dams," wrote Roderick Haig-Brown in *The Living Land,* published in 1961.[10] While his fears have not yet materialized the statement is still true.

At the present time the Fraser, which has immense hydroelectric potential, remains a relatively natural and undisturbed river except in the rapidly growing Vancouver area, around Prince George and elsewhere. To safeguard the rivers for the benefit of the anadromous fishes requires eternal vigilance. Power promoters naturally have their eyes on the Fraser. The nature of British Columbia streams and terrain, points out Haig-Brown, requires the use of very high dams and often a series on the same stream, and thus colossal amounts of electricity could be generated and sold not only in Canada but south of the border, especially in California, using the federal transmission system in Washington and Oregon as a conveyance belt.

In the early 1950s plans were unveiled by the British Columbia Electric Company, later expropriated by the provincial government, for a series of dams to harness parts of the Fraser watershed. The kingpin in this scheme was 720-foot Moran dam, which could be built twenty miles north of Lillooet on the main stem of the Fraser, 220 miles from Vancouver. The plan also included Cottonwood dam 250 feet high and Lillooet dam 130 feet high. In addition, storage projects were planned at Stuart Lake, Babine Lake, and Chilko Lake, all abounding with salmon.

Outlining the plan at the fifth annual National Resource Conference, held at Victoria in 1952, the power company spokesman let his imagination roam. He foresaw the possibility "as yet unexplored, of diverting portions of the Peace, Parsnip and Finlay Rivers into the Fraser at Prince George." This would store a fantastic volume of water to generate electricity in amounts comparable to those of the Columbia River dams. There would also be the benefits of flood control, a navigation channel for a considerable distance on the Fraser, irrigation water for 30,000 acres of land, etc. Cost of the Moran project alone was then estimated at $500 million.

As for the fishery, the speaker admitted there would be problems. But "I am confident," he said, "that, given the money, our fishery and engineering experts can find a way of surmounting the resulting difficulties which admittedly today appear all but insurmountable." [11]

Little more was heard of the scheme for years.

In May 1970 the British Columbia Chamber of Commerce passed a resolution urging the provincial government, which had almost unlimited authority to undertake vast public work schemes, to carry out a feasibility study of the Moran site. This announcement prompted Gerry Kidd, editor of *Western Fisheries,* the industry's trade paper, to comment: "Today, when ecologists are warning of environmental collapse around the corner and conservationists are predicting the extinction of many species of birds, fish and animals in the next 30 years, it is disheartening to hear these quick-buck boomers seriously advocate walling up one of the world's last great salmon rivers." [12]

In October 1971 the federal Department of Fisheries and the International Pacific Salmon Fisheries Commission published the results of a two-year study of what might be called "the folly of Moran dam." This megalith would wall up a canyon through which about 60 percent of the Fraser River water flows. It would have a maximum head of 730 feet and create a 170-mile reservoir that might be drawn down at times as much as 290 feet. At maximum operation the plant would have 3.6 million kilowatts of capacity or twice that of the original Grand Coulee dam. It would however prevent 44 percent of the sockeye and much of the chinook, coho, and steelhead from reaching their spawning grounds. The dam would create staggering fishery problems such as engineers and biologists have never before struggled with.

The report concluded that "there is no precedent for facilities to pass such large numbers of salmon that would have to be passed at Moran and there is no precedent for preservation of any salmon resource upstream from a dam as high as that suggested for Moran." [13] Fortunately for the fishery the Social Credit party, which ran the British Columbia government for twenty years during which it did much to exploit the province's natural resources, especially in building the Peace River power project, was driven from office in 1972. The new government, according to Haig-Brown, a member of the IPSFC, "are committed to opposition to the Moran dam or any damage to fish on the Fraser — and I hope elsewhere." [14]

In an attempt to boost natural production and level out fluctuations in output, international and federal agencies have launched a program of artificial salmon production. The Salmon Commission has built spawning and incubating channels in the Fraser River watershed and the federal Department of Fisheries has undertaken similar projects in other areas, as discussed in Chapter XIX.

On October 6, 1972, Minister of the Environment Jack Davis opened the Capilano fish hatchery on the Capilano River, the first new salmon hatchery built in forty years and the first of a half dozen now under construction. It is capable of holding 2,000,000 eggs and the ponds will carry 1,500,000 fry. Biologists estimate the survival to adult stage will total 68,000 coho, 3000 chinook, and 3200 steelhead trout. Allowing for escapement, this will mean an annual catch of 50,000 salmon starting in 1975 when the cycle is complete, or ten times more than the pre-dam production of the Capilano River.

Sport Fishing

The increase of personal incomes and leisure time has resulted in a growing demand for salmon and steelhead angling in British Columbia. Most of the fishing occurs in tidal waters, in the Strait of Georgia, around the Gulf Islands, and the bays and coves of Vancouver Island and the lower mainland. The tidal fishery is a boat fishery; in summer, from June to early September the clear waters are dotted with thousands of motor craft and sailboats from which men, women, boys, and girls fish with hook and line. The sun shines almost every day, skies are blue, winds calm, and the air is like a tonic to the nerves. On a Sunday one may see thousands of craft, from twelve-footers to oceangoing cruisers, drifting with the tides. Cottony clouds scud across the sky, the hilly islands are green with fir and madroña trees; blue and white ferries going by do not disturb the fishermen, nor do the gulls screeching and diving on the waters. All afternoon the fishermen sit in their boats, and only the approach of night drives them into port. Marinas and public docks are full, women are cooking the freshly caught fish for supper, while others, who made no catch that day, are preparing hamburgers or steaks on charcoal broilers.

Throughout the summer many communities hold salmon derbies to stimulate interest in the sport. For example, Galiano Island held a salmon derby from July 1 to 31, 1971, that was sponsored by the Community Club; all cash and merchandise prizes were donated by the merchants. It was a modest affair, with only $100 for the grand prize, compared to the derby sponsored by a Vancouver newspaper that offered a grand prize of $25,000 and $30,000 in lesser prizes for the largest salmon caught during the weekend of August 15–16, 1971, in an area of 400 square miles of sheltered waters in Howe Sound and English Bay immediately adjacent to the city of Vancouver. About 5000 boats participated.

The number of sportsmen in these paradisaical waters increases each year. Fishing effort in the Strait of Georgia and adjoining bays rose from 189,000 boat-days in 1960 to 265,000 in 1968 (one boat-day is equivalent to two and a half angler days). The sport catch in this period averaged 102,000 coho, 46,000 chinook, and 106,000 grilse.

Sport fishing is also booming in nontidal waters. Most of the coastal streams on Vancouver Island and the mainland contain natural populations of steelhead trout, coho or chinook, and sometimes two or three species. Coho is far more numerous than chinook (called "springs" in British Columbia), but chinook are trophy fish and hence draw many anglers to the Campbell, Bella Coola, Bulkley, Morice, and other rivers. Chinook are caught in early summer, cohos mainly in late summer and early fall, winter steelhead from December through May. Some streams have runs of summer steelhead from June through August. Unusually large steelhead are frequently taken in the Kispiox near Hazelton, and in the Brem, Dean, and other rivers that are accessible only by boat or aircraft. The Thompson River is a well-known summer and fall steelhead stream.

The sport fishery produces considerable economic benefits to the province. According to the Department of Fisheries, "a superficial estimate indicates an annual value [for the recreational fishery] in the Fraser system alone is in excess of $40 million." The department is now engaged in a study to assess the value accurately.

Haig-Brown chastised the Canadian government for its neglect of sport fishing opportunities in an address to the 15th British Columbia Natural Resources Conference in 1962:

> For some reasons, in spite of their tangible yields to the economy and their tangible yields to the entire society, we continue to be unable to take the outdoor recreational resources seriously. The game fish resource is no exception . . . We have no accurate count of our summer steelhead streams and we know nothing of the varying life histories of the runs that frequent them. We do not know with any certainty which salmon stocks contribute most to the sport fishery. We have only the vaguest ideas of the needs and preferences of the people who use the resource and make no attempt to differentiate in providing for them . . . No other resource is so casually regarded by government today and no other is so starved for research and administrative funds. Yet we are using the resource with steadily increasing intensity, in the face of steadily increasing competition from other water users, and in some instances, the most intense commercial competition for the fish themselves.

Since 1962 competition for the salmon and steelhead has accelerated, but little has been done to take the steps suggested by Haig-Brown. Both commercial and sport fishermen find that too many boats are chasing too few fish.

In an effort to relieve the too-many-boats-chasing-too-few-fish situation, the federal government has instituted a policy of reducing commercial fishing licenses. In 1968 7000 vessels were fishing for salmon, but 70 percent of the catch was made by a third of the 10,000 fishermen. In that year the Department of Fisheries instituted a license-control program designed to eliminate the less efficient boats in the interest of conservation and better distribution of returns to fishermen.

*

The Summing Up

If we compare the Canadian experience in handling its Pacific salmon with the American certain conclusions are evident. Thanks mainly to the slower pace of economic development, the Canadians have up to now been able to save a larger proportion of their original stocks than the Americans did in California, in the Columbia River and Oregon's coastal streams, or in Puget Sound. The Canadian record is much better on the west coast than on the east coast. Canadian landings of Pacific salmon exceed that of the United States, excluding Alaska.

In 1971 Rod Hourston, Pacific Area Director of the Department of Fisheries, reported that "despite increasing catches by commercial fishermen, stiff regulations in some seasons and the recent complaints concerning threats to spawning grounds by industry and land settlement, British Columbia's salmon resources have increased by 13 percent during the past decade . . . During the past 10 years, commercial fishermen caught 230 million salmon, compared to 206 million in the previous decade." Hourston added that since 1950 the department has carried out an $18 million resource development program, and the cooperation of the pulp and paper industry in setting high pollution standards in new mills has played a part in the increase of production.[15]

British Columbia is the second largest canner of salmon in North America, exceeded only by Alaska. As Appendix Table 11 shows, output in 1970 and 1971 was about 1.4 million cases each year and the trend has been fairly stable since 1955, though down from the levels of the previous fifteen years.

As a wave of nationalism sweeps over Canada, especially in the western provinces, Canadian fishermen are pressing for a greater share of the salmon in national waters, particularly those produced in the Fraser River system. Intermittent meetings have been held by Canadian and American fishery representatives seeking solutions to salmon problems of mutual concern. The Law of the Sea Conference, scheduled to be held in Chile in 1974, is expected to deal with salmon problems on a global scale.

The Canadians exert tight controls on newer pulp mills and other polluting industries. The Canadian Fisheries Act as amended in 1970 strengthened the national government's hand against polluters of waters frequented by fish by making each offense punishable with a fine of up to $5000 a day, a sum that deters even the wealthiest corporations. The Department of Fisheries requires all industrial effluents to be nontoxic before they can be discharged into rivers. No pulp mill can obtain a construction permit unless it can prove it will not harm the fishery and operations are closed down if something goes wrong.

There are eleven pulp mills now in British Columbia. In 1970 Jack Davis, then Minister of Fisheries, said that most of them were well equipped to take care of their wastes, but "a few are in difficulties with my department because they have not met our standards." Three new mills in the Prince George area in 1969 exceeded the Fisheries Department's limits for suspended solids in their waste emissions and steps were taken to have the situation corrected. The national government also keeps a close eye on sawmills to prevent their piling up sawdust in the streams. Log driving and timber cutting in sensitive watersheds are subject to strict regulation by the Fisheries Department. All this has helped to augment productivity of the rivers.

On Vancouver Island late in 1972 an action group called Save Our Salmon Committee from Tofino and Ucluelet, comprising mainly members of the troll fleet, protested the logging practices in their areas, where creeks and rivers were desecrated and logjams sometimes over a mile long were preventing fish from reaching their spawning grounds. Since repeated protests to the provincial Forest Service and federal Fisheries Service were futile the group decided to come en masse to the capital at Victoria in a caravan of trucks and cars, with their wives and children, and put their case before the provincial Minister of Lands, Forests and Waters. The result was that all logging operations in the area were stopped. The minister promised that a more enlightened policy would be developed and the logging companies would be forced to abide by it. He concluded: "The proper utilization of our valuable resources is a key policy question for the Government. Such proper use must include all our resources, with a full and proper concern for each — for our fish, for our wildlife — and not just for our forests."

Indians and Salmon
in British Columbia

Cedar and Salmon People

BEFORE WHITE SETTLEMENT the land of British Columbia belonged to the Indians: the Tsimshian, Salish, Nootka, Haida, and other tribes. They had been there for innumerable centuries before Captain Cook landed at Nootka on Vancouver Island in 1778 and exchanged gifts with Chief Mokwina. There were then probably 10,000 Nootka-speaking persons on this largest island in the eastern North Pacific, and an equal number of Tlingit and Tsimshian on the mainland.

The natives were well organized socially and even had confederacies of local tribes who shared summer villages close to the outer coasts, convenient to whaling grounds, for hunting the sea otter (then numerous) and seals and fishing for salmon and halibut. In winter they occupied more permanent homes, well-built cedar structures, and enjoyed the refined arts of a leisure-rich people.

These Neolithic folk, like other natives on the North Pacific coast, had developed a rare sense of unity with nature, untrammeled by the technology that has created enormous difficulties in modern life. Nature was infinitely kind to them. The sea and the rivers provided much of their food, to be had for the taking. Deer and other game were plentiful, but the forests were so dense that they did not care much to hunt except to obtain hides and sinews. The climate, though wet in the coastal regions, was relatively mild so that little clothing was needed.

The Haida, who lived on the Queen Charlotte Islands, the Kwakiutl, the Salish, and other tribes might be called the "cedar and salmon" people, for these were the twin gifts of nature that made possible the creation of one of the richest aboriginal cultures in North America by people who did not have such rudimentary elements of

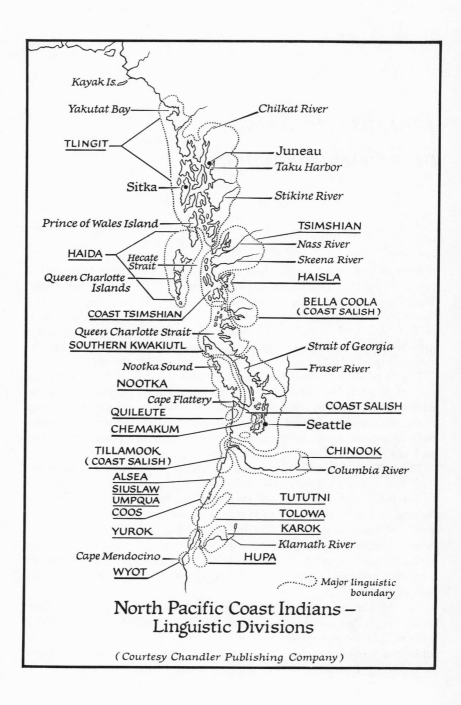

Kayak Is.
Yakutat Bay
Chilkat River
TLINGIT
Juneau
Taku Harbor
Sitka
Stikine River
Prince of Wales Island
TSIMSHIAN
Nass River
HAIDA
Hecate Strait
Skeena River
Queen Charlotte Islands
HAISLA
COAST TSIMSHIAN
BELLA COOLA (COAST SALISH)
Queen Charlotte Strait
SOUTHERN KWAKIUTL
Strait of Georgia
Nootka Sound
Fraser River
NOOTKA
Cape Flattery
COAST SALISH
QUILEUTE
CHEMAKUM
Seattle
TILLAMOOK (COAST SALISH)
CHINOOK
Columbia River
ALSEA
SIUSLAW
UMPQUA
COOS
TUTUTNI
TOLOWA
YUROK
KAROK
Klamath River
Cape Mendocino
HUPA
WYOT
Major linguistic boundary

North Pacific Coast Indians – Linguistic Divisions

(Courtesy Chandler Publishing Company)

technology as metalworking, the wheel, or pottery making. Cedar trees in the surrounding forests provided the wood for houses in the villages fronting the beaches or streams; salmon supplied a large part of their food supply.

Their artistic development was among the most advanced of any prehistoric group in North America. Their basketry, house posts and totem poles, richly decorated boxes and bowls, eating utensils, carved mauls, blankets and armor designed with rich colors and finesse of decoration, and their wonderful painted masks all betokened a people of high intelligence and sensitivity. Philip Drucker's *Cultures of the North Pacific Coast* offers one of the best introductions to their way of life and achievements. The roots of this society, as archeological discoveries in the Fraser River canyon suggest, go back at least 9000 years.

In sum, the aborigines would surely have endorsed Alexander Pope's eulogy to nature in his "Essay on Man":

> For me kind Nature wakes her genial pow'r,
> Suckles each herb, and spreads out ev'ry flow'r;
>
> . . .
>
> For me, health gushes from a thousand springs;
> Seas roll to waft me, suns to light me rise;
> My foot-stool earth, my canopy the skies.

Salmon fed not only the coastal and island dwellers but their relatives who lived inland on the banks of the Fraser, Skeena, Nass, and their tributaries. For instance, in 1904 a fishery inspector made a trip up the Skeena to its confluence with the Babine River. At one place he saw sixteen Indian houses, each thirty by twenty-seven feet and eight feet high, filled with tiers of drying salmon, and in addition there were acres of racks loaded with fish drying in the sun. Since a family used about a thousand sockeye every winter, the inspector estimated that some 750,000 fish were caught annually at the two barricades in the rivers, and this probably had been going on for centuries.[1]

It is estimated that there were perhaps 80,000 people in the entire British Columbia region before the white man came, and some areas like the windswept coast of Vancouver Island had more inhabitants in Captain Cook's time than today.

Around the southern coast of Vancouver Island lived the Coast Salish. At the mouth of the Fraser and along its lower banks were also groups of Salish, enjoying the perennial and unfailing runs of salmon and other fishes. Here in summer, where skies are blue and cloudless day after day, the firs and madroña trees fill the air with sweet smells, the sea is calm and the weather delightfully cool, came hundreds of natives in their canoes to fish. "They formed barges by lashing planks between the canoes 10 to 12 feet apart and sailed up the murky waterway to below the first rapids where they scooped out the salmon with long, slender dipnets or speared them with deft jabs of the harpoon." [2] At the rapids they took enormous quantities, fishing from rickety platforms protruding from the banks or from rocky causeways built out into the swift-flowing river.

Sometimes there were brawls between bands that led to bloodshed. For example, the Fort Langley *Journal* of October 19, 1827, reported a war party returning from the fishery with a victim's head impaled on the stern board of their canoe!

Inlets, bays, and rivers yielded ample bounties of fish and shellfish. The Interior or "Stock" Indians, as they were called, might suffer privations when the upriver runs failed, but they usually had access to the stores of their neighbors, for there seems to have been considerable trade in dried and smoked fish.

Nature was good to these folk and they in turn venerated nature and did not, like advanced modern societies, abuse it. To the Kwakiutl, says the anthropologist Franz Boas, "all nature, the heavenly bodies, rocks and islands, waterfalls, animals and plants were beings of supernatural power." Therefore a man must approach them with prayer: he can ask them for help and also he must express his thanks. For example, when he went out to fish he prayed to the sun: "Welcome, Great Chief, Father, as you come and show yourself this morning. We come and meet alive. Oh, protect me and let nothing evil befall me today, Father."

The salmon was affectionately called "Swimmer" and the eulachon (candlefish) "Chief-of-the-Upper-side-of-the-world."

When a fisherman dipped his net into the water he said: "Go on and gather yourself the fish, that you may be full when you come back, friend! Now go into the water where you may stay, friend." [3]

With the arrival of the first salmon the prayers offered by the people not only expressed gratitude to the salmon spirit but hope that they might meet again the next year, for the bounties of nature were not to be taken for granted.

Salmon were prominent in the myths and ritual dances of the Kwakiutl. Thus a masked dancer chanted at the weir a refrain resembling a chorus of a Greek tragedy, expressing a feeling of hope and fulfillment:

Many salmon are coming ashore with me.
They are coming ashore to you, the post of our heaven.
They are dancing from the salmon's country to the shore.
I come to dance before you at the right hand side of the world,
    overtowering, outshining, surpassing all;
I the salmon.[4]

In the mythology of the north-coast peoples there are many stories about the salmon spirit. One of the most moving is "The Tsimshian and the Salmon Woman," found in different versions among several tribes and recounted here in the version given by Franz Boas:

Tsimshian was a hungry and distressed fisherman. He went down to the beach and built a small house, made a canoe and a spear. One calm day he went out to try to spear a fish. A fog arose on the surface of the water. When it cleared away Tsimshian beheld a bright and fair woman sitting on the bow of his canoe. It was Bright Cloud the Salmon Woman.

He smiled at her and she smiled at him. "I wish to marry you," he said. She replied, "Just take care, Giant! I am the Salmon Woman. Do not do me any harm." Tsimshian replied: "Come, mistress, let us go to our house."

When he entered the house he begged his wife to cause the salmon to appear in the brook flowing at the right side of the little house. Early the next morning she went quietly down to the creek and put her toes in the water. Immediately many spring salmon jumped in the water.

She returned and awoke her husband and he went down to see the fish and was glad. Then she called him to comb his hair, and as she combed it way down his back it changed from black to blond. She also made his skin white and smooth.

The couple lived happily. Every spring the salmon returned to the river at her behest. There were so many that the creek almost dried up.

One day as he went to get wood to smoke his wife's salmon he saw ravens flying over him because they noticed salmon in his canoe. He took out one of his eyes to watch the salmon, saying, "If any ravens should come to the canoe, call me, and I will come and drive them away."

As soon as he left the ravens came and his eye shouted, "My eye, my eye! These ravens are about to devour me." Tsimshian returned quickly and shouted, "My eye, my eye! hide under the stern-board." But both his eye and his salmon were gone. He lost everything.

Bright Cloud Woman consoled him, washed his eye and made a new and better one for him. He was happy again and she loved him until their salmon was all dried.

When the spring came again he went into the river and clubbed salmon, while his wife dried and roasted them, and they filled three houses.

One day Tsimshian became angry at his wife and spoke sharply to her, suspecting that she was visited by a man while he was away.

Bright Cloud Woman said to her husband, "Have pity on me, my dear! No stranger has done any mischief to me. I love you most." But he was not satisfied. In the evening he came home in a rage.

One day Tsimshian dressed up. He was going to take a walk. His wife combed his hair with the backbone of a spring salmon, as she did every morning. But the comb stuck in his hair and he scolded it. Then he took it and threw it into the corner of the house, saying, "You come from the naked body of a woman and you catch my hair." His wife just hung her head and cried but he laughed and went out.

The same incident was repeated when his wife combed his hair the next time. But now she arose and said to the dried salmon, "Come, my tribe, let us go back!" She stood up and whistled and all the salmon flew out of the house. Tsimshian's hair became scorched and returned to its natural color and his rough skin came back again, and he was uglier than before.

Then Bright Cloud Woman led her tribe, the dried salmon, to the water. Tsimshian tried to put his arms around her but her body was like smoke, for she was a cloud.

Tsimshian became very poor and had nothing to eat and was very hungry. He was all alone, with no one to comfort him. He sat down in the house, weeping and sorrowing for the things he had lost.[5]

✿

Decay of Indian Culture

The white man's development of the land and other natural resources had the effect of ultimately destroying the Indian way of life, as in the United States, by alienating the natives from nature and substituting a mode of living largely based on industrial and technological artifacts.

Canadians acquired complete control of Indian lands, says Forrest E. LaViolette, "in a manner consistent with British colonial policy — by some negotiation but chiefly by occupation, by settlement, and by reservations." [6] The colonies of Vancouver Island and British Columbia, united in 1866, followed a policy that ignored, or even denied, there was any native title to the lands and therefore treaties with the Indians were unnecessary. Each local band was allotted small reserves over which it had control.

Little by little the Indians were assimilated to the white man's civilization and its bounties and infirmities, including diseases with which they could not cope and which killed many of them. An influx of missionaries imbued with fanatical zeal to Christianize the heathens hastened their cultural collapse. It is true that the missionaries sought to have the lands restored to the natives, but they were unsuccessful.

A system of Indian agents created in the early 1880s kept watch over the natives; the reserves were formally transferred to the Dominion of Canada, and a Department of Indian Affairs was established to look after them. This had the effect of preventing the complete loss of Indian fishing rights on lands they had long inhabited. Except for limited sections of the coast, there were for a long time relatively few white settlers in British Columbia. Although the land technically no longer belonged to the natives, as long as it was not settled or logged they had the use of it.

Yet the natives increasingly found themselves in a confused and bewildering world. The estimated population fell from 70,000 in 1835 to only 28,000 in 1885; not massacres, as in the United States, but smallpox, influenza, venereal disease, and tuberculosis were primarily responsible for their decline. Survivors had to adapt themselves as best they could. But Neolithic skills that produced the elaborate houses, basketry, totem poles, and splendid works of art such as masks, boxes, feast bowls, spoons, etc., were lost when metal tools came into use. Tailored clothes replaced garments made of bark, wool, or skins. New types of fishhooks were introduced, and linen nets replaced nets made of bark or cedar root. The paddle gave way to sail and later to the powered engine, and the fishing canoe was eventually replaced by the troll, gill netter, or seine boat.

Accompanying the changes in the native economy was a vast social revolution. Traditional religious rites had to be abandoned, the potlatch was outlawed, and social hierarchies broke down. "The chiefs became chiefs only in name," said the anthropologist Diamond Jenness, "for the real authority had passed forever from their hands; and the Europeans who usurped their lands recognized no distinction of rank, but brushed aside every Indian alike with feelings of mingled pity and contempt." [7]

Understandably salmon ceremonials and dances died out or became lifeless vestiges of the rich past. Many things become obsolete and useless (but treasured by the whites, who collected them and placed them in museums): the equipment and fantastic costumes of warriors and shamans and all their curious paraphernalia. The totem poles of which the people were proud, and which formed a kind of "literature," fell into disrepute, and the art of carving them was virtually lost. Saddest of all, perhaps, fish and game became, as to the white man, commodities that could be sold, and the inherent conservation instinct born of a deep respect for nature tended to wither away under the struggle to survive in a cash economy.

As populations declined the villages along the coasts of the mainland and the islands fell into ruins. Houses stood unroofed and unshuttered; totem poles fell to the ground or if still standing were eroding from wind and rain. Only here and there can some bits of Haida, Nootka, Salish, Tlingit, and other cultures be seen in their original settings; for the most part, they may be observed in such places as the Provincial Museum in Victoria, the Art Museum in Portland, Oregon, and the Sheldon Jackson Museum in Sitka.

Some modern Indian villages in British Columbia, however, recall the ancient ones in their prefabricated houses that are set in a row facing the beach, as in aboriginal times, without gardens or fences, for these people have no tradition of growing food nor of delimited property lines. There may even be dugout canoes along the beach, but they are not the handsomely decorated craft of ancient times. However, one may see smokehouses as of old for curing fish and racks for air-drying salmon, herring, and seaweed.[8]

Indian Fishing

A considerable number of Indians are still associated with the fishing industry of British Columbia. In 1883 almost all the 3000 fishermen employed by the canneries were natives; in 1962 only 2300 of the 15,000 commercial fishermen in the province were of Indian blood. The type of fishing has changed considerably from the days of the lonely canoe man who rowed many miles to make a decent catch. Trolling is now done from boats that cost up to $40,000, equipped with hydraulically operated gurdies; nylon nets cost from $700 to $1000 or more, and a fisherman may need several for taking different species of salmon in different fishing areas.

Purse seining requires much more capital. Some of the vessels are 90 feet long and cost $75,000; a new seine net may require an investment of $10,000. The owner of such a costly vessel must employ it the year round and fish for salmon, herring, halibut, etc., to capitalize fully on his investment. Relatively few Indians can command so much capital; hence they must work for the canneries who supply the boat and gear. Yet there are "highliners" among them. Finally, no longer is the entire coast of British Columbia open to the fisherman; some inlets and channels that used to provide entire villages with food have been so depleted they are closed indefinitely to fishing. And drifts that were fished by an Indian family for generations are now usurped by the white man.

How the Indians Live

Marjorie Matley, writing in *Geographical Magazine* (January 1968), provides a vignette of a typical Niska village in the forested Nass River valley. These people make their living by logging and fishing. During the salmon runs many of the men leave the woods and return to the river that was their ancestral home to engage in subsistence fishing. To many, these fish are a vital portion of their annual food supply. Of 650 persons on the tribal roll, 450 live on the reserve and the remainder dwell elsewhere.

In summer some families go to the coast where the men work as fishermen and their wives and daughters are employed in the cannery at Prince Rupert. They live in houses provided by the company. The old women, and sometimes the old men, baby-sit and prepare the family meals.

Social life among the Niska is still to some extent influenced by the salmon runs. Weddings, feasts, and sport events (which play a big role in their lives) are never held during the salmon season. Funerals are held months after a death to allow relatives to save money to do justice to the occasion. The money is usually earned by fishing or working in a cannery when it does not come from work in the woods.

The American anthropologists Ronald P. and Evelyn C. Rohner spent a year among the Kwakiutl on Gilford Island off the northwestern coast of British Columbia. The lives of these folk too are regulated by hunting, fishing, and gathering activities. There are clamming and trolling in winter, gill netting in February and March, salmon fishing from July through October, deer hunting throughout the year but chiefly in October and November, and duck hunting in November and December. Commercial fishing is carried on around Rivers Inlet, about a day's voyage from Gilford Island.

The men work on purse seiners or operate gill-net boats. Only gill nets are permitted to fish in the Inlet itself. Most of the Gilford Island men own, or at least operate a gill netter; few care to work a seine boat, although most of them have done so at one time or another. The chief of the village told the Rohners that not many Indians have enough business sense to operate their own boats, for the returns are uncertain and the government enforces strict limitations on the time and place where fishing is permitted.

Altogether commercial fishing provides only a small portion of the cash income needed by most Gilford Island families, yet few other opportunities for earning money are open to them except logging, in which some of the men are reluctant to engage. About half the families therefore depend upon unemployment insurance, welfare payments, and family allowances to supplement their earnings. Like other Indians, however, these people tend to be improvident. They spend their money on liquor and frivolous purchases and hence must go on welfare part of the year, if they can get it. During the summer of 1962 one of the men made $3100 from commercial fishing but spent $200 on beer, paid the fish company for a new net, net repairs, and other supplies, and ended the season with a gain of $37.00. "This is not unusual," said the Rohners.[9]

Vicissitudes of the Alaska Salmon Fisheries

The Cornucopia

THE 586,400 SQUARE MILES of Alaska, about a fifth the size of the continental United States, is salmon country as Hawaii is pineapple country. Nowhere on earth have these fishes chosen a more picturesque or generally more favorable habitat.

The main body of Alaska measures about 750 miles across east and west, bounded on the north by the Arctic Ocean, the south and southwest by the Pacific, the west by the Bering Sea, and the east by Canada. In each direction innumerable rivers flowing out of glaciers, mountains, tundra, and taiga carry along in their cold waters shoals of young salmon rushing to the sea and adults returning to their spawning grounds and have done so for countless millennia.

There are at least 2000 streams that support significant runs of salmon and/or steelhead trout, but actually no complete count has yet been made. Many of them have no name and have not even been surveyed. Numerous travelers who visited Alaska, from Georg Wilhelm Steller and Vitus Bering in 1741 down to our own day, have commented on the cornucopia of fishes. Thus John Muir, apostle of the wilderness, described a stream draining into Fanshaw Bay in southeastern Alaska in 1890:

> As we neared the mouth of the well-known salmon-stream where we intended making our camp, we noticed jets and flashes of silvery light caused by the startled movement of the salmon that were on their way to the spawning grounds . . . The stream was so filled with them there seemed to be more fish than water in it, and we appeared to be sailing in boiling, seething silver light marvelously relieved in the jet darkness.

A dozen fish were caught in a few minutes with a large hook fastened to the end of a pole. "They were so abundant that [the fisherman] simply groped for them in a random way, or aimed at them by the light they furnished themselves. That food to last a month or two may thus be procured in less than half an hour is a striking illustration of the fruitfulness of these Alaskan waters." [1] This scene can be re-enacted today on many streams despite the fact that much of the cornucopia has been emptied after a century of intense commercial exploitation.

Salmon may be seen almost everywhere in Alaska's rivers and lakes, in estuaries and bays swimming like eager brides and grooms to their mating streams, piled high in cold storage plants, and jammed together on the floors of canneries, still bearing the silvery sheen of the sea, waiting to be sliced, packed, sealed, cooked, and put into tin cans.

Flying in a floatplane the panorama of the salmon world spreads before you. Rivers curve and twist around bleak mountains on Kodiak Island, through the tundra of the Nushagak Peninsula, and wind in corkscrew fashion around the dense forests of Baranof Island. Except for the Yukon and Kuskokwim, there are very few long and complex river systems. Most of the streams are relatively short, but they may be incredibly rich in salmon.

Fish, fish talk, and fishing boats are the most vivid impressions of a visit to Alaska in addition to the staggering beauty of the land. Halibut and salmon are the major commercial species, but the greatest romance is in salmon fishing. In almost every port, which may be only a village sitting at the edge of a fjord or a small town nestling at the foot of a mountain or on an island, trollers, seiners, and gill netters crowd the wharves in summer. The boats bear such names as *Irene G., Peggy Jo, George W., Lucky Star, Trinity,* and they smell of fish and the sea. Their tanned skippers are repairing nets, getting ready for the next run. Fishing may be profitable or not, but the lure of the sea is in their blood. During the pink salmon run of 1949 in southeastern Alaska the purse seiners *ARB #6* and *Melody* each caught some 50,000 salmon. It took eighteen hours to get the fish aboard with the help of nearby vessels. [2] Such catches, however, are uncommon because fishermen avoid making sets in excess of their boats' capacity, which is usually 2000 to 15,000 fish; large catches endanger the nets if fishermen cannot brail the catch.

You cannot sail in Alaskan waters anywhere during the summer without encountering fishermen — in quiet inlets a purse seiner with

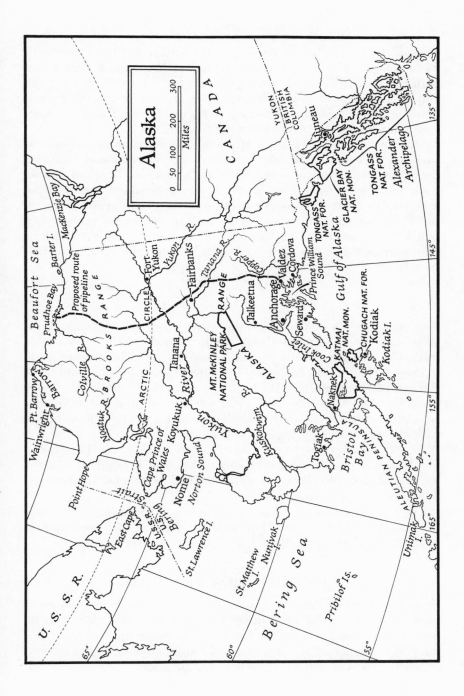

Alaska

Miles
0 50 100 200 300

CANADA

Beaufort Sea

Mackenzie Bay
Barter I.
Prudhoe Bay
BARROW
Pt. Barrow
Wainwright

Colville R.

Noatuk R.

Proposed route of pipeline

BROOKS RANGE

ARCTIC

Fort Yukon
Yukon R.
CIRCLE
Fairbanks
Tanana R.

YUKON
BRITISH COLUMBIA

Juneau

TONGASS NAT. FOR.

Alexander Archipelago

135°

GLACIER BAY NAT. MON.
TONGASS NAT. FOR.

Cordova
Valdez
Prince William Sound

Gulf of Alaska

145°

Copper R.

Talkeetna
Anchorage
ALASKA RANGE
MT. McKINLEY NATIONAL PARK

Seward
Cook Inlet

Tanana
Koyukuk
River
Yukon
Kuskokwim R.

KATMAI NAT. MON.
CHUGACH NAT. FOR.
Kodiak
Kodiak I.

155°

Point Hope

Cape Prince of Wales

Bering Strait

Nome
Norton Sound

Naknek

Togiak

Bristol Bay

ALASKA PENINSULA
ALEUTIAN

East Cape
U.S.S.R.
U.S.

U.S.S.R.

St. Lawrence I.

St. Matthew I.
Nunivak I.

Bering Sea

Pribilof Is.

Unimak I.
165°

60°

65°

55°

the spidery lines of his net floating on the surface, a gill-net boat with its orange marker float vivid against the twilight sea, a scow laden with fish in its deep hold moving to the cannery, a skiff drawing the end of a seine net toward the purse vessel while the sun sets in a blaze of fire, a fisherman standing in his boat gazing at a 200-foot-high glacier that seems to be moving toward him . . .

Most memorable of all is the spawning journey of masses of salmon in a wilderness river or lake, of the water churning and tumbling down the rocks while the red fishes thrash and mill around, falling back and leaping again, and finally reaching the quiet waters above and dashing for their spawning beds. And the harbor seals swimming in the estuary, close together, on the tails of a school of salmon they will kill and eat, and lastly brown bears coming out of the brush to take salmon out of the water and dash back again with fish in their mouths.

Salmon and the Natives

Relatively little is known about the earliest Indians in Alaska. Until they came into contact with the white men they were a Neolithic folk. The tools used by the Haida, Tsimshian, and Tlingit were made of stone. They had lived in the area a long time before Captain Cook discovered them and brought back reports of their way of life. They occupied sites where fish and game were plentiful and developed a seacoast way of life along the deeply indented shores of the mainland and islands.

When the Russians entered southeastern Alaska the Tlingit and Haida had been there for millennia. They had a highly structured society divided into clans, and each clan had its own fishing, hunting, and gathering preserves.

The Eskimos lived in a more hostile area and depended less on fishing than the Indians did. They took the chum salmon in Kotzebue Sound and in the rivers, though char was more abundant.

Commercial Exploitation Begins

From the time of Vitus Bering's discovery until its sale to the United States in 1867, Alaska was a fief of the Czars exploited chiefly for its furs by the Russian-American Company, a counterpart of the Hudson's Bay Company. The Russians did considerable salting of salmon, which mostly was sent to western Russia by a long sea route.

Ivan Petroff in his report on Alaska for the Tenth Census of the United States (1880) noted that "the once-famous Redoubt of deep-lake salmon fishery on Baranof Island, which at one time during the Russian rule supplied this whole region, and whence 2,000 barrels of salmon were shipped in 1868, now lies idle." Hubert H. Bancroft in his *History of Alaska* says that the king salmon was in such demand by the Russians that several barrels of salted fish were shipped every season to Saint Petersburg for the use of officials of the Russian-American Company.[3]

The first cannery was built in 1878 at Klawock on the west coast of Prince William Island. Thereafter the industry grew rapidly despite the remoteness of the territory and the difficulty of transporting supplies, workmen, and equipment by sea from Seattle, Portland, or San Francisco. All five species of *Oncorhynchus* are found in Alaska; pinks and sockeye (here called reds) are by far the most abundant, chum next. Coho and chinook (here called kings) are much less plentiful. Reds and pinks are the favored canning fish, and reds fetch the highest prices.

Before the end of the nineteenth century the canning industry had become established in the southeast along the Copper River, Cook Inlet, on Afognak Island, Kodiak Island, both the south and Bering Sea sides of the Alaska Peninsula, and in the Bristol Bay area.

Alaska's bountiful salmon runs lured many people who had made fortunes on the Columbia, the Sacramento, in Puget Sound, the Fraser, and elsewhere. Hither came the Columbia River Packers Association, a combine from Astoria; R. D. Hume built a cannery; other packers came from Portland, Seattle, San Francisco, Tacoma, Chicago, and even from Europe. There was more money to be made here than on the Columbia after the turn of the century, or on the Fraser after the Hell's Gate disaster. Here were numerous "gold mines" capable of being tapped forever without restraint by government, for the government of Alaska until statehood was achieved in 1959 was a vague and shadowy thing.

As the canneries multiplied, says John N. Cobb, the salteries declined in importance, for the "heavy demand for fresh salmon induced most [of them] to sell their high grade fish to the canneries and pack only the cheaper grades. Many of them quit the business as a result of competition, while others were forced out by the low prices prevailing at times for salted salmon."[4]

The size of the pack rose in meteoric fashion. In 1889 there were thirty-seven canneries that produced 720,000 cases against a total of

478,000 cases in California, Oregon, and Washington combined. A half century later there were 156 canneries. Alaska was feeding innumerable workers in American and European factories with inexpensive protein food and also sending large quantities to Australia, New Zealand, and elsewhere.

Astonishing production records were made on some rivers. Between 1894 and 1917 the Kvichak and Nushagak flowing into Bristol Bay produced some 10 million sockeye annually, compared with 8.2 million for the Fraser. Production of sockeye in the Karluk River on Kodiak Island surpassed all Bristol Bay streams combined for a time, but the pace could not be continued and the runs on the Karluk, as on scores of other hard-fished streams, withered away in time.

Although usually assured of ample supplies, the early canning industry faced difficult problems of logistics. The nearest American port was Seattle, from which machinery, tin plate, and other supplies as well as the labor force (Chinese, Filipinos, Japanese, and others) had to be sent weeks in advance of the runs. At most a cannery operated for two months and the rest of the year it was closed. Since little was known about the size of the runs, the investment might be a foolish gamble or extremely profitable. There were no forecasts that could be used as a guide to production as there are now. Many plants built on remote rivers operated for a few years, or until the runs were exhausted, and then were abandoned. Their rotting hulks may still be seen in inlets and coves throughout Alaska.

Sometimes the cannery "was destined to be the kernel from which a community would spring," says Ernest Gruening. "A store to supply the workers, as well as the nearby native fishermen, and to run a sideline in the fur trade or in native curios — baskets, wooden implements, moccasins, silver and ivory handicrafts — was invariably the first step in such expansion. It invited settlement nearby if the terrain was favorable." [5] In this manner arose Ketchikan, originally a tiny Indian settlement on the banks of a stream of the same name emptying into Tongass Narrows, one of the principal channels for Alaskan steamers. Ketchikan was destined to process more salmon than any community on earth and called itself the "world's salmon capital."

Many of the canneries were built by men who had worked on the Columbia, like Mont Hawthorne, who, as he says in his memoirs, "got in on most everything up north except the profits." In certain parts of southeastern Alaska Haidas and Tsimshian did much of the fishing and were glad to get a nickel for each fish. In central and western Alaska Indians did not comprise a substantial portion of the fishermen until sea otter hunting ceased in 1911; here whites from San Francisco, Astoria, and Seattle were the dominant element.

Waste of fish was often prodigious since there was no limit on the number that could be taken. Who could imagine that the cornucopia would ever diminish? When a law was passed by Congress in 1896 requiring weekend closures, it was generally ignored. There were very few government inspectors to execute this or any other conservation legislation.

Fishing Gear

Purse seines and gill nets were the main gear in the early days of the fishery. Purse seines did not come into extensive use until the advent of powered fishing craft around World War I. Before that, seines were the hand-operated variety, pulled by horses like those on the Columbia River. Later horses were replaced by donkey engines on skids on the beach. Gill nets were used from the earliest days where shallow waters enabled them to operate, such as Copper River, on Kodiak Island, Cook Inlet, and Bristol Bay.

Traps were introduced in the 1890s. When this contraption was perfected for Alaskan waters, notably in the form of a floating trap, it became the major type of gear except where gill netting was cheaper or water conditions posed special problems. By the late 1920s traps accounted for well over 50 percent of the total catches. A large portion of those in use in southeastern Alaska and Prince William Sound were the floating type. Fish wheels were used on some of the larger rivers like the Yukon.

The trap consisted of a wooden structure 100 by 50 feet, fixed on piles or floating logs, with the bottom of its pot and spillers sealed by netting, attached to the shore by a leader of webbing several hundred and even up to a thousand feet long, extending at a right angle from the land. Placed along the path of the salmon returning to their rivers, the leader was a barrier to the fish who were lured into an outer V-shaped heart and thence into an inner V-shaped heart from which they were guided to the pot and then through a narrow web of enclosed tunnels to the spillers. In a good location a trap could take up to 50,000 fish a day and was thus not only more efficient than the purse seine or gill net but cheaper to operate, for it fished automatically and could be emptied at the cannery's convenience.

A watchman's cabin was usually mounted on the trap with frequently an emergency cabin ashore for refuge from severe storms. A heavy work skiff was moored nearby. Every day the fish were brailed if the weather was favorable and a scow came to collect the catches. Trap robbing was such a widespread (and lucrative) activity that in 1919 the industry, in the absence of a local constabulary, asked the United States Navy for assistance, and a gunboat and subchaser were dispatched to Alaska. However, piracy and poaching continued to be rampant. Some plants did not hesitate to buy fish from pirates when their own supplies were scarce, and it was said that sometimes they actually organized these operations. According to the federal government's annual reports on Alaska fisheries, more than 10 percent of the total catches were taken illegally around 1920. The number of convictions was quite small.

Traps, seines, gill nets, and other gear multiplied as the salmon pack doubled and doubled again. Jefferson Mosher, who investigated the fishery for the federal government in 1899 in a summer's voyage that took him from southeastern Alaska to Dutch Harbor in the Aleutians, reported that numerous streams were blockaded by permanent barriers so that "any fish that escaped the fishermen had to spawn below the barrier or not at all." In addition "many streams were virtually sealed off by nets across the mouths, by the use of leads for a trap, or by diverting channels. In the face of this kind of 'fishing' one can only wonder how any fish survived."

An important part of the harvest consisted of chinook caught by trollers off southeastern Alaska — these were mainly fish who had migrated up from the Columbia or Fraser Rivers. Trolling began in the early 1900s as a single line fished from a rowboat. In the next decade powerboats came into use. In the 1920s power gurdies were introduced, permitting the use of steel lines, heavier weights, and more lures per boat. With time, vessels increased in size and efficiency until trollers averaged over forty feet in length and had such aids to navigation as the radio-telephone, direction finders, and echo sounders. The fleet became highly efficient and mobile, able to dash to new fishing grounds as schools of salmon were located. They could stay out two weeks at a time and transport their catches to distant buyers. Even the weather did not stop them, for the use of stabilizers allowed them to work in moderately stormy seas.

Since chinook are the largest of Pacific salmon and bring the highest prices, trolling proved to be a profitable activity. In 1918 the troll harvest reached 8.2 million pounds in southeast Alaska, climbing to 17 million pounds in 1937; after that production fluctuated but dropped to about 9 million pounds in the mid-1950s. The decline was attributable mainly to depletion of Columbia River chinook by destruction of spawning and rearing areas as a result of dams and other disturbances to the watershed.

The Cornucopia Diminishes

That much damage was done to the Alaska fishery by overfishing is proven by the downtrend in catches and packs. A peak of 101 million salmon were caught in 1918, when 6.7 million cases were packed. In the next ten to fifteen years the output dropped but reached new heights in the 1934–1938 period. An all-time record was established in 1936 when 129 million fish were harvested and 8 million cases produced — the bulk of the salmon then (as now) went into tins and only a small proportion was sold as mild cure or fresh. During World War II Alaska accounted for 85 percent of the nation's canned salmon and over 70 percent of North America's. About 25,000 persons were then employed in the fishing industry.

Catches held up fairly well until 1941 (Appendix Table 12) after which they tobogganed, averaging only 41 million in 1951–1959, or about 40 percent of the peak years. In 1967 only 1.5 million cases were packed — the industry had reached its nadir. Many canneries were closed and numerous companies combined in order to gather strength for continuing operations.

Appendix Table 13 shows the Alaska salmon pack from 1940 to 1971.

What caused such a debacle in a land that was still almost entirely wilderness, where the rivers ran pure and clear? The population

THE PACK OF CANNED SALMON IN ALASKA, 1878–1971
IN MILLIONS OF CASES

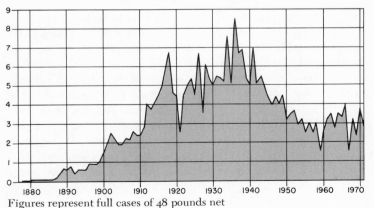

Figures represent full cases of 48 pounds net

numbered 72,000 in 1939 and only 128,000 in 1953 (0.5 persons per square mile). There were few industries, cities, or towns. Except for some gold and copper mining, there was little disturbance to the rivers.

The explanation for this paradox may be quite simple, although there are differing opinions. The consensus is that the industry collapsed because of ineffective regulation of fishing and lack of protection of seed stocks. Also, inadequate scientific knowledge of the races, due to lack of research, seriously handicapped the authorities responsible for managing the fisheries. There may have been other causes. Dr. William F. Thompson, founder of the Fisheries Research Institute of the University of Washington, an organization financed by the Alaska fishing industry that concentrated its work on Alaska salmon research, said: "The assumption, that overfishing is the cause of all declines in abundance, cannot be accepted as long as the relative effects of natural and fishery factors are confused, as they yet are. All over the world the abundance of fish undergoes great natural fluctuations beyond the control of men, as we have recently seen in our tuna, herring and sardine fisheries. We still have to determine the effect of the great environmental changes in the ocean and over the land. Some of these are world-wide. It will be very strange indeed, if, as a result, natural changes in abundance are not found in salmon."

In the ocean fish die from predation, parasites, disease, etc., which scientists are trying to evaluate. Yet the evidence points strongly to reckless exploitation as the major cause of the Alaskan disaster. This was forecast as far back as 1889 by Tarleton H. Bean in his report to the federal government on the Alaskan fisheries:

> Whether these fisheries shall continue to furnish the opportunity for profitable enterprise and investment depends upon the policy to be inaugurated and maintained by the government. Under judicious regulation and restraint these fisheries may be made a continuing source of wealth to the inhabitants of the territory and an important food resource to the nation; without such regulation and restraint we shall have repeated in Alaskan rivers the story of the Sacramento and the Columbia; and the destruction in Alaska will be more rapid because of the small size of the rivers and the ease with which salmon can be prevented from ascending them.

His words went unheeded by the industry.

Politics and Fish

The fate of the fishery was associated with the struggle of the people of Alaska to gain control of their resources. Here large-scale corporate enterprise used the political power that money buys in a democracy to thwart any real restraints on their activities. For example, at one time the J. P. Morgan–Guggenheim interests, which controlled Alaska's copper and coal mines, owned twelve canneries that produced one eighth of the total pack. Since the territory was a ward of Congress the packers achieved their goal by persuading congressmen either to kill fishery conservation legislation or when such laws were passed to deny appropriations for adequate enforcement. Thus the salmon runs were mined like the pine forests in Maine and the Great Lake States in the nineteenth century.

The history of Alaska fishery administration before statehood shows that the packers fought virtually every conservation proposal submitted to the Congress and yielded to compromise only after bitter struggles. Meanwhile they pre-empted numerous streams and paid minimal taxes (which nevertheless comprised the bulk of the territorial taxes), low prices to the fishermen until they organized strong unions, and low wages to the cannery workers until they too organized unions. They took from the rivers their great wealth, while the needs of the people, especially the natives, were largely ignored. They simply subscribed to the popular saying in the territory, "Get in, get it and get out!"

Around 1900 the salmon industry produced $8 million worth of commodities, but Alaskans benefited very little from it. The industry was owned mainly by outside corporations and workmen came from the "lower 48" and returned there after the season; only a small portion of their wages stayed in Alaska.

In his book *The State of Alaska* Ernest Gruening describes with understandable bias, since he was governor of the territory for fourteen years, the struggle of Alaskans to curb overexploitation of the fisheries and gain control of them. Until statehood all regulations were shaped by acts of Congress and executed by federal agencies.

As J. A. Crutchfield and Giulio Pontecorvo put it, the legislation and regulations "were indicative of congressional intent rather than operational programs." [6] The first law passed in 1889 prohibited the barricading of streams and authorized the Secretary of the Treasury, then in charge of the fisheries, to appoint an inspector at $1800 per annum and two assistant inspectors at $1600 plus travel expenses. In his report for 1897 the territorial governor John G. Brady described the problem of maintaining any kind of supervision over the industry with this minuscule force:

> Now, here are 4,735 miles an agent must travel to reach the different canneries. But that is only half the story, for each cannery is supplied with fish from a number of streams, some of them more than 150 miles from the place of cooking . . . An agent is appointed . . . told to proceed to Alaska . . . and finding a folder of the Pacific Coast Steamship Company wrestles with the Alaska route until he believes he understands it. Finally, he arrives at Sitka . . . He inquires how far is the nearest cannery, and how he can get there. It is forty miles, there is no regular boat running there. The only way to get there is to hire a canoe or wait until the cannery steamer, the *Wigwam,* happens to pass by. There is no boat of any kind belonging to the fish inspector, nor has the collector a boat he can loan; so all he can do is wait and take the next mail steamer for Karluk, seven hundred miles west of Sitka. When he reaches there the cannery people will show him every courtesy and see that he has a boat to get around in. Can anything be more humiliating to a government officer appointed to carry out an important duty? [7]

The next important legislation was passed in 1896. Among other provisions it prohibited netting above tidewater on rivers less than 500 feet wide, and nets, traps, or other gear could not blockade more than one-third the width of a channel. (Later legislation forced fishermen to go farther out into the bays and away from the estuaries.) In 1900 the Act of 1896 was modified and extended. Canneries were required to establish hatcheries for propagating red salmon and return the young to the spawning grounds at the rate of four times the number of adult fish of this species taken during the preceding season. This law was impossible to enforce — in fact, it was absurd — and nearly all the packers ignored it. Those who maintained hatcheries obtained tax concessions.

In 1903 the Alaska seal and salmon fisheries were transferred from the Treasury to the Bureau of Fisheries in the newly created Department of Commerce and Labor. From 1906 to 1924 extensive refinements and extensions of basic regulations were promulgated, often on the basis of sound biological data, but as the well-known French saying goes, "The more things changed, the more they were the same." The bureau developed a corps of competent biologists who sought to introduce sensible controls on the industry, but it was often stymied by political pressures and also lack of knowledge.

Thus in 1908 John N. Cobb and Millard C. Marsh reported that "in view of the reports . . . that the trap-net fishermen were not going to observe the law, the waters of southeast Alaska were very thoroughly patrolled this year and a cruise by the assistant agent in Stephens Passage, Lynn Canal, Chatham and Icy Straits . . . covering some 300 miles and including visits to 38 traps, complete and in process of construction, disclosed a most remarkable condition of affairs. Of the 34 traps operating, 29 were brazenly violating the law, 4 were guilty of minor or technical violations and but one trap was confining strictly to the letter of the law." [8]

From 1892 to 1910 there was but one agent and an assistant in all of Alaska responsible for fishery law enforcement; by 1913 the staff had risen to four.

The next step in regulation was the White Act of 1924, inspired by investigations of previous years and extensive congressional hearings at which the industry invariably denied there was any real depletion of the stocks. The act provided that 50 percent of every salmon run should be permitted to escape, a stipulation that was neither biologically sound nor enforceable.

In 1939 the Bureau of Fisheries was transferred to the Department of the Interior as part of the Fish and Wildlife Service and renamed the Bureau of Commercial Fisheries. There followed more congressional investigations and massive reports, but the runs continued to decline. C. H. Gilbert and Henry O'Malley of the Bureau of Fisheries had described the philosophy of the industry as far back as 1919 in their report on *The Alaska Fishery and Fur-Seal Industries* for the Bureau of Fisheries:

> The sequence of events is always the same. Increased production is accomplished by increase of gear. Fluctuations in the seasons become more pronounced. Good seasons will appear in which nearly maximum packs are made. But the poor seasons become more numerous. When poor seasons appear no attempt is made to compensate by fishing less closely. On the contrary, efforts are redoubled to put up the full pack. The poor years strike constantly lower levels, until it is apparent to all that serious depletion has occurred.

"Not any fishermen, not even I, had either the will or the grace to exercise moderation on the sea," says Clark Spurlock, a onetime gill-net fisherman, "but instead took more than was wise. We hastened to do this partly because other equally ignorant or selfish men — freshwater and sports fishermen, lumber men, pulp-mill owners, and the like — were busy as we were destroying these marvelous fishes within the rivers and streams forming the Northwestern watersheds of the continent where, in waters rising a little nearer the sun, the salmon's life cycle ends and begins." [9]

Disinheritance of the Natives

Occupation of Alaska by the Russians for about two centuries disturbed the long-rooted cultures of the Haida and Tlingit but little. These people regarded the Russians as visitors whom they tolerated for the sake of having a constant supply of trade goods. "Russian cultural influence was comparable to that of the trading ships, in which the diffusion of culture, mainly in the acquisition of trade goods, was dictated by native choice." [10] At times the two peoples came into violent conflict and the natives, being outgunned, naturally suffered most.

American sovereignty drastically altered the natives' position. "The United States," Andrew P. Johnson of Sitka, descendant of a Tlingit chief, told me, "vowed it would protect us and our aboriginal rights. Now, instead of taking our game and fish on our own lands we have to buy fishing and hunting licenses though we can take salmon for subsistence. The Redoubt River belonged to me by right of inheritance. But neither I nor my sons can fish it."

In contrast to American and British policy, the Russians made no treaties with the Indians and never defined their status. This situation was allowed to prevail when the United States acquired sovereignty until in 1924 federal legislation granted citizenship to all Indians in the states and territories. But in the intervening fifty-seven years after the purchase of Alaska the aborigines had been deprived of much of their landed heritage, their cultures and folkways were gravely undermined, and their economic system, which did not recognize fish or game as commodities for sale, was rendered obsolete so that many families were barred from their own fishing grounds and were forced to work in canneries or on fishing boats, though they could take fish for subsistence.

As the number of canneries increased the outline of the future became clear: they not only took fish hitherto available to the natives but prevented them from using the streams. The advent of a mining industry had the same effect, for it too barred the natives from the streams running through the mining sites. Resistance was futile, for the Americans were merciless in punishing trespassers.

Systematically, lands and rivers were withdrawn from the Indians' use, while hunting and trapping regulations were imposed. In time the usurpation of Indian property rights was given a kind of legal status. Thus the first Organic Act for Alaska (1884) extended the United States mining laws to the territory, thereby causing the withdrawal of large areas and restricting Indian rights on them to merely homesites and gardens. White men posted a mining claim, staked off and recorded a tract of land, and established "squatters' rights." Although these claims had no legal standing, for title could not be obtained, they were the means whereby the canneries acquired exclusive use of salmon streams.

"A prospective cannery operator would stake off and post his 160 acres, the maximum permitted under the mining laws, 80 on either side of the river mouth, and record his claim in the Land Office. And on that basis he prohibited as trespass entry of any other person who wanted to fish the stream. Then he built his cannery and went into production. When his cannery floor was full of fish, if he wished to allow some Indians to fish the stream, he would do so; if not, he drove them off." Natives were not permitted to file squatters' claims or own a mineral development, on the ground that they were wards of the government and therefore "legally incompetent to perform the duties or enjoy the rights of bona fide citizens."

The Act of March 3, 1891, which extended the general land laws of the United States to Alaska, combined with later laws, further reduced the areas open to native fishing, hunting, and gathering activities. No reservations were created. A pattern of survival developed: the men fished for the companies and the women worked inside the canneries. Shacks were built for them for summer occupancy. A cannery store sold provisions and supplies on credit. Many families became indebted to the companies and had to fish or work for them the following season to pay off their debts.

Tlingit and Haida villages underwent radical transformation. Clan houses were allowed to decay, totem poles faded away, and no new ones were carved. Cedar dugouts along the village beach were replaced by skiffs. The mission church became the center of the village's social and spiritual life, and pagan rituals, like those associated with the salmon, went underground or disappeared.

In 1912 a group of Indians in Sitka organized the Alaska Native

Brotherhood, dedicated to recognition of native citizenship rights, education, and ironically abolition of aboriginal customs. Later it concentrated on fighting for Indian rights in Congress and the courts. It has remained a strong grass-roots organization with considerable influence among its own people and in Congress.

In contrast to the Indians, the Eskimos occupied areas mainly outside commercial fishing regions. The first cannery in Eskimo territory was erected near the mouth of the Wood River in 1884 at Old Nushagak, close to the Russian-American Company's post at Alexandrofski. The first real large-scale operation appeared in 1886 near the mouth of the Wood River. Eventually canneries dotted the banks of all the major rivers flowing into Bristol Bay.

For a long time there was a reluctance to hire Eskimos as cannery workers or as fishermen because they were not accustomed to disciplined labor and the white man's sense of time or to a cash economy. Jefferson Mosher in his report on the salmon and salmon fisheries to the federal government in 1898 said:

> When the cannery ships arrive in the spring the native [Eskimo], having struggled through a long, severe winter, is hungry and has many wants. He greets the cannery ships with childish glee and wishes work. It is given him, his hunger is appeased from the overflowing cannery table, his daily wages soon supply the few luxuries he desires, and then he no longer cares for work. Why should he work? Hunger no longer worries him, his immediate wants are satisfied, and he has no others! . . .
>
> Money seems to have no value to the native except to satisfy his immediate wants, and the traders cater to their taste for gewgaws by supplying them with things for which they have no use. They have a fancy for cuckoo clocks and watches, though they cannot read the time; cheap jewelry and perfume . . . One woman was noticed wearing the usual skin trousers and boots, and over all a velveteen dress, well tucked up, and as greasy as if it had been soaked in a pot of rancid oil . . .

The white men and Chinese introduced liquor to the Eskimos and taught them how to distill it, with disastrous results. In 1900 a Moravian missionary in Nushagak complained "that the great curse of the natives is still drink. It is considered amusing to drink until they lie around like dogs . . . The people earn so much at the canneries that they do not know what to do with their money." Some Eskimos "found it easier to utilize the waste of the canneries than make their own fish traps to secure their winter's supply of fish." [11]

Eventually a few Eskimos became commercial fishermen, using gear and sailboats supplied by the companies, and others worked inside the plants. World War II brought more of them into the industry as white labor became scarce. Bristol Bay canneries drew heavily from nearby communities as well as villages in the north as far away as Kotzebue and Point Hope. Eskimos were accepted by the fishermen's unions and shared their privileges.

In a few instances the government undertook to protect the food supply of the natives. In 1918 the Carlisle Packing Company of Seattle built a floating cannery at Andreafsky, the first on the Yukon. It raised considerable opposition because the 1917 catch had been poor and the future looked dismal for the upriver natives who needed the fish for themselves and their dogs. In 1919 fishing was consequently limited to the mouth of the river or offshore; the next year the company took advantage of the regulation to fish outside this area and made a record catch of 470,000, of which the bulk were chum salmon. This touched off a protest from ecclesiastical spokesmen for the Indians and commercial fishing was forbidden inside the river mouth and in fact eliminated entirely from 1925 to 1931. In 1932 fishing was resumed with two salteries in operation, increasing in number in later years, plus two or three hand-pack or one-line canneries. The number of fish taken by the natives in the Yukon, mainly with fish wheels, held up consistently after 1919 as the upriver runs were given protection.[12]

In 1926 the Kuskokwim was entirely closed to commercial fishing; the order was modified in 1930 to permit some operations in part of Kuskokwim Bay at the request of local residents, who felt it would give employment to the natives and not take an undue proportion of the runs. Displacement of dog teams by an airplane service had actually reduced the market for dried fish. The new regulations provided for the taking of 250,000 king salmon yearly for salting and mild curing. Owing to opposition and reduced runs, this quota was later curtailed. There has never been a cannery on the Kuskokwim or its estuary.

After many years of legal and political pressure by the Alaskan Federation of Natives, Congress at the end of 1971 passed the Alaska Native Claims Settlement Act. Now any United States citizen who is at least one-fourth Eskimo, Aleut, or Alaskan Indian is entitled to share in a settlement that includes 40 million acres of land, an area roughly the size of the state of Washington, and a cash settlement of almost $1 billion. (In 1968 village Alaskans owned in fee less than 500 acres of the 375 million acres of their native land, said a report of the Federal Field Committee for Development Planning in Alaska.) By June 1972 more than 45,000 persons had enrolled under the Native Claims Act and a total of 55,000 to 60,000 persons were expected to enroll inside Alaska and another 15,000 to 20,000 would sign up elsewhere.

Under the settlement about 220 native villages will receive title to the land on which they are located and every individual will be able to gain title to the land he lives on, up to 160 acres. What it will mean in terms of economic benefits to the natives cannot yet be determined.

Salmon and Statehood

Agitation for statehood gained momentum during the 1940s as a result of the influx of soldiers in Alaska. Opposition to federal control expressed itself most against absentee ownership. For a long time Congress ignored it. In 1949 the territorial legislature created a Department of Fisheries, which had little power but could assist the Bureau of Commercial Fisheries by supplementing its appropriations and by doing research. It also provided a training ground for the men who were to take over management of the fisheries when statehood was achieved.

In a referendum in 1952 Alaskans voted 20,500 to 5500 to request Congress to give them control of the fisheries on the grounds that local management was best for the resource. Federal regulation had obviously failed as the industry declined in the 1940s and 1950s. Decisions made in Washington by people remote from the scene, even though advised by competent men in the field, were not often effective. Principles of management that worked well on the Fraser or Columbia Rivers could not be applied without knowledge of the runs, yet relatively little was known about the Alaskan stocks. Expenditures for research by the federal government were a pitiful $100,000 annually until 1948, reaching $250,000 in 1956, $1 million in 1959. The industry relied on its own research arm, the Fisheries Research Institute, which studied biological and management problems, especially in Bristol Bay. Besides niggardly funds for research, Congress continually shortchanged Alaska on appropriations for law enforcement, as Secretary of the Interior Julius Krug told a congressional committee in 1947.

Federal regulation was opposed and sometimes arrogantly defied "by an industry gambling with a large investment and in quest of immediate profits," says Gruening. Typical was the testimony of Nick Bez, a prominent packer, in 1936: "I went to see Secretary [of Commerce] Roper [then in charge of the fisheries] and saw him right in his office. . . . I told him to take his regulation book and throw it in the Potomac River." [13]

After Alaska achieved statehood on January 3, 1959, the picture changed considerably. Nineteen fifty-eight was the last year that fish traps were permitted to operate.

At the twenty-fifth annual meeting of the Pacific Fishery Biologists in 1960 Dr. William F. Royce of the Fisheries Research Institute outlined the principles of management as they were applicable to Alaska:

> The purpose of any regulation is [first] to provide fish for orderly fishing . . . The second reason for regulation is conservation of the resource.
>
> Salmon are valuable, scarce and very vulnerable to fishing as they seek their spawning streams. In order to protect them from extinction, the regulations in the United States have always been drawn to provide escapement while allowing orderly fishing.
>
> [A third objective is] wise use or more specifically . . . maximum sustained yield. This means not only protection from overfishing, but also prevention of underfishing. In our salmon fisheries, it means allowing optimum escapement and cropping the excess. In these highly fluctuating fisheries such excess may be tremendous in the big "cycle years" and here is the most obvious way in which production may be immediately increased.

Royce added that historically regulations in Alaska that have provided orderly fishing and attempted to preserve salmon runs from extinction have been determined essentially by political factors. Such methods of regulation served well during the long period of growth and prosperity of the fishery, which ended about 1941. Following this it became evident that something was seriously wrong. Overall production declined radically during the 1940s due to virtual disappearance of some runs. Other runs continued to produce heavily and constantly and erratically.

> Now it becomes necessary to provide nearly complete protection for some runs and at the same time catch large parts of others . . . These needs require regulation for maximum sustained yield . . . With the increase in knowledge of the effect of fishing on salmon stocks that has been developed since 1945 it appears possible to attain this objective.
>
> Only in our major red salmon runs have the races been defined and satisfactory catch and escapement statistics [become] available. In only these runs have we any scientific forecasts of the size of the run to be expected [but] our knowledge of the optimum escapement is inadequate.
>
> We have something like 10,000 units of spawning salmon, for each of which there must be a division of catch and escapement. This division can be achieved in a practical way by combining and defining major races.[14]

There was need for accurate data for each river and each race, and to this gigantic task (which may be impossible to accomplish) the newly created Alaska Department of Fish and Game dedicated itself. What are the results?

Under state management some major stocks have improved since 1960. In Bristol Bay restoration of the sockeye began in 1960; the scientific work of the Bureau of Commercial Fisheries, the Fisheries Research Institute, and the Department of Fish and Game paid off handsomely in the record sockeye runs in 1965 and 1970. In Alaska sockeye have a dominant five-year cycle; that is, the heaviest runs occur every five — and sometimes every four — years. In Cook Inlet, by contrast, which had a stabilized fishing industry for eighty years, there was a drastic reduction after statehood and the runs continued to go downhill — as they did in southeast Alaska.

Excitement at Bristol Bay

In order to see management in action, let us betake ourselves to Bristol Bay during the great sockeye run of 1970. In 1965 53 million sockeye returned from the sea, one of the largest runs on record, of which 44 million were produced in the Kvichak-Naknek River systems. In

1970 a run of 56 million was forecast by the Fish and Game Department.

When I arrived on June 25 in the decrepit village of King Salmon, where the Department has its headquarters, the fishing season was just starting. Biologists were monitoring the catches and escapement almost hourly; each of the thirteen canneries in the district was contacted at least twice a day for reports on production. On the rivers draining lakes, men in lofty towers were counting fish moving to the spawning beds, while out at sea others were test fishing to get an idea of the strength of the runs before they ran the gauntlet of 900 gill netters waiting for them at the mouths of the rivers and hundreds of set netters along the banks of the rivers. At departmental headquarters biologists were making up tables, drawing charts, correlating data for each stream with meticulous care including the 65-mile Kvichak, 30-mile Naknek, 30-mile Egegik, 40-mile Togiak, and 100-mile Nushagak. On the basis of these data they determined where fishing should be temporarily halted or accelerated, for a balance between catches and escapement had to be attained. The massive sockeye run would pass through the fishing grounds within three weeks; over 2 million were arriving daily, and 800,000 to 900,000 fish were being caught and processed every twenty-four hours.

Excitement mounted as the days passed. The question in everybody's mind was: how close would the run come to the forecast? Canneries were overwhelmed. Some men fished around the clock and slept three hours in twenty-four. They could be seen in restaurants and bars with unkempt beards, bleary eyes, soggy clothes. Some of them would make $20,000 to $30,000 during the season, while in a lean or nonpeak sockeye year like 1968 they did not earn enough to pay their way home to the "lower 48." "Feast or famine" is the saying up and down Bristol Bay.

The runs could best be seen from the air: millions of gleaming fish moving up the crystalline rivers, not yet in their full spawning livery, hugging the shores, heading for the lakes where their bodies would turn red and heads green and they would spawn in August or September. Once they passed the gill nets in open water and set nets on the banks there was nothing to interfere with their marital journey. No human habitations could be seen, no boats on the river or lakes. The tundra looked brown and sere, dotted with dwarf trees and clumps of bushes; strangely beautiful.

In the clear and quiet waters of the broad bay gill netters were spread over a long distance. So many fish were running that they hit the nets as soon as they went out — 4000 could be taken in one day in a small boat, each worth about $1.25. Tenders, mostly power scows, were anchored in strategic positions to receive the catches. A Japanese freezer ship stood by to collect and process fish and take them to Japan. There was a cool easterly blowing; fleecy clouds filled the sky. To the northeast were the snow-capped Chigmit Mountains, in the southwest the battlements of the Alaska Peninsula, and far off faint smokes were visible from fumeroles in the Valley of Ten Thousand Smokes.

Generally commercial fishing is not permitted inside the rivers in Alaska. Those fishermen who sneak into the rivers and are caught — they are called "creek robbers" — are heavily fined.

Canneries worked night and day, and yet they could not keep up with the catches. Some of the companies were limiting their contract fishermen to twelve hours daily, others allowed them to fish for twenty-four hours and rest for twenty-four. Fatigue was overtaking many workers, especially older people, some of whom were dropping out to be replaced by recruits from Eskimo villages.

In the one restaurant at King Salmon one heard many rumors. It was said that some fishermen, not under contract to any company, were dumping their salmon into the river because they could find no buyers. Fish were being given away to all comers gratis. In other years the village was full of buyers looking for fish, but this year independent fishermen were frantically seeking buyers. On the King Salmon-Naknek road I saw an abandoned truckload of sockeye, freshly caught, worth several hundred dollars.

There were many disappointed fishermen, gamblers who staked their savings on getting a jackpot. An Indian from the Quinault Reservation on the Olympic Peninsula said to me, "I came to make a few thousand dollars to put clothes on my children's backs but I had to dump my fish in the river." An old-timer confided, "The fish are there to be taken but we have no commitments and that's our misfortune."

As the days passed and the run approached its peak panic swept Bristol Bay. There were far more fish than the packers could handle, although when the forecasts were published months before they had announced they were ready to process the largest sockeye run in history. Alaska newspapers carried sensational headlines about the glut of fish. Since this was an election year many politicans descended upon Bristol Bay, men running for the United States Senate, United States House of Representatives, governor, etc., seeking to make political capital out of the mess.

An emergency meeting was called by the industry to discuss ways and means of handling the glut, but little came of it. Fishermen's representatives charged the industry with inefficiency and indifference, while industry spokesmen claimed they were doing all they could to process the catches. Meanwhile, with the help of the Alaska Fish and Game Department an Anchorage businessman organized a fish lift, the first ever attempted in Bristol Bay. Soon word spread there was a buyer paying the going price. A string of skiffs appeared at the dock behind the department's headquarters in King Salmon, and for days fish were packed in wooden boxes, iced, and loaded on trucks that took them to the local airport where Hercules cargo planes flew them to Anchorage and other cities for canning. In this manner 200,000 sockeye were saved from destruction.

On July 15 the season ended. Instead of 56 million only 39.6 million fish had shown up, of which 21 million were caught and canned and 18.6 million were allowed to escape. The combined Kvichak-Naknek run, the largest component of the Bristol Bay area, totaled 32.9 million, compared with 44.4 million in 1965, the previous dominant sockeye year.[15]

The 1970 season showed that marketing and processing arrangements in Bristol Bay were inadequate to handle runs of the magnitude forecast. Some people said the industry had played it cool. Canners made a great deal of money, but many fishermen were disappointed. For example, Indians working set nets in the rivers were sometimes left stranded when the company's tender stopped coming to their stations; if they could not get their fish to the cannery they had no market. Contract fishermen fared better but some of them complained they were not allowed to fish as much as they wished.

Many suggestions were made for improving arrangements in peak years. Companies could organize more fish lifts to move surpluses to other parts of Alaska or British Columbia, and even to the Puget Sound area. The state could build a freezing plant in the Bristol Bay area — none yet existed. The number of fishermen could be reduced. And so on. The test would come in 1974 or 1975, the next dominant year for sockeye, provided survival of the huge 1970 spawn is normal.

Summarizing the 1970 season, it was clear that the resource in Bristol Bay had made a remarkable comeback since the state took over management in 1960. A. C. Hartt of the Fisheries Research Institute comments: "The catch versus escapement was much better balanced in 1970 than in the previous cycle year, and the escapement in 1970 was about equal to that of 1960 which produced the all-time record sockeye run of 53.2 million. Thus the Fish and Game Department probably achieved a good escapement-catch ratio and the industry processed the optimum number of fish. The 1970 escapement of 19 million will probably produce more sockeye in the next cycle year — 1974 or 1975 — than the 29 million escapement did in 1965, if fresh water conditions are favorable." [16]

The 1970 harvest in all of Alaska totaled 66.1 million fish, the best since 1949, including 30.2 million pinks, 27.5 million sockeye, 6.6 million chum, 1.2 million coho, and 600,000 chinook. Regionally major producers were as follows: Bristol Bay 21.8 million, Southeastern 13.0 million, and Kodiak 13.9 million. However, in 1973 the Bristol Bay catch was about 1.25 million, and the pack only 75,000 cases, lowest since 1887.

Naknek

How does the wealth of the rivers affect the natives?

To answer this question we visited the village of Naknek, which is situated on the Naknek River and boasts of two large canneries. It is an ancient Eskimo settlement now inhabited chiefly by Indians. The permanent population is about 400. Like all Indian villages in western Alaska, the local economy is dependent on the fish runs.

Naknek is typically a mean, dilapidated community with unpaved streets that are former caribou trails. Its dwellings consist mostly of tumbledown shacks and some quonset huts. Few of them have lawns or plantings of any kind. There are no sidewalks nor many street lights. In front of some houses lie old tires, parts of dismembered cars, and other litter and junk.

The village has two liquor stores, five bars, a Russian Orthodox and a Pentecostal Mission church, a new schoolhouse, and a borough building that is the court and administrative center. There is one general store, owned by a cannery, where prices are even higher than usual in Alaska, a state that has the highest cost of living in the nation.

Naknek reminds one of mining towns in West Virginia or Kentucky. An air of dereliction and despair hangs over it. Many homes display broken windows, doors askew, and rickety steps. Only the Pentecostal Mission, schoolhouse, and company store show signs of recent painting. There is but one hotel, a dilapidated single story frame building also housing a liquor store. A small diesel plant provides the town's electricity. The only road runs about fifteen miles to King Salmon, beyond which is the endless tundra.

As in other villages, the Naknek people work hard during the season, but the money they earn is usually quickly dissipated. It is not used to paint houses or beautify surroundings, to buy new furniture or other necessities; much of it is spent on alcohol, boats, television sets, airplane rides, and other frivolities. For two months the people are well off, but the rest of the year they live in poverty and are assisted only by the Bureau of Indian Affairs, which arranges for unemployment compensation and welfare grants and performs other paternalistic chores.

To a visitor the most lasting impression of Bristol Bay is the poverty and dereliction of the people contrasted with the wealth of the rivers and the profits made by the packers and some fishermen. Once the Eskimos and Indians were proud and self-reliant folk who lived off the land. Now they are mostly dispirited pawns of the industrial economy and dependents of the federal government. Many are permanently in debt to the companies. Alcoholism is rife in the community.

The companies, in sum, have only a vague connection with the natives. They are owned and managed chiefly by outsiders who care little for Alaska and come there only during the fishing season. The welfare of the natives does not trouble them — they need them only as a labor supply. Yet Naknek is much better off than other villages. It derives over 90 percent of its taxes from the canneries and business associated with fishing and has one of the best-financed school districts in Alaska.

Kodiak

Kodiak Island, now the second largest producer of salmon in Alaska, is about 100 miles long and 60 miles wide. Afognak Island lies to the northeast and the two, with many nearby islets, form a chain of about 160 miles that screens from a distance the entrance to Cook Inlet. There is but one city, Kodiak, which has 6850 persons (including the suburbs). The islands are indented by many bays and in their interior are mountains rising to over a 4000-foot elevation.

From the air the island seems like a crazy quilt of lagoons, lakes, serpentine rivers, creeks, and rivulets flowing into numerous arc-shaped bays. The surface of the land is green and mostly treeless and one imagines that in some distant geologic age it was broken by a mighty force into a thousand pieces separated by watery passages. Mountains are the dominant feature of the landscape. In nearly every substantial body of running water there are salmon, and here a stream may provide spawning space for 20,000 fish to the mile.

Except for the city of Kodiak and a few Indian villages, the island is almost devoid of human settlement. You may come upon a guide's cabin hidden in the brush or a hermit's lair. There are no roads except around Kodiak and the nearby naval base. The northeastern tip supports a forest chiefly of white spruce; westward from this point some deciduous trees are found in protected valleys. Parts of the island support a rich growth of grass that furnishes pasture for cattle on a few ranches.

Afognak Island is well timbered and forms part of the Chugach National Forest. It once had a federal salmon hatchery. Now there is a hatchery on Kitoi Bay, used more for experimentation than production. Salmon have the limpid streams to themselves except for brown bears. Once past the fleet of purse seine and gill-net boats and set nets on the beaches, the spawning fish can make their way easily to their natal gravels. There is little traffic on the waterways.

As you alight on Kodiak Island the air seems scented. Even the myriads of mosquitoes can be ignored as you marvel at the lonely splendor of an island set in an emerald sea. The hills are rich with blue lupine and red fireweed. Ptarmigan run in the grass and brown bear prowl the streams, red foxes lurk in the brush, and on the ponds green-headed mergansers swim nonchalantly, assured of their daily morsels of small salmon and other fish. In surveying streams it is not unusual to see twenty bears in three miles, and at the peak of spawning bears swarm in the rivers.

Kodiak Island used to be renowned for sockeye, but since depopulation of the Karluk River it is more famous for massive runs of pinks. In 1970 12 million of these fish were caught in addition to 900,000 sockeye, an equal number of chum, and some 65,000 coho. Kodiak waters are also famous for crabs, halibut, and shrimp.

The pink salmon congregate in the shallow waters of the bays before ascending the rivers; 50,000 may school up in a small area. They show up first around Narrow Cape off the northeast coast, which is a kind of staging area, and from there disperse to the bays and inlets preparatory to going up the streams. These migrations attract a large number of fishermen who use mostly purse seines.

Pinks spawn in numerous small streams, while chum do well in larger bodies of water. Coho mate further upstream than the other species. The canneries are located on uninhabited bays such as Uyak and Uganik. On the Karluk River, once a beehive of activity, only the pilings of canneries may still be seen; none has been in operation since the 1940s.

In the small hatchery at Kitoi Bay sockeye were reared for planting

Five Pacific Salmon: Sockeye, *Oncorhynchus nerka;* Chinook, *O. tsha-wytscha;* Coho, *O. kisutch;* Pink, *O. gorbuscha;* Chum, *O. keta.*

Celilo Falls was an Indian fishing rendezvous for countless centuries before it was drowned out by The Dalles Dam in 1957. The agile Indians fished the churning waters from rickety platforms with dip nets.

Supersaturated nitrogen in the dammed Columbia River induces bubble disease, which has killed millions of salmon. Efforts to eliminate this evil have so far been largely unsuccessful.

During the sockeye run in Bristol Bay rivers, biologists make daily surveys of the escapement, measuring a sample of the run for age-composition, net marks, sex, and other characteristics.

Indians are still permitted to operate fish wheels on the Yukon River, Alaska.

The Puget Sound salmon fleet at Fishermen's Wharf, Seattle.

Crew of the seiner *Adriatic Sea* brailing salmon.

The Fraser produces more sockeye than any river in North America and is also a scenic delight.

The fishways at Hell's Gate on the Fraser enable the salmon to make their way upstream under varying flow conditions. In this canyon the river level may fluctuate 6 or 7 feet in one day and up to 100 feet during the year.

Sport fishing is exciting in the
Alberni Canal on Vancouver Island.

The Columbia is a mighty river and, despite great setbacks, is still one of
the most productive salmon streams on the continent.

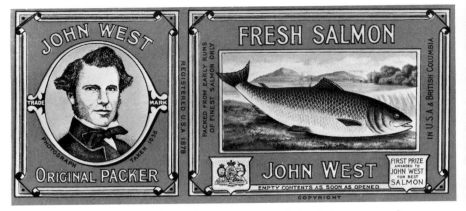

John West, a Liverpool distributor, was one of the first to import Oregon canned salmon in England.

The "iron chink" revolutionized the salmon canning industry by making it possible to cut, slice, and "slime" the fish automatically.

One of the numerous fish wheels owned or leased by the Seufert Canning Company on the mid-Columbia before it went out of business in 1957.

The Bonneville fish ladders are the prototype of all ladders at Columbia River dams.

Visitors watching egg-taking from ripe female salmon at the Idaho Power Company's hatchery on Rapid River. The hatchery was built to compensate for fish losses above the company's dams on the Snake River. Note the automatic devices that drop feed to the fingerlings.

in Frazer Lake, featured in a television documentary by Jacques Cousteau. Formerly a barren lake, installation of a fish ladder at its river outlet has resulted in the creation of a substantial fishery. The escapement reached a peak of 52,000 sockeye in 1971, while the catch was estimated at 50,000.[17]

The Summing Up

Fishing is the most important economic activity in Alaska, the top state in the union in the value of the commercial catch. In 1970 the Alaska pack salmon alone was valued at $130 million wholesale and in 1971 at $111 million.

Since the state took over management of the fisheries in 1960 considerable progress has been made toward their rehabilitation although setbacks occur, as in 1972. In an article in *National Fisherman* (April 1970) Dr. W. F. Royce summed up the problems involved and the policies followed:

> Soon after the Alaska salmon industry started in the 1880's there were cries from conservationists about the practices. They condemned much of what they saw and correctly foretold the eventual decline of Alaska salmon.
>
> But they cried doomsday 40 years too soon and could not explain the continuing increases in production and the apparent health of the salmon runs for several decades. They recommended salmon hatcheries, but these were abandoned within a few years when they ruined the runs they were trying to augment.
>
> They recommended the White Act which required 50 per cent escapement. This was wrong biologically because no uniform percentage escapement is desirable. It can either cause a gross waste of salmon or the ruin of weak segments of the runs. The act was also wrong politically because it gave everyone the impression that the salmon were safeguarded when, in fact, it could not work and was applied to only a few streams in Alaska . . .
>
> They could not explain the decline of the runs. They were demanding more and more escapement, and there were abundant examples of large escapements which did not return the expected numbers of salmon.
>
> The industry turned to Dr. W. F. Thompson at the Univer-

sity of Washington . . . [He] formed the Fisheries Research Institute on the basis of the industry's support . . . Thompson demanded and got freedom to plan his studies and call the shots as he saw them . . . He wanted to know where [the fish] were caught, how many were caught, how many spawned, what factors influenced their survival during the winter, what returns came back from the sea and where the salmon went at sea.

The answer to the conservation problem was simple in concept but difficult in practice. It was as plain as the well-known ability of the salmon to return from the sea to find its own spawning ground and do so on a remarkably close schedule.

The answer was in the individuality of the salmon runs and the need to control them separately, not on a regional basis. There are hundreds of major salmon runs in Alaska. The decisions about the amount of fishing have to be made before the fishing takes place . . .

Each run must be fished, and each must contribute spawners, else the spawning grounds will not be utilized. This is the tough part of salmon management . . . Good forecasts are essential, not only so the fishery agency can make the decisions on time but also to allow the fishermen and industry to prepare for the big runs or small runs . . .

The answers are not all in yet. Too many errors still occur in the regulation. We need better information on optimum escapement goals, more accurate forecasts up and down the coast, and improved survival of the salmon in fresh water. We need to understand why some runs remain small despite large escapements. But now we have confidence that answers can be found and — equally important — put to use.

Nineteen seventy-one was a better than average year for the fisheries: 45.7 million salmon were caught (compared to 66 million the previous year), making the average annual catch since statehood 52 million compared with 44 million in the last decade of federal management. This is a measurable improvement but far below the 92 million average in the 1930s. Nineteen seventy-two was a disastrous year. The canned salmon pack was 1,667,000 cases, one of the poorest in the century (Appendix Table 13).

What is the future of the fisheries? The fabulous stocks have experienced extraordinary vicissitudes in less than a century of exploitation. They were pillaged for a long time; prime rivers were badly depleted or fished out. Yet so rich are the wilderness rivers that with the institution of more scientific management based on the better knowledge of the runs, some of the most abused stocks have shown signs of building back. The fisheries have a long way to go to reach the plenteous state of their heyday, but the Department of Fish and Game, which has managed them since 1960, has, on the whole, made considerable progress — the task is herculean.

In a country as rich in salmon habitat and resources as Alaska, it comes as a surprise to learn that the state is planning to build a series of hatcheries to supplement natural production. The first is being built on Blind Slough near Petersburg at a cost of $2 million. Initial production will be king and coho and rainbow trout. Operation is scheduled for the fall of 1973, and the output will be used to replenish selected streams in southeastern Alaska, one of the areas where natural production has declined most seriously.

Commenting on this new development John Wiese, fishery editor of *Alaska Industry*, says: "It disturbs me because it implies that we must take it for granted that natural occurences of salmon must diminish and also because there is an unfortunate conviction (usually among the least experienced) that this artificial production is as good as what nature gave us. I can't agree to either. Only where an emergency situation exists should this be resorted to . . . One of the biggest problems now is still the need to get the public to understand that much remains to be done in salmon research in order to obtain a good level of management." The resource is so vast, he adds, in geographic extent and volume, that the impetus to survey streams, monitor the runs, and understand where work on the environment is needed to improve the stocks, and where fish may be transplanted, must not slow down.[18]

Threats on the Horizon

Now Alaska seems on the verge of becoming a "developed" land. Much of its wilderness is being invaded and the fish and wildlife face increasing pressures from proposed pipelines and dams, pulp mills, timber cutting, sawmills, urban spread, and other disturbing activities. In the fragile tundra and subarctic terrain some of these developments can be disastrous to the biotic community even with the best ecological safeguards.

One of the foremost threats to the wilderness is the projected tapping of the extensive oil fields on the North Slope of the Arctic, leased to the oil companies by the state in 1969 for $900 million with a guarantee of royalties calculated at $200 to $250 million annually when a pipeline is built to carry the petroleum across the state to Valdez in Prince William Sound, a distance of 789 miles, and thence by tanker to refineries in Puget Sound, and in the San Francisco and Los Angeles areas. Already the considerable drilling and other activities have left indelible scars on the landscape. The pipeline was stalled by court action launched by the Sierra Club, the Wilderness Society, other conservation organizations, and a small group of natives.

The pipeline will cross two major rivers, the Yukon and Copper, and numerous smaller streams that breed migratory fowl and support stocks of char and salmon. What worries the fishing industry and conservationists is the potential danger from breaks in the line with oil moving at temperatures of about 170° F. Some of the line will be buried in permafrost and some of it will be above ground; a break would be ecologically disastrous either way. When the oil is moved to supertankers in Prince William Sound the traffic is expected to reach a peak of a million barrels daily. The Sound teems with marine life, which suffered heavily during the 1964 earthquake. Two hundred eighty-four salmon streams empty into the Sound. Because some salmon spawn in the intertidal areas, any spill or collision could wipe them out. The young fish that hug the shores when they first enter saltwater to work their way to the sea would also be in jeopardy from oil washed onto the beaches and/or emulsified by wave action.

The impact report issued by the Department of the Interior, on March 20, 1972, admits that the major threat of the trans-Alaska pipeline and tanker delivery would be oil spillage. It says there can be no assurance of "perfect no-spillage" performance during the lifetime of the pipeline and estimates an average annual loss of 140,000 barrels of oil as a result of tanker accidents. It says salmon and other fishery resources would be especially vulnerable to such spills. In fact, the report confesses that the effects on the salmon fishery would be felt all along the Pacific coast, down to San Francisco Bay; in addition there would be serious losses from such accidents to Pacific Coast oyster and clam beds.

The impact study considered for the first time alternative routes to move the oil but avoided a clearcut decision. A representative of the Wilderness Society exclaimed at a court hearing, "Oil pollution could turn Puget Sound into a Dead Sea!" This fear has reverberated throughout the nation. Yet the Nixon administration, anxious to please the oil companies who had made large contributions to the campaign for re-election, granted the Alyeshka Pipeline Service Company a permit to build the pipeline, alleging that the "national interest" and the vital needs "to deliver this oil to our West Coast as promptly and as safely as possible" as overriding all environmental considerations. Political crassness can go no further. The interveners lost their suit to bar the pipeline in the District Court but appealed to a higher court.

Settlement of the native land claims by Congress, after many years of agitation, is believed also to have been partly inspired by the desire to overcome native objections to the pipeline. And here too one sees portents of danger to the environment and natural resources.

The Indians will obtain title to 40 million acres of land, much of which will be vital to the fisheries. "The settlement in no way turns salmon resources over to the natives," says John Wiese. "Monies from the settlement could, however, provide financing for added fishing pressures and without some compensating action (like limitation of fishing entry) all that may follow would be excessive harvesting. Processing plant operators have also expressed fears that they might face ruinous competition from native canneries or similar enterprises which could generate a chaotic situation. All of this adds to the need for vigorous attention to research in the various phases of utilization of the stocks — biological, social and economic."

There are other sources of anxiety. Timber cutting and processing is now Alaska's second largest industry. Logs for pulp mills and sawmills come almost entirely from the Chugach and Tongass National Forests. Much of the logging is around streams abounding with salmon or steelhead, and the fallers' chain saws sometimes do irreparable damage to the aquatic environment. For example, residents of Petersburg, at the head of Wrangell Narrows, are at loggerheads with the Forest Service, which often is insensitive to ecological values, because it plans to run a logging road through a popular recreation area that contains coho and steelhead. The stepped-up pace of logging in the Tongass in southeastern Alaska has already perceptibly damaged streamflow in many areas and impaired the habitat of anadromous fishes, although the Forest Service is reluctant to admit it.

Professor Robert B. Weeden of the University of Alaska lists other developments that may have adverse effects: explorations along the Bristol Bay coast of the Alaska Peninsula "where discovery of the commercial oil reserve could lead to serious economic losses to the area's world famous salmon fishery"; enticing oil prospects in the Chukchi Sea adjacent to the northwest coast "where oil spills could cause heavy mortality in migrating whale, seal, walrus and polar bear populations"; advent of a petrochemical industry in the wake of oil developments; the plan of the Alaska Highway Commission to push roads into hitherto undisturbed regions such as the northern part of the Alaska Peninsula where huge salmon populations propagate and are safe from human interference; and soon with road building would come settlement, tourist developments, urbanization, population increase — in short, civilization: the enemy of salmon.

All this, says Weeden, "assumes the continued ascendancy of the frontier mythology in Alaskan government . . . [Yet] it is also possible that new environmental perceptions could make themselves felt politically . . . and lead to significant shifts in economic and social policies." [19] To this author such shifts seem quite remote.

The slump in the salmon runs has considerable political reverberations, accentuated by the delay in construction of the pipeline across the state to bring North Slope oil to market. In the summer of 1972 the hardworking and competent Commissioner of the Fish and Game Department, Wallace Noerenberg, resigned, reputedly under pressure from Governor William Egan, and was replaced by one of his subalterns, James Brooks, a wildlife biologist.

Blame for the downturns in Bristol Bay runs, which comprise a substantial portion of the total Alaska catches, was cast by Governor Egan on the Japanese high seas fishery. At the November 1972 meeting of the International North Pacific Fishery Commission in Vancouver, British Columbia, the Japanese refused as usual to move the abstention line westward so as to permit more Alaska sockeye to escape their nets, although it was shown that the declining runs in the previous two years may have been due to unusually severe winters that reduced the freshwater and marine survival of juvenile fish.

To satisfy the demands of the Bristol Bay and other salmon fishing groups the governor asked the legislature for funds to launch two experimental rearing programs along the Naknek and Nushagak Rivers in an effort to produce faster-growing juveniles. A move was also made to reduce entry into the fishery, as Canada has done, so as to increase the harvests among participants.

On February 9, 1973, the oil industry and its numerous supporters, which include not only the bulk of the politicians but virtually all the chambers of commerce in Alaska, big business organizations, and the newspapers generally, received a "shock" when the United States Appeals Court overturned a lower court decision by ruling that an extra-wide federal land corridor generously granted by the Department of the Interior for the proposed pipeline was illegal — it violated the Mineral Leasing Act of 1920. "This is the worst possible opinion that could have come," said an aide to the governor. But conservationists throughout the nation rejoiced, for now it seemed that the federal government might have to consider an alternate route for tapping the Alaska oil bonanza and getting it to United States markets. The most talked-of alternate would be through Canada; this would ease the minds of fishery and wildlife men and conservationists generally.

In August 1973, however, in the wake of an alleged gasoline shortage believed to have been artificially precipitated by the oil companies, Congress was stampeded into passing a bill that removed all legal barriers to granting the Alyeshka Company a permit to build the pipeline. Spearheading the stampede was Senator Henry Jackson of Washington, aided by the indefatigable congressmen from Alaska. Jackson, author of the monumental Environmental Policy Act of 1969, even acquiesced in a provision of the bill permitting the Alyeshka Company to bypass this act, thus making court action to stall construction impossible.

President Nixon dutifully signed the pipeline bill, and the battle to save the fragile Alaskan landscape, and the wildlife and fisheries that would be imperiled by the extraction and transportation of the oil, seemed hopeless.

Part Four

The
Asian
Resource

XXIV ~⌇

Asian Salmon Resource

ALL SIX SPECIES of Pacific salmon are found in varying abundance in Asian rivers flowing into the Pacific from latitudes 35° to 70° north, that is, from Korea to the Chukotski Peninsula and in the numerous islands off the coast, including Japan. Lesser numbers dwell in the Arctic watersheds of eastern Siberia.

Setting

The great bulk of Asia's salmon are found in the far-eastern region of Soviet Russia, which covers about 1 million square miles, or twice the size of Alaska, and comprises the former provinces of Amur, Primorje (including Sakhalin), Transbaikalia, and Kamchatka (including the Commander Islands). It extends from 42° to 70° north latitude — from Manchuria to the Arctic Coast and from Lake Baikal to the Pacific. The northern parts of this vast region and Sakhalin are mainly tundra; most of the rest is mountainous, watered by innumerable rivers of considerable length. There are parallel mountain ranges along the coast including the Sikhote Alin, Aldan, Anadyr, Stanovoi, and Kamchatka Mountains, many of which are drained by salmon streams.

The major salmon rivers flowing northward to the Arctic are the 1110-mile Kolyma, 850-mile Indigirka, 750-mile Yana, and the mighty Lena, longer than the Mississippi, which follows a course of 3000 miles from the vicinity of Lake Baikal to the Laptev Sea. Among rivers flowing eastward the Amur, 1770 miles long with numerous lengthy tributaries, is the most important for production of anadromous fishes. It drains an area of 1,200,000 square miles, five times the size of the Columbia watershed, emptying into the Sea of Okhotsk. A large part of the Amur, including its tributary the Ussuri, forms the border with China, thus giving the Chinese an opportunity to harvest the salmon that come up that far. Another major salmon river flowing eastward is the Anadyr, which rises in the Kolyma Mountains and empties into the Bering Sea after a run of 450 miles.

In the tundra the subsoil is permanently frozen and when the ground thaws during the short summer bogs and shallows are formed and plants, including dwarf trees, grow profusely. South of the tundra is the taiga, a forest belt some 3000 miles long and 1000 miles wide, stretching from Finland across the Soviet Union to the Pacific Ocean. In the northern portion of the taiga the forests mainly support conifers, while in the southern part there are chiefly hardwoods.

The far-eastern area proliferates with wildlife — fox, wolf, bear, mountain goat, polar fox, spotted deer, marten, lynx, panther, and the famous jungle tiger. As may be expected, the leading exports from the region, apart from minerals, are fur, fish, and timber. Along the Pacific coast roam sea lions, seals, whales, walrus, and swarms of fish, of which the salmon are the most valuable. Around the coast of Kamchatka and the Kurile Islands there is a great salmon bank, as in Bristol Bay and to a much smaller degree around southwestern Greenland.

In the Arctic zone eternal frost and ice mark the seasons except for a brief summer respite. North of the Amur the growing season is less than three months. In the Amur Valley summer is warm and humid but winters are severe, for cold dry winds blow in from the north. The coastal areas are often shrouded in fog; as much as 70 percent of the days of the year may be sunless; snow lies on the ground for seven or eight months in places and temperatures of minus 50° F. may last for weeks, and even 90° below occasionally occurs. In the Sea of Okhotsk ice flows may be thick in early summer, and salmon live beneath them.

The Kamchatka Peninsula, incredibly rich in salmon as Steller discovered, is 750 miles long and 80 to 300 miles wide. Its terrain is mostly flat tundra with two chains of volcanoes running through it, some of which are still active. The highest peak, Mount Klyuchevskaya, rises to almost 16,000 feet. The Kamchatka River, longest in the peninsula, flows for 335 miles in a longitudinal valley and then, bending suddenly to the east, pierces the volcanic chain. Rain, snow, or fog occurs on about 320 days of the year, and there are only two seasons, a short summer and a long winter.

Sakhalin is a mountainous, eel-shaped island 600 miles long and 16 to 105 miles wide, so rich in fishes it has been coveted by both Japan and Russia and therefore has changed hands a few times. Its three mountain ranges are 2000 to 5000 feet above sea level. The climate is harsh and of great variation: in summer the temperature may rise to 80° F. and in winter drop to 40° below zero. Thick clouds shut out the sun most days of the year, while cold currents from the Sea of Okhotsk, aided by strong winds, bring immense ice flows to the east coast even in summer. Men move from one settlement to another on the ice.

In 1890 Anton Chekhov visited Sakhalin, then used as a penal colony by the Czarist government, and with a naturalist's eye described the teeming salmon in the rivers:

> The mass of fish . . . is so great and its run is so precipitous and so extraordinary that anyone who has not seen this magnificent phenomenon cannot actually understand it. The swiftness and density of the run can be judged by the surface of the water, which seems to be seething. The water has a fishy taste, the oars are jammed, and the blades propel the obstructing fish into the air.[1]

The Amur, which the Chinese call Black River, and many of its tributaries cut through mountainous terrain. After the river emerges from the Little Khingan Mountains, it waters a broad fertile plain. The climate is continental with long cold winters and short rainy summers. Grains such as barley, oats, wheat, rye, and rice are grown and cattle are produced. The Amur region is rich in minerals, including coal, iron ore, gold, tungsten, and lead, all vital to the industrialized economy of the Soviet Union.

Despite its generally hostile climate, about 5 million persons now live in Russia's far-eastern area compared with 300,000 in Alaska, which has roughly comparable terrain and climate; the disparity is due principally to the intense development of Siberia's mineral resources by the Communists. Ninety percent of the inhabitants are found along the Trans-Siberian Railroad, which connects European Russia with the Far East, and along the Amur-Ussuri Rivers.

Originally much of Japan with its splendid and numerous rivers offered favorable habitat for anadromous fishes. Now the crowded islands have been largely deserted by wild salmon and replaced by hatchery stock. Their present southern range is Chiba Peninsula near Tokyo, but in the past they were reported from as far south as the island of Kyushu.

Masu and chum salmon formerly inhabited many rivers in Korea, as far west as the Kanjin Chun. They were especially plentiful in the Tumen River, 220 miles long, which forms the border between Korea and China as well as Korea and the U.S.S.R. Biologists say that since the runs in Korea are at the extreme southern limit of their range, their existence is apt to be marginal.

Species

Pinks, chum, and sockeye are the most numerous of the genus *Oncorhynchus* in Asia; chinook and coho, though highly prized for their nutritive qualities, are much less abundant. Some measure of the relative importance of the different species is given by catch statistics. Japanese commercial landings (of which the great bulk are Russian fish) in the years 1957–1969 (see Appendix Table 15) averaged 65,000 metric tons of pinks annually, 47,000 tons of chum, 24,600 tons of sockeye, 7000 tons of coho, and 1060 tons of chinook. The Russians reported a yearly catch in the period 1962–1970 of 21.3 million pinks, 6.2 million chum, 1,150,000 coho, about 1 million sockeye, and a few hundred thousand chinook. Masu or cherry salmon found in Russian, Japanese, and Korean rivers are sometimes more plentiful than coho or chinook.

Almost everywhere in the salmon's range one comes upon rivers containing runs of chum salmon, also called "keta" or "Siberian salmon." According to the Russian ichthyologist Leo S. Berg, they are abundant in the Anadyr, in the Bering Sea, in Kamchatka (particularly west-coast rivers), Sakhalin, the Kurile Islands, and the rivers of Hokkaido. Small numbers are found in Arctic watersheds — the Kolyma, Indigirka, Yana, and lower reaches of the Lena.[2]

Chekhov was fascinated by these fishes in the rivers of foggy Sakhalin:

> The keta are healthy and strong when they enter the mouth of the river, but the constant struggle against the fierce current, the compact throng of fish, hunger, friction, collision with bushes and rocks, all these exhaust them; they become gaunt, their bodies are covered with bruises, the meat becomes white and flaccid, and the teeth protrude. The keta so completely change their characteristics that the uninitiated assume they become another fish and call them not keta but lancet fish.

The keta slowly weaken and can no longer battle against the current. They submerge or hide behind bushes with their mouths buried in the soil. At such times you can pick them up with your hands; even a bear can reach them with his paw. Finally, exhausted by their sexual cravings and by their hunger, they die. By this time many dead fish can be seen halfway along the stream, but the banks of the upper reaches of the rivers are covered with dead fish exuding a foul stench. All the sufferings endured by the fish during their erotic journey culminate in a nomadic thrust towards death . . . Not a single fish returns to the ocean; all perish in the rivers.[3]

There are distinct summer and fall runs of chum; the former attain a maximum length of one meter (3.3 feet) and the latter about eighty centimeters (2.67 feet). They average nine or ten pounds. In Japan a large part of the catch is sold in fresh markets, especially in eastern Hokkaido, where it is a common food of the local people, usually smoked.

Chum migrate considerable distances in the ocean. Summer chum

Schematic Diagram of Distribution and Migration of Mature Chum Salmon in Pacific Ocean by local stocks.

which issue from the Amur River, from streams emptying into the Sea of Okhotsk, and from Western Kamchatka, forage chiefly in the Sea of Okhotsk. Fall chum, in contrast, feed primarily in the ocean proper, as far away as the Gulf of Alaska, where they mingle with schools of Alaskan salmon.[4] The Japanese biologist Seiji Machidori examined the stomach contents of chum salmon caught in the northwestern Pacific Ocean and found they comprised small fish, euphausiids, pteropods, and jellyfish.

Chum return to the rivers after spending one to three winters in the sea. They are known to make long journeys to their spawning grounds: for example, they ascend the Amur River for over 700 miles, clocking about twenty-five miles per day at a steady pace. By the time they reach their destination they have lost much of their fat and flavor and can only mate quickly and expire.

Catches of summer and fall chum are subject to wide fluctuations, due partly, according to the Russian biologist I. B. Birman, to periodic shifts in the Kuroshio Current, which causes cooling and warming of the waters and corresponding changes in the meteorological regime of neighboring parts of the sea and land. During periods of warmer water the species increases in abundance, says Birman, because warming of the sea is favorable to the survival of the eggs in the gravels, while during periods of colder water they decrease. "High winter air temperatures and abundance of early snowfall reduces to a minimum . . . freezing of the spawning beds which, in other winters, causes a rather large part of the eggs laid by salmon to perish."[5] Chum are the major salmon species bred in Japanese hatcheries.

Humpback or pink salmon with two-year lives throng innumerable rivers along the mainland coast from the Bering Strait to Korea and in the long string of islands from the Commanders to Honshu. In some regions they are plentiful in odd-numbered years and sparse in even-numbered, as along the eastern coast of Kamchatka, the Pimori district of Sakhalin, and Hokkaido; in the Nikolaevsk region of the Amur the reverse is true.

Usually the pinks weigh only about four pounds at maturity, yet they manage to wander over a large portion of the Pacific as far as the mid-Aleutians. They generally spawn in the lower reaches of the rivers for they have little time to spare, yet they are seen in the Khungari, a tributary of the Amur, 360 miles from the sea. Typically they enter freshwater about the time the drifting ice disappears, at first one by one, then in the middle of June in vast multitudes, continuing until the middle of July; thereafter stragglers arrive until mid-August.

At times they are so numerous as to cause consternation to fishermen. Thus on July 30, 1926, the Bolshaya River on the west coast of Kamchatka presented an amazing spectacle. "Although the weather was calm and sunny, an extraordinary noise could be heard coming from the middle of the river between its main two channels . . . The population of the fishing camps rushed out to the river bank. Standing there, the fishermen feasted their eyes upon a tremendous school of fish, which went up the river, making a very loud noise, as if a new river had burst into the Bolshaya; the fish jumped out of the water continually. The noisy stretch of water was at least one verst long (1.1 mile) and not less than 100 meters (330 feet) wide, so that the size of the school could be estimated at several million specimens, which all got to the spawning grounds upstream, having passed the fishing camps completely unimpeded." [6] Dead fish appeared in the river by the middle of August.

Sockeye are found over a smaller range in Asia than pinks or chum — from the Gulf of Anadyr to Hokkaido. The Kamchatka Peninsula, however, produces about 80 percent of these red fishes: it seems to have the requisite environments, including lakes for rearing. Sockeye undertake extensive oceanic migrations after spending a

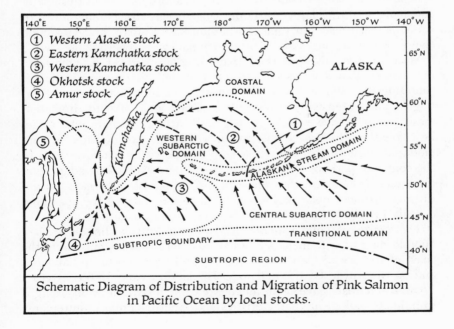

Schematic Diagram of Distribution and Migration of Pink Salmon in Pacific Ocean by local stocks.

year or two in freshwater and are four to five years old when they return to spawn. Members of the eastern Kamchatka stock go as far as the outermost Aleutians, where they mingle with fish from western Alaska. Dwarf-size sockeye (similar to kokanee) are found in the landlocked lakes in Japan and Kamchatka.

In some ways masu or cherry salmon, unknown in North America, are the most interesting of the Asian species. In coloration they resemble coho but are smaller, usually weighing five or six pounds in Japan. Berg, however, reports that in the Tumen River there are female masu weighing four kilograms (8.8 pounds) and males five and a half kilograms (12 pounds). When ready to spawn the females turn from silver to white, while the males, with hook jaws and tremendous teeth, develop large humps like the pinks. Both sexes have eight to eleven light crimson transverse bands (hence are called "cherry salmon"), dark in spawning fish and usually brighter in males than females.

The young stay in the river one year and then descend to the ocean; they attain maturity in their third or fourth year and head for home waters. Most of them remain during their feeding years in the protected Sea of Japan and do not venture further. Many of the parr, as among the Atlantic salmon, become sexually mature in freshwater and mate with the larger seagoing fish. Dwarf-size nonmigratory or resident masu occur in some Formosan, east Korean, and Hokkaido rivers. Masu are successfully bred in Japanese hatcheries.

Masu salmon raise questions that cannot be answered. One must not assume that scientists have yet dispelled all the mysteries surrounding the salmon despite the fact that no genus has been so thoroughly and extensively investigated. One would like to think that masu, as Dr. Neave says, were originally Atlantic salmon who somehow found a Northwest Passage in a distant geologic age, accommodated itself to the new continent, prospered, and multiplied. In the course of perhaps a half-million years there evolved by adaptation to new environments other species closely resembling *Salmo salar* yet distinct in one crucial way — their inability to survive the spawning ordeal. Proof of this assumption is of course in the future.

The range of coho salmon in Asia is relatively limited. They abound mainly in Kamchatka, but there are runs in streams along the coast of the Sea of Okhotsk, in the River Tym in northern Sakhalin, and on the Kurile Islands and some Hokkaido rivers. In recent years Russian scientists have done much work on this species and brought to light its biological characteristics and environmental requirements in Asian waters. Tagging by American scientists show that Kamchatka coho migrate as far as Adak Island in the Aleutians, 900 miles from home. They usually arrive in their rivers later than the other salmon, have a more prolonged run, and spawn from about August 20 to mid-March.

In Kamchatka there are generally early (fall) and late (winter) runs. As in North America, the young usually spend one or two years in freshwater. A. I. Smirnov, who has written a comprehensive report on the coho, says that "before migration the young fish become streamlined, the relative sizes of the fins become reduced . . . the intensive deposition of guanine almost completely obscures the speckled coloration of the body, their behavior changes." [7] Almost all Asian coho spend two winters in the ocean and upon their return (to Kamchatka rivers) average about 3½ kilograms (7.7 pounds).

So far as is known, the lordly chinook are not only the least numerous of the salmon species in Asia but also have the most limited range. They inhabit the Anadyr and some rivers in Kamchatka, are rare in the Amur but somewhat more common in northern Hokkaido streams. In Kamchatka they are prominent in the Bolshaya and Kamchatka Rivers, averaging about eighteen pounds (roughly the same as in the Columbia). Some specimens are reported to attain fifty-five pounds.

Chinook appear in the Kamchatka River in large numbers from the middle of August and ascend over 300 miles, virtually to the headwaters. In the frigid climate the eggs take 110 days to incubate. The Japanese are trying to breed these valuable fishes artificially in Hokkaido hatcheries, using eggs brought from the state of Washington.

Tokyo's Fish Market

One may usually see all six Pacific salmon species and hundreds of other fishes in the wholesale fish market in Tokyo, largest in the world. Here on a May morning, in the company of Dr. Tokiharu Abe, I saw piles of pinks from Hokkaido, cherry salmon from northern Honshu, chum caught in China and shipped from Mukden, chinook air-freighted from Alaska, and sockeye that probably also came from Alaska. Only coho were missing that day.

Every morning except holidays, and regardless of the weather, the tall hatless Dr. Abe, who is inspector of poison fishes for the Tokyo market (they require special handling in order to remove the poison glands and make them edible), arrives about 6 A.M. and after finishing his duties moves with never-ending wonder along the numerous stalls piled with fishes brought from the four ends of the world. All the dealers know him and when a new species is on hand they make it a point of showing it to him. He makes a note of it and when he sees the Emperor, a personal friend who is also a keen ichthyologist, reports his find to him.

That morning at breakfast Dr. Abe told me wistfully about the Sumida River, which once ran pure and clear through the city of Tokyo, much as in Hiroshige's drawings of the "Fifty-Seven Stations on the Tekaido Road" where it seems to flow across a green and mystic landscape with white-mantled Mount Fuji as a backdrop. Servants of the Imperial household used to hook salmon within the purlieus of the palace and present them to the Emperor as fish of rare delicacy. Now the Sumida carries the offal of the world's largest metropolis and runs a sickly yellow. The fairylike landscape of Hiroshige's day has utterly vanished, along with the anadromous fishes. Mount Fuji can rarely be seen because of the haze that covers the sky. Tokyo is a city of Babylonian towers and streets crowded and congested almost to suffocation with automobiles and human beings. Where once salmon was so cheap that poor people could occasionally eat it, it is now a luxury food available only in western-style hotels and restaurants and is more likely than not imported from Alaska.

Russia's Salmon Wealth
and Its Exploitation

The Primitive Peoples

WHEN THE RUSSIANS REACHED the Amur River in their conquest of Siberia they found groups of people speaking strange tongues, in a Neolithic stage of development. These included the Yakuts, Yukagirs, Oroks, Orochi, Nivkhi, Evens, Evenks, Koryaks, Gilyaks, and others who belonged to three broad linguistic stocks: the Turkic, which now comprise 58 percent of the natives of Siberia; the Mongolic, which account for 28 percent; and the Tungusi-Manchurian, 5 percent.[1] Extensive archeological studies have revealed the outlines of their cultures, of peoples living for millennia along the Siberian rivers.

Typical of Siberian primitives were the Nivkhi, who lived on the lower reaches of the Amur River and spoke a language related to that of the Manchurians. When the first Russian, Vasily Poyarkov, visited them in 1643–1646 they were dwelling in villages of wooden winter houses, wore clothing made of fish skins and animal pelts (a cultural trait the Alaskan Indians probably brought from their homeland), kept many dogs, engaged mostly in fishing, and naturally ate fish most of the time. They caught salmon in nets and with seines paid out from a boat and a kind of trap called a "zayezdok."

The Nivkhi also harpooned sturgeon in the estuary of the Amur and hunted sea lions and seals. When the bears came down to the rivers the natives waited for them with bows and arrows. In the winter they hunted sable for its valuable golden brown fur with traps along the rivers and on fallen trees that served the animals as crossings. Squirrels and foxes were hunted with dogs.

The Nivkhi had boats hollowed out of poplar trees, which could be easily carried across shallows and isthmuses and propelled by oars or poles. Footwear, robes, and overcoats were wrought from specially prepared skins of salmon, carp, and pike as well as from seal and elk skin and dog fur. Men did the hunting and fishing while the women made the clothing and utensils, gathered plants, and took care of the dogs. The staple of their diet was always fish, dried, jerked, or as "eukola" made from lightly smoked fish spread out to dry in the sun.

"A favorite delicacy was *mos'*, prepared with fish skins, seal-fat, berries, rice, and sometimes crumbled eukola. Another favorite dish was *talkk* — a salad of raw fish, garnished with wild garlic." [2] When the Nivkhi made contact with the Chinese and traded with them, they became acquainted with rice, millet, and tea, and after the Russians appeared in the Amur River area they began to use small quantities of salt, sugar, and bread made with local grain and water.

Like the American Indians, the Siberian natives regarded the rivers, waters, trees, earth, and animals as having anthropomorphic qualities. The bear cult was a feature of their folkways.

On the upper Amur dwelt the Ulchi, who lived off the sturgeon, carp, smelt, salmon, and other fishes with which the waters teemed — the Amur is said to have at least a hundred species of fish. "The salmon catch and stocks of eukola made of salmon determined the prosperity of Ulchi families for a whole year . . . The waste left from the preparation of eukola was cured and served as feed for the dogs." [3] Salmon were caught with small traps made of stakes and twigs like those of the Nivkhi, with float nets and small thrown seines. Elk, deer, and bear meat filled out their diet along with some wild plants.

Fish provided not only food but skins for raiment. One of the chief occupations of the women was to prepare the skins for clothing, a process that required considerable ingenuity. After the skin was carefully removed from the fish it was dried for several days either indoors or in the shade outdoors, then hammered with a wooden mallet on a special wooden stand. After that wormwood was wrapped in the slightly moistened skin and several hours later it was stretched on a special board and hung near the hearth, where it was allowed to smoke for about two weeks until it turned yellow, when it was considered suitable for use. Clothes made by American Indians from salmon skins may be seen in the Sheldon Jackson Museum in Sitka, Alaska.

The Nanays, who also lived in the Upper Amur area, had contacts with the Manchu and Chinese peoples, with whom they traded sturgeon, valuable not only for its savory white flesh but for its cartilage and spinal cord. As the sturgeon stocks were exhausted salmon became a basic item of trade. Similarly, as the sable were exterminated squirrel pelts became important trade items.

Summer chum come into the rivers in Nanay territory in the middle of July and autumn chum in large numbers between the end of August and mid-September. The humpback salmon were much less numerous. The entire population of the village participated in the fishing.

The Gilyaks were residents of the island of Sakhalin. Chekhov made a study of these primitive folk in 1890. They were then scarcely touched by Russian influence, for the Czarist government was almost completely indifferent to their welfare. They were a polite, cheerful, and friendly people, said Chekhov. "A Gilyak's face is round, flat, moonlike, of yellowish cast, with prominent cheek bones, dirty, with slanting eyes and a barely visible beard. His hair is smooth, black, wavy, gathered in a braid at the nape of the neck. His facial expression is not savage, it is always intelligent, gentle, naively attentive."

The Gilyaks were strong, stocky, muscular persons, of medium stature. "All [the Gilyak's] fat is used for the warmth which a man on Sakhalin must generate in his body in order to compensate for the heat loss caused by the low temperature and the excessive humidity . . . He eats fatty seal meat, salmon, sturgeon, and whale fat. He also eats meat in large quantities in raw, dry and frozen form."

A peculiarity of the Gilyaks was their aversion to water. They never washed their bodies nor their garments or footwear, and "the close proximity of their [dugout] dwellings is indicated by the foul and almost unbearable odor of drying fish and rotting fish waste." [4]

George Kennan, a member of the Western Union Telegraph Expedition that laid out an overland route (which was never used) across Asia to Europe in 1865–1867, provides a picture of the Koryaks of northern Kamchatka. They are the "Kamchadales" described by Steller. In this area the salmon entered the rivers early in June and "were caught by the natives in gillnets, baskets, seines, weirs, traps and a dozen other ingenious contrivances." Kennan saw dozens of small streams choked with dead, dying and decayed fish. Even in little mountain brooks, so narrow a child could step across them, "18 to 20 inch salmon were working their way upstream in water not deep enough to cover their bodies . . . We frequently waded in and threw them out by the dozen with our bare hands . . . If it were not for the abundance of fish the entire country would be uninhabited except by the reindeer people." [5]

❖

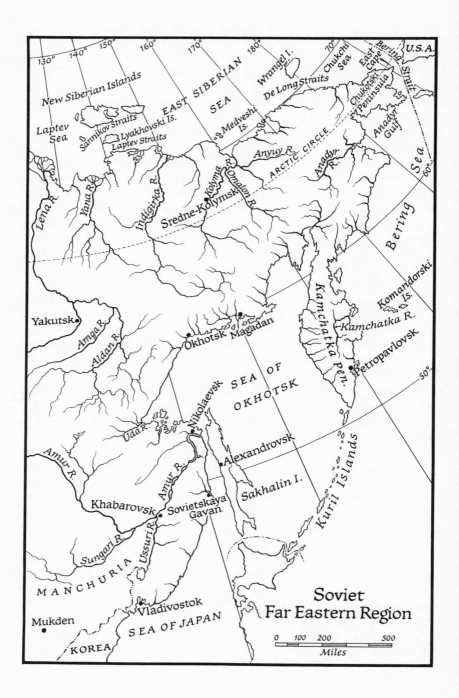

Soviet
Far Eastern Region

0   100   200   500
Miles

The Early Fishery

It was the Japanese who first exploited the salmon runs of the islands off the Siberian coast. In 1752 the feudal Baron of Matsumae had three fishing stations in Sakhalin (called Oku-Ezo by the Japanese). In 1773 the third Baron of Fukuyama started large-scale fishing on this island, taking cod, herring, and salmon; he operated the fishery for seventeen years.[6]

When the Russian-American Company established a post on Sakhalin in 1853 it found Japanese fishermen on the southern extremity of the island and offered them protection. With the emergence of Nippon from its cocoon after the Meiji restoration in 1868, systematic exploitation of the fisheries began. In 1875 under the treaty of Saint Petersburg, Japan ceded Sakhalin to Russia in exchange for the nearby Kurile Islands, but Japanese vessels and merchants retained their privileges on Sakhalin. Chekhov noted that the Japanese were earning half a million rubles annually from fishing its rivers, selling their catches in China and Japan.

The Russian settlers on the island, who were mainly former convicts, were lazy, demoralized, and incompetent. "They do not know how to fish or how to cure fish, and nobody teaches them," said Chekhov. "According to the present custom the prison takes over the best fishing grounds and the settlers are left with rapids and shallows, where their cheap home-made nets are torn to pieces by bushes and rocks." The convicts were catching fish for the prison, and fortunately one of them had been a fisherman in Tagonrog. He managed the saltery. "It would seem that if [he] had not happened to be convicted nobody would know how to handle the fish."

While the convicts were taking gaunt, half-dead salmon in the upper reaches of the Tym, the Japanese were fishing at the mouth of the river after blockading it with palings. In the lower reaches the Gilyaks were catching fish, "which were healthier and tastier than those which were being salted in the Tymor district for the settlers," [7] for their dogs. Meanwhile the Japanese were loading junks and larger vessels with bright silvery salmon and taking them to Hokkaido.

In 1892 the Japanese entered the Amur district, where they were permitted to lease salting stations below the city of Nikolaevsk. These privileges were later extended to Sakhalin and Kamchatka. In 1899 there were 222 Japanese stations on Sakhalin operated by fifty-two companies. In 1900 a flotilla of fifteen Japanese freighters and thirty fishing vessels began to operate in Kamchatka waters under a joint Russian-Japanese management scheme. The Japanese gradually expanded their fishing in Russian territory; catches mounted rapidly along the Siberian coast, at the mouth of the Amur, in southern Sakhalin and in the Kuriles. In the decade 1898 to 1907 their landings averaged 80 million pounds a year in the Amur district alone, over twice as much as was then being taken out of the Columbia River; 70 percent of the catch was exported to Japan.

Thus, as Clinton E. Atkinson says, "it is obvious that the Japanese developed the salmon fisheries of the Far East. Their right to fish in Russian waters was firmly established by the Saint Petersburg Treaty of 1875. Their fisheries were recognized by many Russian regulations. The Japanese were permitted to lease sites for processing salmon (both salteries and canneries). They operated many fisheries jointly with the Russians. Finally, the Russians were almost entirely dependent on the Japanese for their markets in the early years." [8]

From the Russo-Japanese War to World War II (1904–1945)

Once emerged from hibernation, Japan expanded economically and militarily with explosive energy. Copying the industrial and scientific knowhow of the west, down to the details of building a salmon hatchery, Japan rapidly industrialized and acquired markets and access to raw materials in neighboring lands. Since domestic food resources were inadequate to feed a swiftly growing population, the Japanese strove to acquire a greater hold on the Siberian fishery. Canned salmon also brought foreign exchange needed for the grand scheme of industrialization.

Greater access to the Siberian fisheries was one reason the Japanese suddenly attacked Russia's far-eastern garrison without a declaration of war in 1904. By the Treaty of Portsmouth, signed on September 5, 1905, after the rout of the Russian armies and navy in the Far East, Russia ceded to Japan the southern part of Sakhalin (renamed by the victors Karafuto). A convention signed by Japan and Russia on July 28, 1907, stipulated that:

> Japanese subjects are authorized to engage in fishing and the preparation of fish and aquatic products, extending both on the sea and on shore from lots which will be sold by lease at public auction without discrimination between Russian and

Japanese subjects; . . . the Japanese subjects will enjoy under this relationship the same rights as the Russian subjects, having taken their share of fish in the regions specified.

Japanese companies established shore-based stations in Kamchatka and the Maritime Provinces of Siberia. They adopted "a modern type of floating trap which could be completely removed at the end of each fishing season, stored and installed again the following season, or even at a different site," says Atkinson. This kind of trap is still widely used at the mouths of the far-eastern rivers. They also employed large beach seines like those used in Alaska, set by skiffs across the current and drifted downstream and hauled ashore by human hands or with the help of horses. The fishermen, all Japanese, about a dozen to each boat, hauled in the fish with special net bags, each containing about 1500 salmon. The sockeye, chinook, and silvers (coho) were taken to the canneries, while the chum and pinks were split and disemboweled and put in boxes weighing 100 to 150 pounds that were slung on the backs of carriers who marched off to the salting piles.[9]

The Russians also fished for salmon, using 400- to 700-foot seines. They disposed of their catches to the Japanese, for there were scarcely any local markets and shipment to the western part of the country was too expensive. The Japanese pack of canned salmon jumped from 10,000 cases in 1910 to almost 1.5 million cases in 1929, when twenty-nine canneries were in operation in Russian territory. Thus Japan, with relatively little supplies of her own, became a major factor in the world's salmon industry, a position she has held ever since despite considerable vicissitudes.

Having entered World War I on the Allied side, Japan took advantage of the Russian Revolution and the confused period that followed in the Far East to seize control of Sakhalin and other Siberian territory, principally by supporting the White counterrevolutionary armies. When the Communists consolidated their rule in the Far East they ousted the Japanese invaders. A new era then began in the history of the fisheries.

After many abortive attempts to revive the 1905 fishery convention, a new eight-year treaty signed by Japan and Russia came into force in 1928. Japanese concessions continued in Siberian coastal waters but on a decreasing scale as the Soviets expanded their own fishing industry. Japanese catches in the U.S.S.R. fell from an average of 66 million salmon in the period 1908–1924 to 53 million in 1937–1944.[10]

As they found themselves confronted by a resurgent Russia determined to ease them out of the mainland and island fisheries, the Japanese as early as 1927 turned to the sea and launched a mother-ship fleet, taking salmon with huge gill nets on their feeding grounds and processing them on the spot. These fleets could stay out for weeks at a time, for the factory ships were equipped with canning and freezing equipment. In 1933 they also started a land-based drift gill-net and trap-net fishery in the North Kurile Islands, which they then controlled. Japanese also fished in the rich waters along the coast of Kamchatka. These operations resulted in enormous hauls: between 1933 and 1945 they totaled on the average 55 million salmon per year. (Combined Japanese and Russian catches in the coastal areas of the Far East are shown in Appendix Table 14.)

In 1937 the Japanese attempted to extend their lucrative fishing eastward near the North American continent. They offered to cooperate in joint ventures with American fishing companies, but American policy was (and is) opposed to harvesting salmon on the feeding grounds. A Japanese fleet was actually sent to Bristol Bay to take salmon but so fierce was the Alaskan reaction that it turned back.

After Russia declared war on Japan in 1945 the Japanese companies were no longer permitted to fish in Russian territorial waters. At the Yalta Conference in February 1945 the Allied powers promised Russia that Sakhalin and the Kuriles would be returned to her, presumably if she entered the war against Japan. Accordingly, after the war Soviet troops occupied these bleak areas and most of the Japanese settlers, including fishermen, were evacuated to their homeland.

Japan's High Seas Fishing

Japan's fishing fleet was destroyed in World War II. By 1952, however, she had substantially recovered from the war with American aid, rebuilt her fleet, and launched a drive to harvest the fishes of the seven seas.[11]

As Japanese floating canneries appeared in the North Pacific in growing numbers, taking many Alaska salmon, the alarmed Alaskan fishing industry reacted by urging the United States government to set limits to these depredations. As a result, a treaty was negotiated between the United States, Canada, and Japan in 1952 that became effective in June 1953 and required Japan to abstain from fishing east of a line drawn through longitude 175° west, passing through

Adak Island in the Aleutians. This was a provisional line subject to confirmation and adjustment as more information was obtained about the migratory habits of the Alaska salmon. Pursuant to the treaty, the International North Pacific Fisheries Commission was created with a secretariat in Vancouver, British Columbia, to conduct suitable studies to determine the line, or lines, which best divide the salmon of Asian from those of American origin. The treaty was to run for ten years and thereafter could be abrogated by each signatory on one year's notice. As it turned out, large numbers of Bristol Bay sockeye were being taken by Japanese nets west of the provisional line, but efforts to have it moved westward so as to eliminate American fish have met with stubborn Japanese opposition.

The Japanese high seas fleet grew from three mother ships and 57 catcher boats in 1952 to 14 mother ships and 407 catchers in 1955 when 162,000 tons of salmon were harvested that were converted into 1,600,000 cases of canned fish, 19,500 tons of salted fish, over 19,000 tons of frozen fish, and 1000 tons of roe (sold as a delicacy in Japan).

The Russians also became alarmed at such monumental landings. The ichthyologist Peter Moyseev warned that "the uncontrolled Japanese salmon fishing on the high seas which reached great proportions in recent years is not adjusted to conditions of stocks of Pacific salmon and has already caused a sharp decline in abundance of these valuable species. It could rapidly undermine their stock." [12] Accordingly in March 1956 Russia announced the closure of a large section of the international waters of the north Pacific to Japanese fishing vessels. Despite Japan's protest that this was a violation of the freedom of the seas, a delegation was sent to Moscow to negotiate a fisheries treaty. As Russia had become the dominant power in the northwest Pacific and Japan was militarily impotent, a convention was rapidly negotiated and signed in May 1956. It banned Nipponese fishermen from large areas in the Sea of Okhotsk, around the Kuriles, and off the east coast of Kamchatka. The treaty provided for annual quotas and other regulations on Japanese fishing to be determined annually by a Soviet-Japanese commission.

The commission meets every year and decides on quotas, usually after lengthy and hard bargaining. To enforce the regulations Soviet vessels patrol the area of Japanese operations and Russian inspectors are allowed to board the fishing boats and factory ships.

Mother-ship fishing for salmon is permitted by the Russian-Japanese treaty in an area north of 45° north latitude and west of the abstention line (designated as Area A on the map on page 456). A land-based

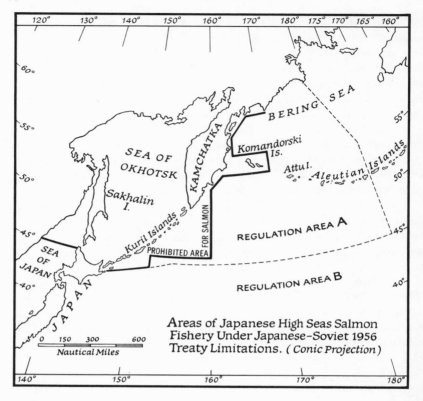

Areas of Japanese High Seas Salmon
Fishery Under Japanese–Soviet 1956
Treaty Limitations. (*Conic Projection*)

Japanese fishery for salmon, without mother ships, using drift nets and longlines is permitted in Area B, south of 45° north. Quotas for both areas are set by the Soviet-Japanese commission. The effect of these curbs has been to reduce Japanese ocean catches from almost 200,000 tons of salmon in 1958 to an average of 100,000 tons annually in the 1960s. Quotas set by the Russian-Japanese negotiators have been steadily reduced.

Japanese Fleet in Action

In 1969 eleven mother ships accompanied by 369 catcher boats fished in Area A; 1706 drifters and long liners, based on Hokkaido ports, were operating in Area B; and 280 drifters and long liners were taking salmon in the Sea of Okhotsk (not subject to treaty limitations). Altogether a fleet of 2715 vessels was engaged in scouring the waters of the North Pacific and its total harvest was 126,000 metric tons of salmon. By virtue of these hauls Japan (which produces a relatively small amount of salmon) has been in first or second place in the world salmon landings since 1955, as the table below shows.

The mother-ship fleet operating in Asia usually leaves its home port Hakodate on the island of Hokkaido on May 15. It operates under rigid rules, as described by Francis M. Fukuhara of the U.S. National Marine Fishery Service: "Since most of the mothership fleets are competitive (with quotas assigned to each), regulations are necessary to avoid conflicts between fleets for preferential fishing grounds. The requirement for minimum spacing between catcher boats stipulated by the Japan-Soviet Fisheries Commission must also be fulfilled. To promote orderly deployment of the fleets, the Salmon Mothership Association subdivided the entire authorized area into 169 subareas called blocks, most of which [are] 3800 to 4000 square miles. On a given day, only the catcher boats of a given fleet [are] permitted to occupy a specific principal block and one-half of an appended block.

"After the first day of fishing, any mothership wishing to move to another area [communicates] its intent to occupy a specific block on a given date by 7 A.M. to either of two motherships which [serves] on a rotational basis as coordinator of fleet deployment. Upon acknowl-

PACIFIC SALMON LANDINGS, 1952–1967							
			Asia			N. America	Grand
	Japan	U.S.S.R.	Total	Canada	U.S.A.	Total	Total
1952	36.5	118.1	154.6	68.3	159.7	258.0	312.6
1953	43.0	190.8	233.8	86.3	141.9	228.2	462.0
1954	76.3	121.6	197.9	82.2	151.2	233.4	431.3
1955	171.8	172.4	344.2	59.5	131.4	199.9	535.1
1956	151.7	160.4	311.1	53.0	137.1	190.1	501.2
1957	184.0	150.0	334.0	61.5	120.3	181.8	515.8
1958	196.6	73.0	269.6	83.9	129.5	213.4	483.0
1959	179.1	94.1	273.2	49.6	92.8	142.2	356.6
1960	144.4	70.0	214.4	35.1	107.1	142.2	356.6
1961	156.2	80.0	236.2	56.8	142.8	199.6	435.8
1962	112.9	60.6	173.5	75.9	142.3	218.2	391.7
1963	148.5	81.1	229.6	56.0	128.5	184.5	414.1
1964	126.5	45.3	171.6	58.4	159.8	218.2	389.8
1965	149.2	87.6	236.8	43.2	148.8	182.0	428.8
1966	128.8	59.7	188.5	76.4	175.9	252.3	440.8
1967	150.3	84.1	234.4	62.9	98.5	161.4	395.8

edgement, that particular area [is] closed to both passage and fishing by vessels of other fleets."

Assignment of the catcher boats is made by the mother ship and master fisherman. Each vessel is positioned by radar and is varied in accordance with the strategy developed by integrating a mass of information received from the scouting vessels (four are assigned to the fleet), catcher boats, samples of landings examined by biologists aboard the mother ships, and data from past fishing experience. The gill nets are set in the direction that, it is believed, will best intercept the shoals of fish moving in the sea, generally from southwest to northeast or vice versa.

Each gill net contains a unit called a "tan," which is about 51 meters (168 feet) at the cork line and 50 meters (165 feet) at the lead line. Mesh sizes are either 4.76 or 5.12 inches and the maximum length of a gill-net string is limited to 6.2 nautical miles west of 175° west longitude and 9.2 miles west of 170° 25' east. About 50 to 100 strings of nets are stacked aboard each catcher boat.

The nets are set at twilight and allowed to drift until 1 A.M., when they are picked up and the fish are brailed onto the boat. By 5 A.M. the well deck is cleared and the long nets are completely retrieved and stacked until set again at twilight.

When most of the catchers have retrieved their nets the mother ship moves into a convenient position for relieving them of their cargoes, which must be done at least once daily except for those that have engine failure or other equipment problems, or badly tangled gear. Some of the catches are immediately frozen and the rest canned. Careful records are kept of the landings by species and by gill-net boats (which are independently owned), with officials of the gill-net vessel owners' association representing the seller and others representing the factory ship owner or buyer. A government inspector certifies to the accuracy of the catches. Usually the fleet operating in Area A is at sea until its quota is fulfilled.

Sockeye, chum, and pink salmon make up about 95 percent of the harvests; the rest are coho and chinook. Species composition varies from year to year due to fluctuations in the numbers spawned in the producing countries, length of freshwater life, and length of sea stay. Catches consist of various age groups. Of the total mother-ship catch of about 93 million sockeye, for example, in the period 1956–1963, about 44 percent had spent two years in the sea and 55 percent three years.[13] The bulk of these fishes came from Russian rivers.

I was in Tokyo in late April 1971 when the Soviet-Japanese commission was coming to the end of its protracted negotiations. At a luncheon I met Dr. Moyseev and Dr. Igor Kurenkov, two of the three Soviet negotiators. They had reached an impasse. "We have done all we could to get an agreement," said Moyseev, "now it's up to Kosygin." A few days before, Japan had sent a special envoy to Moscow to negotiate at the highest levels. Time was getting short, for the Japanese salmon fleet was scheduled to leave soon for the fishing grounds.

On May 1 Tokyo announced that an accord was reached "after two rounds of rough negotiations" between former Agriculture and Forestry Minister Munemori Akagi and Soviet Fisheries Minister Alexander H. Ishkov. Akagi accepted the Soviet demand for a total ban on catching roe-bearing herring (which comes under the 1956 treaty), and Japan's salmon quota was set at 95,000 tons as demanded by the Soviet Union. This was, in fact, 5000 more tons than the 1970 quota. On the very day the agreement was announced a fleet of 114 drift-net boats left Kushiro for operations in Regulation Area B.

On his return to Tokyo Akagi called a press conference. He admitted he was pessimistic about the future of the high seas fishery. "Russia may demand next year that Japan's haul of salmon be drastically cut," he said. For the first time Russia had reserved for itself 15,000 tons of the annual quota, although she does not permit her fleets to take salmon on the high seas. Akagi believed that in the future Moscow would demand that the Russian share be equalized with that of Japan.

The high seas quota for Japanese salmon fishing was 87,000 metric tons in 1972, of which 35,000 tons were taken in Area A (map, page 456) and the rest in Area B. The catch comprised 70 percent chums, 15 percent sockeye, 10 percent pinks, and 5 percent coho and chinook, compared with the 1971 composition of 51 percent chums, 27.5 percent pinks, 17.5 percent sockeye, 3 percent coho, and 1 percent chinook.

A Visit to Hakodate

In the middle of May the eyes of the salmon industry are on Hakodate, the home port of the mother-ship fleet. Built on a rocky peninsula, the city faces the blue waters of Tsugaru Bay where the black factory ships were riding at anchor when I arrived on May 14 and the white catcher boats, scrubbed from stem to stern, were waiting at their wharves for the signal to depart.

Fishing is the economic lifeblood of Hakodate. For six months of the year it is crowded with hundreds of fishing boats chugging in and out of its half-moon harbor. The principal species landed are salmon, cuttlefish, saury, and pike.

As a guest of the Nichiro Fishing Company, which owns four of the eleven mother ships (and which before the last world war had leases on 130 "lots" on Kamchatka), I visited the *Meisei Maru* the day before it sailed. A typical factory ship of 8800 tons, it is served by thirty catcher boats and has facilities for canning and freezing 250 tons of fish. It carries a crew of 35 and 310 factory workers, all men.

The operation lasts sixty to seventy days and may encompass 5000 miles. The men work in foul as well as good weather, which is rare in May and June in the North Pacific. "Swelling seas, storms or high winds do not stop us," said the factory manager. "The best time for catching sockeye is the end of May, pinks from the end of June through July. In July the weather improves and there is more sunshine." Before the invention of modern sounding and weather-forecasting equipment, the voyage was hazardous and sometimes a boat did not come back.

On the morning of May 15 I rose early and reached the Nichiro Company's office at 7 A.M. It was a raw, chilly day. There were about 50,000 people — wives, children, parents, friends — on the wharves to see the 10,000 men who comprised the crews and workers take off. Each boat flew colorful banners, the orange flag of Nippon mingling with the standards of the fishermen's associations. Some had bamboo poles with branches of fresh leaves stuck on them as symbols of good luck. Radios were blaring and TV cameramen and newspaper reporters moved among the crowd. There were young mothers attired in gay western clothes, with babies strapped to their backs and holding young children by the hand; older women in traditional gray or black; and young women in miniskirts. A band played western music intermittently. Firecrackers popped. As each vessel prepared to sail women threw colorful streamers to the crew and held them in their hands until the boat left the dock. No tears were shed, no kissing of loved ones, for the Japanese do not show affection in public.

I accompanied the top officials of the Nichiro Company on their visits to each of their black mother ships, a traditional custom that permits the crew and workers to meet their bosses and drink a toast with them. On each ship the ward room was decorated with artificial flowers (spring had not yet come to Hakodate) and tables were laid for many guests. Three or four of the officials made speeches in Japanese, and although I did not understand the words the emotion in their voices was plain to read. After the speeches young women handed bouquets of fresh flowers to the captain, his mate, and the factory manager, each of whom responded with proper words. Then toasts of beer were drunk to shouts of "Banzai! banzai! banzai!" the traditional good-luck greeting.

As I sat and listened to these festivities I could not help but think that the salmon fishing enterprise was becoming more precarious each year. In reality it is at the mercy of the Soviet Union, whose stocks have been severely depleted by the Japanese and who can effectively curb their harvests, as she has already pushed them out of Siberian waters as well as the grand banks around Sakhalin and the Kuriles. Theoretically international waters beyond claimed territorial limits are open to every nation, but Russia and the United States, with Canada as a partner, have forced the Japanese reluctantly to abstain from taking salmon in parts of the North Pacific and limited their catches.

The livelihood of some 10,000 persons is tied up with the Hakodate salmon fleet. If the Russians reduce the Japanese quotas the companies who own the mother ships would not be perceptibly hurt because they belong to interlocking cartels that profit from a variety of industrial and distributive enterprises. But the fishermen would suffer.

It took several hours for the 350 catcher boats to leave the harbor, moving in single file, their banners flying in the cloudless sky, slowly, majestically; after them came the mother ships. When the last vessel dipped below the horizon the sun disappeared, as if it had done its duty, and white clouds suffused the sky. When the fleet returns in late July with its quota of processed fish the canning equipment will be dismantled and the mother ships will resume their humdrum task of carrying cargo around the world . . . until spring returns to Hokkaido and the salmon fishing season comes round again.

Effects of the Treaties

The 1952 tripartite treaty was a landmark in settling international fishery conflicts because it introduced the unique abstention principle. However, the idea does not sit well with the Japanese, as may be expected. In a symposium on North Pacific fisheries published by the University of Washington School of Law, Professor Shigeru Oda of the Faculty of Law of Tohoku University declared that "the 1952 convention [is] one of the most epoch-making treaties in the history of international law, in that it broke with previous conceptions of the exploitation of marine resources, namely, that all nations concerned should compete with each other on an equal basis to acquire as many resources as possible within limitations (applying equally to all) aimed at conserving those resources."

In his book *International Control of Sea Resources* Oda expands this viewpoint: "It appears to the author that it is not appropriate to define conservation measures only as 'self-denying, restrictive utilization.' It is submitted that the words 'self-denying' do not ring true. In effect, it is only the state which prescribes abstention for others that stands to gain . . . The principle of abstention does not stop at the point of protecting resources from destructive exploitation but goes further and results in exclusion of other nations. It is admitted that some resources artificially cultivated by investment of labor and money should be reserved to those who have invested in the resource. However, regular fishing does not belong to this category."

"Is it reasonable," he asks, "to deprive other states of potential interests in fishing only because they have not engaged in an area previously? If we accept this principle, we are introducing a doctrine very similar to acquisitive prescription into the law of the sea."

Oda is equally opposed to the bilateral treaty of 1956 whereby the Russians regulate and limit the amount of fish the Japanese are allowed to take: "The quota system, like the abstention formula, is ostensibly designed to conserve particular stocks of fish. In fact, these principles seem to provide a scheme whereby the coastal state is able to regulate the high seas fishing of Japan, thereby reducing the Japanese take, while maximizing its own fishery production." [14] The last statement is certainly not true of the salmon, which Japan exploits on the high seas at the expense of Russia and the United States.

Oda skirts the thorny question: who owns the salmon produced at considerable expense in a specific land that are but temporary inhabitants of the ocean? The Russians replied to such arguments as Oda's in the words of the scientist I. I. Lagunov:

> At the present time we think it is well known that the sharp reduction in runs of Pacific salmon, especially to the spawning rivers of the Soviet Far East, is due primarily to the excess catch of salmon on the high seas by the Japanese.

The Japanese are unhappy with the curbs imposed by the abstention line, but they make no attempt to withdraw from the 1952 treaty
for it is to their advantage to retain the good will of the United
States, which is one of their best customers for automobiles, radios,
television components, textiles, etc., and whose raw materials such as
timber and oil feed their industrial machine.

In sum, the treaties seem to have been effective in reducing the
Japanese toll on Soviet and Alaskan salmon stocks. Without them the
anadromous fishes might have been largely swept out of the ocean.

Appendix Table 15 shows Japanese salmon catches in domestic and
international waters in the years 1957–1969.

Decline of Russian Stocks

Japanese operations have seriously encroached upon Russia's fabulous
salmon wealth. To understand what has happened we might look at
the recent history of this resource.

The Russian scientist R. S. Semko divides the history of the salmon
fishery in the northwestern Pacific into four periods:

First, the period 1926 to 1933 when Russian resources were fully
utilized and there was sufficient escapement to sustain the runs into
the Russian rivers.

Second, the years 1934 to 1943 when the fishery developed rapidly;
toward the end of this period coastal catches in Russia declined, despite curtailment of gear, because of intensive Japanese ocean fishing.

Third, from 1944 to 1951 when only stationary nets or beach seines
were used to harvest salmon in the U.S.S.R. and their number
amounted to only half of that in previous peak periods. In this era
the Russian stocks increased partly due to elimination of Japan's fishing fleet during the war

Fourth, in 1952 the picture changed as the Japanese began their
worldwide fishing ventures (while destroying their own salmon rivers
by pollution and other means) and concentrated on fishing the
salmon in the North Pacific until partially halted by treaty, while
Russia, the United States, and Canada refrained from taking salmon
far offshore. In this period the Japanese introduced enormous drift
nets of deadly nylon that, says Semko, they spread over an area of
9000 miles. These were not only effective in catching fish, but a large
proportion of those who escaped suffered injuries and many died without spawning. In the Bristol Bay rivers I saw many sockeye that had
returned from the sea with Japanese net marks on their bodies. In ad-

dition to net fishing Japanese long-line (hook and line) ocean fishing also increased after 1952, taking large numbers of salmon emanating from both continents. Many fish that escaped by throwing their hooks eventually died without spawning.

The advent of high seas fishing introduced a new element, for the stocks could no longer be managed on a scientific basis since returns to the rivers now depended to a considerable extent on how many escaped from the nets. This made it difficult for Russia to manage its own rivers.

Semko underlines this point. "For thirty years," he says, "especially during the first half of this period [1926 to 1960], the salmon runs remained at a high level and the fishery captured mainly mature fish . . . The present high seas fishery for immature fish . . . is irrational, because it captures extremely small fish, which creates serious technical problems and destroys a considerable part of the salmon resources." [15]

Semko's conclusions were substantiated by Dr. William F. Royce in testimony before the Fisheries Subcommittee of the U.S. Senate's Commerce Committee in May 1965: "The decline in Asian salmon catches offers a dramatic example of the detrimental effects of high seas fishing on the salmon runs . . . The Soviet Union suffered a decline in its own salmon production of more than 100,000 tons, or the equivalent of 3 million cases of salmon [annually]. In addition, the spawning stocks of all species in practically all Asian streams are reported to have been extremely poor." [16]

The table opposite shows the precipitous drop between 1940 and 1970 in Soviet salmon catches along the Far East coast, while the table on page 457 shows the total picture of Russian landings in the years 1952 to 1967.

We have other evidence of the fate of the Russian resource in the past twenty-five years. At a symposium held by the Ichthyological Commission in Moscow in 1962 Semko reported that Russian catches of pinks, the most abundant species, fell swiftly between 1951 and 1961, while Japanese hauls of these fish increased rapidly. F. A. Dvinin of the Sakhalin division of the Pacific Fisheries and Oceanographic Institute (TINRO) claimed that the Japanese were responsible for the marked decrease not only in the total salmon catch in Kamchatka but also in the stocks of pinks in waters around Sakhalin and the Kuriles. "In the open part of the Pacific Ocean east of the Kurile Islands and Hokkaido," he said, "where in 1958 we were conducting special studies of the biology of Far-Eastern salmon, the Jap-

SOVIET SALMON CATCHES ALONG THE FAR EAST COAST ° 1940–1969 (million of fish)				
	Pinks	*Chum*	*Sockeye*	*Coho*	*Total*
1940	37.3	17.3	1.3		55.9
1941	57.1	16.8	1.7		75.6
1942	58.6	12.4	2.1		73.1
1943	87.5	19.6	2.9		110.0
1944	78.6	17.3	3.5		96.4
1945	56.4	19.2	4.4		80.0
1946	28.4	21.5	4.9		54.8
1947	98.1	21.7	3.8		123.6
1948	38.7	19.5	2.3		60.5
1949	122.2	24.8	3.3		150.3
1950	27.0	19.2	3.4		49.6
1951	114.7	26.1	2.9		143.7
1952	42.9	13.8	3.4		60.1
1953	105.4	10.6	1.9		117.9
1954	34.2	16.4	1.5		52.1
1955	65.4	20.5	1.1		87.0
1956	53.4	24.2	2.1		79.7
1957	78.8	10.0	1.3		91.1
1958	28.4	8.7	0.4		37.5
1959	34.9	11.9	1.5		48.3
1960	14.5	13.5	1.5		29.5
1961	22.4	11.4	2.9		36.7
1962	10.8	9.2	1.4	1.3	22.7
1963	24.6	9.4	1.9	2.2	37.6
1964	10.6	6.4	1.0	0.3	18.6
1965	34.7	8.5	1.0	1.0	45.9
1966	14.0	7.9	1.5	0.9	24.0
1967	33.1	5.1	1.0	1.0	40.3
1968	10.0	4.4	0.9	1.0	16.4
1969	42.8	1.4	0.6	1.0	46.0
1970	11.1	3.1	1.6	1.6	17.6

Source: Pacific Fisheries and Oceanographic Institute (U.S.S.R.), Petropavlovsk.
° Does not include catches in the rivers.

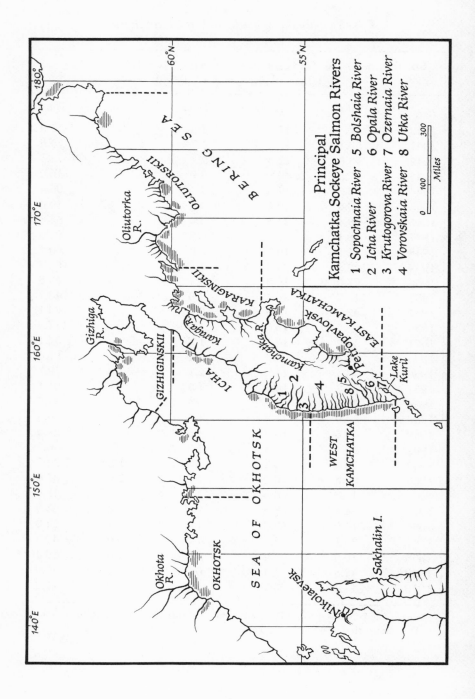

Principal
Kamchatka Sockeye Salmon Rivers

1 Sopochnaia River   5 Bolshaia River
2 Icha River   6 Opala River
3 Krutogorova River 7 Ozernaia River
4 Vorovskaia River   8 Utka River

0   100   300
Miles

anese gangs of drift nets were as much as 9–12 kilometers (5.4–7.2 miles) in length, and the strings of longlines were almost as long . . . In this year here was a particularly large increase in the number of fish captured near home waters which had been injured by longline hooks, also salmon that had ulcerated spots which came from net injuries."

"Fishermen and shore workers in the fishery industry of Sakhalin and the Kurile Islands," he added, "are very uneasy about the future fate of the stocks of Far Eastern salmon."

The biologist Z. I. Petrova studied the stocks in the Bolshoi River in Kamchatka, which used to produce 30,000 tons of salmon annually, mostly pinks and chum. "Until 1954 the runs of pinks fluctuated sharply between odd and even years," she said, "but declined drastically thereafter. In 1954 the catch of pinks amounted to 9,590 tons, but in 1956 the catch was insignificant." In the case of chum "the catch fell from 2360 tons in 1956 to 230 tons in 1960 . . . There are two runs of sockeye, spring and summer. The total catch varied in many years from 65 to 1020 tons. In 1960 it amounted to 95.8 tons, but in 1958, an especially bad year — 25.8 tons. The total yield of all species in 1960 was but 2.5 percent of the 1951 and 1953 levels and the escapement had declined accordingly." [17] Because of the extremely small escapement, large spawning areas in the Bolshoi River were not being utilized and the unused gravels were silted over and covered with vegetation and would soon be of no importance.

The Ozernaya is one of the richest sockeye rivers in Kamchatka, exceeded only in fruitfulness by the Kamchatka River in certain years. It too has been seriously affected by the Japanese fishery. The average sockeye run in this river before high seas fishing began was 5.4 million, of which 70 percent were caught by the Japanese, 10 percent by the Russians, and 20 percent were permitted to escape and produce another generation. In the years 1946–1951, when there was no Japanese fishery, only an exclusive domestic fishery, the escapement averaged 49 percent and the runs began to increase. After the Japanese began to take these fishes on their feeding migrations in the ocean, the escapement fell to 500,000 spawners in 1955, or 7 percent of the total run, and the domestic fishery almost had to cease operations within a few years.[18]

Similar reports of critical drops in abundance were reported by Russian scientists in rivers in Sakhalin, the Okhotsk region, and elsewhere. However, in some cases environmental deterioration was certainly a contributing factor. Thus in his exhaustive report on Kamchatka stocks Semko pinpoints poaching, unfavorable land use, and pollution as factors inimical to anadromous fisheries. "Experience indicates that settlement of people in the valleys of spawning rivers where there are no fish protective enforcement measures brings about rather quickly a decline in the numbers of salmon in those rivers," he said. "In the Kamchatka Peninsula striking examples are the more thickly settled areas of the Kamchatka and Avacha Rivers in which fewer and fewer salmon enter. Here . . . in addition to an intensive fishery, poaching is apparently widespread . . . Large numbers of fish are both openly and secretly trapped throughout the length of the channels where substantial populations are found."

Some of the spawning areas are polluted, indicating that "the laws are not sufficiently enforced." All these factors lead to a curtailment of breeding stock, he concluded. Also, water flow and fish habitat have been impaired by cutting down the forests and by release of waste products from manufacturing plants. Sometimes the spawning rivers and their tributaries are blocked by dams that prevent the fish from reaching their destination.

"In order to maintain the salmon stocks at an adequate level," admonished Semko, "the purpose of fish protection regulations should be to protect the fish against every agency and factor which is likely to adversely affect conditions in the rivers. Furthermore, there must be measures undertaken to increase the productivity of the spawning grounds, particularly by increasing, as has been shown, the return of adult fish from the ocean feeding grounds." [19]

Salmon People Under Soviet Rule

The communist revolution has had profound effects on the seminomadic "salmon people" of the Far East. Siberia's natural resources were almost entirely neglected by the Czars. The remote and inclement territory was used as a dumping ground for political dissenters, thieves, and murderers, who were incarcerated in shabby and cruel prisons or confined to colonies like those described by Tolstoi in his novel *Resurrection* and by Chekhov in *The Island: A Journey to Sakhalin.* The economic and social status of the natives in 1917 was scarcely better than when Steller visited them in 1741.

The Soviet government brought the tribes into the modern world and developed the natural resources of the region. It Sovietized the villages, organized collective farms and fishing cooperatives, introduced modern fishing and farming equipment, built fishing stations and game farms, and uplifted their economic and cultural levels.

Although this revolution was certainly not accomplished without coercion and destruction of the social structure and folk arts and skills, one gathers that the Siberian peoples have been treated with more consideration than was accorded the Eskimos and Indians in Canada and the United States. Instead of being allowed to drift in a confused world of corporate capitalism, propped up by welfare payments, as the Indians and Eskimos are, many debilitated in body and mind, the Siberian tribes have been permitted to share in the wealth of the rivers and the land, and educational and cultural opportunities have been opened to them, although at some sacrifice of their ethnic consciousness.

Typical is the fate of the Ulchi. In the 1920s small fishing cooperatives were established for them and a network of village schools was created. The first communist organization, the Comsomols, also appeared. Institutes of higher education were formed for all northern peoples at Nikolaevsk and Leningrad. These helped to produce an "intelligentsia." The Ulchi language was transformed into a written script, like other Siberian tongues.

The first collectives were organized in 1930–1932 and by 1952 there were eight with a preponderance of Ulchi members and one with mixed Russian-Ulchi persons. Their basic activity is fishing; cattle raising and farming are secondary. "They have large seines, highly productive fish traps of modern construction for catching salmon, cutters and motor boats. Heavy labor is being mechanized. The old fishing implements — floating and fixed nets, and hook and tackle — are also used." It is mostly the Russians who do the fishing, which brings in half the collectives' income, while the Ulchi still hunt as of old.

There are stores in every village where standard foods can be bought, and the women prepare traditional as well as Russian dishes. Old men still make small quantities of eukola every fall as their ancestors did.

In villages like Kolchom, located on a side channel of the Amur River, there are over fifty Russian-type wooden houses (which have replaced the ancient dugout shelters), warm and clean, standing on straight, wide streets, with greenery around them. The streets are lighted by electricity and every house has electric lights and a radio. The village has a primary school, a library with 3000 volumes, a crèche, a health station, and a store. Local "intelligentsia" deliver lectures at the collective farm. Literacy is widespread and many families not only read books at home but according to official Soviet sources subscribe to newspapers and magazines.[20]

In 1948 the Soviet Council of Ministers issued a decree providing free education for the children of northern tribes up to completion of secondary school and, for those qualified, higher education. A medical school was opened in Khabarovsk and hospitals were built to serve the native villages, resulting in a sharp decline in such common diseases as tuberculosis and trachoma and a consequent drop in the death rate.

One could illustrate the beneficial effects of the Soviet rule with many other tribes but let us take note merely of the Evenki, the most numerous and most widely scattered primitives of northern Siberia. Much of the territory they inhabit, the Okhotsk coast, Sakhalin in the north, and the Amur River in the south, is rich in salmon and other freshwater fishes so that originally they depended to a large extent on fishing as well as hunting for sustenance.

Today some of the areas have been greatly transformed by the technological and cultural revolution. Farley Mowat, a Canadian writer who visited Siberia in the late 1960s, describes life in the Magadan district on the Sea of Okhotsk, where the environment is savage. Roads are icy, he says, even in late summer; the sea is "dark, cliff-girt, gale-whipped and fearsome." There are 107 collective and state farms in the district where the natives engage in fishing, fur breeding, trapping, reindeer raising, cattle farming, and mammal hunting in the ocean. "The big cities belong to the whites; the smaller towns are divided between whites and native peoples; and the countryside (apart from mining enterprises) belongs exclusively to the natives."

Mowat visited a typical fishing village operated by the Magadan Fisheries Trust. It had grown in forty years of communist management from a primitive subsistence fishery to a profitable modern enterprise, exploiting mainly herring and some salmon and other fish. The Russian manager claimed that all the small fishing ports in the area "are growing very fast in size and in the quality of life. Specialization and rational use of technology are the answers." Villages and towns have been spruced up. The workers, both native and Caucasian, are trained at the Fishery College at Magadan and are well paid according to their abilities. "The sea," he said, "is a farm, and we must farm it; and the farmers must be well rewarded for their work." [21]

Epilogue

The fate of Asia's Pacific salmon offers a moral if it does not adorn a tale. The moral is that high seas fishing is indiscriminate and wasteful and relentlessly reduces the runs. There is no way to protect the stocks that are being depleted or to accelerate the harvest of those that have overproduced in relation to their spawning areas. In brief, there is no management whatsoever.

Biologists agree that high seas fishing on mixed stocks is not in the interest of good conservation or maximum utilization. This maxim the Japanese ignore. In a visit to fisheries laboratories in Japan, I did not find any work being done on anadromous species with an eye to improving domestic production; all the projects dealt with salmon in the ocean.

It is clear that continuous pressure on Russian (and to some extent Alaskan) stocks through mother-ship fishing has resulted in considerable losses. Only by reducing such pressure can the depleted resources have a chance of revival. Whether this goal will be achieved is a subject that belongs to the realm of geopolitics. It is conceivable, certainly, that the Russians will steadily curtail Japanese quotas and thus make high seas fishing unprofitable for them. Alaskan fishermen would like to have the United States force Japan to accept a westward revision of the abstention line so as to make it impossible to catch Bristol Bay fish — it is estimated that the Japanese are taking an average of 3 million Alaskan sockeye annually.

Our State Department, however, which seems to be subservient to the navy, refuses to consider exerting pressure on Japan to revise the tripartite treaty. It is primarily interested in maintaining harmonious relations with Japan and having the use of air and naval bases there. The salmon fishery is regarded as of little or no importance in naval strategy.

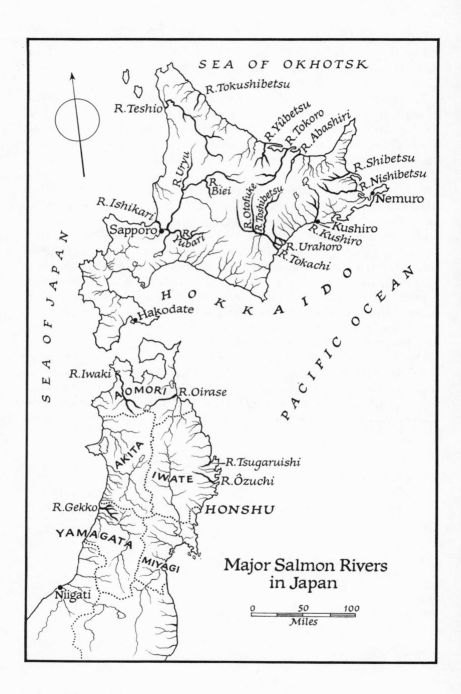

SEA OF OKHOTSK

R.Tokushibetsu

R.Teshio

R.Yûbetsu
R.Tokoro
R.Abashiri

R.Shibetsu
R.Nishibetsu
Nemuro

R.Uryu

R.
Biei

R.Otofuke
R.Toshibetsu

R.Ishikari

Sapporo

R.
Yubari

R.Kushiro
Kushiro

R.Urahoro
R.Tokachi

SEA OF JAPAN

H O K K A I D O

Hakodate

PACIFIC OCEAN

R.Iwaki

AOMORI

R.Oirase

AKITA

R.Tsugaruishi

IWATE

R.Ôzuchi

R.Gekko

HONSHU

YAMAGATA

MIYAGI

Niigati

Major Salmon Rivers
in Japan

0   50   100
Miles

XXVI ∽

Salmon Farming in Japan

JAPAN IS A SLENDER ARCHIPELAGO separated from the Soviet Union and Korea by the Sea of Japan and from China by the East China Sea. Its area is somewhat less than California's, yet it has about 104 million people. The huge population huddles along the narrow coastal strips of the island of Honshu and the less crowded islands of Hokkaido, Shikoku and Kyushu.

As you fly over Honshu the landscape unfolds in an unending pattern of rice paddies rising in tiers, perched in the cups of the hills, or cut out of a patch of woodland. Between the paddies there may be tea or tobacco plantations, bean fields, orange groves, or pear or peach orchards. Only one acre out of seven in Japan is cultivable, but this acre must provide eight times as much food as, for example, it does in France.

Over half the total population lives in a mere 1.25 percent of the country's total area. Cities in Honshu are close together, usually without green belts or buffer zones, forming an endless megalopolis.

The island of Hokkaido, which is a continuation of the Kuriles, has only 5 million persons. Sixty-five percent of Hokkaido is classified as forest (now much denuded) and 15 percent is wilderness graced by volcanic mountains, fumeroles, hot springs, and spectacular scenery incorporated in several national parks. Most of the three-hundred-odd salmon rivers of Japan are in Hokkaido, and the rest are in northern Honshu.

The 220-mile Shinano is the longest river in Honshu, rising at the foot of Mount Kobushi and emptying into the Sea of Japan at Niigata. Most Hokkaido rivers are less than thirty miles long; a dozen or so are about sixty miles, and six are longer. The Ishikari, the longest river in Japan, follows a winding course of 275 miles in western Hokkaido, dropping into Otaru Bay; the Teshio, north of Ishikari, flows for 140 miles into the Gulf of Tatary in the Sea of Japan; the 90-mile Kushiro and the 120-mile Tokachi empty into the Pacific Ocean. All of these streams once produced considerable numbers of salmon but are now generally used for planting artificially bred fish or have been deserted by anadromous species.

The most numerous species of salmon in Japan are chum, pinks, and masu; sockeye, chinook, and coho are not abundant. Chum enter the rivers from September through November and are found as far south as Ibaraki Prefecture in Honshu. Pinks, which arrive from March through May, are most plentiful in Hokkaido, while masu are found mainly in Honshu.

The Ainu

Although some of the islands were occupied in Neolithic times there is little evidence of man's existence in Japan before the Christian era. The Japanese, a Mongolian people, themselves probably emigrated from northeastern and southern Asia and gradually merged into a homogeneous nation. Their cultural influences came from Korea and China. Preceding the Japanese were a taller, more hirsute, and more handsome Mongolian people who have affinities with a similar ethnic group in eastern Siberia — the Ainu. They were originally fishermen dwelling in small villages along the rivers of Honshu and Hokkaido. Bitter wars and savage cruelty of the Japanese greatly reduced their numbers. These are the "salmon people" of Japan.

Terry's Guide Book to the Japanese Empire (1914) describes the Ainu as "expert fishermen . . . Their river canoes are usually dug out of logs . . . [which] may often be seen ascending the rivers, up which the superb salmon goes to spawn in the fresh water near their source. The men spear them with crude, barbed instruments, or catch them in hand-nets. One man usually stands at the stern to propel the boat, while another stands at the bow, harpoon in hand. Torches are used to attract the fish at night." Tourists in those days might come upon the unusual spectacle of a tall, muscular Ainu standing naked in his canoe, "with flowing beard and matted hair," spearing a salmon "under the glare of the sputtering pine torch." Today the Ainu are mostly farmers, but some of them engage in both fishing and farming and are more or less "Japanized" as the newest guidebook published by the Japan Travel Bureau says.

The Ainu used the salmon and other fish to balance their diet of mollusks, seaweed, and occasionally meat, usually bear meat. In fact, they had a bear cult brought from their homeland. Their chants were eulogies of the bear, and in some Ainu villages there are still poles with the fleshless skull of a bear on top and always a wooden cage containing a full-grown bear. Bear cubs roam their filthy huts and are sometimes suckled by the women. Since salmon are avidly eaten by bear, salmon and bear are inextricably associated by the Ainu. In the numerous souvenir shops of Hokkaido the carved wooden figure of a bear with a salmon in its mouth is a ubiquitous item. One stands on my desk as I write.

The Early Fishery

Salmon were regarded as valuable resources by the daimyos in the feudal period of Japanese history, which ended with the Meiji restoration in 1868. They encouraged their tenants to protect the stream beds and spawning stocks, and severe penalties, including capital punishment, were inflicted on those who fished without permission. Salmon were at first taken inside the rivers but with the development of primitive trap nets they were also harvested along the coast.

There are records of commercial salmon fishing in Hokkaido from about 1550 and of coastal fishing in Sakhalin going back to 1752 and in the southern Kurile Islands to 1789. Some of the feudal lords even experimented with artificial propagation of salmon.

Large-scale exploitation of the fishery began with the emergence of Japan as a modern state in the late nineteenth century. In the waters around northern Honshu and Hokkaido the fishes ran by the millions and the shores were dotted with fishing stations. In the autumn they streamed in from the sea and provided a livelihood and food for thousands of people. They were caught near the mouths of the rivers, as on the Ishikari near the city of Sapporo, with huge seines that required scores of men to handle them. Here, according to *Terry's Guide*, 20,000 or more salmon weighing at least ten pounds each were taken in a single day around World War I. Local industries included salting, smoking, canning, and shipping salmon.

There were munificent stocks of salmon on the volcanic and misty Kuriles, then owned by Japan, where the Ainu took them near their spawning grounds in the upper reaches of the rivers. Here also in those days came sportsmen from Japan to fish for salmon. Commercial fishing in the Kuriles was conducted, it seems, on a profligate basis, as a letter of November 30, 1921, from F. S. Booth in

Tokyo to Professor John N. Cobb of the College of Fisheries of the
University of Washington reveals:

> Amongst the narrow chain of scarcely habitable volcanic is-
> lands stretching from Yezo to Kamchatka is one Etorofu.
> Near its southeastern extremity is a long stream famous for
> innumerable fish of a variety unknown elsewhere in Far
> Eastern Waters . . . Here salmon by the myriad, some say
> at least ten million each year, were wont to play about in
> the sea for days near the mouth of the tiny river before the
> procession ahead could pass on upstream and give them
> their turn. So great was the press that steamers passing
> through often were thought to have run aground owing to
> their solid impact. The sea itself all about was white . . .
> with the lashings of these waiting legions.
>
> Equally with the other streams this, once discovered, was
> fished for all that could be gathered and the same fate over-
> took its annually recurring wealth. The topography lent it-
> self to the ravages of human greed. A short distance from
> the river (150 feet) is a basin where fish rest before climbing
> a cataract and on up to the rapids to the lake 2½ miles in-
> land. A light railway was laid along the margin of this basin
> and the fish shoveled out into trucks as fast as these could be
> filled and moved away. Nature gave up the unequal contest
> and the race shrank rapidly towards extinction.
>
> The present owner of this concession . . . has undertaken
> seriously to reestablish the run on his stream by the aid of
> a hatchery.
>
> The lake where the hatchery is located has in times past
> propagated enough sockeye to furnish annual runs of 8 to 10
> million and remains in the same state of nature, without pol-
> lution of the waters.[1]

Deterioration of the Rivers

"Before the Japanese began to lay waste their country in the name
of Westernization," says Bernard Rudofsky in his fascinating book
The Kimono Mind, "it must indeed have been paradise. Visitors grew
rhapsodic over its charms. 'How inviting are the shores with their
cheerful dwellings!' exclaimed Siebold (Japan's Humboldt) when he
first entered Nagasaki Bay . . . The picture one gets from these early

reports resembles nothing so much as archaic Greece . . . Japan was blessed with groves of evergreen cedar, oak and laurel, windswept islands, rocky beaches, and snow-capped mountains." [2]

The prints of Horonobu, Hokusai, Hiroshige, and others depict a kind of lotus-land of exquisite villages and manorial estates, undulating landscapes and dreamlike mountains. Even if these pictures are idealized they delineate an infinitely beautiful country that enraptured western visitors. The official narrative of Commodore Matthew Perry's expedition notes: "All the officers and men were in rapture with the beauty of the country; nothing could be more picturesque than the landscapes wherever the eye was directed . . . a scene of beauty, abundance and happiness, which everyone delighted to contemplate." [3]

Industrialization and population growth spelled the doom of scenic beauty and many rivers. Population jumped from 35 million in 1875 to 53.5 million in 1915; in the next fifty-five years it doubled. There are over a hundred cities with 100,000 or more people and six with over a million, topped by Tokyo with 14 million. Roads are jammed with automotive traffic, cities swarm with human beings, the air is suffused with noxious gases.

During Japan's hectic economic expansion rivers were harnessed for power, tapped for domestic and industrial water supplies, used as sewers, and diverted for irrigation. Flying over Honshu, where the bulk of the Japanese people live, one sees slivers of streams meandering through densely packed cities and towns, estuaries filled with ships and wharves and industrial buildings, rivers flowing yellow with silt and sewage, and a landscape resembling the miasma of the eastern seaboard of the United States, not that of the "Fifty-Seven Stations of the Tekaido Road."

In 1951 Dr. Richard Van Cleve, Dean of the College of Fisheries of the University of Washington, was asked by the Occupation authorities to survey Japan's salmon industry and salmon rivers. He saw nothing but neglect of the fisheries and apathy of local and national governments toward their preservation. "The fisheries have been badly neglected in spite of their relatively high productivity," he said. "In all areas visited where the interests of the fish and power conflict, the record of at least one of the largest power companies is replete with instances of contracts made with fishermen and laws passed by prefectures, providing for proper operation of fishways and maintenance of flows below dams, only to have both contracts and laws disregarded in the interests of more electric power . . . As the company wielded sufficient influence to overwhelm any opposition, no effective maintenance of fish in many areas has been possible except by artificial introduction." [4]

He found that where fishways existed they were bereft of water so that salmon migrating upstream could not reach their spawning grounds, while downstream travelers were killed by unscreened penstocks and diversion canals. Where fishes were able to negotiate the dams, fluctuations in reservoir levels made their migration difficult.

On some Hokkaido rivers Van Cleve discovered that "fisheries officials have taken no interest in providing fish ladders at dams or in screening irrigation canals or power house intakes, and only a passive interest . . . in pollution." [5] They seemed to have adopted the fatalistic attitude that natural spawning was a lost cause and argued that most of the fishes if allowed to migrate up the rivers would be pilfered by the local people. Hence they relied on artificial propagation, reserving certain streams called "salmon culture rivers" solely for the hatchery system. Yet, said Van Cleve, enough salmon escaped over one ladderless dam on the Tokachi River to make it worthwhile to maintain ten weirs for taking fish for the hatcheries. Here 96,000 fish were caught in 1950, of which 20,000 were used for spawning and the rest sold on the market to defray the cost of maintaining the hatchery.

A list of dams higher than fifteen meters (about fifty feet) compiled in 1951 by the Hokkaido prefectural government showed that nineteen out of sixty-eight had fish ladders, but only one of the nineteen was included in Van Cleve's itinerary, and it was not in operation.

Pollution of rivers was widespread in 1951, and "no apparent effort was made by the government toward either preventing or correcting this misuse of the streams." Much damage, for example, was done to the Ishikari River by starch factories, a sugar beet refinery, and an alcohol plant, while the entire upper Sorachi River was made inaccessible to migratory fish by coal mine pollution and a series of unladdered dams. Yet both streams had stretches of excellent gravel that could provide ideal spawning grounds if the salmon were permitted to reach them.[6] To support the hatchery system and safeguard the runs sport and commercial fishing was forbidden in the rivers — and this law is still in force.

I visited Hokkaido in the spring of 1971. Pollution seemed to have increased on a geometric scale in the twenty years since Van Cleve's visit. The Kushiro River may be taken as an example of the new pollution. Pulp mills, fertilizer plants, and other operations dump their wastes into the lower stretches; anadromous fish can no longer live there. The Ishikari is also visibly polluted in and around Sapporo, now a swinging city of 1 million. Natural runs have been abandoned on this stream and a stock of 3000 spawners is maintained by artificial means, a small fraction of the river's original production.

In addition to pollution and blockading of rivers, poaching is still a menace, for every salmon caught may be worth as much as a man can earn in several days of manual labor. Organized gangs operate at night with deadly effectiveness, using radio communications. While several hundred offenders are caught and convicted each year, the maximum punishment of about $60 or six-months imprisonment is rarely imposed.

In a 1966 publication the Japan Fisheries Resource Conservation Association reported that "industrial pollution, transportation of lumber and excavation of river beds for gravel" had ruined many waterways. "Some of the irrigation dams are so large that they prevent, or at least affect migration of the fish. In addition they certainly destroy descending fry by raising water levels and thus misleading them." In Hokkaido there were 178 obstructive developments on seventy-three major rivers, and over a hundred of these presented hazards in various degrees to upstream and seaward migration of fish. There were 2200 starch factories, many power dams, much mining of coal and metals, and other inimical operations.[7]

Thus in a nation dazzled by economic growth, where the Gross National Product is worshiped with a kind of mystical fervor, and where pollution of domestic water supplies with mercury compounds that killed or crippled many people was crassly permitted to continue for years, one cannot expect much consideration for the fishes. In the conflict of fish versus corporate profits the fish have no chance whatsoever.

Aquaculture

Since many of the rivers were ruined for natural spawning the Japanese turned with increasing enthusiasm to artificial production, which they regard as a form of fish farming, an ancient art in the Far East, used as a means of augmenting the nation's food supply.

With little acreage available for meat production, the Japanese rely heavily on fish for the protein of their diet. Of the nation's animal protein intake of twenty-eight grams per capita per day, 60 percent is provided by fish and fish products, including fish sausage, an item one never sees in European or American markets. The Japanese probably catch and eat (often raw) a greater variety of fish and shellfish than any people on earth. On a visit to the wholesale fish market in Tokyo one may see tons of frozen tuna weighing up to 500 and 600 pounds each, from South Atlantic waters, tiny white shrimp, squid, amberjack, porgy, cuttlefish, red octopus, Antarctic whale meat, dried anchovies, tanks with live eels, rainbow trout, ayu (sweet fish), abalone, marlin, rockfish, candlefish from Alaska, scorpion, shark's fins, skates, every species of Pacific salmon, and various shellfishes including oysters, clams, and turtles for Chinese restaurants. The fish come off the boats on the adjoining docks. The market accommodates 1600 brokers, 25,000 buyers, and employs 11,000 people. It handles up to 5000 tons daily, some of which is produced by aquaculture, now successfully pursued in producing salmon, yellowtail, oysters, prawns, and octopus among other species.

Salmon culture goes back a century in Japan. The first hatchery, modeled on the Craig Brook plant at Orland, Maine, was built in 1889, at the headwaters of the Ishikari River, which flows through the Shikotsu-Toya National Park, famous for its volcanoes, caldera lakes with icy-blue waters, and hot springs. The facility was called a central station because it was designed to supply "eyed eggs" for planting in other streams and also served as a technical center to disseminate knowledge and skills of artificial propagation. It has been recently rebuilt and expanded and now has a capacity to incubate 13 million eggs.

Japanese salmon are propagated on a scale eclipsing that of the United States or any other nation. There are some fifty field stations (hatcheries) and seventy-eight egg-collecting stations in Hokkaido alone operated by the Hokkaido Salmon Hatchery system, with a rearing capacity in 1970 of 570 million eggs, and eighty-two hatcheries in northern Honshu with a capacity of 250 million eggs. In 1970 about 600 million fry were sent down to sea, of which 85 percent were chum salmon, 10 percent pinks, and 5 percent masu. Sockeye and chinook are bred only experimentally.

Salmon culture is regarded as a system of sowing a crop and reaping a harvest. When the fish return to the "salmon culture rivers" they are caught near the mouth by fish wheels, bamboo traps, drift nets, or gill nets and kept in holding ponds until they are ready for stripping. Catching the pinks and masu is particularly difficult, for they enter the rivers several months before spawning time and proceed gradually upstream to the uppermost headwaters. Thus "the catching point must be far enough downstream to foil poachers and close enough to headwaters so that the fish will not be caught too long before spawning time. These requirements exist in only a few rivers, and the number of these fish that can be handled are therefore small." [8]

All surplus males and many "green" (unripe) females are killed and sold on the market. Spawned-out carcasses and eggs from unripe fish are also sold and used for food, thus contributing funds to the maintenance of the fish farms.

The eggs are incubated in field stations and when the fry have absorbed their yolk sacs they are moved to outdoor ponds and fed crumbled pellets. It takes the chum about three months to reach seagoing size, about two and a half inches, when they are released into suitable rivers, close to the ocean if possible. The Japanese claim that hatchery operations are more efficient than natural spawning. There is some natural spawning in the salmon culture rivers, but it is more or less accidental. Salmon fishing is lawful only along the shore or in the adjacent waters.

Sport fishermen are denied the pleasure of taking these game fishes and must be content, as the official Japanese tourist guide says, with rainbow or brook trout planted in streams and lakes, or with ayu, a tasty fish that can be caught in the middle reaches of the rivers throughout Japan. Ayu also are fished by means of well-trained cormorants, thus providing a popular spectacle for foreign visitors.

The Kushiro hatchery that I visited is typical of the newer salmon breeding stations. It is located at the headwaters of the Kushiro River close to Akan National Park. It has a 40-million egg capacity, and about 45,000 spawners are needed to supply them.

Here egg taking occurs from September to December and reaches a peak in early November when winter has already set in. The eggs hatch out mostly in February, and the juvenile chum salmon are sent to sea in April or May. There they spend three or four winters (a small proportion extend their stay to five winters) and return weighing on the average 3 kilograms (6.6 pounds). They are taken in the commercial fishery with set nets along the shore; those which escape are used for artificial breeding.

Out of each year's run of salmon into Hokkaido rivers only 3 percent manage to spawn naturally, 57 percent are taken by the hatcheries, and 40 percent are caught in the commercial fishery. The return of chum salmon to Hokkaido rivers from the brood years 1952 to 1963 averaged 1.2 percent or 3,070,000 fish. This means that for every 100 million fry planted in the streams 1.2 million spawners may be expected to return. On this basis the Japanese system of salmon farming is extremely successful from an economic standpoint.

Like other forms of aquaculture, salmon breeding is constantly expanding. The director of the Hokkaido hatchery system told me that he ultimately envisions the production of about 1 billion fry annually. This could make possible the return of about 10 million fish if past averages hold up. The total commercial catch of domestic salmon in Japan is between 4 and 6 million fish a year, providing a livelihood for a few thousand persons.

The eastern and northeastern coasts of Hokkaido are dotted with fishing villages where small boats ride at anchor on the beaches, fish are drying on racks, and wizened fishermen may be seen repairing their nets. As you drive along the coastal road facing the Sea of Okhotsk you pass slender streams with signs that say in Japanese and English, "Salmon Culture Rivers." They belong to the government and trespass is forbidden.

This is a harsh land in winter. The sea is frozen for months at a time and one may walk across the ice to Etorofu, the southernmost of the Kuriles, now Soviet territory. The Japanese are unhappy about the loss of these islands, and on some Hokkaido roads you see signs proclaiming in Japanese "Return the Kuriles," a demand the Russians ignore.

What has become of the 300 or more Japanese rivers that used to teem with salmon? In Hokkaido these fish still spawn in 160 streams and adults are taken for the hatcheries in some fifty-two to sixty-four rivers, of which the most productive are the Tokachi and Nishibetsu, each accommodating 100,000 to 200,000 spawning fish, and the Kushiro, Yubetsu, and Ishikari Rivers, 20,000 to 30,000 fish. Total escapement into Hokkaido rivers is estimated at 500,000 to 900,000 fish annually, of which 300,000 to 500,000 are taken for artificial propagation. In Honshu there are about sixty-five rivers to which salmon return every season. Of these sixty are used to supply eighty-two hatcheries with 150,000 to 200,000 adults.[9] Thus the "fish farms" contribute a substantial portion of the total caught by fishermen along the coast of Japan that goes almost entirely to the domestic market. It is greatly eclipsed by Japanese harvests of Russian and Alaskan fish in the ocean, which for the most part are canned and sold abroad.

Van Cleve pointed out that in contrast to the United States, where catches of salmon are closely regulated, "there is no record that the Japanese have regulated any fishery for the purposes of maintaining yield. Restrictions of their fisheries have been primarily for economic reasons, and controls on fishing intensity seem to have as their primary purpose an adjustment of investment in gear and ships to the expected catch . . . The overfishing of one species will result in its replacement by another species which will maintain the total yield at the same or even higher level." This philosophy animates their global fishing operations.

Currently, the Japanese are putting their faith in an ever-expanding hatchery program to support their domestic salmon industry, which, however, is only a fragment of what it was before the rivers were made available to the polluters and dam builders and the wild stocks were driven out. In the United States salmon hatcheries are used to produce fish to restock rivers depleted of wild stocks.

In short, in Japan the salmon are regarded as a commodity to be produced on a factory basis, supplying the demands of the market. One cannot see their sleek, silvery forms ascend the rivers, battle the currents, and breast the rapids. They are not the dazzling specimens who populate the rivers of Alaska or the Pacific Northwest, nor are they pursued by anglers, for sport fishing is forbidden.

It is worth noting that Van Cleve in his 1951 report pointed out that the capacity of the Hokkaido rivers is being limited to the capacity of the hatcheries, not to the potential of the streams. The Tokachi River alone, he said, if properly developed could handle at least as many salmon as the Hokkaido government planned to introduce in its entire hatchery system by 1954. When the many rivers on the island are considered, said Van Cleve, "the conclusion must be reached that the elimination of natural reproduction and the placing of the entire future of the salmon stocks in the hatcheries alone are reducing the productive capacity of the prefecture to a small fraction of its potential capacity if natural spawning was permitted and protected." This is still true.

The economic basis of hatchery operations seemed strange to Van Cleve, for the Hokkaido Hatchery System was attempting to support itself by competing with fishermen for the fish runs. This is "an unjustifiable use of that resource, . . ." he said. "The fish should be used for the benefit of the people as a whole, not for the support of a government organization that was originally created to protect and conserve that resource." Furthermore, by assuming a monopoly of stream fishing, the prefectural government "seems actually to encourage disrespect for and violation of conservation laws in the streams," and at the same time is "condoning the misuse of the streams by permitting the construction of ladderless dams and by failing to eliminate pollution."

In the two decades since Van Cleve wrote his report, which apparently fell on deaf ears, destruction of the Japanese rivers has proceeded apace with increased industrialization and rapid growth of population, and thus greater reliance is being placed on artificial propagation not only of salmon but many other food fishes.

Part Five

Salmon
for Sport
and Food

Sport Fishing for Salmon and Steelhead Trout

The Mystique of Sport Fishing

THE EARLIEST BOOK on sport fishing in English is *The Treatise of Fishing with an Angle,* published by William Caxton in London in 1496, a book that had been circulating in manuscript for perhaps a century. It is ascribed to Dame Juliana Berners, about whom we know nothing except that she was of aristocratic lineage. In this treatise the techniques of fishing for species commonly found in English rivers are virtually the same as those used today.

The sport was pursued in medieval times by the merchants and other burghers, and perhaps by such landowners as Chaucer's Franklin, though this pastime is not mentioned in *The Canterbury Tales*. A woodcut in Caxton's edition of *The Treatise* shows a solitary angler on the banks of a stream, playing a fish with his long rod held high in his left hand, and a tub filled with his catch on the ground. Fishing was not then a sport of the nobility or royalty, to whom hunting was the only true and noble outdoor pastime down to the time of the French Revolution. In some cases it was about the only outdoor activity of the royal ménage. Louis XVI counted that day lost when he did not have a successful hunt, as on July 14, 1789, when the Bastille fell. That night he noted in his diary, "Nothing happened today."

It was not till the nineteenth century that the democratized monarchs of Europe seemed to take up the bourgeois art of salmon fishing. Edward VII and his son George were keen fishers. This tradition continues. The Queen Mother, now over seventy, casts a line from time to time, and Elizabeth is known to fish for salmon, although her favorite sport is horse racing.

To Dame Juliana "salmon is a noble fish but he is cumbersome to catch. For generally he is only in deep places of great rivers, and for the most part keeps to the middle of the water, so that a man cannot come at him." She tells us that salmon is in season from March to Michaelmas (the end of September) and may be caught with a worm "or with an artificial fly at such times as he leaps, in like manner and way as you catch a trout or a grayling.' [1] The *Treatise* not only contains the essential advice on hooking coarse fish as well as salmon and trout but much else an angler should know. It cautions him "not to fish in any poor man's private water (such as his pond, or tank, or other things necessary for keeping fish in) without his permission and good will" and "not to break any man's fish traps lying in the weirs" nor "take fish caught in them for they are private property."

"I charge you," she says, "that you break no man's hedges in going about your sport, nor open any man's gates without shutting them again. Also, you must not use this . . . artful sport for covetousness, merely for the increasing or saving of your money, but mainly for your enjoyment and to procure the health of your body, and, more especially, of your soul." She urges the angler not to take too many fish at one time, for this "could easily be the occasion of destroying your own sport and other men's also." In short, "when you have a sufficient mess you should covet no more at that time." [2]

Several angling treatises were produced in the reign of Elizabeth I and James I, but they did not advance the art beyond Dame Juliana's methods. The description of a salmon rod and recipe for dressing a fly is first found in Thomas Barker's *Art of Angling* (1657). He discusses fishing for salmon with worms and trolling in the river, presumably the Thames, using gudgeon as bait.

In 1653 Izaak Walton, a retired London merchant with a passion for fishing, published his *Compleat Angler, or the Contemplative Man's Recreation,* a book that went through five editions before his death in 1683, each getting fatter and more prolix. It was not an original work so far as technical matters are concerned, but it elucidated what might be called the mystique of fishing so well that it soon became a classic. Incidentally, Walton knew very little about salmon and probably did not fish for them.

The dialogue format of *The Compleat Angler,* which goes back to the writings of Aelfric, a medieval monk, was a common textbook device. Walton's *dramatis personae* include Piscator (a fisherman), Venator (a hunter), and Auceps (a fowler). Other people come into the picture as the three men set out on a five-day fishing expedition in rural England. Piscator endeavors to instruct his companions in the art of catching trout, bream, chub, grayling, pike, carp, and other fishes, larding his instruction with many philosophical digressions.

Fishing is not only recreation, says Walton, it is an art of the highest sort. "O, sir," says Piscator, "doubt not that angling is an art. Is it not an art to deceive a trout with an artificial fly? a trout that is more sharp-sighted than any hawk you have named. It is an art worth learning, and not to be despised."

"He that hopes to be a good angler, must not only bring an inquiring, searching, observing wit, but he must bring a large measure of hope, and patience, and love and propensity to the art itself." In short, to the devotee "angling will prove to be so pleasant, that it will prove to be like virtue, a reward to itself." [3]

Angling is the best recreation for the busy and harassed man, says Walton, citing his friend Sir Henry Wotton, Provost of Eton and a distinguished diplomat, who said that it "was, after tedious study, a rest to his mind, a cheerer of his spirits, a diverter of sadness, a calmer of unique thoughts, a moderator of passions, a procurer of contentedness: and that it begat habits of peace and patience in those that professed and practised it."

To Walton the joys of angling are not so much in the number of fish caught but in the opportunity to escape from the city (or from one's home) and lead for a time a pastoral existence. "Look," says Piscator to his companions, "under that broad beech tree I sat down when I was last this way a-fishing. And the birds in the adjoining grove seemed to have a friendly contention with an echo, whose dead voice seemed to live in a hollow tree." On another fishing expedition, he recalls, "I sat viewing the silver streams glide silently towards their center, the tempestuous sea; yet sometimes opposed by rugged roots and pebble-stones, which broke their waves and turned them into foam. And sometimes I beguiled me by viewing the harmless lambs; some leaping securely in the cool shade, whilst others sported themselves in the cheerful sun . . . As I thus sat, these and other sights had as fully possessed my soul with content, that I thought, as the poet hath happily expressed it,

> I was for that time lifted above earth
> And possess'd joys not promised in my birth."

Piscator and his friends do not tally the number of fish they catch. The essence of a successful fishing jaunt is to have good fellowship, good food and drink, and the opportunity to shake off the cares of the world. Walton lived thirty years after publishing *The Compleat Angler*, spending a large part of the time fishing such idyllic streams as the Dove in Derbyshire. He died at the age of ninety.

Among the delights of *The Compleat Angler* are the songs, and I

cannot resist quoting one ascribed to Joseph Chalkhill, otherwise unknown, which sums up the eternal joys of fishing:

> O the gallant fisher's life,
>   It is the best of any!
> 'Tis full of pleasure, void of strife,
>   And 'tis beloved by many:
> Other joys
> Are but toys;
>   Only this
>   Lawful is;
>   For our skill
>   Breeds no ill,
> But content and pleasure.
>   . . .
> When we please to walk abroad
>   For our recreation,
> In the fields is our abode,
>   Full of delectation;
>   Where in a brook,
>   With a hook,
>   Or a lake,
>   Fish we take;
>   There we sit,
>   For a bit,
> Till we fish entangle.
>   . . .
> Or we sometimes pass an hour
>   Under a green willow,
> That defends us from a shower —
>   Making earth our pillow;
>   Where we may
>   Think and pray,
>   Before death
>   Stops our breath;
>   Other joys
>   Are but toys,
>   And to be lamented.

Walton was an amiable and gregarious man, much addicted to ecclesiastical friends. He is buried in Winchester Cathedral, and whenever I visit that overpowering edifice I pause at his grave and then
walk over to the pavement where Jane Austen is buried. It is fitting
that these two modest writers, masters of English prose, who have

given so much pleasure to mankind, should be entombed in the same place.

The Victorian scholar and poet Andrew Lang said that "Walton's influence has made almost every poet a bit of a fisherman. And beyond doubt, it has made of every fisherman a bit of a poet." No more fitting tribute can be paid to the London hardware merchant who wrote one of the great classics on the mystique of sport fishing, a book that has never been out of print in the 320 years since its publication.

Angling for Atlantic Salmon

Angling for Atlantic salmon, universally acknowledged to be the prince of game fishes, "is probably the most exclusive sport in the world" says Arnold Gingrich. "One must have leisure time to visit the famous streams because there's no guarantee of success on any particular day or week. In fact, if you can average one salmon per day in a ten-day period the fishing would be rated quite good. If you average two or three salmon per day in the same time — it's exceptional." [4] In short, there is no way to anticipate the quality of angling that will be experienced.

Sport fishing for *Salmo salar* is now concentrated in Norway, Iceland, Scotland, England and Wales, the eastern provinces of Canada (Quebec, New Brunswick, Nova Scotia, and Newfoundland-Labrador), Spain, Finland, and two or three small Maine rivers.

Atlantic salmon are usually fished with the wet fly, although spinning or some form of bait casting is also practiced. Occasionally the dry fly is used. Although salmon do not feed in freshwater, they strike at artificial bait, in anger, or as reflex action.

The most prestigious angler is not only the one who catches trophy-size fish but dresses his own flies. At a game fair I attended at Stanford Park near Rugby in England, the best attended booths were those of the fly tiers.

In rivers where the pools are very wide, as in northern Norway, a boat is required, while on smaller streams bank fishing or wading is possible.

Scandinavia

No matter where it occurs, salmon fishing in Europe is an expensive pastime, for the rivers are usually privately owned and to gain access one must hire a beat, usually through a hotel, inn, travel agency,

or from the owner. There are, however, places where day or weekly
permits are available.

Norway, famous for gigantic fish, is considered one of the most
prestigious countries to pursue the salmon, although its glory has
somewhat faded in recent years. Its rivers "represent an Olympian
height," says Al McClane's *International Fishing Guide*. Each season fifty- to sixty-pounders are caught on rivers originally fished by
titled Englishmen and other foreign aristocrats. The cost of fishing
in 1970 ranged from $550 per week per person on an average stream
to over $3000. On the Alta beats vary in size from a small pool to
a mile or more of a river. Fishing is confined to the summer months
in northern Norway, where the most productive waters are located.
Evenings on the Driva, says the booklet *Fishing in Norway*, "are
filled with the music of countless waterfalls, spilling down the towering escarpments of the Sunndalen valley to mingle with the river.
Salmon lie in the emerald holding-pools while the fishermen ready
their tackle outside the charming fishing huts at Hev, waiting in a
grove of silver birches for good fishing light, when the sun glides
behind the mountains."

Fantastic records have been set on these northern rivers with their
long twilight and nightless nights. The boatmen warm their hands
over steaming coffee and "later row softly while their fishermen
search the long shallows with their bright-feathered flies."

According to the authoritative magazine *The Field*, the best salmon rivers in northern Norway are the Alta, Malangsfoss, Lakselv,
Reppardfjord, and Stabburselv; the Stjordal, Driva, and Surna in central Norway; the Oerstal, Laerdal, Arøy, and Aurland in central Norway; and the Sand and Suldalslagen in south Norway. The season is
from late May to September 5 and fishing is best in June and July.

Outside of Norway salmon angling is hard to find in Scandinavia.
The Teno, which forms part of the border with Norway, is probably
the best river in Finland. A correspondent writes: "It has recently
been stated that out of every hundred anglers on the Teno, only one
gets a salmon. This may well be true statistically, but hardly gives a
true picture. Most of these hundred anglers are tourists passing by,
who fish from the bank on a day-ticket. Fishing here needs a boat, a
guide, and perseverance . . . Most of the well-known beats are a little
upstream of Levjok." The Teno, he adds, has a few tributaries "worthy of mention, and being easier to fish are often more productive.
Three of them are the Petsikko, the Nuorgam and the Pulmanki." [5]
Another river that offers opportunities for sport in northeast Lapland

is the Näätämö. The largest rod-caught salmon on this river in 1971 weighed forty-nine pounds, but ten pounds is the average.

There is fly-fishing for salmon in Sweden on the Morrum on the south coast and the Atram on the west coast.

Iceland is now in a class with the best countries for Atlantic salmon angling. As in Europe generally, fishing rights go with the land. The fishable sections of the rivers are usually in the agricultural areas and the farmers themselves own the water. As in Norway, the British introduced sport fishing in Iceland. Major General R. N. Stewart, who has fished many Icelandic rivers for over a half century, says: "When I first visited the country in 1912 no Icelander that I heard of fished for sport, except a few boys. This was due to the fact that few of them had leisure, partly to the consideration that fish were food and the less time spent in securing food, the more time there was for attending to more urgent problems." [6] In time the farmers learned they could derive considerable revenue from the foreigners who came to fish their streams. After World War II salmon was declared a "freshwater fish" and netting was restricted to the glacial rivers.

Nowadays fishing associations, whose members own the fishing rights, control the rivers and rent out the fishing to clubs and individuals. The number of rods allowed on each river is determined by the Directorate of Freshwater Fisheries and is kept within reasonable limits so as to ensure good sport. Fishing is permitted twelve hours per day between 7 A.M. and 10 P.M., with a midday break of two or three hours. The angler is usually allowed to retain his catch, and there are no bag limits.

Iceland has many salmon rivers, and some of them are being stocked with hatchery fish. Those of glacial origin become swollen during warm weather. Others are nonglacial and are usually smaller. The best rivers are in the southwestern part of the country, where two thirds of the estimated 30,000 annual rod catch is made.

The most productive river is the Ellidaa, which flows in the outskirts of the capital Reykjavik. In the Arnessysla district there are the Ölfuss-Hvita River complex, while in the Borgarfjordur valley there is another Hvita River system, with Grimsa, Thvera, and Nordura as the most important tributaries. Toward the north of the capital there is Laxa i Kjos, while in the northwest there are the Midfjordara, Vididalsa, Vatnsdalsa, Laxa, and Blanda. The best and largest salmon river in the northeast is the Laxa near the town of Husavik.

Jim C. Chapralis, well-known American angler, fished the Laxa i Kjos in the summer of 1972 and writes: "During my three days' fishing two of us took 37 salmon. We probably hooked over a hundred. In talking to other anglers who had fished other rivers in Iceland they did very well also. In one pool scarcely larger than a football field there must have been a thousand salmon."

Roads are few, but as in Alaska there is charter plane service between cities, and a pony ride may be required to reach the stream. Everywhere in summer one sees ponies and people with tents and fishing rods going into the treeless mountains.

Philip K. Crowe, who has fished Atlantic salmon in almost every country where they are found, says that nowhere has he encountered more beautiful settings than in Iceland. "When the salmon refused to budge from their green depths, I looked for birds. I recognized a variety of waders including redshanks, dunlins, sandpipers, oystercatchers and the black-tailed godwits. A number of ducks flew along the river, among which were Barrow's goldeneye, a red-breasted merganser, and a pair of teal. Three whooper swans sailed by and far up in the sky a wedge of geese winged their way north . . . Except for the little shaggy horses, the fat sheep, and an occasional cow, we saw no animals in Iceland." [7]

Michael Frome, conservation editor of *Field and Stream,* reported on a visit to Iceland in the summer of 1972: "The sport fishing is utterly fabulous. Net fishing is prohibited by law so that rivers may continue to produce large natural runs. Imagine sixty major salmon streams, hundreds of trout and char streams, often in beautiful natural settings, that never muddy up, even in the foulest weather." On the best streams favored by foreign sportsmen, like those near Borgarnes, rates during the peak season in mid-July run as high as $200 to $250 a day. There is of course no catch limit and the number of anglers is carefully adjusted to the stream's salmon population. As prices for fishing rise the native anglers, as elsewhere, lose some of their sporting instincts and take as many fish as they can in order to sell them and recoup their expenses. I found this trend in England and Scotland too.

France and Spain

Once richly endowed with salmon in their numerous rivers, France and Spain now provide meager opportunities for the angler. In France heavy estuary netting permits relatively few fish to escape to their home streams. A dozen small and thinly stocked rivers in Brittany and Normandy and a few *gaves* in the Adour River system may still be fished by sportsmen, but their catches are declining.

Where to Fish, published by the British magazine *The Field,* lists the Gaves d'Oloron, d'Ossau, de Nive, and d'Aspe as streams to fish in the Adour basin of southwestern France; the best months are June to the end of August. The Aulne, which flows into the sea at Brest, the Ellé with its center at Châteaulin, the Laïta and Odet, the Trieux and its tributary the Leff, are recommended in Brittany. The Sée, Sienne, and Sélune in Normandy harbor salmon, "but the fishing is hard to come by, being largely in the hand of syndicates." The Allier, a major tributary of the Loire, flowing through the vineyard country of Auvergne, still attracts salmon anglers.

In Spain no netting is permitted, but the locals tend to monopolize the salmon fishing. Of the dozen or so producing rivers, the best are the national fishing preserves for which permits must be obtained from the State Tourist Department — the Eo in Galicia, and the Deva-Cares and Narcea in Asturias.

In a recent communication Crowe describes a fishing jaunt to the Deva-Cares. Salmon were being caught, he says, in large numbers. "At the Casa Julian in the village of Niserias, we saw no less than eight laid out on the tables in the bar. They were fine firm fish of from ten to fifteen pounds without scars from the nets which disfigure so many Norwegian fish." On this river there are beats reserved for Spanish citizens and for tourists and free beats where anyone may fish. The limit in the reserved beats is three fish per day per beat, but in the free waters there are no limits. On the Deva-Cares General Franco comes to fish each spring, accompanied by an aristocratic entourage.

Gillies are sometimes essential. The fly is preferred, but when the river is muddy the salmon is challenged with bait that consists of "the traditional inhabitants of the garden and of baby shrimps, arranged in a string to cover the single hook." Some beats on the Cares are furnished with footpaths cut from the rock so an angler can follow a running fish down or upstream, but many are not and there one must fight the salmon from a stationary position.

"Lack of sport," says Crowe, "does not spoil the days. There is always the pleasure of enjoying the Spanish countryside and eating at the little river restaurants." Many of the fish caught are sold in the nearby markets, but an angler can have his fish smoked and sent to him, or he can take it to a restaurant and have it grilled and served "accompanied only by a green salad whose olive oil and garlic dressing is memorable," and washed down by a light white wine, and after dinner by "oruja," a fiery liquor that aids digestion.[8]

Spain probably offers the least expensive salmon fishing in Europe. A license costs about $2 a beat on the Cares, a hotel reserved for tourists is $22 a day for two, and the gillies receive about $3 a day plus $1.50 for meals. A hotel provides bed and breakfast for $5.

England and Wales

There are 2 million anglers in Britain. Fishing is stratified — that is, there are two kinds, coarse fishing for roach, dace, barbel, bream, chub, carp, rudd, pike, and tench, which are found in many streams, and salmon and trout fishing, which is more prestigious. Coarse fishing is inexpensive, while trout fishing, at least on private waters, is relatively expensive and is pursued on artificially stocked lakes, ponds, and reservoirs as well as rivers with wild stocks. Good salmon fishing is now confined to a small number of rivers in England and Wales and is usually expensive. Beats may be hired through an angling hotel, or directly from the owners. Many British anglers belong to a club that leases stretches of a river for the benefit of its members.

According to *International Fishing Guide,* the best salmon angling rivers in the south of England are the Hampshire Avon, Itchen, Test, and Frome — these chalk streams are better known as trout streams and in some places are dammed to prevent the salmon from ascending too high and imperiling the trout fishing. The Itchen and Test were made famous by Lord Grey of Fallodon, author of the classic *Fly Fishing.* They are quiet, bucolic rivers, graced by water meadows, easy to fish from the banks. May and June were Lord Grey's favorite season. "This is the time of blossom and promise," he says, "everywhere there should be visible growth . . . a sense of luxuriant and abundant young life all around us." Hampshire chalk streams run brim full at this time of year, "and their valleys are all of water meadows, intersected by streams and runnels and channels and cuts of all sorts and sizes carrying over the land the bounty of water."

Roderick Haig-Brown used to fish the Frome as a boy and remembers it (in *A River Never Sleeps*) as "a slow, deep river in its lower reaches, and the meadows through which it runs wilder and rougher than those farther up . . . The river was not tidal where we fished it, but as I remember it now the country had some measure of the bigness and wildness of the tide flats as the mouths of British Columbia rivers I have known since." Bird life was variegated: ravens, big hawks, ducks, and wading birds of many kinds as well as numerous small birds, such as sedge warblers, reed buntings, pipits, and wagtails. "They sang and mated in the reeds and the rough grass . . .

and always things were happening in the wide meadows and willow beds." The Frome still has salmon and its delightful setting, suggesting a Constable picture, has changed little since Haig-Brown fished it.

In the west country there are the rivers Exe, Dart, Tamar, Tavy, Taw, Torridge, and Teign, each yielding to anglers several hundred salmon per year and sometimes more. The Wye is in a class by itself. Like most English streams, it is relatively narrow, meanders across a wide valley below Hereford, past the ancient· town of Monmouth with a statue of Henry V who was born there gracing the market square, and through a picturesque gorge, wooded in parts and with overhanging crags. In this scenic stretch are the ruins of the medieval Tintern Abbey, which inspired Wordsworth's pantheistic poem, written in 1798. Much has changed since then: a motor road runs through the valley and hordes of visitors wander around the desolate precincts of the Abbey. Most of the nets have been taken out of the Wye and anglers profited hugely; in the years 1965–1969 they took an average of 5520 salmon while the nets took only 750.

In the northwest of England the best-known salmon streams are the Ribble, Lune, Eden, Derwent, and Border Esk, and in the northeast the Tweed (beloved of Walter Scott, whose house, Abbotsford, sits close to its banks), Coquet, and Whitby Esk. I have visited the Eden many times. Issuing from the Pennines in Yorkshire, it flows down the soft-green Westmorland and Cumberland fells. In its sixty-five-mile run the Eden passes many serene villages and castles like Armathwaite and Corby until it receives the flow of the Irthing, then turns west and, acquiring the waters of other small streams, reaches the city of Carlisle and shortly disappears into the Solway Firth. Like most English rivers, the Eden is a small stream, running its placid course to the sea in an unhurried manner. Its setting is typically English; the angler may make his cast in the shadow of a 900-year-old yew whose ancient limbs are propped up by strong posts; he gazes upon "woods patched brown with long straths of larch and green with Scots and Austrian pines, the sheltered oaks wrapped in rustly dead leaves and the sycamores in cloaks of yellow." Anglers have been taking in the neighborhood of 1500 salmon a year on the Eden, one of the five or six best angling rivers in England.

Since the English countryside, except for areas scarred by the Industrial Revolution, is generally scenic and visually exciting, the rivers provide settings that can hardly be matched for natural beauty in the greater part of the United States. For example, the Torridge, as described by Bernard Venables in *The Angler's Companion*, is typical of the Devon-Cornwall area: "It is a small river . . . ; it runs intimately with its landscape rather than with splendor. Its prospects usually are short ones, steep and enclosed. But it has a beauty, of its special Devon kind, to enchant and still a troubled mind. In its deep valley, under the tree hung crests, there is a seclusion as gently rurally perfect as is to be found in England. The river runs quietly, except in spates, swirling a little, in places breaking over the stones, but only seldom being riotous, making a lulling dappling sound."

Fly-fishing is the traditional method; a big wet fly is used early in the year and possibly a smaller wet fly at the season's end. Spinning, worm, shrimp, and prawn fishing for salmon are legal, but they are subject to restrictions; on some waters these baits are banned.

The season differs from river to river, opening as early as January on some waters (such as the Tay) and ending as late as November 31 on the Tweed. The upper reaches of a stream are sometimes fished later than the lower; for example, on the Wye the lower river is fished from March to June and the upper from September to October. The grilse run, which usually comes in summer, is sometimes heavy, especially in recent years when considerable numbers of the larger fish, who have spent more than one winter in the sea, have been taken in nets off Greenland and in Davis Strait.

Although the resource has greatly diminished in England and Wales, the amenities of angling are still considerable despite the growth of population and radical changes in the landscape since Izaak Walton's day. The kind of fishing inns he described are still numerous, and many of them unchanged since Piscator and Venator patronized them. Mine host stands behind the bar with ruddy cheeks and jovial expression as shown in the old sporting prints. The ale that warms the angler after several hours on the river is still delightful, especially when drunk before a wood fire under oaken rafters that have absorbed the smoke of centuries.

Such, for example, are the Anglers Rest at Fingle Bridge on the Teign in Dartmoor National Park and the Anglers Arms Inn at Weldon Bridge in Northumberland, a popular rendezvous for fishermen in Regency days and still going strong. The Anglers Arms attracts fishermen who work the Coquet up to Rothbury and down to Felton. "The old mill race near by," says a writer in *The Field*, "is no longer a mill, and the mill race is dry. Saplings have grown on the banks . . . but the river, clear and fresh from the hills, still gurgles and murmurs with the glad music of nature beneath the arches, over which thunder the coaches and cars of this modern age." [9]

Because of the high cost of fishing salmon and trout, many anglers now sell their catches. "The army of anglers grows each year," says Ian Wood, former editor of *Trout and Salmon.* "There is now too little water, and any stretches that are rented to individuals are very highly priced. This tends to make those who have paid so highly for their privilege fish hard and sell their fish." Owners want large bags in order to increase the value of their fishing and therefore permit the use of whatever bait is successful. Tenants want many fish to help pay their rent. Thus much of the sport fishing is now really commercial.

It was on the Wye that Howard Pashley, a schoolmaster who fished during his vacations, set a record that has probably not been superseded on any British river. In a lifetime of fishing this stream, from 1906 to 1951, he hooked 9800 salmon with the fly. For forty-one successive seasons he caught over a hundred fish. His best years were 1936 when he killed 678; 1933, 461; and 1946, 379.

While English rivers are not as famous for large fish as Scottish streams, giants have appeared from time to time, usually caught by netsmen. A Wye salmon picked up above Hereford in May 1920 was fifty-nine and one-half inches long and thirty-three and one-quarter inches in girth and must have weighed at least seventy pounds; in its mouth was an unfortunate angler's Devon minnow. According to *The Field* of July 16, 1881, a specimen weighing eighty-two pounds and fourteen ounces was shown in a Manchester fishmonger's shop with the notation that it had been netted on the Eden.

Scotland

Scotland has far more salmon rivers and glamorous beats than England and Wales. J. Wentworth Day in his *Angler's Pocket Book* lists 110 rivers and lochs where salmon may be fished. As in England, these waters are usually in private ownership; salmon and trout angling is expensive and hard to obtain on the most productive streams, although day or weekly tickets may be procured on less-known waters.

The major rivers from the border going north are the Tweed, Tay, Dee, and Spey; all of them also have fishable tributaries. *The Fishing Waters of Scotland* by Moray McLaren and William B. Currie provides the most up-to-date information on Scotland's salmon waters, plus excellent maps. Beats may be hired through a hotel, and information may be obtained from the Scottish Tourist Board in Edinburgh.

In addition to the major streams, Scotland offers other rivers and lochs, usually in the picturesque Highlands and less spectacular but beautiful lowlands, where good sport can be obtained. For example, the Nith, a Dunfriesshire river, has spring and autumn runs of salmon (and more sea trout). In 1970 anglers took 1444 salmon and 666 grilse, which compares with the best English or Welsh streams except the Wye, but was probably topped by the Tweed, Tay, Spey, and other larger rivers, though no statistics are available. On the Stinchar, an Ayrshire stream, fairly large salmon enter in autumn, from October onward; these fish are called "grey backs" and they also appear in the Girvan and Doon, both of which flow to the north of the Stinchar.

Salmon may be fished in some of the "burns" (creeks) and innumerable lakes of which Loch Lomond is best known, not only for its "bonnie, bonnie banks" and the backdrop of Ben Lomond but for a kind of "civilized wildness" (it is the playground for the people of Glasgow, Stirling, and other communities). Commercial netting and poaching on Loch Lomond and its outlet the River Leven sadly reduced the stocks in the early part of the century, but they now rate high as game-fishing water. Salmon and sea trout may be caught, as William B. Currie says, by anglers who "know the lies," as around the islands off Balmaha, on trolled bait and less frequently with the fly.

Moving to northern Scotland, we may mention the Ythan, which empties into the North Sea north of Aberdeen, after a run of twenty-six miles "through rich and beautiful farming country, with some pleasant riverside stands of trees." It has a good autumn run of salmon and a modest number of spring fish, which may be caught on association waters and private beats. In Scotland's northernmost county, Caithness, there is (among others) the River Thurso, twenty-five miles long, with an unimpressive flow but a remarkable record of salmon catches owing to excellent management by the laird of the river, Sir Tollemache Sinclair, who a half century ago impounded the waters of Loch More and regulated the flow of the stream by a system of sluices. In this way he could keep up the level of the river during the dry season so as to improve salmon runs and fishing. In 1965 the Thurso yielded 2312 salmon to anglers, much more than any English or Welsh river except the Wye.

There are 787 islands scattered around the coasts of Scotland and in the estuaries ("firths"). In the larger islands, as in the Hebrides and Shetlands, there are lochs and occasionally streams and rivers where one can fish for salmon and sea trout in a setting comparable to Iceland's for stark beauty. These little angling paradises may be reached by ferry, or more expensively by helicopter or amphibian plane.

On the island of Skye, largest of the Hebrides, there is the River Slagachan, where six-pound salmon may be caught. On the southern part of Mull there is one really good sea trout and salmon loch, oddly named Ba; an often productive salmon and sea trout river, the Forsa; a chain of salmon and trout lochs at the head of the Lussa River; and a smallish spate salmon river flowing west, the Caladoir.

These are but samples of the wealth of minor salmon waters on the islands; some of them have immense potentials, like the Grimersta on the island of Lewis. This river is only about a mile long, but in the season hordes of salmon appear, anxious to reach the chain of lochs connected to the stream and their spawning grounds. They go through at a ferocious pace and may be caught quite readily. The record was set in 1888 by a Mr. Naylor, who bagged 214 salmon weighing 1307 pounds in nineteen days in addition to 304 sea trout. In one day he fished for nine hours and quit with an hour and a half of daylight remaining, saying he was tired of the slaughter. In July 1873 five rods took with the fly 913 salmon weighing 6300 pounds along with 1073 sea trout.

Salmon fishing remains one of the main pursuits of many sporting peers who spend much of their lives on their vast estates or those of their friends shooting game birds such as pheasants, grouse, and partridges, hunting (called stalking) deer and elk, and angling for *Salmo salar* in the spring, autumn, or winter. A vivid picture of this kind of life is given in the Duke of Portland's *Fifty Years and More of Sport in Scotland*.

A member of the Bentinck family, the Duke owned the estates of Braemore and Langwell, comprising some 80,000 acres in Caithness, well stocked with game birds bred purely for sport and with deer and elk that roamed the Highland forests as well as with salmon in the Tay and other rivers. The estates were tended by gamekeepers and the hunts led by well-trained stalkers. There was sport for every season. Attempts were made to improve the fishing, including the construction of a hatchery with ova taken from salmon on the River Thurso.

Only the Duke and his family and their guests were permitted to fish and hunt on this duchy. To enter without permission was a serious offense. A list of the people who participated in the various sports at Langwell and Braemore reads like Burke's *Peerage* and includes as well foreign princes, queens, and kings.

Meticulous records were kept of every fish, bird, and game animal killed. For example, the Duke records that in 1929 "Baker Carr killed 32 fish; other rods 36 fish, and I killed 65 fish (on the Tay), making a total of 133 fish weighing 2290 lbs." On March 19, 1930, His Grace caught a salmon of thirty-three pounds and on March 22 another of thirty-five pounds, "which until then was the largest fish I had killed on the Tay until on the 11th of April on the Beachill Beat I was fortunate enough to kill one of 37 lbs. During this season," he proudly adds, "I caught in five weeks 6 fish, each one of them weighing more than 30 lbs."

The largest salmon ever taken on the Duke's waters was by Miss G. W. Ballantine on October 7, 1922, on the Tay, and it weighed sixty-two pounds, was fifty-four inches long, and had a girth of twenty-nine and one-half inches, a head twelve inches, and a tail eleven inches. This was probably the heaviest fish ever caught with rod and line on the Tay and the biggest ever bagged by a woman angler in Britain. It is topped by a sixty-seven-pounder hooked in 1812 by the notorious poacher Jock Wallace (who claimed to have played it for ten hours) and by a specimen of sixty-nine and three-fourths pounds hooked by the Earl of Home about 1730. The heaviest Atlantic salmon taken on a rod was caught by Henrik Henriksen, postmaster of Bodeng in Polmak, Norway, on July 28, 1928; it weighed seventy-nine and one-quarter pounds. Larger fishes, including some weighing over 100 pounds, have been netted.[10]

The Duke of Portland's records show that between 1881 and 1932 he and his guests hooked 3312 salmon, or about sixty-three per year. They also killed ninety royal stags in that period and between 1880 and 1922 43,490 brace of grouse, or over one thousand brace annually. The latter record was far eclipsed by the Marquess of Ripon who between 1867 and 1923 bagged 96,000 grouse (about 1700 per year) in addition to 241,000 pheasants and 124,000 partridges. It is doubtful if the kind of sport enjoyed by the Duke of Portland and his circle will ever again be duplicated, for their way of life was considerably altered by two world wars, which killed many of the younger men, and by the heavy taxation introduced by the Labour governments in an effort to equalize the nation's wealth and democratize British institutions, including those relating to sport.

Ireland

Ireland ranks next to Norway and Scotland in popularity among European salmon anglers, although the troubles in Ulster have deterred many people from going there in recent years. Costs are relatively high. Here are many rivers like the Cork Blackwater, which Stephen Gwynn called "the most perfect type of those Irish rivers whose general direction is eastward, and are rivers proper, not prolongations of lake systems." The setting is often picturesque in the Republic of Eire, whose peaty banks and slow-flowing streams with tawny mountains in the distance, uncrowded roads, and sparse settlements provide an atmosphere of peace and serenity.

There are usually two major runs in Ireland: the "springers," which ascend from January until June, and the smaller grilse, which appear with the first rains in June and continue until October. Some rivers like the Ballynahinch have a summer run of adult fish weighing about twelve pounds on the average, compared with three pounds for grilse. The best spring rivers are the Boyne, Suir, Nore, Slaney, and Munster Blackwater.

Large lakes that form part of a river system in Counties Kerry, Connemara, and Donegal offer good salmon fishing in summer. Here the fish may be taken by trolling with a spoon and often are caught while casting small wet flies for trout.

Other rivers much frequented by salmon anglers are the Shannon, Bandon, Barrow, Carrib, Clady, Lee, Moy, Sligo, and Waterville. Some of the Irish rivers are quite short: the Ballynahinch is only three miles long, compared with the 114-mile Suir and even longer Shannon. In Ulster there are some excellent streams, notably the Bann, Finn, Foyle, Faughan, and Roe.

Irish rivers are not as noted for their large fish as the Scottish streams. There are exceptions, of course. The famous Careysville beat on the Cork Blackwater between Fermoy and Lismore, owned by the Lismore Estates Company, has produced salmon over fifty pounds, and before the hydroelectric project impaired the fishing on the Shannon it too sometimes yielded monsters. Occasionally a huge salmon is taken by a rod on the Suir.

Fishing in Connemara, according to Arnold Gingrich, is somewhat like that in Iceland, "for the wild and rugged aspect of its landscape, and for the quick comings and goings of its showers and sunshines . . . [The] bright interval between the overcast and the showers would seem to wake [the fish] up like an alarm clock, and as the sun broke through you'd tend to grip your rod a little tighter, bracing for the sudden savage pull." There are wonderful amenities for the fisher in Ireland, pubs everywhere, with jolly barmen, and the delight of hearing our language spoken in a mellifluous voice, contrasting with the Scottish burrs and flat sounds of the American.

Gingrich suggests a schedule of Irish salmon fishing as follows: first a week out of either the neo-Gothic Ashford Castle or Ballynahinch near the river of that name; second, a week on the Blackwater anywhere from Mallow to Lismore; third, a week on the River Currane out of the Butler Arms hotel in Waterville, County Kerry; and finally a week on the Ilen, at Skibbereen, "if only for the piquancy it would lend to your future small talk, to be able to refer to 'one time at Skibbereen.'" A fifth possibility is a week on the River Maigue, fishing out of the hotel at Adare, County Limerick, close to the Shannon, a divine village and quaint hotel such as you often see driving through the remoter parts of Ireland.[11]

Information on fishing in Ireland may be obtained from the Irish Tourist Board in Dublin and for Northern Ireland from the Fisheries Branch, Ministry of Agriculture, York Buildings, Belfast.

There are no bag limits in the British Isles, although in some instances an angler may be required to give his catch to the hotel that arranged his holiday or to the club that leases the waters. He may of course return the fish to the water as many sportsmen do or sell them to recoup part of his expenses.

Canada

In North America angling for Atlantic salmon is confined almost entirely to Canada. The runs in Maine have failed to come back in appreciable numbers despite the expenditure of millions of dollars on river restoration projects, while none of the restoration projects in other New England states have yet yielded any catches.

Americans who wish to pit their skill against *Salmo salar* usually go to Canada. In 1950 there were 222 rivers in eastern Canada with about 3400 miles of fishable waters on which anglers could cast their lines with some chance of hooking a salmon. Quebec had 55 rivers, New Brunswick 28, Nova Scotia 31, and Newfoundland 108.

Many of the rivers are restricted and hence not easily available to the general public. The province of Quebec has opened at least ten rivers, the Little Cascapedia, Matane, Saint Jean, Cap Chat, Sainte Anne, Romaine, Metis, Au Rocher, Escoumains, etc., all of which may be fished for a nominal fee, and plans to open other Crown waters. Most of the open water is in the Gaspé Peninsula, a two-day drive from anywhere in New England. All the rest of Quebec's famous salmon rivers, including the Ristigouche, Moisie, and Grand Cascapedia, are privately held or leased by the government to syndicates or private individuals. On many of these restricted rivers fishing may be obtained on a daily fee basis. Quebec rivers are often swift, and fishing is from a canoe. On some streams like the Matane one may fish from the bank or wade to reach the salmon pools.

About half of the New Brunswick salmon rivers now offer controlled public angling either through outfitters or on government Crown reserves. Some of the famous rivers in northern New Brunswick are the Tobique which flows into the St. John and the Miramichi with its many arms and tributaries. Southern New Brunswick's major river is the St. John, its entire length easily reached by a network of highways. There is a sport fishery for kelts, called "black salmon," on the Miramichi in the spring.

In Nova Scotia all the rivers are open to the public and may be fished upon the purchase of a license that costs $12.50 for a nonresident. The rivers are usually short and slow except in extremely high water, when canoes are required. Guides are recommended. The most promising rivers are the Margaree, Saint Mary's, Medway, Mersey, LeHave, North Stewiacke, and Grand. The open season is from April 15 to October, but August or September is best for taking larger fish.

Newfoundland-Labrador is a province where salmon fishing is democratized and all one needs is a license plus the services of a guide. There are, however, but few fishing camps or other accommodations, although their number increases as the province becomes more accessible by air and surface transportation. In these so-called "democratized" provinces there is a relatively sharp decline in numbers of salmon in comparison to the "undemocratized."

Lee Wulff lists the Eagle as one of the best salmon streams in Labrador; Jim C. Chapralis, who has fished for salmon in Europe and North America, thinks the Pinware River "is ideal for the sportsman who cannot afford a great amount of money to fish the better rivers of Europe or North America." A week's fishing here cost about $400 in 1972. In Newfoundland rivers emptying into the Gulf of Saint Lawrence are most often recommended, such as the Humber, Grand Codroy, and Portland Creek, all reachable by boat or seaplane from Gander.

In 1970 Canadian angling catches were as follows:

	Salmon	Grilse	Total
New Brunswick	5654	22,234	27,888
Quebec	11,446	3400	14,846
Newfoundland	2695	34,560	37,255
Nova Scotia	1591	3344	4935
	21,386	63,538	84,924

In 1971 the total dropped to 65,000 salmon and grilse, but in 1972 there was some improvement.

APPEARANCE OF THE SALMON AND STEELHEAD TROUT IN THE RIVERS	
Atlantic Salmon	Bright steely-blue back, silvery sides, and a light belly; spots and little x-marks on the top and sides. Pink flesh. After a short time in the river the steel-blue gives way to reddish gray. Tail is deeply forked.
Chinook (King) Salmon	Greenish back fading to silver on the sides and belly. Back is almost black, especially during spawning. Black spots above the lateral line.
Coho Salmon	Black spots on body above lateral line as in chinook but not as profuse. Base (caudal peduncle) of tail relatively thicker than in chinook. Lower gum line whitish gray compared to coal black in chinook. General color upon returning from the sea is silvery blue fading off to silver, but during the spawning run changes to a lackluster background, brown or red. Male develops a marked hooked snout with heavy teeth.
Pink Salmon	Superimposed on a slate-blue back are large elliptical black spots, conspicuous in tail. Sides become silvery fading to white on the belly. Scales very small. During spawning the black spots are diffused and tend to melt into the overall color. Male acquires a noticeable hump behind the head and menacing upper jaw in the river.
Chum Salmon	In its prime in saltwater has a slate-blue back with occasional speckling and fins frequently tinged with black. Darkens as it goes up the river. Because of heavy teeth and hooked jaw, which develop in freshwater, it is called "dog salmon."
Steelhead Trout	Like all rainbows, steelhead is silvery in the sea, its caudal fin square and spotted — in freshwater the blue cast of the back and upper sides changes to green and a pinkish tinge emerges from the sides around the lateral line. Spots become darker and more noticeable. At spawning time the pink tinge changes to deep red — hence the appellation "rainbow."

Note: Sockeye salmon is omitted because it is rarely caught by anglers, disdaining lures or baits. For additional information on the appearance of the various species, see Chapter II.

Angling for Pacific Salmon

Angling for Pacific salmon in North America is not only a democratic sport, in contrast to fishing for Atlantic salmon, but is usually relatively inexpensive. There are innumerable well-stocked streams from northern Alaska to central California. Pacific salmon are pursued by sportsmen in the ocean, the estuaries, and even long distances up the rivers. Steelhead trout are seldom caught in saltwater.

In recent years it is estimated that over 2 million anglers annually fished in saltwater off the Pacific coast, mainly for salmon, and over 2 million salmon and steelhead were caught by them in the ocean and the rivers of the United States, including Canada.

Unlike Europe, Pacific salmon rivers are in public ownership in North America and are accessible to anybody who has a valid fishing license and can reach them. In some areas access may be difficult because property lines run to the river bank.

The Great Lakes area has also developed a considerable sport fishery for salmon and steelhead, while some of the New England states are attempting to acclimate the Pacific species in their rivers but so far with relatively little success.

There is little sport fishing for salmon in Japan and information on Russia, which has the largest stocks of these fishes in Asia, is unavailable, although the sport is undoubtedly pursued there.

New Zealand

Chinook salmon have been acclimatized in rivers of South Island, New Zealand, originally with eggs imported about a century ago from the Baird Hatchery in California. There they are called "quinnat," the name for chinook used in early California fishery literature.

Quinnat may be fished in the late summer and autumn months (that is, from mid-December to April 30) in east-coast rivers of South Island, from Oamaru through Canterbury. They usually weigh from ten to fifteen pounds, but there is a fair proportion of twenty- and thirty-pounders and a sprinkling of heavier fish. They are taken with a surf-type rod, monofilament line, and heavy spoon. The major salmon rivers are the Waiau, Hurumi, Waimakariri, Rakaia, Ashburton, Rangitata, and Waitaki Rivers; the last five are the most popular.

Most of the fishing is concentrated at the mouths of the rivers when the tide comes in, and many fish are caught in the surf. The rivers themselves are frequently in spate and therefore unfishable, especially after a northwest rain has fallen in the Alpine Mountains, which frame the streams. When the run has entered and the water is clear the pools are heavily fished up to the cascades.

Fishing spaces are usually crowded. A writer in *Trout and Salmon* (July 1972) recounts his adventure on the Waitaki River: "There was a double line at the mouth, half-a-mile away, where the river joins the Pacific, but I was content to sit on an old apple box with patience and a borrowed rod and lure and to keep casting. The split river was only a good cast wide. Being tired of trout, it was salmon or nothing, but it was early and only here and there was a salmon being taken . . . [Within the week] we only had one fish — 19 pounds — but several between 24 and 30 pounds were taken, and I had the pleasure of seeing mine canned for home consumption."

United States

No fishes take the angler into more spectacular scenery than the Pacific salmon in North America. They may be caught in ice-studded Glacier Bay west of Juneau, Alaska, where the subarctic sun provides twenty hours of daylight in summer; in cold fjord rivers flowing with the "milk" of melting glaciers; at the mouths of rivers that cascade precipitously into saltwater; in streams backdropped by jagged mountains covered with snow in July; and in rivers tumbling down boulder-strewn canyons that are treacherous to fish and anglers alike. Then there are quieter waters such as streams on the Oregon coast or on the mighty but tamed Columbia.

More salmon are taken by trolling from a boat in saltwater than in the rivers, and here (as elsewhere) one must know the fishes' habits to succeed. In the sea the salmon continues to feed, high-balling through schools of small fish, mangling many, then picking up the stragglers. Spoons and other lures used in trolling are therefore designed to resemble crippled fish; behind the lure is bait such as herring, anchovy, or sand lance. When the salmon is attracted by a flasher or dodger it may strike the herring or anchovy trailing on the hook eighteen to thirty-six inches farther back, or the lure resembling them, and be hooked. It fights desperately to break loose and often succeeds — sometimes only to succumb to mortal wounds.

Many anglers dispense with attraction devices and are successful using herring, anchovy, or sand lance only on one or two hooks trailed on a four- to six-foot leader back of a light sinker (one to four ounces). The bait fish is impaled on the hook or hooks in such a manner that it will rotate, wobble, or dart, like a crippled fish that has lost its equilibrium. The angler has good control of the whereabouts of his bait and can occasionally bounce the bottom for the big chinook that like to feed in deep waters. He is likely to get considerable action from the hooked salmon, although chinook or coho do not usually offer the kind of battle that *Salmo salar* does.

Salmon are also fished from the banks, as on Sauvie Island in the Columbia River near Portland.

Chinook are the prime trophies of river and estuary as of ocean fishing, frequently running to twenty pounds and more; in some areas such as the Campbell River in British Columbia a chinook over twenty-five pounds is called "tyee," an Indian word meaning chief. More coho, however, are caught than chinook; these bright silvery fish average ten to twelve pounds as they emerge from the sea. Chinook are available the year round in some areas, but coho are not. Pink salmon, although less esteemed than chinook or coho, are taken by anglers in saltwater in Alaska, British Columbia, and Washington, using herring as bait. There is some sport fishing for the smaller sockeye in Washington and Alaskan lakes and rivers.

SOME OF THE MAJOR SALMON RIVERS FOR SPORT FISHING IN PACIFIC COAST STATES			
California	*Washington*	*Oregon*	*Idaho*
Klamath	Columbia	Columbia	Clearwater
Trinity	main stem	main stem	River system °
Smith	Skagit	Willamette °	Salmon
Eel	Puyallup	Umpqua	River system °
Feather	Nooksack	Rogue	
Sacramento	Green	Alsea	
	Samish	Nehalem	
	Nisqually	Trask	
	Dosewallips	Deschutes °	
	Dungeness	Clackamas °	
	Chehalis	Siletz	
	Hoh	Coos	
	Humptulips	Santiam	
	Cowlitz °	Sandy °	
	Lewis °		
	Toutle °		
	Washougal °		

° Tributaries of the Columbia. Clearwater supports principally steelhead trout.

BRITISH COLUMBIA

Juan de Fuca Strait

Victoria

Bellingham

Neah Bay

Skagit

Cape Flattery

Sekiu

River

La Push

Port Angeles

Hoh River

Seattle

Puget Sound

Grays Harbor

Westport

WASHINGTON

Ilwaco

Astoria

Warrenton

Columbia

Tillamook Bay

Portland

Cape Kiwanda

OREGON

Siletz River

Willamette R.

Depoe Bay

Florence

Winchester Bay

Charleston

Coos Bay

Rogue River

Gold Beach

Pistol River

Brookings

Smith River

Klamath River

Crescent City

Trinidad

Humboldt Bay

Mad River

Eureka

Sacramento River

Eel River

CALIFORNIA

PACIFIC OCEAN

Fort Bragg

Russian River

San Francisco Bay

San Francisco

San Lorenzo River

Santa Cruz

Monterey Bay

Monterey

Sport
Fishing Centers on
Pacific Coast
from Monterey
to Victoria

The map opposite shows the leading ports along the coasts of Washington, Oregon, and California where anglers may fish from charter boats that operate during the season, which commonly begins in May, peaks in August, and tapers off in September. The best time to fish is early morning or late evening and when the sky is overcast, although boats go out at all times of the day in good weather.

Typical of the rivers listed in the table on page 509 is the Rogue, which flows out of Crater Lake National Park and for much of its course is a dazzling, cascaded stream that breeds strong fishes. I drifted down the upper Rogue before it was dammed in a high-prowed boat called a "Rogue Runner," which accommodates three or four persons and in which one can fish standing at the prow. It was a warm sunny day, with few boatmen or anglers on the stream, which in this ten-mile stretch is too powerful for bank fishing or wading. The river is fifty to seventy-five feet wide, broken by numerous rocks down which the waters pour in frothy cascades and swirls, beating angrily at the craft the rivermen try to steer through difficult passes. Along the banks the firs and cedars rise tier-like to the summits of the mountains; few human habitations can be seen, only an occasional cottage or a ranch where meadowland provides forage for a small herd of cattle. It was too early to fish for the spring chinook that lures many anglers. Here a guide is necessary, for he knows the holes where the fish lie and how to attract them, and he can maneuver the boat through the onrushing torrents that may toss the craft into the air and spell disaster. This part of the Rogue, like much of the white-water river, has been a graveyard for boatmen and fishermen.

Many birds darted in and over the water as we pushed along. Water ouzels skimmed the white surface, a lone duck swam past, the sad notes of a killdeer emanated from the brush. We passed a suspension bridge. After ten miles of drifting we beached the boat and hauled it out of the water. This was its maiden voyage and it met the challenge of the defiant river gallantly.

A few weeks later the lordly chinook came in and anglers awaited them, mainly in the quieter waters where their bodies could be seen as through glass. There were steelhead trout too.

Some 20,000 salmon are landed annually by sportsmen in the 200-mile Rogue and sometimes up to 10,000 steelhead trout. No commercial fishing is permitted on this and other Oregon coastal rivers. Unfortunately, the stretch of the Rogue which I drifted in 1972 is now a dreary reservoir behind the Corps of Engineers' Lost Creek dam. Below Grants Pass it is a sanctuary scenic river.

REGULATION	California	Oregon	Washington	British Columbia	Alaska [*]
Season	Oregon, British Columbia, and Alaska permit a year round saltwater sport fishing season, California permits a year round saltwater season north of Tomales Point. Washington limits ocean sport fishing to the same season in effect for commercial trolling, but angling is permitted the year round in inside marine waters.				
Size Limits					
Chinook	22 in.	20 in.	20 in.	12 in.	none
Coho	22 in.	20 in.	20 in.	12 in.	none
Bag Limit					
Daily	3 fish	3 fish	3 fish	4 fish	6 coho; 3 chinook
In possession	1 daily	6 fish in 7-day period	2 daily	2 daily	2 daily
Gear	angling gear only	1 line per fisherman	1 line per fisherman; 2 lines per fisherman in inside marine waters	more than 1 rod and line legal while trolling	1 rod; 1 line per fisherman

OCEAN SPORT SALMON FISHING REGULATIONS IN CALIFORNIA, OREGON, WASHINGTON, BRITISH COLUMBIA, AND ALASKA

[*] Southeastern Alaska only. These are general regulations in effect in 1973. One should consult local regulations for exceptions.

Alaska

Alaska has more salmon rivers and larger stocks than any other state or province. The greatest portion of the catches are made in saltwater, both offshore and in inland waters around the numerous islands and archipelagoes, on the feeding grounds, and as the returning fish mill in the estuaries. According to Ernest A. Brauer, a sport-fishing writer, "It is possible to catch one or more species of salmon at any time during the summer [in Alaska]. Almost all of July is the hot time to be fishing out of Juneau or Auke Bay because this is the period when the largest kings and the greatest number of them seem to be cruising in the sheltered waters of the Inland Waterway." July is also the time when the salmon derbies are held: the Golden North derby at Juneau, for example, offers prizes ranging from Cadillacs to $1000 bills.

King salmon ascend the rivers through June and July and in decreasing numbers in August; silvers come later, usually in August and September, while sockeye run in late June and to mid-July or after. Sockeye are plentiful in the Bristol Bay area and streams of the Alaska Peninsula and according to experienced anglers will strike at almost any spoon, spinner, or fly tossed at them. Chum salmon are the least popular with sportsmen, but since these twelve- to fifteen-pound fish are found close to some of Alaska's highways (of which there is a dearth) they are often snagged.

Unlike Oregon, Washington, and California, there is a shortage of accommodations in Alaska, and most fishable streams are not accessible except by float plane or boat; roads are few and travel between towns and villages is mainly by air or water. Fishing is done from rowboats, outboard-powered skiffs, or inboard-outboard-powered cruisers. Guides are available and boats and tackle can be rented.

In Alaska angling offers an experience not easily matched elsewhere. On the day we sought the salmon in the cold waters around Sitka, the sky was overcast, as it is frequently even in summer. Few boats were out. The fruitless search was compensated by views of winding waterways framed by half-shrouded mountains, some of which, like Mount Edgecumbe, had traces of snow. Indian fishing huts could be seen on the spits, but no human beings were visible. Brown bear, prowling for salmon, their favorite dish, came down to the water's edge. In this area anglers do not go stream fishing without making sure their rifles are working, for a hungry bear might kill a man who competes with him for the salmon. Insects are a nuisance in summer, especially the multitudinous mosquitoes.

British Columbia

There is excellent fishing for chinook and coho in British Columbia. The *International Fishing Guide* says that good coho fishing may be enjoyed in most of the sheltered bays and inlets on either coast of Vancouver Island; the popular centers are Port Alberni, Campbell River, Cowichan, and Comox. The waters around Galiano, Gabriola, Saltspring, and Pender Islands off the southeastern coast of Vancouver Island are rich in salmon during the summer and early fall, and the gentle climate, with endless cloudless days, makes fishing very pleasant.

On the lower mainland coho are found in late summer and early fall in nearly all coastal inlets and bays, such as Howe Sound, Sechelt Inlet, Jervis Inlet, and Powell River. The Queen Charlotte Islands, relatively unknown and somewhat inaccessible except by private boat or plane, has some ideal salmon fishing areas. Al McLane, editor of the *International Fishing Guide,* says the Copper River and Bay on Moresby Island is probably the best coho fishing region in British Columbia.

In contrast to angling in Alaska is fishing for tyee salmon in the Campbell River, British Columbia. "Once you have reached your destination," says Van Campen Heilner, "you will find yourself set down on the shores of beautiful Discovery Passage in the center of some of the most fanatical anglers in the world. They have come from the far corners of the earth . . . for one thing only — tyee. They talk, eat, and practically sleep with tyee during every waking moment of those three tense weeks in August when the run is on. No other topic is discussed, no other topic would be permitted."

Tyee fishing must follow exact rituals and traditions. The first step is to row over to the Tyee Club's headquarters located on a sandspit at the mouth of the river and weigh in your tackle. "Your line must break dry at 25 pounds, and your rod must conform to a complicated diagrammatic chart," says Heilner.

At exactly 3:45 A.M. the guide bangs on the cabin and hands you a thermos of hot coffee and sandwiches. Fishing begins in the cold morning, as the sun slips over the horizon, in a trim little skiff rowed by a guide. Fish with big broad backs and thick heavy tails are rolling in the waters, jumping out sometimes to get rid of their sea lice. There are forty boats within the radius of the river's mouth; many of the anglers are women shivering in the cold.

By 7:00 A.M. the tide is out and fishing ceases. The fishers return to the lodge for an enormous breakfast, then go to sleep, waking up to meet the guide at 11:00. The biggest salmon taken that morning weighed fifty-two pounds. "Great stuff," says Heilner, "but yours isn't there this morning and you row in at one for lunch. Out at two and beat, beat, beat until five. Then in for an hour's rest, a shower and a highball and out once more at six. This time the whole fleet's out again with a couple more added."

Thus the days pass. "When your great day comes and you catch a tyee, you get a silver button proudly pinned to your shirt and accept the plaudits of the multitude with blushing modesty." [12]

In 1971 about 540,000 salmon were landed in British Columbia by anglers, including a record coho catch of 295,000.

The Middle West

Salmon angling is a new sport in the Middle West, but it has set the fishing world afire, so to speak. The stocking program has grown rapidly since coho smolts from Oregon eggs were planted in some of the upper waters of Lake Michigan in 1966. Introduced to help control the alewife infestation in the Great Lakes, coho along with chinook and steelhead trout have created a popular sport fishery in Lake Michigan and Lake Superior; in fact, all states bordering the Great Lakes now offer salmon fishing based on plantings of eggs or young fish, but Michigan has the largest fishery.

The advent of a salmon fishery in Lake Michigan set off a craze with disastrous results. "People in the Midwest," said Dr. Wayne Tody, Chief of the Fish Division of Michigan's Department of Conservation, in 1967, "who never fished before in their lives (and who had never seen a salmon) are now buying rods and reels and are confirmed coho addicts." Around Labor Day 1967 thousands of anglers flocked to the mouth of the Manistee River, where the salmon had been planted the year before and were expected to return as adults. They came by boat from Chicago, Milwaukee, and other cities hundreds of miles away. The single airline serving the area was loaded with passengers and the highways were jammed with cars and campers, many trailing boats. Some people had to sleep in their boats. Gas stations and grocery stores ran out of supplies and restaurants had long lines of waiting customers. It was the same story at the mouth of the Platte River.

The fact that Lake Michigan could be dangerous for small craft was unfortunately ignored by many people. Storm warnings went unheeded as men in twelve- and fourteen-foot boats, in small canoes, and even in rubber rafts continued to pursue the salmon as much as seven miles from shore. The Coast Guard, state police, and sheriff's deputies could not force anglers off the treacherous waters.

Suddenly, as I have seen it when I used to vacation on Lake Michigan many years ago, the sky darkened and a strong wind blew up. Waves began to rise, but not many boatmen took heed in time. As the fury of the lake slammed into their craft they started their engines and headed for port. Panic ensued. At least 200 boats capsized during the squall; fishing gear, life jackets, clothes, and boat cushions were floating in the water or scattered along the shore. Seven persons were drowned and dozens were injured. After this disaster state officials tightened up boat safety regulations and safety patrols were added to keep Michigan's growing salmon craze under better control.

The best area for salmon fishing in Lake Michigan is along the eastern shore from south of Muskegon to north of the city of Manistee. At the end of summer and into fall good fishing for both coho (by far the more numerous) and chinook is north from Muskegon to Little Traverse Bay at Petoskey. Dr. Tody, who has fished for coho in the Pacific, says that the sporting value of Great Lakes coho is equal to that of their ocean cousins, and often provides spectacular runs and aerial acrobatics.

In spring and summer coho are found in open lake waters near concentrations of alewives or smelt upon which they feed. As the fall season approaches they crowd the mouths of the rivers and are there caught in large numbers, hitting any offering, often with reckless abandon. Some time in September they ascend the rivers. Lake fishing ends that month, but some of the larger streams are open to anglers through October and even November. Bag limits are somewhat more generous than on the Pacific coast, and the minimum size fish that can be kept is ten inches rather than twenty; however, coho caught in Lake Michigan average slightly larger than their Pacific counterparts.

Angling for Steelhead Trout

Steelhead trout closely resembles Atlantic salmon not only morphologically but in its reputation as a game fish. It is found in hundreds of rivers and small streams in North America emptying into the Pacific Ocean and often ascends for hundreds of miles. "From the steelhead's southernmost range in California to the far inlets of Alaska," says Joe Brooks, "when this unique fish comes home to his river to spawn he stirs anglers to a frenzy." [13] Steelhead anglers are now so numerous in the Pacific Northwest that they have formed an organization, Northwest Steelheaders, affiliated with Trout Unlimited, with numerous chapters devoted to the protection and preservation of this resource.

There are usually two distinct runs of steelhead (but many streams do not have both): the winter fish that return to their natal rivers from the middle of November to March, with the heaviest run in December, and the summer steelhead that ascend in the spring, summer, and fall. Oddly enough, both types spawn about the same time, in later winter and early spring, in the case of the summer steelhead, in the spring of the year following the summer entry into the river. Like Atlantic salmon, a small percentage recover from the mating ordeal, return to the sea, and then spawn again. Three- and four-time spawners occasionally occur and seem to be more numerous than among Atlantic salmon. Anglers encounter the kelts usually in March and April as they descend to the ocean. The upper reaches of many streams are closed throughout the winter or early spring angling season, or earlier than in the lower reaches, in order to protect the spawning and spent fish.

Steelhead do not reach the proportions of Atlantic salmon or chinook. The largest specimen ever caught by sportsmen weighed forty-two and a half pounds, but the average is two to ten pounds.

Steelhead fishing is quite different from salmon angling — it is pursued almost entirely in freshwater and mainly in rivers marked by riffles, pools, and white water, which can be worked from the shore or by wading, or from a river boat (also known as a drift boat). To catch a steelhead one must search a great deal of water, wading and walking in the cold river, avoiding deep holes, and as Frank Amato, editor of *Salmon Trout Steelheader,* says, "forming an intimate friendship with the river." There is considerable danger too, for one may slip on a rock and get an unexpected cold bath or have his boat overturned by the churning waters. Each year the rivers take their toll of steelhead fishermen who never return to their homes.

The setting for steelhead fishing in the Pacific Northwest and Alaska is often reminiscent of Scotland or Norway. Typical is the Rogue, where steelhead are fished below Medford. Here the river runs more placidly than upstream, between the mountains and meadows that are green in winter and spring and brown and serene in summer. More dramatic is the North Umpqua, also an Oregon river, flowing north and west to join the main stem, which drops into the ocean at Winchester Bay after a journey of some 200 miles. Between Soda

Springs and Rock Creek the North Umpqua is the fly-fisherman's dream as it descends over many rocky formations, in a gently meandering pattern; the mossy rocks, glittering pellucid waters, and numerous riffles are dotted with anglers on a summer's day. The lofty firs and pines on both banks cast their friendly shadows and the fishermen, oblivious to the noise of the logging trucks on the highway, stand in their waders and hobnailed boots and wait or move gingerly to persuade the fish to rise to their flies. This stretch of the North Umpqua is reserved for fly-fishers only.

Winter steelhead fishing is a challenge that can hardly be matched. "The weather is cold, the rivers are full, the fish are moving," says Amato. The angler rises at 5 A.M. hoping that his favorite river will not be out of its banks, drives up to 100 miles or more on a rain-slickened highway, sometimes iced, "to be greeted by a blast of cold wind and rain as he opens his car door next to the river. He pulls on his hip boots or waders, slips into his fishing vest and dons his rain parka wind breaker." His weapon is a bait casting or spinning rod, and the lure is a cluster of eggs or spinner, or a spoon. Success depends on his ability to read the water and to disregard the punishment of rain and cold wind.

Summer steelheading is more pleasant, although the fish are usually less abundant and the anglers more numerous, for the water is clearer and lower. Only streams that have adequate flows in summer are fishable and this means that the geographic scope of the summer steelhead is much restricted. Summer steelhead are taken in the same way as winter fish; many are caught fly-fishing with sinking lines. Boats are needed on some rivers, others are fishable by wading among the white cascading waters.

There are at least ninety-five steelhead rivers in Washington, fifty in British Columbia, seventy in Oregon, fifty in California, a score or more in Idaho (all tributary to the Snake), and maybe hundreds in Alaska. In general, the fish can be found in any stream that salmon enter, and in some waters they succeed in ascending past natural obstacles that salmon cannot surmount. Some of these once pristine rivers where the "shining pink and silver" fishes — as Zane Grey described them — crowded the waters have been irremediably ruined by civilization and exploding human populations. In Idaho mining companies operating without environmental restraints, logging and irrigation practices, and especially power dams, destroyed much habitat; California streams are afflicted with the same evils; some rivers in Oregon and Washington have also suffered, but here much good steelheading water remains. British Columbia rivers have also been adversely affected by logging and impassable dams.

In the state of Washington, where steelhead is by law a game fish that cannot be sold in commercial channels, the best rivers are the main stem of the Columbia and its tributaries, the Cowlitz, Snake, Toutle, Kalama, Lewis, and Klickitat; the Skagit, Puyallup, Skykomish, Humptulips, Chehalis, Nisqually, Samish, and Hoh. In Oregon the top rivers are the Columbia and its tributaries, the Deschutes, Clackamas (which Rudyard Kipling once fished and eulogized in his *American Notes*), Big Creek, and John Day; and the coastal streams, Rogue, Umpqua, Nestucca, Wilson, Siletz, Coquille, Siuslaw, Trask, Nehalem, Salmon, Illinois, and Chetco.

In 1972 the following were the most productive Oregon steelhead rivers in terms of fishes caught by anglers: the Rogue, 22,800; Umpqua, 18,300; Columbia, 17,500; Nestucca, 17,300; Deschutes, 16,100; Wilson, 14,700; Sandy, 10,400; Coquille, 8000; Siuslaw, 7500; Clackamas, 7000; Trask, 6800; Nehalem, 5500; and Salmon, 5500.

The best steelhead waters in Idaho, where the resource has been severely reduced in recent years by nitrogen supersaturation, are in the Snake and its Clearwater and Salmon River drainages. In California the best rivers for winter steelheading are the Eel, Trinity, and Klamath. Almost every section of Alaska except north of the Alaska Peninsula has excellent steelhead fishing.

According to Roderick Haig-Brown, winter steelhead fishing in British Columbia is recommended on the Vedder and Thompson Rivers, tributaries of the Fraser, on most of the east coast rivers of Vancouver Island, and on the Gold River on the west coast. On the mainland the Atnarco has a late winter run, the Dean a summer run, and the Kispiox and Sustut late summer and early fall runs. The Thompson also has a summer run.

For Further Reading

There is a mountain of books on angling for salmon and steelhead trout, as well as an infinite number of fishermen's reminiscences. To make a selection is difficult. The following list is supplied because it has been useful in the preparation of this chapter:

Bradner, Enos, *Northwest Angling*, Portland, Binfords & Mort, 1950.

Calcott, Ian, *The Art of Salmon Fishing*, Edinburgh, Oliver & Boyd, 1963.

Combs, Trey, *The Steelhead Trout,* Portland, Northwest Salmon Trout Steelheader, 1971.

Crowe, Philip K., *Out of the Mainstream,* New York, Scribner, 1970.

Gingrich, Arnold, *The Well-Tempered Angler,* New York, Knopf, 1966.

Grey, Sir Edward, *Fly Fishing,* London, Dent, 1928.

Grey, Zane, *Tales of Fresh-Water Fishing,* New York, Grosset & Dunlap, 1928.

Haig-Brown, Roderick, *Fisherman's Fall,* New York, Morrow, 1964; *A Primer of Fly-Fishing,* 1964; *A River Never Sleeps,* 1946.

Heilner, Van Campen, *Salt Water Fishing,* New York, Knopf, 1953.

Hewitt, Edward R., *A Trout and Salmon Fisherman for Seventy-Five Years,* New York, Scribner, 1950.

McDonald, John, *The Origins of Angling, and A New Printing of "The Treatise of Fishing with An Angle,"* Garden City, N.Y., Doubleday, 1963.

Rauensdale, Tom, *Understanding Salmon and Trout,* London, John Gifford, 1972.

Ritz, Charles, *A Flyfisher's Life,* New York, Holt, 1959.

Stewart, R. N., *Rivers of Iceland,* Reykjavik, Iceland, Tourist Bureau, 1950.

Van Fleet, Clark C., *Steelhead to a Fly,* Boston, Little, Brown, 1954.

Walton, Izaak, *The Compleat Angler,* ed. Richard LeGallienne, London, John Lane, 1904.

Weeks, Edward, *The Moisie Salmon Club,* Barre, Mass., 1971.

Wulff, Lee, *The Atlantic Salmon,* New York, Barnes, 1963.

Van Dyke, Henry, *Little Rivers,* New York, Scribner, 1903.

XXVIII ~⌒

Salmon — Our Earliest Gourmet Food

Indian Cookery

THE CULINARY ARTS of the Indians were quite simple. Food was boiled in watertight boxes or baskets or was steam-cooked with hot stones in large shallow pits or outside their dwellings. Fish and meat were also broiled over an open fire or bed of coals, or they were smoked. Pacific-coast Indians still use these ancient methods of preparing salmon, and the result is a nutritious and flavorsome dish.

Salmon was also eaten fresh by the aborigines, as the Japanese do now. If it was to be dried it underwent special treatment in order to produce slices thin enough to dry effectively. Usually the fish was cured for preservation at the fishing camp. The rich oil that trickled from the salmon was collected and stored since sources of edible oil were scarce. The roe was regarded by the Indians as a delicacy, as it is in Japan today, and was often smoked.

New England salmon provided food for the Indians, who taught the colonists how to fish for them and prepare them in their fashion, although many British people came from regions well endowed with *Salmo salar*. The fishes, which were sometimes so thick in the rivers that they overturned small boats, were probably as vital to the aborigines as the wild turkey that has received so much publicity.

To an extraordinary extent salmon served the Indians as the staple of their diet, much as meat does in ours, and potatoes in the Irish diet. The nutritional value of the various species, as shown in the table on page 527, indicates that 30 to 33 percent of the salmon consists of protein and fat, enough to provide considerable caloric substance. Chinook has the highest food value, followed by sockeye, coho, pinks, and chum.

✻

Medieval Cookery

During the Middle Ages salmon was often served at noblemen's banquets, which consisted of numerous courses and lasted for hours. It was customary to cook the fish in wine and dress it up for visible as well as gustatory delight. It was served in its silvery coat, head and eyes intact, and brought on a pewter plate to the sound of trumpets, a fitting tribute to its qualities. Servants handed round sauces or spices and the fish was washed down with wine.

The earliest known English salmon recipe is found in the *Noble Book of Cookery* (1500), which stipulates that the fish should be roasted on a gridiron in small pieces, with wine, onions, pepper, and salt. It was also customary to serve salmon grilled and unsauced. Generally it was rich man's food, for during the Middle Ages the artisans in the towns and yeomen in the country, at least in England, had to be content with a diet of black bread, milk, cheese and eggs, and an occasional bit of chicken or bacon, washed down with ale. The poorer peasants had little meat and much bread.

On the manor fish was eaten on Fridays and during Lent. Meat was scarce, especially in winter, because not enough fodder was grown to fatten cattle. The fish eaten by the common folk consisted mostly of salted hake and stockfish (dried cod). It is doubtful that many of them ever tasted much salmon unless they purloined it from the river.

In the ecclesiastical establishments the monks and nuns dined well, and since there were many days in the year when meat was forbidden they subsisted to a considerable extent on fish. Salmon was certainly in high repute, especially in areas where it was abundant.

In the medieval era fish were preserved by salt-pickling in barrels topped up with brine. Powdered salmon preserved by dusting with crushed salt was eaten in London in the fifteenth and sixteenth centuries, but it was not a common food. There was also smoked salmon, "hard and salty, like red herring, and in no way similar to the present day mild cured products," says the authoritative Charles Cutting.[1] Kippered (spawned-out) salmon is mentioned in the household book of King James V of Scotland (1512–1542) and in the records of the monastery of Cupar in Fife. These lean fish, really kelts, were turned into a kipper by being split and smoked.

✿

French Cookery

Gourmet cookery as we know it is basically the invention of French chefs in the eighteenth and nineteenth centuries, using ideas imported by Italian cooks during the Renaissance. "The dishes of the 17th century were very plentiful, very varied, and very complicated, but they were neither delicate in flavor, wholesome nor appetizing," says Paul Lacroix in his book on eighteenth-century French customs, institutions, and costumes.[2] Another authority says that under Louis XIV "cooking was spectacular and ostentatious rather than fine and delicate."[3]

The meals served in royal and noble households were staggering in volume and variety. Nicolas de Bonnefons in *Delights of the Country* (1652) described a feast of eight courses that starts with a variety of *potages,* then a variety of ragouts, followed by a big roast (poultry, partridge, pheasant), a small roast, and in the fifth course fish (salmon, trout, carp, pike, or various fish pies), succeeded by numerous side dishes, fruit, and a windup of sweets (marzipans, musk pastilles, or sugared almonds flavored with musk and amber).[4] Fish has always been a side dish, not a main course, in French and continental cuisine.

Under Louis XV and Louis XVI, who were more delicate in their tastes than Louis XIV, French cooking moved toward greater refinement and showed extraordinary inventiveness. Not only the chefs but the courtiers vied with each other to create new dishes, and eating often became a ritual marked by conversation about other meals. Thus Madame de Sévigné in one of her letters remarks: "We are still on the chapter of peas (imported from Italy); the impatience to eat them, the pleasure of having eaten them, and the joy of eating them again are the three main points our princes have been dwelling on in the last few days."

An attitude developed that made of eating not a chore or mechanical act (as it is now) but an art; an entire literature developed around the mystique of cookery and its role in civilization. As interpreted by some of the masters, like Marie-Antoine Careme, who had been chef to the Rothschilds, Talleyrand, and other nobles, and who was the author of a stupendous work on gastronomy, cooking was like painting and music: "The first, by the richness of its colors, produces the great paintings that seduce the sight and the imagination; the musician, by the combination of his notes, produces harmony, and the sense of hearing receives the sweetest sensations that melody can produce; our culinary combinations are of the same nature; the gourmet's palate and sense of smell receive sensations similar to those of the connoisseurs of painting and music." [5]

Fish, fowl, and meat were honored with a variety of elegant recipes. The results are enshrined in *Larousse Gastronomique*, the bible of modern French cookery. Eight pages are devoted to salmon, indicating the prestige of this fish among *artistes de cuisine*. The entire gamut of salmon preparation with its attendant sauces, garnishes, and other accouterments is expounded in this work. No other fish is so fully treated nor so artistically handled. Ironically, since there is very little salmon left in France, one may travel extensively in that country and dine in good restaurants without finding it on the menu — not even in establishments honored with three stars in the *Michelin Guide*. One may surmise that French chefs, deprived of the native salmon they regard as superior to all others, refuse to accept fish from other countries. For tinned salmon they have nothing but contempt.

The Age of Abundance

Until the nineteenth century Atlantic salmon was fairly abundant and inexpensive in both Europe and North America. Development of methods of shipping fish in ice opened up distant markets. According to the *Edinburgh Review* of April 1814, icing was "the mode of preserving fish now adopted in all the eastern rivers and coasts of Scotland (and the west country), and we believe, in some parts of Ireland, by which means salmon is conveyed fresh to the capital of the empire . . . Every salmon fishery is now provided with an ice house, for laying in a stock during winter. The salmon are packed in large oblong wooden boxes, with pounded ice interspersed betwixt them; and in this manner they are conveyed to London as fresh as when they were taken out of the water." [6]

In 1817 7200 hundred-weight boxes of iced salmon were shipped to London from the Rivers Dee and Don alone, and in later years the shipments were much larger. By 1838 a regular steamer service was taking the iced fish to Edinburgh and London from Scottish rivers; there it could be kept fresh for eight to ten days and in summer six to eight days. About 60 percent of the Scottish catch was exported.

In Ireland the great bulk of the catches was also exported. Few families below the gentry class ate much salmon, or even knew how to prepare it.

During the age of abundance salmon was the rich man's delicacy, but it was also the common man's food. All the farmhouses in the Vale of Tweed, said Richard Kerr in his *General View of the County of Berwick* (1809), depended upon the salmon for their winter's food supply. In Norway, as in New England and upper New York state, local people took as many salmon out of the rivers as they could and stored them for the winter. Knut Dahl, the Norwegian biologist, said that in the Trondheim district he met old people who remembered that whenever the inhabitants of a farm in the Lower Gula valley fancied some salmon, they brought out their boat and seine and fished until their needs were satisfied. In the autumn men, women, and children would band together and empty every pool in the small rivers that flowed through the valley. Catches were divided equally among the participants, a custom that existed for centuries. In a country where good agricultural land and cattle were scarce, fish in the rivers were a valuable food supply.

The role that salmon played in peasant diets in Scandinavian countries is told by Uno Lappea, a fishery officer in Lulea in north Sweden. In his native village of Kengis it was not uncommon for a single family to consume fifty salmon a year (as much as 900 pounds). They were salted down in wooden barrels upon being taken from the river; after a couple of days the mucus and brine were scraped off and the fish were removed from the barrels and salted again in large, well-cleaned vats kept in cellars specially built for that purpose. The supply usually lasted until the hay harvest was completed the next summer.

Salmon were prepared in rather simple ways by Scandinavian housewives: baked or partly steamed on top of potatoes in a boiling pot. Kidneys and liver were ground up into a pudding and the roe was salted and eaten. Such dishes harked back to Viking days.

As with any savory food, one can quickly tire of it if eaten too often. The tales of apprentices who refused to work unless their salmon ration was reduced to two or three times a week are found in nearly every country where the fish were abundant (including the United States).

The coming of steamboats and railroads made it possible to transport fish rapidly over long distances and thus further enlarged the markets. In *The Pickwick Papers* (1836) Dickens says that pickled salmon was a popular and inexpensive morsel; bracketed with oysters, it was associated by Sam Weller and his father with mean streets and poverty. In contrast, boiled salmon with lobster sauce appeared among the fish courses in upper-class households along with oysters and turbot. Since English cooking is more prosaic than French, no outstanding salmon dishes seem to have been invented.

Advent of a canning industry in North America and Asia provided a new source of supply, although canned fish was (and is) regarded as unsuitable for high cuisine. This product, however, introduced the delectable fish to countries and peoples — as in the southern hemisphere — who have no supply of their own. It was cheap and abundant and quickly entered working-class households.

Francis Seufert, last president of the Seufert Canning Company on the Columbia River, told me that the bulk of their pack was sold in New York City and other east-coast markets where it was consumed by people working in sweatshops and other factories. In the early days of the Columbia River and Oregon coastal fishery much of the pack was exported to Great Britain where it was also welcomed among the working class. As late as the 1930s, when I lived in Manhattan, the windows of grocery stores and delicatessens were piled high with canned salmon emanating from Astoria, Oregon. It was then quite inexpensive and enormously popular for snacks and other meals. Today it is so expensive as to be out of the reach of lower-income and even middle-income folk.

Salmon Markets

Thanks to air transport, fresh-frozen salmon is available almost anywhere in the world — for a price. One may eat Alaska king salmon in a Tokyo restaurant or in a posh restaurant in Rio or Johannesburg.

Some conception of the size of the market is given by an analysis of the annual harvest and its distribution. In 1971 228 million pounds of Pacific salmon were canned in North America, about 40 million pounds were sold as fresh-frozen, and 3.6 million pounds were mild cured. Fresh chinook commands the highest prices with coho next. Chum, sockeye, and pinks are mainly canning fish in North America, while in Japan chum — usually smoked — is the main and usually the only species found in retail markets.

Growth of demand for mild-cure salmon (lox) indicates its gourmet status; in fact, it is now the most expensive form of salmon in the United States, selling for up to $5 a pound. This product was introduced to both England and the United States by Russian Jewish immigrants. One of the first commercial enterprises devoted to mild curing was founded in London in 1879; 90 percent of the output was then consumed by the Jewish community. Gradually it found its way to the pubs and restaurants, served not only as *hors d'oeuvre* but in sandwiches. It was especially "recommended by doctors to patients who have inhospitable stomachs." [7]

In the United States mild-cure salmon was introduced on the Pacific coast in 1889 but did not attract attention until the end of the century when two small plants were opened on the Columbia River. A few tierces were occasionally packed in Alaska before 1906, when it was established on a commercial basis. Today it is a major industry, and the chief markets are cities with large Jewish populations such as New York, Philadelphia, Chicago, Miami, Los Angeles, etc. Epicures prefer their lox to come from Nova Scotia, Scotland, Ireland, or Scandinavia — that is, Atlantic salmon with its gentle curing, lovely pale color, and beautiful texture cut in paper-thin slices against the grain and preferably eaten between two halves of a bagel topped with cream cheese.

NUTRITIONAL VALUE OF SALMON				
Species	Total solids (percent)	Fat (percent)	Protein (percent)	Ash (percent)	Food value per pound (calories)
Chinook	36.8	15.7	17.7	1.2	991
Sockeye	35.2	11.2	20.8	1.2	860
Coho	32.5	8.5	21.1	1.2	750
Pink	30.2	7.0	21.4	0.8	696
Chum	30.0	6.7	20.7	1.0	514

In the United States average annual consumption is about 0.7 pound of canned salmon per capita — or 7 percent of our total fish consumption. According to industry spokesmen, demand always exceeds the available supply. In 1971 North American packers produced 4,770,000 forty-eight one-pound cases worth $208 million wholesale, of which 1,970,000 cases were sockeye, 1,670,000 cases pinks, 655,000 cases chum, 395,000 cases coho, and 80,000 cases chinook and steelhead; about 11 percent of the pack was exported and the remainder sold in domestic markets. In that year the United States exported almost 33 million pounds of fresh and frozen salmon worth $21.2 million. Salmon imports totaled 9.2 million pounds (canned and fresh and frozen).

Because of small harvests, there is no canning of Atlantic salmon.

Salmon Cookery Today

As one travels around the world, he encounters salmon prepared in myriad ways. The amiable Escoffier, prince of chefs, says in his *Cook Book* that salmon should be served as plainly as possible, either boiled, cold or hot, grilled, or *à la meunière* (that is, cooking the slices or fillets in the frying pan with very hot butter) and that it should always be accompanied by cucumber salad. "In addition to these three methods of serving salmon," he says, "the fish lends itself to a whole host of preparations which are of the greatest value in the varying of menus." He offers over a score of recipes: salmon kedgeree, salmon cutlets, salmon loaf in brioche paste, salmon *à la Chambord*, Lucullus salmon cut, Nesselrode salmon cut, *Saumon royal*, *Valois, mousseline,* etc. One need not take seriously Escoffier's recommendation that cucumber salad must always go with salmon.

One cannot live in Oregon, as I do, without becoming fond of salmon, but it must be properly prepared. I have eaten it grilled, broiled, cooked, poached, smoked, "moussed," and even in gefüllte fish. One of the most popular methods of preparing it is Indian fashion. The fish is split and put between the branches of a sapling, the twigs tied so as to hold the fish in a kind of cage, then hung over an outdoor fire and slowly cooked and smoked at the same time. For a sauce lemon butter is used.

Grilled salmon garnished with lemon butter is my favorite among the wide variety of salmon dishes. I have eaten it not only on the west coast and in Alaska but in Spain and Japan, grilled to a delicate turn that brings out its full flavor.

One can also highly recommend poached salmon. It must be prepared, as James Beard suggests, in the form of steaks lightly dusted with flour, sautéed in butter, and flavored with sherry — a wonderful dish, served hot or cold.

In Sweden one is served "gravad lax," literally buried salmon, for which (as for eels) one must cultivate a taste. It is a lightly salted fish, buried in tubs and kept there until the flesh becomes "clear," a process that takes a month or two. Despite its smell it is highly prized by gourmets.

In Japan, where raw fish — sashimi — is a commonplace food, salmon is sometimes placed before you in this form. It is also featured in teriyaki dishes, that is, marinated in a soy-based sauce and broiled, steamed, fried, or sautéed — a much more acceptable dish than sashimi. One may also encounter in Japan a dish called "yamakawi-yaki," which is salmon broiled after soaking half a day in thick sweet sake or in a fermented rice drink called "amazake."

For those who live near a fishing center the best time to buy fresh salmon is in late spring and summer. Broiled in a preheated pan and spread with butter and lemon juice, this is one of America's supreme fish dishes. Many anglers in the Pacific Northwest smoke their own salmon; others have them canned in custom canneries.

Another favorite is braised *Saumon à l'Americaine,* cooked in white wine, as recommended by James Beard (a native of Astoria, Oregon) in his *Fish Cookery,* which contains the largest collection of salmon recipes of any American cookbook I have seen.

Promising developments in aquaculture may greatly augment the world's supply of salmon for the table and restaurant trade. The first crop of 12- to 14-ounce salmon produced in saltwater cages was marketed in the fall of 1971 by a Washington state firm, and initial reactions were quite favorable. This experiment, if successful, will make available to housewives "a fish that spans the diameter of a plate and offers from one-half to one pound of meat in one or two fish." [8] Promoters envisage the growth of an industry comparable per- haps to that of salmon canning; hence it is not far-fetched to imagine that the day may soon arrive when one finds in the market not only full-grown salmon fattened on the natural food of the sea but dwarf- size fish grown entirely on artificial feed yet tasting quite as good.

EPILOGUE ∼◡

Man and the Salmon:
A Problem in Coexistence

I

THE SALMON as we know them probably preceded man upon the earth. *Salmo salar* is believed to be the progenitor of all the salmon species and existed in its present form half a million years ago when the advanced anthropoid apes were on their way to evolving into humanoids. The two — man and the salmon — had a harmonious relationship as determined by the food chain. Only since the advent of the Industrial Revolution has the relationship changed as man increasingly usurps or destroys the salmon's environment and decimates the stocks as well.

In this book we have examined the long history of man's use of the fishes on three continents, from the Stone Age to the present. We have considerable knowledge of primitive man's use of the salmon in distant times. Excavations by Professor L. S. Cressman of the University of Oregon along the Columbia River show that salmon was a common food among the Indians 11,000 years ago. In Europe salmon vertebrae have been found in caves inhabited during the Magdalenian period some 15,000 to 20,000 years ago. These peoples had mastered the art of freshwater fishing and depended upon it as a source of their food supply.

We know little about the European cave dwellers except what we can glean from their polychrome paintings on limestone walls, their sculptures on cavern floors, and other artistic objects they left behind. They frequently depicted the salmon and other fishes with meticulous fidelity. These remarkable works are believed to have had a twofold purpose. The artists created them for esthetic satisfaction, but they may also have been magicians, as Henri Breuil says, hoping by their work, "to increase and multiply the game they wanted, to make the hunt (and fishing) more fruitful, and to destroy harmful beasts."

The Indians of the North Pacific coast, whom we call "the salmon people," supply us with considerable information recorded by anthropologists (they had no written language) about their attitude toward the animal world, and especially about the salmon, which was the mainstay of their food supply. The fishes crowded the streams and returned with astonishing regularity to the mouths of the rivers; after a brief rest they moved upstream to their spawning grounds. They knew exactly where they were going and could not be deterred by foaming waterfalls, cataracts, or other obstructions. Nature had given them the stamina of race horses (although some of them weighed but six or seven pounds) and the ability to jump ten or eleven feet to overcome natural obstacles. Hence the Romans called the fish *salmo,* the leaper. After spawning the fishes died and their discolored and decaying bodies drifted downstream. The next year they reappeared in the rivers.

What could primitive people who were pantheists like the ancient Greeks make of this phenomenon? They had a rather vague idea of the cosmos or Creator, but they believed in the immortality of the animals by whom they were surrounded. Just as Christians believe that Christ, an immortal, came down to earth to sacrifice himself for the benefit of man, so the Indians believed that the salmon spirits returned each year to sacrifice themselves for the sake of man in order to prevent his starvation, died, and returned the following year. They believed the fishes lived in great houses under the sea and when the time came for the run they dressed in garments of salmon skins. Around these beliefs the Indians wove elaborate and poetic myths and rituals, as the Greeks did about the return of the wine god Bacchus every spring.

II

I think we have much to learn from the primitive peoples' attitudes toward their food animals. They lived in a pristine environment where fish and game were abundant, yet they exploited these resources with restraint, out of an inherent conservation instinct coupled with religious awe. This was made clear to me by Andrew P. Johnson, descendant of Tlingit chiefs, who said: "The Great Creator, my father told me, sees everything. The undying Creator created the fish for the benefit of the human beings but we must not take them except for food."

"The white man," he added, "is a great wastrel. In Sitka they used to destroy three scows of salmon at a time when canneries could not handle them — thousands of fish. We were taught it was a sin to kill off the seed stock but the white man killed the seed stock and depleted the rivers."

It is important to note that primitive folk did not regard fish or game as salable commodities until they came in contact with white men. They bartered pulverized salmon (pemmican) with other tribes for things they desired but there was no cash involved. As they were driven from their ancestral homes and forced into reservations many Indians had to fish commercially in order to eke out a livelihood. Thus a cash nexus entered and in time they overfished some of the rivers as the white men did. Greed replaced religious veneration.

III

The Indians did not have our anthropocentric conception of the world. Their cosmology was more like that of the Deists as expressed in Alexander Pope's *Essay on Man*. The Creator, he says, recognizes

> . . . no high, no low, no great, no small;
> He fills, he bounds, connects, and equals all!

Under the Judao-Christian ethic man is placed at the top of the pyramid. We are told in Genesis (I, 26):

> Then God said, "Let us make man in our image, after our likeness; and let them have dominion over the fish of the sea, and over the birds of the air, and over all the earth, and over every creeping thing that creeps upon the earth."

Consciously or not, this verse has influenced man's onslaught on the animal world, which has resulted in the extermination of many species — for profit or the mere lust to kill.

As lord of creation man believes that all nature is at his mercy and the right of any species to coexistence, on any terms, does not enter his consciousness if it conflicts with his economic or other values. This attitude, which Scott Paradise, writing in the *Nation* of December 29, 1969, terms "the vandal ideology," is of course not confined to Christian peoples.

It arises, he says, from the premise "that man is the source of all value, and the universe exists only for man's use . . . It narrows the meaning of value to that which has calculable value. Thus if the world's whaling fleets find profit in exterminating the last of the great whales, the whales must go. No argument about either the rights of whales or their ecological value will be admitted. The only argument that can possibly have effect contends that more profit might be made if whaling were limited so as to guarantee a perpetual harvest of blubber and meat."

This example fits the present plight of the salmon, who are being fished on their feeding migrations in the Atlantic, and on a much larger scale in the Pacific, and almost everywhere are harried by man, who takes them in excessive numbers or impairs or destroys their habitats.

The Atlantic salmon have been reduced to a small fraction of their original abundance. Pacific salmon are much more numerous, but this abundance is bound to diminish under present policies, despite conservation programs in existence.

IV

What is the future of the salmon?

The Industrial Revolution has everywhere wrought a radical change in man's attitude toward nature. As industries spread, people moved from their rural homes to cities where they lost touch with nature. Rivers were (and are) regarded as arteries of transportation, sources of water for domestic and industrial uses, and often as depositories of sewage and wastes. Often the needs of fishes for clean and well-aerated water have been ignored where economic values are at stake.

In the industrialized nations economic progress is worshiped by rich and poor alike and in its name much of the beauty of the land, along with the fish and game and other wildlife, has been sacrificed. Indeed, no sacrifice of the environment and natural resources is deemed by most people, especially politicians, economists, bankers, industrialists, and the like, as too great if thereby the nation's stock of goods — automobiles, appliances, clothing, paper, and what not — is increased. Efforts to combat this ingrained trend by passage of wise conservation laws seem to do little good.

The Gross National Product is a veritable god and when it increases the priestlike economists, politicians, and businessmen proclaim that the nation is becoming richer, and therefore happier. The adverse impact on the environment is seldom mentioned except by ecologists and conservationists.

More and more people, in the United States and other western countries, however, are beginning to realize that the Industrial Revolution and its creator, technological man, have gone too far. The effects on the biosphere, they claim, have created an environmental crisis. They question the value of unrestrained economic progress and unbridled technology, which they believe can only lead to continued environmental destruction and may imperil man's very survival on our fragile planet.

An editorial in the British magazine *Ecologist* (July 1971) sums up their arguments:

> Eventually, when all the basic requirements of life are furnished by machines, when the water we drink, the food we eat, the air we breathe, are all furnished by factories of different sorts, the instability of our society will be such, that the slightest technical hitch, the unavailability of some key resource, an industrial dispute, an act of sabotage — any one of these could lead to the collapse of the whole caboodle.

The virtues of a simpler and less machinelike existence, less harmful to the environment and the biotic community, are gaining wider acceptance. Those who feel that man's arrant assumption of hegemony over the animal world has already done far too much damage urge the rejection of the biblical injunction. In fact, they think it is nonsensical. They argue that a world in which salmon and whales and condors and other endangered species cannot live may be a world in which man himself cannot live.

The environmental revolution offers hope, but as yet it has scarcely gathered any real momentum in any nation. "Most of the politicians of the so-called developing countries insist on industrializing in order to achieve progress," says the *Ecologist*, "and they think they can do it and at the same time avoid the terrible social and ecological problems that industrialized countries are encountering . . .

"These are sheer illusions. It is precisely progress that is causing all our problems, and they cannot be solved save by foregoing it" — by ending the pollution of rivers, lakes, estuaries, and oceans; by stopping the damming of streams harboring valuable fishes for the sake of generating electricity to make beer cans, paper for trashy newspapers and magazines, chemicals for plastics, detergents, plutonium for atomic bombs, and the like.

Only a deceleration of industrial activity, coupled with something like the Indians' awe and veneration of the wondrous animals who supply us with food, can ultimately save the salmon and other endangered species.

Appendix Tables
Notes
Bibliography
Index

Appendix Tables

1. LANDINGS OF ATLANTIC SALMON, 1964–1970, IN THOUSAND METRIC TONS							
	1964	1965	1966	1967	1968	1969	1970
Total	14.0	12.0	12.0	14.0	13.0	13.0	13.0
Denmark	1.7	2.0	1.7	2.0	2.3	2.0	1.8
Greenland	1.5	0.9	1.2	1.3	1.2	2.2	2.2
Canada	2.1	2.2	2.4	2.8	2.1	2.0	2.2
Finland	0.5	0.3	0.3	0.4	0.5	0.5	0.5
West Germany	0.3	0.2	0.2	0.2	0.2	0.2	0.2
Iceland	0.2			0.1	0.1	0.1	0.2
Ireland	1.6	1.5	1.2	1.5	1.4	1.7	1.8
Norway	1.9	1.7	1.6	1.7	1.6	1.3	1.0
Poland	0.4	0.2	0.1	0.1	0.1	0.2	0.1
Sweden	0.7	0.6	0.5	0.5	0.7	0.7	0.6
Russia	0.9	0.8	0.8	1.0	1.0	0.5	0.6
United Kingdom							
England & Wales	0.3	0.3	0.4	0.4	0.3	0.4	0.5
Scotland	1.9	1.6	1.6	2.1	1.9	1.4	1.3
Northern Ireland	0.4	0.3	0.3	0.4	0.3	0.3	0.3
Faroe Islands			0.1	0.2	0.1	0.2	0.3

Sources: *Yearbook of Fishery Statistics,* Food and Agriculture Organization, and International Commission for Northwest Atlantic Fisheries.

2. CATCHES OF ATLANTIC SALMON IN HOME WATERS (EXCLUSIVE OF HIGH SEAS FISHING), 1960–1971, IN METRIC TONS

	Russia	England & Wales	Ice-land	Ire-land	Northern Ireland	Norway	Canada	Scot-land
1960	1100	283	100	743	139	1659	1635	1436
1961	790	232	127	707	132	1533	1580	1196
1962	710	318	125	1459	356	1935	1717	1740
1963	480	325	145	1458	306	1786	1848	1698
1964	590	307	135	1617	377	2147	2066	1914
1965	590	320	133	1457	281	2000	2113	1602
1966	570	387	106	1238	287	1791	2356	1624
1967	883	420	146	1463	449	1960	2859	2133
1968	827	282	162	1413	312	1514	2104	1563
1969	360	377	133	1730	267	1383	1957	1941
1970		527	195	1787	297	1171	2097	1424
1971		425	204	1635	191	1185	1837	1310

Source: International Commission for Northwest Atlantic Fisheries.

3. LANDINGS OF PACIFIC SALMON, 1952–1970, IN THOUSAND METRIC TONS

Year	Total	United States	Canada	Russia	Japan
1952	412.6	159.7	68.3	118.1	36.5
1953	462.0	141.9	86.3	190.8	43.0
1954	431.3	151.2	82.2	121.6	76.3
1955	445.1	131.4	59.5	172.4	171.8
1956	501.2	137.1	53.0	160.4	151.7
1957	515.8	120.3	61.5	150.0	184.0
1958	483.0	129.5	83.9	73.0	196.6
1959	415.6	92.8	49.6	94.1	179.1
1960	356.6	107.1	35.1	70.0	144.4
1961	435.8	142.8	56.8	80.0	156.2
1962	391.7	142.3	75.9	60.6	112.9
1963	414.1	128.5	56.0	81.1	148.5
1964	382.7	159.8	56.2	46.9	119.8
1965	430.2	148.2	43.2	89.8	149.0
1966	430.6	175.8	76.5	59.7	128.6
1967	396.5	98:2	62.9	84.2	151.2
1968	385.5	148.5	82.7	39.3	115.0
1969	380.6	121.5	37.7	78.2	143.2
1970	414.2	180.1	71.7	42.7	119.7

Source: *Yearbook of Fishery Statistics,* Food and Agriculture Organization.

4. LANDINGS OF PACIFIC SALMON, 1964–1970, BY SPECIES, IN THOUSAND METRIC TONS

Species	1964	1965	1966	1967	1968	1969	1970
Pinks	144	161	175	169	156	195	134
Chum	120	100	123	127	129	68	110
Sockeye	54	104	79	50	46	65	104
Chinook	22	21	21	20	19	22	24
Coho	44	45	43	32	36	32	43
Total	384	431	441	398	386	382	415

Source: *Yearbook of Fishery Statistics,* Food and Agriculture Organization.

5. CALIFORNIA COMMERCIAL SALMON LANDINGS, 1916–1970, IN POUNDS

Year	Coastal Ports	Sacramento Area Ports	Coastal Rivers	Total
1916	5,592,216	3,450,786	1,896,592	10,939;594
1917	6,085,997	3,975,487	999,097	11,060,581
1918	5,933,346	5,938,029	1,221,813	13,093,188
1919	7,208,382	4,529,222	1,408,123	13,145,727
1920	6,066,190	3,860,312	1,207,317	11,133,819
1921	4,483,105	2,511,127	996,700	7,990,932
1922	4,338,317	1,765,066	1,131,741	7,235,124
1923	3,736,924	2,243,945	1,109,391	7,090,260
1924	6,374,573	2,640,110	1,000,586	10,015,269
1925	5,481,536	2,778,846	1,265,371	9,525,753
1926	3,863,677	1,261,776	958,626	6,084,079
1927	4,921,600	920,786	669,543	6,511,929
1928	3,444,306	553,777	480,483	4,478,566
1929	4,033,660	581,497	429,714	5,044,871
1930	4,085,650	1,213,698	703,546	6,002,894
1931	3,666,841	941,605	686,065	5,294,511
1932	2,649,204	1,264,987	703,990	4,618,181
1933	3,657,661	454,253	446,520	4,558,434
1934	3,921,530	397,572	—	4,319,102
1935	4,773,112	888,868	—	5,661,980
1936	4,093,475	949,179	—	5,042,654
1937	5,934,996	974,871	—	6,909,867
1938	2,170,921	1,668,376	—	3,839,297
1939	2,238,755	496,933	—	2,735,688
1940	5,160,393	1,515,588	—	6,675,981
1941	2,946,030	844,963	—	3,790,993
1942	4,063,306	2,552,944	—	6,616,250
1943	5,285,527	1,295,424	—	6,580,951
1944	7,021,848	3,265,143	—	10,286,991
1945	7,912,754	5,467,960	—	13,380,714
1946	7,196,527	6,463,245	—	13,659,772
1947	8,104,297	3,380,484	—	11,484,781
1948	5,860,915	1,939,801	—	7,800,716
1949	5,531,021	899,090	—	6,430,111

(contd.)

Year	Coastal Ports	Sacramento Area Ports	Coastal Rivers	Total
1950	5,867,346	1,202,890	—	7,070,236
1951	5,849,530	1,343,171	—	7,192,701
1952	6,536,890	738,081	—	7,274,971
1953	7,136,223	869,696	—	8,005,919
1954	8,599,579	900,961	—	9,500,540
1955	9,656,996	2,320,746	—	11,977,742
1956	10,274,902	1,139,585	—	11,414,487
1957	5,176,909	321,824	—	5,498,733
1958	3,656,841	—	—	3,656,841
1959	6,768,699	463	—	6,769,162
1960	6,221,445	—	—	6,221,445
1961	8,637,907	—	—	8,637,907
1962	6,672,861	—	—	6,672,861
1963	7,859,186	—	—	7,859,186
1964	9,481,215	—	—	9,481,215
1965	9,737,775	—	—	9,737,775
1966	9,446,995	—	—	9,446,995
1967	7,401,729	—	—	7,401,729
1968	6,951,931	—	—	6,951,931
1969	6,150,906	—	—	6,150,906
1970	6,611,552	—	—	6,611,552

Source: California Department of Fish and Game.

6. LANDINGS OF SALMON AND STEELHEAD TROUT FROM THE COLUMBIA RIVER, 1866–1970, BY SPECIES, IN THOUSANDS OF POUNDS

Year	Chinook	Sockeye	Chum	Coho	Steelhead Trout	Total
1866	272	—	—	—	—	272
1867	1,224	—	—	—	—	1,224
1868	1,904	—	—	—	—	1,904
1869	6,800	—	—	—	—	6,800
1870	10,200	—	—	—	—	10,200
1871	13,600	—	—	—	—	13,600
1872	17,000	—	—	—	—	17,000
1873	17,000	—	—	—	—	17,000
1874	23,800	—	—	—	—	23,800
1875	25,500	—	—	—	—	25,500
1876	30,600	—	—	—	—	30,600
1877	25,840	—	—	—	—	25,840
1878	31,280	—	—	—	—	31,280
1879	32,640	—	—	—	—	32,640
1880	36,040	—	—	—	—	36,040
1881	37,400	—	—	—	—	37,400
1882	36,808	—	—	—	—	36,808
1883	42,799	—	—	—	—	42,799
1884	42,160	—	—	—	—	42,160
1885	37,658	—	—	—	—	37,658
1886	30,498	—	—	—	—	30,498
1887	24,208	—	—	—	—	24,208
1888	25,328	—	—	—	—	25,328
1889	18,135	1,211	—	—	1,727	21,073
1890	22,821	3,899	—	—	2,912	29,632
1891	24,066	1,053	—	—	2,010	27,129
1892	23,410	4,525	—	284	4,920	33,139
1893	19,637	2,071	157	1,979	4,435	28,279
1894	23,875	2,979	—	2,908	3,565	33,327
1895	30,253	1,225	1,530	6,773	3,378	43,159
1896	25,224	1,155	—	2,999	3,377	32,755
1897	29,867	882	—	4,137	3,138	38,024
1898	23,180	4,554	—	4,449	1,787	33,970
1899	18,771	1,630	774	2,013	816	24,004

(*contd.*)

Year	Chinook	Sockeye	Chum	Coho	Steelhead Trout	Total
1900	19,245	895	1,203	3,055	1,401	25,799
1901	—	—	—	—	—	—
1902	23,034	1,159	707	716	584	26,200
1903	27,917	570	680	828	493	30,488
1904	31,783	878	1,407	2,125	671	36,864
1905	33,029	528	1,751	1,824	668	37,800
1906	29,971	531	1,891	2,818	442	35,653
1907	24,250	374	1,534	2,159	403	28,720
1908	19,743	584	1,148	2,137	729	24,341
1909	17,119	1,704	1,668	2,868	1,175	25,534
1910	25,326	424	4,525	4,687	370	35,332
1911	36,602	407	3,636	5,400	584	46,629
1912	21,388	558	1,272	2,165	2,147	27,530
1913	19,384	758	905	2,786	2,168	25,996
1914	25,409	2,401	3,351	4,744	1,908	37,813
1915	32,127	371	5,884	2,267	2,690	43,339
1916	31,992	257	5,288	3,542	1,581	42,660
1917	29,522	542	3,649	4,372	2,233	40,318
1918	29,249	2,573	2,030	6,674	3,023	43,549
1919	30,325	494	5,133	6,170	1,900	44,022
1920	31,094	178	1,278	1,838	1,166	35,554
1921	21,552	411	328	2,338	1,021	25,660
1922	17,915	2,091	601	6,150	2,163	28,920
1923	21,578	2,605	1,735	6,965	2,684	35,567
1924	22,365	501	3,927	7,796	3,193	37,782
1925	26,660	384	3,795	7,937	2,907	41,682
1926	21,241	1,478	2,234	6,606	3,843	35,402
1927	24,011	468	4,655	5,209	3,147	37,490
1928	18,149	327	8,497	3,723	2,160	32,856
1929	18,151	685	3,714	6,701	2,871	42,122
1930	20,079	668	773	7,737	2,404	31,661
1931	21,378	281	239	2,714	2,126	26,738
1932	16,001	190	1,174	4,097	1,432	22,894
1933	19,528	471	1,659	2,702	1,958	26,318
1934	18,788	467	1,663	4,775	1,919	27,612
1935	15,206	46	810	2,684	1,764	20,510
1936	15,960	302	1,142	1,739	2,304	21,447

(*contd.*)

Year	Chinook	Sockeye	Chum	Coho	Steelhead Trout	Total
1937	18,653	335	1,910	1,842	1,933	24,673
1938	12,418	425	1,915	2,311	1,764	18,833
1939	13,499	270	1,174	1,530	1,438	17,911
1940	13,516	362	1,253	1,373	2,825	19,329
1941	23,239	506	4,150	1,045	2,663	31,603
1942	16,689	192	5,191	645	1,839	24,556
1943	11,426	146	960	706	1,514	14,752
1944	14,060	55	275	1,533	1,720	17,583
1945	12,973	9	589	1,835	1,964	17,370
1946	14,278	128	887	1,059	1,725	18,077
1947	17,310	718	496	1,498	1,649	21,671
1948	17,352	96	1,045	1,173	1,579	21,245
1949	10,769	24	545	899	814	13,051
—	—	—	—	—	—	—
1954	5,313	243	320	303	1,467	7,647
1955	8,582	200	125	599	1,297	10,804
1956	8,179	287	46	460	812	9,783
1957	5,919	240	32	391	741	7,323
1958	6,434	724	89	168	700	8,114
1959	4,594	636	43	120	673	6,065
1960	3,928	394	15	159	723	5,219
1961	4,160	158	17	383	716	5,434
1962	5,467	52	48	600	723	6,890
1963	4,346	49	15	501	972	5,883
1964	4,484	68	24	1,964	425	6,965
1965	6,143	23	6	1,902	510	8,584
1966	3,612	17	11	4,389	393	8,423
1967	4,974	195	10	3,819	445	9,442
1968	4,097	90	3	962	428	5,580
1969	5,776	104	4	1,663	490	8,034
1970	6,480	56	4	5,738	310	12,588

Sources: Reports of Oregon Fish Commission; *Pacific Fisherman Yearbooks;* John N. Cobb, *Pacific Salmon Fisheries* (1917).

Year	Plants	Chinook	Sockeye (Blueback)	Coho	Chum & Pink	Steelhead Trout	Total

7. COLUMBIA RIVER CANNED SALMON PACK, 1940–1971, NUMBER OF CANNERIES AND 48 1-LB. CASES

Year	Plants	Chinook	Sockeye (Blueback)	Coho	Chum & Pink	Steelhead Trout	Total
1940	11	244,570	23,974	59,737	25,282	33,436	386,999
1941	11	328,609	33,070	35,727	83,144	33,162	513,712
1942	12	274,750	23,256	26,541	118,051	21,803	464,401
1943	11	130,373	2,880	5,707	12,439	16,261	167,660
1944	10	163,047	758	12,210	1,525	19,222	196,762
1945	8	132,014	112	22,154	1,032	19,314	175,670
1946	11	159,872	9,726	6,883	15,617	17,373	209,471
1947	10	250,318	15,079	42,789	17,121	21,999	347,306
1948	12	235,310	3,339	39,425	26,201	19,977	324,242
1949	12	133,347	6,630	16,740	12,386	9,019	178,122
1950	11	136,635	3,630	29,507	12,952	10,266	192,990
1951	10	143,046	4,552	29,099	11,566	14,862	203,125
1952	9	95,353	9,824	29,701	13,759	18,979	167,616
1953	8	97,320	3,014	24,219	9,775	19,420	153,748
1954	8	71,993	8,485	12,670	12,530	13,379	119,057
1955	8	117,882	3,010	20,254	6,774	13,737	161,557
1956	8	112,076	19,346	22,031	5,497	8,171	167,121
1957	8	87,420	8,496	28,725	5,770	7,605	138,016
1958	7	82,786	44,129	9,917	6,113	6,313	149,258
1959	10	70,149	18,069	14,931	6,250	9,847	118,246
1960	8	50,285	8,650	5,202	2,459	6,174	72,770
1961	8	56,351	4,463	24,723	3,675	6,839	96,051
1962	8	64,437	1,289	15,178	5,355	5,785	92,044
1963	8	52,213	2,583	17,299	2,625	7,654	82,374
1964	8	52,620	3,038	30,478	2,090	—	88,226
1965	8	72,550	1,257	46,216	3,701	3,747	127,471
1966	7	42,099	3,466	51,586	184	2,875	100,210
1967	6	42,768	5,086	48,612	7,438	2,072	105,476
1968	6	25,678	4,385	26,778	1,602	2,846	61,290
1969	5	29,057	6,627	10,452	8,222	2,994	57,352
1970	6	21,025	1,910	38,698	4,469	254	66,356
1971	7	38,247	37,007	45,573	32,634	2,495	155,946

Source: *National Fisherman Yearbooks.*

8. SALMON COUNTED AT BONNEVILLE DAM, 1938–1970

Year	Chinook	Steelhead Trout	Sockeye (Blueback)	Coho	Chum	Pink	Total
1938	271,799	107,003	75,040	15,185	2,117		471,144
1939	286,189	122,032	73,382	14,383	1,168		497,154
1940	391,587	185,174	148,807	11,917	1,729		739,214
1941	461,443	118,089	65,741	17,911	5,269	4	668,457
1942	401,942	151,800	55,464	12,402	1,865	11	623,484
1943	313,123	92,133	39,845	2,547	788		448,436
1944	240,764	100,518	15,072	4,207	954	1	361,516
1945	297,478	120,133	9,501	790	728	1	428,631
1946	446,052	142,807	74,376	3,898	1,178	2	668,313
1947	480,377	135,444	171,139	11,174	199	3	798,336
1948	419,555	139,062	131,541	4,081	3,636	2	697,877
1949	277,697	119,285	51,444	1,004	2,028	6	451,464
1950	357,375	114,087	77,993	10,151	1,069	8	560,683
1951	331,788	140,689	169,428	5,201	1,044	7	648,157
1952	420,879	260,990	184,645	7,768	1,505	9	875,796
1953	332,479	223,914	235,215	13,018	1,728	10	806,364
1954	320,947	176,260	130,107	4,062	1,569	4	632,949
1955	359,853	198,411	237,748	3,725	318	9	800,064
1956	300,917	131,116	156,418	6,127	693	4	595,275
1957	403,286	139,183	82,915	4,675	569	12	630,640
1958	426,419	131,437	122,389	3,673	455	6	684,379
1959	345,028	129,026	86,560	2,695	906	22	564,237
1960	256,049	113,676	59,713	3,268	1,026		433,732
1961	281,980	139,719	17,111	3,456	896	12	443,174
1962	286,625	164,025	28,179	14,788	1,013	27	494,657
1963	278,560	129,418	60,319	12,658	739	34	481,728
1964	344,422	117,252	99,856	53,602	632	45	615,809
1965	317,957	166,453	55,125	76,032	496	64	616,127
1966	340,111	143,661	156,661	71,891	872	58	713,254
1967	366,237	121,872	144,158	96,488	352	50	729,157
1968	341,154	106,974	108,207	63,488	79	21	619,923
1969	507,543	140,782	59,636	49,378	143	86	757,568
1970	384,780	113,510	70,762	80,116	209	150	649,526
Total	11,592,395	4,635,935	3,254,497	685,759	37,972	668	20,207,225
33-Year Average	351,285	140,483	98,621	20,781	1,151	20	612,340

Source: U.S. Army Corps of Engineers.

9. CATCHES OF SALMON ON PUGET SOUND, 1913–1966, IN NUMBERS OF FISH, NET GEAR ONLY

Year	Chinook	Chum	Pink	Coho	Sockeye	Total
1913	290,044	604,857	15,907,710	1,225,115	21,598,964	39,626,690
1914	425,979	1,686,137	75,491	1,499,306	3,451,402	7,138,315
1915	301,174	1,884,144	7,368,713	1,108,896	804,385	11,467,312
1916	301,178	1,884,147	68,098	1,108,898	804,387	4,166,708
1917	419,072	1,094,465	13,343,892	878,162	4,960,987	20,696,578
1918	452,789	1,156,451	77,821	1,531,119	560,898	3,779,078
1919	328,421	1,475,044	4,667,522	1,363,153	745,698	8,579,838
1920	265,578	683,086	18,899	521,403	652,405	2,141,371
1921	265,366	267,992	4,401,087	735,559	1,135,473	6,805,477
1922	207,671	502,230	32,289	869,134	505,551	2,116,875
1923	224,299	637,866	5,533,262	853,137	482,387	7,730,951
1924	242,680	859,983	100,045	908,326	746,839	2,857,873
1925	283,370	534,812	6,665,247	848,036	1,241,858	9,573,323
1926	250,761	1,063,610	24,372	681,023	431,702	2,451,468
1927	285,892	526,868	6,524,566	1,005,325	987,648	9,330,299
1928	241,563	1,044,094	9,453	742,159	608,458	2,645,727
1929	310,276	1,486,410	7,430,802	787,640	1,247,690	11,262,818
1930	277,500	1,011,336	17,365	559,355	3,237,423	5,102,979
1931	206,742	682,482	8,130,875	506,212	723,225	10,249,536
1932	179,374	1,092,309	8,839	453,747	818,561	2,552,830
1933	210,534	504,139	6,039,735	531,056	1,575,236	8,860,236
1934	200,145	866,826	13,032	438,467	2,648,295	4,166,765
1935	91,700	818,730	5,810,779	1,014,344	615,551	8,351,104
1936	85,163	784,075	24,432	459,097	454,078	1,806,845
1937	103,238	774,345	5,069,137	608,663	898,311	7,453,694
1938	58,478	802,177	7,893	326,048	1,409,251	2,603,847
1939	63,388	331,366	4,058,885	563,145	557,019	5,573,803
1940	75,114	565,195	25,895	388,344	656,721	1,711,269
1941	83,715	672,733	2,016,469	602,495	1,560,467	4,935,879
1942	59,754	643,976	1,896	212,533	2,936,030	3,854,189
1943	69,547	396,240	970,459	493,406	244,320	2,173,972
1944	68,977	320,694	4,262	300,454	326,236	1,020,623
1945	90,360	421,096	5,891,223	500,482	190,169	7,093,330
1946	62,600	1,250,821	218	205,969	3,552,981	5,072,589
1947	42,505	595,408	9,362,248	561,986	90,112	10,652,259
1948	41,976	940,771	201	381,232	1,089,824	2,454,004
1949	52,815	439,980	7,586,986	607,420	1,065,771	9,752,972

(*contd.*)

Year	Chinook	Chum	Pink	Coho	Sockeye	Total
1950	47,553	886,591	9,856	673,409	1,221,691	2,839,100
1951	54,316	796,321	5,660,184	488,228	1,137,483	8,136,532
1952	60,704	772,973	1,714	777,071	1,114,649	2,727,111
1953	61,812	346,365	5,932,065	465,467	2,032,493	8,838,202
1954	58,892	422,783	223	227,010	4,804,061	5,512,969
1955	58,951	215,616	5,096,317	416,306	1,008,214	6,795,404
1956	50,359	105,905	699	570,472	907,417	1,634,852
1957	48,623	103,495	2,986,258	293,949	1,688,945	5,121,270
1958	50,446	421,393	2,907	352,175	5,254,738	6,081,659
1959	55,323	361,913	2,427,036	347,820	1,807,862	4,999,954
1960	64,719	135,017	305	103,787	1,190,726	1,494,554
1961	81,096	133,244	688,237	384,415	1,377,712	2,664,704
1962	48,207	173,681	121	414,208	754,488	1,390,705
1963	94,007	295,362	5,671,717	232,822	1,314,725	7,608,633
1964	75,448	247,345	490	401,991	508,914	1,234,188
1965	96,297	191,684	624,177	405,060	1,022,984	2,340,202
1966	102,827	402,012	809	633,825	1,338,518	2,477,991

Source: Washington Department of Fisheries.

10. PUGET SOUND SALMON PACK, 1940–1971,
NUMBER OF CANNERIES AND 48 1-LB. CASES

Year	Plants	Sockeye	Pink	Chum	Coho	Chinook	Total
1940	9	62,748	2,947	23,405	30,654	1,674	121,428
1941	9	110,758	153,924	25,423	46,213	4,769	341,087
1942	10	258,488	851	2,223	6,862	1,204	269,628
1943	10	19,149	62,129	243	26,292	2,864	110,677
1944	3	37,214	299	—	373	1,064	38,950
1945	6	53,532	305,245	1,184	18,802	3,639	382,402
1946	20	271,311	91	47,099	7,118	6,841	332,460
1947	25	7,516	639,426	139,131	79,450	29,143	894,666
1948	22	91,268	4,645	245,133	70,659	27,043	438,748
1949	23	94,627	557,740	162,532	55,910	8,594	879,403
1950	20	128,385	2,277	512,997	116,655	8,215	768,529
1951	25	156,461	441,605	233,468	88,511	11,275	931,320
1952	20	114,707	817	292,318	172,910	7,869	588,621
1953	22	164,848	440,860	144,542	54,901	3,974	809,125
1954	21	507,719	1,429	272,455	29,252	5,054	815,909
1955	23	81,913	411,280	88,672	63,526	10,177	655,568
1956	15	70,285	320	47,068	59,481	3,582	180,736
1957	20	189,406	228,930	88,623	87,339	6,497	600,795
1958	19	415,645	2,374	145,715	38,351	2,106	604,191
1959	23	134,739	184,448	156,074	76,377	10,221	561,859
1960	21	122,317	3,776	48,003	11,286	2,535	187,917
1961	22	140,478	95,242	87,032	58,515	4,633	385,900
1962	21	84,218	56,043	53,044	35,788	2,872	231,965
1963	24	119,045	385,562	25,903	17,921	5,439	553,870
1964	20	58,196	11,831	19,499	23,551	4,872	117,949
1965	12	107,420	65,004	19,718	32,293	8,814	233,249
1966	18	144,299	52,588	25,174	36,747	5,885	264,693
1967	17	175,616	280,832	18,453	23,656	2,752	501,309
1968	14	83,547	23,405	23,003	17,440	458	147,853
1969	12	108,581	68,642	889	24,310	6,946	209,826
1970	13	108,588	9,159	12,385	37,570	788	168,490
1971	18	245,844	146,930	16,564	41,538	4,692	455,550

Source: *National Fisherman Yearbooks.*

11. British Columbia Salmon Pack, 1940–1971, in 48 1-lb. Cases

Year	Sockeye Fraser River	Sockeye Other Districts	Total Sockeye	Chinook (Spring)	Coho & Blueback	Steelhead Trout	Pink	Chum	Total Cases
1940	86,215	280,188	366,403	17,741	224,524	1,205	213,911	643,443	1,467,227
1941	149,715	305,582	455,297	50,476	391,407	3,454	427,766	920,470	2,248,870
1942	418,491	248,080	666,571	24,745	211,139	4,649	270,622	633,834	1,811,560
1943	72,507	92,382	164,889	10,658	186,042	3,095	530,188	363,348	1,258,221
1944	107,431	140,283	247,714	19,362	183,546	3,926	389,692	255,316	1,097,557
1945	122,384	205,617	329,001	12,800	218,887	2,922	825,512	350,188	1,739,311
1946	381,580	161,447	543,027	8,100	100,154	4,115	116,607	576,133	1,348,138
1947	91,238	195,259	286,497	10,017	146,293	3,268	600,787	486,615	1,533,478
1948	83,986	176,656	260,642	16,438	207,116	5,665	321,721	496,553	1,308,137
1949	116,171	143,649	259,821	21,163	215,376	2,374	709,992	227,737	1,436,464
1950	239,333	168,708	408,041	9,133	116,642	3,243	446,516	498,984	1,482,560
1951	260,258	168,041	428,299	13,698	312,845	3,656	736,093	461,806	1,956,397
1952	213,408	235,766	449,174	9,064	64,095	3,752	675,836	91,514	1,293,435
1953	176,097	334,050	510,147	13,048	110,164	3,031	794,764	394,113	1,825,267
1954	486,805	193,913	680,718	14,080	128,080	3,734	335,550	580,574	1,742,736
1955	95,377	149,444	244,821	17,853	185,723	1,590	831,253	124,860	1,406,100

Year	Sockeye Fraser River	Sockeye Other Districts	Total Sockeye	Chinook (Spring)	Coho & Blueback	Steelhead Trout	Pink	Chum	Total Cases
1956	84,296	320,096	404,392	11,671	217,915	1,254	363,633	203,710	1,202,575
1957	101,716	126,736	228,452	10,481	217,915	1,125	751,608	239,539	1,449,120
1958	420,000	659,155	1,079,155	10,475	132,403	1,213	455,518	229,292	1,908,056
1959	123,248	132,922	256,170	15,231	213,106	866	458,596	133,128	1,077,097
1960	97,000	129,844	226,844	5,916	91,504	504	219,564	86,818	631,150
1961	116,231	281,974	398,205	7,921	241,378	978	666,290	95,385	1,410,157
1962	78,047	219,669	297,716	7,174	187,735	815	1,188,661	134,483	1,816,584
1963	32,418	125,957	158,375	10,000	146,099	771	757,452	119,190	1,191,887
1964	44,000	299,358	343,358	9,127	204,732	1,262	464,107	232,722	1,255,308
1965	89,738	156,060	245,798	18,891	295,284	843	287,925	65,216	913,957
1966	133,653	274,296	407,949	14,585	281,623	2,480	951,794	160,784	1,819,215
1967	157,590	401,302	558,892	14,679	146,677	1,296	650,142	94,022	1,465,708
1968	77,090	533,921	611,011	7,416	187,594	933	669,347	270,688	1,746,989
1969	141,623	217,985	359,608	5,301	57,947	585	154,188	46,524	624,153
1970	146,033	249,573	395,606	10,024	114,555	531	660,389	242,389	1,423,882
1971	285,000	283,638	568,638	11,800	220,953	1,288	504,280	98,193	1,405,152

Source: *National Fisherman Yearbooks.*

Appendix Tables

	12. ALASKA COMMERCIAL SALMON CATCHES, 1906–1970, IN MILLIONS OF FISH					
Year	Total	Sockeye	Pink	Chum	Coho	Chinook (King)
1906	31.9	19.6	7.7	3.3	1.0	0.3
1907	34.9	19.2	12.7	1.8	0.9	0.3
1908	43.3	25.0	15.1	2.2	0.7	0.3
1909	34.4	23.0	9.5	1.2	0.6	0.4
1910	34.7	23.0	9.5	1.2	0.6	0.4
1911	33.6	19.2	10.7	2.3	1.0	0.4
1912	61.0	28.6	24.0	6.4	1.5	0.5
1913	59.9	28.6	27.0	3.0	0.8	0.5
1914	54.7	29.8	16.7	6.3	1.3	0.6
1915	63.5	25.9	30.9	4.8	1.3	0.6
1916	72.0	29.7	31.8	7.4	2.4	0.7
1917	92.6	36.5	44.9	8.5	2.1	0.6
1918	101.5	35.3	48.3	14.2	2.9	0.8
1919	58.2	16.7	25.9	12.2	2.4	1.0
1920	65.1	20.2	32.1	10.1	1.9	0.8
1921	37.9	26.1	7.1	2.6	1.3	0.8
1922	72.4	33.9	30.6	5.3	1.8	0.8
1923	77.4	26.9	42.3	5.7	1.8	0.7
1924	79.5	19.0	49.1	8.7	1.9	0.8
1925	64.2	15.2	34.7	11.5	2.0	0.8
1926	96.9	30.4	53.0	10.8	2.1	0.6
1927	48.2	17.6	21.2	5.7	2.7	1.0
1928	89.4	27.5	47.5	10.1	3.7	0.6
1929	72.0	19.2	40.4	9.4	2.2	0.8
1930	82.9	11.0	60.4	6.6	4.0	0.9
1931	73.8	23.1	41.4	6.6	2.0	0.7
1932	75.7	26.9	36.2	9.6	2.1	0.9
1933	81.9	31.6	39.8	7.9	2.0	0.6
1934	116.6	32.2	73.0	8.1	2.7	0.6
1935	73.3	10.5	50.2	9.4	2.3	0.9
1936	129.4	35.6	78.0	12.1	2.8	0.9
1937	109.3	31.0	66.2	9.0	2.0	1.1
1938	103.0	35.3	55.2	8.5	3.1	0.9
1939	79.3	24.6	44.7	7.6	1.6	0.8

(*contd.*)

Year	Total	Sockeye	Pink	Chum	Coho	Chinook (King)
1940	85.9	11.9	60.2	10.1	3.1	0.6
1941	108.4	15.4	80.3	7.6	4.0	1.1
1942	83.2	12.9	55.5	10.0	4.0	0.8
1943	85.8	26.3	46.7	9.7	2.5	0.6
1944	72.5	20.2	38.9	10.5	2.4	0.5
1945	78.0	15.1	50.5	8.2	3.6	0.6
1946	75.5	14.5	48.9	7.5	3.8	0.8
1947	70.2	25.9	34.9	6.3	2.4	0.7
1948	60.1	19.7	28.4	8.3	3.0	0.7
1949	78.7	11.8	57.2	5.8	3.1	0.8
1950	46.0	13.8	21.4	7.7	2.5	0.6
1951	49.5	9.7	28.4	6.6	4.0	0.8
1952	48.1	16.9	19.9	8.2	2.4	0.7
1953	37.0	11.8	15.7	7.2	1.6	0.7
1954	43.1	9.4	22.2	8.4	2.5	0.6
1955	38.5	8.5	24.1	3.5	1.8	0.6
1956	49.3	14.6	25.5	7.2	1.5	0.5
1957	33.6	9.7	13.5	8.3	1.6	0.5
1958	40.9	6.1	26.1	6.6	1.6	0.6
1959	25.0	8.0	10.9	4.0	1.5	0.6
1960	42.4	17.8	16.1	6.6	1.4	0.5
1961	45.0	16.1	21.5	5.6	1.3	0.5
1962	63.9	9.3	43.9	7.1	3.6	—
1963	47.4	6.2	34.3	4.4	2.0	0.5
1964	66.1	10.0	45.3	7.3	2.6	0.9
1965	56.3	30.0	20.3	3.4	2.0	0.6
1966	64.0	15.1	40.0	6.5	1.9	0.5
1967	21.0	8.6	6.6	3.7	1.5	0.6
1968	62.4	8.2	44.7	6.1	2.8	0.6
1969	42.5	11.9	25.7	3.2	1.0	0.7
1970	66.1	27.5	30.2	6.6	1.2	0.6

Sources: U.S. Fish and Wildlife Service and Alaska Department of Fish and Game.

13. PACK OF ALASKA CANNED SALMON BY SPECIES, 1940–1971, IN 48 1-LB. CASES					
Year	Sockeye	Pink	Chum	Coho	Chinook (King)	Total
1940	953,381	2,908,025	860,539	284,130	22,303	5,028,378
1941	1,164,888	4,636,649	710,507	356,213	38,246	6,906,503
1942	912,006	2,818,650	942,789	372,537	43,137	5,089,109
1943	1,982,175	2,322,057	882,578	158,734	50,965	5,396,509
1944	1,580,757	2,087,322	985,725	187,053	36,939	4,877,796
1945	1,173,356	2,239,282	688,485	195,860	41,709	4,338,692
1946	1,065,898	3,057,121	617,155	193,061	37,874	3,971,109
1947	1,876,239	1,723,617	500,211	148,715	53,684	4,302,466
1948	1,635,463	1,304,044	774,661	241,799	54,645	4,010,612
1949	967,636	2,682,330	499,226	192,352	50,007	4,391,541
1950	1,166,052	1,095,534	780,684	191,501	54,321	3,288,092
1951	816,831	1,559,748	721,152	345,159	91,425	3,534,315
1952	1,181,162	1,172,168	966,660	197,004	56,970	3,573,964
1953	994,293	955,528	800,882	127,676	56,222	2,934,601
1954	804,194	1,149,422	1,029,295	171,643	52,600	3,207,154
1955	661,607	1,270,303	363,657	114,584	47,818	2,457,969
1956	1,015,558	1,116,769	675,034	95,940	47,053	2,950,354
1957	763,030	713,774	829,816	87,290	47,984	2,441,894
1958	488,354	1,547,651	754,806	101,991	51,778	2,944,580
1959	584,503	634,945	415,326	98,298	45,267	1,778,339
1960	1,166,000	731,000	626,971	77,978	46,870	2,648,819
1961	1,295,545	1,265,481	515,404	81,848	53,684	3,211,962
1962	754,586	1,893,285	702,307	112,354	48,580	3,511,112
1963	479,441	1,570,291	432,695	130,286	37,486	2,650,199
1964	716,481	1,927,783	688,591	164,831	37,684	3,535,370
1965	1,942,751	932,366	289,181	96,997	48,769	3,310,064
1966	1,234,131	2,008,802	583,449	115,728	34,847	3,976,957
1967	684,341	328,817	343,715	66,667	45,261	1,468,801
1968	627,138	1,746,832	640,910	122,950	42,813	3,180,643
1969	787,378	1,223,424	181,888	24,340	34,992	2,252,022
1970	1,794,402	1,326,334	471,763	56,186	27,019	3,675,704
1971	1,096,438	1,017,653	557,357	76,174	31,535	2,779,157

Source: *National Fisherman Yearbooks.*

	Pink	Chum	Sockeye	Coho	Total

14. SALMON CATCHES (BY JAPANESE AND RUSSIANS) FROM COASTAL AREAS OF THE SOVIET FAR EAST, 1909–1944, IN MILLIONS OF FISH

	Pink	Chum	Sockeye	Coho	Total
1909	13.8	25.7	—	—	39.5
1910	14.8	41.7	1.7	—	58.1
1911	47.2	30.8	3.2	0.7	81.9
1912	26.6	24.3	2.4	0.4	53.8
1913	39.0	31.7	2.4	0.3	73.4
1914	73.9	20.0	1.6	0.4	95.8
1915	46.0	13.8	2.9	0.3	63.1
1916	84.5	8.0	6.2	0.6	99.3
1917	92.5	14.1	3.6	0.6	110.8
1918	75.4	15.7	4.1	0.7	95.9
1919	57.5	15.4	6.9	1.6	81.4
1920	82.6	16.2	7.2	1.5	107.6
1921	62.7	10.8	3.0	0.6	77.1
1922	93.9	15.3	6.0	0.9	116.6
1923			NA		
1924			NA		
1925	NA	12.0	6.2	1.4	NA
1926	125.8	14.7	8.8	1.1	150.0
1927	35.0	15.4	9.3	1.4	61.1
1928	112.8	25.2	15.4	1.3	155.6
1929	14.9	28.8	11.2	1.1	56.0
1930	100.1	29.4	12.4	2.7	144.8
1931	36.9	32.8	9.7	1.0	80.4
1932	114.8	27.2	9.0	0.6	151.8
1933	40.5	22.3	5.9	0.5	69.2
1934	137.7	34.8	12.5	0.9	186.0
1935	90.7	28.6	4.8	1.1	125.2
1936	73.0	42.0	7.9	3.2	126.2
1937	97.1	26.2	9.3	2.1	134.7
1938	101.3	30.2	11.3	1.7	144.5
1939	129.3	27.1	8.4	1.2	166.0
1940	118.0	26.6	5.0	1.3	151.0

(*contd.*)

1941	131.1	26.2	5.6	0.9	163.9
1942	89.1	16.0	5.7	2.0	112.9
1943	79.1	22.2	5.3	0.8	107.5
1944	115.6	17.8	4.9	1.0	139.3

Source: International North Pacific Fisheries Commission and Clinton E. Atkinson.

15. JAPANESE COMMERCIAL SALMON CATCHES IN DOMESTIC AND INTERNATIONAL WATERS, BY SPECIES, 1957–1969, IN METRIC TONS

Year	Sockeye	Chum	Pink	Coho	Chinook	Total
1957	43,329	40,400	95,435	2,173	202	181,539
1958	25,609	68,113	91,376	11,166	366	196,630
1959	19,738	51,598	101,038	6,157	530	179,061
1960	30,575	48,592	60,586	5,977	1,117	146,847
1961	36,738	38,991	73,525	4,286	506	154,045
1962	24,836	41,993	36,597	8,368	1,083	112,878
1963	19,105	44,099	71,439	9,493	877	145,013
1964	14,306	50,558	35,475	12,517	2,072	114,928
1965	25,016	45,739	62,991	7,196	1,059	142,001
1966	16,599	57,527	43,177	4,683	1,336	123,322
1967	20,493	51,630	64,481	3,851	1,053	141,508
1968	16,766	42,519	42,787	5,551	1,488	109,111
1969	15,502	30,171	69,520	9,558	1,569	126,320

Source: Japan Fishery Agency.

Year	Sockeye	Pink	Chum	Coho	Chinook	Total

16. SALMON CATCHES BY JAPANESE MOTHER-SHIP FISHERY IN THE PACIFIC OCEAN, 1952–1968, IN THOUSANDS OF FISH

Year	Sockeye	Pink	Chum	Coho	Chinook	Total
1952	738	698	629	24	1	2,091
1953	1,534	2,892	2,678	307	3	7,414
1954	3,382	2,698	8,254	675	57	15,071
1955	9,456	9,108	14,012	1,467	43	34,164
1956	8,702	6,589	15,316	3,393	117	34,170
1957	19,403	17,204	8,877	193	25	46,042
1958	10,708	7,859	14,048	3,106	38	35,832
1959	9,125	18,642	12,856	1,388	63	42,326
1960	12,879	1,826	10,517	862	180	26,324
1961	12,998	3,226	6,128	281	31	22,704
1962	10,590	1,011	6,372	1,531	122	19,755
1963	8,902	6,242	5,858	1,890	88	23,475
1964	7,097	2,198	8,640	3,533	410	21,964
1965	12,038	4,238	6,037	1,173	185	23,864
1966	7,254	2,457	8,562	466	208	19,046
1967	8,087	7,698	6,848	225	127	23,060
1968	6,373	3,609	8,107	805	362	19,563

Source: International North Pacific Fisheries Commission.

Notes

CHAPTER I (*pages 3–10*)
Evolution and Distribution of the Salmon

1. J. M. Macfarlane, *The Evolution and Distribution of Fishes*, p. 358.
2. G. V. Nikolsky, *The Ecology of Fishes*, p. 236.
3. "Origin and Speciation of *Oncorhynchus*," *Trans. Royal Society Canada*, Vol. 52, Series 3, June 1958. Dr. Neave points out that "Oncorhynchus has never reached the Atlantic (under its own steam), for the changing climates of the Pleistocene did not produce a favorable combination of circumstances (such as the absence of a Bering land bridge plus a mild climate)."
4. Sven Ekman, *Zoogeography of the Sea*, p. 162.
5. Personal communication.
6. Edouard Le Danois, *Fishes of the World*, p. 32.

CHAPTER II (*pages 11–32*)
Life History and Migrations

1. R. E. Foerster, *The Sockeye Salmon*, p. 67.
2. Lynwood S. Smith, "The Pacific Salmon's Long Voyage," University of Washington, School of Fisheries publication.
3. R. E. Foerster, personal communication.
4. Roderick Haig-Brown, *Fisherman's Fall*, p. 77.
5. Ferris Neave, "A Review of the Life History of the North Pacific Salmon," p. 72, Bulletin 18, International North Pacific Fisheries Commission.
6. Smith, "The Pacific Salmon's Long Voyage."
7. This account of the oceanic migrations of Pacific salmon is based chiefly on William F. Royce, Lynwood S. Smith, and Alan C. Hartt, *Models of Oceanic Migrations of Pacific Salmon and Comments on Guidance Mechanisms*.
8. A. C. Hartt, in Bulletin 19, International North Pacific Fisheries Commission.
9. See Trey Combs, *The Steelhead Trout*, pp. 33–38.

10. Ferris Neave, "Ocean Migrations of Pink Salmon," 1964.
11. Royce, et al., *Models of Oceanic Migrations.*
12. T. A. Stuart, *The Leaping Behavior of Salmon and Trout at Falls and Obstructions.*
13. Charles H. Gilbert, "The Salmon of the Yukon River," 1920, pp. 319–26.
14. *Pacific Salmon*, Circular 24, Fish and Wildlife Service, 1953, p. 5.
15. This account of the spawning process is based on Leonard P. Schultz, "The Breeding Habits of Salmon and Trout," and Brian Curtis, *The Life Story of the Fish.*
16. J. A. Hutton, *Wye Salmon and Other Fish*, p. 142.
17. J. W. Jones, *Atlantic Salmon*, p. 22.

CHAPTER III (*pages 35–43*)
Primitive Man and the Atlantic Salmon

1. Gavin de Beer, *A Handbook on Evolution*, p. 90.
2. For an interesting account of the evolution of primitive fishing devices, see A. Thomazi, *Histoire de la Pêche: Des Âges de la Pierre à Nos Jours.*
3. Grahame Clark, *World Prehistory: An Outline*, p. 70.
4. I. W. Cornwall, *Prehistoric Animals and Their Hunters*, p. 110.
5. Cornwall, p. 109.
6. Henri Breuil and Raymond Lantier, *The Men of the Old Stone Age*, p. 117.
7. Cornwall, p. 108.
8. *The Sunday Times* (London), February 2, 1969.
9. A. and G. Sieveking, *The Caves of France and Northern Spain*, p. 42.

CHAPTER IV (*pages 45–90*)
Salmon in Great Britain

1. E. W. Hunter-Christie, "The Trent," in *Portraits of Rivers*, ed. Eileen Molony, p. 28.
2. Brian Waters, *Portraits of Rivers*, pp. 92–93.
3. Roderick Haig-Brown, *A River Never Sleeps*, p. 100.
4. Fraser Darling and J. Morton Boyd, *The Highlands and Islands of Scotland*, p. 266.
5. James R. Coull, "Salmon Fishing in the North-East of Scotland Before 1800," *Aberdeen University Review*, Vol. XLII, No. 137, Spring 1967; reprinted in the *Salmon Net*, 1969, published by the Salmon Net Fishing Association of Scotland.
6. Charles L. Cutting, *Fish Saving*, p. 83.
7. Daniel Defoe, *A Tour Thro' the Whole Island of Great Britain*, Vol. II, p. 797.
8. Defoe, *Tour*, Vol. I, p. 258.
9. M. Dorothy George, *London Life in the 18th Century*, p. 162.
10. Peter Lord, *The River Trent*, p. 43.

11. James Ritchie, *The Influence of Man on Animal Life in Scotland*, p. 386.
12. Thomas Tod Stoddard, *Art of Angling*, p. 96.
13. George Bompas, *Life of Frank Buckland*, p. 245.
14. G. H. O. Burgess, *The Eccentric Ark*, p. 151.
15. *Eighth Report of the Inspectors of Salmon Fisheries*, pp. 69–71.
16. This account of the Thames salmon is mainly adapted from A. Court-ney Williams, *Angling Diversions* (London, Herbert Jenkins, n.d.).
17. H. A. Herbert, *Tale of a Wye Fisherman*, p. 84.
18. Alex Russel, *The Salmon*, p. 99.
19. Archibald Young, *Salmon Fisheries*, p. 232.
20. Sir Edward Grey, *Flyfishing*, p. 184.
21. *Salmon and Freshwater Fisheries in Scotland*, November, 1971, Edin-burgh, H.M.S.O.

CHAPTER V *(pages 91–109)*
Salmon in Ireland

1. Alfred S. Moore, *The Irish Salmon Industry*, unpublished.
2. Grenville A. J. Cole, *Ireland: The Land and Its Landscape*, Dublin, 1914, p. 50.
3. A. E. J. Went, "A Short History of the Fisheries of the River Nore," *Journal of Royal Society of Antiquarians of Ireland*, Vol. LXXXV, 1955.
4. Quoted by Went, "The Fisheries of the River Lee," *Journal of the Cork Historical and Archaeological Society*, Vol. LXV, 1960.
5. Helen Landseth, *Dear Dark Head*, p. 101.
6. Fynes Moryson, *Itinerary*, p. 231.
7. Cecil Woodham-Smith, *The Great Hunger*, p. 76
8. A. E. J. Went, *The Pursuit of Salmon in Ireland*, p. 202.
9. Went, p. 214.
10. Augustus Grimble, *The Salmon Rivers of Ireland*, p. 66.
11. Grimble, pp. 200–201.
12. Personal communication from J. F. Williams, Fisheries Manager, Elec-tricity Supply Board, May 26, 1970.
13. *Irish Fishery Investigations*, Series A, No. 7, 1971, p. 6.
14. John Reader, *Ireland of the Welcomes*, Vol. 16, No. 6.
15. Peter Liddell, *The Salmon Rivers of Eire*, paragraph 179.
16. Personal communication, June 1971.

CHAPTER VI *(pages 111–132)*
Iberian and French Salmon

1. Personal communication, February 18, 1966.
2. Marzales, in *El Salmon y Su Pesca en España.*
3. Personal communication, January 22, 1968.
4. Personal communication, December 22, 1969.
5. Personal communication, April 11, 1971.

6. L. de Boisset, preface to *Le Saumon: Poisson Royal,* by Louis Carrère, p. 12.
7. R. Bachelier, "L'Histoire du Saumon en Loire," p. 3.
8. Louis Roule, *Étude sur le Saumon des Eaux Douces en France,* 1920.
9. Henri Boyer, *Le Saumon dans le Haut-Allier,* p. 26.
10. Boyer, p. 26.
11. Yves Gestin, *Histoire du Chateaulin,* p. 87.
12. R. Vibert and L. de Boisset, *La Pêche Fluviale en France,* pp. 12–14.
13. International Atlantic Salmon Foundation, *Newsletter,* December 1971.
14. Personal communication, Summer 1971.

CHAPTER VII (*pages 133–139*)
Demise of the Meuse and Rhine Rivers

1. *Standard Encyclopedia of Rivers and Lakes,* ed. R. Kay Greswell and Anthony Huxley, p. 165.
2. A. E. Gathorne-Hardy, *The Salmon.*
3. *Reports of the Inspector of Salmon Fisheries for England and Wales for 1886,* p. 32.
4. *Reports,* p. 32.
5. Personal communication from Roger Bachelier.

CHAPTER VIII (*pages 141–153*)
Norwegian Successes and Setbacks

1. Magnus Berg, *Salmon and Salmon Fishing,* p. 24.
2. W. J. M. Menzies, *The Stock of Salmon,* p. 66.
3. Anders Hagen, *Norway,* p. 75.
4. Magnus Berg, "The Norwegian Salmon Fishery," *Atlantic Salmon Journal,* No. 4, 1970.
5. Berg, "The Norwegian Salmon Fishery."
6. Fraser Sandeman, *Angling Travels in Norway,* p. 174.
7. John Dean Caton, *A Summer in Norway,* p. 28.
8. *Salmon and Sea Trout Fisheries,* Oslo Central Bureau of Statistics, 1971.
9. Personal communication.
10. Berg, "The Norwegian Salmon Fishery."

CHAPTER IX (*pages 155–168*)
Baltic and Arctic Salmon

1. Borje Carlin, *Lectures Delivered for the Atlantic Salmon Association,* p. 14.
2. Carlin, *Lectures.*
3. Carlin, *Lectures.*
4. Dr. Arne Lindroth points out that we can not compare yearly hauls without considering the long-term fluctuations in the stock due to unknown but natural causes (personal communication, December 22, 1970).

5. Andrew C. O'Dell, *The Scandinavian World*, p. 74.
6. T. H. Jarvi, "On the Productivity of Salmon Reproduction in the Northern Baltic Area," ICES, 1948.
7. Seppo Hurme, "Kaakaman Lohipadon Saalisvaihtelut," 1966.
8. Seppo Hurme, "Lounais-Suomen Lohija Taimenjoet," p. 16.
9. Demel Kazimierz and Stanislaw Rutkowicz, *The Barents Sea*, pp. 196–98.
10. Nikolai T. Kozhun, "Atlantic Salmon in the U.S.S.R.," *Atlantic Salmon Journal*, June 1964.
11. Arne Lindroth, "The Baltic Salmon," p. 396.
12. Personal communication, September 10, 1972.

CHAPTER X *(pages 169–189)*
The American Experience

1. James A. Tuck, "An Archaic Indian Cemetery In Newfoundland," *Scientific American*, June 1970.
2. Ernest Poole, *The Great White Hills of New Hampshire*, p. 360.
3. Charles E. Goodspeed, *Angling in North America*, p. 65.
4. Quoted by George B. Goode, *Food and Game Fishes of North America*, p. 443.
5. Henry B. Bigelow and William C. Shroeder, *Fishes of the Gulf of Maine*, p. 125.
6. Henry David Thoreau, *A Week on the Concord and Merrimack Rivers*, pp. 39–40.
7. Timothy Dwight, *Travels in New England and New York*, Vol. II, p. 307.
8. Philip K. Crowe, *Out of the Mainstream: Fishing Reminiscences Around the World*, pp. 167–68.
9. C. G. Atkins, "Local History of Salmon and Salmon Fishing in New England Rivers," p. 290.
10. Atkins, in George B. Goode, *The Fisheries and Fishery Industries of the United States*, p. 727.
11. Goode, *Fisheries*, p. 727.
12. Thoreau, *The Maine Woods*, pp. 3–4.
13. Richard E. Cutting and W. H. Everhart, *The Penobscot River*, p. 16.
14. Goode, *Fisheries*, p. 718.
15. Henry P. Wells, *The American Salmon Fisherman*, p. 10.
16. American Fisheries Society Newsletter, January–February 1972.
17. M. C. Edmunds, "Obstructions to the Ascent of Fish in the Tributaries of Lake Champlain," pp. 624–25.
18. Richard E. Cutting and W. H. Everhart, *The Penobscot River*, p. 21.
19. *Hearings before the Committee on Energy, Natural Resources and the Environment*, 91st Congress, 1st and 2nd Sessions, 1970, p. 250.
20. International Atlantic Salmon Foundation Newsletter, December 1972.
21. Personal communication from Richard E. Griffith, Regional Director of the Bureau of Sport Fisheries and Wildlife in Boston, January 1972.
22. Personal communication, Griffith.

CHAPTER XI (*pages 191–211*)
The Canadian Experience

1. Wilfred Carter, "The Straight Edge of the Curve," paper presented at International Salmon Conference, London, April 15, 1969.
2. Genio Scott, *Fishing in American Waters,* p. 216.
3. Richard Nettle, *The Salmon Fisheries of the St. Lawrence,* p. 26.
4. Nettle, p. 27.
5. Nettle, p. 31.
6. Nettle, p. 70.
7. Nettle, p. 85.
8. Nettle, p. 89.
9. Nettle, pp. 116–17.
10. Address to the International Salmon Conference, London, April 15, 1969.
11. Henry P. Wells, *The American Salmon Fisherman,* p. 19.
12. N. E. J. MacEachern and J. R. MacDonald, "The Salmon Fishery in Nova Scotia," *Canadian Fish Culturist,* Oct. 1962.
13. Scott, pp. 399–400.
14. Thad. Norris, *The American Angler's Guide,* pp. 399–400.
15. Norris, pp. 399–400.
16. Edward Weeks, *The Moisie Salmon Club,* p. 3.
17. W. J. M. Menzies, *A Report on the Present Position of the Atlantic Salmon Fisheries of Canada,* p. 13.
18. International Atlantic Salmon Foundation Newsletter, May 1972.

CHAPTER XII (*pages 213–221*)
The Greenland Fishery — Final Catastrophe?

1. Report from the American Embassy, Copenhagen, December 18, 1969.
2. International Council for the Exploration of the Sea, *Cooperative Research Report,* Series A, Nos. 8 and 24.
3. Wilfred Carter, "The Greenland and the Highseas Atlantic Salmon Fishery," International Atlantic Salmon Foundation, April 1970.
4. Quoted by Francis T. Christy, Jr., and Anthony Scott, *The Common Wealth in Ocean Fisheries,* p. 155.
5. Personal communication, July 7, 1972.

CHAPTER XIII (*pages 225–234*)
Discovery of the Pacific Salmon

1. Peter Lauridsen, *Vitus Bering,* p. 136.
2. F. A. Golder, *Bering's Voyages,* Vol. II, p. 5.
3. Quoted by Leo S. Berg, *Freshwater Fishes of the USSR and Adjacent Countries,* pp. 194–95.
4. Golder, II, p. 48.

5. Sven Waxell, *The American Expedition*, p. 72.
6. Waxell, pp. 213–14.
7. Stepan P. Krashnennikov, *The Natural History of Kamchatka*, pp. 144–46.
8. Krashnennikov, p. 146.
9. Krashnennikov, p. 147.
10. Alan Villiers, *Captain James Cook*, p. 248.
11. *The Journals of Captain Cook*, Part I, p. 374.
12. *The Journals*, I, p. 439.
13. Villiers, p. 251.
14. *The Journals*, I, p. 674.

CHAPTER XIV (*pages 235–262*)
The Destruction of California and Its Salmon

1. Carl Meyer, "The Yurok of Trinidad Bay," in *The California Indians*, p. 263.
2. John E. Skinner, *A Historical Review of the Fish and Wildlife Resources of the San Francisco Bay Area*, p. 27.
3. A. L. Kroeber, "Yurok National Character," in *The California Indians*, p. 387.
4. E. H. Erikson, "Observations on the Yurok: Childhood and World Image," *California University Publications in American Archeology and Ethnology*, Vol. 35, p. 257.
5. Adapted from *Yurok Narratives*, by Robert Spott and A. L. Kroeber, *California University Publications in American Archeology and Ethnology*, Vol. 35, pp. 171–199.
6. T. T. Waterman and A. L. Kroeber, "The Kepel Fish Dam," *California University Publications in American Archeology and Ethnology*, Vol. 35, p. 50.
7. Skinner, p. 59.
8. Joel W. Hedgpeth, "California's Forgotten Fish," *Outdoor America*, January 1942.
9. Joel W. Hedgpeth, "The Passing of the Salmon," *Scientific Monthly*, Vol. 59 (1944).
10. See Richard J. Hallock, Robert F. Elwell, and Donald H. Fry, Jr., *Migrations of Adult King Salmon in the San Joaquin Delta*.
11. Raymond F. Dasmann, *The Destruction of California*, p. 146.
12. For a penetrating critique of the Bureau of Reclamation, see *Damming the West*, by Richard L. Berkman and Kip Vicusi (New York, Grossman Publishers, 1971).
13. *An Environmental Tragedy*, Report to the Department of Fish and Game, Sacramento, March 15, 1971.
14. *Wild Rivers Reporter*, issued by the Committee of Two Million, Spring 1972.
15. *National Fisherman Yearbook*, 1971, p. 85.

CHAPTER XV (*pages 263–291*)
The Dammed Columbia and Unlucky Salmon — Part 1

1. Personal communication from Ivan Donaldson, December 12, 1970.
2. Quoted in Olin D. Wheeler, *The Trail of Lewis and Clark*, Vol. 2.
3. L. S. Cressman, *The Sandal and the Cave*, p. 21.
4. Quoted in Wheeler, Vol. 2, p. 139.
5. Wheeler, Vol. 2.
6. Craig and Hacker have a detailed account of the Indian fishery in their *History and Development of the Fisheries of the Columbia River*.
7. Adapted from Ella E. Clark, *Indian Legends of the Pacific Northwest*, pp. 95–98.
8. Philip Drucker, *Indians of the Northwest Coast*, pp. 154–55.
9. Personal communication, July 10, 1970.
10. Martha Ferguson McKeown, *The Trail Led North: Mont Hawthorne's Story*, pp. 1–11.
11. Personal communication from Francis Seufert.
12. *First and Second Annual Reports of the Game and Fish Protector*, 1894, p. 7.
13. Willis H. Rich, *The Salmon Runs of the Columbia River in 1938*, p. 40.
14. Corps of Engineers, *Columbia River and Tributaries* (House Doc. 531, 81st Cong., 2nd session), Vol. VII, p. 2863.
15. This statement obviously cannot be documented but from conversations with many people who followed those events carefully, I am convinced it is true.
16. Personal communication, December 1, 1970.

CHAPTER XVI (*pages 292–310*)
The Dammed Columbia and Unlucky Salmon — Part 2

1. *Hearings Before the Subcommittee of the Committee on Appropriations*, House of Representatives, 82nd Congress, 2nd sess., Part 2, p. 879.
2. C. H. Clay, *Design of Fishways and Other Fish Facilities*, p. 57.
3. William E. Pitney, *Oregon Game Commission Bulletin*, September 1970.
4. Howard L. Raymond, "Migration Rates of Yearling Chinook Salmon in Relation to Flows and Impoundments in the Columbia and Snake Rivers," Washington Dept. of Fisheries, 1968.
5. Donald L. Park, "Seasonal Changes in Downstream Migration of Age-Group O Chinook Salmon in the Upper Columbia River," 1969.
6. Press release, U.S. Environmental Protection Agency, July 18, 1972.
7. Federal Power Commission, *Initial and Reply Brief of Commission Staff Counsel*, Snake River dams, Washington, D.C., October 22, 1970.
8. Quoted in a letter from the Regional Solicitor, Department of the Interior, to Frank H. Bellman, October 12, 1970, Departmental files.
9. Memorandum by George W. Snyder, Biological Laboratory, National Marine Fisheries Service, Seattle, 1970.
10. *Columbia River Gillnetter*, October 1971.

CHAPTER XVII (*pages 311–322*)
Death and Revival of the Willamette River

1. William D. Welsh, *A Brief History of Oregon City and West Linn* (Crown-Zellerbach Co., West Linn, n.d.), p. 7.
2. G. S. Holland, J. E. Lasater, E. D. Neumann, and W. E. Eldridge, *Toxic Effects of Organic and Inorganic Pollutants on Young Salmon and Trout*, p. 10.
3. Holland et al., p. 253.
4. Federal Water Pollution Control Administration, "Summary of Water Quality Control and Management: Willamette River Basin," p. 3.
5. FWPCA, "Pollution Control," p. 6.
6. FWPCA, "Willamette River: An Example of a River Being Cleaned Up," Portland, September 1970.
7. Oregon Fish Commission press release, September 20, 1972.

CHAPTER XVIII (*pages 323–333*)
Oregon's Coastal Streams

1. *Oregon Guide*, pp. 33–34.
2. R. D. Hume, *Salmon of the Pacific Coast*, p. 23.
3. *First and Second Annual Reports of the Game and Fish Protector*, p. 11.
4. John T. Gharrett and John I. Hodges, *Salmon Fisheries of the Coastal Rivers of Oregon South of the Columbia*, p. 16.
5. Oregon Fish Commission, "Spawning Fish Surveys in Coastal Watersheds, 1969," June 1970.
6. *Oregon Game Commission Bulletin*, August 1970.

CHAPTER XIX (*pages 334–346*)
Breakthrough in Salmon Culture

1. Joel Hedgpeth, "The Passing of the Salmon," *Scientific Monthly*, Vol. 59, p. 373.
2. Personal communication.
3. Oregon Fish Commission report, unpublished, 1968.
4. Roger E. Burrows and Bobby D. Combs, "Controlled Environments for Salmon Propagation," p. 123.
5. L. E. Perry, Address to the Pacific Marine Fisheries Commission, November 21, 1968.
6. W. P. Wickett, "Production of Chum and Pink Salmon in a Controlled Stream," Fisheries Research Board of Canada, Progress Reports, Pacific Coast Station, 1952.
7. International Pacific Salmon Fisheries Commission, *Report for 1969*, p. 4.
8. Washington Department of Fisheries, *Report for 1969*, pp. 83–84.
9. Personal communication, December 20, 1971.

CHAPTER XX (*pages 347–365*)

The Puget Sound Fishery

1. Edmond L. Meany, *Vancouver's Discovery of Puget Sound*, p. 62.
2. J. A. Crutchfield and Giulio Pontecorvo, *The Pacific Salmon Fisheries*, p. 130.
3. *The Pacific Tourist*, ed. F. E. Shearer, 1970 reprint, p. 326.
4. Ralph W. Hidy, Frank Ernest Hill, and Allan Nevins, *Timber and Men*, p. 212.
5. Henry O. Wendler and Gene Deschamps, "Logging Dams on Coastal Washington Streams."
6. *Pollutional Effects of Pulp and Paper Mill Wastes in Puget Sound*, Federal Water Pollution Control Administration, Portland, Oregon, March 1967, p. 92.
7. FWPCA, p. 421.
8. Quoted in Portland *Oregonian*, February 16, 1970.
9. Portland *Oregonian*.
10. Crutchfield and Pontecorvo, pp. 152–53.
11. "Recreational Use of Surplus Hatchery Coho Salmon," *Transactions American Fisheries Society*, 1969, No. 3.
12. Earl Clark, "A New Salmon Run in the Northwest," *Pacific Discovery*, March–April 1970.

CHAPTER XXI (*pages 367–390*)

Vicissitudes of the British Columbia Fisheries

1. *Western Fisheries*, May 1972.
2. Hugh McKervill, *The Salmon People*, p. 26.
3. Roderick Haig-Brown, *The Living Land*, p. 145.
4. Quoted by Cecily Lyons, *Salmon: Our Heritage*, pp. 674–76.
5. A. V. Hill, *Tides of Change*, p. 146.
6. W. F. Thompson, "Effect of the Obstruction at Hell's Gate on the Sockeye Salmon of the Fraser River," p. 169.
7. John N. Cobb, *Pacific Salmon Fisheries*, p. 507.
8. Annual Report, 1971, International Pacific Salmon Fisheries Commission, pp. 22–23.
9. See "Salute to the Salmon," published by the International Pacific Salmon Fisheries Commission, 1958.
10. Haig-Brown, p. 158.
11. *Transactions of the Fifteenth British Columbia Natural Resources Conference*, p. 257.
12. *Western Fisheries*, May 1970.
13. Quoted in *Western Fisheries*, October 1971.
14. Personal communication, September 8, 1972.
15. Reported in *National Fisherman*, August 1971.

CHAPTER XXII (*pages 391–400*)

Indians and Salmon in British Columbia

1. Hugh McKervill, *The Salmon People*, pp. 10–11.
2. McKervill, p. 16.

3. Franz Boas, *Kwakiutl Ethnography*, pp. 155–57.
4. Franz Boas, *The Social Organization and the Secret Societies of the Kwakiutl Indians*.
5. Adapted from *Tsimshian Mythology* by Franz Boas, pp. 76–79.
6. Forrest E. LaViolette, *The Struggle for Survival*, p. 11.
7. Diamond Jenness, *The Indians of Canada*, p. 258.
8. Wilson Duff, *The Indian History of British Columbia*, Vol. I, pp. 77–79.
9. Ronald P. and Evelyn C. Rohner, *The Kwakiutl Indians of British Columbia*, p. 46.

CHAPTER XXIII (*pages 401–433*)
Vicissitudes of the Alaska Salmon Fisheries

1. John Muir, *Travels in Alaska*, pp. 256–57.
2. *Pacific Fisherman*, October 1949.
3. Quoted by John N. Cobb, *Pacific Salmon Fisheries*, p. 441.
4. Cobb, p. 449.
5. Ernest Gruening, *The State of Alaska*, pp. 74–75.
6. J. A. Crutchfield and Giulio Pontecorvo, *The Pacific Salmon Fisheries*, p. 71.
7. Quoted by Gruening, pp. 248–49.
8. Millard C. Marsh and John N. Cobb, *The Fisheries of Alaska in 1908*.
9. Unpublished manuscript.
10. Philip Drucker, *Cultures of the North Pacific Coast*, p. 205.
11. James W. Van Stone, *Eskimos of the Nushagak River*, pp. 76–77.
12. "Arctic-Yukon-Kuskokwim Area Salmon Fishing History," Alaska Fish and Game Department, Informational Leaflet 70, December 21, 1965.
13. Quoted by Gruening, p. 400.
14. W. F. Royce, University of Washington College of Fisheries, Contribution No. 121, 1960.
15. Alaska Fish and Game Department, Informational Leaflets 136 and 149.
16. Personal communication, March 13, 1972.
17. Personal communication from Wallace Noerenberg, formerly Commissioner of Fish and Game.
18. Personal communication, March 6, 1972.
19. "Oil and Wildlife: A Biologist's View," paper delivered to the North American Wildlife Conference, March 1971, Portland, Oregon.

CHAPTER XXIV (*pages 437–446*)
Asian Salmon Resource

1. Anton Chekhov, *The Island: A Journey to Sakhalin*, p. 273.
2. Leo S. Berg, *Freshwater Fishes of the U.S.S.R. and Adjacent Countries*, p. 182.
3. Chekhov, p. 273.
4. G. V. Nikolsky, *Special Ichthyology*, p. 156.
5. I. B. Birman, "More About the Influence of the Kurosio Current on the

Dynamics of Abundance of Salmon," tr. Fisheries Research Board of Canada.

6. I. F. Pravdin, quoted by Berg, pp. 194–95.
7. A. I. Smirnov, *The Biology of Reproduction and Development of the Coho.*

CHAPTER XXV (*pages 447–471*)
Russia's Salmon Wealth and Its Exploitation

1. *Peoples of Siberia,* edited by M. G. Levin and L. P. Potapov, p. 2.
2. Levin and Potapov, p. 771. It is probable that the Indians, who were descendants of Siberian people, arrived in North America complete with "Siberian" fishing skills and perhaps also with the knowledge of making pemmican.
3. Levin and Potapov, p. 722.
4. Anton Chekhov, *The Island: A Journey to Sakhalin,* p. 148.
5. George Kennan, *Tent Life in Siberia,* pp. 166–67.
6. Mitsuo Konda, *Studies on the Optimum Mesh of Salmon Gill Net,* p. 5.
7. Chekhov, p. 275.
8. Clinton E. Atkinson, *The Salmon Fisheries of the Soviet Far East,* p. 11.
9. Rupert L. Purdon, "World Trade in Canned Salmon," pp. 43–44.
10. Figures taken from Bulletin No. 12, International North Pacific Fisheries Commission, 1961.
11. See Georg Borgstrom, *Japan's World Success in Fishing,* 1964.
12. Quoted by Atkinson, p. 53.
13. This account of mother-ship operations is taken from Francis M. Fukuhara, *An Analysis of the Biological and Fishery Statistics of the Japanese Mothership Salmon Fishery.*
14. Shigeru Oda, "Japan and International Conventions Relating to North Pacific Fisheries," *Washington Law Review,* October 1967, p. 69.
15. R. S. Semko, "The Current Condition of Stocks of Pacific Salmon, Rate of Exploitation, and Future Utilization," in *Salmon Fishing of the Far East,* ed. E. N. Pavlovskii, pp. 13–14.
16. *Hearings,* 89th Congress, 1st Session, May 11–12, 1962, p. 80.
17. In *Salmon Fishing of the Far East,* ed. E. N. Pavlovskii, p. 26.
18. Pavlovskii, p. 32.
19. R. S. Semko, *The Stocks of West Kamchatka Salmon and Their Commercial Utilization.*
20. This account of the sovietization of native life is taken from Levin and Potapov, pp. 732–36.
21. Farley Mowat, *The Siberians,* p. 349.

CHAPTER XXVI (*pages 473–484*)
Salmon Farming in Japan

1. Unpublished Ms. in College of Fisheries, University of Washington.
2. Bernard Rudofsky, *The Kimono Mind,* p. 15.
3. Quoted in Rudofsky, p. 16.

4. Richard Van Cleve, "Japanese Freshwater Fisheries and Water Use Projects," p. 19.
5. Van Cleve, p. 20.
6. Van Cleve, p. 20.
7. *The Propagation of Chum Salmon in Japan,* Japan Fisheries Resource Conservation Association, p. 24.
8. Van Cleve, p. 23.
9. Van Cleve, p. 23.

CHAPTER XXVII (*pages 487–520*)
Sport Fishing for Salmon and Steelhead Trout

1. *The Origins of Angling, and A New Printing of "The Treatise of Fishing with An Angle,"* ed. John McDonald, p. 56.
2. *Origins of Angling,* p. 66.
3. Walton's *The Compleat Angler,* edited Richard Le Gallienne, p. 41.
4. Arnold Gingrich, in McClane's *Standard Fishing Encyclopedia,* p. 70.
5. Personal communication from Michael McBreen, September 6, 1970.
6. R. N. Stewart, *Rivers of Iceland,* p. 143.
7. Philip K. Crowe, *Out of the Mainstream,* p. 100.
8. Personal communication, June 8, 1972.
9. C. R. Denton, "A Regency Angling Club," *The Field,* August 26, 1965.
10. See A. Courtney Williams, *Angling Diversions,* pp. 142–48.
11. Arnold Gingrich, *The Well-Tempered Angler,* p. 179.
12. *Salt Water Fishing* by Van Campen Heilner, pp. 224–34.
13. Joe Brooks, "Steelhead or Atlantic Salmon?" *Outdoor Life,* September 1971.

CHAPTER XXVIII (*pages 521–529*)
Salmon — Our Earliest Gourmet Food

1. Charles Cutting, *Fish Saving,* p. 85.
2. Paul Lacroix, *France in the 18th Century,* p. 367.
3. *Larousse Gastronomique,* p. 299.
4. *Larousse Gastronomique,* pp. 93–94.
5. Sanche de Gramont, *The French,* p. 370.
6. Cutting, pp. 215–16.
7. Andre Launay, *Posh Food,* p. 39.
8. *National Fisherman Yearbook,* 1972, p. 92.

Bibliography

CHAPTER I

Evolution and Distribution of the Salmon

Berg, Leo S., *Freshwater Fishes of the U.S.S.R. and Adjacent Countries,* translated from Russian, National Science Foundation and Smithsonian Institution, Washington, D.C., 1962.

Ekman, Sven, *Zoogeography of the Sea,* London, Sigdwick & Jackson, 1953.

Foerster, R. E., *The Sockeye Salmon,* Ottawa, Fisheries Research Board of Canada, Bulletin 162, 1968.

Le Danois, Edouard, *Fishes of the World,* London, Harrap, 1957.

Macfarlane, John Muirhead, *The Evolution and Distribution of Fishes,* New York, Macmillan, 1923.

Neave, Ferris, "Origin and Speciation of *Oncorhynchus,*" *Transactions Royal Society of Canada,* Vol. 52, Series 3, June 1958.

Nikolsky, G. V., *The Ecology of Fishes,* London, Academic Press, 1963.

Power, G., "The Evolution of the Freshwater Races of the Atlantic Salmon (*Salmo salar*) in Eastern North America," *Arctic,* Vol. 11, No. 2 (1958).

Rostlund, Erhard, *Freshwater Fish and Fishing in Native North America,* University of California Publications in Geography, Vol. 9, 1952.

Tchernevin, V., "The Origin of Salmon: Is Its Ancestry Marine or Freshwater?", *Salmon and Trout Magazine,* No. 95, 1939.

CHAPTER II

Life History and Migrations

Blair, A. A., "Atlantic Salmon Tagged in East Coast Newfoundland Waters at Bonavista," *Journal Fisheries Research Board of Canada,* 13 (2), March 1956.

Brett, J. R., "The Swimming Energetics of Salmon," *Scientific American,* August 1965.

Combs, Trey, *The Steelhead Trout,* Portland, Ore., Northwest Salmon Trout Steelheader Co., 1971.

Curtis, Brian, *The Life Story of the Fish,* New York, Dover, 1961.

Foerster, R. E., *The Sockeye Salmon*, Ottawa, Fisheries Research Board of Canada, Bulletin 162, 1968.
Gilbert, Charles H., "The Salmon of the Yukon River," Washington, D.C., Bulletin of the Bureau of Fisheries, Vol. XXXVIII, 1921–1922.
Hagen, William, Jr., *Pacific Salmon*, U.S. Fish and Wildlife Service, Circular 24, 1953.
Haig-Brown, Roderick, *Fisherman's Fall*, New York, Morrow.
Hasler, Arthur D., *Underwater Guideposts: Homing of Salmon*, Madison, University of Wisconsin Press, 1966.
Healey, M. C., "Orientation of Pink Salmon During Early Migration from Bella Coola River System," *Journal Fisheries Research Board of Canada*, 24 (11), November 1967.
Huntsman, A. G., *Return of the Salmon from the Sea*, Ottawa, Biological Board of Canada, 1936.
Hutton, J. Arthur, *Wye Salmon and Other Fish*, Altrincham, Sheratt & Son, 1949.
International North Pacific Fisheries Commission, Bulletin 16, "Coho, Chinook and Masu Salmon in Offshore Waters," Vancouver, B.C., 1965.
——, Bulletin 18, "A Review of the Life History of North Pacific Salmon," 1966.
——, Bulletin 20, "Sockeye Salmon in Offshore Waters," 1966.
——, Bulletin 23, "Spawning Populations of North Pacific Salmon," 1967.
Jackson, P. A., and D. I. D. Howie, "The Movement of Salmon (*Salmo salar*) Through an Estuary and a Fish Pass," *Irish Fisheries Investigations*, Series A, No. 2, 1967.
Johnson, W. E., and C. Groot, "Observations on the Migration of Young Sockeye (*Oncorhynchus nerka*) Through a Large, Complex Lake System," *Fisheries Research Board of Canada*, 20 (4), 1963.
Jones, J. W., *Atlantic Salmon*, London, Collins, 1959.
Krashnennikov, Stepan P., *Explorations of Kamchatka*, translated by E. A. P. Crownhart-Vaughn, Portland, Oregon, Oregon Historical Society, 1972.
Moriarity, G., "Movements of Salmon Around Ireland from the North Mayo Coast," *Proceedings of the Royal Irish Academy*, Vol. 66, Section B, No. 1, January 1968.
Neave, Ferris, "Ocean Migrations of Pink Salmon," *Journal Fisheries Research Board of Canada*, 21 (5), 1964.
Netboy, Anthony, *The Atlantic Salmon: A Vanishing Species?* Boston, Houghton Mifflin, 1968.
Nikolsky, G. V., *The Ecology of Fishes*, New York, Academic Press, 1963.
Pyefinch, K. A., "A Review of the Literature on the Biology of the Atlantic Salmon," Edinburgh, Scottish Home Department, 1955.
Royce, William F., Lynwood S. Smith, and Alan C. Hartt, *Models of Oceanic Migrations of Pacific Salmon and Comments on Guidance Mechanisms*, U.S. Fish and Wildlife Service, Fishery Bulletin 66 (3), 1968.
Schultz, Leonard P., "The Breeding Habits of Salmon and Trout," Smithsonian Report for 1937, reprinted in *Earth and Life*, Vol. II, *Smithsonian Treasury of Science*, Washington, D.C., Smithsonian Institute, 1960.

Scottish Fisheries Bulletin, Department of Agriculture and Fisheries for Scotland, Edinburgh, No. 35, June 1971.

Stuart, T. A., *The Leaping Behavior of Salmon and Trout at Falls and Obstructions,* Department of Agriculture and Fisheries for Scotland, Edinburgh, 1962.

Went, A. E. J., "Irish Kelt Tagging Experiments, 1961/62 to 1966/67," *Irish Fisheries Investigation,* Series A, No. 5, Department of Agriculture and Fisheries, Dublin, 1969.

——, *The Irish Salmon and Salmon Fisheries,* London, Edward Arnold, 1955.

Wagner, Harry H., "A Summary of Investigations on the Use of Hatchery-Reared Steelhead in the Management of a Sport Fishery," Corvallis, Oregon State University, Fishery Report No. 5, January 1967.

Wilimovsky, N. J., ed., *Symposium on Pink Salmon,* University of British Columbia, Vancouver, Canada, 1962.

CHAPTER III

Primitive Man and the Atlantic Salmon

Breuil, Henri, and Raymond Lantier, *The Men of the Old Stone Age,* London, Harrap, 1965.

Cave of Altamira and Other Caves, Santander, Patronato de las Cuevas, 1961.

Childe, V. Gordon, *What Happened in History,* London, Penguin Books, 1967.

Clark, Grahame, *World Prehistory: An Outline,* Cambridge University Press, 1962.

Cole, Sonia, *The Neolithic Revolution,* 4th ed., London, British Museum, 1967.

Concise Encyclopedia of Archaeology, ed. Leonard Cottrell, New York, Hawthorn Books, 1960.

Cornwall, I. W., *Prehistoric Animals and Their Hunters,* London, Faber, 1968.

de Beer, Gavin, *A Handbook on Evolution,* 3rd ed., London, British Museum, 1964.

Sieveking, Ann and Gale, *The Caves of France and Northern Spain: A Guide,* London, Vista Books, 1962.

Thomazi, A., *Histoire de la Pêche: Des Ages de la Pierre à Nos Jours,* Paris, Payot, 1907.

CHAPTER IV

Salmon in Great Britain

Ashworth, Thomas, *The Salmon Fisheries of England,* London, Longmans, Green, 1868.

Bompas, G. C., *Life of Frank Buckland,* London, Nelson, n.d.

Burgess, G. H. O., *The Eccentric Ark: The Curious World of Frank Buckland,* New York, Horizon Press, 1967.

Calderwood, W. L., *The Salmon Rivers and Lochs of Scotland*, London, Edward Arnold, 1921.

Cornish, C. J., *Wild England of Today*, London, Nelson, 1895.

Cutting, Charles L., *Fish Saving*, London, Leonard Hill, 1955.

Darling, F. Fraser, and J. Morton Boyd, *The Highlands and Islands of Scotland*, London, Collins, 1964.

Day, Francis, *Salmonidae of Britain and Ireland*, London, Williams and Norgate, 1887.

Defoe, Daniel, *A Tour Thro' the Whole Island of Great Britain*, London, Everyman's Library, 1928.

Francis, Francis, *Reports on Salmon Ladders*, London, Horace Cox, 1870.

Fort, R. S., and J. D. Brayshaw, *Fishery Management*, London, Faber, 1961.

George, M. Dorothy, *London Life in the 18th Century*, New York, Harper, 1964.

Grey, Sir Edward, *Flyfishing*, London, Dent, 1928.

Grimble, Augustus, *The Salmon Rivers of England and Wales*, London, Kegan, Paul, 1913.

———, *The Salmon Rivers of Scotland*, London, Kegan, Paul, 1913.

Haig-Brown, Roderick, *A River Never Sleeps*, New York, Morrow, 1946.

Herbert, H. A., *Tale of a Wye Fisherman*, London, 1953.

Historical Works of Giraldus Cambrensis, ed. Thomas Wright, London, Bonn, 1863.

Hutton, J. Arthur, *Development of Our Salmon Fisheries*, Manchester, Sharrat & Hughes, 1917.

Lord, Peter, *The River Trent*, London, Robert Hale, n.d.

McLaren, Moray, and William B. Currie, *The Fishing Waters of Scotland*, London, John Murray, 1972.

Mantoux, Paul, *The Industrial Revolution in the 18th Century*, New York, Harper, 1961.

Mellanby, Kenneth, *Pesticides and Pollution*, London, Scientific Book Club, 1967.

Menzies, W. J. M., *The Salmon: Its Life History*, Edinburgh, Blackwood, 1925.

———, *The Stock of Salmon*, London, Edward Arnold, 1949.

Mills, Derek, *Salmon and Trout*, Edinburgh, Oliver and Boyd, 1971.

Netboy, Anthony, *The Atlantic Salmon: A Vanishing Species?*, Boston, Houghton Mifflin, 1968.

Portraits of Rivers, ed. Eileen Molony, London, Dobson, 1963.

Report of the Freshwater Fisheries Laboratory, Pitlochry, for 1969, Edinburgh, Department of Agriculture and Fisheries.

Report of the Inspectors of Salmon Fisheries (England and Wales) for 1868, London, H.M.S.O., 1869; *for 1887, 1888*.

Ritchie, James, *The Influence of Man on Animal Life in Scotland*, Cambridge University Press, 1920.

Russel, Alex, *The Salmon*, Edinburgh, Edmonston and Douglas, 1864.

Scrope, William, *Days and Nights of Salmon Fishing in the Tweed*, London, Arnold, 1898.

Seaman, Kenneth, "When Salmon Ran Up the Trent," *Trout and Salmon*, March 1969.

Stoddard, Thomas Tod, *The Art of Angling*, Edinburgh, Chambers, 1836.
Turing, H. D., "Pollution Affecting Rivers in England and Wales," British Field Sports Society, London, 1947.
Waters, Brian, *Thirteen Rivers to the Thames*, London, Dent, 1964.
Wykes, Alan, *An Eye on the Thames*, London, Jarrolds, 1966.
Young, Archibald, *Salmon Fisheries*, London, Stanford, 1877.

CHAPTER V

Salmon in Ireland

Day, Francis, *Salmonidae of Britain and Ireland*, London, Williams and Norgate, 1887.
Foyle Fisheries Commission, 19th Annual Report, 1969–1970.
Grimble, Augustus, *The Salmon Rivers of Ireland*, London, Kegan, Paul, 1913.
Illustrated Guide to the Counties of Ireland, Dublin, Irish Tourist Board, n.d.
Irish Fisheries Investigations, Series A (Freshwater), Department of Agriculture and Fisheries, Dublin, No. 7, 1971.
Landseth, Helen, *Dear Dark Head: An Intimate Story of Ireland*, New York, McGraw-Hill, 1936.
Liddell, Peter, *The Salmon Rivers of Eire*, A Report to the Irish Tourist Board, February 1971.
Moore, Alfred S., *The Irish Salmon Industry*, 1929, unpublished.
Salmon Research Trust of Ireland, 1971 Annual Report.
Went, A. E. J., *The Irish Salmon*, London, Edward Arnold, 1955.
——, *Lectures for Atlantic Salmon Association*, Montreal, 1970.
Young, Archibald, *Salmon Fisheries*, London, Stanford, 1877.
——, "The Pursuit of Salmon in Ireland," *Proceedings of the Royal Irish Academy*, Vol. 63, Section 6, No. 6, 1964.

CHAPTER VI

Iberian and French Salmon

Bachelier, R. "L'Histoire du Saumon en Loire," *Bulletin Français de Pisciculture*, Paris, Nos. 211–212.
Boyer, Henri, *Le Saumon dans le Haut-Allier*, Paris, 1930.
Carrère, Louis, *Le Saumon: Poisson Royal*, Paris, Librairie de Champs Élysées, 1943.
Gestin, Yves, *Histoire du Chateaulin*, 1946.
Latour, Commandant, *Le Saumon dans les Courses d'Eau Breton*, Paris, 1928.
Moreau, Emile, *Histoire Naturelle de Poissons de la France*, Paris, Masson, 1881, Vol. 3.
Penn Ar Bed, a Regional Journal of Geography, "The Salmon in Brittany," Natural Science and Nature Protection, Brest, December 1968.
Report of the Inspector of Salmon Fisheries for England and Wales, London, H.M.S.O., 1887.
St. Prix, C. de, *Question de Pisciculture en Basse Bretagne*, Morlaix, 1862.

El Salmon y su Pesca, La Direccion General del Turismo, Madrid, 1945.

Vibert, Richard, and L. de Boisset, *La Pêche Fluviale en France,* Paris, Librairie de Champs Élysées, 1944.

CHAPTER VII

Demise of the Meuse and Rhine Rivers

Boisset, Louis de, and Richard Vibert, *La Pêche Fluviale en France,* Paris, Libraire de Champs Elysées, 1944.

Gathorne-Hardy, A. E., *The Salmon,* London, Longmans, Green, 1898.

Hoek, P. P. C., *Propagation and Protection of the Rhine Salmon,* Washington, D.C., Bureau of Commercial Fisheries, 1910.

Moreau, Emile, *Histoire Naturelle de Poissons de la France,* Paris, Masson, Vol. 3. *Rivers and Lakes,* ed. R. Kay Greswell and Anthony Huxley, New York, Putnam, 1965.

Vibert, Richard, "La Regression du Saumon du Rhin," *Bulletin Francaise de Pisci-Culture,* No. 156.

CHAPTER VIII

Norwegian Successes and Setbacks

Berg, Magnus, *Laks og Laksefiske (Salmon and Salmon Fishing),* Bergen, Universitets Forlaget, 1963, unpublished translation.

Caton, John Dean, *A Summer in Norway,* Chicago, Jensen McClurg, 1875.

Crowe, Philip K., *Out of the Mainstream: Fishing Reminiscences Around the World,* New York, Scribner, 1971.

Curry-Lindahl, Kai, *Europe: A Natural History,* New York, Random House, 1964.

Dahl, Knut, *Salmon and Trout: A Handbook,* London, Salmon and Trout Association, 1914.

———, and Sven Sømme, *Experiments in Salmon Marking,* Oslo, 1936 and 1942.

Hagen, Anders, *Norway,* New York, Praeger, 1967.

Løchen, Gudny, *Laksefiske I Meraker,* Elverum, Norsk Skogbrukmuseum, 1970.

Menzies, W. J. M., *The Stock of Salmon,* London, Edward Arnold, 1949.

Report on Industrial Hydroelectric Power Developments in Norway and Sweden, Committee on Public Works, U.S. Senate, Washington, D.C., Government Printing Office, 1961.

Rosseland, Leiv, "Norwegian Statistics for the Salmon and Sea-Trout Fishery," 1876–1965, International Council for the Exploration of the Sea, Charlottenlund, Denmark, 1966.

———, *Salmon and Sea-Trout Fisheries,* Oslo, Central Bureau of Statistics, 1971.

U.S. Fish and Wildlife Service, Foreign Fisheries Leaflet 183, "Atlantic Salmon — High Seas Fisheries Outlook," Washington, D.C., March 1970.

CHAPTER IX
Baltic and Arctic Salmon

Carlin, Borje, *Lectures Delivered for the Atlantic Salmon Association,* Montreal, 1969.
Christensen, O., "The Danish Salmon Fishery in the Eastern Baltic in the Season 1967–68," International Council for the Exploration of the Sea, Charlottenlund, Denmark, 1968.
Hurme, Seppo, "Suomen Itameren Puoleiset Lohija Taimenjoet," *Ylipainos Eramies,* No. 11/66.
——, *The Anadromous Fishes in the Baltic Side-Rivers of Finland,* paper published in Helsinki, Department of Agriculture, 1962.
——, "Kaakaman Lohipadon Saalisvaihtelut," *Ylipainos Eramies,* No. 9/66.
——, "Salmon and Trout Rivers in Southwestern Finland," Helsinki, 1967.
Kazimierz, Demel, and Stanislaw Rutkowicz, *The Barents Sea,* U.S. Department of the Interior and National Science Foundation, Washington, D.C., 1966.
Lindroth, Arne, "The Baltic Salmon: Its Natural and Artificial Regulation," *Mittelung, Intl. Verein. Limm.,* Stuttgart, 1965.
Netboy, Anthony, *The Atlantic Salmon: A Vanishing Resource?,* Boston, Houghton Mifflin, 1968. See Bibliography, pages 394–96.
O'Dell, Andrew C., *The Scandinavian World,* London, Longmans, Green, 1957.

CHAPTER X
The American Experience

Atkins, C. G., "Local History of Salmon and Salmon Fishing in New England Rivers," in *Report of the U.S. Commissioner for Fish and Fisheries for 1872–73,* Washington, D.C., 1874.
Bigelow, Henry B., and William C. Shroeder, *Fishes of the Gulf of Maine,* Fishery Bulletin 74, U.S. Fish and Wildlife Service, 1953.
Blair, A. A., "Scales of Lake Ontario Salmon Indicate a Landlocked Form," *Copeia,* No. 4, 1938.
Crowe, Philip K., *Out of the Mainstream: Fishing Reminiscences Around the World,* New York, Scribners, 1971.
Cutting, Richard E., and W. H. Everhart, *The Penobscot River,* Penobscot Conservation Association, February 1968.
Cutting, Richard E., and Alfred E. Meister, "Marine Migrations of Atlantic Salmon Kelts Tagged in Maine, U.S.A.," International Commission on North Atlantic Fisheries, Research Document 67, 1957.
Edmunds, M. C., "Obstructions to the Ascent of Fish in the Tributaries of Lake Champlain," *Report of the U.S. Commissioner of Fish and Fisheries for 1872–73,* Washington, D.C., 1874.
Elson, P. F., and C. J. Kerswill, "Developing Criteria for Pesticide Residues Important to Fisheries," Canadian Fisheries Reports No. 9, Department of Fisheries, Ottawa, July 1967.

Fishes of the Western North Atlantic, Part 3, No. 1, Memoir, Sears Foundation for Marine Research, New Haven, Conn., 1963.

Goode, George B., *Food and Game Fishes of North America*, Washington, 1887.

———, *The Fisheries and Fishery Industries of the United States*, Washington, 1887.

Goodspeed, Charles E., *Angling in America*, Boston, Houghton Mifflin, 1939.

Ingstad, Helge, *Westward to Vineland*, London, Jonathan Cape, 1969.

Jordan, David S., and Barton W. Evermann, *American Food and Game Fishes*, New York, Doubleday, Page, 1908.

Kendall, William C., *The Fishes of New England: The Salmon Family*, Part I, Boston, Natural History Society, 1935.

Meister, Alfred L., "The Work of the Atlantic Sea-Run Salmon Commission of the State of Maine," a paper delivered at the International Atlantic Salmon Conference, London, April 15–16, 1969.

Poole, Ernest, *The Great White Hills of New Hampshire*, Garden City, Doubleday, 1946.

Rostlund, Erhard, *Freshwater Fish and Fishing in Native North America*, University of California Publications in Geography, Vol. IX, 1952.

Scott, Genio, *Fishing in American Waters*, New York, American News Company, 1875.

Seccombe, Joseph, *A Discourse Utter'd in Part at Ammauskeeg Falls in the Fishing-Season: 1739*, Barre, Mass., 1970.

Storer, David H., *A History of Massachusetts*, Cambridge, Welch and Bigelow, 1867.

Thoreau, Henry David, *The Maine Woods*, Boston, Houghton Mifflin, 1893.

———, *Walden*, New York, New American Library, 1960.

———, *A Week on the Concord and Merrimack Rivers*, Boston, Houghton Mifflin, 1893.

Wells, Henry P., *The American Salmon Fisherman*, New York, Harper, 1886.

CHAPTER XI

The Canadian Experience

Blaisdell, Harold F., *The Philosophical Fisherman*, Boston, Houghton Mifflin, 1969.

Canada's Atlantic Salmon, Ottawa, Department of Fisheries, November 1954.

Huntsman, A. G., *The Maritime Salmon of Canada*, Ottawa, Biological Board of Canada, Bulletin XXI, 1931.

Menzies, W. J. M., *A Report on the Present Position of the Atlantic Salmon Fisheries of Canada*, Montreal, Atlantic Salmon Association, October 1951.

Nettle, Richard, *The Salmon Fisheries of the St. Lawrence*, Montreal, 1857.

Norris, Thad., *The American Angler's Guide*, Philadelphia, 1864.

Saunders, Richard L., "Contributions of Salmon from the Northwest Mira-
michi River, New Brunswick, to Various Fisheries," *Journal of the
Fisheries Research Board of Canada,* 26: 269–78, 1969.
———, and John R. Sprague, "Effects of Copper-Zinc Mining Pollution on a
Spawning Population of Atlantic Salmon," in *Water Research,* London,
Pergamon Press, 1967.
Scott, Genio, *Fishing in American Waters,* New York, American News
Company, 1875.
Weeks, Edward, *The Moisie Salmon Club,* Barre, Mass., 1971.
Wright, Esther Clark, *The St. John River and Its Tributaries,* 1966.

CHAPTER XII
The Greenland Fishery — Final Catastrophe?

Christy, Francis T., Jr., and Anthony Scott, *The Common Wealth in Ocean
Fisheries,* Baltimore, Johns Hopkins Press, 1965.
International Council for the Exploration of the Sea, *Cooperative Research
Report,* Series A, No. 8, October 1967; No. 12, February 1969; No.
24, May 1971, Charlottenlund, Denmark.
"Japan and International Conventions Relating to North Pacific Fisheries,"
Washington Law Review, Vol. 43, No. 1, University of Washington,
Seattle, October 1967.
Nielsen, Jørgen, *Contributions to the Biology of the Salmonidae in Green-
land, I–IV,* Copenhagen, 1961.
*Report of the ICES/ICNAF Joint Working Party on North Atlantic
Salmon,* Dublin, 21–24, ICNAF Res. Doc. 72/32, March 1972.
Sosin, Mark, "Greenland Salmon," *Field & Stream,* May 1970.
Stefansson, Vilhjalmur, *Greenland,* New York, Doubleday, 1947.
U.S. Fish and Wildlife Service, Foreign Fisheries Leaflets: #92 and 92A,
"Greenland Fisheries Series," February 1969; #183, "Atlantic Salmon
— High Seas Fisheries Outlook," March 1970; #167, "Danish View-
point on High-Seas Fishing for Atlantic Salmon," November 1968,
Washington, D.C.

CHAPTER XIII
Discovery of the Pacific Salmon

Berg, Leo S., *Freshwater Fishes of the U.S.S.R. and Adjacent Countries,*
Washington, D.C., National Science Foundation, 1962.
Golder, F. A., *Bering's Voyages,* Vol. II, New York, American Geographical
Society, 1925.
Journals of Captain Cook on His Voyages of Discovery, 1776–1780, ed.
J. C. Beaglehole, Parts I and II, Cambridge, Hakluyt Society, 1967.
Krashnennikov, Stepan P., *The Natural History of Kamchatka and the Ku-
rilski Islands With the Countries Adjacent,* tr. James Grieve, reprinted
by Quadrangle Books, Chicago, 1962.
Lauridsen, Peter, *Vitus Bering: The Discoverer of Bering Strait,* tr. Julius
E. Olsen, Chicago, Griggs & Co., 1889.

Stejneger, Leonhard, *George Wilhelm Steller*, Cambridge, Harvard University Press, 1936.
Villiers, Alan, *Captain James Cook*, New York, Scribners, 1967.
Waxell, Sven, *The American Expedition*, London, William Hodge, 1952.

CHAPTER XIV
The Destruction of California and Its Salmon

California Fish and Wildlife Plan, Vol. II, Part B, "Inventory of Salmon and Steelhead and Marine Resources," California Fish and Game Department, October 1, 1965.
The California Indians, ed. R. F. Heizer and M. A. Whipple, 2nd ed., University of California Press, Berkeley, 1971.
California University Publications in American Archeology and Ethnology, Vol. 35, University of California Press, Berkeley.
Clark, G. H., *Sacramento–San Joaquin Salmon Fishery in California*, California Fish and Game Department, 1920.
Dasmann, Raymond F., *The Destruction of California*, New York, Collier Books, 1966.
Fry, Donald H., Jr., and Eldon P. Hughes, *The California Salmon Troll Fishery*, Bulletin 2, Pacific Marine Fisheries Commission, Portland, Ore., 1951.
Hallock, Richard J., Robert F. Elwell, and Donald H. Fry, Jr., *Migrations of Adult King Salmon in the San Joaquin Delta*, California Fish and Game Department, 1970.
Hanson, Harry A., Osgood R. Smith, and Paul R. Needham, *An Investigation of Fish-Salvage Problems in Relation to Shasta Dam*, Bureau of Fisheries, Special Scientific Report No. 10, 1940, processed.
Hedgpeth, Joel W., "The Passing of the Salmon," *Scientific Monthly*, Vol. 59 (1944).
Kroeber, A. L., and S. A. Barrett, *Fishing Among the Indians of Northwestern California*, University of California Press, Berkeley, Anthropological Records 21:1, 1960.
Leitritz, Earl, *A History of California Fish Hatcheries, 1870–1960*, Department of Fish and Game, Fish Bulletin 150, 1970.
Rolle, Andrew F., and John Gaines, *The Golden State: A History of California*, New York, Crowell, 1965.
Rostlund, Erhard, *Freshwater Fish and Fishing in Native North America*, Berkeley, University of California Publications in Geography, Vol. 9, 1952.
Skinner, John E., *A Historical Review of the Fish and Wildlife Resources of the San Francisco Bay Area*, California Fish and Game Department, June 1962.
Sumner, F. H., and Osgood R. Smith, "A Biological Study of the Effect of Mining Debris Dams and Hydraulic Mining on Fish Life in the Yuba and American Rivers in California," Stanford University, California, May 1, 1939, processed.

CHAPTERS XV—XVI
The Dammed Columbia and Unlucky Salmon
Parts I and II

A Summary of Recent Columbia River Salmon and Steelhead Runs and Harvest, Portland, Oregon Game Commission, 1973.

Bell, Milo, *Fisheries Handbook of Engineering Requirements and Biological Criteria,* Portland, Corps of Engineers, 1973.

Bessey, Roy F., *Pacific Northwest Regional Planning — A Review,* Olympia, Washington Department of Conservation, 1963.

——, *The Public Issues of Middle Snake Development,* Olympia, Washington Department of Conservation, 1964.

——, "Public Issues on the Middle Snake," in *Symposium on Reservoirs, Problems and Conflicts,* Oregon State University, Water Resources Research Institute, 1969.

Biological Implications of the Nuclear Age, U.S. Atomic Energy Commission, December 1969.

Bonneville Power Administration, *Fact Book,* Portland, 1968.

——, 1969 Annual Report, 1969.

——, Regional Advisory Council, Conference Proceedings, January 9, 1970.

——, "Ten Year Hydro-Thermal Power Program for the Pacific Northwest," January 1969.

——, "Thirty Years of Service," n.d.

Chapman, W. M., "Fish Problems Connected with Grand Coulee," Oregon Fish Commission, Contribution No. 2, 1940.

Clay, C. H., *Design of Fishways and Other Fish Facilities,* Ottawa, Department of Fisheries, 1961.

Cobb, John N., *Pacific Salmon Fisheries,* Appendix III to Report of U.S. Fish Commissioner, 1930.

Columbia River Fishery Development Program, Bureau of Commercial Fisheries, Circular 192, 1964.

Craig, J. A., and R. L. Hacker, *History and Development of the Fisheries of the Columbia River,* Bureau of Fisheries, 1940.

De Loach, Daniel B., *The Salmon Canning Industry,* Oregon State College Press, Corvallis, 1939.

Donaldson, Ivan J., and Frederick K. Cramer, *Fishwheels on the Columbia,* Portland, Binfords & Morts, 1971.

Drucker, Philip, *Indians of the Northwest Coast,* Garden City, N.Y., Natural History Press, 1963.

Ebel, Wesley J., "Dissolved Nitrogen Surveys of the Columbia and Snake Rivers," Bureau of Commercial Fisheries, Seattle, August 1970.

——, "Supersaturation of Nitrogen in the Columbia River and Its Effect on Salmon and Steelhead Trout," Fish and Wildlife Service, *Fishery Bulletin,* Vol. 68, No. 1 (1969).

Elling, Carl H., and Gerald B. Collins, "Summary of Progress in Fish-Passage Research," 1964 and seq., Bureau of Commercial Fisheries, Seattle.

Environmental Protection Agency, "Columbia River Thermal Effects Study," Portland, January 1971.

Fish and Game Protector, *First and Second Annual Reports*, Salem, Oregon, 1891; *Third and Fourth Annual Reports*, 1894; *Fifth and Sixth Annual Reports*, 1898.

Fisheries Statistics of Oregon, ed. F. C. Cleaver, Oregon Fish Commission, 1951.

Fulton, Leonard A., *Spawning Areas and Abundance of Chinook Salmon . . . in the Columbia River Basin — Past and Present*, Fish and Wildlife Service, Special Scientific Report, No. 571, October 1968.

Goode, George B., *Fishery Industries of the United States*, Washington, D.C., 1887, Section V.

Gordon, R. N., "Fisheries Problems Associated with Hydroelectric Developments," *Canadian Fish Culturist*, October 1965.

Hearings before the Subcommittee of the Committee on Appropriations, House of Representatives, 83rd Cong., 1st sess., Part 1, and 2nd sess., Part 2.

Holbrook, Stewart, *The Columbia*, New York, Farrar and Rinehart, 1957.

Laythe, Leo L., *The Fishery Development Program in the Lower Columbia River*, Bureau of Commercial Fisheries, 1948.

McDonald, Lucille, *A History of Southwest Washington*, Portland, Binfords & Mort, 1966.

McKeown, Martha Ferguson, *The Trail Led North: Mont Hawthorne's Story*, New York, Macmillan, 1948.

McLellan, Sister Mary de Sales, "The Beginning of the Commercial Salmon Fishery on the Columbia River," *Oregon Historical Quarterly*, Vol. XXXV, No. 3 (1964).

Morgan, Murray, *The Columbia: Powerhouse of the West*, Seattle, Superior Publishing Company, 1949.

Needham, Paul R., "Dam Construction in Relation to Columbia River Salmon Fisheries," *North American Wildlife Conference Transactions*, 1949.

Netboy, Anthony, *Salmon of the Pacific Northwest: Fish vs. Dams*, Portland, Binfords and Mort, 1958.

Ocean Migrations and Exploitation of Northwest Pacific Salmon Stocks of Chinook and Coho to 1964, Pacific Marine Fisheries Commission, Portland, Part I, 1969.

Peery, W. K., *And There Were Salmon*, Portland, Ore., Binfords and Mort, 1949.

Pruter, A. T., *Commercial Fisheries of the Columbia and Adjacent Ocean Waters*, Bureau of Commercial Fisheries, Fishery Industrial Research Reprint 42, n.d.

Raymond, Howard L., "A Summary of the 1969 and 1970 Outmigration of Juvenile Chinook Salmon and Steelhead Trout from the Snake River," Seattle, Bureau of Commercial Fisheries, September 1970.

Rich, Willis H., *The Present State of the Columbia River Salmon Resources*, Oregon Fish Commission, Contribution No. 3, 1941.

——, *The Salmon Runs of the Columbia River in 1938*, Fish and Wildlife Service, 1942.

Status of Columbia River Salmon and Steelhead Trout, Vancouver, Wash., Pacific Northwest River Basins Commission, May 1972.

Status Report, Columbia River Fish Runs and Commercial Fisheries,
   1938–70, Fish Commission of Oregon and Washington Department of
   Fisheries, January 1972.
Transactions of the American Fisheries Society:
   Raymond, Howard L., "Effect of John Day Reservoir on the Migration
      Rate of Juvenile Chinook Salmon in the Columbia River," Vol. 98,
      No. 3 (July 1969).
      "Migration Rates of Yearling Chinook in Relation to Flows and
      Impoundments in the Columbia and Snake Rivers," Vol. 97, No. 4
      (October 1968).
      ———, and Wallace W. Bentley, "Passage of Juvenile Fish Through
      Orifices in Gatewells of Turbine Intakes at McNary Dam," Vol.
      98, No. 4 (October 1969).
   Park, Donald L., "Seasonal Changes in Downstream Migration of Age-
      Group O Chinook Salmon in the Upper Columbia River," Vol. 98,
      No. 2 (April 1969).
Wheeler, Olin D., *The Trail of Lewis and Clark,* New York, Putnam, 1904.
Winther, Oscar Osburn, *The Great Northwest,* New York, Knopf, 1952.
———, *The Old Oregon Country,* Lincoln, University of Nebraska Press,
   1969.

CHAPTER XVII

Death and Revival of the Willamette River

Federal Water Pollution Control Administration, "Summary of Water Qual-
   ity Control and Management: Willamette River Basin," Portland, Janu-
   ary 1967.
———, "Willamette River: An Example of a River Being Cleaned Up," Port-
   land, September 1970.
Gleeson, George W., *The Return of a River: The Willamette River, Ore-
   gon,* Corvallis, Oregon State University Press, June 1972.
Holland, G. S., J. E. Lasater, E. D. Neumann, and W. E. Eldredge, *Toxic
   Effects of Organic and Inorganic Pollutants on Young Salmon and
   Trout,* Olympia, Washington Department of Fisheries, January 1964.

CHAPTER XVIII

Oregon's Coastal Streams

Dodds, Gordon B., *The Salmon King of Oregon,* Chapel Hill, University of
   North Carolina Press, 1959.
———, ed., *A Pygmy Monopolist: The Life and Doings of R. D. Hume,
   Written by Himself,* Madison, State Historical Society of Wisconsin,
   1961.
First and Second Annual Reports of the Fish and Game Protector, Salem,
   Oregon, 1889, 1891.
Gharrett, John T., and John I. Hodges, *Salmon Fisheries of the Coastal Riv-
   ers of Oregon South of the Columbia,* Oregon Fish Commission, Con-
   tribution No. 13, December 1950.

Oregon Guide, Portland, Binfords & Mort, rev. edition, 1951.
Peterson, Emil R., and Alfred Powers, *A Century of Coos and Curry,* Portland, Binfords & Mort, 1952.
Report of the Commissioner for Fish and Fisheries for Year Ending June 30, 1896, Washington, D.C., 1898.

CHAPTER XIX

Breakthrough in Salmon Culture

Burrows, Roger E., and Bobby D. Combs, "Controlled Environments for Salmon Propagation," *Progressive Fish-Culturist,* Vol. 30, No. 3, July 1968.
———, "The Influence of Fingerling Quality on Adult Salmon Survivals," *Transactions of the American Fisheries Society,* Vol. 98, No. 4, October 1969.
———, "Water Temperature Requirements for Maximum Productivity of Salmon," Proc. 12th Pacific Northwest Symposium on Water Pollution Research, *Water Temperature — Influences, Effects, and Controls,* Corvallis, Oregon, Public Health Service, 1963.
Donaldson, Lauren, and Deb Menasveta, "Selective Breeding of Chinook Salmon," *Transactions American Fisheries Society,* Vol. 90, No. 2, 1961.
"Hatcheries in British Columbia — Part I," a digest of the report by Resource Development Branch of the Department of Fisheries, Vancouver, B.C., *Western Fisheries,* April 1971.
Hedgpeth, Joel W., "The Passing of the Salmon," *Scientific Monthly,* 59 (1944).
Idyll, C. P., *The Sea Against Hunger,* New York, Crowell, 1970.

CHAPTER XX

The Puget Sound Fishery

Avery, Mary W., *Washington: A History of the Evergreen State,* Seattle, University of Washington Press, 1965.
Crutchfield, J. A., and Giulio Pontecorvo, *The Pacific Salmon Fisheries,* Baltimore, Johns Hopkins University Press, 1969.
Haw, Frank, Henry O. Wendler, and Gene Deschamps, "Development of Washington State Salmon Sport Fishery Through 1964," Washington Department of Fisheries, Research Bulletin No. 2, May 1967.
Hidy, Ralph W., Frank Ernest Hill, and Allan Nevins, *Timber and Men: The Weyerhaeuser Story,* New York, Macmilln, 1963.
Junge, Charles O., Jr., "Commercial Salmon Fishing Intensity in Puget Sound, 1939–1955," Fisheries Research Papers, Washington Department of Fisheries, Vol. 2, No. 2, April 1959.
Meany, Edmond L., *Vancouver's Discovery of Puget Sound,* New York, Macmillan, 1907.
Pollutional Effects of Pulp and Paper Mill Wastes in Puget Sound, Portland, Federal Water Pollution Control Administration, March 1967.

Readings in Pacific Northwest History, ed. Charles M. Gates, Seattle, University Bookstore, 1941.
Research Report on the Washington State Offshore Troll Fishery, Portland, Pacific Marine Fisheries Commission, 1951.
Shearer, F. E., ed., *The Pacific Tourist,* New York, Crown, 1970 reprint.
Uncommon Controversy: Fishing Rights of the Muckleshoot, Puyallup and Nisqually Indians, Seattle, University of Washington Press, 1970.
Washington: A Guide to the Evergreen State, Portland, Binfords & Mort, 1950.
Wendler, Henry O., and Gene Deschamps, "Logging Dams on Coastal Washington Streams," Washington Department of Fisheries, Fisheries Research Papers.
Wright, Samuel G., *The Origin and Migration of Washington's Chinook and Coho Salmon,* Washington Dept. of Fisheries, October 1968.

CHAPTER XXI

Vicissitudes of the British Columbia Fisheries

Cobb, John N., *Pacific Salmon Fisheries,* Report of the U.S. Commissioner of Fisheries, Appendix iii, 1930 (originally published in 1917).
Foerster, R. E., *The Sockeye Salmon,* Ottawa, Fisheries Research Board of Canada, Bulletin 162, 1968.
Gregory, Homer E., and Kathleen Barnes, *Pacific Fisheries,* San Fancisco, Institute of Pacific Relations, 1939.
Haig-Brown, Roderick, *The Living Land,* Toronto, Macmillan, 1961.
Hill, A. V., *Tides of Change: A Story of Fishermen's Cooperatives in British Columbia,* Prince Rupert, B.C., 1967.
International North Pacific Fisheries Commission, "Pacific Salmon in Canada," Bulletin 23, Vancouver, B.C., 1967.
International Pacific Salmon Fisheries Commission, Annual Reports, 1957–1971.
Large, R. Geddes, *The Skeena: River of Destiny,* Vancouver, B.C., Mitchell Press, 1958.
Lyons, Cecily, *Salmon: Our Heritage,* Vancouver, B.C., 1969.
Mackay, Douglas, *The Honorable Company,* Toronto, McClelland and Stewart, 1966.
McKervill, Hugh W., *The Salmon People,* Sidney, B.C., Gray's Publishing Company, 1967.
Royce, William F., "On the Possibility of Improving Salmon Spawning Areas," *Transactions North American Wildlife Conference,* 1959.
Thompson, William F., "Effect of the Obstruction at Hell's Gate on the Sockeye Salmon of the Fraser River," International Pacific Salmon Fisheries Commission, New Westminster, B.C., Bulletin 1, 1945.
Transactions of the Fifteenth British Columbia Natural Resources Conference, Victoria, B.C., 1962:
"Effects of Man-Made Environmental Changes and Public Access Problems on Use of the British Columbia Sport Fishery," by F. D. Maher.

"Non-Tidal Sport Fishery" by S. B. Smith.
"Tidal Sport Fishery" by A. L. W. Tuomi.
"Sport Fisheries — General Evaluation," by Roderick Haig-Brown.
Van Cleve, Richard, "The International Pacific Salmon Fisheries Commission and Conservation of the Fraser River Salmon Runs," *Transactions North American Wildlife Conference*, 1949.

CHAPTER XXII
Indians and Salmon in British Columbia

Boas, Franz, *Kwakiutl Ethnography*, ed. Helen Codere, University of Chicago Press, n.d.
——, *Social Organization and the Secret Societies of the Kwakiutl Indians*, Washington, D.C., Government Printing Office, 1897.
——, *Tsimshian Mythology*, University of Chicago Press, 1916.
Duff, Wilson, *The Indian History of British Columbia*, Vol. I, Victoria, B.C., Provincial Museum, 1965.
Jenness, Diamond, *The Indians of Canada*, 2nd ed., Ottawa, National Museum of Canada, Bulletin 65, n.d.
La Violette, Forrest E., *The Struggle for Survival*, Toronto, University of Toronto Press, 1961.
McKervill, Hugh, *The Salmon People*, Sidney, B. C., Gray's Publishing Company, 1967.
Rohner, Ronald P. and Evelyn C., *The Kwakiutl Indians of British Columbia*, New York, Holt, Rinehart and Winston, 1970.

CHAPTER XXIII
Vicissitudes of the Alaska Salmon Fisheries

"Arctic-Yukon-Kuskokwim Area Salmon Fishing History," Alaska Fish and Game Department, Informational Leaflet 170.
Bancroft, Hubert H., *History of Alaska*, San Francisco, 1886.
Cobb, John N., *Pacific Salmon Fisheries*, 4th edition, Washington, D.C., 1930.
Cooley, Richard A., *Politics and Conservation: The Decline of the Alaska Salmon*, New York, Harper, 1963.
Crutchfield, J. A., and Giulio Pontecorvo, *The Pacific Salmon Fisheries*, Baltimore, Johns Hopkins Press, 1969.
Dall, William H., *Alaska and Its Resources*, Boston, Lee and Shepherd, 1870.
Drucker, Philip, *Cultures of the North Pacific Coast*, Scranton, Pa., Chandler, 1965.
Effects of Clearcutting on Salmon Habitat of Two Southeast Alaska Streams, U.S. Forest Service, Juneau, 1969.
Gilbert, C. H., and Henry O'Malley, "Special Investigations of the Salmon Fishery in General in Western Alaska," in *Alaska Fishery and Fur Seal Industries in 1919*, Washington, D.C., 1920.
Gruening, Ernest, *The State of Alaska*, New York, Random House, 1968.

Jordan, David S., and Barton W. Evermann, *Preliminary Report of the Alaska Salmon Commission*, House Doc. 477, 56th Congress, 2nd session, 1906.
"King Salmon and the Ocean Troll Fishery of Southeastern Alaska," Research Report No. 1, Department of Fisheries, Juneau, September 1956.
Laycock, George, *Alaska: The Embattled Frontier*, Boston, Houghton Mifflin, 1971.
McKeown, Martha Ferguson, *Alaska Silver*, New York, Macmillan, 1951.
Marsh, Willard C., and John N. Cobb, *The Fisheries of Alaska in 1908*, Bureau of Fisheries, Document No. 645, 1909.
Mathews, Richard K., *The Yukon*, New York, Holt, Rinehart and Winston, 1968.
National Resources Committee, *Regional Planning*, Part VII, *Alaska, Its Resources and Development*, Washington, D.C., 1937.
Oswalt, Wendell H., *Alaskan Eskimos*, San Francisco, Chandler, 1967.
Rogers, George, *The Future of Alaska, Economic Consequences of Statehood*, Baltimore, Johns Hopkins Press, 1962.
Smith, Howard, Allyn H. Seymour, and Lauren R. Donaldson, "The Salmon Resource," in *Environment of the Cape Thompson Region, Alaska*, ed. N. J. Wilimovsky and John N. Wolfe, Atomic Energy Commission, Oak Ridge, Tenn., January 1966.
Sundborg, George, *Opportunity in Alaska*, New York, Macmillan, 1945.
Underwood, John J., *Alaska, an Empire in the Making*, New York, Dodd, Mead, 1925.
Van Stone, James W., *Eskimos of the Nushagak River*, Seattle, University of Washington Press, 1967.

CHAPTER XXIV

Asian Salmon Resource

Berg, Leo S., *Freshwater Fishes of the U.S.S.R. and Adjacent Countries*, tr. from the Russian, Washington, D.C., National Science Foundation, 1962.
Chekhov, Anton, *The Island: A Journey to Sakhalin*, New York, Washington Square Press, 1967.
Futaki, Hiroshi, "Notes on the Migration of the Masu Salmon in the Japan Sea," Bulletin of the Japan Sea Regional Fisheries Research Laboratory, No. 18, August 1967.
International North Pacific Fisheries Commission, Bulletin 6, "Movement of Salmon in the North Pacific Ocean and Bering Sea as Determined by Tagging, 1956–1958," by A. C. Hartt, Vancouver, B.C., 1962.
——, Bulletin 15, "Salmon of the North Pacific Ocean: Offshore Distribution of Salmon," by J. I. Manzer, T. Ishida, A. E. Peterson, and M. G. Hanavan, 1965.
——, Bulletin 16, "Coho, Chinook and Masu Salmon in Offshore Waters," by Harold Godfrey, J. E. Mason, and Shichi Tanaka, 1965.
——, Bulletin 18, "Sockeye Salmon in the Far East," by N. Hanamura,

"Pink Salmon in the Far East," by T. Ishida, and "Chum Salmon in the Far East," by S. Sano, 1966.

——, Bulletin 20, "Sockeye Salmon in Offshore Waters," by L. Margolis, F. C. Cleaver, Y. Fukuda, and H. Godfrey, 1966.

——, Bulletin 22, "Pink Salmon in Offshore Waters," by Ferris Neave, Teruo Ishida, and Sueto Murai.

Mori, Tamezo, *Check List of the Fishes of Korea*, Hyogo University of Agriculture, Sasayama, 1952.

Nikolsky, G. V., *Special Ichthyology*, Washington, D.C., National Science Foundation, 1961.

Smirnov, A. I., *The Biology of Reproduction and Development of the Coho*, tr. Fisheries Research Board of Canada, Series No. 287, 1960.

Survey of the Salmon and Trout Resources of the Republic of Korea, U.S. Agency for International Development and Republic of Korea, Seoul, June 30, 1967.

CHAPTER XXV

Russia's Salmon Wealth and Its Exploitation

Atkinson, Clinton E., *The Salmon Fisheries of the Soviet Far East*, M.S. thesis, University of Washington, 1964, unpublished.

Borgstrom, Georg, *Japan's World Success in Fishing*, London, Fishing News, 1964.

Chekhov, Anton, *The Island: A Journey to Sakhalin*, New York, Washington Square Press, 1967.

Chitwood, Philip E., *Japanese, Soviet and South Korean Fisheries Off Alaska*, U.S. Fish and Wildlife Service, Bureau of Commercial Fisheries, Circular 310, 1969.

Christy, Francis T., Jr., and Anthony Scott, *The Common Wealth in Ocean Fisheries*, Baltimore, Resources for the Future, 1965.

Dvinin, P. A., "Causes of the Decrease in Abundance of Sakhalin Pink Salmon in 1958," tr. W. E. Ricker, Fisheries Research Board of Canada, Nainamo, B.C., 1960.

Fukuhara, Francis M., *An Analysis of the Biological and Fishery Statistics of the Japanese Mothership Salmon Fishery*, Ph.D. thesis, University of Washington, unpublished.

International North Pacific Fisheries Commission, Bulletin 12, "Salmon of the North Pacific Ocean," Part I, 1963.

——, Bulletin 16, 1965, Part IV.

——, Bulletin 18, 1966.

——, Statistical Yearbook, 1967.

Johnston, Douglas M., *The International Law of Fisheries*, New Haven, Yale University Press, 1965.

Konda, Mitsuo, *Studies on the Optimum Mesh of Salmon Gill Net*, Hokkaido University, December 1966.

Kurenkov, I. I., "On the Causes of the Marked Decline in Kamchatka Salmon Populations," tr. R. E. Foerster, Fisheries Research Board of Canada, Nainamo, B.C., 1960.

Mowat, Farley, *The Siberians*, Boston, Little, Brown, 1971.

National Fisherman Yearbook, 1971.
"North Pacific Fisheries Symposium," *Washington Law Review,* School of
    Law, University of Washington, October 1967.
Oda, Shigeru, *International Control of Sea Resources,* Netherlands, A. W.
    Sythoff, 1963.
Pacific Salmon, Selected Articles from Soviet Periodicals, National Science
    Foundation, Washington, D.C., 1961.
Pares, Bernard, *Russia,* New York, Mentor Books, 1963.
Peoples of Siberia, ed. M. G. Levin and L. P. Potapov, tr. Stephen Dunn,
    University of Chicago Press, 1964.
Purdon, Rupert L., "World Trade in Canned Salmon," U.S. Department of
    Commerce, Promotion Series No. 14, 1925.
Salmon Fishing of the Far East, Ichthyological Commission (Moscow), ed.
    E. N. Pavlovskii, tr. Fisheries Research Board of Canada, 1964.
Semko, R. S., *The Stocks of West Kamchatka Salmon and Their Commer-
    cial Utilization,* tr. R. E. Foerster and Leda V. Sagan, Fisheries Re-
    search Board of Canada, Nainamo, B.C., 1960.
Van Cleve, Richard, and Ralph W. Johnson, *Management of the High Seas
    Fisheries of the Northeastern Pacific,* Contribution No. 160, Seattle,
    College of Fisheries, University of Washington, November 1963.

CHAPTER XXVI

Salmon Farming in Japan

Borgstrom, Georg, *Japan's World Success in Fishing,* London, Fishing
    News, 1964.
Ienago, Saburo, *History of Japan,* Tokyo, Japan Travel Bureau, 1962.
Konda, Mitsuo, *Studies on the Optimum Mesh of Salmon Gill Net,* Hok-
    kaido University, December 1966.
New Official Guide to Japan, Tokyo, Japan Travel Bureau, 1968.
Official Guide to Eastern Asia, Vol. III, *Northeastern Japan,* Tokyo, Japa-
    nese Government Railways, 1914.
Propagation of Chum Salmon in Japan, Japan Fisheries Resource Conser-
    vation Association, Tokyo, 1966.
Rudofsky, Bernard, *The Kimono Mind,* Garden City, N.Y., Doubleday,
    1965.
Van Cleve, Richard, "Japanese Freshwater Fisheries and Water Use Proj-
    ects," Supreme Commander for the Allied Powers, mimeographed,
    Tokyo, July 1951.

CHAPTER XXVII

Sport Fishing for Salmon and Steelhead Trout

Calcott, Ian, *The Art of Salmon Fishing,* Edinburgh, Oliver & Boyd, 1963.
Canadian Fisherman's Handbook by Jeremy Brown and John Power, Win-
    nipeg, Ontario, Greywood, 1970.
Day, J. Wentworth, *Angler's Pocket Book,* London, Evans Brothers, 1966.
Gingrich, Arnold, *The Well-Tempered Angler,* New York, Knopf, 1965.

Luch, Bill, and Frank W. Amato, *Steelhead Drift Fishing and Fly Fishing*, Seattle, Craftsman & Met Press, 1970.

McLaren, Moray, and William B. Currie, *The Fishing Waters of Scotland*, London, John Murray, 1972.

Ravensdale, Tom, *Understanding Salmon and Trout*, London, John Gifford, 1972.

CHAPTER XXVIII
Salmon — Our Earliest Gourmet Food

Beard, James, *James Beard's Fish Cookery*, New York, Paperback Library, 1969.

Brown, Dale, *American Cooking: The Northwest*, New York, Time-Life, 1970.

Cutting, Charles, *Fish Saving*, London, Leonard Hill, 1955.

Escoffier, A., *A Guide to the Fine Art of Cookery*, New York, Crown, 1948.

Gavin, Fernande, *The Art of French Cooking*, New York, Bantam Books, 1969.

Gramont, Sanche de, *The French*, New York, Putnam, 1969.

Hume, Rosemary, and Downes, Muriel, *Penguin Cordon Bleu Cookery*, Baltimore, Penguin Books, 1963.

Lacroix, Paul, *France in the Eighteenth Century*, New York, Ungar, 1963.

Larousse Gastronomique, New York, Crown, 1961.

Launay, Andre, *Posh Cooking*, Baltimore, Penguin Books, 1964.

Madame Prunier's Fish Cookery Book, London, Arrow, 1967.

Tannahill, Reay, *Food in History*, New York, Stein and Day, 1973.

Index

Adamson, William Agar, 195
Adour River (France), 120–21
Agaki, Munimori, 459
Age of Fishes (Devonian period), 3
Ainu ("salmon people") of Japan, 474–75
Alain (Count of Brittany), 122
Alaska: suitability of, for salmon production, 401–4; native peoples of, 404; start of commercial exploitation in, 404–7; fishing gear used in, 407–9; decline in salmon fishery, 409–10; impact of politics on salmon industry of, 411–14; Act of 1896 (Alaska fishery legislation), 412; impact of American sovereignty on natives of, 414–18; effect of statehood for, on salmon resource, 418–20; 1970 sockeye run at Bristol Bay, 420–24; impact on natives in Naknek, of salmon wealth, 424–25; salmon production on Kodiak Island, 425–27; current status of salmon production in, 427–29; threat of oil industry to salmon rivers in, 429–33; estimate of sockeye of, taken by Japan, 471; ocean sport salmon fishing regulations in, 512; sport fishing for Pacific salmon in rivers of, 513; commercial salmon catches (1906–70), 554–55; canned salmon pack (1940–71), 556
Alaska Native Brotherhood, 415–16

Alaska Native Claims Settlement Act (1971), 417–18
Alaskan Federation of Natives, 417
Alfonso el Sabio (King of Spain), fishery legislation, 113
Altamira cave (Spain), 41–43
Aluminum smelter, proposed construction of, on Columbia River, 308–9
Amato, Frank, 517–18
America, North (U.S.): Atlantic salmon in colonial era, 169–73; Atlantic salmon migrations and spawning in, 173–74; depopulation of New England rivers of, 174–80; Penobscot and other Maine rivers, 180–82; sport fishing for Atlantic salmon in, 182–83, 508–11, 515–16; decimation of Lake Ontario and Lake Champlain salmon in, 183–86; efforts to revive New England rivers in, 186–89
American Fishery Society, 249
Amur River, 439
Anadromous Fisheries Act (U.S.), 261
Anadromous fishes, defined, 4
ANDRS, see National Association for Protection of Salmon Rivers
Anglers' Cooperative Association (England), 80, 89
Angling, see Sport fishing for salmon
Anza, Juan Bautista de, 239

Appert, François, 276

Aquaculture: Pacific salmon, 342; Atlantic salmon, 343–44; in Japan, 489–94

Arctic Ocean, 162; Russian salmon rivers flowing into, 166–68

Armstrong, Rev. Benjamin, 70–71

Artedi, Peter (ichthyologist), 231

Artificial propagation of salmon: need for large-scale program of, in Great Britain, 88–89; Canadian interest in, 211; R. D. Hume's methods of, 325; early efforts at, 334–36; breakthrough in, 336–37; cycle of reproduction in, 337–39; effects of hatchery operations on salmon runs, 339–40; spawning channels for, 340–41; use of saltwater culture for, 342–44; in Japan, 479–84

Asia: major salmon rivers of, 437–40; species of salmon found in, 440–45; salmon landings of (1952–67), 457; future of Pacific salmon in, 470–71. *See also* Japan; Russia

Astoria, Oregon, 281, 308; as center of canning industry, 276, 277–78, 526

Atkins, Charles G., 179–80, 181, 182

Atkinson, Clinton E., 452, 453

Atlantic salmon (*Salmo salar*): origin of, 4; relationship of, to Pacific species, 7–8; range of, 9–10; catches of (1964–70), 10, 539; biological stages of, 11, 14; spawning of, 11, 31; life in the river of, 12–13; ocean life of, 21; life span of, 32; sport fishing for, 491–506; appearance of, 506; landings (1964–70), 539; catches in home waters (1960–71), 540

Atlantic Salmon Association (Canada), 202, 207, 219

Atlantic Salmon Research Trust (England), 87, 89

Atlantic Sea-Run Salmon Commission of Maine, 173, 186

Atomic Energy Commission, 307

Ausonius, 118

Austen, Jane, 490–91

Ayala, Don Pedro de, 57

Bachelier, Roger, 122, 124–25, 127

Backman, Kenneth, 317

Baltic Sea: fishes, 155–56; fishery, 158–60; Swedish river, emptying into, 160–62; Finnish rivers flowing into, 162–65; increasing pollution in, 165; Danish and Polish contributions to, 165–66; Russian rivers flowing into, 166, 168

Bancroft, Hubert H., 405

Barents Sea, 166, 167, 168

Barker, Thomas, *Art of Angling*, 488

Barnaby, Tom, 335

Barrington, A. D., 137

Bean, Tarleton H., 410

Beaufort, Duke of, 72

Bede, the Venerable, 45

Behr bill (California), 259

Bell, Frank, 287

Bell, Milo, 287, 288

Belloni, Judge Robert C., 303, 365

Belton, William, 146, 148

Bentley, Dr. William (of Salem, Mass.), 172–73

Beresford, Lord William, 146

Berg, Leo S. (ichthyologist), 440, 444

Berg, Magnus, on Norwegian salmon, 142, 144, 150, 153, 343

Bering, Vitus, 231, 234, 401, 404; expedition of, 225–26, 230

Berlingske Tidende (Copenhagen newspaper), 147

Berners (or Barnes), Dame Juliana, *The Treatise of Fishing with an Angle*, 75, 487–88

Bernhold, Dr. Jurgen, 138

Bez, Nick, 419

Birman, I. B., 442

Bismarck, Prince Otto von, 136

Blair, A. A., 184

Blood, Henry, 287

Boards of Conservators (Ireland), 107–8
Boas, Franz, 394, 395–96
Boece, Hector, 56
Boisset, L. de, 121, 126, 127
Bonaparte, Napoleon, 136, 276
Bonnefons, Nicolas de, 523
Bonneville dam (Columbia River), 285–89, 292, 295; salmon counted at (1938–70), 548
Bonneville Power Administration (BPA), 297, 308
Booth, F. S., 475–76
Borland, Joseph, 81
Borrell, Max, 113–17
Boyle, Richard (Earl of Cork), 92
Bradner, Enos, 519
Brady, John G., 412
Brauer, Ernest A., 513
Breuil, Henri, 40, 530–31
Brian Boru (King of Ireland), 98
Bridges and Roads, Bureau of (France), 127
British Columbia, 367; salmon rivers of, 368–69; salmon runs of, 369–71; early traders and canners of, 371–75; commercial salmon fishing in, 375–76; salmon disaster at Hell's Gate in, 376–80; Adams River in, 380, 383–84; controversy over damming of Fraser River, 384–86; sport fishing in, 386–88, 514; salmon situation in, summarized, 389–90; "cedar and salmon" people of, 391–96; destruction of Indian culture in, 397–98; Indian fishing in, 398–99; Indian way of life in, 399–400; ocean sport salmon fishing regulations in, 512; salmon pack (1940–71), 552–53
Brooks, James, 432
Brooks, Joe, 516
Buchanan-Smith, Alick, 85, 89
Buck, Richard A. (CASE), 188, 218
Buckland, Frank T., 65–66, 67–68, 71
Buffon, Count Georges Louis, 334
Bulleid, M. J., 88, 89

Burney, Fanny, 234
Burney, James, 234
Burrows, Roger E., 337

Cabot, John and Sebastian, 171
Caesar, Julius, 45, 134
Calcott, Ian, 519
California: decline of the salmon in, 235–36; species of salmon in rivers of, 236–38; aboriginal population of, 239–40; and Yurok first salmon ceremony, 240–44; Yurok Indians of, 240–47; and construction of Kepel dam by Yurok, 244–46; commercial fishing in, 247–49; effects of hydraulic mining on salmon runs, 250; commercial salmon landings (1916–70), 542–43; environmental destruction in, 249–56; effects of Central Valley Project, 252–56; Water Code, 261; conservation efforts in, 256–62; Advisory Committee on Salmon and Steelhead Trout in, 257–58, 260–62; major salmon rivers for sport fishing in, 509; ocean sport salmon fishing regulations in, 512
Canada: Atlantic salmon rivers of, 191–94; Atlantic salmon rivers for sport fishing, 504–5; exploitation of Quebec fishery, 194–97; exploitation of maritime fisheries, 197–200; rise of sport fishing in, 200–202; 504–6; efforts to halt decline of Atlantic salmon stock, 202–7; impact of Greenland fishery on Atlantic salmon of, 207–8; curtailment of commercial fishing for Atlantic salmon in, 208–11; Pacific salmon landings of (1952–67), 457
Canadian Fisheries Act, 389–90
Canadian National Railroad (formerly Canadian Northern), 376
Canadian Pacific Railroad, 373, 376
Canning industry, salmon: California, 248–49; Columbia River, 276–

Canning industry, *contd.*
78; Oregon coastal rivers, 325–28; British Columbia, 371–75; Alaska, 405–7, 409, 416–17; Japan, 453, 454, 455

Carlin, Borje, 157

Carlos IV (King of Spain), 114

Carter, Wilfred, 191–92, 199, 207, 208, 210, 217

Cartwright, John and Edmund, 193

CASE, *see* Committee for the Atlantic Salmon Emergency

Caxton, William, 487

Celilo Falls (Columbia River): Indian fishery at, 269–71, 302, 303; first salmon ceremonies at, 273–74, 290–91

Central Valley Project (CVP), California, 252–56, 261

Chalkhill, Joseph, 490

Chambers, E. D. T., 197

Champlain, Lake, decimation of salmon in, 183, 185

Chapman, Dr. Carleton B., 71

Chapralis, Jim C., 493–94, 505

Charles II (King of England), 69, 97

Chaucer, Geoffrey, 49, 487

Chekhov, Anton, 439, 440–41, 449, 451, 468

Cherry salmon (*Oncorhynchus masu*), 8, 10; biological data for, 29; in Asia, 444; in Japan, 474

Chinese, employment of, in Columbia River canneries, 277; in Fraser River canneries, 374

Chinook Indians (Columbia River), 267; lore of, 271–73; first salmon ceremonies of, 273–74, 290–91

Chinook (king) salmon (*Oncorhynchus tshawytscha*), 9–10, 11, 16; return of, to the river, 25, 26; upstream journeys of, 28; biological data for, 29; life span of, 32; of Kamchatka (called *chavitcha*), 229–30; in California, 236–38; in the Columbia River, 265–66, 304–5; in Willamette River, 312, 314–15, 319–20, 321; in Oregon's

Chinook (king) salmon, *contd.*
coastal streams, 328, 330–31; artificial propagation of, 339, 340; transplantations of, 344–45; in Puget Sound, 358–59, 360–61; in British Columbia rivers, 369–71; in Alaska (called kings), 405, 408–9, 424; in Asia, 440, 445; appearance of, 506; in New Zealand (called "quinnat"), 507; in North America, 509; food value of, 521, 527

Chorpening, Gen., 292–93

Christensen, Ole, 215

Christy, Francis T., Jr., 219

Chum salmon (*Oncorhynchus keta*), 10, 12, 13, 15, 19; return to the river of, 25, 26, 28; biological data for, 29; in Kamchatka (called *keta*), 230; in the Columbia River, 265, 266, 305, 306; in Oregon's coastal streams, 330; transplantation of, 345; in Puget Sound, 358; in British Columbia rivers, 369–70; in Alaska, 405, 424, 426; in Asia, 440–42; Soviet catches of along Far East coast (1940–69), 465; in Japan, 474; appearance of, 506; food value of, 521, 527

Clark, Elisha, 184

Clark, Ella E., 271–72

Clark, Grahame, 37–38

Clay, C. H., 287, 294

Clean Rivers (Estuaries and Tidal Waters) Act of 1960 (England), 79

Clean Water Act of 1965 (U.S.), 318–19

Clerke, Capt. Charles, 233, 234

Clyde River (Scotland), 50, 63

Cobb, John N., 283, 351, 379, 405, 413, 476

Coble, use of, in salmon fishing, 56, 86, 87

Coho (silver) salmon (*Oncorhynchus kisutch*), 15, 16, 23; biological data for, 29; in California, 236, 238; in the Columbia River,

Coho (silver) salmon, *contd.*
265, 266, 305–6; in the Willamette River, 319–20; in Oregon's coastal streams, 328, 330; artificial propagation of, 339–40; transplantations of, 344–45; in Puget Sound, 358–59, 360–61; in British Columbia rivers, 369–71; in Alaska, 405, 424, 426; in Asia, 440, 444–45; Soviet catches of, along Far East coast (1940–69), 465; appearance of, 506; in Lake Michigan, 515–16; food value of, 521, 527

Colbert, Jean Baptiste, 125

Cole, Grenville, 92

College of Fisheries (University of Washington), 342

Columbia River (Canada-U.S.): described, 263–65; salmon runs in, 265–66; Indian fishery of, 267–74; first salmon rites at Celilo village on, 273–74, 290–91; arrival of white settlers and commercial fishermen, 274–76; canning industry of, 276–78; fishing gear and fishermen of, 279–81; fishing regulations of, 281–83; effect of development of watershed on salmon runs of, 283–85; impact of dam construction on fish populations of, 285–90, 292–97; Fishery Development Program of, 297–98; taming of, 298–300; resurgence of Indian fishery in, 302–3; commercial versus sport fishing on, 303–4; current status of fishery of, 304–7; future of fishery of, 307–10; landings of salmon and steelhead trout (1866–1970), 544–46; canned salmon pack (1940–71), 547

Columbia River Packers Association, 405

Combs, Trey, 519

Commercial Fisheries, Bureau of (U.S.), 296, 297, 413, 418, 420

Commercial salmon fishing: need for curtailment of, in Great Britain,

Commercial salmon fishing, *contd.*
89; need for regulation of, in Ireland, 108; Eastern Canadian curtailment of, 208–11; in California, 247–49; banning of, in Oregon coastal rivers, 328–29

Committee for the Atlantic Salmon Emergency (CASE), 188, 218

Committee of Two Million (California), 258–59

Connecticut River (New England), destruction of, 177–78; restoration efforts, 187–88

Conservation programs in Great Britain, 64–68, 76–82; in Norway, 145; in Canada, 208–11; in California, 256–62; in Columbia River, 297–98

Cook, Capt. James, 347, 391, 393, 404; discoveries of, 231–34

Cookery, salmon: French, 122–23, 523–24; Indian, 521; medieval, 522; abundance of salmon for, 524–26; present status of, 528–29

Cookson, Col. Fife, 76

Cornwall, I. W., 40

Corps of Engineers, U.S. Army, 357; and California rivers, 256, 258, 259; "308 Report" on Columbia River, 285; and dams built on Columbia River, 285–87, 289–90, 307; on Willamette River, 311, 318; on Oregon's Rogue River, 331; and Oregon's estuaries, 332, 333

Corte-Real, Gaspar and Miguel, 171

Couch, Capt. John, 274

Coull, James R., 55–56

Cousteau, Jacques, 426–27

Coxon, Richard, 70

Coyote (mythological god), 271–73

Cressman, L. S., 267, 530

Cro-Magnons, 35–36

Crowe, Philip K., 168, 519; on salmon fishing in Spain, 117, 495; on Norwegian sport fishing, 152; on the Connecticut River, 178; on Iceland, 494

Crutchfield, J. A., 351, 358–59, 411

Culture, salmon, *see* Artificial propagation of salmon
Curraghs, use of, in Irish salmon
fishing, 101, 105–6
Currie, William B., 50–51, 80, 82,
499, 500
Cutting, Charles, 522

Daggett, Ezra, 276
Dahl, Knut (Norwegian ichthyolo-
gist), 142, 149, 525
Dalles dam, The (Columbia River),
290, 292, 295, 296, 302
Dams, effects on salmon stocks of:
in Scotland, 81–82; in Ireland,
101–3; in Iberian peninsula, 114–
15; in France, 125, 126; in Nor-
way, 152; in Sweden, 156–58; in
the United States, 177–78; on Co-
lumbia River, 285–90; 292–97; in
California, 250–56; in Japan,
477–78
Daniel, William B., 95
Darling, Fraser, 52
Dart River (England), 49
Darwin, Charles R., 7, 8
Dasmann, Raymond, 255
Davidson, William, 193
Davis, Jack, 209, 386, 390
Day, Francis, 4
Day, J. Wentworth, 499
DDT, damage to fishes from Can-
adian forest spraying of, 204–6
Deelder, C. L. (on Rhine salmon),
137
Dee River (Scotland), 50, 51
Defoe, Daniel, 49, 57–58
Dempster, George, 58–59
Denisoff, Count Nicholas, 147
Denmark, salmon fishing in, 155,
165–66
Dery, Louis, 196
Devonshire, Duke of, 92, 100
Dickens, Charles, on salmon crisis,
64–65; 525
Dingell-Johnson Anadromous Fish
Act (U.S.), 187

Disease, salmon, *see* U.D.N.
Domesday Book, salmon fisheries
listed in, 45
Dominis, Capt. John, 274
Donaldson, Lauren, 339
Don River (Scotland), 50, 51
Dordogne River (France), 120
Douglas, David, 267
Drake, Sir Francis, 347
Drucker, Philip, 270, 273, 393
Dudley, Earl of, 148
Durand, Peter, 276
Dvinin, F. A., 464–67
Dwight, Timothy, 177
Dysart, George, 303

Eastwood, John F., 80
Ecologist, quoted, 534
Eden River (England), 46, 497
Edward I (King of England), 54
Edward III (King of England), 69
Edward IV (King of England), 53
Edward VII (King of England),
487
Egan, William, Governor of Alaska,
432–33
Ekman, Sven, 7–8
Électricité de France (EDF), 127
Electricity Supply Board (ESB), Ire-
land, 102, 108
Elizabeth I (Queen of England),
96–97, 488
Elizabeth II (Queen of England),
487
England: salmon rivers of, 46–49,
54–55, 83–85; despoiling of, 60–
62, 65–67, 78–80; sport fishing in,
496–99. *See also* Great Britain
Environmental Protection Agency
(U.S.), 181, 297, 315, 319
Environmental Quality Commission
(U.S.), 319
Ericson, Leif, 169, 171
Escoffier, Auguste, 528
Evans, Nicholas, 215, 216
Evolution of the salmon, 3–4; origin
(freshwater versus marine), 4–7;

Evolution of the salmon, *contd.*
    evolution of Pacific species, 7–9;
    range of the salmon, 9–10
Ewan, Alexander, 372
Exe River (England), 49

Fairchild, C. G., 265
Feather River project (California),
    256
Federal Power Act (U.S.), 261
Federal Power Commission (U.S.),
    262, 301–2
Federal-Provincial Coordinating
    Committee on Atlantic Salmon
    (Canada), 202
Federal Water Pollution Control
    Administration (now Environ-
    mental Protection Agency)
    (U.S), 315–16, 356
Federal Water Project Recreation
    Act (U.S.), 261
Field, The, 76, 492, 495, 499
Field and Stream, quoted, 206, 494
Fiennes, Celia, 58
Finland: salmon fishing in, 155, 156,
    162–65; sport fishing for salmon
    in, 492
Finnish Water Law, 165
Fish and Game Code (California),
    262
Fish and Game Commission (Cali-
    fornia), 248, 254
Fish and Game Department of
    Alaska, 420–21, 423
Fish and Game Department of Cali-
    fornia, 258, 259, 260, 261–62
Fish and Game Department of
    Idaho, 341
Fish and Wildlife Service, U.S., 289,
    336
Fish Commissioners, Board of (Ore-
    gon), 327
Fish Commission of Oregon, 282,
    283, 302–3, 320, 321; status re-
    port on stocks in Columbia River,
    305–6; and rehabilitation of Wil-
    lamette River, 319; annual
    spawning survey of coastal

streams, 329, 330; work of, in
    artificial propagation, 336, 339
Fish Commission of Washington
    State, 282, 302–3
Fish Commission, U.S., 334
Fisheries, Washington Department
    of, 314, 341, 351, 355, 360, 379
Fisheries Research Board of Canada,
    203
Fisheries Research Institute (Uni-
    versity of Washington), 410, 418,
    419, 420, 428
Fisheries Resource Conservation As-
    sociation (Japan), 479
Fishing gear and methods: evolu-
    tion of, 36–39; history of Irish,
    97–99; on Columbia River, 279–
    81; Alaskan, 407–9
Fish wheels, described, 280
Fitzdavid, Milo, 94
Fly Fishers Club, 80
Foerster, R. E., 8, 13, 16, 20, 25
Food, *see* Cookery, salmon
Forest Practice Act (California), 261
Foyle Fisheries Commission (Ire-
    land), 103
Framboisière, Abraham de la, 123
Frame, George W., 17
France: salmon rivers of, 118–21;
    abundance of salmon in, before
    Revolution of 1789, 121–22; salm-
    on as dietary staple in, 122–23;
    scarcity of salmon in, 123–26; cur-
    rent status of salmon, 126–32;
    sport fishing for Atlantic salmon,
    494–95
Francis, Francis, 70
Franck, Richard, 57
Franco, Gen. Francisco, 114, 117,
    495
Fraser, T. B., 207–8
Fraser River (British Columbia):
    described, 368; salmon runs in,
    369–71; discovery of gold in, 372;
    canneries of, 372–74; Hell's Gate
    salmon disaster on, 376–80; man-
    agement of salmon resource, 380–
    83; controversy over damming of,
    384–86

Frome, Michael, 494
Frome River (England), 48–49, 496–97
Fukuhara, Francis M., 457–58
Fukuyama, Baron of, 451
FWPCA, *see* Federal Water Pollution Control Administration

Garonne River (France), 120
General Electric Company (Portland, Oregon), 307
George, Dorothy, 58
George I (King of England), 54
George III (King of England), 193
George Red Hawk, 288
Germany, salmon fishing in, 155, 166
Gesner, Konrad von, 4
Gestin, Yves, 124
Gharrett, John T., 329
Gilbert, Charles H., 28, 413
Gilbert, Sir Humphrey, 96–97
Gingrich, Arnold, 491, 503–4, 519
Giraldus Cambrensis (Gerald the Welshman), 45, 92
Gladstone, William E., 75
Gmelin, Georg, 226
Godfrey, Harold, 370–71
Golder, F. A., 227
Goodspeed, Charles E., 182
Gooking, Daniel, 172
Gordon, Duke of, 55
Grand Coulee dam (Columbia River), 285, 289
Great Britain, 45–46; salmon rivers of England and Wales, 46–49, 83–85, 496, 497; salmon rivers of Scotland, 49–52, 73–74, 85–87; fishing rights in, 52–53; protection of salmon in, 53–55; history of salmon fishing in, 55–59; impact of Industrial Revolution on salmon rivers in, 59–64, 497; salmon conservation legislation in, 64–68, 76–82; destruction of the Thames River, 68–72; resuscitation of the Wye River, 72–73; growth of sport fishing in, 74–76,

Great Britain, *contd.*
496–502; future of the salmon in, 87–90
Greenland salmon fishery, 213–16; impact on Maine salmon runs of, 187; impact of, on Atlantic salmon resource in Canada, 207–8, 209; accelerating conflict over, 216–17; efforts to curtail, 217–19, 220–21; problem of ownership of the salmon, 219–20
Grenfell, Sir Wilfred, 199
Grey, Sir Edward (Viscount of Fallodon), 75, 107, 496, 519
Grey, Zane, 331, 518, 519
Grieve, James, 231
Griffiths, Roger, 70
Grimble, Augustus, 47, 100, 107
Grotius, Hugo, 219–20
Gruening, Ernest, 406, 411, 419
Guggenheim interests in Alaska canneries, 411
Guidance mechanisms for salmon ocean migrations, 21–25
Gunther, A., 4
Gwynn, Stephen, 94, 503

Haig-Brown, Roderick, 15, 374; on the Frome River, 48–49, 496–97; on damming the Fraser River, 384, 386; on British Columbian sport fishing, 388, 519
Hall, Wade B., 302
Hapgood, Andrew, 247, 276
Hardy, Sir Alister, 213
Harley, Robert (Lord Oxford), 57
Hartt, A. C., 423–24
Hasler, Arthur D., 23, 156
Hatcheries, salmon: early, 334–36; development of, 337–39; effects on salmon populations, 339–40
Hawthorne, Mont, 277, 406
Healey, M. C., 23
Hedgpeth, Joel, on California salmon, 250, 252
Heilner, Van Campen, 514, 520
Hell's Canyon (Snake River), 301

Hell's Gate (Fraser River), 368; salmon disaster at, 351, 372, 374, 376–80
Hennessy, David, 372
Henri IV (King of France), 121
Henriksen, Henrik, 502
Herbert, H. A., 72
Hewitt, Edward R., 520
Higden, Ranulf, 45
High Mountain Sheep dam (Snake River), proposed and rejected by U.S. Supreme Court, 301
High seas fishery: Norwegian, 149–53; curtailment of Canadian, 209, 211; Japanese, 456–61
Hill, A. V., 375
Hiroshige, 446, 477
Hodges, John I., 329
Hoek, P. P. C., 137
Hokusai, 477
Hollbrook, Stewart, 279, 281
Holm, Don, 332
Holmes, Harlan B., 287
Home, Earl of, 502
Hoover, Herbert, 313
Horonobu, 477
Hourston, Rod, 389
Housekeeper's Manual, on sport fishing, 183
Hudson's Bay Company, activities in eastern and western Canada in relation to salmon resources, 194, 195, 274, 318, 371
Humboldt, Alexander von, 476
Hume, George W. and William (early salmon canners), 247, 276, 350
Hume, R. D. (salmon canner), 325, 331, 405
Hunter, Robert, 365
Hunter Committee (Scotland), 90
Hurme, Seppo (Finnish biologist), 162, 163–65
Hutton, J. A., 31–32

Iberian peninsula: salmon rivers and fishing in, 111–15; sport fishing in, 115–18

Ice Harbor dam (Snake River), 292–94, 295, 296
Iceland, sport fishing for Atlantic salmon in, 493–94
ICNAF, *see* International Commission for North Atlantic Fisheries
Idaho, major salmon rivers for sport fishing in, 509
Idyll, C. P., 345
Indian Affairs, Bureau of (U.S.), 425
Indian Affairs, Department of (British Columbia), 397
Indians, importance of salmon to: in California, 239–47; on Columbia River, 267–74, 290–91, 302–3; on Oregon coastal rivers, 324; and fishing controversy on the Columbia River, 302–3; in Puget Sound, 364–65; in British Columbia, 391–400; in Alaska, 404
Ingstad, Helge (discoverer of Vinland), 169
Initiative 77, passage of, by Washington legislature, 351–52
International Atlantic Salmon Foundation, 87, 128, 209, 211
International Commission for North Atlantic Fisheries (ICNAF), 209, 216, 218, 220
International Commission for the Protection of the Rhine Against Pollution, 138
International Council for the Exploration of the Sea, 133, 163, 166, 168
International North Pacific Fishery Commission, 432, 455
International Pacific Salmon Fisheries Commission (IPSFC), 341, 371, 383; creation of, 379–80; on proposed Moran dam (Fraser River), 385–86
Ireland: early fisheries of, 91–92; salmon rivers of, 92–96, 503; history of salmon use on, 96–97; fishing methods of, 97–99; problem of overfishing in, 99–101; impact of dams on salmon in,

Ireland, *contd.*
101–3; current status of salmon in, 103–6; sport fishing in, 106–9, 502–4
Irish Inland Fishery Commission, 100
Irish Salmon Research Trust, 89, 104
Ishkov, Alexander H., 459

Jacobi, Lieutenant (first salmonid culturist), 334
James I (King of England), 488
James III (King of Scotland), 55
James V (King of Scotland), 522
Japan: 438–39; yearly salmon catch of, 440; Tokyo fish market, 445–46; exploitation of Russia's salmon runs by, 451–54; effects of Japanese-Soviet treaties with, on Soviet salmon stocks, 452–55, 459, 461–63; high seas fishing by, 454–56; salmon landings of (1952–67), 457; Hakodate's salmon fleet, 459–61; estimate of Alaskan sockeye taken by, 471; salmon rivers of, 473–74, 482; "salmon people" of, 474–75; early fishery, 475–76; deterioration of rivers of, 476–79; artificial propagation, 479–84; commercial salmon catches (1957–69), 558; mother-ship fishery catches (1952–68), 559
Japan-Soviet Fisheries Commission, 457, 459
Jarvi, T. H., 163
Jeffries, Ernest, 335–36
Jenness, Diamond, 398
John Day dam (Columbia River), 290, 292, 295, 296, 297, 298
Johnson, Andrew P., 275, 414, 531–32
Juan II (King of Portugal), 113
Juan de Fuca Strait, 347, 348, 350; trolling in, 351, 354, 375; effects of pulp mills on salmon in, 355; sport fishing in, 359, 360

Kamchatka Peninsula (U.S.S.R.), 225–29, 438, 467–68; account of Pacific salmon in *Natural History of Kamchatka*, 229–31; Capt. Cook's stay in, 234
Kamchatka River (U.S.S.R.), 227, 228, 229, 438, 445; species of salmon in, 443–45; decline of salmon stocks in, 467–68
Kask, J. L., 203–4
Kasimierz, Demel, 168
Kennan, George, 449
Kerr, Richard, 524–25
Ketchikan, Alaska, called "world's salmon capital," 406
Kidd, Gerry, quoted, 385
King salmon, *see* Chinook salmon
Kodiak Island (Alaska), salmon production on, 425–27
Kokanee (sockeye salmon), 9, 362, 444
Korea, salmon in rivers of, 440
Korn, Lawrence, 295–96
Kosygin, Aleksei, 459
Krashnennikov, Stepan P., *Natural History of Kamchatka*, 228, 229, 230, 231
Kroeber, A. L., 239, 240
Krug, Julius, 419
Krupp, Alfred A., 134
Kurenkov, Igor, 459

Lacroix, Paul, 123, 523
Lagunov, I. I., 462
Landseth, Helen, 96
Lang, Andrew, 75, 491
Lantier, Raymond, 40
Lappea, Uno, 525
La Rocque, Joseph Felix, 194
Larousse Gastronomique, 524
LaViolette, Forrest E., 397
Law of the Sea Conference (scheduled for 1974), 389
Lawson, Christopher, 173
Le Danois, Edouard, 9
Leicester, Earl of, 146
Le Mercier and Le Moyne, Jesuit Fathers, 183–84

Lever Brothers (aquaculture experiment), 344
Lewis and Clark expedition, 267–68, 270, 290, 298
Liddell, Peter, 107–9, 215
Lindroth, Arne (Swedish biologist), 161, 166, 168
Linnaeus, Carolus, 230
Lipton, Sir Thomas, 147
Locke, David O., 187
Loggie, Alexander (early British Columbia canner), 372
Logging industry, contribution of, to pollution of Puget Sound rivers, 354–55
Loire River (France), fishery, 120
"Lords' rivers" (Norway), 146–49
Louis XIV (King of France), 123, 125, 136, 523
Louis XV (King of France), 123, 523
Louis XVI (King of France), 523
Lovat, Lord, 51
Lox (mild-cure salmon), demand for, 526–27
Lune River (England), 46–47, 49

McCall, Tom, Governor of Oregon, 308, 321
McClane, Al, 492
McDonald, John, 520
McDonald, Lucille, 281
Macfarlane, J. M., 4–6
McKay, Douglas, 294
McKean, John, 320
McKenna, Joseph, 275
McKervill, Hugh, 372
McLaren, Moray, 50, 499
McLoughlin, John, 312
McMillan, Archibald, 371
McNary dam (Columbia River), 290, 292, 295, 298
Mactaquac dam (New Brunswick), effect on salmon of, 206
Magnuson, Warren, 293
Maine, salmon rivers of, 178–82
Maine Water Improvement Commission, 181

Malcolm II (King of Scotland), 53
Marine, Ministry of (France), 127
Maritime fisheries, *see under* Canada
Marsh, Millard C., 413
Martensen, Capt. Ole, 215–16
Marzales, Marques de, 114–15
Mascall, Leonard, 54
Masu, *see* Cherry salmon
Matley, Marjorie, 399
Matsumae, Baron of, 451
Meader, J. W., 176
Meister, Alfred L., 186
Menzies, W. J. M., 21, 81, 202–3, 213
Merced Irrigation District (California), 260
Merced River (California), 259–60
Merrimack River (New England), 172, 176–77, 182
Mesolithic (Middle Stone) Age, 36; fishing gear in, 37–38
Meuse River (Western Europe), demise of, 133
Michigan, Lake, sport salmon fishing craze in, 515–16
Migration of salmon: juvenile life in the river, 11–15; ocean life, 15–21; guidance mechanisms for, 21–25; return to the river for reproduction and death, 25–32
Miramichi Salmon Association (Canada), 219
Mitchill Samuel Latham, 172, 177
Mokwina, Chief, 391
Molina, Tirso de, *Trickster of Seville*, quoted, 112
Moore, Alfred, 91, 97
Moreau, Émile, 125
Morgan, J. P., 411
Morse, Senator Wayne, 293
Mortimer, John and Festy, 105–6
Moryson, Fynes, 96
Moselle River (France), 118
Mosely, Sir Oswald, 60
Mosher, Jefferson, 408, 416
Moss, Frank, 177
Mowat, Farley, 470
Moyseev, Peter (Russian ichthyologist), 455, 459

Muir, John, 401–2
Müller, G. F., 226

Nader, Ralph, 255
National Association for Protection
of Salmon Rivers (ANDRS),
France, 128
National Environmental Council
(Great Britain), 88
National Marine Fisheries Service
(U.S.), 296, 307, 339, 342
National Waters Restoration League
(Ireland), 108–9
National Wildlife Federation (U.S.),
331
Neave, Ferris, 7–9, 23–24, 35, 444
Neolithic (New Stone) Age, 36;
fishing gear in, 37, 38
Nets: use of, in medieval period, 56;
British regulation or suppression
of fixed, 65; Scottish use of bag
and fly, 86–87. *See also* Fishing
gear and methods
Nettle, Richard, on St. Lawrence
salmon rivers, 195–99
Neuberger, Richard L., 288
Nevins, Allan, 354
New England rivers, interest in re-
vival of, 186–89
New Zealand, sport fishing for Pa-
cific salmon in, 507–8
Nichiro Fishing Company (Japan),
460–61
Nielsen, Jørgen, 213
Nikolsky, G. V. (Russian ichthyolo-
gist), 6
Nixon, President Richard M., 218,
431
NMFS, *see* National Marine Fish-
eries Service
Noerenberg, Wallace, 432
Norris, Thad., 201
North American Atlantic Salmon
Council, 209
Northumberland, Duke of, 66
Northwest Estuary and Coastal Zone
Symposium (U.S.), 358

Northwest Steelheaders (U.S.), 516
Norway: salmon rivers of, 141–42,
492; salmon migration patterns
in, 142–43; history of salmon
fishery in, 143–45; salmon conservation in, 145; sport fishing in,
145–49, 492; high seas fishery in,
149–53; achievements in saltwater culture, 342–44
Nuclear power industry, effect on
salmon in Columbia River, 307–
10

O'Dell, Andrew C., 162
Oglesby, Arthur, 82
Oil industry, threat to Alaska salm-
on by, 430–33
Olin, John M., 221
Olsen, Rolf, 153
O'Malley, Henry, 413
Oncorhynchus gorbuscha, see Pink
salmon
Oncorhynchus keta, see Chum salm-
on
Oncorhynchus kisutch, see Coho
salmon
Oncorhynchus masu, see Cherry
salmon
Oncorhynchus nerka, see Sockeye
salmon
Oncorhynchus species (Pacific salmon): 4, 231; evolution of Atlantic
salmon into, 8–9
Oncorhynchus tshawytscha, see
Chinook salmon
Ontario, Lake, decimation of salmon
in, 183–85
Oregon: salmon in coastal streams of,
323–24; aborigines of, 324; assault on fishery of, 324–28; closure of coastal rivers to commercial fishing, 328–29; sport fishing
in, 330–31, 509; and abuse of the
estuaries, 331–33; ocean sport
salmon fishing regulations in, 512
Oregon Boundary Treaty of 1846,
311, 348

Oregon Dunes Recreational Area, 333
Oregon Fish and Game Protector, report of, 282–83
Oregon Game Commission, 320–21, 329–30, 341
Oregonian (Portland), 277, 332
Oregon State University, 336
Organic Act for Alaska (1884), 415
Ormond, Duke of, 94
Ottar, Brynjulf, 153
Overnetting, problem of, in Ireland, 99–101

Pacific Coast Biological Station (British Columbia), 340
Pacific Fisheries and Oceanographic Institute (TINRO), U.S.S.R., 464
Pacific Marine Fisheries Commission (U.S.), 352
Pacific salmon (*Oncorhynchus*): origin of, 4; range of, 5, 9–10; evolution of, 7–9; catches of (1964–70), 10; biological stages of, 11, 14; juvenile life in the river of, 12–13; ocean life of, 16–20; biological data for, 29; life span of, 32; scientific and local names of, 231; sport fishing for, 507–16; landings (1952–70), 541; by species (1964–70), 541
Pacific Tourist, 235
Paleolithic (Old Stone) Age, 35–36; fishing gear in, 37; *Salmo salar* and the cave men in, 39, 41
Pallas, Peter Simon, 230
Paper and pulp mills, contribution to pollution of Willamette River, 312–14; in Puget Sound, 355–57
Paradise, Scott, quoted, 532–33
Park, Donald L., 296
Parker, Sir Hyde, 146, 148
Pashley, Robert, 73, 76, 499
Payne, John, 250
Pearson, Anthony, 78–79
Peery, William K., 271
Pennant, Thomas, 230–31

Penobscot River (Maine), 180–182; sport fishing in, 182–83; interest in revival of, 186–87
Pentelow, F. T. K., 78
Perry, L. E., 297, 340
Perry, Commodore Matthew, 477
Peters, Samuel A., 174
Peter the Great, 225
Petroff, Ivan, 405
Petrova, Z. I., 467
Phelipot, Pierre, 128–29, 131
Philip II (King of Spain), 96, 113
Pickernell, Clarence, 364
Piggins, David, 89, 104, 109
Pink (or humpbacked) salmon (*Oncorhynchus gorbuscha*), 10, 230; juvenile life in the river of, 12, 13, 15; life span of, 18, 19; migrations of, 23; physiological changes in, 26; biological data for, 29; in the Columbia River, 265, 266, 306; in the Willamette River, 315; transplantation of, 345; in Puget Sound, 351, 358–59, 360, 361; in British Columbia rivers, 369–71; in Alaska, 405, 424, 426; in Asia, 440, 442–43; Soviet catches of, along Far East coast (1940–69), 465; in Japan, 474; appearance of, 506; food value of, 521, 527
Pitney, William E., 295
Pliny the Elder, *Natural History*, 118
Poaching: in Scotland, 63–64; penalties in Ireland compared with England, 107–8; in Spain, 117; in France, 122, 129–31; Canadian, 206; in Alaska, 408; in Japan, 479
Poland, salmon fishing in, 155, 156, 166
Polarlaks (cutter), 215–16
Pollexfen, George, 100
Pollution: effects on British salmon fishing, 60–63, 65–66, 71–72, 78–81; relative absence of, in Ireland, 103, 109; in Iberian peninsula, 115; in French rivers, 126; in the Rhine River, 138–39; in Norwe-

Pollution, *contd.*
gian rivers, 153; in the Baltic Sea, 165; in American rivers, 177–78, 180–81, 183, 185–89; impact on Canadian salmon runs, 203–6; in Willamette River, 313–20 *passim;* of Puget Sound, 354–58; in Japanese rivers, 478, 483–84; need for deceleration of industrial activity to conquer, 534–35
Pontecorvo, Giulio, 351, 358–59, 411
Pope, Alexander, quoted, 393, 532
Portland, Duke of, 501–2
Portugal, salmon rivers of, 111–13
Pottinger, Sir Henry, 146
Poyarkov, Vasily, 447
Pravdin, I. F., 227
Primitive man: relationship of salmon and, 35–43 *passim,* 530–33; first record of salmon and, in North America, 169–70; of Russia, 447–49
Puget Sound: discovery of, by Vancouver, 347–48; timber and fish of, 348–54; pollution in, 354–58; downward trend in fisheries of, 358–59; sport fishery in, 359–62; and Lake Washington's sockeye fishery, 362–64; and Indian fishing controversy, 364–65; salmon catches (1913–66), 549–50; salmon pack on (1940–71), 551
Purchase, Thomas, 173

Quebec fishery, *see under* Canada
Quinault River Treaty, 349

Rabaut, Congressman, 292–93
Raleigh, Sir Walter, 92
Raymond, Howard L., 296
Reader, John, 105–6
Reagan, Ronald, 259
Reclamation, Bureau of (California), 258, 259, 260; Central Valley

Reclamation, Bureau of, *contd.*
Project of, 252–56; and Grand Coulee dam, 285; and Snake River dams, 300; and Columbia River, 307
Reed, George, 333
Refuse Act of 1899 (U.S.), 313, 357
Requart, Sañez, 113
Research, salmon: need for long-term, in Great Britain, 88, 89; Ireland's program of, 104
Restoration of Atlantic Salmon in America, Inc. (RASA), 188–89
Rhine River (Western Europe), demise of, 133, 134–39
Ribble River (England), 46–47, 49
Rich, Willis H., report on Columbia River runs, 283
Richard, René, 131
Richard II (King of England), 54
Richard the Lion-hearted, 53
Richmond, H. Russell (Bonneville Power Administration), 308
Ripon, Marquess of, 502
Ritchie, James, 63
Ritz, Charles, 520
River Boards Act of 1948 (England and Wales), 77
Rivers (Prevention of Pollution) Act of 1951, 1960, and 1961 (England and Wales), 77, 79
Rivers, salmon: England and Wales, 46–49, 54–55, 60–62, 65–67, 83–85; Scotland, 49–52, 62–64, 73–74, 85–87; Ireland, 92–96; Spain and Portugal, 111–13, 115–18; France, 118–21; Norway, 141–42, 146–49, 151–53; Sweden, 160–62; of United States, depopulation of, 174–80; New England, interest in revival of, 186–89; Canada, 191–94, 504–5; California, 236–38; Oregon, 324–29; British Columbia, 368–69; Alaska, 401–4; Soviet Far East, 437–40; China, 439; Korea, 440; Japan, 473–74, 476–79, 482. *See also names of individual rivers*
Robert III (King of Scotland), 55

Roberts, Jim, 308–9
Rogers, William G., Jr., 308
Rogue River (Oregon), 324–25, 328, 331, 511
Rohner, Ronald P. and Evelyn C., 400
Rook, Roger, 320–21
Roosevelt, President Franklin D., 285
Roosevelt, President Theodore, 354
Roper, Daniel C., 419
Rosseland, Leiv, 143
Rostlund, Erhard, 170
Roule, Louis, 122
Rousseau, Rollie, 331–32
Roxburgh, Duke of, 146, 147
Royal Commission of Inquiry (Great Britain), 65
Royal Greenland Trading Company, 214
Royce, Dr. William F., 18, 20, 419–20; on salmon navigational ability, 23, 24; on Alaska salmon industry, 427–28; on decline of Asian salmon, 464
Rudofsky, Bernard, 476–77
Rudy, Paul, 332
Russel, Alex, 73
Russia: Atlantic salmon rivers, 166–68; salmon rivers in Far East, 437–40; primitive peoples of, in Far East, 447–49; early fishery for Pacific salmon, 451–52; exploitation of salmon runs of, by Japanese, 451-54, 461; effects of treaties with Japan on salmon stocks of, 452–55, 459, 461–63; effects of Japan's high seas fishing, 454–59; Pacific salmon landings (1952–67), 440, 457; decline of salmon stocks of, 463–68; salmon catches of, along Far East coast (1940–69), 465; effect on native peoples of Soviet rule, 468–70; future of Pacific salmon in, 470–71; salmon catches in Far East (1909–44), 557–58
Russian-American Company, 404, 416, 451

Rutkowicz, Stanislaw, 168
Ryan, Colonel R. M., 85

Sage, Dean, 183
St. John, Sir Walter, 69
Saint Lawrence River (Canada) salmon fisheries, 192–93, 194–95
Sakhalin Island (U.S.S.R.) fisheries, 438–39, 451, 452, 453, 454
Salmo gairdneri, see Steelhead trout
Salmon and Freshwater Fisheries Act of 1923 (England and Wales), 76
Salmon and Trout Association (England), 78, 89, 219
Salmon and Trout Magazine, 6
Salmon ceremonies, first: Yurok (California), 240–44, 273; at Celilo Falls (Columbia River), 273–74, 290–91
Salmon-Cultural Laboratory (Washington), 337
Salmon Fisheries Act of 1861 (England and Wales), 65, 72, 99
Salmon Fisheries Act of 1863 (Ireland), 98, 99
Salmon Fishery Acts of 1862 and 1868 (Scotland), 74
Salmon Mothership Association (Japan), 457
"Salmon people," 531; of British Columbia, 391–96; under Soviet rule, 468–70; of Japan (the Ainu), 474–75
Salmon River (Idaho), 301
Salo, E. O., 358
Sandeman, Fraser, 146
Sanitary Authority, Oregon (now Department of Environmental Quality), 314, 319
San Luis project (California), 256
Save Our Salmon Committee from Tofino and Ucluelet (Vancouver Island), 390
Scandinavia: history of salmon fishery in, 143–45; sport fishing for Atlantic salmon, 491–94; salm-

Scandinavia, *contd.*
  on cookery in, 525. *See also* Finland; Norway; Sweden
Schultz, Leonard P., 30
Scotland: salmon rivers of, 49–52, 85–87, 499–500; despoiling of, 62–64, 80–82; decline of, 73–74; sport fishing, 499–502. *See also* Great Britain
Scott, Anthony, 219
Scott, Genio, 194, 200
Scott, Sir Walter, 63–64, 497
Scrope, William, 64
Seafield, Countess of, 82
Sea Fishery Industry Acts of 1959 and 1962 (Scotland), 86
Seaman, Kenneth, 60
Sea Pool Fisheries, 342
Seattle, Chief (Duwamish tribe), 349–50
Seccombe, Rev. Joseph, 172
Seiji Machidori, 442
Seine River (France), 120
Semko, R. S., 463–64, 468
Seufert, Francis, 300, 526
Seufert Canning Company, 280, 290, 300, 526
Severn River (England), 48, 49
Sévigné, Madame de, quoted, 523
Shakespeare, William, quoted, 48, 54
Shannon River (Ireland), 94; scheme (hydroelectric project), 101–2
Shigeru Oda, 462
Siebold, Philipp Franz van, 476
Sierra Club, 430
Silver salmon, *see* Coho salmon
Simison, Herbert E., 316–17
Sinclair, Sir Tollemache, 500
Smirnov, A. I., 445
Smith, Donald A. (later Lord Strathcona), 194
Smith, Lynwood S., 13, 15
Snake River (U.S.), 263–64; controversy over dam construction on, 292–94, 295, 297, 300–302
Social Credit party (British Colum-

Social Credit party, *contd.*
  bia), attitude toward Fraser River, 386
Society for the Preservation of Salmon in Brittany and Lower Normandy, 127
Sockeye salmon (*Oncorhynchus nerka*), 10, 230; spawning of, in lakes or streams, 11, 15; migrations of, 19; return of, to the river, 25, 26; observations of, ascending waterfall, 27–28; biological data for, 29; in the Columbia River, 265, 266, 305, 306; spawning channels for, 341; in Puget Sound, 351, 358–59; Lake Washington's, 362–64; in British Columbia rivers, 369–71, 380–84; death of, at Hell's Gate, 376–80; in Alaska (called reds), 405–6, 420–24, 426, 427; in Asia, 440, 443–44; Soviet catches of, along Far East coast (1940–69), 465; food value of, 521, 527
Sømme, Sven, 142, 149
Southgate, B. A., 78
Spain: salmon rivers of, 111–13; sportsmen's rivers of, 115–18, 494–96
Spawning: effect of, on Pacific and Atlantic salmon, 4; and return of the salmon to the river, 25–26; physiological changes prior to, 26–28; and reproduction and death, 28–32
Spenser, Edmund, 69
Spey River (Scotland), 50, 51, 62
Sport Fisheries and Wildlife, Bureau of, 188, 336, 337, 338
Sport fishing for salmon: growth of British, 74–76, 496–99; in Ireland, 106–7, 502–4; in Spanish rivers, 115–18, 494–96; in Norwegian rivers, 145–49, 492; in United States, 182–83, 508–11; rise of Canadian, 200–202, 504–6; versus commercial fishing in Columbia River, 303–4; in Oregon's coastal

Sport fishing for salmon, *contd.*
streams, 330–31; in Washington state, 359–62; in British Columbia, 386–88, 514; mystique of, 487–91; in Scandinavia, 491–94; in Iceland, 493–94; in France and Spain, 494–96; in Scotland, 499–502; in New Zealand, 507–8; in Alaska, 513; in Middle West (U.S.), 515–16; for steelhead trout, 516–19
Spott, Robert, 240
Spurlock, Clark, 414
Steelhead trout (*Salmo gairdneri*): origin of, 4; range of, 5, 10; spawning of, 11, 31; juvenile life in the river of, 13; transition between freshwater and seawater for, 16; ocean life of, 20–21; return of, to the river, 25; in California, 236, 238; in the Columbia River, 265, 266, 306–7; in Willamette River, 311–12, 319–20; in Oregon's coastal streams, 328, 330–31; artificial propagation of, 339–40; in Washington rivers, 360; in British Columbia rivers, 369–70; appearance of, described, 506; sport fishing for, in Oregon, California, Washington, British Columbia, and Alaska rivers, 516–19; food value of, 521
Steller, Georg Wilhelm, 226, 401, 449, 468; explorations and discoveries of, 227–29, 231, 438
Stevens, Gov. Isaac Ingalls, 275, 349
Stewart, R. N., 493, 520
Stilwell, E. M., 179
Stoddard, Thomas Tod, 64
Stone, Livingston (fish culturist), 249–50, 334–35
Stuart, T. A., 27
Suatuola, Don Marcellino de, 41
Suckley, George, 231
Supreme Court, United States, 302; decision on High Mountain Sheep dam, 301
Sutherland, Countess of, 82

Sutter, John, 247
Sweden: salmon fishing in, 155, 156, 493; hydroelectric development in, 156–58; river fisheries of, 160–62
Swedish Salmon Research Institute, 160
Swedish Water Law, 157, 165

Tay River (Scotland), 50, 51, 63
Tchernavin, V., 6
Tennessee Valley Authority, 78
Terry's Guide Book to the Japanese Empire, 474, 475
Tetreault, Bertrand, 207
Thames Conservancy, 79
Thames River (England), destruction of, 68–72
Thames Salmon Association, 71
Thompson, Daniel P., 185
Thompson, David, 267
Thompson, Henry, 291
Thompson, Tommy, 290–91
Thompson, W. F., 378, 380, 381, 410, 427–28
Thoreau, Henry David, 172, 176–77, 180–81
Thyssen, Fritz, 134
Tinker, Jon, 138
Tocqueville, Alexis de, 97
Tody, Dr. Wayne, 515, 516
Tokiharu, Abe, 445–46
Tollefson, Roger, 357
Tollefson, Thor, 361–62
Tolstoi, Leo, 469
Transplantations of salmon to new parts of the world, 344–46
Treaty of Medicine Creek, 349
Treaty of Point Elliott, 349
Treaty of Portsmouth, 452
Treaty of Saint Petersburg, 451, 452
Treaty of Walla Walla, 275
Trent River (England), 47, 60–61, 62
Trojan nuclear power plant (Oregon), 307
Trout and Salmon, 60, 508

Trout Unlimited, 516
Tuck, James A., 170
Tweed Acts of 1857 and 1859 (Scotland), 64, 73
Tweed River (Scotland), 50, 51, 62, 64
Tyne River (England), 67, 83

U.D.N. (ulcerative dermal necrosis), 51, 82, 86, 89–90, 102; first appearance of, in Ireland, 104–5; presence of, in Spain, 116; presence of, in France, 131
Union Carbide Corporation, 342
U.S. Fish and Wildlife Service, 289, 336
U.S. Fish Commission, 334
U.S.S.R., *see* Russia

Van Cleve, Richard, report on Japan's salmon rivers, 477–78, 482–84
Vancouver, Capt. George, discovery of Puget Sound, 347–48
Van Drimmelen, D. E., on Rhine River salmon, 137
Van Dyke, Henry, 520
Van Fleet, Clark C., 520
Van Stahlin, Jacob, 231
Venables, Bernard, 498
Verhoeven, Leon, 20
Vibert, Richard, 126, 127
Victoria (Queen of England), 75
Vieth, F. H. D., 199
Vinland colony, 169, 171
Vladimiriskaya, N. M., 166–67

Wade, Charles, 84–85
Wagner, Richard, 136
Walbaum, Johann Julius, 231
Wales, salmon rivers of, 46–49, 54–55, 83–85; despoiling of, 65–67; sport fishing in, 496–99. *See also* Great Britain

Wallace, Jock, 502
Walton, Izaak, 60, 498; *The Compleat Angler*, 70, 75, 488–91, 520; Izaak Walton League, 304, 318, 331
Washington: major salmon rivers for sport fishing in, 509; ocean sport salmon fishing regulations in, 512
Washington, Lake, sockeye fishery, 362–64
Water Resources, Department of (California), 259, 260, 262
Water Resources Act of 1963 (England and Wales), 77
Waterman, T. T., 244
Waters, Brian, 48
Waters and Forests, Bureau of (France), 125, 127
Watson, Winslow C., 185
Waxell, Sven, 228–29, 230
Weeden, Robert B., 431–32
Weeks, Edward, 201–2, 520
Weir, Tom, 86–87
Wells, Henry P., 183, 199
Wendler, Henry O., 355
Went, Dr. A. E. J., 32, 104; on salmon in Ireland, 91–92, 94, 96; on sport fishing, 106
Westminster, Duke of, 146, 147
Weyerhaeuser timber empire, 354–55
White Act of 1924 (Alaska), 413, 427
Whitman, Dr. and Mrs. Marcus, 275
Wickett, W. P., 341
Wiese, John, 429, 431
Wilderness Society, 430–31
Wildlife Federation, Oregon, 333
Wilhelm, Kaiser, 136
Willamette Greenway Committee, 317–18
Willamette River (Oregon): settlement on banks of, 311–12; pollution of, 312–14; effects of pollution of, on the fishery, 314–16; viewed by Simison (FWPCA), 316–17; viewed by Greenway Committee, 317–18; rehabilitation of, 318–20; downstream fish mi-

Willamette River *contd.*
gration problems in, 320–21; future outlook for, 321–22
Willard Laboratory (Washington), 336
Williams, A. Courtney, 69
Williams, S. W., 280
William the Conqueror, 45
Wilmot, Samuel, 184
Wise, James, 372
Wood, Ian, 499
Wood, Joe, 250
Woodham-Smith, Cecil, 97
Wordsworth, William, 47–48, 497
Wotton, Sir Henry, 489
Wulff, Lee, 505, 520

Wye Board of Conservators, 72
Wye Fisheries Association, 72
Wye Preservation Society, 72
Wye River (Wales and England), 47–48, 49, 497, 499; resuscitation of, 72–73
Wyeth, Capt. Nathaniel, 274

Yeats, William Butler, 95, 100
Young, Archibald, 62, 74, 99–100
Yurok Indians (California): first salmon ceremony of, 240–44, 273; construction of Kepel dam by, 244–47

THE SALMON

THEIR FIGHT FOR SURVIVAL
by ANTHONY NETBOY

Here is the complete story of the world's most spectacular and valuable family of fishes. It traces the evolution and life history of the Pacific and Atlantic salmon, their extraordinary migrations, and their relations with man from the Stone Age to the present. Country by country, Professor Netboy examines the all-out conservation battles, won or lost, and the international agreements that now give the Pacific fishery — and to a lesser extent the Atlantic resource — a measure of protection.

Salmon once thronged the rivers in North America, Europe, and Asia in such numbers that spawning runs would cause the waters to overflow the banks and sometimes would upset small boats. They were an abundant source of cheap food. Then in the nineteenth century, and continuing to the present day, overfishing, pollution, dam building, and other uses of the rivers destroyed the runs in countless streams.

This book has the authority of firsthand knowledge. It is the first in any language that traces the fate of both the Pacific and Atlantic salmon on every continent where they are found.

In his pursuit of the fascinating salmon, Anthony Netboy has traveled widely, has studied the fish climbing the ladders at Bonneville dam on the Columbia, explored the very Spanish streams where the ancient cave painters took their fish, and watched the runs come in on the bleak shores of eastern Hokkaido.

In *The Salmon: Their Fight for Survival* he has given us a highly readable and vital case history of the struggle to create a viable balance between technology and nature, to translate the biologists' understanding of the salmon's needs into political fact. "A world in which the salmon cannot live," warns the author, "may be a world in which man cannot live either."

0174

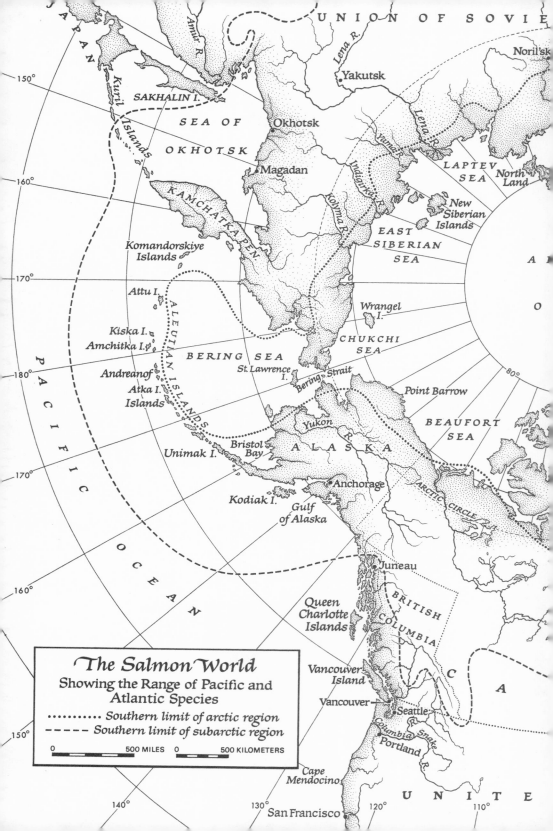

The Salmon World
Showing the Range of Pacific and Atlantic Species

·············· Southern limit of arctic region

---- ---- Southern limit of subarctic region

0   500 MILES   0   500 KILOMETERS